Principles of Money, Banking, and Financial Markets

Principles of Money, Banking, and Financial Markets

THIRD, REVISED AND EXPANDED EDITION

Lawrence S. Ritter

&

William L. Silber

Basic Books, Inc., Publishers   *New York*

Copyright © 1974 by Basic Books, Inc.
Copyright © 1977, 1980 by Lawrence S. Ritter
and William L. Silber
Library of Congress Catalog Number: LC 79–3139
ISBN: 0–465–06339–X
Printed in the United States of America
All rights reserved
Designed by Vincent Torre
10 9 8 7 6 5 4 3 2

"... be careful in teaching,
for error in teaching amounts
to deliberate sin."

The *Mishnah*
Pirkei Avot, 4

1981 Supplement: Legal and Regulatory Developments

Congressional legislation and Federal Reserve administrative changes during 1980 have significantly altered the institutional framework of our financial system. We think these developments are sufficiently important to warrant a special bulletin for users of this book. We have, therefore, prepared the following concise summary of these changes, together with their implications for principles of money, banking, and financial markets.

Definitions of Money (Chapter 1)

In 1980 the Federal Reserve completely revamped its money supply definitions. Table 1 on page 5 is revised below to incorporate the Fed's new money supply definitions. Note that the new M1B is the same as the old M1, so throughout the book whenever we refer to the money supply we mean M1B unless otherwise specified.

TABLE 1
Four Definitions of the Money Supply
(mid-1980)

M1A *	Currency outside banks ($110 billion) plus demand deposits at commercial banks ($260 billion)	$ 370 billion
M1B *	Add checking-type accounts at thrift institutions and automatic transfers from savings to demand deposits ($20 billion)	390 billion
M2	Add passbook savings deposits ($380 billion) and small-size time deposits ($720 billion) at both commercial banks and thrift institutions, shares in money market mutual funds ($75 billion), and bank overnight repurchase agreements ($25 billion)	1,590 billion
M3	Add large-size ($100,000 and over) time deposits ($230 billion)	1,820 billion

SOURCE: *Federal Reserve Bulletin.*
NOTE: Money market mutual funds and bank repurchase agreements are discussed in subsequent chapters.

Reserve Requirements (Chapters 3 and 12)

Congressional passage of the Depository Institutions Deregulation and Monetary Control Act of 1980 marks the most important banking legislation since the 1930s. The Act provides that reserve requirements will

* Wall Street Journal 1/5/82, pp 43 - the Fed announced that it will go to a single M1 money supply measure beginning tomorrow.

vii

now be uniformly applied by the Federal Reserve to *all* transactions or checking-type desposits at all depository institutions, *regardless of Federal Reserve membership or type of institution.*

Transactions deposits include demand deposits, NOW (negotiable order of withdrawal) accounts, automatic transfers from savings to demand deposits, and similar accounts at all commercial banks, savings banks, savings and loan associations, and credit unions. The Act provides for an eight-year gradual phase-in period for the reserve requirements of nonmember banks and thrift institutions. By the end of that period (i.e., by 1988), all depository institutions—member and nonmember, commercial bank and thrift—will have to hold reserves of 3 percent against that portion of their transactions accounts below $25 million, and 12 percent (the Fed can vary this between 8 and 14 percent) against the portion above $25 million.

For time and savings deposits, reserve requirements are being eliminated entirely against personal or individual deposits. Against business time deposits, all depository institutions will have to hold reserves of 3 percent (the Fed can vary this between 0 and 9 percent).

Thus Federal Reserve membership has been made essentially irrelevant and the perennial problem of dropouts from the Federal Reserve System (pages 33, 159–162) has finally been resolved.

Discounting (Chapters 3 and 13)

In return the Act provides that nonmember banks and thrift institutions will now have the same access to borrowing from the Federal Reserve Banks as member banks have, and on exactly the same terms.

Deposit Interest Rate Ceilings (Chapters 7 and 9)

Regulation Q's ubiquitous interest rate ceilings on time and savings deposits appear, at long last, to be on their last legs. The Act phases them out as economic conditions warrant and within a six-year period. However, don't cheer too soon: Congress could always change its mind at the last minute.

And the ban against paying interest on demand deposits has disappeared: the Act permits all depository institutions nationwide to offer NOW accounts—interest-bearing checking accounts—starting on January 1, 1981.

Deposit Insurance (Chapter 8)

Finally, federal deposit insurance has been raised from $40,000 to $100,000 at commercial banks, savings banks, savings and loan associations, and credit unions.

About the Authors

LAWRENCE S. RITTER is Professor of Finance and Economics and Chairman of the Finance Department at the undergraduate and graduate Schools of Business of New York University. A former Chief of the Domestic Research Division of the Federal Reserve Bank of New York, he has served as a consultant to the U.S. Treasury, the Federal Deposit Insurance Corporation, the Board of Governors of the Federal Reserve System, the American Bankers Association, and the Association of Reserve City Bankers. He has been the Editor of the *Journal of Finance* and is a past President of the American Finance Association. Professor Ritter is the author of numerous articles in professional journals, as well as of *The Glory of Their Times* (1966), a best-selling book about the early days of baseball, and of *The Image of Their Greatness: An Illustrated History of Baseball from 1900 to the Present* (1979).

WILLIAM L. SILBER is Professor of Economics and Finance at the Graduate School of Business Administration at New York University. A former Senior Staff Economist with the President's Council of Economic Advisers, he has served as a consultant to the Board of Governors of the Federal Reserve System, the President's Commission on Financial Structure and Regulation, the U.S. Senate Committee on the Budget, the House Committee on Banking, Currency and Housing, the Justice Department, the Federal Reserve Bank of New York, the Federal Home Loan Bank Board, the National Commission on Electronic Funds Transfers, and the Department of Housing and Urban Development. He is an Associate Editor of the *Review of Economics and Statistics* and is the author of *Portfolio Behavior of Financial Institutions* (1970), *Financial Innovation* (1975), and *Commercial Bank Liability Management* (1978), as well as of numerous articles in professional journals.

Contents

PART I
The Basics

PART II

Intermediaries and Banks

Contents

PART III

The Art of Central Banking

PART IV

Monetary Theory

PART V

The Monetarist-Keynesian Debate and Its Policy Implications

PART VI

The Effectiveness of Monetary Policy

PART VII

Financial Markets and Interest Rates

Contents

PART IX

The Past and the Future

Notes to Instructor:
Possible Course Outlines

The organization of this textbook reflects the way we would teach a course, in Money and Banking or Money and Financial Markets. However, we realize that there are alternative ways to organize such a course, ways that would involve a different ordering of chapters. We have, therefore, written the book with the ideal of flexibility in mind. The only constraint is that Part I (Chapters 1 through 6) should be assigned at the beginning, since it lays the basic foundations regardless of eventual topic emphasis. Even there, however, some might want to move the Appendix to Chapter 3 back into Part III. The book is written so such a move will not interfere with comprehension.

While every teacher can best structure his or her own course, here are some illustrative examples of the ways this book can be adapted to different approaches.

The two major types of course organization are (1) a financial institutions and markets and central banking emphasis, and (2) a monetary theory and policy emphasis. The ordering of the chapters as they appear in the Table of Contents reflects the first type of approach: financial institutions and markets and central banking. Even within each of these categories, it is possible to emphasize different subjects. Here are some suggestions:

1. *Financial institutions and markets and central banking*: After the Basics in Part I, Parts II and III present a comprehensive analysis of the business of financial intermediaries—with emphasis on commercial banking—and the art of central banking. A limited amount of theory on the role of money in the economy is given in

Chapters 1 and 4 to provide the proper framework for the discussions of central banking. When the formal presentation of monetary theory begins, in Part IV, it is possible to reduce the emphasis on theory by eliminating Chapters 19 and 22 and the Appendix to Chapter 23. These sections construct and then apply IS-LM analysis, but the rest of the book is written so that the omission of this material will not interrupt its continuity or intelligibility. It is also possible to move more quickly into financial markets by going directly to Part VII ("Financial Markets and Interest Rates") after Part I or after any subsequent part. Many professors seem to prefer teaching Parts I, II, and III in sequence, and then moving to Part VI or VII before returning to Parts IV and V.

2. *Monetary theory and policy:* After Part I is completed, monetary theory can be introduced immediately by going directly to Part IV. This can be followed with the Monetarist-Keynesian debate in Part V and the discussion of the effectiveness of monetary policy in Part VI. One can then backtrack to Parts II and III, which discuss financial institutions and central banking, and then continue with Part VII ("Financial Markets and Interest Rates"). In fact, Chapters 29 and 30 in Part VII ("Forecasting Interest Rates" and "The Structure of Interest Rates") could be brought into a theory-oriented course much earlier, right after Part V (the Monetarist-Keynesian debate).

3. *History and international aspects:* It is possible to put all of Part VIII ("International Finance") virtually anywhere one wishes, provided the basics in Part I have been covered. The international chapters, for example, could easily follow Part III ("The Art of Central Banking") or Part VI ("The Effectiveness of Monetary Policy"). Although there is only one chapter devoted explicitly to history (Chapter 37), historical materials are interspersed throughout the book—especially in Chapters 7-10, on financial intermediaries and banks; in Chapters 11-13, on central banking; and in Chapter 34, on international financial crises.

An Instructor's Manual and Student Workbook are available from Basic Books. Write for them if you wish. Also note that we have sprinkled a few news clippings through the text to help illustrate the relevance of the material.

Acknowledgments

The first two editions of this book generated a number of unsolicited communications from students and teachers. Some were favorable, others critical, but all helped us prepare this third edition. We would like to thank the following for taking the time and effort to help improve this revision:

John A. Carlson, *Purdue University*
Robert M. Domine, *University of Michigan*
James S. Earley, *University of California, Riverside*
William P. Field, Jr., *Nicholls State University*
Stanley Fischer, *Massachusetts Institute of Technology*
Jerry W. Gustafson, *Beloit College*
John B. Guerard, Jr., *University of Texas*
Philip J. Hahn, *Youngstown State University*
Gabriel Hawawini, *Baruch College of City University of New York*
Naphtali Hoffman, *Elmira College*
Edward J. Kane, *Ohio State University*
Jimmie King, *Tuskagee Institute*
Robert L. Moore, *Harvard University*
Alan Rabin, *University of Tennessee*
Deborah E. Robbins, *Wellesley College*
John M. Sapinsley, *Rhode Island College*
Edward Shapiro, *University of Toledo*
Thomas J. Shea, *Springfield College*
Cathy Sherman, *University of Texas*
Milton H. Spencer, *Wayne State University*
Joan Walters, *Fairfield University*
Stuart Wood, *Tulane University*

PART I

The Basics

Chapter 1

Money and the Economy

T HE *LACK* OF MONEY is the root of all evil," said George Bernard Shaw. While that might be somewhat of an exaggeration, there have been numerous periods in history when it appeared to be more true than false. There have also been rather lengthy episodes when the opposite seemed true: when economic disruption apparently stemmed not from too little money, but from too *much* of it.

From this line of thought, the question naturally arises: What is the "right" amount of money? Not too little, not too much, but just right. And how can we go about getting it?

Questions of this sort used to be considered heresy, back in the days when the economy was viewed as a marvel of perpetual motion, sparked by divine inspiration in the form of gold (which gave money intrinsic value) and human intelligence (which told us to stay out of the way and let things work out by themselves). Flanked by the twin eternal verities—the gold standard and the balanced budget—laissez-faire reigned supreme. Let nature take its course, and everything will turn out for the best in this best of all possible worlds.

Today we are no longer so sure. Aggregate spending on the nation's output of new goods and services—the economy's gross national product (GNP)—is no longer seen as inevitably producing full employment, stable prices, a high rate of economic growth, balance in international payments, and all the other things we expect our economy to yield. We have experienced too many instances of GNP falling short of the mark, or overshooting it, to retain blind faith in any built-in self-correcting thermostat. So today we deliberately try to influence the course of economic events. We tinker, meddle, turn switches, push buttons, pull levers, and try to make things better.

But are they really any better? The answer is far from clear. Nevertheless, for most people the issue now is not *whether* the government should intervene, but how, when, and to what extent. The ends are not particularly new—high employment, price stability, economic growth, and balance of payments equilibrium—but the means are. The means most frequently used today to influence the economy's direction are *monetary policy*, with which this book is directly concerned, and *fiscal policy*, about which we will also have a fair amount to say. How well do they work? Are they appropriate to achieve their purposes? Can they be improved?

As a first approximation, monetary policy involves regulating the money supply and conditions in financial markets in order to achieve the goals of national economic policy. Fiscal policy involves changing government spending and tax rates for similar purposes. Let's set the stage for exploring these issues by providing a first look at the supply of money and its relationship to economic activity.

The Supply of Money

What *is* money, anyway? And how much of it do we actually have?

Money is just what you think it is—what you spend when you want to buy something. The Indians used beads, Eskimos used fishhooks, and we use *currency* (coins and dollar bills) and, most of all, *demand deposits* in banks (checking accounts).

Money is used (1) as a means of payment—a medium of exchange—but it has other functions as well. It is also used (2) as a store of value, when people hold on to it, and (3) as a standard of value (a unit of account) when people compare prices and thereby assess relative values. But most prominently money is what you can spend, a generally acceptable medium of exchange that you can use to buy things or settle debts.

How large a money supply do we have? It amounted to $360 billion at the end of 1978, roughly $95 billion in the form of currency and $265 billion in demand deposits at banks. This definition of money —currency outside banks plus demand deposits—is frequently called M1 (to distinguish it from three other definitions of money, M1+, M2, and M3, which we will get to in a moment). If you want to know what the money supply is *today*, add about 5 or 6 percent per annum to that figure since the end of 1978 and you probably won't be far off. Or else do what we did: Look it up in the latest issue of the *Federal Reserve Bulletin*.

Since currency and checking accounts are spendable at face

value virtually anywhere, at any time, they are the most "liquid" assets a person can have. A liquid asset is something you can turn into the generally acceptable medium of exchange quickly without taking a loss—as compared with "frozen" assets, for example, which can be sold or liquidated on short notice only at a substantially lower price. Money is the most liquid asset you can have (because it *is* the medium of exchange), but it is not the only one. Savings deposits and government bonds are rather liquid, although not quite as liquid as money because you can't spend them. To spend them, you first have to exchange them for money. At the other extreme, real estate and vintage automobiles typically rank fairly low on the liquidity scale: If you have to sell quickly, you're likely to take a beating on the deal.

Thus liquidity is a continuum, ranging from currency and demand deposits at the top of the scale to a variety of frozen assets at the bottom. As a result, what we call "money" is not a fixed and immutable thing, like what we call water (H_2O), but to a great extent is a matter of judgment; there are several different definitions of money, each of which drops one notch lower on the liquidity scale in drawing the line between "money" and "all other assets". Table 1 summarizes four different definitions of the money supply.

TABLE 1

Four Definitions of the Money Supply
(End of 1978)

M1	Currency outside banks ($95 billion) plus demand deposits at both commercial banks ($260 billion) and at thrift institutions ($5 billion)	$360 billion
M1+	Add passbook savings deposits at commercial banks ($235 billion)	595 billion
M2	Add passbook savings deposits at thrift institutions ($290 billion)	885 billion
M3	Add time deposits at both commercial banks ($365 billion) and at thrift institutions ($325 billion)	1,575 billion

Source: Federal Reserve Bulletin.
Note: These definitions reflect proposals made by the Federal Reserve in the January 1979 issue of the *Federal Reserve Bulletin.* They are currently being revised to include other assets which are also used as media of exchange. Money market mutual funds and bank repurchase agreements, both of which are discussed in subsequent chapters, will be included in some of the new definitions (see *Federal Reserve Bulletin,* February 1980).

M1 refers to the most liquid assets of all—currency and checking accounts. Until recently, commercial banks were the only financial institutions permitted to issue checking accounts, and they are still responsible for the overwhelming proportion of them. However, the financial system is constantly changing, innovating, and evolving— an observation that will become increasingly familiar as you turn the pages of this book. One recent change occurred a few years ago, in the 1970s, when thrift institutions—mutual savings banks, savings and loan associations, and credit unions—also began issuing demand deposits. Since there is no meaningful difference between a checking account at a commercial bank and one at a thrift institution, they are all included in M1. As Table 1 indicates, the great bulk of checking accounts is still in commercial banks ($260 billion out of $265 billion), but savings banks, savings and loan associations, and credit unions are newcomers to the field. As they gain both experience and greater public acceptance of their checking account facilities they are likely to increase their share. Since M1 is confined to the most highly liquid assets, those commonly used as a means of payment, it is the narrowest definition of the money supply (as well as the most traditional one, by the way).

M1+ drops a rung lower on the liquidity ladder to include passbook savings deposits at commercial banks, which amounted to $235 billion at the end of 1978. You can't spend a savings deposit directly, but you can exchange it for cash pretty quickly at a guaranteed dollar amount with no risk of loss.

M2 drops just a shade lower on the liquidity scale by adding passbook savings deposits at savings banks and similar deposits (usually called shares) in savings and loan associations and credit unions. The distinction between M1+ and M2 is hard to see, since savings deposits at thrift institutions are clearly just as liquid as at commercial banks. There is some evidence, however, suggesting that people are possibly a bit more willing to withdraw funds from a savings account at a commercial bank than from one at a thrift institution. If this is so, then it is reasonable to distinguish between M1+ and M2. But if this difference in people's behavior fades over time, as is likely, then M1+ will become redundant and can be dropped, because it will be conceptually indistinguishable from M2.

M3 consists of M2 plus all *time* deposits, regardless of whether they are at commercial banks or at thrift institutions. Unlike passbook savings deposits, time deposits have a scheduled maturity date—like six months or two years—and if you want to withdraw your funds earlier, you suffer a substantial penalty by having to forfeit part of the accumulated interest. Thus time deposits are less liquid than savings deposits.

So what is the money supply in the United States? Is it $360 billion (M1) or $1,575 billion (M3), or something in between? Each definition of money has its adherents, but by and large most economists prefer the narrow definition of the money supply—M1—because that and only that is generally acceptable as a means of payment. Once you go beyond currency and checking accounts, it is hard to find a logical place to stop, since many things (bonds, stocks, waterbeds) contain liquidity in varying degree. Throughout this book, therefore, we will for the most part stick to the narrow definition of money—currency plus demand deposits.[1]

Who Determines Our Money Supply?

Why do we have $360 billion of money in the United States? Who, or what, determines how much there will be?

Regardless of what you might have heard, the amount of gold does *not* determine the money supply. Indeed, it has very little influence on it. In 1968 the last remaining link between the money supply and gold was severed when a law requiring 25 percent gold backing behind most of our currency was repealed. If that is all news to you, it is a good indication of just how unimportant the connection between gold and money has always been, at least in our lifetime.

Both currency and demand deposits can be increased (or decreased) without any relation to gold. Does that disturb you? Does it lead you to distrust the value of your money? Then send it to us. We'll be delighted to pay you ninety cents on the dollar, which should be a bargain if you believe all you read about a dollar being worth only sixty cents, or fifty cents, or whatever the latest figure might be.[2]

If gold is not the watchdog, then who (or what) does determine how much money we will have?

The monetary authority in most countries is called the central bank. A central bank does not deal directly with the public; it is rather a bank for banks, and it is responsible for the execution of national monetary policy. In the United States the central bank is the Federal Reserve, created by Congress in 1913. It consists of 12 district Federal Reserve Banks, scattered throughout the country, and a Board of Governors in Washington. This hydra-headed monster, which some

[1] Which is not to say that M1 is a perfect measure of how much of the means of payment is in existence. As just two examples of its shortcomings, notice that M1 does not include travelers checks outstanding, nor any estimate of existing bank "overdraft" facilities (which are arrangements that allow people to write checks—legally—even when they don't have enough in their checking accounts to cover them). These as well as other funds available for immediate payment are not included in M1 mainly because of the absence of reliable data on them.

[2] Actually, when you read that the dollar is worth only fifty cents it provides a clue to why gold has little to do with the *value* of money, in addition to having little to do with determining the amount outstanding. Money is valuable only because you can buy things with it—like clothes and books and stereos. The value of a dollar is, therefore, determined by the prices of the things we buy. When people say a dollar is worth only fifty cents they mean that a dollar can now buy what only fifty cents could have bought a few years ago (because prices have doubled).

view as benign but others consider an ever-lurking peril, possesses ultimate authority over the money supply.

As noted above, the money supply (M1) consists of currency and
demand deposits. *Currency* is manufactured by money factories—the
Bureau of Engraving and Printing and the Mint—and then shipped
under heavy guard to the U.S. Treasury and the Federal Reserve for
further distribution. For the most part it enters circulation when people
and business firms cash checks at their local banks. Thus it is the
public that ultimately decides what proportion of the money supply will
be in the form of currency, with the Federal Reserve Banks whole-
saling the necessary coins and paper to local banks. The Federal Reserve is not particularly concerned with the fraction of the money
supply that is in one form or another, but rather with the *total* of demand deposits plus currency.[3]

As Table 1 shows, most of the money supply (three-quarters of
it) is in the form of *demand deposits*, and most of the demand deposits
(98 percent of them) are in commercial banks. Demand deposits in
commercial banks come into being, as we shall see in Chapter 2, when
commercial banks extend credit—that is, when they make loans or
buy securities. Demand deposits vanish, as silently as they came, when
banks contract credit—when bank loans are repaid or banks sell securities. It is precisely here, through its ability to control the behavior
of commercial banks, that the Federal Reserve wields its primary
authority over the money supply and thereby implements monetary
policy.

This process of money creation by commercial banks, under the
influence of the Federal Reserve, will be discussed at greater length in
the following chapters. But before we get into the details, we should
back off for a moment and ask why all the fuss? Why is money so
important to begin with?

---

[3] Just in case you're curious, here are some miscellaneous facts about coins
and currency: Coins are manufactured by the U.S. Mint, which has production
facilities in Philadelphia, Denver, and San Francisco. All currency is manufactured by the U.S. Bureau of Engraving and Printing in Washington, D.C.
The largest denomination of currency now issued is the $100 bill; there used to
be $500, $1,000, $5,000, and $10,000 bills in circulation, but they were all
discontinued in 1945. The average life of a $1 bill is about a year and a half,
before getting torn or worn out, which is why the government started issuing the
new Susan B. Anthony dollar coins in 1979. Coins last much longer than currency. Banks send worn-out bills back to the Federal Reserve, which destroys
them. The $95 billion of currency and coin in circulation in the United States at
the end of 1978 amounted to about $430 on average for every man, woman, and
child—or $1,720 on average for a family of four. Which means, if you stop to
think about it, that there must be an awful lot of hoarding going on *somewhere*.

The Importance of Money I: Man Beats Barter

What good is money in the first place? To appreciate the importance of money in an economic system, it is instructive to speculate on what the economy might look like without it. In other words, why was money invented (by Sir John Money in 3016 B.C.)?

For one thing, without money individuals in the economy would have to devote more time to buying what they want and selling what they don't. In other words, people would have less time to work and play. A barter economy is one without a medium of exchange or a unit of account (the measuring rod function of money). Let's see what it might be like in a barter economy.

Say you are a carpenter and agree to build a bookcase for your neighbor. Your friend happens to raise chickens and pays you with 17 pounds of feathers and a dozen eggs. You decide to make one pillow for yourself, so you now have 16 pounds of feathers to exchange for the rest of the week's groceries, and hopefully something left over to pay the plumber for fixing the leaky outhouse. All you must do is find a grocer whose wife just gave birth and therefore needs a few extra pillows (hopefully she had triplets), and you still have to look around for a plumber with similar needs.

What's more, you have to remember that a loaf of bread exchanges for six ounces of feathers (it also exchanges for eleven books of matches or three boxes of crayons or one Yankee Yearbook, but never mind because you don't have any of these things to spare). And of course all the other items on the grocer's shelf have similar price tags—the tags are bigger than the items.

Along comes money and simplifies matters. Workers are paid in something called money, which they can then use to pay their bills and make their purchases (medium of exchange). We no longer need price tags giving rates of exchange between an item and everything else that might conceivably be exchanged for it. Instead, prices of goods and services are expressed in terms of money, a common denominator (unit of account).

The most important thing about the medium of exchange is that every person must be confident that it can be passed on to someone else—that it be generally acceptable in trade. Paradoxically, a person will accept the medium of exchange only when certain that it can be passed on to someone else. One key characteristic is that the *uncertainty* over its value in trade must be very *low*. People will be more willing to accept the medium of exchange if they are certain what it is worth in terms of things they really want. The uncertainty of barter transactions makes people wary of exchange: If I want to sell my house and buy a car and you want to do just the reverse, we might be able to strike a deal except for the fact that you've got shifty eyes and are likely to rip me off by passing me a lemon; hence no deal; I'm uncertain about the value of the thing I accept in exchange. The medium of exchange, which is handled often in many transactions, becomes familiar to us all and can be checked carefully for fraud, thereby reducing uncertainty in trading.

Closely related to the low-uncertainty-high-exchangeability syndrome is the ability to hold on to the medium of exchange without its deteriorating in value. It must be a good store of value; or, as soon as I accept the medium of exchange I'll try to get rid of it, lest it be worth fewer and fewer goods and services tomorrow or the day after. If I have little confidence that the medium of exchange will hold its value. I'll be reluctant to accept it in exchange; in other words, it won't be the medium of exchange for very long.

The medium of exchange also usually serves as a unit of account. In other words, the prices of all other goods are expressed in terms of, say, dollars. Without such a unit of account, you'd have to remember the exchange ratios of soap for bread, knives for shirts, and bookcases for haircuts (and haircuts for soap). The unit of account reduces the information you have to carry around in your brain—freeing that limited space for creative speculation.

So money is a good thing. It frees people from spending too much time running around bartering goods and services, and allows them to undertake other endeavors—production, relaxation, contemplation, and temptation.

It is important to emphasize that people hold the medium of exchange—money—not because it has any intrinsic value but because it can be exchanged for things to eat, drink, wear, and play with. The *value* of a unit of money is determined, therefore, by the prices of each and every thing—more accurately, the average level of all prices. If prices go up, a unit of money (a dollar) is worth less because it will buy less; if prices go down—use your imagination—a dollar is worth more because it will buy more.

The Importance of Money II:
Financial Institutions and Markets

Money also contributes to economic development and growth, by stimulating both saving and investment and facilitating transfers of funds out of the hoards of savers and into the hands of borrowers who want to undertake investment projects but do not have enough of their own money to do so. Financial markets give savers a variety of ways to lend their savings to borrowers, thereby increasing the volume of both saving and investment and encouraging economic growth.

People who save are often not the same people who can see and exploit profitable investment opportunities. In an economy without money, the only way a person can invest (buy productive equipment) is if he himself consumes less than his income (saves). Similarly, in an economy without money the only way a person can save—that is consume less than his income—is by acquiring real goods himself.

The introduction of money, however, permits separation of the act of investment from the act of saving: money makes it possible for a person to invest without first refraining from consumption (saving), and likewise makes it possible for a person to save without himself investing. People can now invest who are not fortunate enough to have their own savings.

In a monetary economy, a person simply accumulates his saving in cash (money is a store of value). Through financial markets, he can lend his surplus cash to a business firm borrowing the funds to invest in new equipment, equipment it might not have been able to buy if it did not have access to borrowed funds. Both are better off— the saver because he receives interest payments, and the business firm because it presumably would not borrow and invest the money unless it expected to earn a return over and above the interest cost. And the economy is also better off: the only way an economy can grow is by allocating part of its resources to the creation of new and better productive facilities.

In an advanced economy such as ours, this channeling of funds from savers to investors, through financial markets, reaches highly complex dimensions. A wide variety of financial instruments, such as stocks, bonds, and mortgages, are utilized as devices through which borrowers can gain access to the surplus funds of savers. Various markets specialize in trading one or the other of these financial instruments.

And financial institutions have sprung up—such as commercial banks, savings banks, savings and loan associations, credit unions, insurance companies, mutual funds, and pension funds—that act as middlemen in transferring funds from ultimate lenders to ultimate borrowers. Such financial institutions, or financial intermediaries, as they are often called, themselves borrow from saver-lenders and then turn around and lend the funds to borrower-investors. They mobilize the savings of many small savers and package them for sale to the highest bidders. In the process, again both ultimate saver-lenders and

11

ultimate borrower-investors gain: savers have the added option of acquiring bank deposits or savings and loan shares, which are less risky than stocks or bonds, and business firm borrowers can tap large sums of money from a single source.

None of this would be possible were it not for the existence of money, the one financial asset that lies at the foundation of the whole superstructure. But once we have this unique thing called money, we also have the problem of controlling it.

Uncontrolled, it may cause hyperinflation or disastrous depression, and thereby cancel its blessings. If price inflation gets out of hand, for example, money ceases to be a reliable store of value and therefore becomes a less efficient medium of exchange. People become reluctant to accept cash in payment for goods and services, and when they do accept it, they try to get rid of it as soon as possible. As we noted above, the value of money is determined by the price level of the goods money is used to purchase. The higher the prices, the more dollars one has to give up to get real goods or buy services. Inflation (rising prices) reduces the value of money. Hyperinflation (prices rising at a fast and furious pace) reduces the value of money by a lot within a short time span. Hence, people don't want to hold very much cash—they want to exchange it for goods as quickly as possible. Thus, if money breaks down as a store of value, it starts to deteriorate as a medium of exchange as well, and we start to slip back into barter. People spend more time exchanging goods and less time producing, consuming, and enjoying them. Severe depression causes different but no less serious consequences.

So once we have money, the question constantly challenges us: *How much* of it should there be?

How Large Should the Money Supply Be?

In theory, the answer is simple enough. Presumably, the supply of money affects the rate of spending, and therefore we should have enough money so that we buy, at current prices, all the goods and services the economy is able to produce. If we spend less, we will have idle capacity and idle men; if we spend more, we will wind up with higher prices but no more real goods or services. In other words, we need a money supply large enough to generate just the right amount of spending to give us a GNP that represents full employment at stable prices. More money than that would mean more spending and inflation, and less money would mean less spending and recession or depression.

In practice, unfortunately, the answer is not nearly that simple. Decisions about the appropriate level of the money supply are precisely what countercyclical monetary policy is all about. That is, monetary policy consists of varying the amount of money in the economy, presumably increasing it (or, more realistically, increasing the rate at which it is growing) during a recession, to stimulate spending; and decreasing it (or increasing it at a less than normal rate) during a boom, to inhibit spending.

But whether just changing the money supply really can influence people's *spending* in any consistent way is not that obvious. What a change in the money supply can do is alter people's *liquidity*. Money, after all, is the most liquid of all assets. A liquid asset, as mentioned above, is something that can be turned into cash—that is, sold or "liquidated"—quickly, with no loss in dollar value. Money already *is* cash. You can't get more liquid than that!

Since monetary policy alters the liquidity of the public's portfolio of total assets—including, in that balance sheet, holdings of real as well as financial assets—it should thereby lead to portfolio readjustments that involve spending decisions. An increase in the money supply implies that the public is more liquid than formerly; a decrease in the money supply implies that the public is less liquid than before. If the public had formerly been satisfied with its holdings of money relative to the rest of its assets, a change in that money supply will presumably lead to readjustments throughout the rest of its portfolio.[4]

In other words, these changes in liquidity should lead to more (or less) spending on either real assets (cars and television sets) or financial assets (stocks and bonds). If spending on real assets expands, demand for goods and services increases, and GNP is directly affected. If spending on financial assets goes up, the increased demand for stocks and bonds drives up securities prices. Higher securities prices mean lower interest rates. The fall in interest rates may induce more

[4] Of course, if monetary policy could increase the money supply while all other assets of the public remained unchanged, people would not only be more liquid but also wealthier. As we will see in Chapter 3, however, monetary policy can only alter the composition of the public's assets but cannot change its total wealth *directly*.

spending on housing and on plant and equipment (investment spending), thereby influencing GNP through that route.[5]

Underlying the effectiveness of monetary policy, therefore, is its impact on the liquidity of the public. But whether a change in the supply of liquidity actually does influence spending depends on what is happening to the demand for liquidity. If the supply of money is increased but the demand expands even more, the additional money will be held and not spent. "Easy" or "tight" money is not really a matter of increases or decreases in the money supply in an absolute sense, but rather increases or decreases relative to the demand for money. In the past decade we have had few periods in which the money supply actually decreased, yet we have had many periods of tight money because the *rate* of growth was so small that the demand for money rose faster than the supply.

If people always respond in a consistent manner to an increase in their liquidity (the proportion of money in their portfolio), the Federal Reserve will be able to gauge the impact on GNP of a change in the money supply. But if people's spending reactions vary unpredictably when there is a change in the money supply, the central bank will never know whether it should alter the money supply a little or a lot (or even at all!) to bring about a specified change in spending.

The relationship between changes in the money supply and consequent changes in spending brings us to the speed with which money is spent, its rate of turnover or velocity. When the Federal Reserve increases the money supply by $1 billion, how much of an effect will this have on people's spending, and thereby on GNP? Say we are in a recession, with GNP $20 billion below prosperity levels. Can the Fed induce a $20 billion expansion in spending by increasing the money supply by $2 billion? Or will it take a $10 billion . . . or a $15 billion . . . increase in the money supply to do the job?

---

[5] Since it will come up again and again, it is worth devoting a moment to the *inverse* relationship between the *price* of an income-earning asset and its effective *rate of interest* (or yield). For example, a long-term bond that carries a fixed interest payment of $10 a year, and costs $100, yields an annual interest rate of 10 percent. However, if the price of the bond were to rise to $200, the effective rate of interest would drop to 10/200, or 5 percent. And if the price of the security were to fall to $50, the yield would rise to 10/50, or 20 percent. Conclusion: A rise (or fall) in the price of a bond is reflected, in terms of sheer arithmetic, in an automatic change in the opposite direction in the effective rate of interest. To say the price of bonds rose or the rate of interest fell are two different ways of saying the same thing. We will return to this concept in Chapter 5.

"Frank, how did you ever find this guru?"

Drawing by D. Fradon; © 1968 The New Yorker Magazine, Inc.

Velocity: The Missing Link

Clearly, this is the key puzzle that monetary policy must solve if it is to operate effectively. After all, the central bank is not in business to change the money supply just for the sake of changing the money supply. Money is only a means to an end, and the end is the total volume of spending—which should be sufficient to give us high employment but not so great as to produce excessively rising prices.

When the Federal Reserve increases the money supply, the recipients of this additional liquidity *probably* spend some of it on goods and services, increasing GNP. The funds thereby move from the original recipients to the sellers of the goods and services. Now *they* have more money than before, and if they behave the same way as the others, they too are *likely* to spend some of it. GNP thus rises further, and at the same time the money moves on to a still different set of owners who, in turn, *may* also spend part of it, thereby increasing GNP again. Over a period of time, say a year, a multiple increase in spending and GNP could thus flow from an initial increase in the stock of money.

This relationship between the increase in GNP over a period of time, and the initial change in the money supply, is important enough to have a name: the velocity of money. Technically speaking, velocity

15

is found, after the process has ended, by dividing the cumulative increase in GNP by the initial increase in the money supply.

We similarly can compute the velocity of the *total* amount of money in the country by dividing total GNP (not just the increase in it) by the total money supply. This gives us the average number of times each dollar turns over to buy goods and services during the year. In 1978, for example, with a GNP of $2,100 billion and an average money supply of $350 billion, the velocity of money was 2,100 divided by 350, or 6 per annum. Each dollar, on the average, was spent 6 times in purchasing goods and services during 1978.

With this missing link—velocity—now in place, we can reformulate the problem of monetary policy more succinctly. The Federal Reserve controls the supply of money. Its main job is to regulate the flow of spending. The flow of spending, however, depends not only on the supply of money but also on that supply's rate of turnover, or velocity, and this the Federal Reserve does *not* have under its thumb. Since any given supply of money might be spent faster or slower— that is, velocity might rise or fall—a rather wide range of potential spending could conceivably flow from any given stock of money.

If it weren't for the complications introduced by velocity, decisions regarding the appropriate money supply would be fairly simple, and there would be little disagreement among rational people. However, complications there are, and a central problem of monetary theory is the exploration of exactly what determines the velocity of money—or, looked at another way, what determines the volume of spending flowing from a change in the supply of money. As we shall see, disagreements over the determinants and behavior of velocity underlie much of the dispute between those who favor monetary policy and those who prefer to rely on fiscal policy in stabilizing the level of economic activity.

A Preview

We now have an overall view of the role of money in economic activity. To help you keep track of where we'll be going, here is how the remainder of the book is arranged. Each of the remaining chapters of this introductory section (Part I, "The Basics") corresponds to more detailed discussions that appear later on in the book.

Chapter 2 introduces the fundamentals of commercial banks and money creation. Correspondingly, all of Part II is devoted to a more comprehensive analysis of what financial institutions do and how they work, with special emphasis on commercial banks. Similarly, Chapter

3 introduces the Federal Reserve, and Part III provides an in-depth view of Federal Reserve policy-making.

This chapter's theme of money and economic activity is carried a bit further in Chapter 4, which provides the basics of GNP analysis. Part IV is devoted to the somewhat broader subject of monetary theory. Parts V and VI continue along these lines, going into the celebrated debate between the Monetarists and the Keynesians regarding the effectiveness of monetary policy and into the impact of monetary policy on the economy as a whole and on specific sectors (like the stock market and housing).

The basis for understanding the financial system in general is set forth in Chapters 5 and 6. On that groundwork, a more detailed analysis of financial markets is presented in Part VII; here the structure of interest rates and the interrelationships among markets is given extensive treatment.

In Part VIII we look at the role of money in international finance for the first time. The balance of payments enters the picture here, as well as exchange rates and the function of gold in the world's monetary system. While we have relegated the foreign sector to a separate section, the feedbacks to domestic markets and monetary policy are important and are explicitly discussed in that section.

The book ends (Part IX) with a historical review that will help put everything into perspective. Just for good measure, we follow our historical survey with a peek into the future of money and finance.

Suggestions for Further Reading

An excellent summary of money in exchange systems is Chapter 2 of Mark J. Flannery and Dwight M. Jaffee, *The Economic Implications of an Electronic Monetary Transfer System* (Lexington, Mass.: Lexington Books, 1973). The book by Charles A. E. Goodhart, *Money, Information, and Uncertainty* (New York: Barnes & Noble, 1975) discusses the role of money with special emphasis on risk and uncertainty. Renewed focus on the foundations of money is indicated by Robert Clower's collection of essays, *Monetary Theory: Selected Readings* (New York: Penguin, 1970). His introduction is especially good.

If you want to step back a bit and view things from a broader perspective, we recommend Norman Angell, *The Story of Money* (New York: Frederick A. Stokes Co., 1929); and Paul Einzig, *Primitive Money*, 2d edition (New York: Oxford University Press, 1966). For a fascinating illustration of the need for money, and the functions it performs, read R. A. Radford, "The Economic Organization of a P.O.W. Camp," *Economica* (November 1945).

Commercial Banking and Deposit Creation

THE BIBLE BEGINS with the creation of heaven and earth. Money and banking textbooks also begin with creation—the creation of money by commercial banks. Creation *ex nihilo* is the favorite explanation in both cases. Unable to demonstrate the Biblical creation "out of nothing," we'll do the next best thing: show how banks create money out of nothing. To see how it works, let's go into the banking business ourselves.

The Business of Banking

Commercial banks, as we saw in the previous chapter, are the habitat of almost all of the country's demand deposits (checking accounts). Since demand deposits are money, that looks like an intriguing business to get involved in. First we'll have to get together enough of our friends to back us, since you need a lot of money to begin with before you can start a bank. Poor people don't open banks (at least not legally).

While we're dreaming, we might as well go all out and assume we can raise $5 million, that the various legal formalities are satisfied, and that our bank is chartered as a member of the Federal Reserve

System. For $1 million we buy a building and refurbish it like a spooky castle in Transylvania, hire six tellers and talk them into wearing monster masks (like Dracula, Frankenstein, and Ritter and Silber), and employ a sour-faced accountant who graduated from embalming school and knows more about formaldehyde than accounts receivable. One overcast and gloomy day we open our doors for business. The accountant reluctantly stops reading *Horror Comics* long enough to show us the bank's balance sheet on opening morning:

Assets		Liabilities and Net Worth	
Cash	$4,000,000	Net Worth	$5,000,000
Building, etc.	1,000,000		

This looks nice, but it could be better. Too much cash. Doesn't earn any interest. So we immediately take three-quarters of the cash and buy government bonds with it. The T-account, showing the *changes* that occur in our balance sheet, looks like this:

A		L & NW
Cash	−$3,000,000	
Government bonds	+ 3,000,000	

Next, for purposes that will become clear shortly, we take another $900,000 and ship it to our regional Federal Reserve Bank, to open up a deposit in our bank's name:

A		L & NW
Cash	−$900,000	
Deposit in Fed	+ 900,000	

During the course of the first few days, we gleefully welcome long lines of new depositors who open up accounts with us by depositing $2 million worth of checks drawn on *other* banks—where they are closing out their accounts, because they like our ambience better. Our T-account for these deposits is as follows:

A		L & NW	
Cash items in process of collection	+$2,000,000	Demand deposits	+$2,000,000

A demand deposit in a bank is an asset for the depositor. It is part of his wealth. For the bank, however, it is a *liability,* a debt, because we are obligated to pay it—indeed, to pay it *on demand*. A demand deposit must be paid any time the depositor wishes, either by handing out currency across the counter or by transferring the funds to someone else upon the depositor's order. That is precisely what a

19

*"Come right in. What makes you think we're not a member
of the Federal Reserve System?"*

check is: A depositor's order to a bank to transfer his funds to whoever
is named on the check, or to whoever has endorsed it on the back.

We now have $2 million of checks drawn on other banks that
our new customers have deposited with us. We have to "collect" these
checks—so far they are just "cash items in process of collection." If
we had the time, we could take each check to the bank on which it
is drawn, ask for currency over the counter, and then haul it back
to our own bank. Since this would get tedious if we had to do it every
day, what we do instead is what all the other banks do—rely on the
Federal Reserve to help us in the check collection process. Federal
Reserve Banks play a pivotal role in collecting checks, so vital that we
must disgress a moment to see how they do it.

There are twelve Federal Reserve Banks located around the
country—in New York, Atlanta, Dallas, Minneapolis, San Francisco,
and so on. Every commercial member bank is affiliated with one of
them. The Federal Reserve Banks themselves have little direct contact
with the public; mostly they deal with the government and with com-

20

mercial banks. Through facilities provided by them, however, checks are efficiently collected and funds transferred around the country. The primary collection vehicle is the deposit that each member bank maintains with its regional Federal Reserve Bank, which is one reason we deposited $900,000 in our Federal Reserve Bank two T-accounts back.

Let's see how the collection process works. We take the $2 million worth of checks our new customers have deposited, checks drawn on other banks, and ship the whole batch of them to the Federal Reserve Bank. The Fed credits us with these checks by increasing our "deposit in the Fed" by that amount. At the same time, it *deducts* $2 million from the "deposits in the Fed" of the banks on which the checks were drawn. It then sends these checks to the appropriate banks, with a slip notifying them of the deduction, and the banks in turn deduct the proper amounts from their depositors' accounts. The T-accounts of the whole check collection process look like this, with the arrows showing the direction in which the checks move:

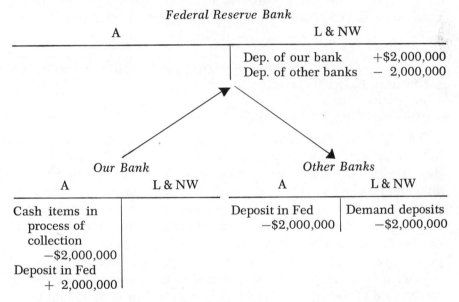

We can summarize this collection process in a few words: When a bank receives a check drawn on another bank, it gains deposits in the Fed equal to the amount of the check. Conversely, the bank on which the check was drawn loses deposits in the Fed of the same amount.[1] We will see soon that deposits in the Fed are part of a bank's *reserves*. We can rephrase the above into an important banking prin-

---

[1] Notice that the deposits of member banks in the Federal Reserve Bank are *liabilities* of the Federal Reserve Bank (although assets of the commercial banks), just as deposits of the public in a commercial bank are liabilities of the bank (although assets of the depositors).

ciple: *When a bank receives a check drawn on another bank, it gains reserves equal to the amount of the check. Conversely, the bank on which the check was drawn loses reserves of the same amount.*

Two minor complications. One: what if one of the commercial banks involved is not a member of the Federal Reserve System, and thus doesn't have to keep a deposit in the Fed? No problem. Some nonmember banks hold such a deposit anyway, even though they are not required to, just for convenience in clearing checks; those that don't have such a deposit clear through arrangements with other banks that do. Two: what if the two commercial banks involved are in different Federal Reserve Districts, so they have deposits in two *different* Federal Reserve Banks? Again no problem. The Federal Reserve has its own Inter-District Settlement Fund, where the twelve Federal Reserve Banks all hold accounts, and they settle up in such cases by transferring balances among themselves on the books of the Inter-District Settlement Fund.

So where do we stand now? Let's take a look at our bank's balance sheet, after all the above transactions have been incorporated into it:

A		L & NW	
Cash	$ 100,000	Demand deposits	$2,000,000
Deposit in Fed	2,900,000	Net worth	5,000,000
Government bonds	3,000,000		
Building, etc.	1,000,000		

Looking at this balance sheet reminds us that it is time to bring into the picture the fact that commercial banks have to hold part of their assets in the form of *reserves*. Member banks like ours are required to hold reserves—*in the form of either cash or deposits in the Fed*—as specified by the Board of Governors of the Federal Reserve.

In particular, the Fed's regulations require that member banks must hold cash and/or deposits in the Fed at least equal to a designated percentage of their demand deposit liabilities—7 percent of demand deposits on the first $2 million of deposits, 9½ percent on from $2 to $10 million of deposits, 11¾ percent on from $10 to $100 million of deposits, 12¾ percent on from $100 to $400 million of deposits, and 16¼ percent on all additional demand deposits. These figures can be changed by the Federal Reserve without getting the approval of Congress, provided the required percentages stay between 7 and 22 percent.

How does our bank stand with respect to reserves? To simplify matters, let's assume from here on that all banks, ours included, have to hold reserves equal to a flat 10 percent of demand deposits, regardless of how much demand deposits they have. According to actual regulations, we should hold reserves of only 7 percent, since we haven't exceeded the $2 million deposit level yet; but let's assume, for illustrative purposes, that instead of a sliding scale for reserve requirements it is simply 10 percent for all banks.

We *have* reserves—cash and/or deposits in the Fed—of $3 million. With demand deposits of $2 million, we *need* reserves equal to 10 percent of that figure, or $200,000, to satisfy our legal obligation. Thus we have *excess* reserves of $2.8 million. That simple calculation, computing the amount of a bank's excess reserves, is crucially important in the banking business.

What should we do now? Unfortunately, with this balance sheet we are not too profitable. We have a lot of excess reserves that are earning no interest, and not enough earning assets. All we have in the way of interest-bearing assets is the $3 million of government bonds we bought practically before we opened our doors. Banks make profits mostly by making loans. Surely we can hustle up some good loans—preferably to people who don't need the money, because they are obviously the ones who deserve it most (and are most likely to pay us back).

Let's assume we can find enough creditworthy borrowers who want to take out loans. Then a big question faces us: *How much can we safely lend?*

Deposit Expansion: The Single Bank

To answer the question of how much we can safely lend, we need to know two things: (1) how much excess reserves we have, and (2) what happens when we make a loan. We already know how much excess reserves we have—$2.8 million. So let's take a moment to examine what happens when we make a loan.

When a bank lends, the borrower does not ordinarily take the proceeds in hundred dollar bills; he or she takes a brand-new checking account instead. On the bank's balance sheet, loans (an asset) and demand deposits (a liability) both rise. A bank *creates* a demand deposit when it lends. In effect, since demand deposits are money, banks create money.

How much, then, can we lend? Since the only limit on our creation of demand deposits appears to be the requirement that we have a 10 percent reserve, a superficial answer would be that we can lend—and create demand deposits—up to a limit of ten times our excess reserves. We have excess reserves of $2.8 million, so why not lend ten times that, or $28 million? If we did, here is what would happen:[2]

A		L & NW	
Loans	+$28,000,000	Demand deposits	+$28,000,000

And our new balance sheet would look like this:

A			L & NW	
Reserves { Cash	$	100,000	Demand deposits	$30,000,000
Deposit in Fed		2,900,000	Net worth	5,000,000
Government bonds		3,000,000		
Loans		28,000,000		
Building, etc.		1,000,000		

We now have some good news and some bad news. First the good news: We have a fairly large amount of demand deposit liabilities—$30 million—and our reserves, at $3 million, are legally sufficient to support them. It appears we have found a veritable gold mine. In business hardly a month, only a $5 million investment, and here we are collecting the interest on $3 million of government bonds *and* $28 million of loans.

But wait a minute, because here comes the bad news: We haven't really looked into what happens *after* a borrower takes out a loan. Most borrowers don't take out loans, and pay interest on them, just to leave the funds sitting there. They want to *spend* the money. (Gulp!) And when they do, they'll write checks on those brand new demand deposits, the checks will probably be deposited in *other* banks by their recipients, and when they clear through the Federal Reserve we'll *lose reserves*. (Remember that a bank on which a check is drawn loses reserves equal to the amount of the check.) Thus, for our bank:

A		L & NW	
Deposit in Fed	−$28,000,000	Demand deposits	−$28,000,000

If our deposits in the Fed are only $2.9 million to begin with, we can hardly stand by calmly while they fall by $28 *million*. We'll wind up in jail instead of on the Riviera. Something has clearly gone very wrong. What has gone wrong, obviously, is that we miscalculated our lending limit, the amount we could safely lend—"safely" meaning without endangering our legal reserve position.

What, then, is our safe lending limit? It is the amount of reserves we can afford to lose, and we already know what that is: our *excess* reserves. *A single commercial bank can lend up to the amount of its*

---

[2] Actually, a bank would typically "discount" the loan—that is, deduct the interest in advance, giving the borrowers somewhat less than $28 million. For the sake of convenience, let's ignore this detail.

excess reserves, and no more. If it tries to lend more, it will find itself with inadequate reserves as soon as the borrowers spend the proceeds of the loans and the checks are collected through the Federal Reserve's check collection facilities.

So let's start over again. Our excess reserves are $2.8 million. If we lend that amount, our balance sheet entry is:

A		L & NW	
Loans	+$2,800,000	Demand deposits	+$2,800,000

When the borrowers spend the funds, assuming the checks are deposited in other banks, we have:

A		L & NW	
Deposit in Fed	−$2,800,000	Demand deposits	−$2,800,000

Which leaves our balance sheet as follows:

A			L & NW	
Reserves { Cash	$	100,000	Demand deposits	$2,000,000
Deposit in Fed		100,000	Net worth	5,000,000
Government bonds		3,000,000		
Loans		2,800,000		
Building, etc.		1,000,000		

Now, after all checks have cleared, we end up with deposits of $2 million and reserves of $200,000, which is right on the dot—our reserves equal one-tenth of our deposits. But notice that we got there by shrinking our reserves, *not* by blowing up our deposits (as in the previous disastrous example). We shrank our reserves by lending an amount equal to the excess, which resulted in an equivalent reduction in our reserves in the ordinary course of events.[3]

Notice also that the purchase of securities would have the same effect on reserves as lending, except it would probably occur more rapidly. If we bought securities for the bank, we would generally not open a deposit account for the seller, but simply pay him with a check drawn on the bank (payable via our account at the Fed). As soon as the check cleared, our reserves would fall by that amount.

The conclusion of this section is worth emphasizing: A single

[3] Calculation of excess reserves to estimate our lending ability should always be made *prior* to extending new loans, without including the reserves needed to support the new loan-created deposits. For example, after we made the $2.8 million of loans noted above, demand deposits went up by the same amount, so that required reserves rose by $280,000. But that $280,000 increase in required reserves does not affect our lending ability, because so long as those $2.8 million of deposits are there, our reserves are more than ample. It is not until those loan-created deposits disappear—when the borrowers write checks on their new deposits—that our reserves will drop, as the checks are collected in favor of other banks through the Federal Reserve. By that time, however, we won't need reserves against those deposits, since they will no longer be on our books.

commercial bank cannot safely lend (or buy securities) in an amount greater than its excess reserves, as calculated *before* it makes the loan. But it *can* lend or buy securities up to the amount of its excess reserves without endangering its legal reserve position.

The individual bank can therefore create money (demand deposits), but only if it has excess reserves to begin with. As soon as it has created this money—in our case, $2.8 million—it *loses* it to another bank when the money is spent. This is the key to the difference between the ability of a single bank to create money as compared with the banking system as a whole.

Deposit Expansion: The Banking System

When we loaned our $2.8 million and created demand deposits of that amount for the borrowers, they soon spent the funds, and we lost both the newly created deposits and reserves of a like amount. That ended *our* ability to lend. But in the check-clearing process, some other banks *gained* $2.8 million of deposits and reserves, and those other banks can expand *their* lending, for now *they* have excess reserves.

Let's simplify our calculations at this point and assume that instead of having excess reserves of $2.8 million, and lending that amount, we had excess reserves of only $1,000, and had loaned that. Just to make the numbers easier to work with. When the checks cleared, some other banks would have gained $1,000 of deposits and reserves, and those other banks could now continue the process, for they now have excess reserves. If the entire $1,000 were deposited in one bank (Bank B), that Bank's T-account would look like this:

Bank B

A		L & NW	
Deposit in Fed	+$1,000	Demand deposits	+$1,000

Bank B can now extend credit and create additional demand deposits. Assuming it were all loaned up (zero excess reserves) before it received this deposit, how much could Bank B lend? Less than we did, because its excess reserves are not $1,000 but only $900—it has new reserves of $1,000, but it needs $100 additional as reserves against the $1,000 deposit.

If Bank B does indeed make a $900 loan, we should start to sense what is going to happen: Its loans and deposits will both rise by $900, and when the borrowers spend the funds its *reserves* and deposits will both fall by the same amount. Net result: Its demand deposits will drop back to $1,000, its reserves to $100, and its lending (and money-creating) ability will be exhausted.

However, when Bank B's borrowers spend their $900, giving checks to people who deposit them in other banks (such as Bank C), the very clearing process that takes reserves and deposits away from Bank B transfers them *to* Bank C:

Bank C

A		L & NW	
Deposit in Fed	+$900	Demand deposits	+$900

Now Bank C can carry the torch. It can lend, and create new demand deposits, up to the amount of *its* excess reserves, which are $810. As the process is repeated, Bank D can lend $729 (creating that much additional demand deposits), Bank E can lend $656.10, Bank F $590.49, and so on. Because the reserve requirement is 10 percent, each bank in the sequence gets excess reserves, lends, and creates new demand deposits equal to 90 percent of the preceding one. If we add $1,000 + $900 + $810 + $729 + $656.10 + . . ., the summation of the series approaches $10,000.

When expansion has approached its $10,000 limit, the banking *system* will have demand deposits that are a multiple of its reserves —demand deposits will be $10,000 on the liabilities side and reserves $1,000 on the asset side for all banks taken together. (At the same time, of course, banks will also have $9,000 in other assets—loans in our example.) For the banking system, this final stage is reached not by shrinking reserves, as in the case of a single bank, but by blowing up deposits. The key: While each individual commercial bank loses reserves after it lends—in the check-clearing process—some bank always gains the reserves another bank loses, so reserves for the entire banking system do not change. They just get transferred from bank to bank. However, as banks lend more and more, demand deposit liabilities grow, thereby reducing *excess* reserves even though the total reserves of the system do not change. This continuous decline in excess reserves eventually sets a limit on further expansion. (Although we promised creation *ex nihilo*, we didn't say it could go on forever.)

In more general terms, how much can the banking system expand demand deposits? While a single commercial bank can lend (and create demand deposits) only up to the amount of its excess reserves, the banking *system* can create demand deposits up to a *multiple* of an original injection of excess reserves.

The particular expansion multiple for the banking system depends on the prevailing required reserve ratio. In our example, with a reserve requirement of $1/10$, the multiple is ten (an original increase of $1,000 in excess reserves can lend to an eventual $10,000 increase in demand deposits). If the reserve requirement were $1/5$, the multiple would be five (an original increase of $1,000 in excess reserves could lead to a potential $5,000 increase in demand deposits). In general, *the multiple is always the reciprocal of the reserve requirement ratio*. In brief, for the entire banking system:

$$\text{original excess reserves} \times \frac{1}{\text{reserve ratio}} = \frac{\text{potential change in demand}}{\text{deposits}}$$

We can derive this formula more formally. We have been assuming that each bank lends out all of its excess reserves. The process of deposit expansion can continue until all excess reserves become required reserves because of deposit growth; then no more deposit expansion can take place. At that point, total reserves (R) will equal the required reserve ratio on demand deposits (r_{dd}) times total demand deposits (DD). That is:

$$R = r_{dd} \times DD$$

Dividing both sides of the equation by r_{dd} (which is a legal operation even in the banking business) produces:

$$\frac{R}{r_{dd}} = \frac{r_{dd} \times DD}{r_{dd}}$$

or

$$R \times \frac{1}{r_{dd}} = DD$$

Using the familiar delta sign to denote change-in, we have:

$$\Delta R \times \frac{1}{r_{dd}} = \Delta DD$$

where the change in reserves initially produces excess reserves in that amount until demand deposits are created in sufficient magnitude by the banks to put all the reserves in the required category.[4]

[4] An even more formal derivation of the relationship between changes in reserves and changes in deposits uses the formula for the sum of the (geometric) series discussed above in the text. In particular, the change in demand deposits due to an increase in reserves can be expressed as follows:

$$\Delta DD = \Delta R \left[1 + (1 - r_{dd}) + (1 - r_{dd})^2 + \ldots + (1 - r_{dd})^n \right]$$

There is a formula (white and bubbly) which gives the sum of the geometric progression within the brackets. As n gets infinitely large, the formula becomes:

$$\frac{1}{1 - (1 - r_{dd})} = \frac{1}{r_{dd}}$$

or, believe it or not:

$$\Delta DD = \Delta R \times \frac{1}{r_{dd}}$$

Deposit Contraction

A change in demand deposits can, of course, be down as well as up, negative as well as positive. If we start with a *deficiency* in reserves in the formula, a negative excess, the potential change in demand deposits is negative rather than positive. Instead of money being *created* by banks when they lend or buy securities, money is *destroyed* as bank loans are repaid or securities sold.

When someone repays a bank loan, the bank has less loans outstanding and at the same time deducts the amount repaid from the borrower's demand deposit balance. There are fewer demand deposits in existence; money has disappeared. Similarly, if a bank sells a bond to one of its own depositors, it takes payment by reducing the depositor's checking account balance. If it sells a bond to a depositor in another bank, the other bank winds up with fewer demand deposit liabilities.

The potential multiple contraction in demand deposits follows the same principles discussed above for the potential expansion of demand deposits, with one exception: the entire downward multiple change in demand deposits could conceivably take place in one single bank.

Say that a bank has a $1,000 reserve deficiency. It is then faced with two stark alternatives: It must either (a) increase its reserves by $1,000 or (b) decrease its demand deposits by ten times $1,000, or $10,000 (assuming a reserve requirement of 10 percent).

Let's take the second alternative first. The bank could decrease its demand deposits by the entire $10,000 by demanding repayment of that many loans, or by selling that many securities to its own depositors. Loans (or bonds) would drop by $10,000 on the asset side, demand deposits would drop by the same amount on the liabilities side, and the reserve deficiency would be eliminated. In this case, the single bank alone bears the entire multiple decrease in the money supply.

It is more likely that the bank will choose the first option, increasing its reserves by $1,000. One way it could go about this is by borrowing $1,000 in reserves from the Federal Reserve, an alternative we will discuss more fully in Chapters 3 and 13. Another way is by selling $1,000 of bonds on the open market, making the reasonable assumption that they will be bought by depositors in other banks (our bank being just a little fish in a veritable sea of banks). After the checks are cleared, its deposits in the Fed will be $1,000 higher and its reserves will be adequate once again.

But the reserves gained by Bank A will be another bank's loss.

Some other bank—the bank where the purchaser of the bond kept his account—has lost $1,000 of deposits and $1,000 of reserves. Assuming that this second bank, Bank B, had precisely adequate reserves before this transaction, it now has a $900 reserve deficiency. It has lost $1,000 of reserves, but its requirements are $100 lower because it has also lost $1,000 of demand deposits, so its deficiency is only $900.

Bank B will now have no choice but to (a) get $900 in additional reserves, or (b) reduce its demand deposits by ten times $900, or $9,000. If it sells $900 of bonds to depositors in other banks, it gets its reserves, but in doing so it puts the other banks $810 in the hole. Thus the multiple contraction process continues very much like the multiple expansion process ($1,000 + $900 + $810 + $729 + $656.10 + . . .), and the summation of the series again approaches $10,000. At each stage, the bank that sells securities gains reserves, but at the expense of other banks, since the buyers of the bonds pay by checks that are cleared via the transfer of reserves on the books of the Federal Reserve Banks. Reserve deficiencies are shuffled from bank to bank, just as in the expansion process reserve excesses are shuffled from one bank to another.

There is a difference, however. When banks get *excess* reserves, they *may* lend more and increase the money supply. When they have *deficient* reserves, they *must* reduce their demand deposits.

Control over bank reserves thus gives the Federal Reserve considerable power over the money supply. If the Fed can inject excess reserves into the banking system, it can *permit* commercial banks to expand the money supply by a multiple of the injection. If it can impose a deficit reserve position on the banking system, it can *force* a multiple reduction in the money supply.

We now turn to the Fed's tricks of the trade. After seeing how the Fed operates, we will return to bank deposit creation in an Appendix to the following chapter, adding to the picture a few complicating elements we have so far ignored in the interest of simplicity.

Suggestions for Further Reading

In case you feel you don't have a firm grasp of the basic principles underlying deposit expansion and contraction, try pp. 2–13 in Dorothy M. Nichols's excellent pamphlet, *Modern Money Mechanics: A Workbook on Deposits, Currency, and Bank Reserves*, which is available free from the Federal Reserve Bank of Chicago (P. O. Box 834, Chicago, Illinois, 60690).

Chapter 3

A Bird's-Eye View of the Federal Reserve

THE FEDERAL RESERVE—twelve regional Federal Reserve Banks and a Board of Governors in Washington—possesses ultimate control over bank lending and the money supply. It exercises this authority through its power to alter bank reserves, whether the banks like it or not. The Fed manipulates bank reserves in several different ways, none of which—contrary to what you might have heard—are particularly dramatic.

It is *not* true, for instance, that the Federal Reserve has experienced safecrackers scattered throughout the United States, whose job it is to break into vaults in the dead of night and remove stacks of hundred-dollar bills when the Fed wants to reduce reserves, or add stacks of the same when it wants to increase them. That is simply not the way the Federal Reserve operates. Besides, it would foul up everybody's bookkeeping, and since the whole monetary system is based on bookkeeping, as you're starting to see, it would be self-defeating.

Neither is it true that the Fed places self-destruct tape recordings in secret hiding places, instructing undercover agents to undertake perilous missions designed to confuse bank presidents so that they think they have more (or less) excess reserves than they actually have. The Federal Reserve has denied these rumors as total fabrications.

The central bank's methods are more prosaic (at least so far as we know). It alters bank excess reserves either by changing reserve *requirements* relative to deposits, or by changing the actual *amount* of reserves the banks hold. In this chapter we will take a first look at these methods, and then go into them in greater depth in Part III.

Reserve Requirements

Within boundaries established by Congress, the Federal Reserve's Board of Governors can specify the reserve requirements that member banks must hold against deposits. Congressional limits are that reserves must be between 7 and 22 percent of demand deposits, and between 3 and 10 percent of time and savings deposits. Such reserves, as we have seen, must be held in the form of vault cash and/or deposits in a regional Federal Reserve Bank.

Lowering the demand deposit reserve requirement—for example, from 20 to 10 percent—does two things. First, it instantly and automatically increases banks' excess reserves, since less reserves are now required against any given volume of demand deposits. A bank with demand deposits of $1,000 and reserves of $200 would be all loaned up were the reserve requirement 20 percent; lowering it to 10 percent suddenly provides $100 of excess reserves. More excess reserves, of course, enable banks to make more loans, buy more securities, and expand demand deposits.

In addition, lowering the required reserve ratio also increases the demand deposit expansion *multiplier* for the entire banking system, since, as we saw in Chapter 2, the multiplier is, in fact, the reciprocal of the required reserve ratio. The smaller the ratio, the larger its reciprocal. Thus a decrease from 20 percent to 10 percent would raise the deposit expansion multiplier from five to ten.

Raising reserve requirements—for example, from 10 to 20 percent—would have the opposite effects. It would create reserve deficiencies, or at least reduce excesses, *and* lower the potential for multiple expansion. Putting banks into a deficit reserve position would *force* them to call in loans and sell securities, bringing about a reduction in demand deposits, while smaller excesses would at least restrain lending and deposit creation.

The Federal Reserve has not used its authority to change reserve requirements very frequently, partly because the effects are so powerful. It is difficult to make fine adjustments with so blunt an instrument.

Another reason it has been employed sparingly, perhaps even more important, is that a change in the Fed's reserve requirements affects only banks that are members of the Federal Reserve System. Thus, raising reserve requirements is somewhat inequitable in its impact; it penalizes member banks but does not touch nonmembers. About 70 percent of all bank deposits in the country are in member banks. Nevertheless, if the Fed's reserve requirements were to become too burdensome, many banks that are now members might decide to drop out and become nonmembers, which could impair the Federal Reserve's effectiveness.[1]

Discounting and the Discount Rate

The Federal Reserve may also alter bank excess reserves by changing the actual amount of reserves banks hold. One way this is accomplished is through the discount mechanism—which amounts to lending reserves, temporarily, to commercial banks. The Fed charges an interest rate, known as the discount rate, on such loans. In other words, member banks faced with reserve deficits can temporarily borrow reserves from their regional Federal Reserve Bank at a price (the discount rate).

Say that a bank in Cucamonga, California, has deficient reserves of $1,000 (it needs $1,000 more reserves than it has). Rather than take the drastic step of calling in loans, and preferring not to sell securities, it can borrow the reserves it needs from the Federal Reserve Bank of San Francisco at the prevailing discount rate. If it did so, the T-accounts would look like this:

Federal Reserve Bank

A		L & NW	
Loan to Cucamonga Bank	+$1,000	Deposit of Cucamonga Bank	+$1,000

Cucamonga Commercial Bank

A		L & NW	
Deposit in Fed	+$1,000	Due to Fed	+$1,000

[1] In recent years many banks have been leaving the System. We will discuss the issue of commercial bank membership in the Federal Reserve System more fully in Chapter 12. Nonmember banks must also satisfy legal reserve requirements, as set by the state in which the bank is chartered, but these are typically less onerous than the Fed's reserve requirements.

When a businessman borrows from a commercial bank, he receives a brand new deposit at the bank. A commercial bank is in the same position relative to the Federal Reserve: when it borrows from its friendly neighborhood Federal Reserve Bank, it receives a brand new deposit at the Fed which augments its legal reserves.[2] The ability to borrow these reserves—to discount from the Fed—means that the Cucamonga bank does not have to call in loans or sell securities, and the money supply can remain unchanged.

A bank might also be more aggressive and borrow enough reserves to move into an *excess* reserve position, to make additional loans and thereby increase the money supply. The Fed generally frowns on such behavior, and tries to discourage it by establishing ground rules as to when it is proper for banks to utilize the discount facility. In general, it is OK if a bank does so only once in a while in order to adjust a deficit reserve position. It is not OK if a bank does so frequently, and in order to *expand* its earning assets.

More important, the Federal Reserve tries to influence the willingness of member banks to borrow reserves by manipulating the interest rate it charges on such loans (the discount rate). A lower discount rate will make the borrowing of reserves more attractive to commercial banks, and a higher discount rate will make it less attractive.

Two shortcomings of the discount mechanism for injecting or withdrawing reserves are: (1) it only applies to member banks, since under ordinary circumstances nonmember banks cannot use it; and (2) the initiative as to whether or not to borrow from the Fed rests not with the Fed but with the member banks.

Member banks will want to borrow reserves only when they need them. If they already have ample reserves, there is no reason for them to borrow more no matter how low the discount rate. During the 1930s and 1940s, for example, when banks generally had substantial excess reserves, the discount mechanism rusted from disuse, and changes in the discount rate became irrelevant. In recent decades, however, excess reserves have declined and discounting has once again become common, so that changes in the discount rate are more important as a tool of Federal Reserve policy. Nevertheless, since the initiative still rests with the commercial banks rather than the Fed, the discount process is not a very efficient instrument for the Federal Reserve to use in injecting or withdrawing reserves when *it* wishes to do so.

---

[2] Notice again that the Cucamonga bank's deposit in the Fed is an asset of the Cucamonga bank, but a liability of the Fed (just as your deposit in a local bank is your asset but the bank's liability).

Open Market Operations

The most important way the Federal Reserve alters the actual amount of reserves the banks hold is not by discounting, but by frequent buying and selling of government securities—better known as open market operations. Undertaken at its own initiative, likely to affect nonmember as well as member banks, usable in small or large doses and therefore capable of fine tuning, open market operations are the mainstay of Federal Reserve policy.

About $500 billion worth of marketable government securities are outstanding. They are held as investments by the public—by individuals, corporations, financial institutions, and so on. About $115 billion are held by the Federal Reserve System. These government securities came into being when the United States Treasury had to borrow to finance past budget deficits. Some are long-term bonds, running fifteen or twenty years until maturity, and others are shorter term, all the way down to government securities called Treasury bills that are issued for only a few months. The existence of this pool of widely held marketable securities, with many potential buyers and sellers, offers an ideal vehicle through which the Federal Reserve can affect bank reserves. Federal Reserve purchases of government securities increase bank reserves, and Federal Reserve sales decrease them. Here's how it works:

When the Federal Reserve *buys* $1,000 of government securities, much as you might buy a stock or a bond on one of the stock exchanges, it pays with a check drawn on itself. *If the Fed buys the securities directly from a commercial bank*—say from a bank in Succasunna, N.J.—the Succasunna bank sends the Fed's check to its regional Federal Reserve Bank (the Federal Reserve Bank of Philadelphia), and has its deposit at the Fed—its reserves—increased by $1,000. Its excess reserves rise by the full amount of the transaction, and with more excess reserves it can make more loans and increase its demand deposits.

The T-accounts for a Federal Reserve purchase of government securities directly from a commercial bank are:

Federal Reserve

A		L & NW	
Govt. securities	+$1,000	Deposit of Succasunna Bank	+$1,000

Succasunna Commercial Bank

A		L & NW	
Deposit in Fed	+$1,000		
Govt. securities	− 1,000		

But what the central bank giveth, the central bank can taketh away. When the Federal Reserve *sells* government securities out of its portfolio, it *gets paid* for them, and everything is completely reversed. Say the Fed sells $1,000 of government securities directly to our friendly Succasunna bank—the Succasunna bank now has gained $1,000 worth of securities, which is good, but it has to pay for them, which is bad. The Fed takes payment by deducting that sum from the Succasunna bank's deposit at the Federal Reserve, thus diminishing its reserves. If you were to draw up the T-accounts for the transaction, everything would be exactly the same as the T-accounts above, except that every plus sign would become a minus and every minus sign a plus. The Succasunna bank's excess reserves fall by the full amount of the transaction; if it had no excess reserves, now it has a $1,000 reserve deficiency.

Note that the Federal Reserve could achieve the same ends— that is, change bank reserves—by buying or selling any asset, such as record albums or any type of bond or stock. The reason for limiting its open market operations to the purchase and sale of government securities is quite obvious: Who would determine whether the Federal Reserve should buy Bob Dylan or Barry Manilow? General Motors stock or IBM? The Federal Reserve is smart enough, at least in this respect, to keep its hands out of the public hair.

Of course, when the Federal Reserve buys (or sells) government securities, it has no assurance that a commercial bank will be the other party to the transaction. But it doesn't really matter very much whether the securities the Fed buys are being sold by a commercial bank or by someone else, nor is it especially important whether the securities the Fed sells are ultimately bought by a commercial bank or by someone else. In either case, when the Fed buys, bank reserves go up, and when the Fed sells, bank reserves go down.

For example, *suppose that when the Fed bought $1,000 of government securities, the seller of the securities wasn't the Succasunna bank but an insurance company in Mishawaka, Indiana.* It wouldn't matter if the insurance company were in Chillicothe, Ohio, Waxahachie, Texas, Tallahatchie, Mississippi, or even Punxsutawney, Pennsylvania. However, *this* insurance company happens to be in Mishawaka, Indiana. In any case, when the Fed buys it still pays for the securities with a check drawn on itself. When the insurance company deposits the $1,000 check in its local commercial bank, the Mishawaka bank now has the Federal Reserve's check (an asset), and it gives the insurance company a demand deposit (a liability to the bank, although an asset of the insurance company). In turn, the Mishawaka bank sends the check to its regional Federal Reserve Bank (the Federal Reserve Bank of Chicago), and receives in exchange a $1,000 addition to its reserves.[3]

The T-account for the insurance company shows that it now has $1,000 less in government securities, and $1,000 more in its demand deposit account at its local commercial bank. For the Federal Reserve and the Mishawaka bank, the T-accounts for such a Federal Reserve purchase look like this:

Federal Reserve

A		L & NW	
Govt. securities	+$1,000	Deposit of Mishawaka Bank	+$1,000

Mishawaka Commercial Bank

A		L & NW	
Deposit in Fed	+$1,000	Demand deposit of Ins. Co.	+$1,000

Notice that in this case the commercial bank's excess reserves go up, but not by the full amount of the transaction. The bank has $1,000 more of reserves, but it needs $100 more (assuming a 10 percent reserve requirement) because its deposits have gone up by $1,000; thus its *excess* reserves have risen by $900. However, the money supply has *already* risen by $1,000, so the ultimate potential effect on the money supply is the same regardless of who the Fed buys its securities from:

If the Fed buys $1,000 of government securities directly from commercial banks, bank excess reserves rise by the full $1,000 and the banking system can then create $10,000 of new money (assuming a 10 percent reserve requirement);

If the Fed buys from nonbanks, bank excess reserves rise by only $900 and the banking system can create $9,000 of new money—but the money supply has already gone up by $1,000, and $9,000 + $1,000 also equal $10,000. So, in the end, the ultimate effect on the money supply of either type of open market purchase turns out to be the same.[4]

[3] Speaking of place names reminds us of Zzyzx Road (believe it or not), which you will encounter on Interstate 15 between Barstow and Las Vegas.

[4] Similarly, were the Fed to *sell* securities to an insurance company, everything would be exactly the same as the T-accounts immediately above, except the signs would be reversed. Our Mishawaka bank would find its excess reserves diminished by $900 (not by $1,000, because although its reserves would be $1,000 lower, its deposit liabilities would also be that much lower). When the Fed sells securities directly to commercial banks, on the other hand, bank excess reserves fall by the full amount of the sale. However, in both cases the ultimate potential effect on the money supply is the same.

Commercial banks are unable to do anything to offset these measures. If the Fed wants to reduce bank reserves by open market sales, there is nothing the banks can do about it. By lowering its selling price, the Fed can always unearth a buyer. Since it is not in business to make a profit, the Fed is free to alter its selling price as it wishes. And while any single commercial bank can replenish its own reserves by selling securities to other banks—or to individuals who keep their accounts in other banks—the reserves of the other banks will then decline. Reserves replenished by one bank are lost by others. Total bank reserves must fall by the value of the securities sold by the Federal Reserve.

As suggested in Chapter 1 (see footnote 4 in that chapter), it should now be clear why a contraction or expansion in the money supply via pure monetary policy does not change the total size of the public's portfolio (its wealth) directly. The public gives up an asset, or incurs a liability, as part of the very process through which currency or demand deposits rise; the reverse occurs when demand deposits decline. For example, if the money supply is increased by Federal Reserve open market purchases of securities, the increased demand deposit acquired by the public is offset by the reduction in its holdings of government securities (they were purchased by the Federal Reserve). In any subsequent expansion of demand deposits by bank lending or security purchases, the public acquires an asset (demand deposits) but either creates a liability against itself in the form of a bank loan or sells to the bank an asset of equal value, such as a government bond.

A Step Back

It's time to step back a moment to see just where we are. We've seen that the central bank can affect the ability of commercial banks to lend and buy securities, and thereby to create (or destroy) money. It can do this by changing bank required reserve ratios, or by changing the actual amount of bank reserves—by altering the discount rate and, most importantly, by open market operations. When banks are put in a deficit reserve position, they *must* take steps to reduce their demand deposit liabilities; when banks are given excess reserves, on the other hand, they *may* lend more, buy more securities, and increase the money supply—but the Fed cannot compel them to do so.

Why does the Fed engage in all these shenanigans? Because the money supply is important. Changes in the money supply alter people's liquidity and probably affect their spending, and spending helps determine whether we're going to have recession or inflation (or both!). In addition, by changing the ability and eagerness of banks to lend and buy securities, the Fed affects the terms on which banks lend— the interest rate. And this also influences spending by consumers and business firms: higher interest rates discourage borrowing and spending, while lower rates do the opposite.

Schematically, the Federal Reserve's game plan, at least as a first approximation, looks something like Chart 1.

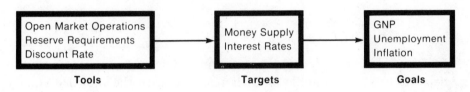

CHART 1 / The Fed's Game Plan

The job of the Federal Reserve looks rather simple. In fact, it is far more complex than it appears, as we shall see in Part III. The Appendix to this chapter gives an idea of some of the complications involved; you may want to read it now or perhaps wait until you reach Part III. In either case, don't ignore the details. It helps to know about trees to get through the forest.

Appendix

The Fed and the Money Supply: Three Complications

In Chapter 2 we discussed how commercial banks create demand deposits in some multiple of their reserves, with the multiple equal to the reciprocal of the required reserve ratio. In Chapter 3 we have just seen that the Fed controls both the required reserve ratio *and* the volume of bank reserves. Under the circumstances, it would seem a cinch for the Federal Reserve to generate any money supply it wants. But things are never that simple. Let's see why.

By way of review, in terms of our formula from Chapter 2, a change in bank reserves (ΔR) times the reciprocal of the demand deposit reserve ratio (r_{dd}) gives us the maximum potential change in demand deposits (ΔDD).[1] Say the reserve requirement against demand deposits is 10 percent, the figure we have been using for illustrative purposes, and the Fed increases bank reserves by $1,000:

$$\Delta R \times \frac{1}{r_{dd}} = \Delta DD$$

$$\Delta R \times \frac{1}{.10} = \Delta DD$$

$$\Delta R \times 10 = \Delta DD$$

$$\$1,000 \times 10 = \$10,000$$

The actual change in demand deposits will reach the maximum of $10,000 as long as banks lend out all of their excess reserves. If we were to draw up a consolidated T-account for the entire banking system following this $1,000 injection of reserves, showing the changes that take place in the balance sheets of all banks taken together, our formula tells us it would look like this:

---

[1] See p. 28 in Chapter 2.

Final Position, All Banks Taken Together
($1,000 change in reserves; $r_{dd} = 10\%$)

A		L & NW
Reserves (cash + deposit in Fed)	+$1,000	Demand deposits +$10,000
Loans and securities	+ 9,000	

Even before we get to the real complications, we should note that this deposit expansion multiplier of 10 is misleadingly large. We have been assuming a reserve requirement ratio of 10 percent because it simplifies our calculations, but actually at the present time the average demand deposit reserve requirement is about 15 percent. The larger the reserve ratio, the smaller the potential multiple expansion of demand deposits; the reciprocal of 15 percent is only 6⅔. Thus an injection of $1,000 of reserves in the real world would produce an eventual maximum increase of only $6,667 in demand deposits:

$$\Delta R \times \frac{1}{r_{dd}} = \Delta DD$$

$$\Delta R \times \frac{1}{.15} = \Delta DD$$

$$\Delta R \times 6\text{-}2/3 = \Delta DD$$

$$\$1,000 \times 6\text{-}2/3 = \$6,667$$

If, as above, we were to draw up a consolidated T-account for all banks under these conditions, following a $1,000 addition to reserves, it would look like this:

Final Position, All Banks Taken Together
($1,000 change in reserves; $r_{dd} = 15\%$)

A		L & NW
Reserves (cash + deposit in Fed)	+$1,000	Demand deposits +$6,667
Loans and securities	+ 5,667	

But this is just an amendment to what we have been saying, in terms of more realistic numbers, and poses no problem for the Federal Reserve as long as it controls the reserve requirement.[2] Looking a bit deeper, we find that more fundamental difficulties face the Fed in its efforts to control the money supply, even with our precision-like formulae. These can be categorized into three main complications.

    1.   *Up to now, we have abstracted from the fact that, as demand*

---

[2] Actually, the Fed doesn't completely control the required reserve ratio since, as we saw in Chapter 2, there are different reserve requirements for banks of different sizes. Hence r_{dd} is really a weighted average of these, and the weights can change as deposits shift from one bank to another.

deposits expand, the public is likely to want to hold part of its increased money supply in the form of currency. About one-quarter of our money supply is in the form of currency, three-quarters in the form of demand deposits. When people need more currency, they simply go to their bank and cash a check. On the bank's balance sheet, both cash (an asset) and demand deposits (a liability) fall. The bank's excess reserves also fall by 85 percent of the withdrawal, assuming a 15 percent reserve ratio.

Notice that a $100 currency withdrawal does not directly change the public's money holdings; it simply switches $100 from demand deposits to dollar bills, leaving the total money supply unaltered. But it *does* deplete bank excess reserves by $85, because a $100 demand deposit uses up only $15 in reserves, whereas a $100 cash withdrawal subtracts a full $100 of reserves (remember that cash in bank vaults counts as reserves). Draining of currency into the hands of the public thus depletes bank reserves dollar for dollar and thereby cuts back the expansion potential of the banking system.

For every $1 in demand deposits, the public seems to want currency holdings of about 30 cents. That is, the ratio of currency to demand deposits (c/dd) appears to be about 30 percent. This, of course, alters our demand deposit expansion formula. It is fairly easy to see the changes that are necessary: What we have to do is incorporate the currency/demand deposit ratio into the formula.

We continue to assume that banks lend out all their excess reserves. We saw in Chapter 2 that demand deposits could expand until all excess reserves become required reserves (because of deposit growth)—that is, until the demand deposit reserve requirement (r_{dd}) times the growth in demand deposits (ΔDD) equals the change in reserves (ΔR). But now, when reserves rise initially by ΔR, not only will they be absorbed by demand deposit growth, but in addition some of these reserves will *leave* the banking system as the public holds more currency (equal to c/dd times the growth in demand deposits). Although banks will still expand their demand deposits until all reserves are in the required category, *they will be unable to retain all of the initial change in reserves.* Since the initial injection of reserves eventually winds up as either required reserves or as currency held by the public, we have:

$$\Delta R = (r_{dd} \times \Delta DD) + (c/dd \times \Delta DD)$$

Factoring out the ΔDDs gives us:

$$\Delta R = (r_{dd} + c/dd) \times \Delta DD$$

and finally:

$$\Delta R \times \frac{1}{r_{dd} + c/dd} = \Delta DD$$

where the *initial change* in reserves (ΔR) is no longer fully retained within the banking system, because part leaks out into currency holdings outside the system. This total—bank reserves plus currency outside the banks—is important enough to deserve a name of its own: *The monetary base* (B), also known as high-powered money. When the Federal Reserve injects reserves, it is really adding to the monetary base, since some of these reserves will shift over into the form of currency holdings outside the banking system.

Let us now return, with our new formula, to our illustrative example. Assume a currency/demand deposit ratio of 30 percent, along with our good old 15 percent demand deposit reserve requirement, and our even more familiar injection of $1,000 of reserves by the Fed. However, due to the currency drain, the $1,000 of additional reserves are not all kept by the banks, so that in our new formula we should properly refer to a $1,000 increase in the monetary base (B) rather than reserves. What we get, after all is said and done, is a multiple expansion potential for demand deposits that is considerably smaller than before—now it is not 6.67, but only 2.22:[3]

$$\Delta B \times \frac{1}{r_{dd} + c/dd} = \Delta DD$$

$$\Delta B \times \frac{1}{.15 + .30} = \Delta DD$$

$$\Delta B \times \frac{1}{.45} = \Delta DD$$

$$\Delta B \times \quad 2.22 \quad = \Delta DD$$

$$\$1,000 \times \quad 2.22 \quad = \$2,222$$

The magic is evaporating! Now an initial $1,000 injection of reserves produces an eventual maximum increase in demand deposits of only $2,222. If we again drew up a consolidated T-account for all banks, following a $1,000 initial boost to reserves, the final results would look like this:

Final Position, All Banks Taken Together
($1,000 initial change in reserves; $r_{dd} = 15\%$;
and now adding cash drain: $c/dd = 30\%$)

A		L & NW	
Reserves (cash + deposit in Fed)	+$ 333	Demand deposits	+$2,222
Loans and securities	+ 1,889		

Memorandum: currency drain (i.e., currency outside the banks, held by the public): + $667

---

[3] This multiplier is strictly correct only if ΔB is initially all reserves.

Notice that, because of the currency drain, the banking system *retains* as reserves only $333 of the original $1,000. With a 15 percent reserve requirement, this can support demand deposits of only $2,222. The other $667 has moved *out* of the banking system into the hands of the general public, on the premise—which appears valid in fact—that the public wants to hold 30 cents more currency when it gets $1 more demand deposits (667 = 30% of 2,222).[4]

2. *In the second place, we have to recognize that banks have time and savings deposits as well as demand deposits among their liabilities, and that these also require reserves.* At the end of 1978, commercial bank time and savings deposits added up to about $600 billion, well in excess of their 260 billion demand deposits. The average reserve requirement on such deposits is about 4 percent. While this is not as large as the reserve requirement against demand deposits, it does serve to absorb bank reserves and thereby further reduce the demand deposit expansion potential of the system.

In the past two decades, commercial bank time and savings deposits have grown much more rapidly than demand deposits. The ratio of commercial bank time and savings deposits to demand deposits (sd/dd) appears to be about 2.3 to 1. Since the reserve requirement against such deposits (r_{sd}) averages 4 percent, this has to affect our demand deposit expansion formula. Using the same logic as

---

[4] The total change in the *money supply* due to the *initial* change in reserves (= change in the monetary base) is the sum of the change in demand deposits and the change in currency. We have just seen that currency goes up by 30 percent of 2,222, or more generally:

$$\Delta \text{ currency} = c/dd \times \Delta DD = c/dd \times \frac{1}{r_{dd} + c/dd} \times \Delta B$$

Hence, the total change in the money supply (ΔM) due to the initial change in reserves is:

$$\Delta M = \Delta DD + \Delta\text{currency} = \frac{1}{r_{dd} + c/dd} \times \Delta B + \frac{c/dd}{r_{dd} + c/dd} \times \Delta B$$

which simplifies to:

$$\Delta M = \frac{1 + c/dd}{r_{dd} + c/dd} \times \Delta B$$

Using our numbers, the money supply multiplier is 2.889:

$$\Delta M = 2.889 \times \$1,000 = \$2,889$$

which is $2,222 in demand deposits and $667 in currency.

before, the new demand deposit multiplier turns out to be 1.845:[5]

$$\Delta B \times \frac{1}{r_{dd} + c/dd + sd/dd(r_{sd})} = \Delta DD$$

$$\Delta B \times \frac{1}{.15 + .30 + 2.3(.04)} = \Delta DD$$

$$\Delta B \times \frac{1}{.15 + .30 + .092} = \Delta DD$$

$$\Delta B \times \frac{1}{.542} = \Delta DD$$

$$\Delta B \times 1.845 = \Delta DD$$

$$\$1,000 \times 1.845 = \$1,845$$

Taking into account actual average demand deposit reserve requirements, currency drains, and savings deposit growth, we find that the demand deposit multiplier has shrunk all the way to 1.845! The corresponding money supply multiplier—which includes the increase in currency held by the public—is 2.399 (see footnote 5). An increase of $1,000 in the monetary base is likely, realistically, to produce

[5] The derivation is as follows: The initial injection of reserves (ΔB) now gets absorbed by required reserves against demand deposits ($r_{dd} \times \Delta DD$); by currency ($c/dd \times \Delta DD$); and by required reserves against time and savings deposits. The increase in time and savings deposits (ΔSD) equals $sd/dd \times \Delta DD$, and reserves against time and savings deposits equal $r_{sd} \times sd/dd \times \Delta DD$. Therefore, we have:

$$\Delta B = (r_{dd} \times \Delta DD) + (c/dd \times \Delta DD) + (sd/dd \times r_{sd} \times \Delta DD)$$

Factoring out the ΔDDs gives us:

$$\Delta B = [r_{dd} + c/dd + (sd/dd \times r_{sd})] \times \Delta DD$$

and finally:

$$\Delta B \times \frac{1}{r_{dd} + c/dd + (sd/dd)(r_{sd})} = \Delta DD$$

Following footnote 4, we can extend this expression to the money supply as a whole (not just demand deposits) by adding the increase in currency in circulation to the increase in demand deposits:

$$\Delta M = \Delta DD + \Delta currency = \frac{1}{r_{dd} + c/dd + (sd/dd)(r_{sd})} \times \Delta B +$$

$$\frac{c/dd}{r_{dd} + c/dd + (sd/dd)(r_{sd})} \times \Delta B$$

which simplifies to:

$$\Delta M = \frac{1 + c/dd}{r_{dd} + c/dd + (sd/dd)(r_{sd})} \times \Delta B$$

If you work it out, you'll find that this yields a money supply multiplier of 2.399.

an eventual demand deposit increase no larger than $1,845, and a money supply increase no larger than $2,399.[6]

3. *Finally, a last complication: We have been assuming that all banks are willing to expand their loans (or securities purchases) up to the full amount of their excess reserves.* This may not always be so. If some banks don't lend all their excess reserves (perhaps because they cannot find enough creditworthy borrowers), and don't buy additional securities (perhaps because they expect bond prices to fall), the whole sequence of lending and demand deposit creation cannot reach its theoretical maximum, not even the maximum of 1.845 times an initial change in reserves.

Banks that do not fully expand their loans won't lose all their excess reserves to other banks, so the other banks will be unable to lend as much. In addition, banks that do lend are likely to lose some reserves to the nonlenders, thereby rendering such reserves immobile. Thus the potential multiple of 1.845 can only be realized if *all* banks are willing to lend and/or buy securities up to the *full* amount of their excess reserves.

In the 1930s idle excess reserves were plentiful. In the past two

[6] The consolidated bank T-account for an initial $1,000 reserve increase under these circumstances is interesting:

Final Position, All Banks Taken Together
($1,000 initial change in reserves; $r_{dd} = 15\%$;
currency drain $c/dd = 30\%$; and now adding
savings deposit growth: $sd/dd = 2.3$ and
$r_{sd} = 4\%$)

A		L & NW	
Reserves (cash + deposit in Fed) + $ 446.5		Demand deposits + $1,845	
For dem. deposits: + $ 276.75			
For sav. deposits: + 169.75			
Loans and securities + 5,642		Savings deposits + 4,243.5	

Memorandum: currency drain (i.e., currency outside the banks, held by the public): + $553.5 (= 30% of $1,845)

The above proportional relationships among bank balance sheet items are rather realistic relative to each other, although of course the absolute numbers are not. Compare them with the previous T-account and notice that the growth of demand deposits is now less—$1,845 compared to $2,222. However, *total* deposit growth is now $6,088, almost triple what it was before. Similarly, bank lending (including securities purchases) is now much larger—$5,642 compared to only $1,889.

These results—less demand deposits but more total deposits and more bank lending—reflect two things. The currency drain is now less, so the banking system is retaining more reserves. (The currency drain is less even though the c/dd ratio is the same, because currency outflows depend on the growth of demand deposits only.) And savings deposits, while they use up reserves and thereby inhibit potential demand deposit expansion, do not remove reserves from the banking system the way currency drains do; with savings deposits, banks can continue lending, and indeed can lend even *more* than with an equivalent amount of demand deposits, because the reserve requirement against savings deposits is lower.

decades most banks have stayed rather fully loaned up, so this has not been so much of a problem. Unused excess reserves have been small in amount and concentrated in small rural banks.[7] Under the circumstances, since idle reserves are not very significant today, a realistic multiple for demand deposit expansion at the present time is probably not far below our 1.845 figure—about 1.7 or 1.8 would be a reasonable estimate, but only an estimate.[8]

What do all these complications mean for the Federal Reserve, these successive modifications of our original simple demand deposit expansion multiplier? (Remember when it was just the reciprocal of the demand deposit reserve requirement?) They mean, most importantly, that the Fed's ability to control the money supply is not nearly as precise as we had originally thought. As it attempts to control the money supply, the central bank has to worry about currency drains, savings deposit growth, and bank holdings of idle excess reserves. We have used past averages to get numbers for the multipliers, but for the Fed that is simply not good enough. It has to predict with accuracy the various ratios for the coming weeks and months if it is to succeed in making the money supply what it wants it to be.

Suggestions for Further Reading

For a painstaking derivation of the demand deposit multipliers discussed in this Appendix, and a few others as well, see John T. Boorman and Thomas M. Havrilesky, *Money Supply, Money Demand, and Macroeconomic Models* (Boston: Allyn and Bacon, 1972), pp. 10–41. Also see Dorothy M. Nichols' pamphlet *Modern Money Mechanics: A Workbook on Deposits, Currency, and Bank Reserves* (Federal Reserve Bank of Chicago), pp. 29–31. For an advanced treatment with some historical perspective, see Phillip Cagan, *Determinants and Effects of Changes in the Stock of Money, 1875–1960* (New York: Columbia University Press, 1965).

[7] It is quite possible that bank holdings of excess reserves are a function of interest rates, high rates inducing banks to make more loans and hold less excess reserves, and low rates making it less costly for banks to hold excess reserves (they are not giving up much interest income by not lending). This raises the possibility that demand deposits and money supply are a function of interest rates—a subject we return to later in the book. So stay awake—first one to spot it gets a free tune-up.

[8] You might have realized that we were using *average* ratios of currency to demand deposits, and savings deposits to demand deposits, as estimates of the *marginal* relationships (e.g., the *increase* in currency associated with an *increase* in demand deposits). The formula that produced the demand deposit multiplier estimate of 1.845 is properly based on marginal ratios. Since average is not always a good guide to marginal, our estimate is really just that—an estimate. On the other hand, wasn't it Gertrude Stein who said, "An estimate is an estimate is an estimate"?

Chapter 4

Simple Stuff on GNP

THIS CHAPTER is so easy it almost wasn't. In fact, if you look at the pictures and they bring back fond memories of Eco. 1, please do not alert the copyright authorities—we are guilty of using such elementary materials as the circular flow of income and output, the cleavage between saving and investment, and other paradigms of praxeology and catallactic concepts. Of course, if you have forgotten the meaning of some of the simple terms in the last sentence, you may read on to refresh your memory (sorry, but you're going to have to use Webster's *un*abridged dictionary).

The Circular Flow of Spending, Income, and Output

Let's start by taking a simplified view of the economy, dividing its participants into two groups: business firms and households. Firms produce goods and services for sale; households buy these goods and services and consume them. Households are able to buy the goods and

48

services produced by firms because they also supply firms with all of the land, labor, capital and entrepreneurship required for production; hence they receive as income the total proceeds of production. The total value of the goods and services produced is called gross national product (GNP), or more simply national income (Y), and it can be measured by either the total output sold by firms *or* the total income received by households (in the form of wages, rent, interest, and profits).

These relationships are summarized in Figure 1, the inner circle

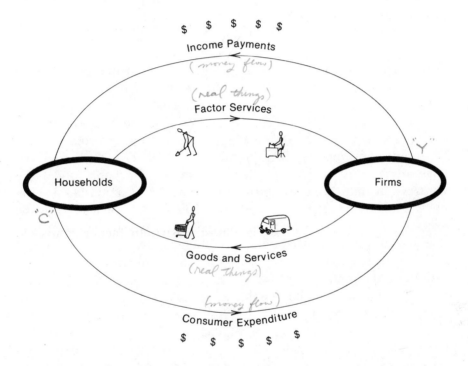

FIGURE 1 / The circular flow of spending, income, and output.

recording flows of *real* things (factors of production to firms and goods and services to households), the outer circle recording the associated *money* flows (income payments to households and money expenditures to firms). The money flow relationship can be written symbolically as $C = Y$, where C stands for household spending on consumer goods and Y stands for national income or GNP.

As long as firms sell all of their output, they will continue to produce at that level. As long as we assume that all of the income received by households is spent on the goods and services produced, production equals sales, output equals demand, and we are in equilibrium (no tendency for anything to change). But if we keep this up much longer, you will have fallen asleep in the very position you are now holding this book (also equilibrium). So we modify things a bit to make our hypothetical economy more like the real one.

Saving and Investment

Households don't spend all of their income; they usually save some fraction. Saving represents a leakage in the circular flow. Total income of households (which is equal to the total value of goods and services produced by firms) does not all return to firms in the form of consumption expenditures. Saving (S) is defined simply as total income (Y) minus consumption spending (C)—i.e., $S = Y - C$. It may not have anything to do with putting the money in a bank, under the mattress (if that's what turns you on), or in the stock market. Households may do any of these things with their saving—that is, with the excess of their income over their spending on consumer goods. For now we are not concerned with their financial transactions, but just with the fact that failure to spend all income implies that total expenditure is less than total income (and total production). If things remained that way, output would exceed sales and firms would want to cut back production.

But all is not lost. Consumer goods are not the only thing that firms produce. Firms themselves add to their stock of production facilities or to inventories—they buy goods and services for their own use, which we call investment spending (I). If firms *want* to *invest* (I) exactly what households *want to save* (S), then all that is produced will once again be sold, but this time to both households (for consumption) and business firms (for investment). And, of course, the level of output will be one of equilibrium (hooray). This happy state of affairs is summarized in Figure 2 and can be represented as $C + I = Y$. Note that we can also describe the situation as one in which the leakage from the household spending stream (saving) is equal to business spending on investment, or, in symbols, $S = I$.

In Figure 2 we have labeled the connecting link between saving and investment the financial markets. Decisions to save are often made by people very different from those who invest—saving is done by all

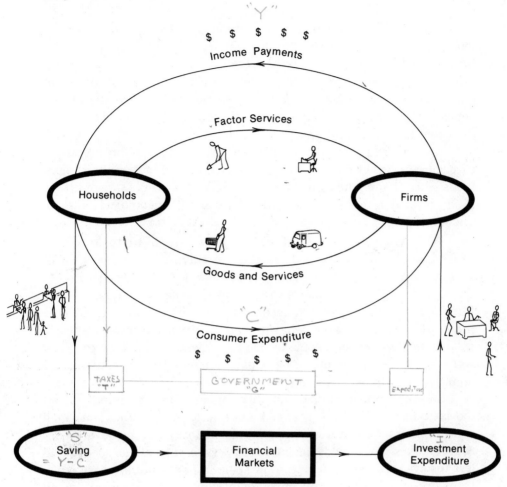

FIGURE 2 / The circular flow including saving and investment.

the little guys in the economy who scrimp to hold their spending down in order to prepare for a rainy day, while investment is done by corporate executives sitting around a huge oval desk with thirteen phones and four secretaries. These seemingly diverse groups are brought together by financial markets, with the savings of the little people borrowed by the corporate executives and then spent on investment goods, so that both groups may continue along their merry way (anybody wanna trade places?).

The word "investment" is frequently confusing because it is used to mean different things. Here it means the purchase of "real" productive facilities, like factories and machine tools, whereas in common usage "investment" often refers to purely financial transactions, like buying stocks and bonds. Buying stocks and bonds can have implica-

51

tions for "real" investment (the purchase of factories and machine tools), but they are clearly different things. We will usually reserve the term "investment" for buying productive facilities, as we are using it here. In later chapters, however, we will occasionally fall into common parlance and use it for buying financial assets, like stocks and bonds; in that case, the purely financial meaning will be clear from the context.

It is important to note that our discussion of equilibrium output as occurring when saving equals investment emphasizes that households *want to save* the same amount as business firms *want to invest*. If financial markets somehow bring this about, income will remain unchanged.

We have to distinguish this condition (where desired S = desired I) from one in which S and I are equal simply by definition. That is, saving is defined as $Y - C$. But $C + I = Y$, so that I also equals $Y - C$. Thus, by definition, S must always equal I, since both equal $Y - C$. But *this* equality is an ex post accounting identity, always true by definition. It is not an ex ante behavior equality arising from what people *want* to do. Only when people *want* to save what firms *want* to invest will income be in equilibrium (remain unchanged). A concrete example is given later in Chapter 18.

So far we have ignored the government (wishful thinking?). It too introduces a leakage between income payments and household consumption expenditures—namely, taxes (T). When the government collects taxes, households have less to spend on consumer goods (and less to save). If some other form of spending does not increase when taxes are levied, production once again would exceed the sum of all types of expenditures, and economic activity would decline. But the government could lend these funds to business firms so they can increase investment spending, or, believe it or not, the government itself can buy goods and services from business firms (where do you think the defense department gets all those guns?).

If *desired* spending in the form of consumption (C), investment (I), and government (G) expenditure equals total output, or $C + I + G = Y$, then that level of production will be maintained. Note that we can also describe the situation as one in which total leakages from the spending stream, saving plus taxes, equals total spending injections in the form of investment and government expenditure, or $S + T = I + G$. For simplicity, we may sometimes refer to the left-hand side as total saving and the right-hand side as total investment.

While we have now relaxed many of the hypothetical assumptions that populated our simple economy, we have still not introduced foreigners—exports and imports. Such a radical step is usually reserved for an entirely separate section in most textbooks. Ours is no exception. We believe (firmly) that the American Way of Life is best preserved when the outsiders are sealed off from the normal folks.[1]

Another Catallactic Concept[2]

We can look at the same subject, total spending in the economy, from a slightly different angle. So far we have viewed total spending as consisting of three categories, $C + I + G$. This breakdown is in terms of who does the spending, consumers, business firms, or government. But total spending could also be viewed as consisting of the quantity of money in existence (M) multiplied by the average number of times each dollar is spent on goods and services during a given period of time, which, as we noted in Chapter 1, is called velocity (V) or the rate of turnover of money.

This way of looking at total spending $(M \times V)$ is in terms of *what* is spent rather than *who* does the spending. An analogy: If two people are alternating driving a car, and one drives 50 miles and the other 30 miles, the total number of miles driven equals 80. A different way of finding the total miles driven is to calculate how many hours were spent driving and the average speed per hour—say, two hours at an average speed of 40 miles per hour. Total: 80 miles. This second way makes who is doing the driving irrelevant, just as with $M \times V$ it is irrelevant who is doing the spending. Since $M \times V$, just as $C + I + G$, equals total spending, we can also equate $M \times V$ with Y (as can be seen in Table 1 below). At times one way of looking at the process $(C + I + G = Y)$ may be more fruitful, and at times the other $(M \times V = Y)$ might be more illuminating. Different economists prefer different formulations (different strokes for different folks).

TABLE 1

Components of Spending = Income, 1955–1975

($ in billions)

Year	C	+	I	+	G	=	GNP	=	M	×	V
1955	$254		$ 70		$ 75		$399		$134		2.98
1965	430		120		138		688		167		4.12
1975	963		206		331		1500		290		5.17

Source: *Annual Reports*, Council of Economic Advisors.

[1] Ancient tablets unearthed by archaeologist Mel Brooks reveal that the first national anthem in the history of the world was *"Let Them All Go to Hell Except for Cave 76."*

[2] Literally: exchange concept. Paradigm of praxeology = model of human action.

Our discussion of Classical and Keynesian macroeconomics in Part IV draws on some of the basic relationships among spending, output, velocity, saving, and investment that have been outlined here. We have not yet tried to use any of these tools for analytical purposes —that will be coming out of your ears soon enough. We have also not burdened you with the details of GNP accounting. Let's just say that you are ready to tackle the issues of *macro*economics that are crucial for a full evaluation of the impact of money and monetary policy on the economy. Before we get there, however, let's expand somewhat on the connecting link between saving and investment. Financial markets are more interesting than most, so don't go away.

Suggestions for Further Reading

For those of you who simply cannot resist knowing the precise definitions of GNP, net national product, national income, personal income, and so on, you can review it all in Paul Samuelson's *Economics*, 10th ed. (New York: McGraw-Hill, 1976), chap. 10, or in a comparable chapter in any basic economics textbook. More advanced discussion on conceptual problems in GNP accounting and an introduction to "sector accounts" (the business sector, the government sector, and so on) can be found in intermediate texts in macroeconomics. Some good examples are: Thomas F. Dernburg and Duncan M. McDougall, *Macroeconomics*, 5th ed. (New York: McGraw-Hill, 1976); Stanley Fischer and Rudiger Dornbusch, *Macroeconomics* (New York: McGraw-Hill, 1978); and Edward Shapiro, *Macroeconomic Analysis*, 4th ed. (New York: Harcourt, Brace, Jovanovich, 1978).

Chapter 5

Financial Markets and Institutions

FINANCIAL MARKETS are basically the same as other kinds of markets. People buy and sell, bargain and hassle, win and lose, just as in the flea markets of Casablanca and Amsterdam or the gold markets of London and Zurich. In financial markets they buy and sell securities—like stocks and bonds—which are less tangible than hot wristwatches or cold gold bars but are no less valuable. Stocks and bonds can be very valuable indeed, even though they are nothing but pieces of paper.

The Function of Financial Markets

Financial markets are the transmission mechanism between saver-lenders and borrower-spenders. They are the connecting link between saving and investment, as we saw in Figure 2 of the previous chapter. Through a wide variety of techniques, instruments, and institutions, financial markets mobilize the savings of millions and channel them into the hands of borrower-spenders who need more funds than they have on hand. Financial markets are conduits through which those who do not spend all their income can make their excess funds available to those who want to spend more than their income.

Saver-lenders stand to benefit because they earn interest or dividends on their funds. Borrower-investors stand to gain because they get access to money to carry out investment plans they otherwise could not finance (and which presumably yield more than the interest they pay). Without financial markets, savers would have no choice but to hoard their excess money, and borrowers would be unable to realize their investment plans except those they could finance by themselves.

Financial markets give savers additional options besides that of simply holding their savings in the form of cash: They can, if they wish, *buy securities* with the money. Similarly, through financial markets borrowers can finance their investment plans even though they may not have previously accumulated funds to draw upon: They can *sell securities* to obtain the funds they need.

Schematically, Figure 1 illustrates in simplified form the flow of funds from ultimate saver-lenders, through financial markets, to ultimate borrower-spenders. Ultimate lenders are on the left, ultimate bor-

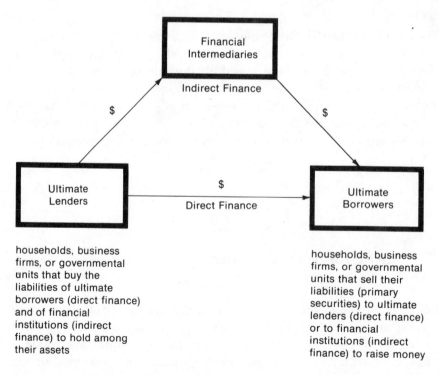

FIGURE 1 / Flows of funds from lenders to borrowers.

rowers on the right. Funds flow from left to right, either directly (straight from ultimate lenders to ultimate borrowers) or indirectly (through financial institutions, such as banks and insurance companies). The liabilities issued by ultimate borrowers, known as *primary securities*, flow in the opposite direction, from right to left, as they are purchased by either ultimate lenders (direct finance) or financial institutions (indirect finance).

Ultimate lenders are typically households, although from time to time business firms and governmental bodies—federal, state, and local —also lend substantial amounts. *Ultimate borrowers* are mostly business firms and governments, although households are also important as consumer credit and mortgage borrowers. The financial market in which the transaction takes place generally takes its name from the borrowers' side of the market, more specifically from the particular kind of primary security involved—the government bond market, the municipal bond market, the mortgage market, the corporate bond market, the stock market, and so on.[1] Sometimes, however, it is the lender who gives the market its name, as, for example, the market for bank loans.

The existence of highly developed, widely accessible, and smoothly functioning financial markets is of crucial importance in transmitting savings into the hands of those desiring to make investment expenditures. Those who can visualize and exploit potentially profitable investment opportunities are frequently not the same people who generate current saving. If the financial transmission mechanism is underdeveloped, inaccessible, or imperfect, the flow of funds from household saving to business investment will be impeded, and GNP will fall below its potential.

While it is true that, for the whole economy, saving must equal investment, ex post, this equality may take place at low or high magnitudes of saving and investment, implying low or high magnitudes of production, employment, and GNP. As we stressed in the previous chapter, the equality between realized (or ex post) saving and investment does not mean that all desired (or ex ante) saving must inevitably flow into or be matched by an equal volume of investment spending.

Assume, for example, that a significant portion of otherwise feasible investment plans is not undertaken because of lack of financing, due to the failure of financial markets to channel funds effectively from savers able to lend to business firms anxious to borrow. The end result of such a curtailment of investment spending is likely to be a

---

[1] Strictly speaking, corporate stocks are not liabilities. They are evidence of ownership and thus do not represent either "lending" or "borrowing." Nevertheless, we will often neglect this distinction, in the interest of simplicity, and speak of bonds and stocks as though they were roughly the same thing.

lower level of GNP, out of which will be generated a reduced volume of saving. Realized (or ex post) saving and investment will be equal, after all is said and done, but at levels far below their potential and at a level of GNP also far below that which could have been reached had financial markets operated more effectively.

A concrete example of the failure of financial markets to channel funds effectively arises when there is a lack of adequate information about borrowers seeking funds and/or lenders wanting to lend them out. This highlights the main function of any market—to bring buyers and sellers together. In financial markets, it is buyers and sellers of credit. If some potential borrowers, for example, are unaware of financial markets—or if knowledge about sources of funds is not widely disseminated—then some investments which could have been undertaken won't be (there are savers who would have willingly loaned the funds at rates of interest equal to, or less than, what investors would have been willing to pay).

A similar situation could arise as far as savers are concerned. Some may not be aware of lending opportunities. Instead of being put to work, funds are put under the mattress and less investment takes place (which in turn lowers saving as income declines). But well-developed financial markets do not permit such waste and inefficiency.

Securities brokers, dealers, and stock exchanges are some of the institutional arrangements that develop to help bring together buyers and sellers of financial assets. In addition to these trading facilities, financial intermediaries also step in to help set matters right.

The Role of Financial Intermediaries

Financial intermediaries are nothing more than financial institutions —commercial banks, savings banks, savings and loan associations, credit unions, pension funds, insurance companies, and so on—that act as middlemen, transferring funds from ultimate lenders to ultimate borrowers. They borrow from Peter in order to lend to Paul. (Actually, that cliché has been around for so long that Paul is way over his head in debt by now; his credit rating is lower than New York City's.) What all financial intermediaries have in common is that they acquire funds by issuing their own liabilities to the public (saving deposits, savings and loan shares), and then turn around and use this money to buy primary securities (stocks, bonds, mortgages) for themselves.

Because these institutions exist, savers who do not want to hoard their cash under a mattress, but who feel hesitant about purchasing corporate bonds or stocks or mortgages (primary securities) because they feel that these assets are perhaps too risky or too illiquid—or because they don't know about the availability of such items—are given a third alternative. They can "purchase" savings deposits or savings and loan shares. In that way they can hold a relatively safe and quite liquid financial asset, yet still earn *some* interest income. At the same time, corporations and potential homeowners can sell their bonds, stocks, and mortgages—to the financial intermediaries rather than to the original savers themselves. Financial intermediaries, in brief, "intermediate" between ultimate saver-lenders and ultimate borrowers.

Financial intermediation, or indirect finance, is precisely the above process: savers deposit funds with financial institutions rather than directly buying bonds or mortgages, and the financial institutions, in turn, lend to the ultimate borrowers. *Disintermediation* is the reverse: savers take funds out of deposit accounts, or reduce the amounts they normally put in, and invest directly in primary securities such as stocks and bonds. (We will encounter financial *dis*intermediation again in Chapter 7.)

Financial institutions are in a better position than individuals to bear and spread the risks of primary security ownership. Because of their large size, intermediaries can diversify their portfolios and minimize the risk involved in holding any one security. They are experts in evaluating borrower credit characteristics. They employ skilled portfolio managers and can take advantage of administrative economies in large-scale buying and selling.

For these reasons, they can afford to receive lower yields on their assets, and will accept them if they have to. Competition among financial intermediaries forces interest rates to the lowest level compatible with their evaluation of the risks of security ownership. These yields are lower than if the primary securities were held by individual investors, who are unable to minimize their risks as efficiently.

The growth in financial intermediaries has been spectacular in the post-World War II period. Time and savings deposits in commercial banks have grown from $30 billion at the end of World War II to $600 billion at the end of 1978, and savings and loan shares have increased from less than $10 billion to over $400 billion.

It is worth noting that since financial intermediation tends to lower interest rates, or at least to moderate any increase, it has been highly beneficial to our rate of economic growth.[2] A high rate of economic growth requires a large volume of real investment. The lower the rate of interest that ultimate borrowers must pay, the greater their expenditure on real investment.

The beneficial effect of intermediation on economic growth can also be seen from the viewpoint of risk bearing. Intermediaries are better able than individuals to bear the risks of lending out capital. As was previously stressed, ability to diversity, economies of scale, and expertise in lending account for this comparative advantage of institutions over individuals. As financial intermediaries own a larger and larger portion of the marketable securities outstanding, the subjective risk borne by the economy is lowered, interest rates are reduced, and more real investment takes place. Funds are channeled from ultimate lenders, through intermediaries, to ultimate borrowers more efficiently than if the intermediaries did not exist.

A brief profile of the major financial institutions is appropriate at this point, to get an overall perspective. Later, in Part II, we will examine the operations of financial institutions—especially commercial banks—in greater detail.

Financial Institutions in Profile

Although all financial institutions have a great deal in common, performing as they do essentially similar functions, there are also substantial differences among them. Ranking them in terms of asset size, for example, as in Table 1, commercial banks are easily the largest, followed rather far behind by savings and loan associations and life insurance companies. Near the bottom are credit unions and money market mutual funds. Don't sell them short, however; both credit unions and money market mutual funds have had extremely vigorous growth rates in recent years.

In addition to sheer size, the *composition* of assets and liabilities also differs significantly from one type of financial intermediary to another. Since we will devote all of Part II to the details, it is enough for now to note that commercial banks are the most widely diversified of all financial institutions in terms of both their assets and their liabilities. Although by law they cannot acquire corporate stocks,

---

[2] In recent years financial intermediation has grown but interest rates have frequently risen, because "all other things" have not remained constant. (In Part IV we discuss these "other things.") Without financial intermediation, interest rates would have risen even higher.

TABLE 1

Financial Institutions, Ranked by Asset Size (end of 1978)

Institution	Asset Size*
Commercial banks	$1,130
Savings and loan associations	520
Life insurance companies	380
Private noninsured pension funds	200
Mutual savings banks	160
State and local government retirement funds	150
Sales and consumer finance companies	140
Property and casualty insurance companies	130
Credit unions	60
Mutual funds	40
Money market mutual funds	10

° Total financial assets, in billions of dollars.
Source: Federal Reserve Flow of Funds Accounts.

they have substantial holdings of government bonds, municipal bonds, business loans, mortgages, and consumer loans among their assets.

Savings and loan associations and mutual savings banks hold primarily home mortgages. There is really very little difference between savings and loan associations and mutual savings banks in terms of what they do and how they operate. Both are frequently referred to as "thrift institutions." Savings and loans are more familiar to many people, since there are about 5,000 of them spread throughout the nation. On the other hand, there are only about 500 mutual savings banks because they are chartered in only seventeen states, mostly in the Northeast.

Life insurance companies, as the name implies, insure people against death, with premiums based on mortality statistics. These premiums are used to buy corporate bonds and stocks and mortgages, especially on industrial properties. Property and casualty insurance companies are the folks who insure homeowners against burglary and fire and insure car owners against theft and collision. With the premiums they receive—big ones from those under twenty-five years of age—they buy high-grade municipal and corporate bonds and blue-chip stocks.

Pension funds provide individuals with a systematic plans to contribute funds during their working years, to be paid out after they retire (called an annuity). Pension funds invest most of the money in stocks and corporate bonds. Mutual funds enable the small saver to buy corporate stock and if he wants to get his money back he doesn't have to wait until retirement, since he can sell his mutual fund shares any time he wants (although not at any price he wants).[3] Credit unions

[3] Money market mutual funds are something else again. They invest mostly in money market instruments, such as Treasury bills and bank negotiable certificates of deposit. We will meet them again in Chapter 7.

*"I'll bet a $5,000 savings and loan deposit
that you've got the Old Maid."*

and finance companies are at the other end of the financial spectrum:
they help individuals spend now and pay later by extending consumer
loans. Thus of all financial institutions, the only ones that spread-
eagle all financial markets are commercial banks (except that they
are not involved in the stock market).

The asset composition of each kind of financial institution reflects three main influences: the nature of its liabilities, tax considerations, and legal constraints. Life insurance companies, for example,
with relatively predictable long-term commitments, can afford to hold

long-term mortgages (which are not very liquid), but property and casualty insurance companies require assets that can be disposed of more rapidly if necessary. Similarly, institutions most subject to federal taxation, such as commercial banks, are most likely to buy municipal bonds, since the interest on municipal bonds is exempt from federal income taxes. With respect to legal constraints, savings and loan associations and savings banks are the prime example—legislation prohibits them from straying very far from residential mortgage lending.

Having surveyed the function of financial markets and the role that financial intermediaries play in those markets, it is time to turn to a brief examination of the markets themselves. Generally, a distinction is drawn between the market for long-term securities (a year or longer in original maturity), called the "capital market," and the market for shorter-term issues, the "money market."

The Capital Market

By far the largest sector of the capital market, in terms of dollar volume of securities outstanding, is the stock market, as Table 2 indicates.[4] About 70 percent of all the outstanding stocks are owned by individuals, without the benefit of financial intermediation; the rest are held

TABLE 2
The Capital Market: Securities Outstanding
(end of 1978)

Type of Instrument	Amount Outstanding*
Corporate stocks (at market value)	$1,100
Residential mortgages	880
Corporate bonds	420
Consumer loans	340
U.S. Government securities (marketable, long-term)	330
Commercial and farm mortgages	290
State and local government bonds	260
Bank business loans	220
U.S. Government Agency securities	140

* In billions of dollars.
Source: Federal Reserve Flow of Funds Accounts and *Federal Reserve Bulletin.*

[4] Corporate stocks represent ownership, not indebtedness. Thus they have no maturity date at all.

by such institutional investors as pension funds, mutual funds, and insurance companies (in that order).

Mortgages are usually divided into residential (one-to-four family homes and multifamily) and commercial and farm mortgages. Most one-to-four family home mortgages—some of which are insured by the Federal Housing Authority or guaranteed by the Veterans' Administration—are financed by savings and loan associations and savings banks, but commercial banks are also important lenders in this area. Multifamily mortgages are purchased mostly by thrift institutions (savings and loan associations and savings banks) and life insurance companies, commercial mortgages mainly by life insurance companies and commercial banks.

In the corporate bond market, life insurance companies are the main lenders (they own more than a third of the corporate bonds), followed by pension and retirement funds and households (direct finance). State and local government bonds, on the other hand, are bought primarily for their tax exempt feature, since their interest is exempt from federal income taxes: Commercial banks own half of the total outstanding, followed by wealthy individuals (again direct finance) and property and casualty insurance companies.

U.S. Government securities are generally bought by a wide variety of purchasers, including the Federal Reserve, commercial banks, individuals, and foreigners. The same is true of the securities of various government agencies (such as the Federal Home Loan Banks, the Federal National Mortgage Association, and the Federal Land Banks); most of these are guaranteed, formally or informally, by the full faith and credit of the federal government.

In many of these sectors of the capital market, active trading takes place daily for outstanding issues—especially for stocks and for U.S. Government securities, to a lesser extent for corporate and for municipal (state and local) bonds. Trading is facilitated by a wide variety of institutions, including securities dealers and brokers, with expensive communications facilities, under the watchful eye of government regulators (such as the Securities and Exchange Commission). We will explore the functioning of all these markets in greater depth in Chapter 31.

In other sectors, such as consumer credit and bank business loans, there is virtually no secondary market at all—i.e., no trading in outstanding securities—so that these securities have little marketability and liquidity. In the residential mortgage market, government-sponsored agencies such as the Federal National Mortgage Association now make a secondary market in mortgages (see Chapter 27), thereby giving home mortgages a degree of liquidity they formerly lacked.

Trading is most active, as noted, in the stock and bond markets, but even there it does not compare with the dollar volume of turnover that daily characterizes the money market, especially with respect to Treasury bills.

The Money Market

In contrast to the capital market, with its long-term securities, the money market specializes in short-term instruments that almost by definition are highly liquid—that is, readily marketable, with little possibility of loss. If you need to raise cash quickly and are forced to dispose of long-term securities, you can take a beating; but if you have short-term securities, chances are you can sell them without taking much of a loss. The short-term securities will mature pretty soon anyway, so if you can hold off a little while you can redeem them at face value when they mature. In addition, it is simply a fact of life, imbedded in the mathematics of bond yields and prices, that for long-term securities a small change in interest rates involves a large change in price, whereas for short-term securities even a large change in yield involves only a small change in price.

Example: A rise in yield from 7 to 8 percent on a $10,000 face value 30-year bond bearing a 7 percent coupon involves a fall in price from $10,000 to $8,870. A similar rise in yield on a three-month security of similar coupon involves a fall in price from $10,000 to only $9,970.[5]

For this reason, business firms and others with temporary surplus funds buy money market instruments rather than long-term securities. They purchase short-term money market securities and thus earn interest without much risk exposure. Commercial banks are particularly important participants in the money market, both as lenders and borrowers, as they adjust their legal reserve positions, invest temporarily idle balances, or sell some of their securities to raise funds in anticipation of forthcoming business demands for loans.

As Table 3 indicates, U.S. Treasury bills are the dominant money market instrument, with about $160 billion outstanding. Treasury bills are short-term debts of the U.S. Government. Typically, they are issued for three months or six months or a year. Treasury bills have been around since 1929. In 1961 they were joined by bank CDs, when the First National City Bank of New York introduced the large-denomina-

[5] For a more general proof, see the last section of this chapter.

TABLE 3
The Money Market: Securities Outstanding
(end of 1978)

Type of Instrument	Amount Outstanding*
U.S. Treasury bills	$160
Negotiable bank CDs (large denomination)	100
Commercial paper	80
Bankers' acceptances	30

° In billions of dollars.
Source: Federal Reserve Flow of Funds Accounts and *Federal Reserve Bulletin.*

tion ($100,000 and over) negotiable certificate of deposit. Negotiable CDs are deposits and thus liabilities of the issuing banks. But they are interest-earning assets to the corporations that hold them; they are attractive to corporate treasurers since they are readily marketable through dealers who specialize in buying and selling them. Thus a corporate treasurer who needs cash quickly can sell off CDs before they mature. The negotiable CD offers corporate treasurers an alternative to Treasury bills or other money market instruments. By raising the rate they pay on CDs, banks can entice corporate surplus funds that might otherwise go into Treasury bills.

Commercial paper is also largely held by corporate treasurers. It represents short-term liabilities of *prime* business firms and finance companies. Bankers' acceptances, the least important of the main money market instruments, arise mostly in the course of international trade transactions.

In addition to the above, the daily purchase and sale of "Federal funds" (member bank reserves at the Federal Reserve Banks) is also of major importance in the money market, particularly with respect to the role of commercial banks. In a typical Federal funds transaction, a bank with excess reserves will sell some of its excess to a bank with deficient reserves, on an overnight basis and at an agreed-upon interest rate. We will encounter Federal funds in a number of chapters; just remember, Federal funds as the term is used here has no necessary connection with the U.S. Treasury.

Asset Prices and Yields

Before leaving this chapter, it is useful to have at least a nodding acquaintance with the calculation of bond prices and yields. For example, suppose you pay $900 for a $1,000-face-value 5 percent-coupon bond that will mature in ten years and that you expect to hold until maturity. *What annual interest rate will you be getting on that security?*

To begin with, you have to be careful to keep clear which interest rate you are talking about. At a minimum, it is important to distinguish between (1) the coupon rate, (2) the current yield, and (3) the yield to maturity.

1. *The coupon rate* is 5 percent, which merely means that printed on the face of the bond is the statement that each year the holder will get a payment equal to 5 percent of the $1,000 face value, or $50. If you had paid the $1,000 face value for the bond, you would indeed be getting 5 percent interest. But bond prices rise and fall. In this case, you are paying only $900; so although the coupon rate specifies 5 percent, you will actually be getting more than 5 percent because you paid less than $1,000. But how much more?

2. *The current yield* is calculated as the annual dollar interest payment divided by the price you paid for the bond, or $50/$900 = 5.56 percent. It looks appealing but actually it is rarely quoted because it is inexact except under rather restrictive assumptions. Specifically, it fails to take into account receipts accruing beyond a one-year time horizon, including the fact that when the bond matures, in ten years, you will have a $100 capital gain. (You paid only $900, but when the bond matures it will be redeemed at its $1,000 face value).

3. *The yield to maturity*—the most widely used interest rate in the bond markets—takes into account the elements that the current yield neglects. To fully understand it, however, we will have to back up a moment and realize the implications of that venerable cliché: *time is money.* Like most clichés, it succinctly expresses a fundamental truth.

If you deposit $100 in a bank at 5 percent annual interest, what is your deposit worth after a year? The answer, of course, is $105. More formally: $100 (1 + .05) = $105. What is it worth after two years? Due to compounding (receiving interest on interest), it becomes $105 (1 + .05) = $110.25. What the second year really amounts to is $100 (1 + .05) (1 + .05), or $100 (1 + .05)^2 = $110.25. On the same basis, after three years the deposit would be worth $100 (1 + .05)^3 and after four years $100 (1 + .05)^4, and so on.

If $100 today at 5 percent interest is worth $105 a year from now, and $110.25 two years from now, we can *work backward* and say that $105 a year from now must be worth only $100 today, and that $110.25 two years from now must also be worth only $100 today. In the previous paragraph, we applied an interest rate to increase a present sum into the future; now, when we work backward, we are *discounting* to reduce a future sum back to its present value (time is money). Putting it a bit more formally, we have simply transposed the previous paragraph's

$$\$100\,(1 + .05) = \$105 \qquad \text{into} \qquad \$100 = \frac{\$105}{(1 + .05)}$$

$$\text{and}\ \$100\,(1 + .05)^2 = \$110.25 \qquad \text{into} \qquad \$100 = \frac{\$110.25}{(1 + .05)^2}.$$

With that as background, we can now understand—at least intuitively—the general formula for the price or present value (P) of a fixed-income security which pays a dollar coupon (C) in each of n years and has a face value (F) which will be paid off at maturity n years from now. The general formula for the present value or price of such a security is:

$$P = \frac{C_1}{(1 + r)} + \frac{C_2}{(1 + r)^2} + \frac{C_3}{(1 + r)^3} + \ \cdots\ + \frac{C_n}{(1 + r)^n} + \frac{F_n}{(1 + r)^n}$$

In our example, we already know the price or present value ($900), the coupon payments ($50), the face value ($1,000), and the number of years to maturity (10). Thus:

$$\$900 = \frac{\$50}{(1 + r)} + \frac{\$50}{(1 + r)^2} + \frac{\$50}{(1 + r)^3} + \ \cdots\ + \frac{\$50}{(1 + r)^{10}} + \frac{\$1000}{(1 + r)^{10}}$$

What we do *not* know is r—the particular rate of discount that will make the sum of all the expected future payments equal to the present value (or price) of $900. That particular r is called the *yield to maturity*. In corporation finance textbooks it is also called the internal rate of return.

What is r in this case?

We could figure it out by trial and error, trying one discount rate (say 5 percent) and then another (6 percent) until we find the one that makes all the terms on the right-hand side of the formula add up to $900. But that would be a time-consuming process. It would be a lot quicker (and easier) to look it up in a book of bond tables, where it is all figured out for us. There the yield to maturity in this particular case turns out to be 6.37 percent. That is the answer we have been searching for: 6.37 percent is the effective annual interest rate you will be getting on this security.[6] Put in terms of our previous forward-looking example: investing $900 at 6.37 percent would generate

[6] Bond tables are generally constructed on the assumption of semiannual interest payments. If you work this problem on a hand calculator, assuming only one interest payment a year, you will get 6.38 percent.

coupon payments of $50 per year for ten years and a $1,000 payment at the end of ten years.

To summarize: A payment that is due to you in one year is discounted by $(1 + r)$, one due in two years by $(1 + r)^2$, one due in three years by $(1 + r)^3$, and so on; with a given r, the longer away the payment the smaller its present value (time is money!). The yield to maturity (or internal rate of return) of 6.37 percent is the rate of discount that will make the sum of the present values of all future payments equal to the price (of $900). The $900 price therefore consists of the sum of the discounted present values of all the expected future payments.

4. We can use this example to illustrate the important *inverse relationship between bond prices and yields.* As early as Chapter 1 (see footnote 5), we mentioned that "a rise (or fall) in the price of a bond is reflected, in terms of sheer arithmetic, in an automatic change in the opposite direction in the effective rate of interest. To say the price of bonds rose or the rate of interest fell are two different ways of saying the same thing."

This is clearly seen by looking at our general formula for the present value or price of a bond. If the coupon (C) and the face value (F) are fixed, a higher price (P) must imply a lower yield to maturity (r). Similarly, a lower P must imply a higher r.

For instance, what if you paid not $900 but $950 for the bond we have been discussing? What yield to maturity would you be getting then? Substitute $950 for $900 in our illustration above. The yield to maturity, according to bond tables, would fall to 5.66 percent. What if you paid only $850? Then the yield to maturity would rise to 7.13 percent.

In our example, we have assumed that we know P and want to find the resulting interest rate. We could do it the other way around: we could assume we want to get a certain target rate of interest and then search for whatever price would provide it. For instance, enter 7 percent as a target rate of interest in the formula above, and then find the price that would provide that yield to maturity (assuming, of course, that C and F are fixed). The answer must be a price *below* $900, since $900 only gives us a 6.37 percent yield. (The answer, according to bond tables, is that in this case a price of $858 would produce a 7 percent yield to maturity.)

In this connection, the special case of a consol—or perpetuity— deserves a paragraph or two of its own because it illustrates this principle so clearly. A consol is a bond with no maturity date at all. It promises that the holder will receive a fixed annual dollar payment forever, with no redemption date. In that case, with n approaching infinity, our general present value formula collapses (you'll have to take our word for it) into simply:

$$P = \frac{C}{r}$$

Here it becomes obvious that, with C given (at say $50), the price (P) and the rate of interest (r) have to move inversely. If P falls, r must rise; and if P rises, r must fall.

5. We can also use our general formula above, for the present value or price of a bond, to explain why *a given change in interest rates affects long-term bond prices so much more than it affects the prices of short-term securities*. In the money market section of this chapter, we noted that "it is simply a fact of life, imbedded in the mathematics of bond yields and prices, that for long-term securities a small change in interest rates involves a large change in price, whereas for short-term securities even a large change in yield involves only a small change in price."

This fact—the longer a bond's maturity, the more its price will be affected by a change in the general level of interest rates—has enormous implications for capital gains and losses. When all interest rates fall, short and long term, long-term securities rise dramatically in price, not short-term ones. Similarly, when all interest rates rise across the board, long-term bonds—not the shorter ones—drop drastically in price. In other words, you could get rich quick with long bonds, but you could also go down the drain.

Our general formula explains why this is so, when the change in interest rates is the same throughout the maturity range. The formula shows that the price or present value of a bond consists of the sum of the discounted present values of all of its future payments. With a short-term security, you will receive only a few future payments; thus a change in the discount factor (r) will have relatively little impact on the price. The longer the maturity of a security, however, the greater will be the impact of a change in r on the price because a larger number of future payments will be discounted, and for a longer period of time. The longer period of time is important: remember that discounting a payment due ten years hence isn't just discounting (dividing) by $(1 + r)$ but by $(1 + r)^{10}$.

6. Finally, a word of warning. Thus far we have talked only about nominal interest rates, but *it is important to distinguish between nominal and "real" rates*. The 6.37 percent yield to maturity on our bond is a nominal rate of interest. The "real" rate of interest is defined as the nominal rate minus the rate of inflation—because inflation means that you will get back dollars that are worth less (in terms of purchasing power) than the dollars you originally paid out. In our

example, if inflation proceeds at a constant rate of 5 percent a year, then the *real* rate of interest is 6.37 percent minus 5 percent or only 1.37 percent. If inflation is *greater* than 6.37 percent per annum, the real rate of interest would actually be *negative*—which was indeed the case in the late 1970s.

With these five chapters as background, we are almost ready to turn to money and the financial system in greater detail. Before we do so, however, let's take a quick look at portfolio theory—at some general principles of which assets to buy (and which to get rid of!). We don't promise to teach you how to get rich quick—we're still trying to figure that one out ourselves—but maybe we can help you go broke more slowly.

Suggestions for Further Reading

The overall perspective of this chapter is derived primarily from John G. Gurley, "Financial Institutions in the Saving-Investment Process," *Proceedings of the 1959 Conference on Saving and Residential Financing* (United States Savings and Loan League, 1959). A very popular introduction to this general area is Dorothy M. Nichols, *Two Faces of Debt* (Federal Reserve Bank of Chicago).

For more on financial institutions, in terms of their activities and the composition of their assets and liabilities, see Robert P. Black and Doris E. Harless, *Nonbank Financial Institutions* (Federal Reserve Bank of Richmond); Raymond W. Goldsmith, *Financial Intermediaries in the American Economy Since 1900* (Princeton, N.J.: Princeton University Press, 1958); and Donald P. Jacobs, Loring C. Farwell, and Edwin H. Neave, *Financial Institutions*, 5th ed. (Homewood, Ill.: Irwin, 1972). For a formal econometric investigation into financial institutions, see William L. Silber, *Portfolio Behavior of Financial Institutions* (New York: Holt, Rinehart and Winston, 1970).

The operations of the money and capital markets are explored in greater depth in *Money Market Instruments* (Federal Reserve Bank of Cleveland); *Instruments of The Money Market* (Federal Reserve Bank of Richmond); Wesley Lindow, *Inside the Money Market* (New York: Random House, 1972); and William C. Freund, *Investment Fundamentals* (Washington, D.C.: American Bankers Association, 1970).

There is also a lot of useful information in Yale L. Meltzer, *Putting Money to Work: An Investment Primer* (Englewood Cliffs, N.J.: Prentice-Hall, 1976); and in Marcia Stigum, *The Money Market: Myth, Reality, and Practice* (Homewood, Ill.: Dow Jones–Irwin, 1978).

On interest, discount, and related matters see Gary E. Clayton and Christopher B. Spivey, *The Time Value of Money* (Philadelphia: W. B. Saunders, 1978).

Chapter 6

Risk and Portfolio Choice

RISK is a double-edged sword: it complicates decision-making but makes things interesting. That is true of life in general and monetary-financial economics in particular. At this point we'll stick to the economic perspective, although the end of our chapter will hint at issues with a broader appeal.

Our main concern is setting the framework for decisions regarding the allocation of wealth among alternative assets. This is what is meant by portfolio selection. In accountants' terminology, we will examine the balance sheet decisions of the individual. The most interesting elements concern how to choose among assets with varying degrees of risk.

Before our foray into risky decision-making, however, let's set the stage by describing the financial sector without risk. It's certainly not the world as we know it, but it is a useful point of departure.

A World of Certainty

Without risk there are no disappointments. All plans proceed as conceived; all expectations are fulfilled; no promises are broken. Life is perfectly predictable, and so is the financial sector.

One person's promise to repay a loan is as good as anyone else's. No one is a welcher—not even your brother-in-law. Under such ideal conditions there is exactly one interest rate applicable to each and every loan. Anyone trying to charge more will not succeed in making a loan; anyone charging less will be deluged with requests for funds. All promissory notes are perfect substitutes for each other; hence they must sell for the same price, which means they offer the same yield. Thus, the interest rate is the same for all—it is the yield earned by lenders on a riskless loan, one that will be repaid in full by all borrowers, without a shadow of a doubt, at a designated time in the future.

Since this is a rather peculiar world, to say the least, it's worth asking whether there will be any borrowing or lending at all, under such mythical conditions? The answer is yes, as long as individuals differ regarding the desired time patterns of their consumption. Those preferring instant gratification (IG) may want to consume more today than their current income, while prudent providers (PP) may want to consume less than their current income. The PPs lend to the IGs at the unique rate of interest. That rate is determined, in fact, by the balancing of the total demand for funds by the IGs with the total supply of funds from the PPs.

The rate of interest doesn't have anything to do with risk since there isn't any. Rather, the interest rate influences people's consumption and investment decisions. If more people want to borrow—either to buy a new hat (consumption) or to build a new factory (real investment)—than want to lend, the rate of interest will be pushed up by the unsatisfied (and still-eager) borrowers. The rise in the rate of interest causes some to rethink their borrowing and spending plans, while others may decide to save and lend more—with a higher interest rate it pays to be a prudent provider. Thus the key decisions influenced by the rate of interest are consumption, saving, and investment. There are no portfolio problems because every financial asset is the same.

Sources of Uncertainty

At the very least, the world, as we know it, is rife with unanticipated disappointment. Borrowers, however well-intentioned, may be simply unable to fulfill their promises to repay borrowed funds. Factories built to produce polyester fabrics might become obsolete because of renewed enchantment with natural fibers. The manufacturer who borrowed funds with every intention of repaying out of expected polyester sales cannot pay the promised interest and/or principal on his loan. Either event is called a default, and the lenders' expected return is either reduced or wiped out.

Default risk is associated with all promissory notes of individuals and private corporations. The obligations of the federal government, on the other hand, are not so flawed. Federal taxing power, together with the authority to coin money, means that payment of interest and principal on federal obligations is never in doubt. There is, however, still another source of uncertainty affecting even the yields of default-free government securities: the risk of fluctuations in the level of the interest rate—sometimes called market risk or capital uncertainty.

A two-year government bond selling for its $1,000 face value and bearing an interest coupon of $60, payable at the end of each year, has an expected yield of 6 percent. There is no question that this bond will yield 6 percent if held to maturity. If you buy it you'll receive $60 per annum plus $1,000 at maturity. That's 6 percent, given the initial $1,000 outlay. But in our world of uncertainty, it's just possible that you will have to sell unexpectedly before maturity—say, at the end of one year. To whom do you sell? To someone else, to someone who wants to lend funds for one year (the original two-year bond now has one year to maturity). At what price? Aha! That's the big question, as we discussed at the end of the last chapter. Can you get $1,000 for the bond, thereby realizing 6 percent, as expected? Not necessarily! It depends on the yield on newly issued one-year government securities. If the going rate of interest on one-year securities is 6 percent, the old bond sells for $1,000 and the yield is as expected. But if, for some reason, yields have risen to 7 percent, so that new bonds bear a coupon of $70 per $1,000, then you'll be offered less. In fact, you'll be offered only $990, or just enough to make the $60 coupon yield 7 percent to the new holder; that, after all, is the going rate of interest.

What has happened to the two-year government bond sold after one year? Instead of yielding 6 percent, the expected yield to maturity, its actual yield turns out to be only 5 percent—the $60 coupon *minus* a capital loss of $10. The *holding-period* yield can be less than the original expected yield to maturity if the level of interest rates rises. Thus bonds that are sold before maturity have uncertain yields even if all coupon payments are made on time and even if the face value is paid at maturity. And, in our uncertain world, it's not unlikely for bondholders to need funds before their investments mature.

Still more uncertainty would be evident if we considered real interest rates rather than nominal yields, as mentioned in the previous chapter. Government bonds do not promise real yields—just nominal payments. But we have already sufficiently complicated our simple world to examine the principles of portfolio choice under uncertainty. Obviously there are many rates of interest on securities that differ with respect to maturity and issuer. Or, more generally, securities have different expected yields and varying degrees of risk. How can or should these securities be combined under rational decision-making? We have already mentioned the principle of diversification in connection with financial intermediaries in Chapter 5 (see page 59). We are also familiar with its usage in everyday discussion. As we will see below, portfolio diversification is desirable under certain circumstances and can be optimally designed given specific interrelationships between securities.

Risk Aversion and Portfolio Analysis

One of the most important *assumptions* of modern portfolio analysis is risk aversion. People are assumed to dislike risk. That doesn't mean they'll never indulge—they will if the price is right. And in the context of securities in a portfolio, the right price translates into a sufficiently high expected yield.

The simplest example illustrating risk aversion is the preference for a security which is certain to pay 5 percent compared with one having an equal chance of paying either 8 percent or 2 percent. The second security has an average return of 5 percent: about half the time its yield is 8 percent, and about half the time its yield is 2 percent. Its *expected* yield is 5 percent, where the formal definition of expectation is: the sum of the possible outcomes multiplied by their respective probabilities: $8\% \times \frac{1}{2}$ plus $2\% \times \frac{1}{2} = 5\%$. Note that the *expected* yield is nothing more than the average yield.

Why does a risk averter prefer the certain return of 5 percent to an equal chance of 8 percent or 2 percent, even though the expected values of the two securities are identical? Simply put, the extra pleasure when the return is 8 percent is less than the additional pain when the return is 2 percent. Sound familiar? It should, because it's nothing more than diminishing marginal utility of money: each additional dollar is worth less (although you always want more!).

Would the risk-averter ever be indifferent between a security paying a fixed yield with certainty, such as a 5 percent savings deposit in a commercial bank, and a bond whose return is uncertain? Yes, but only if the bond had a higher expected return to compensate for the undesirable uncertainty. For example, if the bond's equally probable outcomes were either 10 percent or 2 percent, so the expected return is 6 percent ($10\% \times \frac{1}{2}$ plus $2\% \times \frac{1}{2} = 6\%$), then our risk-averting portfolio manager might be indifferent. If the possible outcomes are 12 percent and 2 percent, so that the expected return is 7 percent, then he might even prefer the risky venture—since the compensation in terms of higher expected yield is enough to induce risk-taking. The required trade-off of higher return per unit of risk—the degree of risk aversion—is a subjective measure, quite different for every individual.

Does all this mean someone who is not a risk averter must have deep-seated emotional problems? Not at all—he or she is simply a risk lover (also known as a compulsive-degenerate gambler). We observe that most people in the real world are risk averters. Not because they tell us so in any direct way, but because most people hold diversified portfolios—many different securities rather than just one with the highest possible return. Diversification is the salvation of the risk averter, but mere child's-play to the risk lover.

Before proceeding to the principles of diversification and portfolio selection, it is useful to note that we have used what is formally called a probability distribution to represent the outcomes of our financial investment. Each of the possible "events" (8% or 2%) has a probability of occurring ($\frac{1}{2}$ in our case) and the sum of the probabilities is unity (at least one of the possible outcomes must occur). Moreover, we have used a statistic called the arithmetic mean (the common average) to summarize the most likely outcome—the expected value. In this vein, we can try to specify more carefully the meaning of risk.

Uncertain outcomes make for risky investments. While the expected value of our equally probable 8 percent and 2 percent investment is 5 percent, sometimes the return will be 3 percent more than the mean and sometimes the return will be 3 percent less. The deviation of actual returns from expected returns is a useful measure of risk. Formal statistical techniques suggest a slightly more complicated approach—just to terrorize the uninitiated. Deviations of actual outcomes from the mean can be either positive or negative. In fact, if one were to add them up, the pluses and minuses would cancel! We could apply either of two arithmetic operations to avoid the canceling problem: (1) take absolute values; (2) square the deviations (recalling that a negative number squared is a positive number). The second is used in calculating what is called the standard deviation, which we now describe in somewhat greater detail.

In addition to the magnitude of the deviation around the expected value, risk should also be related to the probability of such events actually occurring. Thus, if the 2% outcome has only a 1 in 10 chance of actually occurring, this represents less of a risk than if it has a probability of ½. In calculating the standard deviation, the squared deviations around the mean are "weighted" by their probability of occurring; that is, they are multiplied by their respective probabilities. This makes the standard deviation a still more intuitive measure of risk. The final step in the calculation is to restore the numbers to their original scale by taking the square root of the entire mess. In our example, we have the following: $(8 - 5)^2 \times \frac{1}{2} + (2 - 5)^2 \times \frac{1}{2} = 9 \times \frac{1}{2} + 9 \times \frac{1}{2} = 9$, the square-root of which is 3. In particular, for this investment the standard deviation of the probability distribution of returns is 3 percent. With a more complicated probability distribution, the numerical results are not quite so simple.

A potential drawback of the standard deviation is the use of both positive and negative deviations about the expected value. Shouldn't risk measure only the disappointments—that is, when actual outcomes are below expectations? That's a reasonable suggestion. But when the probability distribution is symmetrical above and below the mean, it makes no difference (below the mean is just half the total). Since there is evidence suggesting that security returns have this symmetry (they are normally distributed), and since the standard deviation has nice statistical properties (whatever that means), much of portfolio analysis uses the standard deviation to measure risk.

We are now prepared for one of the most fundamental propositions of modern portfolio theory:[1] An asset may seem very risky when viewed in isolation, but when combined with other assets, the risk of the portfolio may be substantially less—even zero! To illustrate this we also consider the central problem of portfolio analysis: how to choose an efficient portfolio.

Portfolio Selection

Take two assets (please). The first we'll call asset A for Adventure Inc. We're not quite sure what business they're in, but it's a good one. In good times, it pays 16 percent and in bad times it pays 2 percent, clearly a cyclical industry. An expected return of 9 percent—but with fairly large uncertainty over the actual outcome—varying directly with the pulse of economic activity. Now consider asset B for Barbiturates Inc.

[1] The original work on modern portfolio theory is Harry Markowitz, *Portfolio Selection* (New York: Wiley, 1959). Major extensions are summarized in William F. Sharpe, *Portfolio Theory and Capital Markets* (New York: McGraw-Hill, 1970).

We know pretty much what they do. In good times they lose money, producing a return of minus 2 percent. But in bad times they rake it in, earning 12 percent for the misanthropic investors. The expected return is 5 percent, with substantial variance in the actual results. Note, however, that asset B's outcomes are countercyclical—they are better when the economy is worse.

Could it make sense to buy both of these highly risky investments—apparently exposing oneself to all sorts of disappointment? The answer is definitely yes. In fact—dividing your funds equally between assets A and B yields a return of 7 percent, in both good times and bad—there is no uncertainty at all![2]

Does that mean I would definitely prefer the half-and-half combination to either A or B by itself? Well, I know I prefer it to B because B's expected return is only 5 percent and it is uncertain at that, while the half-and-half portfolio gives me 7 percent and no risk. The risk averter clearly chooses the combination portfolio. Less clear is whether he chooses the fifty-fifty strategy or puts all his money in A. While A has uncertainty, it also has a higher expected return (9 percent versus 7 percent). The choice of A versus the combination depends upon the precise nature of the risk averter's preferences—whether the extra 2 percent expected return compensates for the increase in risk.

The principal lesson derived from the example is twofold. First, the uncertainty of return of an individual asset is *not* by itself a measure of its riskiness. Rather it is the contribution of the asset's uncertain return to total portfolio risk that matters. Second, a key determinant of the latter is the interrelationship between the variability of the assets' returns. This is so important it has a name of its own—covariance.[3]

---

[2] Here's the arithmetic: Start with $200. Put $100 in A and $100 in B. In "good times" A pays $16 (= 16 percent of $100) and B loses $2. The investor earns $14 ($16 minus $2) on $200 invested, or 7 percent (14/200). In "bad times" the $100 in A earns $2 while the $100 in B earns $12, for a total of $14, which is once again 7 percent. Note: the standard deviation of the returns on the half-and-half portfolio is zero even though each security's return had a positive standard deviation.

[3] Covariance has a simple intuitive definition: comovement. It also has a precise mathematical measurement. In our case, the deviation of each security's return from its mean is derived; the product of the paired observations is then weighted (as in the standard deviation) by the probability of each of the paired observations actually occurring. Positive covariance indicates that when one security's return is above its mean, so is the other. Negative covariance indicates when one security's return is above its mean, the other is below.

The term "correlation" used in the following sentence of the text also has specific mathematical connotation. It is the covariance divided by the product of the standard deviations. It rescales covariance so that *perfect* comovement is +1.0 and perfectly offsetting movement is −1.0, with intermediate relationships between these two extremes. A zero correlation means that the returns of the two securities are independent.

In the example just given, assets A and B are perfectly negatively correlated: when asset A's realized yield is low, that of B is high, and vice versa; and the magnitudes are such that there is perfect offset. That's why combining the two reduces risk (in this case to zero). Indeed, this *is* the principal of portfolio diversification: hold a number of assets (rather than one) so that the exposure to risk is reduced. An asset such as B, whose returns are countercyclical (high when everything else is low) is an ideal addition to a risk averter's portfolio.

But assets such as B are relatively hard to come by. If portfolio diversification to reduce risk depended on finding assets with "negative covariance of returns" we'd be in for tough times (and lots of risk). But the magic of portfolio diversification extends to other cases as well. In particular, as long as assets do not have *precisely* the same *pattern* of returns, then holding a group of assets reduces risk.[4]

Take the case where each asset yields either 6 percent or 2 percent, but the outcomes are independent of good times or bad times, *and of each other*, like the flip of a coin. Does dividing the portfolio between two such assets, X and Y, reduce risk? Well, if I hold both X and Y and *both* happen to yield 6 percent or both happen to yield 2 percent, I'm in the same situation as with holding just one. But it's also possible, in fact *just* as possible, that when X is yielding 6 percent, Y yields 2 percent, or when X yields 2 percent, Y yields 6 percent. In these cases, uncertainty is zero and the return is the average—4 percent. In fact, if I held many, many such assets, all with an equal chance of 6 percent or 2 percent, and the outcome of one is *independent* of every other asset, then I'd be virtually certain of always earning 4 percent. About half of the outcomes would be 6 percent and half would be 2 percent.

You should recognize that the key condition in this last example is the word "independence." When asset returns are relatively independent (zero covariance), putting many together tends to produce the average return just about all of the time. Risk is thereby reduced to zero. Does that mean that most people who, in fact, hold diversified portfolios have zero risk? No it doesn't, because most assets are affected in a systematic way by economic conditions—hence most asset returns are not completely independent of each other.

---

[4] The same pattern of returns translates into a correlation coefficient of +1.0 (the returns on all assets are above or below their respective means at the same time and are proportional to their standard deviations).

Summary Principles

The examples of portfolio diversification just given permit some refinement in the first principles discussed earlier. The standard deviation of returns is a good measure of risk when analyzing a security
by itself. It is also a good measure of risk for an entire portfolio. But
it is a relatively poor measure of the risk-contribution of a single
security to an entire portfolio. That depends much more on the covariance of returns with other securities; more precisely, the *average
covariance* of a security's returns with all others. The reason lies in
the magic of diversification: the risk-contribution to a portfolio of a
security's returns that are substantially independent of all other returns is nearly zero. This *nonsystematic* risk is diversified away as the
number of securities held increases (as in our coin flipping example).
Only the *systematic* movement of the return on a security with all
others adds to portfolio risk.

If most asset holders are risk averse, then it also follows that
they will demand extra compensation—higher expected returns—in
proportion to the systematic risk of a security. The excess return on
a risky security compared with a risk-free asset must be related to its
average covariance with all other securities.

This information is just about all that is necessary for the first
step in portfolio decision-making: separate *efficient* from *inefficient*
portfolios. In fact, in our earlier example, asset B was ruled out because it had the same risk as the half-and-half portfolio (zero) but
yielded less (5 percent versus 7 percent). A portfolio consisting only
of asset B is inefficient. More generally, efficient portfolios have the
following characteristics: greatest possible return for a given risk;
lowest risk for a given return.

After calculating the various combinations of assets that produce
efficient portfolios, investors choose that portfolio which matches
their risk-return preferences. In our earlier example, we could not
say whether asset A (yielding 9 percent with risk) dominated the half-
and-half combination (yielding 7 percent and no risk). Both of these
are efficient portfolios. Which is preferred depends upon the subjective trade-off between risk and return demanded by an individual.

Actually, the final choice of portfolio composition can be separated into two distinct decisions: first, derive the efficient combination of risky securities and second, determine how much cash to hold
versus the risky assets. We discuss the second issue in Chapter 18
under the demand for money while the first will be dealt with in
Chapter 30 within the context of the structure of interest rates.

It's worth emphasizing at this point that all of our analysis holds only for risk averters. For risk lovers, this has been a classroom exercise, useful primarily in preparation for the final exam. How many of you are really risk lovers? Although it sounds like an enjoyable avocation, fewer people than you think actually meet the standard.

The fact that most people hold many financial assets supports the assumption of risk aversion. A risk lover would not find it sensible to hold a diversified portfolio. He would choose to invest in one asset with large possible capital gains (and losses, although he usually puts the latter in parentheses). That doesn't necessarily mean that people won't gamble occasionally: putting down a dollar in a lottery for a one-in-two-million chance of winning a million dollars has some psychic appeal (the mere thought of winning is enough to make you buy two tickets). An occasional trip to Las Vegas—while not an appropriate risk-averter activity—has its other compensations. But when it comes to putting *all* your assets to work—would you take a fifty-fifty chance of doubling your money or losing it all? If your answer is no, you're a risk averter; if the answer is yes, you're a risk lover. If you are the former, then some of the principles of diversification suggested here can help in deciding on the assets you should place in your portfolio. If you are the latter—see you on the next junket to Vegas (bring all of your money and jewelry and clothes and whatever else you can muster up and join the ASCPA—Anonymous Spurners of Conventional Portfolio Analysis).

Suggestions for Further Reading

The seminal book by Harry Markowitz, *Portfolio Selection* (New York: Wiley, 1959) is still the best place to start. For a masterful introduction see William J. Baumol, *Portfolio Theory: The Selection of Asset Combinations* (New York: General Learning Corp., 1970). A leading text on investments is, William F. Sharpe, *Investments* (Englewood Cliffs, N.J.: Prentice-Hall, 1978).

PART II

*Intermediaries
and Banks*

Chapter 7

Financial Intermediation in Practice

IN CHAPTER 5 we saw what financial intermediation was all about and took an overall look at financial institutions and markets. In Chapter 6 we surveyed some of the fundamentals of portfolio theory. It is time to pull all this together and inquire more closely into how the major financial institutions operate—how they acquire funds, what they do with the money once they've got it, and how the profit motive and the regulatory environment influence their behavior. We will look at the major financial institutions in this chapter and then, in the following three chapters, zero in on the largest—commercial banks—and explore their structure and decision making in greater detail.

The Major Financial Institutions

The bird's-eye view of the major financial institutions in Chapter 5 permits us to concentrate now on the ways in which each *intermediates* between saver-lenders and borrower-spenders. What that means is paying special attention to the composition of their liabilities and assets, because they acquire funds from saver-lenders by "selling" their own liabilities, and then turn around and obtain assets when they disperse the funds to borrower-spenders. By paying a lower interest rate when acquiring funds than they charge when dispersing them, financial institutions make a profit on the differential.

    1. *Commercial banks* are the most prominent of all financial institutions. There are almost 15,000 of them, ranging from the Bank of America (with over $75 billion in total deposits) to thousands of small banks scattered throughout the country (many of which have less than $5 million in deposits).

Banks' major source of funds used to be demand deposits, but in the past ten or twenty years savings and time deposits—including large-size negotiable certificates of deposit—have grown relatively more important than demand deposits. With these funds, they buy a wide variety of assets, ranging from short-term government securities to long-term business loans and home mortgages. Since we will devote all of the next three chapters to commercial banks, it is enough for now to simply say that they are the most widely diversified of all financial institutions in terms of both assets and liabilities.

2. *Savings and loan associations* have been primarily savings deposit–oriented on the liabilities side and home mortgage–oriented on the asset side. This was their original purpose—to encourage family thrift and home ownership—and for the most part they are still legally required to adhere to those goals, although changes are in the making.

There are about 5,000 savings and loan associations in the United States, extending from coast to coast. They are supervised by the Federal Home Loan Bank Board in Washington. Deposits (called shares) are insured up to $40,000 per depositor by the Federal Savings and Loan Insurance Corporation, which is to S&Ls what the better-known Federal Deposit Insurance Corporation (FDIC) is to commercial banks and mutual savings banks. Although the bulk of their funds comes from passbook deposits and savings certificates, they can also borrow when necessary from the Federal Home Loan Bank of their district (there are twelve of them, just like the regional Federal Reserve Banks). At times, when savings inflows have dried up, this source of funds has assumed considerable importance.

Savings and loan associations have encountered severe financial problems because such a large proportion of their liabilities is in the form of savings deposits—which are in effect payable virtually on demand—while a large proportion of their assets consists of long-term mortgages, many of which were acquired years ago. Typically, they pay a fixed interest rate for their savings deposits—say 6 percent—and then turn around and make home mortgage loans at a higher rate—say 8 percent. The 2 percent differential is their profit. However, imagine the problems they face when short-term interest rates rise to 9 percent: they are caught in a profit squeeze because they find it necessary to pay 9 percent to get new money (and also to prevent an outflow of their existing deposits), while their assets are still yielding only 8 percent because most of them were acquired long ago. This is exactly what has happened during periods of tight money and rising short-term interest rates, a subject we will return to shortly.

3. *Mutual savings banks* are identical to savings and loan associations in most respects, except that there are only about 500 of them

and they are concentrated mostly in New England and the mid-Atlantic states. As with S&Ls, they obtain most of their funds in the form of savings deposits and receive significant tax incentives to invest them primarily in home mortgages.

As their name implies, mutual savings banks are legally structured as "mutuals" or "cooperatives," with the depositors or shareholders "owning" the institution. Many S&Ls are also mutual associations, although a significant proportion are stockholder-owned. Mutual savings banks are state-chartered institutions, with supervision and insurance provided by the FDIC.

Since mutual savings banks are so similar to S&Ls, they face identical problems when short-term interest rates rise: they have to pay more to obtain new money (and to retain a lot of what they have), but the return they get on most of their assets fails to rise correspondingly since they are long-term mortgages acquired years ago.

4. *Life insurance companies* rank third in total size, after commercial banks and S&Ls. They can predict with a high degree of actuarial accuracy how much money they will need to pay out in benefits this year, next year, even ten and twenty years from now; and they invest accordingly, aiming for the highest yield consistent with maximum safety. A high proportion of life insurance company assets thus consists of long-term corporate bonds and mortgages (although the mortgages are primarily on commercial rather than on residential properties).

CHART 1 / Asset composition of selected financial institutions (end of 1978). Source: *Federal Reserve Bulletin.*

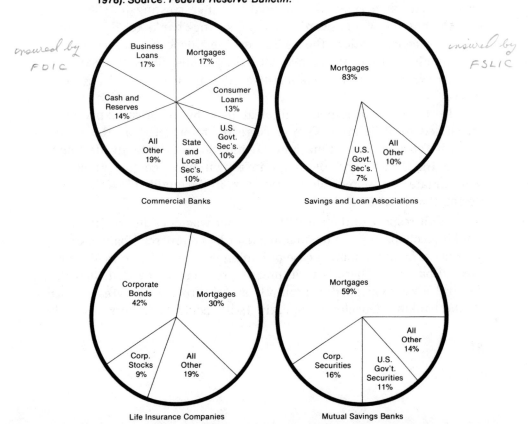

Deposit Rate Ceilings and Financial Disintermediation

Before proceeding further, an essential ingredient has to be brought into the picture, one that has played an important (and controversial) role in the financial system for many years. That ingredient is interest rate ceilings on deposits—more familiarly known as Regulation Q.

The Federal Reserve sets the legal maximum interest rates—through what is called Regulation Q—that commercial banks are allowed to pay on their time and savings deposit liabilities. The maximum interest rates that savings banks and savings and loan association may offer depositors are also regulated. In addition, banks have been prohibited from paying any interest at all on *demand deposits*—in effect, a demand deposit interest rate ceiling set at zero.

Regulation Q was enacted in the Banking Act of 1933, on the grounds that excessive interest rate competition for deposits during the 1920s had undermined the soundness of the banking system. It was believed that competition among commercial banks for funds had driven deposit rates up too high. To cover their costs, banks acquired high-yielding but excessively risky low-quality assets. This deterioration in the quality of bank portfolios, it was said, contributed to the collapse of the banking system in the early 1930s. Abolition of interest rate competition for deposits, by setting rate ceilings, was seen as rooting out the basic element weakening the banking system.

Similar arguments were responsible for the imposition of comparable ceilings over S&Ls and savings banks starting in 1966. Although, in an effort to reward S&Ls and savings banks for their home mortgage concentration, the ceiling on their deposit rates is set ¼ percent higher than at commercial banks. Thus, S&Ls and savings banks have been given a competitive edge in attracting depositors' funds.

In retrospect, it is not at all clear that the historical experience which led to Regulation Q was correctly interpreted at the time. Interest rates on bank time and savings deposits actually declined during the 1920s, and thorough investigation since has failed to substantiate any appreciable deterioration in the quality of bank assets during that period.

With respect to the early 1930s, what was once interpreted as a banking collapse due to mismanagement by commercial bankers now appears to be much more a case of banking collapse due to inadequate *central* banking. There is widespread agreement today that, had the Federal Reserve stepped in promptly and vigorously, the greater part of the banking debacle of the early 1930s could have been avoided.

Whatever the logic of such ceilings in 1933, after thousands of bank failures, there are far fewer grounds for continuing them today. Bank failures are now rare—over the past quarter century they have averaged less than six a year—and those that have occurred have generally been attributable more to embezzlement or other fraudulent practices than to excessive competition of any kind. In any case, the reason so few banks have failed is not due to Regulation Q, but to the existence of the Federal Deposit Insurance Corporation.

Regulation Q *has* effectively prevented aggressive, well-managed banks from offering depositors more attractive interest rates than the bank next door. Aggressive banks that would like to compete for funds by bidding more for deposits have been legally prohibited from doing so, which also means, of course, that depositors have simultaneously been deprived of the enlarged options that more vigorous price competition among banks would offer them. It is true that banks have been known to give away toasters, radios, and a two-year subscription to *Playboy* in order to attract deposits. But how do banks reach those who don't eat bread, can't stand the radio, and have foresworn serious reading?[1]

Regulation Q has also caused intermittent financial *dis*intermediation—as during the tight-money episodes of 1966, 1969, and 1973–1974. During those periods, money market interest rates rose to what were then record levels, but deposit interest rates lagged behind. With deposit interest rates substantially below open market rates, savers stopped moving funds *into* financial institutions—instead, they moved them *out*. People took money out of savings accounts and put funds directly into primary securities, thereby bypassing the intermediaries.

This behavior is known as financial disintermediation. Financial intermediation describes savers depositing funds with financial institutions, which then turn around and buy primary securities (such as bonds, stocks, and mortgages). Financial disintermediation is the reverse: savers take funds *out* of their deposit accounts, or reduce the amounts they normally put in, and directly buy the primary securities themselves.

This put the intermediaries under severe pressure. With substantial withdrawals and minimal inflows of new funds, their profit position was threatened, their solvency was endangered, and their ability to lend evaporated. They reacted as financial institutions will—

---

[1] In addition, Regulation Q discriminates against the small saver. Higher interest rates are permitted on large deposits (over $100,000) than on small ones. See Edward J. Kane, "Short-Changing the Small Saver," *Journal of Money, Credit and Banking* (November 1970).

by pulling in their horns, trying to retrench, and running to Congress for help.

What happened? What caused the usually smoothly functioning financial system to start to come apart at the seams?

What happened was that market interest rates went so high so fast that the intermediaries, for both internal and external reasons, could not raise the rates they pay depositors high enough or fast enough to stay competitive. Disappointed depositors drowned their sorrow by going out and buying high-yielding primary securities on their own.

Two reasons prevented the intermediaries from adjusting their deposit rates sufficiently to stay competitive with open market rates on primary securities. *Internally,* they felt they could not afford to. The assets of most intermediaries are predominàntly long-term; most were bought some time ago, at considerably lower yields. The average rate of return is thus heavily weighted by the past. The purchase of new, higher-yielding securities will only slightly increase the overall yield on the total portfolio. On the other hand, if they increase their passbook savings deposit rates to attract new money, they have no choice but to pay the new higher rates to *all* passbook savings depositors.[3]

In 1966 and again in 1969 and 1973–1974, market rates moved up so far and so rapidly that most financial institutions felt, after a brief attempt to stay in the race, that it was too costly to continue. They had, to put it bluntly, been priced out of the market.

But there was another reason why they did not stay in the race, an *external* one. Namely, Regulation Q. Some intermediaries—perhaps the better managed ones—were all for posting higher passbook savings deposit rates and going after new business. But they couldn't. The legal deposit rate ceilings imposed by the Federal Reserve, the Federal Home Loan Bank Board and other supervisory agencies prevented them from raising deposit rates further once the maximum limits had been reached.

Indeed, in mid-1966 the deposit rate ceilings were actually rolled back to lower levels, forcing many institutions that had posted higher interest rates to reduce them. With market rates still rising, it is no wonder many depositors withdrew their money and went directly into the securities markets themselves.

The disintermediation effects of Regulation Q have been softened in the last few years by several regulatory changes. In 1970 the Federal Reserve eliminated the rate ceilings on large-size ($100,000 and over) negotiable CDs that mature in less than three months, in order to ease money market pressures stemming from the collapse of the Penn

Central Railroad. And in 1973 the Fed eliminated the ceilings on longer-maturity large-size CDs as well.

Equally important, especially in forestalling disintermediation during the tight-money episode of 1978–1979, was a newly permitted six-month money market time certificate that commercial banks and thrift institutions were allowed to issue starting in mid-1978. The interest rate on these is tied to the Treasury bill rate, so that depositors could receive high money market yields without withdrawing their funds from the depository institutions. They can merely shift their funds for six months in the same bank or S&L from a passbook savings account to a money market time certificate. So far, however, these are not permitted in denominations below $10,000, leaving smaller depositors out in the cold.

Money market mutual funds are the private sector's answer to this under-$10,000 gap. They are a new kind of financial institution that has arisen in recent years in response to the restrictions imposed by Regulation Q. With large depositors able to get the benefits of high money market rates—since large CDs of $100,000 and over were freed from deposit rate ceilings in 1970 and 1973, and with money market time certificates available in denominations of $10,000—there was room for ingenuity and innovation on behalf of small depositors. This ingenuity was provided, beginning in the early seventies, by money market mutual funds: they gather together the funds of many small savers, in batches as small as $1,000 and $2,000, and then proceed to buy high-yielding large-size CDs and other money market instruments, such as commercial paper, in denominations of $25,000, $50,000, and $100,000. By pooling their funds, small savers are thus able to gain access to money market yields that Regulation Q would otherwise prevent them from realizing. Remember however, these money market funds are not insured by any Federal agency. Nevertheless, by late 1979 the money market mutual funds had grown to nearly $40 billion in total assets. And much to the government's consternation, no one regulates them (at least not so far).

Financial Institutions Are Becoming More Alike

So far in this chapter we have stressed the differences among financial institutions; traditional distinctions that have deep historical and institutional roots. But in recent years these differences have been eroding, making depository institutions increasingly alike. By the 1990s it may be difficult to tell them apart.

Consider the following:

1.   Traditionally, commercial banks have not been permitted to open savings accounts for business firms. If a business wanted a passbook savings deposit, it had to be at a mutual savings bank or a savings and loan association. Beginning in 1975, however, commercial banks were allowed to accept savings deposits from business firms, up to $150,000 per depositor per bank.

2.   Traditionally, demand deposits have been the province of commercial banks, with other deposit-type financial institutions legally barred from offering checking account facilities. In 1972, however, NOW (negotiable order of withdrawal) accounts were introduced by a Massachusetts savings bank—the Consumers Savings Bank of Worcester—and by 1978 such accounts were permitted for thrift institutions in six New England states and in New York. For all practical purposes, a NOW account is a checking account. Since early 1978 credit unions throughout the country can also offer checking accounts, called credit union share drafts.

3.   Traditionally—at least since the Banking Act of 1933—interest on demand deposits has been prohibited. NOW accounts, however, at mutual savings banks and at savings and loan associations, are not only checking accounts but *interest-bearing* checking accounts to boot. Beginning in 1978, commercial banks in six New England states and in New York were likewise permitted to offer NOW accounts —interest-bearing checking accounts. Credit union share drafts also bear interest.

4.   Closely related to NOW accounts—which in effect pay interest on transactions balances—are automatic transfer services (ATS), which have been authorized nationwide for commercial banks and thrift institutions since late 1978. With ATS, funds are transferred automatically from a savings account to a checking account whenever the checking account balance falls below an agreed-upon level. Overdrafts (writing a check for more than is in the checking account) can thus be covered by automatic transfers from the savings account. In effect, interest can be earned on transactions balances by holding funds in your savings deposit until you are ready to spend them. (Other recently developed means of immediately transferring funds from savings to checking accounts include telephone transfers and plastic "debit" cards inserted in automated teller machines.)

An indication of the somewhat chaotic state of affairs, a ruling by the courts in early 1979 has questioned the legality of ATS accounts. There may be no choice but to seek congressional legislation to make *de jure* interest-bearing accounts out of these *de facto* innovations.

5. Traditionally, mutual savings banks and savings and loans have specialized almost exclusively in mortgage lending. They are presently lobbying vigorously, however, for the right to make consumer loans. They also want to issue variable-rate mortgages, where the mortgage interest rate would rise or fall depending on market interest rate fluctuations. This would alleviate the profit squeeze that typically grips them during tight-money periods, when they have to pay more for funds but their returns are frozen at past levels because so much of their portfolio is extremely long term. Consumer loans and variable-rate mortgages would help their income rise along with their costs, permitting them to attract deposits by offering competitive yields.

6. Traditionally, credit unions have specialized almost exclusively in consumer loans. In 1977, however, they were given the right to make long-term mortgage loans.

The net result of all these innovations and related developments is that the traditional specialization of financial institutions is breaking down. Financial institutions are becoming more general and more alike. In a sense, they are all in the process of becoming commercial banks—dealing in checking accounts and becoming more diversified in both their assets and their liabilities.

Are Commercial Banks Different?

Throughout this chapter we have mentioned the profits earned by financial institutions on the differential between interest rates on assets and liabilities. If asked what determines the optimal level of savings and loan shares, or savings bank deposits, from the viewpoint of management, we would discuss the interest rate earned on assets and the rate paid on liabilities. At some point, for example, it would no longer pay savings institutions to attract deposits—namely, when the interest return on their assets no longer exceeds the rate paid on their liabilities. Only if the rate earned on assets goes up will they raise deposit rates; only then will they want to attract liabilities—and this is as it should be. A financial institution is like any other firm. The level of operations (deposits or loans) should be determined by the familiar marginal-revenue-equals-marginal-cost condition of traditional price theory.

Back in Chapter 3, however, when discussing the level of demand and time deposits for commercial banks we hardly mentioned the rate of interest. Instead, the level of demand deposits supplied by commercial banks was given by the volume of reserves times the deposit multiplier (the reciprocal of the required reserve ratio). The deposit multiplier approach assumes that an increase in reserves will always be loaned out, until all reserves wind up in the required category. A lower required reserve ratio means more demand deposits, and more reserves mean more demand deposits.

It is obvious that we cannot apply the deposit multiplier analysis to savings institutions. If we did, it would suggest that the level of their liabilities should be infinite—a required reserve ratio of zero and one divided by zero is infinity—a ridiculously unrealistic proposition that even an economist could not promote with a semiclear conscience. Clearly, therefore, the marginal-revenue-marginal-cost approach is correct for nonbank financial institutions: that is what sets the upper limit to savings bank size, just as it sets the upper limit to the size of any firm in the economy. So why not for commercial banks, at least as they are traditionally described?

The only justification for using the deposit multiplier approach for commercial banks is when marginal-revenue-marginal-cost calculations are not relevant.[2] We can count on commercial bankers lending out all of their reserves, until none are in the excess category, only if they are in a position where marginal revenue *exceeds* marginal cost. That has been true because of two traditional legal regulations: no interest is permitted on bank demand deposits, and bank required reserves must be held in a form (cash and deposits at the Fed) that earn the banks no interest. The former holds down the marginal cost of demand deposits, while the latter means that revenues are earned on only a fraction (85 percent if the required reserve ratio is 15 percent) of assets. Banks would love to increase their loans and deposits until marginal revenue falls to the point where it equals marginal cost. For every additional dollar loaned out in such circumstances, profits go up. Why don't they do it? Because they are constrained by the required reserve ratio and the fixed volume of reserves.

The truth about the determination of the volume of demand deposits lies somewhere between the basic deposit multiplier approach and the marginal-revenue-equals-marginal-cost approach. As we hinted in the Appendix to Chapter 3 (see footnote 7), the level of demand deposits (and the money supply) can also be a function of interest

---

[2] These arguments follow those set forth by James Tobin, "Commercial Banks as Creators of Money," in *Banking and Monetary Studies,* ed. Deane Carson (Homewood, Ill.: Irwin, 1963).

rates. For example, we pointed out that commercial banks will borrow reserves from the Fed when the interest rate on bank loans (marginal revenue) goes up. Similarly, if rates fall to low enough levels, banks may just sit with excess reserves rather than incurring any risks by making loans or buying securities. And this situation occurred quite dramatically in the 1930s.

A *compleat* treatment of the determination of the supply of demand deposits is basically similar to savings deposits and savings and loan shares. The credit multiplier approach is, indeed, oversimplified. Demand deposits depend on the volume of reserves but also on interest rates. Past estimates have put this interest-sensitivity at rather small magnitudes, suggesting that the traditional multiplier approach may be a fair approximation to the real world. However, the changing financial environment discussed in this chapter suggests that the continued viability of the multiplier approach may be short-lived. Moreover, the view that commercial banks are different *in principle* from other financial institutions cannot be supported. Marginal-cost-marginal-revenue calculations are relevant even though traditionally blunted by legal and administrative regulations.

All of this suggest that it is crucial to examine more closely commercial banks and how they conduct their business. That will take us through the next three chapters.

Suggestions for Further Reading

Two classics on financial intermediaries are the book by John G. Gurley and Edwin S. Shaw, *Money in a Theory of Finance* (Washington, D.C.: Brookings Institution, 1960), and the article by James Tobin, "Commercial Banks as Creators of Money," in *Banking and Monetary Studies*, ed. Deane Carson (Homewood, Ill.: Irwin, 1963).

If you want to know more about the administration of Regulation Q over the years, a convenient source is the article by Adrian W. Throop which takes up just about the whole November 1974 issue of the Federal Reserve Bank of Dallas *Business Review*. You can find the current Regulation Q rate ceilings in the statistical section in the back of any recent *Federal Reserve Bulletin* (usually they are on page A10 in a table labeled "Maximum Interest Rates Payable on Time and Savings Deposits at Federally Insured Institutions"). With respect to demand deposits, see Bryon Higgins, "Interest Payments on Demand Deposits: Historical Evolution and Current Controversy," Federal Reserve Bank of Kansas City *Monthly Review* (July-August 1977).

For a careful survey of recent legislative developments regarding financial institutions, see Jean M. Lovati, "The Growing Similarity Among Financial Institutions," Federal Reserve Bank of St. Louis *Review* (October 1977).

Chapter 8

The Regulation and Structure of the Banking Industry

COMMERCIAL BANKS are the most important financial institutions in the United States. At the end of 1978 they had over a trillion dollars in total assets, compared with about $500 billion for savings and loan associations, $400 billion for life insurance companies, and $150 billion for savings banks. An industry this size, particularly one so intimately involved with the monetary and payments system, clearly occupies a key role in the functioning of the economy.

Is the banking industry so structured as to best provide the financial services needed by a changing and growing economy? Is there enough competition in banking to make it a dynamic and innovative industry, responsive to private needs and public goals? Are banks safe places in which to put your money? Who supervises banks, in what ways, and for what purposes?

The Dual Banking System

The American banking system is known as a "dual" banking system, not because its origins have anything to do with the historic encounter between Alexander Hamilton and Aaron Burr in 1804, but because its main feature is side-by-side federal and state chartering (and supervision) of commercial banks. It has no counterpart in any other country. Indeed, it arose quite by accident in the United States, the unexpected result of legislation in the 1860s that was intended to shift the authority to charter banks from the various state governments to the federal government.

The National Currency Act of 1863, the National Bank Act of 1864, and related post–Civil War legislation established a new federally chartered banking system, under the supervision of the Comptroller of the Currency (within the U.S. Treasury). The idea was to drive the existing state-chartered banks out of business by imposing a prohibitive tax on their issuance of state banknotes (currency issued by state-chartered banks), which in those days was the principal form of circulating money. However, the plot was foiled in the nick of time and state-chartered banks survived and eventually flourished—because public acceptance of demand deposits in lieu of currency enabled the state banks to make loans and create money, despite their inability to issue banknotes.

Thus today we have a dual banking system: federally chartered banks, under the aegis of the Comptroller of the Currency, and state-chartered banks, under the supervision of each of the various states in which they are located. Federally chartered banks are for the most part larger institutions, but state-chartered banks are more numerous. In mid-1978, as Table 1 indicates, roughly two-thirds of the commercial banks had state charters, but the one-third with national charters held over half the deposits in the banking system.

In 1913, with the passage of the Federal Reserve Act, another supervisory layer was added as national banks were required to be-

TABLE 1
Status of Commercial Banks, 1978
($ in billions)

All Commercial Banks	Number of Banks 14,698		Total Deposits $966	
	No.	%	Amount	%
National banks	4,616	31	$527	55
State banks	10,082	69	439	45
F.R. member banks	5,621	38	694	72
Nonmember banks	9,077	62	272	28
FDIC insured banks	14,381	98	946	98
Noninsured banks	317	2	20	2

Source: *Federal Reserve Bulletin.* Data for June 30, 1978.

come member banks of the Federal Reserve System, while state banks were permitted the option of joining or not. At present, as shown in Table 1, most state banks are not members of the Federal Reserve System. Nevertheless, member banks, both state and national, hold about 70 percent of the total deposits in the banking system.

An additional supervisory structure was laid atop the edifice with the establishment of federal deposit insurance in the 1930s. All Federal Reserve member banks, which includes all national banks, are required to be insured by the Federal Deposit Insurance Corporation (FDIC), while state nonmembers retain the option of having federal deposit insurance or not. Virtually all banks, however, have chosen federal deposit insurance coverage, as Table 1 indicates. (We will return to the FDIC later in this chapter.)

As matters now stand, a national bank is subject to the supervisory authority of the Comptroller of the Currency, the Federal Reserve, and the FDIC. A state member bank that is insured is subject to the regulatory authority of the state in which it is located (usually exercised through a state banking commission), the Federal Reserve, and the FDIC. A state bank that is not a member of the Federal Reserve, but is insured, is subject to its state's regulations plus the FDIC. A unique feature of the system is that the regulated can choose their regulator: state banks can shift to national charters and vice versa, state member banks can shift to nonmember status and vice versa. An economic historian might be able to detect the application of Gresham's law to bank supervision: bad regulators drive out good regulators.[1]

To some extent—in bank examinations, for instance—the degree of overlap is more apparent than real. National banks are subject to examination by the Comptroller's office, the Fed, and the FDIC, but in

[1] Since every money and banking textbook should tell you what Gresham's law is—and since this is as good a chance as any—here it is. Sir Thomas Gresham (1519–1579), financial adviser to Queen Elizabeth I, is said to have coined the phrase "bad money drives good money out of circulation"—meaning that if two types of money of the same denomination serve as media of exchange, one containing less valuable (or debased) metal and the other containing more valuable metal, the coins containing the less valuable metal will remain in circulation while the more valuable coins will be hoarded. The bad money (less valuable intrinsic content) will drive the good money (more valuable intrinsic content) out of circulation, because everyone will try to hold on to the more valuable and pass on the less valuable.

Concrete examples of Gresham's law occur daily. Dimes and quarters minted in 1965 and after have been 75 percent copper and 25 percent nickel bonded to a pure copper core; previously they had been 90 percent silver and 10 percent copper. In light of the relatively high price of silver, the intrinsic value of a coin minted in 1965 or after is much less than one minted before 1965. The result, à la Gresham, is that post–1964 dimes and quarters remain in circulation while an estimated $2½ billion of the more valuable earlier coins have disappeared into private hoards.

practice the latter two do not exercise their authority, accepting the Comptroller's examinations as adequate. Thus national banks, in practice, have but one examining authority over them, while virtually all state banks have two. A state member bank is subject to examination by the state, the Fed, and the FDIC; in this case, though, the FDIC gives way, accepting the reports of the Federal Reserve. A state non-member insured bank entertains state and FDIC examiners.

The justification for the dual banking system—side-by-side federal and state bank regulation—is that it is supposed to foster change and innovation by providing alternative routes through which banks can seek charters and do business. It is claimed that a dual banking system is more responsive to the evolving banking needs of the economy than a single system could be:

> The dual system fosters innovation by permitting either the state or the federal governments to experiment with and to develop new approaches to satisfying the banking needs of the public. The existence of two systems of banks, state and national, with individual banks free to move from one system to the other, encourages a wholesome competitive spirit among the banks. Furthermore, the dual system imposes upon those responsible for law-making and supervision an attitude of reasonableness and flexibility in the regulation of banks, an attitude that a monolithic system would be less likely to foster.[2]

The validity of these arguments is difficult to assess, but whatever their merits no one has been marching in the streets demanding change in the status quo. The dual banking system seems to be working tolerably well, regardless of its logic, except for the problem of dropouts from Federal Reserve membership—and the consequences of that could be nullified by simply requiring all banks, whether members or not, to hold reserves as specified by the Fed (as will be discussed in Chapter 12).

Multiple Federal Authorities

The dual banking system, whatever its faults, has aroused considerably less controversy than the existence of multiple and often conflicting supervisory authorities at the federal level. Dispute among the federal banking agencies was especially marked during the regime of James J. Saxon as Comptroller of the Currency, from late 1961 to late 1966. The Comptroller repeatedly sought to depart from estab-

[2] *First Report* of the Advisory Committee on Commercial Bank Supervision, submitted to the Superintendent of Banks of the State of New York (December 1965), pp. 2–3.

*The Comptroller repeatedly sought to depart
from established precedent.* . . .

lished precedent, only to be met by resistance from the more con-
servative Federal Reserve and FDIC.

Conflict erupted in the mid-1960s over such issues as whether
certain kinds of bank liabilities should be considered as deposits for
purposes of reserve requirements (the Comptroller said they should
not be considered as deposits, the Fed said they should); whether
national banks should be permitted to underwrite municipal revenue
bonds (the Comptroller said that they should be permitted to do so,
the Fed said no); and whether national banks could establish subsidiaries to engage in bank-related functions (the Comptroller ruled
that they could, the Federal Reserve that they could not). Most of these
disputes were settled by some form of compromise. Nor were relations
strained only between the Comptroller's office and the Federal Reserve.
Cooperation between Comptroller Saxon and the FDIC became minimal as well, even though the Comptroller is one of the three members
of the FDIC's Board of Directors. Amity was not furthered by the
Comptroller's refusal, after a while, to attend FDIC Board meetings
in person.

Different interpretations of the same statutes, and ensuing dissension that has punctuated relations among the federal supervisory agencies, has led many to recommend that all federal chartering, examination, and supervisory responsibilities should be combined in a single agency. The proposal has always foundered, however, on lack of consensus as to which agency—the Federal Reserve, the FDIC, or the Comptroller of the Currency—is most appropriate. Notice that consolidation at the federal level would not affect the dual banking system, since state chartering and supervision would continue to exist.

The Commission on Money and Credit, for example, recommended in 1961 (before Mr. Saxon took office) that the Comptroller of the Currency and the FDIC be abolished as independent agencies and their functions transferred to departments within the Federal Reserve.[3] However, five of the twenty Commission members dissented from this proposal, not on the grounds that unification was undesirable, but because they viewed the Fed as the wrong agency in which to consolidate authority. Four of the five implied that the proper place to unify all federal examination and supervisory power—aside from monetary policy powers—would be not the Federal Reserve but the FDIC. In their view, the conduct of monetary police alone is sufficiently demanding to fully absorb the time and energy of the Fed; supervisory responsibilities should be divorced from monetary policy responsibilities and placed solely in the hands of the FDIC or the Comptroller.

Despite the fact that one study group after another has seen fit to recommend increased unification at the federal level—disagreeing only in how that unification might best be achieved—the existing tripartite arrangement remains. It was modified slightly in 1978 when Congress attempted to achieve some coordination by establishing a five-member Federal Financial Institutions Examination Council. The Council consists of a member of the Federal Reserve Board, the Comptroller of the Currency, and the chairmen of the FDIC, the Federal Home Loan Bank Board, and the National Credit Union Administration. Its purpose is to try to develop uniform reporting, examination, and supervisory standards for all financial institutions supervised by federal agencies.

The present system is defended by some on the grounds that divided federal authority, like the dual banking system, provides an element of flexibility, fostering innovation and change, that would be lacking were all federal banking powers concentrated in one agency. On the other hand, if there is to be federal supervision of banking at all, it would appear axiomatic that it be consistent in application and

---

[3] See *Money and Credit* (Englewood Cliffs, N.J.: Prentice-Hall, 1961), pp. 174–175.

operated at minimum cost—which implies that one supervisory body is preferable to three, especially when they tend to disagree among themselves.

It has to be admitted, however, as an argument in favor of the status quo, that federal regulatory agencies, in general, have not compiled a particularly outstanding record for imaginative leadership, for stimulating innovation, or even for protecting (not to mention furthering) the public interest. While a forward-looking, able, and conscientious single federal banking authority would undoubtedly be an improvement over present arrangements, lack of these qualities in a consolidated agency might only make matters worse.

Deposit Insurance and the FDIC

It is time for more detail on the Federal Deposit Insurance Corporation (FDIC) and its crucial role in banking today. Although it may be hard to believe nowadays, bank failures were a common event before the FDIC was established on January 1, 1934. During the 1920s bank failures averaged about 600 a year, and during the years 1930–1933 over 2,000 a year! Read that sentence over again, so you really appreciate how huge those numbers are, and so you get some idea of how many people lost their life savings as bank after bank disappeared. The gory details on bank failures are in Table 2. At the end of 1933 there were fewer than 15,000 commercial banks remaining out of 30,000 that had been in existence in 1920. Since the end of World War II, on the other hand, bank failures have averaged less than six a year. On the basis of that record, the FDIC is probably the most successful and worthwhile government agency ever established.[4]

The Banking Acts of 1933 and 1935 accomplished many things, including the creation of the FDIC to insure deposits (demand, passbook savings, and time) at commercial and mutual savings banks. Companion legislation created the Federal Savings and Loan Insurance Corporation to do the same for savings and loan associations, and in 1970 the National Credit Union Administration initiated deposit in-

[4] The typical point of view of the banking community in 1933, with respect to the feasibility of federal deposit insurance, was summarized in the gloomy conclusion that "the plan is inherently fallacious . . . one of those plausible, but deceptive, human plans that in actual application only serve to render worse the very evils they seek to cure." (*The Guaranty of Bank Deposits*, Economic Policy Commission, American Bankers Association, 1933, p. 43.) On this basis, organized banking groups generally opposed legislation establishing the FDIC.

TABLE 2
Bank Failures, 1920–1933

Year	No. of Bank Failures*
1920	170
1921	510
1922	370
1923	650
1924	780
1925	620
1926	980
1927	670
1928	500
1929	660
1930	1,350
1931	2,290
1932	1,460
1933	4,000

* Rounded to the nearest 10.
Source: Historical Statistics of the United States, pp. 636–637.

surance for federally chartered credit unions. FDIC deposit insurance became effective in 1934, with coverage limited to $2,500 per depositor per bank. This was raised to $5,000 in mid-1934, $10,000 in 1950, $15,000 in 1966, $20,000 in 1969, and $40,000 in November of 1974.

According to FDIC survey data, the present $40,000 coverage provides full insurance for about 99 percent of the *depositors* in insured banks. With respect to the dollar volume of deposits, however, the 1 percent of depositors not fully covered hold *uninsured* balances that constitute 36 percent of the dollar value of total deposits.[5] In other words, although almost all depositors are fully insured (i.e., they have less than $40,000 in their accounts in any single bank), over a third of the deposits in terms of dollar volume are not insured. A $100,000 negotiable certificate of deposit (CD), for example, would be insured for $40,000, and uninsured for the $60,000 balance.

Although nominal insurance coverage is $40,000 per depositor per bank, in fact actual coverage may be greater (never less), depending on the procedure used by the FDIC in taking over a failed bank. The FDIC may allow the bank to go into receivership, the so-called "payoff" method. In such cases the FDIC sends its agents to the bank, verifies the deposit records, and then pays out funds directly to each depositor up to a limit of $40,000. Thereafter the FDIC shares, on a pro rata basis with the claims of depositors in excess of their insurance and with the other creditors, in the residual proceeds realized from

[5] See 1975 *Annual Report* of the Federal Deposit Insurance Corporation, pp. xiv–xvi.

liquidation of the failed bank's assets. The FDIC reports that, after liquidation, those with deposits in excess of the insurance limit have usually received back over ninety cents on the dollar, but often only after a wait of several years.

Alternatively, the FDIC may succeed in merging the failed bank with a healthy one, the so-called "assumption" method. The deposits of the failed bank are assumed by another bank into which the distressed one is merged, and made available in full to the depositors. The FDIC may assist in this procedure by making loans to the bank taking over, or relieving it of some of the weaker assets of the failed bank. In such cases the FDIC has in effect completely insured all depositors to the *full* amount of their deposits, regardless of the technical insurance coverage limit.

The original capital of the FDIC was provided by a levy on the Treasury and the Federal Reserve Banks, amounting to $289 million, which was fully repaid in 1948. In addition, insured banks are assessed annually one-twelfth of 1 percent of their *total* deposits (not just their insured deposits). With continued growth of the insurance fund to about $9 billion, the effective rate of these assessments has been reduced by rebates which the FDIC annually returns to the banks. Thus the effective assessment rate in recent years has generally been no more than about one-thirtieth of 1 percent of a bank's total deposits.

Were the banking system to collapse, an insurance fund of $9 billion is obviously insufficient to pay off several hundred billion dollars of currently insured deposits. The FDIC has additional legislative authority to borrow up to $3 billion from the U.S. Treasury in case of emergency, but such numbers are really meaningless. The reasoning underlying the FDIC does not involve calculations of actuarial probability, but rather the basic premise that the very existence of federal deposit insurance eliminates the possibility of large-scale bank failure. By insuring deposits under the auspices of the Federal Government, with the implied support of the United States Treasury to whatever extent necessary, the FDIC has successfully eliminated the old-fashioned "run on the bank" by frightened depositors that formerly heralded another bank failure. If people hear their bank is "in trouble" now, they hardly pay attention. They're insured, so who cares? Thanks to this simple but effective device, savings have been made safe and the banking system has prospered in the last 45 years as never before.

However, a word of caution. Although apprehensive depositors no longer form long lines waiting to withdraw their funds from a bank that is rumored to be "in trouble," a less obvious but very large deposit drain can still occur through the failure of corporate treasurers to renew outstanding large-size negotiable certificates of deposit (CDs).

Corporate treasurers are exceedingly careful about which banks they put their funds in, since large-size CDs ($100,000 and over) are only insured up to the $40,000 insurance limit. Similarly, large corporate checking accounts will be transferred quickly from a bank in trouble to one that is safe.

For example, New York's Franklin National Bank lost half a billion dollars of CDs between May and October of 1974—the five-month interval between when it first became known that the bank was in trouble and when it was finally officially declared insolvent by the Comptroller of the Currency and the FDIC. When Franklin National's CDs came due, corporate treasurers simply failed to renew them (they let them "run off"), so that $500 million in deposits left the bank silently and invisibly, without any line at all forming in front of the tellers' windows. So a "run on the bank" is not entirely a thing of the past, after all! It should be noted, however, that in this case the infection did not spread, and there was no financial panic; no other bank was affected by Franklin National's difficulties.[6]

Bank Size Distribution

The objectives of bank supervision, regulation, and insurance are to protect the safety of depositors' funds and promote a viable and smoothly functioning banking system—one that will encourage saving, channel funds from savers to borrowers, enable borrowers to get funds on reasonable terms, and foster economic stability and growth. All of this means that the objectives of bank supervision, regulation, and insurance are to make sure that banks are both safe and competitive. The FDIC and bank examinations are designed to ensure safety, while other aspects of supervision are intended to promote competition.

In down-to-earth terms, competitive conditions mean that customers can shop around—that they have alternatives. For example, are the opportunities open to depositors sufficiently varied to give them

[6] Nor did any Franklin National depositor lose a penny when the bank folded (although the bank's stockholders lost plenty). With over $2 billion in deposits in May 1974, Franklin National was the largest bank ever to fail in U.S. history. The institution was taken over by the European-American Bank, which is owned by a consortium of six large European banks. As far as depositors were concerned, the only difference was that their new checks were baby blue instead of passionate pink. This is an example of the assumption method of handling a failed bank, as described above.

an array of choices with respect to deposit terms and yields, so they can pick those that best fit their particular needs? Similarly, do borrowers who are refused a loan at one bank have alternatives open to them—other banks to which they can turn? Do banks actively seek customers, either depositors or borrowers, by offering more service or better terms than rival banks are offering?

As we have mentioned before (in Chapter 7), probably the most competition-inhibiting element in banking at the present time is Regulation Q, which prohibits banks from paying depositors more than specified maximum interests rate on deposits. But Regulation Q is run a close second by the prevailing network of laws and regulations regarding branch banking, laws that have resulted in a size-distribution of commercial banks that is unique to this country.

With over 14,000 commercial banks in the United States, there would appear to be, on the face of it, a high degree of robust competition in banking. However, as Table 3 indicates, a large percentage of

TABLE 3

Size Distribution of Insured Commercial Banks

(end of 1977)

Deposit Size	No. of Banks	% of Total Banks	% of Total Deposits
Less than $10 million	3,790	26	2
$10–25 million	4,911	34	8
$25–50 million	2,980	21	10
$50–100 million	1,485	10	10
$100–500 million	981	7	18
$500 million– 1 billion	124	1	8
Over $1 billion	141	1	44
TOTALS	14,412	100	100

Source: FDIC and *The American Banker.*

banks are very small institutions, with less than $25 million deposits per bank. Indeed, about 8,700 of the banks in the country—60 percent of them—are that small (see lines 1 and 2 in the table). These 8,700 banks hold only 10 percent of the aggregate deposits in the banking system. Most of them are located in small, one-bank towns.

At the other end of the scale, about a thousand large banks (the last 3 lines of Table 3), only 9 percent of the total, hold 70 percent of all bank deposits. Moreover, fewer than 300 banks hold over half of the deposits.

These inverse pyramids, involving numbers on the one hand and deposit size on the other, raise two important questions bearing on the allocation of financial resources. *Are there too many small banks?* And, at the other extreme: *Are the few Giant Banks too large for comfort?*

The traditional American reaction to these questions has been to ignore the first and assume the worst regarding the second. The small unit bank, like the Family Farm, is generally embraced as an integral part of the American Way of Life, regardless of whether or not it has the economic strength to stand on its own two feet in terms of costs and revenues. Conversely, bigness is typically equated with monopoly and evil, especially where financial institutions are concerned.

Are There Too Many Small Banks?

If this large number of very small banks were the product of natural evolution, it would indicate that the optimum (low-cost) size bank is probably a very small institution, with less than $25 million in deposits. Their large numbers would attest to their competitive viability.

However, the reason there are so many very small banks in this country does not have much to do with their successful adaptation to changing economic needs or their innovative capabilities. It is simply because most of them are *sheltered* from competition by state anti-branching statutes, to which the federal banking authorities defer. Many very small banks would be unable to remain in business were a large bank to open up a branch next door. The fact that in many states the large bank is legally prohibited from doing so is what permits many small banks to survive—and to saddle their communities with high-cost banking.

The National Bank Act of 1864 totally prohibited national banks from branching, either within a state or across state lines. This was amended by the McFadden Act in 1927, and the Banking Act of 1933, to permit national banks to branch within a state to whatever extent state-chartered banks can branch in that state. At present, about one-third of the states, mostly in the Midwest, permit only unit banking—that is, no branches at all are allowed. Another third of the states, mostly in the East, allow only some limited form of branching. The remaining states, largely in the West, permit unlimited statewide branching. In summary: *federal regulations require that a federally chartered bank abide by the branching laws of the state in which it is headquartered, and interstate branching is prohibited everywhere* (for national banks by the National Bank Act and for state banks by the laws of the fifty states).[7]

The result is that state antibranching statutes, not economic circumstances, are the principal determinant of the number of banks in the United States. The fact that there are over 14,000 independent commercial banks bears witness to the *absence*, not the presence, of vigorous competition. If there were fewer banks, and more of them were close to optimum size, the general public would be better served. The proof is that over half the banks in the country are located in the no-branching states, where the average bank size is only about one-fifth that in unlimited branching states.

Most state legislatures that have maintained strict antibranching statutes have done so in the face of considerable evidence that branching would be more efficient and more viable than many small independent unit banks in providing the financial services needed by a dynamic economy. This has become more important with the introduction of large-scale computerized technology into banking; even present, not to mention future, technology cannot be utilized advantageously by small unit banks, where the costs are too great because volume is too small. However, the political influence of the banking industry on the state level has repeatedly outflanked the interests of the (unorganized) general public, a process that has been facilitated by the tactic of playing on the deep-seated American fear of bigness, especially in banking.

Closely related to the branching issue is that of new entry into the banking industry. By law, both federal and state banking authorities typically evaluate a number of conditions before chartering a new bank. These include the adequacy of its capital structure, the general character of its management, its future earnings prospects, and the convenience and needs of the community it proposes to serve. (Fur-

---

[7] Exactly what is a branch? Is a remote-service unit a branch (such as an automated-teller machine that accepts deposits and dispenses cash around the clock)? In 1974 the Comptroller of the Currency ruled they are *not* branches, thereby opening the way for national banks to install them regardless of state branching statutes. But since then a number of state courts have held they *are* branches, and in 1976 the Supreme Court in effect upheld the state courts by refusing to review those decisions. At latest count, eighteen states have enacted laws saying they are not branches, fourteen states say they are, and the remaining eighteen states haven't made up their minds.

Similar problems afflict bank "loan production offices." Such offices have been established, primarily by large banks, to solicit loan business and prepare loan applications. They do not accept deposits, and technically the parent bank —not the loan production office—makes the final loan decision and disburses the funds. Are they branches? In 1966 the Comptroller of the Currency ruled they are not, but in 1979 a federal court said they are. So if you want to give *the* correct answer on the final, you'd better keep a lookout for the latest decision.

ther, the well-known liquidity index is given due consideration: namely, the number of state legislators on the bank's board of directors multiplied by the number of Little League baseball teams it proposes to sponsor.)

Few would dispute the necessity of maintaining standards of capital adequacy, or the need for determining that the management of a proposed new bank, and their backers, are honest people, without underworld connections. (Not to mention the desirability of a rating higher than 3_π on the liquidity index.) But the other two elements in the screening process, the future earnings prospects of a proposed new bank and the convenience and needs of the community in which it would be located, in effect shield existing banking institutions from the rigors (and vitality) of competition more than they serve the interests of the public at large.

The purpose of both an earnings prospects criterion and a convenience and needs criterion is supposedly the prevention of bank failures. But measures that insulate all banks from the slightest chance of failure are also measures that inhibit risk-taking, discourage financial innovation, circumscribe management decision-making, and stifle the benefits to the general public that can flow from competitive rivalry. These are high costs to pay, particularly when federal deposit insurance protection has eliminated the widespread distress that bank failures formerly caused.[8]

Do the Giant Banks Pose a Monopoly Threat?

So far we have emphasized that there are probably too many very small banks in the United States, too small for efficient operation. What about the other end of the scale—where a few Giant Banks each has over $7 *billion* in deposits? This handful of banks, one-tenth of 1 percent of all the banks in the country, holds one-fourth of all the banking system's deposits. Do these 18 Giants, listed in Table 4, pose a clear and present monopoly danger?

[8] Peltzman has concluded, for example, that in recent decades regulatory restriction has reduced the rate of entry "by a third to a half below what it otherwise would have been." See Sam Peltzman, "Bank Entry Regulation: Its Impact and Purpose," in *Studies in Banking Competition and Banking Structure* (Comptroller of the Currency, 1966).

TABLE 4

The Eighteen Giants

Bank	Deposits*
Bank of America (San Francisco)	$76.8
Citibank (New York)	61.6
Chase Manhattan (New York)	49.5
Manufacturers Hanover (New York)	32.1
Morgan Guaranty (New York)	28.6
Chemical (New York)	24.9
Continental Illinois (Chicago)	20.9
Bankers Trust (New York)	18.4
First National (Chicago)	17.5
Security Pacific (Los Angeles)	17.0
Wells Fargo (San Francisco)	14.8
Marine Midland (Buffalo)	11.4
Crocker (San Francisco)	11.2
United California (Los Angeles)	10.2
Irving Trust (New York)	9.5
Mellon (Pittsburgh)	8.5
First National (Boston)	7.6
National Bank of Detroit	7.0

° In billions of dollars, end of 1978.
Source: The American Banker.

Opinions differ on this, of course, but at this stage in history the Giant Banks appear to be more benign than malignant. Not because they are particularly generous, home loving, or patriotic—at least no more so than any of us—but simply because, large as they are, they still face sufficient competition to keep them in line. Close on their heels are another two dozen banks with deposits between $3 and $7 billion, and close behind *them* come another hundred with deposits between $1 and $3 billion.

The monopoly threat is further ameliorated in this country by legislation that forbids banking and industrial operations by the same firm. In some other countries—Japan is the outstanding example— giant banks are affiliated with giant manufacturing firms under common ownership, representing a vast concentration of economic power. If Chase Manhattan Bank, Xerox, and IBM could merge into a huge combine, as is permissible in Japan (where they are called *zaibatsus*), then we would really have something to worry about. Moreover, as is evident in the accompanying news item, in the United States there has been direct competition between banks and corporations in the lending of funds to other corporations. This, too, has kept the banks in line.

None of the above should be taken to advocate complacency. Advances in technology are likely to increase the optimum size of bank in the future, as well as generate powerful economic incentives for mergers between banks and other kinds of business—especially with those involved in data transmission and communications. Nevertheless, so long as existing antitrust statutes are enforced, fears of the dangers of banking monopoly appear to be unrealistic, at least for the time being.

Suggestions for Further Reading

On the problems of bank regulation, Marriner Eccles's analysis of many years ago still sounds up-to-date; it is in his autobiography, *Beckoning Frontiers* (New York: Knopf, 1951), pp. 266–86. Also, the Autumn 1966 issue of Duke University's *Law and Contemporary Problems* contains an outstanding collection of articles in the general area of bank regulation.

The literature on bank structure is extensive. The classic in the field is David A. Alhadeff's *Monopoly and Competition in Banking* (Berkeley: University of California Press, 1954). A good jumping-off point for more recent developments is Alfred Broaddus, "Banking Structure: What It Means and Why It Matters," *Monthly Review* of the Federal Reserve Bank of Richmond (November 1971). Also Jerome C. Darnell, "Does Banking Structure Spur Economic Growth?," *Business Review* of the Federal Reserve Bank of Philadelphia (November 1972). Interesting applications of theory are in the December 1972 issue of the Philadelphia Reserve Bank's *Business Review:* "Changing Pennsylvania's Branching Laws: An Economic Analysis," by Ronald D. Watson, Jerome C. Darnell, Cynthia A. Glassman, Marylin G. Mathis, Donald J. Mullineaux, and George S. Oldfield. See also Ernest Bloch, "Changes in the Structure of Bank and Nonbank Competition in the United States," *Banco Nazionale del Lavoro Quarterly Review* (March 1968).

For good surveys of the literature, see Jack M. Guttentag and Edward S. Herman, *Bank Structure and Performance* (New York University, Institute of Finance, 1967), and Larry R. Mote, "The Perennial Issue: Branch Banking," Federal Reserve Bank of Chicago's *Business Conditions* (February 1974). Also see *Studies in Banking Competition and Banking Structure* (Comptroller of the Currency, 1966), and Neil B. Murphy and Frederick W. Bell, *Economics of Scale in Commercial Banking* (Federal Reserve Bank of Boston, 1967). Regarding bank entry, see Donald R. Fraser and Peter S. Rose, "Bank Entry and Bank Performance," *Journal of Finance* (March 1972), and David A. Alhadeff, "Barriers to Bank Entry," *Southern Economic Journal* (April 1974).

Closely related to structure and regulation is the role of bank examination. On this see George J. Benston's monograph, *Bank Examination* (New York University, Institute of Finance, 1973). Also, while you're at it, make sure to see W. C. Fields (as Egbert Sousé) in the movie *The Bank Dick*. Franklin Pangborn plays the part of the bank examiner (J. Pinkerton Snoopington).

Banks Lose Out in Surge Of Lending by Companies

By HENRY SCOTT-STOKES

A fierce battle is in progress between commercial banks and industrial corporations in the hot competition to lend cash to, oddly enough, other industrial companies. Since a decade ago, when short-term lending by one corporation to another was a mere $757 million, this business has soared to $15.5 billion, cutting out the banks along the way.

This boom in the commercial paper market, as it is known, where companies serves as both lender and borrower, using corporate i.o.u.'s, is a source of deep concern to bankers. Their lending to industry is still much bigger than the commercial paper market, but they have been losing customers rapidly to their nonbanking competitors, fundamentally because the bankers' interest rates are higher than those of industry.

The bankers are still a long way ahead, with short-term lending to industry of $123 billion, but their loan totals have barely changed in two years, while lending through the commercial paper market has shot up by 50 percent during this period.

Interest Rate Gap

Recently the struggle between the banks and industry has seemed almost one-sided. The heart of the banks' problems has been the gap between the interest rates they offer to charge and the lower rates charged by industry through the dealers who act as intermediaries in the commercial paper market. These are investment banks such as Goldman, Sachs & Company, the First Boston Corporation, A. G. Becker and Salomon Brothers.

The banks charge at least their prime rate, which is 7.75 percent at present, and also ask for a compensating deposit of at least 10 percent of the total borrowed, which raises their effective interest rate to close to 8.5 percent. In the commercial paper market, 30-to-60-day cash is obtainable at 6.4 percent plus a one-eighth of 1 percent commission for the dealer.

However, the real interest gap between the banks and the industrial lend-lenders may not be as high as it might appear, since the banks have ways to cut their rates and to help favored clients. But the gap remains. And any corporate treasurer who ignores this gap is costing his company money.

Outsiders may well ask why industrial companies do not all switch their borrowing from the banks, which stands at $123 billion, to borrowing from other corporations with cash in hand.

Banks Offer Services

The reasons are:

¶Banks offer services.

¶They cater to concerns too small for the paper market, which accepts only big companies.

¶Banks have cut interest rates.

The banks have cut their margins to the bone. This was the significance of an announcement last month by Morgan Guaranty Trust Company, according to which rates of under 7 percent are offered on cash loans for up to 10 days. This represented a reduction of more than 0.75 percent from the prime.

Morgan Guaranty, according to its president-elect, Lewis T. Preston, in a telephone interview, is bringing its rates closer in line with those already offered by its closest competitors.

"There's been much under-the-table cutting of interest rates," said Mr. Preston. "Morgan hasn't been doing that; it likes to be straightforward. We have been reacting to the cutting."

Mr. Preston saw the move as defensive and not as an aggressive onslaught on the paper market.

"Bankers have got to learn to live with the paper market," he said. "We want to provide a facility which will be useful to customers and we are not aiming to replace the paper market."

A bank stock analyst commented: "The Morgan move has not been made to attract loans from the commercial paper market, but that is not saying that commercial paper has not been gaining ground at the expense of the banks. Morgan's is a very special move, just 10-day money and for the select few—and still priced above commercial paper rates. It is not an inducement to borrowers."

A Citibank spokesman said that the announcement, which was followed by a similar move by the Wells Fargo Bank of San Francisco, would have no impact on industrial paper issued by industrial corporations, but only on financial paper, which is also issued by finance companies through the commercial paper market, and accounts for three quarters of the $64 billion total paper market.

The volume of financial paper vastly exceeds that of industrial paper, and stood at $48 billion at the end of November. Finance companies, such as G.M.A.C. (the General Motors Acceptance Corporation), and Ford Credit, have long borrowed from the paper market in preference to obtaining short-

NEWS ITEM / Banks Find Lending Highly Competitive

SOURCE: *New York Times*, December 19, 1977

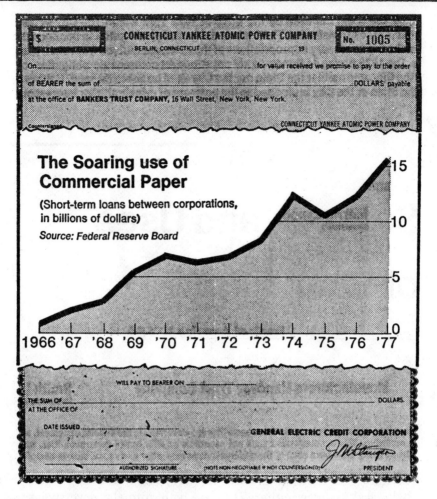

The Soaring use of Commercial Paper

(Short-term loans between corporations, in billions of dollars)

Source: Federal Reserve Board

term loans from the banks. Morgan thus sought to protect its links with finance companies.

In the fierce competition for business loans, real interest rates are being driven down by eager banks with sluggish portfolios of borrowers, struggling with one another for few clients. The situation is exacerbated by foreign banks, of which over 100 have offices in New York, who are also seeking scarce business and are pushing downward on short-term interest rates, cutting the profits of American banks.

The foreign banks do not make many loans here but they press hard. C. Edward McConnell, a vice president of the stock analysis firm of Keefe, Bruyette & Woods Inc., said that Japanese banks were alleged to have offered short-term money at one-eighth of 1 percent over cost, well below 7 percent and a very low level indeed.

However, analysts say it would be wrong to blame Japanese and other foreign banks for the heavy pressure on interest margins. This pressure has been created by a combination of low commercial paper rates, cheap loans priced below the prime by domestic banks and the use by foreign bankers of overseas money markets, notably the Euromarket, to offer very cheap loans here.

"It is becoming harder and harder to separate the New York and London markets," said Mr. McConnell. He referred to the $350 billion money market which is based mainly in London and dominates international finance outside the United States.

A German banker added: "Competition is very hot and it's driven rates down. So many banks have opened here, especially the Germans, and they are bringing down short-term rates towards Eurodollar margins—margins have been cut in half in a year from 1 percent to ½ percent. There's desperate search for borrowers."

An American bank stock analyst said: "The bankers are speechless. They don't know what to do. There have been three years of no loan demand at New York banks; loans are at a lower level than three years ago. One has to wonder whether this is a secular trend or whether this is just a cycle which will end."

George Salem, an analyst at Reynold Securities, said that the trend was secular: "There's a change in the borrowing and spending habits of corporations; they are generating more of their funds internally, and they are using more nonbank external sources of funds — such as the paper market."

However, the bottom line is that for the time being, bank profit margins are under pressure.

Chapter 9

Sources and Uses
of Bank Funds

BANKS are business firms. Banks might not look like Frisbee factories, but then King Kong doesn't look much like Rudolph the Red-nosed Reindeer either. They are both animals, nevertheless.

Like Frisbee manufacturers, bankers buy inputs, massage them a bit, burn a little incense, say the magic words, and out pops some output from the oven. If their luck holds, they can sell the finished product for more than it cost to buy the raw materials and process them through the assembly line.

For a banker, the raw material is money. He buys it at a long counter he sets up in the store, then rushes around to the back, polishing it on his sleeve as he goes, sits down behind a huge desk (a little out of breath), and sells it as soon as he can to someone else. If he's really good at his business, sometimes he can even sell it back to the same person he bought it from (a trick bankers picked up from Los Angeles used car salesmen, who first perfected the art of selling a customer back his own trade-in).

About the only way you can tell whether a banker is buying money or selling it is to observe him in his native habitat and see whether he's standing up or sitting down. For some unknown reason, probably an inherited trait, bankers always stand up when they buy money (take your deposit), but invariably sit down when they sell it (make loans or buy securities). In the first part of this chapter we'll look at what happens when they're standing up, and then at what they do when they sit down.

Sources of Bank Funds: Major Trends Since 1950

Tables 1 and 2 show the major trends over the last quarter century in sources of bank funds. Table 1 contains the dollar amounts and Table 2 the relative percentages of the various sources of funds. Notice first how demand deposits, which used to be the major source of bank

TABLE 1

Liabilities and Capital of Insured Commercial Banks,
1950–1978
(in billions of dollars)

	1950	1955	1960	1965	1970	1978
Demand deposits	$117	$141	$156	$184	$247	$400
Passbook savings deposits	28	38	55	93	99	221
Time deposits*	8	12	18	39	110	295
Large-size negotiable CDs	0	0	0	16	26	100
Miscellaneous liabilities	3	3	6	13	54	170
Equity capital	11	15	21	30	40	87
TOTAL	167	209	256	375	576	1,273

* Excluding large-size ($100,000 and over) negotiable certificates of deposit. For the years prior to 1965, the breakdown between time deposits proper and passbook savings deposits has been estimated by the authors.
Source: FDIC *Annual Reports* and *Federal Reserve Bulletin.* All figures are as of year end.

TABLE 2

Liabilities and Capital of Insured Commercial Banks,
1950–1978
(percentage distribution)

	1950	1955	1960	1965	1970	1978
Demand deposits	70%	68%	61%	49%	43%	32%
Passbook savings deposits	17	18	22	25	17	17
Time deposits	5	6	7	11	19	23
Large-size negotiable CDs	0	0	0	4	5	8
Miscellaneous liabilities	2	1	2	3	9	13
Equity capital	6	7	8	8	7	7
TOTAL	100	100	100	100	100	100

Source: Table 1.

funds—70 percent in 1950—have slipped in importance, declining to 32 percent by 1978. The steady decline in the importance of demand deposits is not easily visible in Table 1, since their dollar amount has continued to grow; but Table 2 clearly shows how much they have diminished in relative significance.

This decline is traceable to the legal prohibition against banks paying interest on demand deposits, combined with the general increase in interest rates on other types of assets over the postwar period. Individuals and business firms are reluctant to hold any more demand deposits than they really need for their day-to-day payments. They have learned that it pays to economize on their checking accounts, since to hold more than is absolutely necessary means sacrificing interest income.

Savings and time deposits, on the other hand, have expanded from only 22 percent of bank funds in 1950 to 48 percent in 1978. Savings and time deposits are frequently lumped together, but in the tables we have disaggregated them into three components: passbook savings deposits, time deposits (not counting large-size negotiable certificates of deposit), and large-size ($100,000 and over) negotiable CDs. One reason for the separation is that their relative growth rates have differed considerably over the period.

Passbook savings deposits are the traditional form of savings account, held mostly by individuals and nonprofit organizations. A little blue (sometimes green) passbook has been the standard symbol of a savings account for generations, and until the late 1960s such passbook accounts represented the bulk of total commercial bank savings and time deposits. As late as 1960, as Tables 1 and 2 indicate, passbook savings deposits were more than three times as large as time deposits. The latter consist of certificates of deposit with a scheduled maturity date, and are held by business firms as well as by individuals. They have swept well ahead of passbook savings deposits in recent years.

With passbook savings accounts, funds can be withdrawn from the savings account at any time. Technically, thirty days' notice is required prior to a withdrawal, although this requirement is universally waived. On the other hand, if depositors want to withdraw funds from a time deposit before the scheduled maturity date they are subject to substantial penalties, such as the forfeiture of interest. Why, then, have time certificates of deposit become so popular in recent years?

The reason is our old friend, Regulation Q. Banks are permitted to offer higher yields on time certificates than on passbook savings. In early 1979, for example, a commercial bank could legally offer a po-

*"And here's an extra 'substantial penalty' for the early
withdrawal of your time deposit!"*

Drawing by D. Fradon; © 1975 The New Yorker Magazine, Inc.

tential depositor only 5 percent interest on a regular passbook savings
account. But it could offer up to 6½ percent on a small (less than
$100,000) certificate of deposit maturing in 2½ years or up to 7¾
percent on one maturing in eight years or more. Because of such interest differentials, time deposits have grown more popular than the
traditional passbook savings account in recent years, as Tables 1 and
2 indicate.

The growth of time deposits was given particular impetus by the
"invention" of the negotiable certificate of deposit in 1961. Usually
issued in denominations of $100,000 and over, the negotiable CD can
be sold if one has to raise cash before it matures. Thus it serves as an
alternative to Treasury bills for the corporate treasurer with excess
funds to invest for a short time. At the end of 1978, $100 billion of
corporate funds were invested in large-size negotiable CDs, a money
market instrument that had not even been in existence in 1960.

Until Regulation Q's rate ceilings on large-size CDs were completely suspended in 1973, such certificates of deposit had been a
mixed blessing for the banking community because they were a particularly unstable source of funds. When market interest rates rose
above Regulation Q ceilings, corporate treasurers promptly shifted
over to Treasury bills to get the higher yields. For instance, there were
$24 billion in large-size CDs outstanding in late 1968, but only $10
billion in early 1970 (after 1969's tight money and high interest rates),
and then a resurgence to $26 billion by the end of 1970 (after mone-

tary policy had eased and interest rates declined). The lifting of rate ceilings on large-denomination CDs since mid-1973, however, has resulted in greater stability in this source of funds.

Tables 1 and 2 also show a substantial increase in "miscellaneous" liabilities over the past ten or fifteen years. Such miscellaneous liabilities include a wide variety of nondeposit sources of funds: borrowings from the Federal Reserve; borrowings in the Federal funds market; borrowings by banks from their foreign branches; transactions among banks, their parent holding companies, and their subsidiaries; and sales of securities and loans that banks have agreed to buy back at a later date (which are called repurchase agreements).[1]

Many of these nondeposit sources flourished for the first time in the hothouse tight money atmosphere of 1966 and 1969. Squeezed by a shortage of deposit funds relative to loan demands, banks devised all sorts of ways to expand their access to funds.

The formation of one-bank holding companies, for example, was greatly stimulated during the 1960s. We will return to one-bank holding companies later in the chapter; at the moment, we want to call attention only to their fund-raising role. What happened was that many banks reorganized their corporate structure into holding .company form, and the holding company then "owned" the bank. The parent corporation, not the bank, would sell commercial paper in its own name, thereby avoiding regulatory restrictions (such as Regulation Q and reserve requirements) that would apply were a bank to do the same thing.

The holding company would then use these funds to purchase assets from its bank's portfolio, in that way giving the bank additional cash with which to make more loans. Holding companies were also used as an umbrella under which various bank lending operations were spun off into subsidiary corporations, such as a consumer loan firm, a mortgage financing company, and so on. These companies proceeded to finance themselves by selling their own securities or commercial paper to the public.

[1] When banks sell securities to corporations under agreements to repurchase (RPs), the banks commit themselves to buy the securities back on a specified future date—often the next day—at a predetermined price. In effect, the bank is borrowing funds with the securities as collateral; the interest rate for such borrowings is determined by the difference between today's selling price and tomorrow's higher repurchase price. With overnight RPs, the bank gains access to short-term funds, which it hopes to employ profitably, and the corporation earns interest while sacrificing virtually no liquidity. When such a transaction is made, the bank balance sheets show a rise in borrowings and a corresponding drop in demand deposit liabilities (which means the money supply falls). The widespread growth of overnight RPs in recent years has increased scepticism regarding the value of the money supply figures as a reliable measure of liquidity in the economy. See William L. Silber, *Commercial Bank Liability Management* (Chicago: Association of Reserve City Bankers, 1978), pages 42–45, and Gillian Garcia and Simon Pak, "Some Clues in the Case of the Missing Money," *American Economic Review* (May 1979).

The Federal Reserve, having caught the banks *flagrante delicto*, countered in 1970 by imposing reserve requirements on bank-related commercial paper, the proceeds of which accrue to the bank involved. In effect, such funds were classified as "deposits" for reserve requirement purposes.

Finally, it is important to call attention to a traditional nondeposit source of funds that has been missed because so far we have looked only at the liabilities side of the balance sheet. That source is the *sale of assets* on the open market—usually short-term government securities, sometimes longer-term governments as well—when money tightens and banks feel reserve pressures. Traditionally, commercial banks sell government securities in the upswing of the business cycle, when loan demand is vigorous and they need more funds to satisfy it than are flowing in from normal channels. They generally buy their governments in the downswing of the business cycle, when loan demand is weak. This is a cyclical phenomenon and to see it we would have to look at the asset side of the balance sheet, especially at its cyclical fluctuations rather than the broad secular trends we have been observing. And it is to the asset side that we now turn.

Uses of Bank Funds: Major Trends Since 1950

So far we have looked only at the liabilities side of bank balance sheets, at their sources of funds. Now we turn to the asset side, to their uses of funds. Having acquired money in one way or another (we firmly resist the temptation to say by hook or by crook), banks proceed to use it to buy financial assets for the purpose of making a profit on the turnaround.

Tables 3 and 4 show the major trends over the last quarter century in uses of bank funds. Table 3 contains the dollar amounts and Table 4 the relative percentages of the various uses of funds. It is clear that banks have cut way back on the proportion of their funds in cash assets (which includes their deposits at the Fed) plus holdings of government securities—from 61 percent of total assets in 1950 to only 24 percent in 1978. These assets have been replaced by state and local government securities, mortgages, and loans of all sorts, up from 36 percent of total assets in 1950 to 68 percent in 1978.

Between 1950 and 1978 the biggest upsurge was in business loans, followed by mortgages, consumer loans, and state and local government securities in that order. The heavy emphasis on business

TABLE 3

Assets of Insured Commercial Banks, 1950–1978
(in billions of dollars)

	1950	1955	1960	1965	1970	1978
Cash assets	$40	$47	$52	$60	$93	$178
U.S. govt. and agency securities	61	61	61	64	75	132
State and local govt. securities	8	13	17	38	69	124
Other securities	4	4	3	1	3	13
Business loans	22	33	43	71	112	223
Mortgage loans	13	21	29	49	73	214
Consumer loans	10	17	26	45	66	168
Other loans	7	10	19	37	63	135
Miscellaneous assets	2	3	6	10	22	86
TOTAL	167	209	256	375	576	1,273

Source: FDIC *Annual Reports.* All figures are as of year end.

TABLE 4

Assets of Insured Commercial Banks, 1950–1978
(percentage distribution)

	1950	1955	1960	1965	1970	1978
Cash assets	24%	23%	20%	16%	16%	14%
U.S. govt. and agency securities	37	29	24	17	13	10
State and local govt. securities	5	6	7	10	12	10
Other securities	2	2	1	—	1	1
Business loans	13	16	17	19	19	17
Mortgage loans	8	10	11	13	13	17
Consumer loans	6	8	10	12	11	13
Other loans	4	5	8	10	11	11
Miscellaneous assets	1	1	2	3	4	7
TOTAL	100	100	100	100	100	100

Source: Table 3.

loans reflects the dominant role of commercial banks in the area of business finance, while the expansion in mortgages, consumer loans, and municipal securities reflects the growth of home building, consumer spending, and state and local government spending over most of the period since the end of World War II.

Holdings of U.S. government securities increased least of all.[2] Is this because bankers don't like Uncle Sam? Are they unpatriotic? We don't know about that, but the actual reason is because in 1950, so soon after World War II, bank portfolios were still swollen with far more government securities than banks ordinarily hold, due to financ-

[2] Bank holdings of short-term government securities are frequently called "secondary reserves," because they are highly marketable and can be liquidated on short notice.

ing the war. When Pearl Harbor was bombed in December 1941, commercial banks held only about $20 billion of government securities, roughly a quarter of their total assets. By the end of 1945, when the shooting stopped (for a while), their portfolio of governments had skyrocketed to $90 billion, equal to 55 percent of total assets, the result of huge government bond flotations to raise funds for war finance. (So they really are patriotic after all.) In 1950 banks still held far more governments than usual, so the ensuing relative decline was to some extent expected.

In the years since 1950, banks have shied away from governments, but not always. They generally dump government securities, as mentioned above, when business is expanding and loan demand is strong. But they typically buy some of them back in the downswing of the business cycle, when opportunities to make good loans diminish. Thus bank holdings of U.S. government securities show a counter-cyclical pattern, falling when the business cycle is on the upswing and rising when business conditions decline. Loans in general, and business loans in particular, move in the opposite direction—i.e., in harmony with the business cycle. Government securities thus appear to be a residual use of bank funds, not as desirable as other earning assets when the others are available, but preferable to cash when the others are not available.

In fact, commercial banks would have even fewer government securities than they now have—and to some extent fewer municipals as well—were it not for legal requirements that force them to hold such securities as collateral against the deposits of federal, state, and local governments. By statute, all U.S. government deposits must be fully matched on the asset side of the bank balance sheet by "pledged assets." Such "pledged assets" have to be in the form of U.S. Government or high-grade municipal bonds. State and local governments generally have similar requirements. In case of bank failure, governmental deposits are thereby fully protected. It is estimated that at the present time at least a third of all the securities in commercial bank portfolios are required as pledged collateral against governmental deposits.[3]

Why is it that no *stocks* are included among bank assets? Why no GE, IBM, GM, or TWA? (Not to mention NYU, UCLA, and SMU, none of which has had a decent football team for years.) The reason is that commercial banks have traditionally been barred by law from owning stocks, on the grounds that they (the stocks) are too risky.

---

[3] The literature on pledging is sparse. By far the most comprehensive analysis of the facts and issues involved is by Charles F. Haywood, *The Pledging of Bank Assets* (Chicago: Association of Reserve City Bankers, 1967).

This prohibition dates from the National Currency Act of 1863 and the National Bank Act of 1864, and has been reaffirmed repeatedly in subsequent legislation. Banks *do* buy billions of dollars worth of stocks, but not for themselves—they buy them for the trusts, estates, and pension funds that they manage for others. Such trust department holdings are not included among a bank's own assets.

The Banking Act of 1933 took matters one step further by forcing commercial banks out of the investment banking business. Investment banking consists of "underwriting" new securities issues, which means selling and distributing new stock and bond offerings to ultimate buyers. Commercial banks had become deeply involved in underwriting in the 1920s, not always with happy results. There were suspicions that banks on occasion dumped bonds that they couldn't sell to anyone else into trust funds that they managed. To avoid such conflicts of interest, the Banking Act of 1933—often called the Glass-Steagall Act—divorced commercial from investment banking; banks that had been involved in both areas were forced to choose one or the other. As a result, commercial banks now cannot distribute any securities except those of the U.S. Government and "full faith and credit" general obligations of state and local governments.[4]

Bank Capital

When we discussed sources of bank funds earlier in this chapter, we neglected to call attention to one particular source of bank funds: equity capital. We did not discuss it at that time because it is best considered not by itself but in conjunction with the overall balance sheet. The function of equity capital is to serve as a buffer, so that if a bank experiences hard times depositors will not be affected immediately. As with equity capital in any business, it serves as a cushion against adversity. (In return, of course, stockholders also get the fruits of prosperity.)[5]

---

[4] The Banking Act of 1933 is called the Glass-Steagall Act after its two principal sponsors, Senator Carter Glass of Virginia and Representative Henry B. Steagall of Alabama. While we're at it, Representative Louis T. McFadden was from Pennsylvania. Quick now: what was the McFadden Act? (Check the previous chapter.)

[5] By equity capital, we mean the difference between total assets and total liabilities on a bank's balance sheet. In that sense it is a buffer protecting depositors in case the value of assets declines. This measure of equity capital has no necessary connection with the value of a bank as measured by the price of its stock in the stock market. Accountants and finance majors worry about such discrepancies, but we don't have to.

As Table 2 shows, equity capital has held at a stable 7 or 8 percent of total sources of funds ever since 1955. But meanwhile the overall riskiness of bank assets has increased. Bank examiners measure the riskiness of bank portfolios by subtracting cash assets and U.S. government securities from total assets. Thus, as Table 4 shows, 39 percent of bank assets were risk assets in 1950, 56 percent in 1960, and 76 percent in 1978. The ratio of the dollar amount of equity capital to risk assets (from Tables 1 and 3) is shown in Table 5.

TABLE 5

Equity Capital to Risk Assets, 1950–1978*

		1950	1955	1960	1965	1970	1975
(1)	Equity capital	$ 11	$ 15	$ 21	$ 30	$ 40	$ 87
(2)	Risk assets	$ 66	$101	$143	$251	$408	$963
	(1) ÷ (2)	17%	15%	15%	12%	10%	9%

° Equity capital and risk assets in billions of dollars.
Source: Tables 1 and 3.

It is clear from Table 5 that the ratio of equity capital to risk assets has been generally declining since 1960. This has led many bank regulators to question the adequacy of bank capital today, and to suggest that banks go about rebuilding their capital positions (by retained earnings and new stock flotations) so as to regain the levels of capital relative to risk assets that were typical fifteen or twenty years ago.

Bankers, on the other hand, typically prefer to operate with less rather than more equity. Because equity is usually more expensive than deposits or other short-term borrowed funds, a bank's profitability is enhanced the less it relies on equity and the more on deposits and other debt. As a result, there is constant conflict between bankers and the supervisory authorities as to how much bank capital is appropriate.

One-Bank Holding Companies: What Is the Business of Banking?

Within the context of how banks employ their funds, the recent growth of one-bank holding companies deserves special mention, particularly since it indicates possible developments in banking over the coming years.

Actually, one-bank holding companies have been a part of the American banking scene for a long time. Macy's department store has had its own bank for many years, as have the United Mine Workers, the Amalgamated Clothing Workers, Goodyear Tire and Rubber, and Montgomery Ward. But mostly these were just isolated curiosities until the late 1960s. In 1965 there were over 500 such one-bank holding companies in existence, but they had only 5 percent of the total deposits in the banking system.

In the late 1960s, however, virtually all the nation's larger commercial banks converted their corporate structure to holding company form, so that by the early 1970s one-bank holding companies had increased to over 1,500 institutions, and had more than one-third of the deposits in the banking system. By the late 1970s that figure had grown to two-thirds. What factors account for so many commercial banks joining the one-bank holding company parade? How justified is the frequently expressed concern that they represent a dangerous and unhealthy mixture of banking and commerce?

The primary motivation for the growth of one-bank holding companies was *not,* as is sometimes alleged, an attempt to form vast financial-industrial combines, like Japan's *zaibatsus.* The underlying reasons were much more mundane: an effort on the part of American banks to evolve into new functional areas—such as data processing activities, insurance services, mutual fund sales, investment advisory services, and so on—in which, *as banks*, they could not fully participate. Faced with legal and regulatory constraints on their ability, as banks, to move into diversified financial activities, they turned to the holding company format as a way out. The holding company becomes an umbrella, sheltering under a single corporate structure the bank *and* various affiliated subsidiaries that can legally offer an array of financial services.

The question of what particular functions are or are not appropriate for banks to engage in first came to the fore in the early 1960s, when Comptroller of the Currency James J. Saxon adopted a broad interpretation of what banks could do on the basis of the "incidental powers necessary to carry on the business of banking" clause in federal statutes. The clause is traceable back to the National Currency Act of 1863, and has been repeated in virtually all federal banking legislation since. According to the statutes, banks can accept deposits, make loans, and so on, *and* can engage in such other incidental activities as are "necessary to carry on the business of banking."

The Comptroller ruled, on the basis of this clause, that banks could engage in a wide variety of "bank-related" financial activities, but other federal regulatory agencies, with a narrower interpretation of the same clause, contested these rulings. In addition, legal challenges arose in the courts, initiated by nonbank businesses (such as insurance companies) that were already engaged in those fields and weren't all that happy about the new competition. It was then that the banks turned to the one-bank holding company form, using it as an instrument for establishing a firmer legal base on which to develop new financial activities.

The apparition of potential *zaibatsus* was put to rest once and for all by Congressional legislation in 1970 regulating one-bank holding companies. That legislation specified that one-bank holding companies must confine their activities to fields "so closely related to banking as to be a proper incident thereto." The supervisory body is the Board of Governors of the Federal Reserve System. Thus one-bank holding companies cannot engage in manufacturing, communications, or any other industry not "closely related" to banking.

The future activities of one-bank holding companies are still unclear. The Federal Reserve, pursuant to the 1970 legislation, has ruled that they may engage in certain specified activities, such as some forms of insurance underwriting, acting as an investment or financial adviser, and providing bookkeeping or data processing services. But litigation continues in the courts; for example, in 1971 the Supreme Court decided that one-bank holding companies could not operate their own mutual funds, and in 1976 the Federal Reserve decided that they should not be permitted to operate travel agencies, because that activity is not "closely related" to banking. The outcome of other suits, still pending, will be a crucial factor in deciding the shape of banking in the future.

One thing that has already happened, however, is that the venerable geographic restrictions that have inhibited banking for so long appear to have been irrevocably breached. National banks still cannot branch across state lines—and indeed cannot branch in a state except as that state's laws permit its state-chartered banks to branch. However, the geographic limitations that the McFadden Act and the Banking Act of 1933 placed on branches do not apply to nonbank subsidiaries. Under the one-bank holding company umbrella, both national and state banks can now establish bank-related subsidiaries and affiliates anywhere in the country. New York banks now have mortgage company affiliates in Florida, and California banks have finance company affiliates in Texas. Whether this breakdown of traditional geographic restrictions will eventually extend to banks themselves, resulting in nationwide commercial bank branching, remains to be seen. But the first step in that direction has definitely been taken.

Suggestions for Further Reading

On nondeposit sources of funds, a useful review is the four-part series by Robert E. Knight, "An Alternative Approach to Liquidity," in the *Monthly Review* of the Federal Reserve Bank of Kansas City (December 1969 and February, April, and May 1970). A good bibliography on the subject of bank capital can be found in Ronald D. Watson's informative "Insuring Some Progress in the Bank Capital Hassle," Federal Reserve Bank of Philadelphia's *Business Review* (July/August 1974). In addition, the entire September 1976 issue of the Federal Reserve Bank of Chicago's *Business Conditions* is devoted to Harvey Rosenblum's "Bank Capital Adequacy."

If you want to learn more about one-bank holding companies, a good place to start is William F. Upshaw's series of three articles, "Anti-Trust and the New Bank Holding Company Act," in the *Monthly Review* of the Federal Reserve Bank of Richmond (February, March, and April 1971). Also see his three-part series on "Bank Affiliates and Their Regulation," in the same *Review* (March, April, and May 1973). You can then turn to Harvey Rosenblum's three-part series on bank holding companies in the Federal Reserve Bank of Chicago's *Business Conditions* (August 1973 and February and April 1975). For more recent developments, see *The Bank Holding Company Movement to 1978: A Compendium* (Washington: Board of Governors of the Federal Reserve System, 1978).

Chapter 10

Bank Profitability: Liquidity Versus Earnings

BANK MANAGEMENT is a never-ending tug of war—between liquidity and safety, on the one hand, and earnings and profitability on the other. The reason: The more liquid an asset, the less it is likely to yield. But banks are business firms, with stockholders; presumably, they want to earn profits. Why not forget about liquidity, then, and buy only high-yielding (less liquid) assets? Because, due to the unique structure of their liabilities, banks *need* liquidity—that is, they need assets that are quickly convertible into cash, with little or no loss in value. So bank management faces an endless conflict (a conflict of interest?).

The nature of bank liabilities confirms their need for liquidity on the asset side. Demand deposits, for example, are all payable, as their name implies, on *demand*. And so are passbook savings deposits, for all practical purposes; even though the law provides that a 30-day waiting period could be invoked before a savings account can be withdrawn, this provision is almost never exercised. Thus a far larger proportion of commercial bank liabilities is payable on demand than is the case with any other type of business. But, of course, if a bank holds only highly liquid assets to meet any conceivable volume of withdrawals, it will probably not cover its costs and will have to go out of business.

Liquidity and Profitability: 1950-1978

The asset composition of all insured commercial banks (Table 3 in Chapter 9) illustrates bankers' adaptation to liquidity needs in light of the shifting composition of their liabilities (Table 1 in Chapter 9). The end results in terms of profitability are shown in Tables 1 and 2 below. Table 1 shows the dollar amounts of income and expenses, and Table 2 the percentage distributions.

Notice that, over the 28 years covered by Tables 1 and 2, interest earnings on loans have grown greatly relative to all other sources of income. On the cost side, however, interest payments—on time and savings deposits and on other borrowed funds—have become the main cost element, now well in excess of wages and salaries (compare 1978 with 1950 in this respect).

Having to *pay out* so much in interest puts added pressure on bank portfolio decision-makers to acquire assets that *return* enough in interest to make the bank a profitable enterprise. This illustrates concretely the dilemma constantly facing bankers: They must maintain liquidity (because of the nature of their liabilities), and yet they are always tempted to reduce liquidity (to generate profits).

By almost any measure, bank liquidity has indeed declined substantially over the years 1950–1978. One traditional rule-of-thumb measure that is widely used as a rough gauge of bank liquidity is the ratio of total loans to total deposits. A lower loan/deposit ratio indicates a rise in bank liquidity, a higher loan/deposit ratio a decline in bank liquidity. If you compare the data on Tables 1 and 3 in Chapter 7, you will find that the loan/deposit ratio rose from 34 percent in 1950 to 51 percent in 1960 and to 73 percent in 1978.[1]

The extent of this decline in liquidity is somewhat misleading, since banks were excessively liquid by historical standards at the end of World War II—their portfolios swollen by the huge amount of government securities they acquired in the process of war finance. Nevertheless, the decline in liquidity since 1950 has been far greater than had been anticipated. Faced with rising costs and a generally strong demand for loans over the postwar period, banks have deliberately cut back sharply on their liquidity to maintain their profitability.

For the banking *system,* all the banks taken together, ultimate liquidity is provided by the Federal Reserve, as we shall see. But what about an *individual* commercial bank: How can a single commercial

---

[1] For 1950, 52/153 = 34% ; for 1960, 117/229 = 51% ; for 1978, 740/1016 = 73%. These figures are for all insured commercial banks. Larger banks typically have higher loan/deposit ratios than smaller ones.

TABLE 1

*Operating Income, Expenses, and Net Income of Insured
Commercial Banks, 1950–1978*
(in billions of dollars)

	1950	1955	1960	1965	1970	1978
Operating Income						
Interest on loans	$2.0	$3.7	$6.8	$11.2	$24.0	$86.6
Interest on securities	1.2	1.7	2.3	3.5	6.5	16.5
Service charges and fees	.3	.5	.8	1.1	2.0	4.9
Trust department income	.2	.3	.5	.8	1.1	2.1
Other operating income	.2	.2	.3	.2	1.1	3.5
TOTAL	3.9	6.4	10.7	16.8	34.7	113.6
Operating Expenses						
Salaries and wages	1.2	1.9	2.9	4.4	7.7	18.7
Interest on deposits	.3	.7	1.8	5.1	10.5	50.2
Interest on other borrowed funds	—	—	—	.2	2.0	8.8
Other operating expenses	.9	1.4	2.2	2.8	7.4	20.8
TOTAL	2.4	4.0	6.9	12.5	27.6	98.5
Net Operating Income	1.5	2.4	3.8	4.3	7.1	15.1
Securities gains (losses)	(.1)	(.5)	(.4)	(.8)	(.1)	(.1)
Taxes	.4	.8	1.4	1.0	1.9	4.2
Net After-Tax Income	1.0	1.1	2.0	2.5	5.1	10.8

Source: FDIC *Annual Reports.*

TABLE 2

*Operating Income and Expenses of Insured Commercial Banks,
1950–1978*
(percentage distribution)

	1950	1955	1960	1965	1970	1978
Operating Income						
Interest on loans	51%	58%	63%	67%	69%	76%
Interest on securities	31	26	21	21	19	15
Service charges and fees	8	8	8	6	6	4
Trust department income	5	5	5	5	3	2
Other operating income	5	3	3	1	3	3
TOTAL	100	100	100	100	100	100
Operating Expenses						
Salaries and wages	50	48	42	35	28	19
Interest on deposits	13	17	26	41	38	51
Interest on other borrowed funds	—	—	—	2	7	9
Other operating expenses	37	35	32	22	27	21
TOTAL	100	100	100	100	100	100

Source: Table 1.

bank best provide for its liquidity needs? Views on this have changed over time, from the traditional precepts of the commercial loan theory in the 1920s, to the "shiftability" thesis in the 1930s, to the doctrine of "anticipated income" in the 1940s and 1950s, to the newfangled (but short-lived) panacea of exclusive reliance on "liability management" in the 1960s. Let's take a look at each of these approaches to bank management.

The Commercial Loan Theory of Banking

The commercial loan theory—or the real bills doctrine, as it was also called—insisted that commercial banks, because of the nature of their liabilities, should make only short-term, self-liquidating, productive loans. Since the bulk of commercial bank liabilities are payable on demand, it was argued that assets should similarly be as short-term as possible. The ideal asset was seen as the short-term business loan for working capital purposes, with a maximum maturity of about three months. Loans or investments of longer duration should not be made, it was said, except to the extent of a bank's capital accounts, and per-haps—this was never fully resolved—its savings deposits.

The "self-liquidating" aspect of the commercial loan theory meant that the funds for a borrower to repay a loan were supposed to arise out of the very transaction being financed by that particular loan. A loan to finance inventories, the classic example, would be repaid by the businessman out of his receipts from the sale of those very inventories. The sale proceeds from the transaction being financed would give rise to the *automatic self-liquidation* of the bank's assets.

Commercial banks, of course, no longer follow the tenets of the commercial loan theory, if indeed they ever really did. Securities, mortgage loans, and consumer loans are all beyond the pale, as are business "term loans"—with an original maturity of one year or longer —which nowadays comprise about half of all bank business loans. Although it is hard to believe today, commercial banks made virtually no consumer loans or business term loans prior to the 1930s.

The reason banks have abandoned the commercial loan theory was not because it contained theoretical defects, but simply because it was (and is) impractical: if banks want to stay in business in a competitive environment, they have to supply what borrowers want. And borrowers are not that anxious to acquire funds for only three months and for such restrictive purposes. The greatest borrower demand in the past four or five decades has been for mortgage loans, consumer loans, and business term loans, and banks have consequently altered their attitudes and policies to adapt to the realities of the market.

However, the real bills doctrine does indeed contain theoretical defects, and recognition of these flaws has led to its abandonment as a theoretical ideal as well as a guide to practical operations (which means that banks no longer give it lip service, which they used to do even when they weren't abiding by its precepts). The fundamental fallacy in the commercial loan theory is that no loan is, in itself, automatically *self*-liquidating. A loan to a retailer to purchase inventories is supposed automatically to yield sufficient funds to pay off the loan when the goods are sold to consumers. *But* if the inventory is not successfully sold to consumers the loan cannot be automatically liquidated. In every case, liquidation depends on the successful completion of plans which necessarily involve third parties other than the lender and the borrower. In this example, the third parties are the retailer's consumer customers.

In addition, the commercial loan theory fails to distinguish adequately between the individual bank and the banking system. To the individual banker, many loans appear to be highly liquid which, from the point of view of the banking *system,* are not liquid at all—because the repayment of one loan often requires the extension of another. The ability of a retailer to repay his inventory loan often depends ultimately on the extension of consumer loans to his customers. Since each loan is negotiated by different people, probably at different banks, without any apparent connection between them, an illusion of self-liquidation prevails. What actually happens is that one loan is repaid because another has been extended to someone else. Were the consumer loan not extended, the inventory loan could not be repaid. In effect, the burden of repayment is continuously shifted from one borrower to another—and from the point of view of the banking system as a whole no *net* liquidation takes place.

The shortcomings of the commercial loan theory, in both theory and practice, led to the development of more realistic views as to how a bank might best provide for its liquidity needs. At first, the commercial loan theory was supplanted by the "shiftability" thesis—the view that the best way to safeguard liquidity was to buy assets that could be readily *sold* to others when funds are needed. This was replaced in turn by the doctrine of "anticipated income."

The Shiftability Thesis

The idea of liquidity through shiftability—through the ability to sell off (or shift) assets to others—changed the emphasis for the source of liquidity from the loan portfolio to the securities portfolio. This has particular applicability to short-term open market investments, such as Treasury bills, which generally can be promptly sold whenever it is necessary to raise funds.

It is no accident, by the way, that the view that liquidity could be provided via shiftability paralleled the growth of money market instruments, which are especially suited for that role. Until the 1920s bankers had always looked to their loan portfolio for their liquidity, simply because there was no other place to find it. Prior to World War I the federal debt was less than $1 billion, very little of it in short-term form. The volume of commercial paper and bankers' acceptances was correspondingly small. Short-term open market securities of high quality did not exist in sufficient volume before the late 1920s to serve as a meaningful source of bank liquidity.

Treasury bills, first introduced in 1929, provided the perfect shiftability instrument. They are of high quality, they usually can be sold quickly without taking a loss, and they are in abundant supply. Since their growth in the 1930s coincided with a dearth of opportunities to make good business loans—because of the Great Depression—it was not unnatural that the concept of providing for liquidity by holdings of short-term securities gained wide sanction. (Necessity is the mother of invention, especially for theories.) By World War II, money market securities had all but completely replaced the loan portfolio as the source of bank liquidity, both in practice and in theory.

However, the shiftability theory will work—that is, will provide a bank with liquidity when it needs it—only if everyone is not utilizing the same channels at the same time. One bank, or a few banks, can always obtain funds on short notice by selling off Treasury bills in the open market. At times many banks can do so, provided households or corporations are buying. But *everyone* cannot be a seller simultaneously. There have to be buyers to whom sellers can sell (remember that—it is one of the most profound ideas economics has to offer).

Thus the shiftability theory contains the same defect that plagued the commercial loan theory—it inevitably relies on the actions of a third party. It will work for one bank, or a few banks, but it cannot be relied upon as a source of liquidity for a large number of banks in times of widespread emergency. On such occasions, the liquidity of short-term money market instruments evaporates for lack of sufficient buyers. *Only the Federal Reserve can provide liquidity under such circumstances,* by stepping in as a ready buyer of securities, willing to accommodate all sellers.

The Doctrine of Anticipated Income

A third view of how to provide for bank liquidity developed in the late 1940s and 1950s. Known as the doctrine of anticipated income, it reverted to the loan portfolio as the source of liquidity. Not surprisingly, in the pragmatic American environment, once again practice preceded theory.

During the Depression and World War II, the heyday of the shiftability theory, bank securities holdings grew larger than their loans. But once the war had ended, the trend began to reverse itself and bank loans expanded at a rapid rate; by 1956 loans once again exceeded securities holdings. Today, bank portfolios show more than $2 of loans for every $1 of securities. But the bulk of these loans—unlike the situation before 1930—are consumer loans, mortgage loans, and business term loans. These are not easily shiftable, and they are the direct antithesis of the short-term business loan favored by the commercial loan theory.

Bankers evidently require theoretical justification before they can feel entirely comfortable in accepting the earnings yielded by such assets, and the doctrine of anticipated income provided that justification. It was (and still is) reasoned that the way in which most loans are liquidated should be faced squarely: They are not inherently self-liquidating, but rather are paid off out of the earnings that accrue to the borrower from transactions with numerous third parties. Strictly speaking, no loan automatically generates its own repayment, as the commercial loan theory had claimed. *All* loans, in one way or another, get repaid out of the future income of the borrower, income which arises from a number of sources, some of which may be only remotely connected with the transaction being financed by the loan itself.

Realizing this, consumer loans, mortgage loans, and term loans to business are then seen as fundamentally no different from the traditional short-term business loan that finances inventories. In addition, to the extent that they are amortized, as most loans are today—that is, they are repaid periodically, in installments, instead of in a lump sum at the maturity of the loan—such loans provide a continuous cash inflow similar to a spaced series of short-term loans, thereby contributing regularly to liquidity.

All of which is well and good, except that the doctrine of anticipated income, by itself, does not fill the entire bill. What it really amounts to is a method for analyzing borrower creditworthiness: it gives the lender criteria for evaluating the potential of a borrower to successfully repay (or liquidate) a loan of a given amount on schedule. Bank liquidity, however, is more than that. It also refers to the ability of a bank to raise cash quickly when needed. Installment repayments provide a regular stream of liquidity, but are not adequate to meet extraordinary emergency cash needs. If the doctrine of anticipated income is looked upon as what it is—a method of evaluating borrower creditworthiness (can he meet his loan repayments on time?) and scheduling inflows of funds over time—then it is properly seen as complementary to, rather than competitive with, other theories of bank liquidity.

Liability Management

The 1960s witnessed a dramatic change in bank liquidity practices. Until then, provision for liquidity had been sought almost entirely on the asset side of the balance sheet. The commercial loan theory, shiftability, anticipated income—all relied on asset management, in some form, to supply liquidity when needed. The single exception to this principle was occasional resort to Federal Reserve discounting.

Starting in the early 1960s, however, banks began increasingly to draw their liquidity from the *liabilities* side of the balance sheet. *Instead of taking their liability structure as given and tailoring their assets to fit, they began to take a target asset growth as given and adjusted their liabilities to suit their needs.* Liability management became the most important banking development of the 1960s. It was facilitated by the growth of the negotiable CD market, which started in early 1961, and by such related developments later in the decade as the purchase of funds from foreign branches, the growth of the Federal funds market, and the use of the holding company device to raise funds through subsidiaries and affiliates.

More and more during the 1960s, banks—especially the larger ones—came to rely on their ability to buy (borrow) money when necessary as a means of meeting whatever liquidity needs might arise. Why store up liquidity in short-term, low-yielding assets, when it could always be bought in the market when needed? Why try to make any short-term loans, when long-term loans were what borrowers were asking for? Why turn away creditworthy potential borrowers with talk of being "loaned up"—only to see them get loans from competitors—when the necessary funds could always be bought by selling new CDs?

Occasionally a somber note was sounded: What if the Federal Reserve did not keep on raising Regulation Q's rate ceilings? If the ceilings were not raised in tandem with market interest rates, bank CDs would no longer be competitive with Treasury bills, and the funds banks had been attracting would go elsewhere. But such Cassandras were hard to take seriously. After all, hadn't the Fed always raised the rate ceilings when market interest rates rose—in 1957, in 1962, in 1963, in 1964, and in 1965?

But all good things must come to an end. In 1966 and again in 1969 the Fed was not so accommodating, and the new panacea of liability management was deflated to proper proportions. At the beginning of 1966, exclusive reliance on liability management appeared to many bankers to be an easy solution to the perennial dilemma of bank liquidity: namely, don't worry about it until you have to, and then borrow all you need by issuing CDs or some other liability. By the end of 1969, however, they were all too aware that the answer was not that simple. Just as determined Federal Reserve action can drive securities prices down and thereby erode the market for assets, it can also (through Regulation Q) destroy the market for liabilities. And even if the Fed does not use Regulation Q to destroy the market for CDs—as in the 1973–1974 tight money episode, when rate ceilings on large CDs were abolished—the *cost* of raising new funds may go so high as to make it prohibitive.

The expansion of the Federal funds market during the 1960s also played a significant role in the development of bank liability management. In a traditional Federal funds transaction, a bank with excess reserves will sell some of its excess to a bank with deficient reserves, on an overnight basis and at an agreed-upon interest rate. Thus, Federal funds are made available on the same day a transaction is concluded.

For a bank seeking to make up a reserve deficiency, the Federal funds market is an alternative to borrowing from the Federal Reserve through the discount window or to selling off short-term assets. Since borrowing at the discount window is an alternative to buying Federal funds, the interest rate on Federal funds never rose above the discount rate (until the mid-1960s). If the Federal funds rate went above the discount rate, a bank needing reserves would merely use the discount window instead of buying Federal funds from another commercial bank.

Since the mid-1960s, however, the daily Federal funds rate has rarely been *below* the discount rate. This is because in recent years the market has changed its nature. It used to involve only banks making temporary last-minute adjustments in their reserves. Now a number of large banks use the Federal funds market to make virtually continuous net purchases, even when they are not faced with a reserve shortage; they are using the Federal funds market to acquire funds on a more or less permanent basis. Thus, Federal funds are just another bank liability used to expand lending ability.

The paradoxical result is that the shortest of all money market tranactions—the overnight purchase of Federal funds—has become in many respects more like a capital market than a money market instrument. This serves as a good lesson in why you cannot draw a hard and fast line between the two. Virtually all financial markets are interconnected and interrrelated, in one way or another. We will return to these interactions in Chapter 30, when we examine the determinants of the structure of interest rates—why some interest rates are higher than others, and what causes changes in their relationships.

Bank Management with Models and Computers

The 1960s not only saw the rise and fall of excessive emphasis on liability management in banking, but also produced the first applications of computers to aid bankers in their decision making. Unlike the temporary nature of the theories of bank liquidity discussed above, the use of computer models is here to stay (because computers cost more than theories, hence cannot be disposed of so easily).

The theories of bank management we have examined illustrate quite clearly that there are many factors which must enter the portfolio decisions of a bank. Liquidity can be provided in numerous ways. There are many potential assets which yield different returns, depending upon the risks involved (see Chapter 30 for a discussion of yield differentials on different assets). In other words, no single decision-rule can be used for a general approach to bank portfolio selection.

The use of computers and a technique known as linear programming has put some order into the procedure for allocating bank funds, and has also made explicit the costs of high liquidity (in terms of foregone income). Linear programming is a general mathematical procedure that can be used whenever it is desired to maximize something subject to constraints. In the case of a bank, the objective is to maximize profits subject to the constraints imposed by liquidity requirements and the regulatory framework. It is possible to express this profit objective and the constraints in formal mathematical equations. Solving this system of equations provides the bank with actual numbers for how much to invest in (say) Treasury bills, commercial loans, and other assets, and how much to pay for savings deposits, CDs, and so on.

BOOTH

"Our main bank is right near your home, and we have fifteen other handy branches with all the latest push-button systems. We'll give you top interest rates and lollipops on your 'rainy-day' savings account. You can also have a safe-deposit box that no one but you is allowed to open. You'll get free 'stop-and-bank' souvenirs, such as little silver Empire State Buildings and Abraham Lincolns. There is a brand-new playground next to your bank, and you'll get a chance to win one of the grand sweepstakes prizes— hi-fi stereo, color television, or two weeks for two in Mexico City."

We will spare you the details of how to solve such linear programming problems—the most widely used procedure (algorithm) is called the "simplex" method, not because it is a "simple" solution to a "complex" problem (which it is), but because it has something to do with evaluating a simplex, which just happens to be an N-dimensional analogue of a triangle. Understand? Just be aware of the fact that such an approach to bank portfolio management exists, can be used in actual practice, and is indeed used.

While technocrats in operations research departments of large commercial banks have no doubt contributed much to efficient bank management, we must still emphasize that sophisticated mathematical techniques do not, by themselves, insure success, Actual numbers must be put into a linear programming model detailing, for example, prospective yields on alternative bank investments. This information requires the analysis of financial experts and economists (time out for a commercial). In other words, linear programming is an aid to sophisticated bank management, but not a substitute for it.

Discretionary Funds Management

The central focus of bank management today is a modified form of liability management, best described as discretionary funds management. It revolves around the strategic employment of interest-sensitive funds—whether liabilities *or* assets—that can be increased or decreased at the bank's initiative.

Bank management in relatively large institutions meets at least monthly, often weekly, to project expected movements in *non*discretionary funds—anticipated inflows and outflows that are beyond the bank's immediate control. These would include expected extensions or repayments of business loans, projected inflows and outflows of time and savings deposits, and so on. The result of all these nondiscretionary flows is either a projected *net outflow* of funds or a projected *net inflow*, which the bank must accommodate in the short run. An expected net outflow means funds must be raised to fill the gap; an expected net inflow means there are surplus funds to dispose of.

It is the *discretionary* liabilities and assets that will be used to raise funds or dispose of them, as the case might be. If a bank needs to raise funds, it might buy Federal funds, sell Treasury bills, sell securities under repurchase agreements, or borrow through CDs or from the Federal Reserve. If it has funds to dispose of, funds it does not want to keep idle, it might sell Federal funds, buy Treasury bills, lower its CD rate and let CDs run off, and so on. Whether a discretionary item is an asset or a liability is relatively unimportant in the bank's financing decision. The most basic consideration is to raise funds at minimum cost or to allocate a surplus to maximize profits.

These alternative sources of funds all stand on a common

footing in that each of them can—at a price—supply a dollar of liquidity which is just as good as a dollar of liquidity acquired from any other source. The theories of liquidity discussed earlier in this chapter each implied that there was something uniquely beneficial in one or the other of these sources of liquidity, as though it could always satisfy liquidity needs "best." In so doing, they ignored what should be the crucial deciding factor in each particular instance: namely, the relative cost (and availability) of acquiring funds throughout the entire array of potential alternatives, with due consideration paid to the relative risks involved in each alternative and particularly in too extensive reliance on any one of them. In brief, at any one time a choice exists among an array of alternatives as to how liquidity might be acquired. It will be more profitable to make this choice in terms of relative costs and risks than to blindly follow oversimplified theories.

Finally, it must be emphasized that fundamental to the state of bank liquidity are three basic factors that are too often overlooked: (1) federal monetary-fiscal policies, to maintain a prosperous economy in which the anticipated income of borrowers will actually be realized; (2) federal deposit insurance protection, which has successfully eliminated the old-fashioned "run on the bank" that used to spark liquidity crises; and (3) the Federal Reserve itself, in times of unforeseen widespread financial emergency, standing by as a "lender of last resort" through its discount facilities.

Suggestions for Further Reading

The problems of bank liquidity are discussed in surprisingly modern terms in Walter Bagehot's classic *Lombard Street* (New York: Scribner's, 1873; reprinted Homewood, Ill.: Irwin, 1962); and in Lloyd W. Mints, *A History of Banking Theory* (University of Chicago Press, 1945). Also see Herbert V. Prochnow, *Term Loans and Theories of Bank Liquidity* (Englewood Cliffs, N.J.: Prentice-Hall, 1949).

On liability management, see the articles by Robert E. Knight, mentioned at the end of Chapter 9, and Paul S. Nadler, *Commercial Banking in the Economy*, 3rd ed. (New York: Random House, 1979). Also see Stuart A. Schweitzer, "Bank Liability Management: For Better or Worse?" in the Federal Reserve Bank of Philadelphia's *Business Review* (December 1974), and Wesley Lindow, "In Defense of Liability Management," *Journal of Portfolio Management* (Summer 1975). On discretionary funds management, see William L. Silber, *Commercial Bank Liability Management*

(Chicago: Association of Reserve City Bankers, 1978). A useful introduction to linear programming and bank management is Alfred Broadus, "Linear Programming: A New Approach to Bank Portfolio Management;" Federal Reserve Bank of Richmond *Monthly Review* (November 1972). A good summary of the literature is Kalman J. Cohen and Fredrick S. Hammer, eds., *Analytical Methods in Banking.* (Homewood, Ill.: Irwin, 1966); and Kalman J. Cohen and Stephen E. Gibson, eds., *Management Science in Banking* (Boston: Warren Gorham, and Lamont, 1978).

PART III

The Art of Central Banking

Chapter 11

Who's in Charge Here?

MONETARY POLICY is the responsibility of the Federal Reserve, but to whom is the Federal Reserve responsible? We saw in Chapter 1 that the money supply should be set to give us full employment without inflation. The Federal Reserve checks the money supply, but who checks the Fed?

The answer to that question is so complex that if we unravel it successfully (which is not too likely a prospect), we will either have unveiled one of the great socioeconomic creations in the annals of civilization, comparable to the invention of inside plumbing, or unmasked one of the most devious schemes ever contrived by the mind of man to camouflage the true locus of clandestine power.

According to some, the Federal Reserve is responsible to the Congress. But it is the President, not Congress, who appoints the seven members of the Board of Governors of the Federal Reserve System, who occupy the stately building at 20th Street and Constitution Avenue, Washington, D.C. The President also selects from among those seven the Chairman of the Board of Governors, the principal spokesman for the central bank.

On that basis, one might surmise that the Federal Reserve is responsible to the executive branch of government, in the person of the President and his administration. However, since each member serves a fourteen-year term, the current President can appoint only two of the seven-member Board of Governors, unless there are deaths or resignations. Even the Chairman may be the appointee of the previous administration. Furthermore, it is Congress that created the Federal Reserve (not in its own image) in 1913, and it is Congress, not the President, that has the authority to alter its working mandate at any time. In 1935, for example, Congress chose to throw two administration representatives off the Board of Governors—the Secretary of the Treasury and the Comptroller of the Currency, both of whom had been ex officio members—simply because they were representatives of the executive branch.

Others, more cynical, have suggested that the Federal Reserve is mostly responsible to the private banking community, primarily the 5,600 commercial banks that are member banks of the Federal Reserve System. The member banks do in fact choose the presidents of each of the twelve regional Federal Reserve banks, including the President of the most aristocratic of all, the Federal Reserve Bank of New York. It may or may not be significant that the annual salary of the President of the Federal Reserve Bank of New York is $110,000 while that of the Chairman of the Board of Governors in Washington is $57,500.

Who's in charge here? Who, indeed? In Chapter 1 we noted how bank lending and the money supply affect economic activity. In Chapter 3 we showed how the central bank could control bank lending and the money supply (if it wanted to). And we devote all of Part IV to a more detailed discussion of the role of money in economic activity. Before continuing further, however, let's see who should get the accolades for the successes and who should get the blame for the mistakes.

Formal Structure

The statutory organization of the Federal Reserve System is a case study in those currently popular concepts, decentralization and the blending of public and private authority. A deliberate attempt was made in the enabling congressional legislation—the 1913 Federal Reserve Act—to diffuse power over a broad base—geographically, between the private and public sectors, and even within the government —so that no one person, group, or sector, either inside or outside the government, could exert enough leverage to dominate the thrust of monetary policy.

Who's in Charge Here?

As noted in Figure 1, the Board of Governors of the Federal Reserve System consists of seven members, appointed by the President with the advice and consent of the Senate. To prevent presidential board-packing, each member is appointed for a term of fourteen years, with one term expiring at the end of January in each even-numbered year. Furthermore, no two board members may come from the same Federal Reserve District. The Chairman of the Board of Governors, chosen from among the seven by the President, serves a four-year term. However, his term is not concurrent with the presidential term, so an incoming President could find himself saddled with an already appointed Chairman for much of his first term in office. The Board is independent of the congressional appropriations process and partially exempt from audit by the government's watchdog, the

FIGURE 1 / The formal structure and policy organization of the Federal Reserve System.

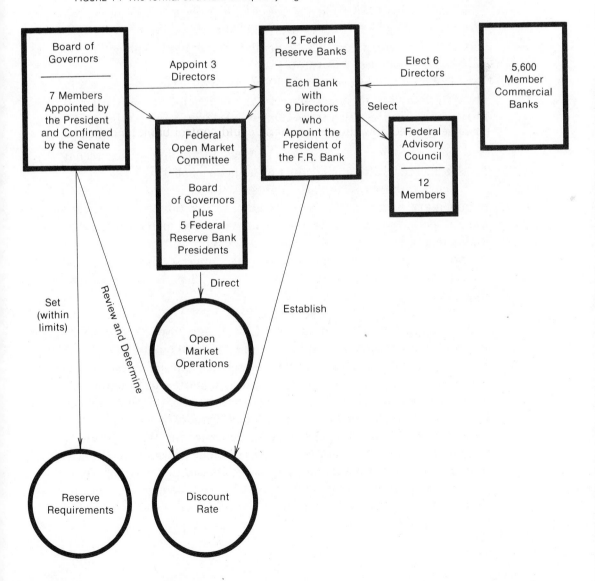

General Accounting Office, since its operating funds come from the earnings of the twelve regional Federal Reserve banks.

The regional Federal Reserve banks, one in each Federal Reserve District, are geographically dispersed throughout the nation—the Federal Reserve Bank of New York, the Federal Reserve Bank of Kansas City, the Federal Reserve Bank of San Francisco, and so on (see Figure 2). Each Federal Reserve Bank is privately owned by the member banks in its district, the very commercial banks it is charged with supervising and regulating. Each member commercial bank is required to buy stock in its district Federal Reserve Bank equal to 6 percent of its own capital and surplus. Of this 6 percent, 3 percent must be paid in and 3 percent is subject to call by the Board of Governors. However, the profits accruing to ownership are limited by law to a 6 percent annual dividend on paid-in capital stock. The member bank stockholders elect six of the nine directors of their district Federal Reserve Bank, and the remaining three are appointed from Washington by the Board of Governors. These nine directors, in turn, choose the president of their Federal Reserve Bank, subject to the approval of the Board of Governors.

The directors of each Federal Reserve Bank also select a person, always a commercial banker, to serve on the Federal Advisory Council, a statutory body consisting of a member from each of the twelve Federal Reserve districts. The Federal Advisory Council consults quarterly with the Board of Governors in Washington and makes recommendations regarding the conduct of monetary policy.

Legal authority is similarly diffused with respect to the *execution* of monetary policy, as Figure 1 indicates. The Board of Governors has the power to set reserve requirements on commercial bank time and demand deposits, for example, but it cannot set them outside the bounds of the specific limits imposed by Congress (between 3 and 10 percent for time deposits, between 7 and 22 percent for demand deposits).

Open market operations are directed by a body known as the Federal Open Market Committee (FOMC), composed of the seven-member Board of Governors plus five of the Reserve Bank presidents. Since the members of the Board of Governors are appointed by the White House, and the Reserve Bank presidents are appointed by the directors of each Federal Reserve Bank, who are (six of nine) elected by the member commercial banks, the diffusion of authority over open market operations spans the distance from the White House to the member bank on Main Street. In addition, although the FOMC directs open market operations, they are executed at the trading desk of the Federal Reserve Bank of New York by a gentleman who appears to be simultaneously an employee of the FOMC and the Federal Reserve Bank of New York.

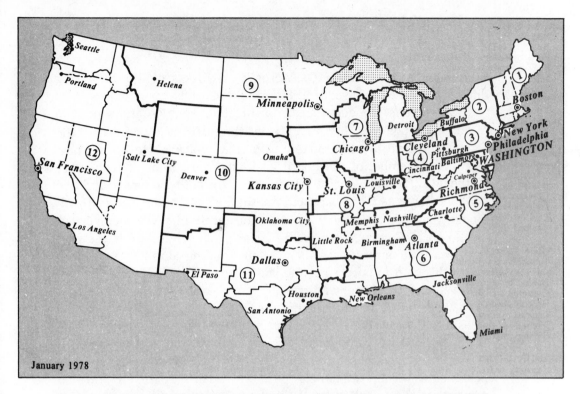

January 1978

BOUNDARIES OF FEDERAL RESERVE DISTRICTS AND THEIR BRANCH TERRITORIES

Legend

───── Boundaries of Federal Reserve Districts   ───── Boundaries of Federal Reserve Branch Territories

⭐ Board of Governors of the Federal Reserve System

◉ Federal Reserve Bank Cities   • Federal Reserve Branch Cities

FIGURE 2 / The Federal Reserve System.

Drawn by R. W. Galvin, Cart. SOURCE: Federal Reserve *Bulletin*.

Source: Federal Reserve Bulletin.
Note: Hawaii and Alaska are in the Twelfth Federal Reserve District.

Legal authority over discount rates is even more confusing. Discount rates are "established" every two weeks by the directors of each regional Federal Reserve Bank, but they are subject to "review and determination" by the Board of Governors. The distinction between "establishing" discount rates and "determining" them is a fine line indeed, and it would not be surprising if confusion occasionally arose as to precisely where the final authority and responsibility lie.

The Realities of Power

So much for the Land of Oz. Actually, the facts of life are rather different, as the more realistic Figure 3 illustrates.

By all odds, the dominant figure in the formation and execution of monetary policy is the Chairman of the Board of Governors of the Federal Reserve System, currently Paul A. Volcker. He is the most prominent member of the Board itself, the most influential member of the FOMC, and generally recognized by both Congress and the public at large as *the* spokesman for the Federal Reserve System. Although the Federal Reserve Act appears to put all seven members of the Board of Governors on more or less equal footing, over the past forty years the strong personalities, outstanding abilities, and determined devotion to purpose of the chairmen—first Marriner S. Eccles, then William McChesney Martin, Jr., later Arthur F. Burns, and now Paul Volcker—have made them rather more equal than the others. As adviser to the President, negotiator with Congress, and final authority on appointments throughout the system, with influence over all aspects of monetary policy in his capacity as Chairman of both the Board of Governors and the FOMC, the Chairman for all practical purposes is the embodiment of the central bank in this country.

The other six members of the Board of Governors also exercise a substantial amount of authority, more so than is indicated in the formal paper structure of the system, because with the passage of time primary responsibility for monetary policy has become more centralized and concentrated in Washington. When the Federal Reserve Act was passed in 1913, it was thought that the Federal Reserve System would be mainly a passive service agency, supplying currency when needed, clearing checks, and providing a discount facility for the convenience of the private commercial member banks. At that time there was no conception of monetary policy as an active countercyclical force. Open market operations were unknown and reserve requirements were fixed by law, with no flexibility permitted. Since then, of course, the central bank has shifted from passive accommodation to active regulation, from the performance of regional service functions to the implementation of national economic policy. This shift has been accompanied, naturally enough, by a rise in the power of the centralized Board of Governors in Washington and a corresponding decline in the role of the regional Federal Reserve Banks and their "owners," the commercial banks.

It would not be unrealistic to describe the central bank today as headquartered in Washington, with twelve field offices located

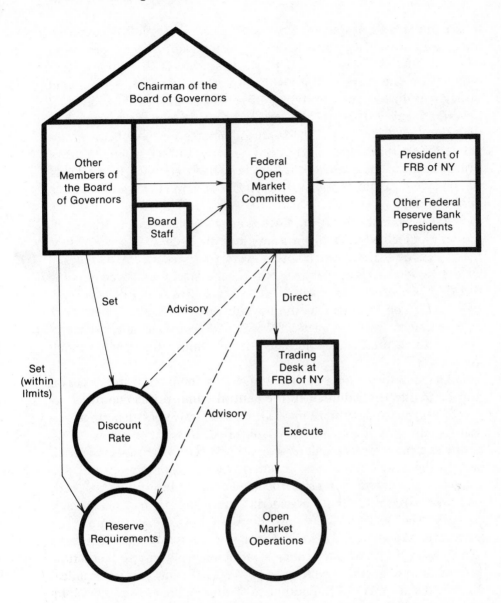

FIGURE 3 / The realities of power within the Federal Reserve System.

throughout the nation. These field offices may be known by the rather imposing name of Federal Reserve Banks, and they do indeed retain a certain degree of autonomy in expressing their views on the wisdom of various policies. But even so they essentially amount to little more than branches of the Washington headquarters.

Closely related to the Board of Governors in the informal power structure, and deriving influence through that association, is the Board's professional staff of economic experts and advisers. The long tenure in the Federal Reserve System of many senior staff economists, their familiarity with Federal Reserve history, and their expertise in monetary analysis give them a power base that is to a large extent founded on the respect with which they, as individuals, are held throughout the System. Through daily consultation with the individual Governors and written and oral presentations before each meeting of the FOMC, staff personnel exert an indefinable but significant influence on the ultimate decision-making process. In fact, in recent years two members of the Board's staff have been elevated to the Board itself, via presidential nomination (Robert Holland in 1973 and Charles Partee in 1976).[1]

Aside from the Board of Governors, its Chairman, and its staff, the only other body playing a major role in Federal Reserve policy-making is the FOMC, which meets every four weeks in Washington. Of the twelve members on the FOMC, a majority of seven are the Board of Governors themselves. The other five are Reserve Bank presidents. The President of the Federal Reserve Bank of New York is a permanent member of the FOMC, and the other eleven Federal Reserve Bank presidents alternate the remaining four seats among themselves.

The statutory authority of the FOMC is confined to the direction of open market operations, but in recent years it has become the practice to bring all policy matters under review at FOMC meetings. Although only five of the Reserve Bank presidents are entitled to vote at any one time, typically all twelve attend every meeting and participate in the discussion. Thus, potential reserve-requirement and discount-rate changes are, in effect, decided upon within the FOMC, with the twelve Reserve Bank presidents participating in an advisory capacity. The Board of Governors, however, always has the final say on reserve requirements and discount rates if matters should come to a showdown, particularly since legal opinion appears to be that, in case of disagreement, the Board's power to "review and determine" discount rates overrides the authority of the indivdual Reserve Banks to "establish" them.

Once the FOMC decides on the appropriate open market policy, actual execution of the policy directive until the next meeting is the responsibility of the Account Manager at the Federal Reserve Bank of New York's trading desk. He is called the Account Manager because he manages the System Open Market Account, which includes all of the securities holdings of the Federal Reserve System. Since the FOMC's instructions are often couched in rather broad language, the Account Manager has to translate these instructions into actual daily

[1] And in 1978, Nancy Teeters became the first woman member of the Board of Governors.

purchases and sales of Treasury securities. In the process, at least a modest amount of leeway and personal interpretation is inevitable, as we discuss further in Chapter 14.

Like the Account Manager, the unique position of the President of the Federal Reserve Bank of New York in the hierarchy also stems from his role and status in the nation's financial center. If he is inclined to use this leverage, as Allan Sproul did a quarter-century ago and Benjamin Strong before him, the President of the New York Reserve Bank can mount a substantial challenge even to the Chairman of the Board of Governors. Since such a challenge would have little legal foundation, it would have to be based on the prestige of the presidency of the Federal Reserve Bank of New York and the forcefulness of the man who holds the position. Both Allan Sproul and Benjamin Strong were men of exceptional ability and personality.

But where, in the corridors of power, does this leave the member banks, the directors of each Federal Reserve Bank, and the Federal Advisory Council? Pretty much shut out, if the truth be known.

The member banks do indeed "own" their district Federal Reserve Bank, but such stockholding is mostly symbolic and carries none of the usual attributes of ownership. The member banks also have a major voice in electing the directors of their Reserve Bank, but the directors in turn have responsibilities that are largely ceremonial. True, they appoint the members of the Federal Advisory Council, but the Federal Advisory Council serves mostly a public relations purpose and has little to do with actual policy-making. The directors of each Federal Reserve Bank also choose the president of their Reserve Bank, subject to the approval of the Board of Governors. But the "subject to approval" clause has meant, in practice, that the most the directors can really do is submit a list of nominees for the position of president. On several occasions, the choice of the directors of a Federal Reserve Bank has not met with approval from Washington; such cases have made very clear exactly where ultimate authority is lodged.

How Independent the Central Bank?

The fact that ultimate authority over monetary policy resides in Washington brings to the fore the relationship between the central bank and the other branches of government also responsible for overall national economic policy—the Congress and the administration, the latter personified by the President.

The Federal Reserve is a creature of the Congress. The Constitution gives Congress the power "to coin money and regulate the value thereof." On this basis, in 1913 Congress created the Federal Reserve as the institution delegated to administer that responsibility on its behalf. Congress requires periodic accountability by the Federal Reserve and has the authority to amend the enabling legislation, the Federal Reserve Act, any time it sees fit.

Essentially, Congress has given the Federal Reserve a broad mandate to regulate the monetary system in the public interest, and then has more or less stood aside and let the monetary authorities pursue this objective on their own and to the best of their abilities. Congress has also attempted to minimize interference on the part of the administration by giving each member of the Board of Governors a fourteen-year term, thereby sharply limiting any single President's influence over the board.

This semi-independent status of the central bank is a source of continuous friction. Some members of Congress believe that the Federal Reserve has carried its "independence" much too far. There has been some concern over its freedom from congressional appropriations and its partial exemption from standard government audit, as noted early in this chapter. Also, the Federal Reserve's responsibility on occasion for tight money and high interest rates has stimulated some intensive questioning at congressional hearings, including frequent scoldings of Federal Reserve officials by populist-minded congressmen who get uptight about tight money.

Others, in Congress and out, have complained that the Federal Reserve simply has not done a very good job, that we would all be better off if Congress laid down some guidelines or rules to limit the discretion available to the monetary authorities in conducting their business. We will discuss such proposals in Chapter 25.)

The relationship between the central bank and the President has also aroused considerable controversy. Many feel that the Federal Reserve should be a part of the executive branch of government, responsible to the President, on the grounds that monetary policy is an integral part of national economic policy. Monetary policy should therefore be coordinated at the highest level (that is, by the President), along with fiscal policy, as a component part of the administration's total program for economic growth and stability.

To do otherwise, it is charged, is both undemocratic and divisive —undemocratic because monetary policy is too important to be run by an elite group of experts insulated from the politcial process, and divisive because monetary and fiscal policy should not work at cross-purposes. Since fiscal policy proposals are clearly within the Presi-

The President holds frequent meetings with the Chairman of the Board of Governors, the Secretary of the Treasury, and the Chairman of the Council of Economic Advisors.

dent's domain, monetary policy should be as well. A Federal Reserve independent of presidential authority conflicts with the administration's responsibilty to promulgate and coordinate an overall economic program.

On the other hand, the case for central bank independence from the President rests on the pragmatic grounds that subordination of the central bank to the executive branch of government invites excessive money creation and consequent inflation. The charge that an independent Federal Reserve is undemocratic is countered by the reminder that the central bank is still very much responsible to Congress, which can alter or amend the Federal Reserve Act anytime it wishes. In addi-

WHITE HOUSE WARNS FED AGAINST LIFTING OF INTEREST RATES

Without Addressing Central Bank, Statement Says Further Rise Could Endanger Recovery

By JOHN H. ALLAN

In an unusual move, the White House yesterday warned the Federal Reserve Board—without addressing it directly—against raising interest rates and thus hurting the economy.

The warning, coming just a short while before the Federal Reserve released banking statistics that strongly indicated further rate increases were imminent, appeared to revive the dormant conflict between the Administration and the nation's monetary authorities.

It also cast doubt on the chances of Arthur F. Burns's reappointment as chairman of the Federal Reserve when his term expires early next year. Even before the White House statement, many businessmen and economists had expressed the opinion that Dr. Burns's reappointment was in danger. Page D1.

White House Issues Notice

The White House made its position known in a "notice to the press" that mentioned the Federal Reserve only in a reference to the central bank's role in setting growth targets for the nation's money supply. The statement, however, cautioned the central bank in unmistakable language.

"Rapid growth of the money supply is a matter of concern when it occurs in the context of very rapid economic expansion, high employment and a worsening out-look for inflation," the statement said. "Those are not the circumstances we face presently," it emphasized.

The statement was written in response to a reporter's request at a news briefing Wednesday for the Administration's views on short-term interest rates and the money supply. Normally, a White House reply would await the next scheduled news briefing, but in this case, the White House chose to distribute its comments in a special, general release.

Dr. Burns, meanwhile, was in Kansas City, Mo., yesterday for a meeting of the directors of the Federal Reserve bank there. A spokesman said that the Fed chairman was aware of the White House statement but would make no comment on it.

The White House warning was one of the most direct of the continuing maneuvers of several branches of the Federal Government to chip away at the independence of the Federal Reserve, an agency that works on its own to promote economic growth while maintaining stability in the purchasing power of the dollar. The Fed's conduct in pursuing these aims affects jobs and inflation, touching everyone in some degree.

In recent years, Congress has moved to circumscribe the Federal Reserve's power by making it report twice a year on monetary policy and its targets for money supply growth.

The Carter Administration has urged that the Federal Reserve chairman's term in office run concurrently with the President's. Mr. Burns, last appointed to the chairmanship in 1974 by former President Nixon, comes up for reappointment in January.

Higher short-term rates, the White House said, could divert money from savings accounts and impair mortgage lending for housing, which has been a particularly strong element in the economic recovery. It noted that higher interest rates had already "unsettled" the stock market, although it conceded that so far they had not "seriously damaged" the overall recovery.

Short-term interest rates have been climbing steadily since late July, largely as the result of the Federal Reserve's effort to slow down expansion of the nation's money supply—the amount of currency in circulation plus the funds on deposit in checking accounts at banks.

NEWS ITEM / Who's in Charge Here?

SOURCE: *New York Times*, October 21, 1977

tion, the President holds frequent meetings with the Chairman of the Board of Governors, the Secretary of the Treasury, and the Chairman of the Council of Economic Advisors.

It is feared by many, and not without historical justification, that if the monetary authority is made the junior partner to the President or the Treasury (the fiscal authority), monetary stability will be sacrificed to the government's revenue needs—the government will be tempted to seek the easy way out in raising funds, by printing money or borrowing excessively at artificially low interest rates, in preference to the politically more difficult route of raising taxes or cutting back on government spending. (Chapter 37 goes into more details on the conflicts between the Treasury and the Federal Reserve during the past thirty-five years.) The sole purpose of an independent monetary authority, in brief, is to forestall the natural propensity of governments to resort to inflation.

Still to Come

The rest of Part III takes an intensive look at Federal Reserve methods of control. Back in Chapter 3 ("A Bird's-Eye View of the Federal Reserve"), we glanced at the three main instruments of Federal Reserve policy—reserve requirements, the discount rate, and open market operations. It's time to revisit each and see more fully how the Fed goes about its business.

These policy instruments do not exhaust the Fed's arsenal of weapons. In addition to the general or quantitative controls, the Fed also exercises some selective or qualitative controls. For example, it sets maximum interest rates banks may pay to depositors, which we examined in Chapter 9. And it regulates margin (or down payment) requirements on stock market credit; we discuss this in Chapter 26. Other selective credit policies—primarily with respect to housing— are analyzed in Chapter 27.

Suggestions for Further Reading

For a formal description of the Federal Reserve's structure, read Chapter 2 of the sixth edition of *The Federal Reserve System: Purposes and Functions* (Washington, D.C.: Board of Governors of the Federal Reserve System, 1974). On the internal workings of the Fed, see C. R. Whittlesey, "Power and Influence in the Federal Reserve System," *Economica* (February 1963); David P. Eastburn, "The Federal Reserve as a Living Institution," in *Men, Money, and Policy: Essays in Honor of Karl R. Bopp* (Federal Reserve Bank of Philadelphia, 1970); and Jane W. D'Arista, *Federal Reserve Structure and the Development of Monetary Policy* (Staff Report, House Committee on Banking and Currency, U.S. Congress, 1971). A particularly interesting study of the internal operations of the Federal Reserve is by Thomas Havrilesky, William P. Yohe, and David Schirm, "The Economic Affiliations of Directors of Federal Reserve District Banks," in *Social Science Quarterly* (December 1973).

On the place of the central bank within the governmental framework, see Miroslav A. Kriz, "Central Banks and the State Today," *American Economic Review* (September 1948), and the "Comment" by Roland I. Robinson in the same *Review* (March 1949). Also see Kenneth E. Boulding, "The Legitimacy of Central Banks," in *Fundamental Reappraisal of the Discount Mechanism* (Board of Governors of the Federal Reserve System, 1969).

Finally, for the real flavor and excitement of central banking, two books are *must* reading: Marriner Eccles's autobiography, *Beckoning Frontiers* (New York: Knopf, 1951); and the *Selected Papers of Allan Sproul*, edited by Lawrence S. Ritter and published by the Federal Reserve Bank of New York in 1980. Marriner Eccles was a member of the Board of Governors from 1934 to 1951 and its Chairman from 1934 to 1948. Allan Sproul was President of the Federal Reserve Bank of New York from 1941 to 1956.

Chapter 12

Reserve Requirements

R EQUIREMENTS OF ANY SORT are generally a drag. Course requirements have to be fulfilled before you can get a degree, licensing requirements have to be met before you can pilot a 747, and reserve requirements have to be satisfied by commercial bankers before they can make loans and accept deposits.

It was thought many years ago that the purpose of bank reserve requirements was to provide for bank liquidity, solvency, and safety. It was believed that if banks held reserves against their deposits, this would make the banks more liquid and depositors' funds more safe.

But reserve requirements, at around 15 percent, are much too low to accomplish these ends, which are better achieved in other ways anyway (as by federal deposit insurance). As seen today, the primary function of bank reserve requirements is to serve as an instrument of monetary control; by varying them, as we know, the Federal Reserve can instantly change the excess reserves of all member banks, and can also change the demand deposit expansion multiplier for the banking system (since the multiplier involves the reciprocal of the required reserve ratio). Such changes are thought to be so powerful that they are used rather sparingly, for fear they may produce too great an effect.

The increase of ½ of 1 percentage point in required reserves against demand deposits in July 1973, for example, immediately shifted $850 million of reserves from the excess category, where they could have been used as a basis for loan and deposit expansion, to the required category, where for all practical purposes they were immobilized. On most occasions when reserve requirements are changed, the Fed finds it necessary to undertake open market operations to blunt the powerful impact of the change. Indicative of all these complications is the fact that between 1952 and 1979 reserve requirements against demand deposits were raised only six times and lowered on about a dozen occasions.

Let us examine the details of reserve requirements as they are structured today and some of the problems they create.

Existing Reserve Requirements

Legal reserve requirements for member banks of the Federal Reserve System must be held in the form of either vault cash or deposits in a bank's regional Federal Reserve Bank. The requirements are set by the Board of Governors of the Federal Reserve System within a range specified by Congress. The specified limits established by Congress are as follows:

Between 3 and 10 percent against savings and time deposits

Between 7 and 14 percent against a bank's demand deposits up to $400 million

Between 10 and 22 percent against a bank's demand deposits over $400 million[1]

In early 1979, the reserves that each member bank was required to hold were as shown in Table 1.

Requirement schedules are graduated for each bank, with each deposit interval applying to that part of a bank's deposits. Basing reserve requirements on deposit size categories is relatively new, dating only from 1966 for time deposits and from 1968 for demand deposits. Until then, reserve requirements were based entirely on geographic location: Banks in larger cities (called reserve cities) had higher reserve requirements than banks in smaller cities (called country banks). From 1966 until 1972 both geographic location and

[1] Banks with demand deposits over $400 million are called "reserve city banks," a term that once referred to geographic location and thus had more meaning than it does today. As it stands now, the definition of a reserve city bank has nothing to do with the city where it is located; a reserve city bank is any bank with demand deposits over $400 million.

TABLE 1

Reserve Requirements in Effect in Early 1979

Type of Deposit	Reserve Requirement
Demand deposits:	
The first $2 million	7 percent
From $2 to $10 million	9½ percent
From $10 to $100 million	11¾ percent
From $100 to $400 million	12¾ percent
Over $400 million	16¼ percent
Passbook savings deposits	3 percent
Time deposits:	
Original maturity 1 to 6 months	
The first $5 million	3 percent
Over $5 million	6 percent
Original maturity 6 months to 4 years	2½ percent
Original maturity 4 years or more	1 percent
Large-size CDs ($100,000 and over)	2 percent additional

Note: The *average* of reserves on all savings and other time deposits, taken in the aggregate, must be at least 3 percent, since this is the minimum prescribed by congressional statute.
Source: Federal Reserve Bulletin.

deposit size were used to determine requirements, and in late 1972 geographic basis was entirely abandoned in favor of requirements determined by the amount of deposits. In addition, starting in 1974 the maturity of time deposits was also taken into account.

Setting reserve requirements by deposit size—which essentially means by bank size—enables the Federal Reserve to allow smaller banks to hold a smaller percentage of their assets in the form of non-interest-bearing reserves, which, of course, increases their earnings. If small banks had to hold the same reserve ratios as larger banks, their profitability would be reduced, since reserve balances earn no interest.

Why are small banks favored in this way? Because small banks generally tend to be less profitable than larger ones to begin with, and the Federal Reserve is fearful that if it sets reserve requirements that are too high on small banks they will all drop out of the Federal Reserve System. This statement calls for a bit of background on the structural organization of banking in the United States today.

The Problem of System Membership

There are approximately 14,700 commercial banks in the United States today, of which about 4,600 are chartered to do business by the federal government (national banks) and 10,100 are chartered to do business by the states in which they operate (state banks). All national banks are *required* to be members of the Federal Reserve System, and thus must abide by the Fed's rules and regulations regarding reserve requirements. State-chartered banks are free to join the system or not, as they wish; if they do not join, their reserve requirements are set by the state in which they operate, usually by a state banking commission under ground rules established by the state legislature. At present only about 1,000 of the 10,100 state banks have chosen to become Federal Reserve member banks, so that less than 6,000 of the 14,700 commercial banks in the country are members.

The reason so few state banks have chosen membership is that most state reserve requirements for nonmember banks are lower than the Fed's requirements for member banks. In addition, in many states the reserve requirements for nonmember banks can be satisfied by the holding of interest-earning assets, such as government securities.

Although most banks are *not* members of the Federal Reserve System, member banks include almost all large banks, and they hold the bulk of the deposits—over 70 percent of the total deposits in the banking system are in the less than 6,000 member banks. The other 9,000 banks, the nonmembers, hold only 28 percent of the total deposits in the country; they are, clearly, the smaller institutions.

Nevertheless, the Federal Reserve is worried; ever since the end of World War II, the percentage of banks that are System members has been declining, as Table 2 indicates. New banks invariably choose a state rather than a national charter, so they do not have to become members, and every year some existing banks with a national charter shift over to a state charter so that they can drop out of the System. Federal legislation requires that national banks be members, but there

TABLE 2

Membership of Commercial Banks in the Federal Reserve System, 1945–1978

End of	Number of Commercial Banks	No. of Banks Members of F.R. System	Members as % of Total No. of Banks	Member Bank Deposits as % of Total Bank Deposits
1945	14,011	6,884	49%	87%
1950	14,121	6,873	49	86
1955	13,716	6,543	47	85
1960	13,472	6,174	46	84
1965	13,804	6,221	45	83
1970	13,686	5,767	42	80
1975	14,633	5,788	40	75
1978	14,719	5,586	38	72

Source: *Federal Reserve Bulletin.*

is no law that says a national bank has to keep that status; state law permitting, it can switch from a national to a state charter and then wave bye-bye to membership in the Federal Reserve System. As Table 2 indicates, over the past thirty years not only has there been a steady decline in member banks as a percentage of total commercial banks, but—more important—there has been a similar steady drop in member bank deposits as a percentage of total commercial bank deposits.

It is because the Federal Reserve does not want this trend to continue that it favors smaller banks in its reserve regulations and is more inclined to lower reserve requirements across the board than to raise them. A continued exodus of banks from System membership raises the possibility that the Fed's effectiveness might eventually be impaired as the central bank loses direct contact with a larger proportion of the nation's money supply. As matters now stand, however, the dropout trend is not likely to stop, since membership imposes a competitive disadvantage relative to nonmembership: member banks have to bear a larger reserve burden than nonmembers, with consequent impact on their earnings. This differential is difficult to justify in light of the fact that the primary function of reserve requirements is to further the implementation of monetary policy, and deposits in nonmember banks are as much a part of the money supply as deposits in member banks.

In response to this problem, it has frequently been recommended that all commercial banks, whether members or not, be required to hold reserves as specified by the Federal Reserve. Three prestigious study groups have come to this conclusion in recent years (the Commission on Money and Credit in 1961, President Kennedy's Committee on Financial Institutions in 1963, and President Nixon's Commission on Financial Structure and Regulation in 1971); since 1964 the Federal Reserve itself has annually recommended to the Congress that legislation along these lines be enacted. So far, however, such recommendations have been without success. In the aggregate, the banking industry prefers the status quo, and the banking industry wields a lot of political clout.

Another alternative, at the opposite extreme, is for the Fed to eliminate its own reserve requirements. If it did so, what would happen? Actually, even without formal reserve requirements the Fed would not be out of business. As long as commercial banks have a demand for claims against the central bank, and as long as the central bank controls the supply of such claims (via open market operations), monetary policy could still work.

Would banks want to hold Federal Reserve Notes (i.e., dollar bills) without a required reserve ratio? Of course they would. Don't you hold them? Holding the medium of exchange as an asset in one's portfolio is rational as long as one needs to carry out transactions and there are risks attached to holding other assets. Would banks still want to hold deposits in the Fed? Again yes, for check clearing purposes. While changing reserve requirements would be out the window as a tool of monetary policy if there were no formal reserve requirements, the Federal Reserve would still be very much in the monetary policy business.

Suggestions for Further Reading

The views of the Commission on Money and Credit on reserve requirements and other matters can be found in *Money and Credit* (Prentice-Hall, 1961). For the conclusions of President Kennedy's Committee on Financial Institutions, see *Report of the Committee on Financial Institutions to the President of the United States* (Washington, D.C.: U.S. Government Printing Office, 1963). For President Nixon's comparable committee, see *The Report of the President's Commission on Financial Structure and Regulation* (U.S. Government Printing Office, 1971).

If you want to pursue the subject of reserve requirements further, you will find the following two articles well worth reading: John H. Kareken, "On the Relative Merits of Reserve Ratio Changes and Open Market Operations," *Journal of Finance* (March 1961); and William Poole and Charles Lieberman, "Improving Monetary Control," *Brookings Papers on Economic Activity* (No. 2, 1972). Also see the articles by Edward G. Boehne and Ira Kaminow in the June 1974 issue of the Federal Reserve Bank of Philadelphia's *Business Review*. For an exhaustive analysis of the Federal Reserve's membership problem, see George Benston, *Federal Reserve Membership: Consequences, Costs, Benefits, and Alternatives* (Chicago: Association of Reserve City Bankers, 1978).

If you want to learn more about the reserve requirements that the various states impose on nonmember banks, you will find a useful compilation in Robert E. Knight's two-part article in the Kansas City Reserve Bank's *Monthly Review* (April-May 1974). For information on reserve requirements in foreign countries, see George Garvy, "Reserve Requirements Abroad," *Monthly Review* of the Federal Reserve Bank of New York (October 1973).

Appendix

Managing a Bank's Money Position

I

The legal obligation to hold reserves leads to the problem of managing a bank's reserve position—usually called managing its "money position." This appendix explains how a bank's required reserves are computed and how a bank's "money desk" manager goes about the job of meeting those requirements.

First, the simple rules of the game:

1. A commercial bank that is a member bank of the Federal Reserve System has to hold required reserves against both its demand and time deposit liabilities. These requirements are graduated according to the amount of a bank's deposits.

2. Only two assets can be used to fulfill these requirements, namely cash in vault and deposits in the regional Federal Reserve Bank. Neither of these earn any interest, so while a bank must hold enough reserves to meet its requirements it has an incentive not to hold any more than that.

II

From here on, however, matters get more complex. The first complication of these simple rules is that reserve requirements are not imposed against a bank's total demand deposits but against its *net* demand deposits. Net demand deposits are a bank's total demand deposit liabilities minus both (a) cash items in process of collection and (b) demand balances due *from* domestic banks. Both of these deductions are *asset* items on a bank's balance sheet. Deducting them from a bank's total demand deposit liabilities avoids requiring reserves twice against what is really the same deposit. In other words, by allowing these two deductions the Fed avoids double counting of demand deposit liabilities of the commercial banking system to the public.

For example, take the asset item "cash items in process of collection." Say you have an account in the King Kong National Bank and you write a check and give it to a storekeeper who deposits it in the Godzilla State Bank on the other side of town. This is a new demand deposit liability for Godzilla, but until the check clears, King Kong still has your demand deposit on its books too. In fact, for the moment King Kong doesn't even know you have written that check, so it is still figuring you have the same demand deposit and is still holding the required reserve against it. If both banks had to hold reserves against these deposits, they would both be holding reserves against what really amounts to one and the same deposit. What Godzilla, the storekeeper's bank, does until the check clears is list an offsetting item on the asset side of its balance sheet, namely "cash item in process of collection." This is subtracted from its total demand deposits when it computes its net demand deposits, so for now only King Kong has to hold reserves against this deposit. Then when the check clears in a day or so, several things happen: the King Kong National Bank receives your check back, cancels it, and removes your demand deposit from its books; and the Godzilla State Bank removes the entry "cash items in process of collection" from its assets (because the check is no longer "in process" of collection—it has actually been collected). Now King Kong no longer has the deposit and no longer has to keep reserves against it. The deposit is now officially at Godzilla and that is the bank that has to hold reserves against it.

Similar logic—avoiding double counting of the banking system's demand deposit liabilities to the public—is also behind the other deduction, "demand balances due *from* domestic banks." These are simply interbank deposits as carried on the books (as assets) of the *depositing* bank. Say you deposit a $100 check in your account at King Kong National. Also let's say that King Kong is a correspondent of a large city bank, the Bank of America (also known as the Mighty Joe Young Bank and Trust Company). A correspondent bank holds deposits with another bank usually to facilitate check clearing and for other services. King Kong therefore may very well make a $100 deposit of its own in the Bank of America. When King Kong does this, it enters an asset on its books "demand balance due from the Bank of America." King Kong deducts this from its total demand deposits when calculating its net demand deposits, because in effect it has shifted the deposit to the Bank of America. It is the Bank of America that must now hold reserves against this $100 deposit.

III

The next complication of the simple rules is that a bank's required reserves are (a) computed on a daily average basis over a weekly interval, and (b) based on its daily average deposits two weeks *earlier*. In other words, a bank's required reserves for Week 3 are calculated on the basis of its daily average deposits during Week 1. Let's take a concrete example. Here are a bank's net demand deposits and time deposits at the close of business each day for a statement week (the first week in January):

First Week in January

	Net Demand Deposits	Time and Savings Deposits
Thursday	$145 million	$ 190 million
Friday	125	195
Saturday	125	195
Sunday	125	195
Monday	130	215
Tuesday	132	208
Wednesday	128	202
	$910 million	$1400 million

Net demand deposits = $ 910 ÷ 7 = $130 million daily average
Time and savings deposits = $1400 ÷ 7 = $200 million daily average

Notice that by convention a statement week begins on a Thursday and ends on a Wednesday. And notice that Friday's closing figures count three times, since they count for Saturday and Sunday also. On the basis of these deposit figures during the first week in January, how much required reserves does this bank have to hold? Given present reserve requirements (see Table 1 on p. 159), it needs to have reserves as follows:

Against demand deposits:

7% against the first $2 million =	$	140,000
9½% against the next $8 million =		760,000
11¾% against the next $90 million =		10,575,000
12¾% against the last $30 million =		3,825,000
		$15,300,000

Against time and savings deposits (assuming a flat 3% requirement):
3% against all $200 million = $6 million
Total required reserves = $21.3 million

IV

So our bank needs reserves of $21.3 million to satisfy its requirements. It needs such reserves in the form of vault cash and/or deposits in the Fed. However, a distinction is made between these two: the vault cash that is used to satisfy these requirements is the cash in vault during the *same* week as the bank's deposit liabilities are figured (that is, the first week in January), but the deposits at the Fed are those that will be held *two weeks later* (the third week in January). This two-week lag permits a bank to know what its reserve target is before it has to hit it.

Here is this bank's vault cash during the first week in January (notice again that Friday's figure counts three times):

First Week in January

	Vault Cash
Thursday	$ 5.1 million
Friday	5.4
Saturday	5.4
Sunday	5.4
Monday	5.0
Tuesday	5.3
Wednesday	5.5
	$37.1 million

Vault cash = $37.1 ÷ 7 = $5.3 million daily average

V

Now the money position manager knows exactly what he (or she) has to do during the third statement week in January. He has to hit a reserve target (in the form of daily average deposits at the Fed) of $16 million—$21.3 million required reserves minus $5.3 million already satisfied by vault cash. If he hits a *higher* figure than that $16 million target he will be penalizing the bank in the form of foregone income, since excess reserves earn no interest. (Neither do required reserves, for that matter, but there is no way to avoid those.) On the other hand, if he winds up with a figure *lower* than $16 million he will also be penalizing the bank, because banks that are deficient in their reserves have to pay a penalty on the deficiency equal to a rate of interest 2 percentage points above the prevailing discount rate.

However, the job isn't *totally* impossible. The Fed's rules permit a bank to run an excess or a deficiency of as much as 2 percent of required reserves and to carry that excess or shortfall over into the following statement week. So if the money manager gets within $426,000 of his target (2 percent of $21.3 million = $426,000), he can apply the excess or make up the deficiency during the following week without penalty. (But a bank cannot carry over an excess or a deficiency more than one week.) This carryover provision, like the two-week lag, was put in to prevent money position managers from going *completely* bananas.

So here is the money desk manager as the third statement week in January begins. Let's say he has the flu (more likely an ulcer) and misses work on Thursday and Friday. He comes in on Monday morning and takes a look at the reports on his desk. They show closing balances on the four days of the statement week already elapsed.

Third Week in January

	Deposit at the Fed
Thursday	$16 million
Friday	12
Saturday	12
Sunday	12
	$52 million

Deposit at Fed = $52 ÷ 4 = $13 million daily average

Since his target is a $16 million daily average for the week, he is already well in the hole. With a four-day daily average of only $13 million, this amounts to a $3 million shortfall per day times four days or a cumulative deficiency of $12 million for the week thus far. That triple counting of Friday's closing balance has fouled things up again! To make up this $12 million cumulative shortfall in the next three days will require averaging $4 million above target each day—in other words, building up the balance in the Fed to average $20 million a day, for the rest of the statement week. To increase the bank's deposit at the Fed, he will start selling assets, like Treasury bills, and borrowing money—in the Federal funds market, via CDs, and maybe, if things get bad enough, at the Fed's discount window.

What if he had arrived on Monday morning and found a healthy surplus already built up? Then he would try to *reduce* his balance at the Fed—by buying Treasury bills perhaps, or selling Federal funds, or maybe by paying off any outstanding indebtedness at the Fed's discount window.[1]

[1] Just to add a little spice to the game, the Fed's rules specify that a bank cannot allow its actual reserves at the close of a day to fall below 50 percent of its required reserves. In this case, for example, the bank cannot let its actual reserves fall below $10.65 million (= 50 percent of $21.3 million). So the money manager doesn't want to build up too large a cumulative surplus early in a week, because this rule could prevent him from running a large enough deficit late in the week to offset it.

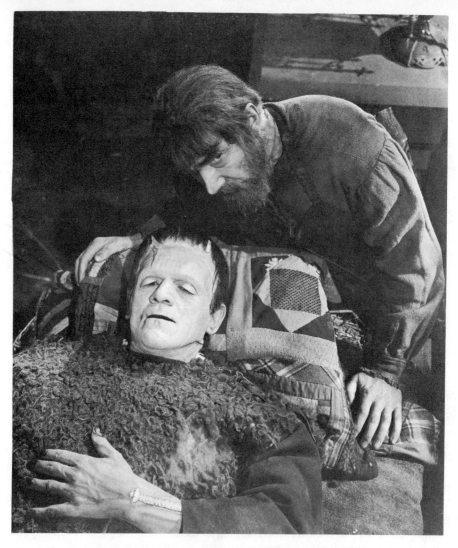

"Psst, it's Wednesday! We need reserves bad . . .
get in there and buy some Fed funds."

Why is the money desk manager's job so difficult? Because so many things that affect a bank's reserve balance are not within his control. After all, every check that is written by a depositor of the bank —or received by a depositor—and that clears through the Federal Reserve alters the bank's reserves. If a large corporate depositor writes a big check, the bank's reserves fall; if many large corporate depositors do so, the bank's reserves fall a lot. The opposite happens if depositors receive checks and send them in to the bank to be credited to their accounts—then the bank's reserves at the Fed rise. A large bank will have thousands of such transactions each day, often with unpredictable net effects on its reserves. You can always tell who the money position managers are in large banks: they have glazed eyes and they twitch a lot. But there are compensations: they get paid well and have long vacations.

168

Chapter 13

Discounting and the Discount Rate

DISCOUNTING was considered the *main* instrument of central banking throughout the nineteenth century and the first three decades of the twentieth. It reached its apogee in terms of prestige in 1931 (the same year that "The Star-Spangled Banner" was declared the national anthem by act of Congress). At that time, England's Macmillan Committee, somewhat carried away by the splendor of it all, reported that the discount rate "is an absolute necessity for the sound management of a monetary system, and is a most delicate and beautiful instrument for the purpose."[1] This was just at the time—1931—when the monetary system of virtually every country was collapsing into ruins, whether it had a "delicate and beautiful" discount rate or not.

It should be mentioned at the start that discount policy has two dimensions: the first is *price*, the discount rate, the rate of interest the Federal Reserve charges commercial banks when they borrow from the Fed. The second dimension has to do with the *quantity* of Federal Reserve lending, including Federal Reserve surveillance over the amount that each bank borrows, the reasons why it borrows, and the collateral it offers in exchange. Let us examine quantity first and price second—each, in its turn, has been credited with the mystique of power that surrounds discounting.

[1] *Report of the Committee on Finance and Industry* (London: His Majesty's Stationery Office, 1931), p. 97.

The Central Bank: Lender of Last Resort

Historically, the primary function of a central bank has been to stand ready to supply liquidity—promptly and in abundance—whenever the economy is in danger of coming apart at the seams because of a shortage of money. While that is no longer its sole function, it is still one of its most important. The central bank is the ultimate source of liquidity in the economy, since its power over bank reserves can increase (or decrease) the ability of the banking system to create money. No one else can do this job, so it is the central bank that must be responsible for supplying funds promptly on those rare but crucial occasions when liquidity shortages threaten economic stability. "Financial panics," the history books call them. Because of this responsibility, the central bank has traditionally been called the "lender of last resort."[2]

When the Federal Reserve Act was passed in 1913, its principal feature was setting up a discounting mechanism—facilities through which member banks could temporarily borrow funds from the Fed. Until that time there had been no such mechanism available (indeed, until then there was no central bank in this country). It is also worth noting that open market operations were unknown then (they were not understood or used until the 1920s), and bank reserve requirements could not be varied by the Federal Reserve (they were fixed by Congress; legislation permitting the Fed to alter reserve requirements, within limits, was not enacted until the 1930s). Thus the *only* monetary policy instrument contained in the original Federal Reserve Act was discount policy.

The new discount facilities were intended to prevent the recurrence of financial panics such as had periodically plagued the United

_____

[2] The principle of the central bank as "lender of last resort" was eloquently articulated as long ago as 1873 by Walter Bagehot in *Lombard Street,* the first full-blown exposition of what central banking is all about. Many of his ideas stemmed from Henry Thornton's *An Enquiry into the Nature and Effects of the Paper Credit of Great Britain,* which was published in 1802 (before most of you were born).

Two relatively recent examples of this "crisis function" of discounting occurred in 1970 and 1974. In 1970, when the Penn Central Railroad went bankrupt, the Fed stepped in and made loans freely available in order to avert a collapse of lending in the short-term money market—a lot of lenders had been afraid that other large firms might go bankrupt also, and were reluctant to make loans without lots of collateral just in case the loans turned sour. And in 1974 the Fed made $1.7 billion of emergency credit available to New York's Franklin National Bank when that institution got into big trouble, and by so doing reassured the public that the entire banking system was not on the verge of collapse. Eventually Franklin National went down the drain anyway, but there was no financial panic and no depositor lost a penny. The Franklin National Bank, with over $2 billion in deposits, was the largest bank ever to fail in U.S. history . . . so far.

"There's a run on the bank!"

Drawn by Robt. Day; © 1969 The New Yorker Magazine, Inc.

States during the 1800s and early 1900s. Such financial crises were typically ignited when some banks failed, and frightened depositors in other banks rushed to exchange their checking accounts for currency. Until 1934 there was no such thing as federal deposit insurance; if your bank went down the drain, you went with it. Faced with a "run on the bank," banks would have to call in loans and sell securities to raise cash to meet depositor withdrawals, which would endanger still other banks. Such infectious liquidity crises often jeopardized the entire financial system, since—as we saw in Chapter 2—calling in loans and selling securities to depositors in other banks merely shifts reserve shortages like a hot potato from one bank to another.

The new discount facilities instituted by the passage of the

171

Federal Reserve Act in 1913 were supposed to provide a vehicle through which the Federal Reserve could quickly inject funds precisely where needed in order to stop a panic from spreading. Banks threatened with cash drains could borrow what they needed from the Fed—the lender of last resort. Thus they could get more reserves without any other bank losing them, and thereby prevent the infection from becoming a plague. (For the T-accounts of discounting, see p. 33.)

However, when the showdown came, after the stock market crash of 1929, the discount mechanism could not stem the tide. In the four years 1930–1933, more than 9,000 commercial banks failed, almost 40 percent of all the banks in the country. Ah, the good old days! Out of 24,000 commercial banks in existence in 1929, less than 15,000 were still present or accounted for at the end of 1933.

What went wrong? Lots of things, including the Federal Reserve's lack of experience in dealing with such a gargantuan economic collapse, its failure to use open market operations in sufficient volume, and the absence of appropriate federal fiscal policies. And last but not least, the failure of the Fed to aggressively assume its role as lender of last resort—largely due to the fact that from the very beginning the discount mechanism, and its crucially important lender of last resort function, had unfortunately gotten all tangled up with an outdated and fallacious theory of commercial and central banking, known as the commercial loan theory (which we've encountered in Chapter 10's discussion of bank management).

Discounting and the Commercial Loan Theory

The Federal Reserve Act did *not* provide that the central bank could or should lend as much as possible to commercial banks in times of financial emergency.[3] Quite the contrary; the 1913 law specified that only certain types of paper (collateral) were "eligible" for discount at the central bank, regardless of economic and financial conditions. Without the appropriate collateral, commercial banks could not borrow from the Federal Reserve, no matter how great their needs might be. The justification for these restrictive "eligibility requirements" was the commercial loan theory of banking—also known as the real bills

---

[3] Despite Bagehot's exposition 40 years earlier.

doctrine—a theory of commercial and central banking that had gained prominence in the nineteenth century and had considerable influence on the framers of the Federal Reserve Act.

The commercial loan theory specified the kind of loans commercial banks should make (to remain appropriately liquid) and how the central bank should conduct its discounting operations (for optimum control of the money supply). Specifically, it held that commercial banks should make only *short-term, self-liquidating, productive* loans.[4] And the central bank, in turn, should only lend to commercial banks on the collateral of such IOUs—thereby insuring that commercial banks would confine their lending to such loans, in order to have assets that would be eligible for use as collateral in borrowing from the Federal Reserve. This simple principle, it was naïvely believed, would ensure the proper degree of liquidity for each commercial bank and the proper money supply for the economy as a whole—proper in the sense of not too big, not too small, but just right, as Goldilocks would say.

Here is the logic: If banks made only this kind of loan, then the increased money supply that accompanies bank lending would always be paralleled by an increased physical volume of goods moving through the channels of trade, with the loans (and the money supply) subject to self-liquidation when the goods were sold. Thus increased bank credit and money would be accompanied by expanded production; when the output was sold to consumers and removed from the market, the loans would be repaid and the money supply would correspondingly shrink. The volume of money was viewed as varying with the "needs of trade" and thus remaining neutral, neither inflationary nor deflationary. By regulating the *kind* of bank credit, its *quality*, it was thought that we could automatically ensure its appropriate *quantity*.

The Federal Reserve participated in this process by augmenting or diminishing bank reserves through the "discount window," accepting only "approved" loans as collateral for *re*discount. When business

---

[4] *Short-term* because the bulk of commercial bank liabilities have traditionally been short-term—mostly demand deposits, subject to immediate call. It was thought that by restricting their assets to short-term loans, commercial banks would thereby be assured of adequate liquidity to meet whatever emergencies might arise. To "borrow short and lend long" was seen as the sure road to perdition, inviting illiquidity and inability to meet one's obligations.

Self-liquidating refers to loans that are supposed to be repaid automatically by the borrower through funds arising from the very transaction being financed. Example: a loan to a retailer to purchase inventories. When the retailer sells those inventories to consumers, he "automatically" receives enough money to repay the loan. Consumer loans and home mortgage loans are not permissible; such loans are not viewed as *self*-liquidating.

Finally, a *productive* loan meant a loan to a business firm to finance the production or marketing of physical goods. Loans to purchase or carry securities were verboten.

expanded and the needs of trade increased, banks could obtain additional reserves by rediscounting eligible paper, the IOUs they acquired when they made loans of the approved sort. When business contracted and the needs of trade subsided, the volume of discounting, the supply of bank reserves, and the amount of bank credit and money would all contract as well. This close connection between the kind of commercial bank lending and the amount of central bank (re)discounting was viewed as the mechanism that would always adjust the volume of bank reserves and the supply of bank credit and money to the amount consistent with economic stability.

Notice the word "*re*discount" in the previous paragraph. It has fallen into disuse, like vaudeville, because it is no longer around. The Federal Reserve Act assumed that all member bank borrowing from the Fed would take a particular form, for which the term "rediscounting" is more accurate than "discounting." When a bank lends to a borrower, it usually *discounts* the borrower's IOU; *that is, it deducts the interest on the loan immediately*. A borrower taking out a one-year $100,000 loan with a 10 percent discount will receive only $90,000 now, although he will agree to repay $100,000 when the note comes due.[5] If the bank, in turn, decides to borrow from the Fed, it could do so by sending this note to the regional Federal Reserve Bank, which would *re*discount it; that is, the Fed would also deduct its interest charge immediately, and give only the balance to the commercial bank. It was assumed in the original Federal Reserve Act that all member bank borrowing from the Fed would take this form—commercial banks would always borrow by rediscounting their customers' notes with the Fed.[6]

The Federal Reserve Act specified that the Fed could only (re)discount eligible collateral—loans of the sort approved by the commercial loan theory—on the assumption that this was a good way to induce commercial banks to make only such loans. However, limiting eligibility for discounting to a certain type of loan obviously runs counter to the lender of last resort principle—that in emergencies the central bank should lend freely to a bank in need, regardless of what kind of collateral the bank might have available.

---

[5] The true rate of interest is not 10 percent but $\frac{10,000}{90,000}$ or 11.1 percent, because you get only $90,000 and you have to pay $10,000 interest.

[6] Nowadays, most bank borrowing from the Fed is accomplished via straight borrowing, without any customer IOUs involved, with the bank usually putting up some government securities as collateral. Technically, this is properly called an "advance" rather than a "discount" or a "rediscount." However, in popular terminology the term "discounting" has come to describe *all* member bank borrowing from the Fed, regardless of the technical details of how it is accomplished.

Fallacies in the Commercial Loan Theory

As a guide for central banks, the commercial loan theory deserved an F minus (and that's grading on a curve). The "needs of trade" are no longer accepted as adequate criteria for central banking, nor is regulating the *kind* of bank credit viewed as an appropriate way to control its amount (although, as we will see in Chapter 27, there *may* be other reasons to try to influence the kind of credit financial institutions create).

If bank credit and money supply are permitted to fluctuate on the basis of the "needs of trade," there is no way for the Federal Reserve to prevent either spiraling recession or inflation. Indeed, monetary policies based solely on the "needs of trade" exacerbate, rather than mitigate, both recession and inflation. If a recession should start, for example, the "needs of trade" automatically decline. A smaller volume of production and sales will be reflected in smaller demands for inventory loans, bank loans will contract, and the money supply will decline. However, this will only reinforce the slowdown in business activity. A central bank acting countercyclically should make every effort to *prevent* a contraction in bank loans and the money supply under such circumstances.

Similarly, when inflationary pressures develop, the "needs of trade" typically expand. Businessmen want larger inventory loans, a perfectly legitimate demand for credit insofar as the commercial loan theory is concerned. But a central bank acting countercyclically should again make every effort to prevent what the "needs of trade" would invite, in this instance an expansion in bank credit and money under inflationary conditions.

According to the commercial loan theory, regulating the purpose for which credit is extended—the kind of credit—will automatically yield the appropriate amount. As these examples show, however, purpose is a poor indicator of proper amount. Thus today the Fed concentrates directly on the total supply of bank reserves and money, and for the most part leaves the form, type, purpose, and composition of bank credit to be determined by the needs and preferences of private lenders and borrowers themselves.

The present approach is additionally justified in that it is only the aggregate amount of bank credit, not its composition or purpose, that the Federal Reserve is really able to control anyway. This is because of the familiar multiple expansion of bank credit. When the Fed extends new reserves through discounting, banks receiving the new reserves might conceivably make only approved types of loans to their customers. When these customers spend the money, however, it soon becomes deposits and reserves in other banks, enabling the other banks to increase loans. These other banks have no way of knowing how their additional reserves originally came into existence, and they couldn't care less. They will make whatever loans they please, regardless of the Fed's intent when it originally injected the reserves.

The turnover of money and bank reserves, from person to person and from bank to bank, makes it impossible for the Fed to control the eventual composition of bank credit merely by controlling the purpose for which reserves are initially created. Therefore today the central bank focuses its attention directly on the *quantity* of money and bank credit—which it can control, within limits—and leaves the purposes for which credit is extended and money is spent—which it cannot control with any of its existing tools—to the interplay of private market forces.

Discounting Today

Remnants of the commercial loan theory are still hanging from the discount window, although not too prominently. The Federal Reserve Act has been amended to permit the Fed to lend to member banks on the basis of just about any collateral, except that when the collateral is not government securities or eligible paper (as traditionally defined) the applicable discount rate *must* be ½ of 1 percentage point above the normal discount rate.

In recent years the Federal Reserve itself has repeatedly urged that the law be amended to eliminate this ½ of 1 percentage point differential on "ineligible" collateral, but without success. Actually, once you think about it, this much of a change would only be going half way: there is really no reason to require *any* collateral whatsoever, whether eligible or ineligible, behind commercial bank borrowing from the Federal Reserve.[7]

Commercial banks make unsecured loans to customers of good credit standing every day, on their customers' signature alone, and there is no reason why banks should be treated any differently when they, in turn, seek to borrow from the Federal Reserve. If a bank is in business, accepting deposits and making loans, and is examined

---

[7] When Walter Bagehot laid down the principle in 1873 that the central bank should be the lender of last resort in financial panics, he stressed that it should lend freely and amply, virtually regardless of the collateral commercial banks might have to offer.

periodically (as all of them are), it should qualify for access to Federal Reserve credit on an unsecured basis and at the regular discount rate. In any event, just about all discounting today is secured by government securities; the borrowing bank sends some of its government securities to its regional Federal Reserve Bank as collateral until the debt is repaid. Technically, as noted in footnote 6, borrowing from the Fed in this manner is called an "advance" rather than a "discount." With the passage of time the words have become practically synonymous.

The Federal Reserve typically lends only to banks that are members of the Federal Reserve System, but in "emergency circumstances" it has the authority to lend to nonmember banks as well. Of course, financial crises do not occur all that frequently, so in the ordinary course of events the Federal Reserve is not often called upon to assume its ultimate lender-of-last-resort role. (One halfway decent panic every four or five years is the most anyone could hope for). For the most part, member bank use of the discount window is rather routine, not at all panic-oriented, with banks borrowing here and there to make short-run adjustments in their reserves with no fuss or bother—as when a bank finds itself with an unexpected reserve deficit and needs to borrow a million or so to tide itself over for a few days.

The Fed has always stressed that ordinary run-of-the-mill borrowing of this sort (as contrasted with crisis situations) should not be used *too* often to get banks out of reserve difficulties. Banks should run their affairs so they do not have to rely on the Fed to bail them out every few weeks. Or, as the Federal Reserve usually puts it, discounting is considered a privilege, not a right, and privileges should not be abused. Federal Reserve surveillance enforces the "privilege not a right" concept by checking on banks that borrow too much or too frequently.[8] A bank is supposed to borrow only on account of *need*, and not go out and make a *profit* on the deal.

In particular, the Fed is sensitive to the possibility that banks may borrow from it and then turn around and use the money to purchase higher-yielding securities, such as a bank borrowing from the Fed at a 7 percent discount rate and then using the funds to buy a short-term security yielding 8 percent. That's a no-no! Nor does the Fed like it when a bank borrows from it too often, in effect using the discount facility as a more or less permanent source of funds.

In practice, it is not always so easy to determine whether a bank is borrowing on account of "need" or to make a "profit." A bank faced

[8] In 1973, however, the Fed introduced a special "seasonal borrowing privilege" that encourages small banks to borrow at the discount window to cover most of their recurring reserve needs arising from seasonal swings in loans or deposits (as happens to banks in agricultural or resort areas).

Fed Reprimands Some New York Banks
For Abusing Their Borrowing Privileges

BY EDWARD P. FOLDESSY
Staff Reporter of THE WALL STREET JOURNAL

The Federal Reserve Bank of New York has reprimanded some large banks in New York for abusing their borrowing privilege at its discount window.

It was learned that the New York Fed has told a number of money-center banks to stay out of the discount window unless there wasn't any reasonable alternative available.

According to sources, the problem arose because of the currently low discount rate, the interest rate charged by the Fed on loans to member commercial banks. That rate has been at 5¾% since August. By contrast, the rate on federal funds, uncommitted reserves banks lend one another, has been hovering around 6½%.

For many banks, the rate differential was too much of a lure. At least some banks, it was understood, borrowed from the Fed at the lower rate and reloaned the money in the federal funds market, a "no-no" by Fed standards.

The Federal Reserve considers discount borrowings as a privilege, not a right. And it expects money market banks to use the federal funds market for their needs when such funds are reasonably available. But many banks had continued to use the discount window when funds were relatively abundant.

The identity of the banks that were reprimanded couldn't be obtained. Figures previously released by the Fed showed that the 10 largest New York banks had borrowed more than $1.1 billion from the discount window last Wednesday, almost a third of the total such borrowings of $3.4 billion from all Federal Reserve district banks. The $3.4 billion borrowing was the largest for any single day since Sept. 25, 1974, when borrowings totaled $5.04 billion.

At least some analysts said the heavy borrowings could force the Fed to boost the discount rate to 6% or 6¼% to bring it closer in line with the federal funds rate.

NEWS ITEM / Discounting: A Right or a Privilege?

SOURCE: *Wall Street Journal*, October 25, 1977

with a reserve deficiency can cover it by borrowing funds from the Fed *or* by selling some securities in the money market. Relative rates of interest will be a determining element in deciding between these alternatives. Say the discount rate is 7 percent and the short-term securities the bank is holding are yielding 8 percent. The bank will be tempted, naturally enough, to utilize the least-cost alternative in adjusting its reserve position—to borrow at 7 percent from the Fed rather than to sell off securities yielding 8 percent. Is this bank borrowing because of "need" or for "profit"? It isn't going out and buying *additional* securities yielding 8 percent; it's just not disposing of the ones it already has. The need is there, but least-cost methods of satisfying it are also relevant.

One Fed method of preventing "abuse" of the discount facility is tighter surveillance procedures. Another way is simply to raise the price of borrowing—which brings us to the discount rate itself.

The Discount Rate and Market Interest Rates

The objective of changing the discount rate is just what the Federal Reserve says it is: A higher discount rate discourages member bank borrowing from the Fed, and a lower discount rate encourages it. These results flow from the least-cost alternatives facing banks with reserve deficiencies. A higher discount rate makes it relatively more advantageous to sell securities to get additional reserves, and a lower discount rate makes it relatively more advantageous to borrow from the Fed. Actually, "higher" and "lower" in absolute terms are not as important as the relationship between the discount rate and market interest rates. Member bank discounting is discouraged (by cost considerations) when the discount rate is *above* other short-term interest rates, and encouraged when it is *below* market interest rates.[9]

In some countries the discount rate is kept above short-term market interest rates at all times (a "penalty rate"), as a means of restraining excessive commercial bank use of the central bank's borrowing facilities. In the United States, on the other hand, the discount rate is usually, although not always, held below the Treasury bill rate, so that the Fed has to rely more on surveillance to prevent "abuse of the discount privilege."

How does a change in the discount rate affect market interest rates? The two are not *directly* connected. A higher or lower discount rate alters member bank borrowing, thereby changing bank reserves, bank lending, the money supply, and finally market interest rates. However, this is a rather weak linkage, since the effects on reserves and the money supply of a change in the discount rate are small compared with the effects of the two other tools available to the Federal Reserve.[10]

[9] See R. Alton Gilbert, "Benefits of Borrowing from the Federal Reserve when the Discount Rate is Below Market Interest Rates," Federal Reserve Bank of St. Louis *Review* (March 1979).

[10] Only a small proportion of member bank reserves is attributable to the discounting process. In early 1979, for example, total member bank reserves were about $43 billion, of which only about $1 billion was acquired through the discount window. During the 1970s, borrowing from the Fed averaged less than a billion dollars annually. Even at its peak of almost $3½ billion in mid–1974, discounting still provided less than 10 percent of total bank reserves, and usually the percentage is much less—on average about 2 or 3 percent.

Changes in the discount rate, however, certainly do *change* the volume of reserves, and it is the changes that are important. Empirical estimates of the impact of a 1 percentage point change in the discount rate (say, from 7 to 8 percent) on the volume of member bank borrowing are diverse, ranging from $100 million to over $500 million. The net effect on the volume of demand deposits, and on the money supply, is small, however. See Robert H. Rasche, "A Review of Empirical Studies on the Money Supply Mechanism," Federal Reserve Bank of St. Louis *Review* (July 1972).

And yet, there does appear to be a connection between the discount rate and market interest rates. As can be seen in Chart 1, a close relationship exists between the discount rate and short-term interest rates, such as the Federal funds rate and the yield on Treasury bills, and also between the discount rate and the prime bank lending rate, the interest rate that banks charge their best business customers.

Careful examination, however, reveals that changes in the Federal funds rate and in Treasury bill yields typically *precede* changes in the discount rate. The Federal funds rate and Treasury bill yields rise, probably because of Federal Reserve open market operations, and then—after they have risen quite a while and often quite a bit—the discount rate moves up. Or bill rates fall and then the discount rate is lowered. In other words, a change in the discount rate is likely to come *after* a basic change in market interest rates has already occurred. This is not *always* true, of course, but it is *generally* the case.

One possible way that changes in the discount rate might directly affect market interest rates is through the "announcement effect" produced when a discount rate change comes unexpectedly. An unanticipated rise in the discount rate is likely to lead bondholders to expect tight money and higher interest rates (lower bond prices). They sell bonds to avoid capital losses, thus hastening the drop in bond prices and the rise in interest rates.

The key is that the rise in the discount rate under such circumstances generates expectations regarding future interest rates. But if the public had already observed tightening in the credit markets prior to the change in the discount rate, due to open market operations, the actual announcement itself would produce very little reaction. In fact, the bond markets might be relieved of uncertainty, and interest rates might fall back a bit. The change in the discount rate thus usually confirms what is going on, but does not initiate it.

Chart 1, which we just mentioned, shows the relationship between the discount rate, the Federal funds rate, the three-month Treasury bill yield, and the prime loan rate during the last half of 1976 and all of 1977. This was a particularly interesting period for two reasons. First, because it shows that there is no fixed relationship between the discount rate and the Federal funds rate or between the discount rate and Treasury bill yields. The three move closely together, but they often change relative positions. Early in the period the discount rate is higher than both the Federal funds rate and the bill rate, in the middle of the period it is between them, and then late in 1977 it falls below both of them.

The second reason Chart 1 is interesting is that it shows a period in which the discount rate was significantly lower than money market

Discounting and the Discount Rate

rates, which led to predictable consequences. In October 1977, when the Federal funds rate was 6½ percent and the yield on Treasury bills 6.2 percent, the discount rate was only 5¾ percent. These differentials produced an irresistible urge for banks to adjust their reserve positions by borrowing from the Fed rather than by borrowing from each other in the Federal funds market or by selling Treasury bills. And sure enough, member bank borrowing from the Fed spurted sharply. Indeed, discounting grew so rapidly in October 1977 that the Fed had to reprimand a number of banks for "abusing their borrowing privilege at the discount window" (see accompanying news item). For many banks, the rate differentials were too much of a lure: they borrowed from the Federal Reserve at 5¾ percent and reloaned the money in

CHART 1 / Togetherness 1976–1977.

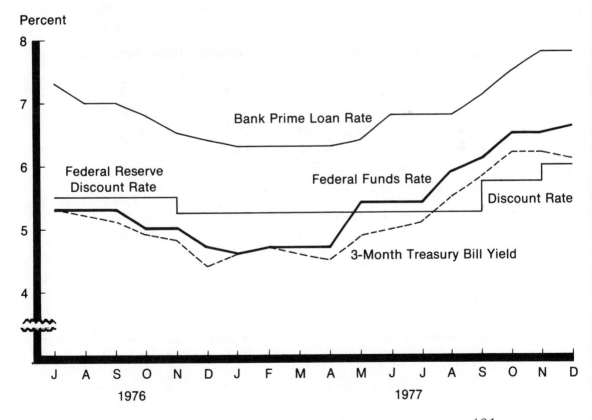

181

the Federal funds market at 6½ percent or bought Treasury bills yielding 6.2 percent—simply disgraceful by Fed standards.

In an effort to keep the discount rate in closer touch with other short-term rates, there was a change in the administration of the discount rate late in 1970. During the 1960s, changes in the discount rate were made infrequently, a pattern that was mirrored by the prime rate charged by commercial banks to their best customers. During the ten years from 1960 until 1970, the discount rate was changed a total of twelve times and the prime rate was changed a total of sixteen times. (In fact, much of the impact of tight money during that period was transmitted to the prime customers of banks by changes in compensating balances—the portion of a loan that must be held on deposit at the bank—that were required of business firms, and by changes in the standards as to who qualified for the prime rate. Thus, the comovement in the discount rate and the prime rate was somewhat illusory, since the effective prime rate changed even though the posted rate was fixed.)

To avoid the uncertain announcement effects associated with large and infrequent discount rate changes, late in 1970 the Federal Reserve embarked on a course of altering the discount rate more frequently and in smaller steps. During the fourteen months from November 1970 through December 1971, for example, the discount rate was changed eight times, only four less than during the entire 1960–1970 period. (Similarly, the prime rate was changed a total of twenty-three times during that period, seven more times than during the entire decade of the 1960s).

The discount rate now follows the movements in short-term rates, especially the Federal funds rate and the Treasury bill rate, even more closely than before. It is clear that the Federal Reserve wants to get changes in the discount rate off the front page of your favorite newspaper and into the anonymity of the interest rate quotations in the financial section (which happens to be close to the sports pages, allowing you to throw away the first section of the paper).[11]

[11] Great Britain's central bank, the Bank of England, has carried this line of thinking to its logical conclusion (almost). Late in 1972 it announced that it would no longer "set" the discount rate, but would let it float ½ of 1 percentage point above whatever the three-month Treasury bill rate happened to be. The Bank of England's discount rate is thus both a penalty rate and a floating rate (except, said the Bank of England, on those occasions when it decides it wants to "lead" market rates up or down, it will then set the discount rate at whatever level it wishes, regardless of the Treasury bill rate).

Suggestions for Further Reading

A good survey of the evolution of thinking behind discounting and the discount rate can be found in Murray E. Polakeff, "Federal Reserve Discount Policy and Its Critics," in *Banking and Monetary Studies*, ed. Deane Carson (Homewood, Ill.: Irwin, 1963). The standard works in this field are W. W. Riefler, *Money Rates and Money Markets in the United States* (New York: Harper, 1930); R. C. Turner, *Member Bank Borrowing* (Columbus: Ohio State University Press, 1938); and Warren L. Smith, "The Discount Rate as a Credit Control Weapon," *Journal of Political Economy* (April 1958). A formal statistical analysis of member bank borrowing is Stephen M. Goldfeld and Edward J. Kane, "The Determinants of Member Bank Borrowing," *Journal of Finance* (September 1966). A recent article that explores in some detail the seminal ideas of Henry Thornton and Walter Bagehot is well worth reading; see Thomas M. Humphrey, "The Classical Concept of the Lender of Last Resort," *Economic Review* of the Federal Reserve Bank of Richmond (January/February 1975).

The Federal Reserve has also conducted a full-scale study of discounting. It published the results in 1971 and 1972 in three volumes under the overall title *Reappraisal of the Federal Reserve Discount Mechanism*. For an intriguing analysis bearing on financial crises, that has implications for the lender of last resort function, see Hyman P. Minsky, "Can It Happen Again?" in Deane Carson, ed., *Banking and Monetary Studies* (Homewood, Ill.: Irwin, 1963).

Speaking of a "run on the bank," by the way, as we were early in this chapter, the most vivid description of what it was like is contained in Marriner Eccles's autobiography, *Beckoning Frontiers* (New York: Knopf, 1951), pp. 54 ff.

Chapter 14

Open Market Operations

AT 11:15 IN THE MORNING of each business day, a long-distance conference call takes place among three men: Peter Stern-light, the manager of the System Open Market Account, who is located in the Federal Reserve Bank of New York; a member of the Board of Governors in Washington, D.C.; and a president of one of the other Federal Reserve banks currently serving on the Federal Open Market Committee (FOMC). The job of the Account Manager is to carry out open market operations for the purpose of implementing the monetary policy directive issued at the last meeting of the FOMC. Each morning he reviews the operations planned for the day via the telephone hookup.

Although we have never listened in to what is said during one of these calls, we can make a pretty good guess at the conversation, much as sports commentators are able to surmise what is said at those all-important conferences between the quarterback and his coach in the closing minutes of a game, or the even more important huddle between a pitcher and catcher with men on second and third and none out. It probably goes something like this:

OPERATOR: Kansas City and Washington are standing by, New York. Will you deposit $3.35, please?

NEW YORK: You mean it's our turn to pay? Hold on a minute, operator, we don't seem to have enough change here.

WASHINGTON: This is Chairman Volcker on the line.

NEW YORK: Sorry, there's no one here by that name.

WASHINGTON: No, you don't seem to understand, I'm Chairman Paul Volcker and I want . . .

NEW YORK: Hello Paul, it's Peter. Sorry for the mix-up, but we've just hired a few Ph.D.s to man the phones, and they haven't gotten the hang of it quite yet.

WASHINGTON: I know just what you mean. Say, we've got a problem here. Our staff says the 6-1/2 to 9 percent range for M1 should replace as the main target the 4 to 6-1/2 percent range on M2. Or is it the other way around?

NEW YORK: Frankly, our people have urged me to look at the M3 numbers, trying to hit the fourth-quarter-to-fourth-quarter growth figures, rather than the two-month targets. They say the M1 ball game is over.

KANSAS CITY: Hello? Hello? When do we start?

If you think we have exaggerated the potential confusion confronting the Account Manager, a reading of some of the FOMC operating instructions should convince you otherwise. The primary thrust of monetary policy is summarized in the FOMC directive. Let's take a detailed look at how it is formulated and the ways in which it can be interpreted. We can then turn to the open market operations used in carrying it out.

The FOMC Directive

The FOMC meets in Washington about once every four weeks. At the beginning of each meeting the staff of the FOMC, comprising economists from the Board of Governors and the district Federal Reserve Banks, presents a review of recent economic and financial developments—what is happening to prices, unemployment, the balance of payments, interest rates, money supply, bank credit, and so on. Projections are also made for the months ahead. In fact, just to give you the flavor of the menu of information prepared by the staff, including how it is served to the FOMC, we reproduce for you some of the charts that decorate the walls of the "boardroom" at the Fed. Charts are the second most important product of the Federal Reserve System (right after reserves).

After the chart show, the meeting proceeds to a discussion among the committee members; each expresses his or her views on the current economic and financial scene and proposes appropriate monetary policies. The FOMC directive, embodying the committee's decision on the desired posture of monetary policy until the next meeting, is voted on toward the end of each meeting, with dissents recorded for posterity. If economic conditions are proceeding as had been expected and the current stance of monetary policy is still appropriate, the previous directive may remain unaltered. If conditions change, the directive is modified accordingly.

In recent years, the FOMC directive has usually contained five or six paragraphs. The first few review economic and financial developments, including the behavior of real output, inflation, monetary aggregates, and interest rates. The fourth or fifth paragraph then turns to a general qualitative statement of current policy goals. For example, at the meeting on February 6, 1979, the goals of the FOMC were set forth as follows:

> Taking account of past and prospective developments . . . it is the policy of the Federal Open Market Committee to foster monetary and financial conditions that will resist inflationary pressures while encouraging moderate economic expansion and contributing to a sustainable pattern of international transactions.

The FOMC discusses the fate of the Account Manager.

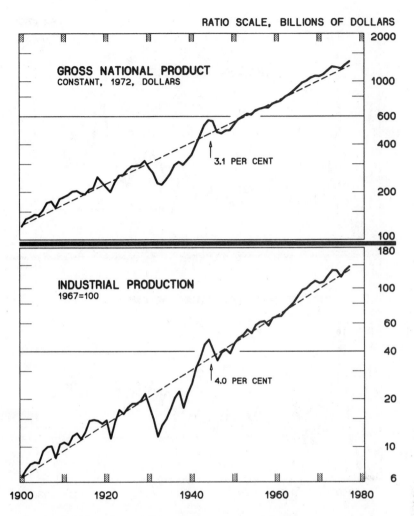

RATIO SCALE, BILLIONS OF DOLLARS

CHART 1 / The Fed's concern with real economic activity is indicated by its monitoring real GNP and industrial production compared with their long-run trends. Source: *Federal Reserve Chart Book.*

While the statement of goals does not contain everything—we know that the FOMC is not trying to eliminate environmental pollution (at least not yet)—it does include virtually every objective of stabilization policy. This general statement of goals is rarely changed significantly. Toward the end of 1975, for example, when in the throes of recession, the phrase "encouraging economic expansion" replaced "inflationary pressures" as the first goal mentioned.

Immediately following this general statement, the directive presents the long-run target ranges for the monetary aggregates that are thought to be consistent with the broadly stated goals. At the meeting of February 6, 1979, the annual targets were stated as follows:

187

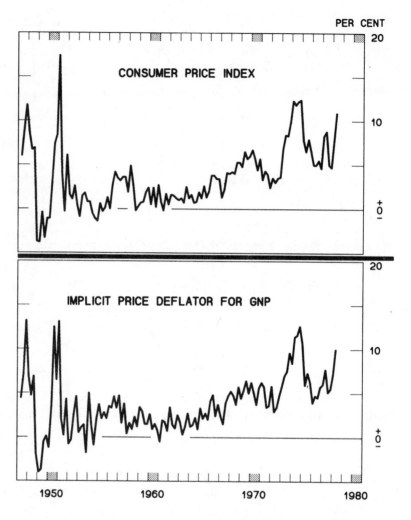

PER CENT

CHART 2 / Central bank preoccupation with inflation is evident from its double-barreled surveillance: annual rates of increase in the Consumer Price Index and the GNP deflator. Source: *Federal Reserve Chart Book.*

The Committee agreed that these objectives would be furthered by growth of M-1, M-2 and M-3 from the fourth quarter of 1978 to the fourth quarter of 1979 within ranges of 1-1/2 to 4-1/2 percent, 5 to 8 percent and 6 to 9 percent.

Two sources of flexibility appear in these annual targets. Obviously they can be changed each quarter. In our illustration, the growth rates are calculated from fourth-quarter 1978 to fourth-quarter 1979, but will then be altered to the first-quarter 1979 through the first-quarter 1980. Moreover, the ranges are rather broad, giving the Fed wide latitude in hitting the targets.

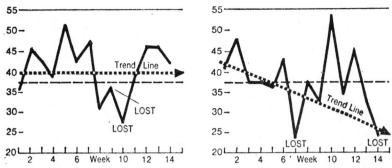

Winning teams control the ball on the ground. Dallas has done this consistently, with 40.3 rushes a game, above the National Football League average. The Cowboys' running suffered in their 10th game, against the Steelers: They ran with the ball only 27 times, and lost. Denver's rushing game weakened as the season progressed. The Broncos opened with two strong games, but these were against the Cardinals and the Bills, notoriously weak against the run. In each of Denver's two losses — to Oakland and Dallas — the Broncos ran only 23 times. Their season's average merely equaled the league's: about 37 rushes a game.

CHART 3 / Any lingering doubts that the Fed carefully prepares a game plan are dispelled by this detailed analysis of the 1978 Super Bowl Teams. This week-by-week and trend line analysis of rushes per game during the season is not released in the Fed's chartbook, but reliable sources insist it is nestled between inflation and short-term funds in the Fed's chartroom.

The last order of business in the FOMC directive is to specify the immediate requirements for the implementation of these longer-run objectives. In our by now familiar meeting of February 6, 1979, the specification was as follows:

In the period before the next regular meeting, System open market operations are to be directed at maintaining the weekly average federal funds rate at about the current level, provided that over the February-March period the annual rates of growth of M1 and M2, given approximately equal weight, appear to be within ranges of 3 to 7 percent and 5 to 9 percent, respectively.

Now we have a second set of monetary aggregate targets, this time specified for a two-month period. These two-month growth rates are altered, both to take into account "special events" as well as to be consistent with the longer-run objectives. Moreover, the Federal funds rate (the interest rate on reserves loaned on an overnight basis between banks) was used as still another short-run guideline, presumably to help the Account Manager hit the aggregate bulls' eye. Unfortunately, the manager's accuracy leaves much to be desired, as we'll see in Chapter 16. Perhaps there are too many numbers and too many targets floating around. It almost guarantees some confusion, as we suggested in our opening conversation.

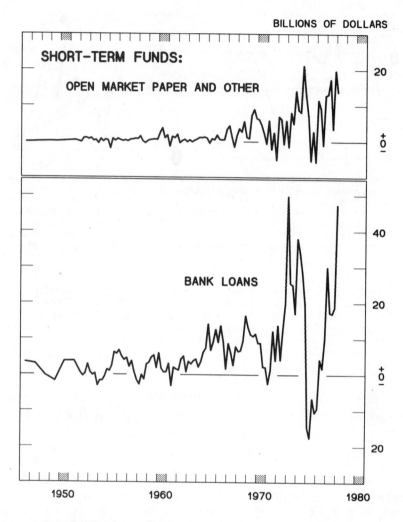

BILLIONS OF DOLLARS

CHART 4 / The Federal Reserve carefully monitors the short-run demands for funds by corporate business, with commercial paper issues (included in the top half) coming to life during the 1970s. Source: *Federal Reserve Chart Book.*

The emphasis in the FOMC directive is clearly on monetary aggregates. It wasn't always that way, as our chapter on Federal Reserve history (Chapter 37) indicates. In fact, until 1966 the directive to the Account Manager was couched solely in terms of money market conditions—easier or firmer. Free reserves (member bank excess reserves less their borrowings from the Fed) and short-term interest rates ruled the day, especially the Treasury bill rate and the federal funds rate.

In 1966, however, the directive was altered to include what was called a proviso clause. The Account Manager was directed, for ex-

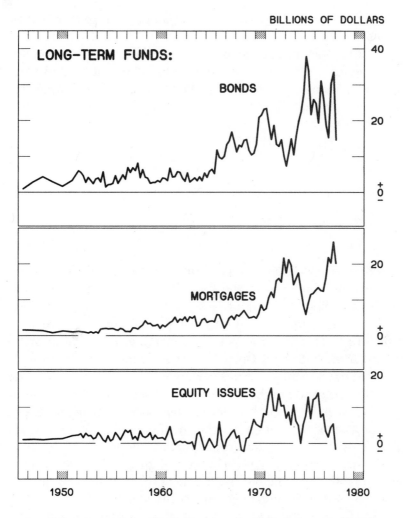

BILLIONS OF DOLLARS

LONG-TERM FUNDS:

BONDS

40

20

+
0
–

20

MORTGAGES

+
0
–

20

EQUITY ISSUES

+
0
–

1950   1960   1970   1980

CHART 5 / Ever-so-careful not to slight anyone, the Fed supplements Chart 4's picture of short-term credit with this set of graphs at the long end.
Source: *Federal Reserve Chart Book*.

ample, "to conduct open market operations with a view towards somewhat firmer conditions in the money market, *provided* [our italics] that bank credit was not deviating significantly from projections." At the first meeting in 1970, the monetary aggregates in the directive were expanded to include money as well as bank credit in the proviso clause. At the third meeting in 1970, the monetary aggregates finally were put on a par with interest rates and money market conditions. The FOMC expressed a desire to seek "moderate growth in money and bank credit over the months ahead" as well as "money market conditions consistent with that objective." Then, early in 1972, the FOMC added reserves as an operating target along with money market conditions.

Both money market conditions, especially the Federal funds rate, and reserves are supposed to be used to achieve a desired pattern of growth in monetary aggregates. Now that we know what must be done, let's see how they do it.

The Operating Room

Open market operations are performed in a well-guarded room within a fortress-like building in the heart of the nation's financial center. The Federal Reserve Bank of New York, designated by the FOMC as its operating arm, is located on Liberty Street, only three blocks from Wall Street. This location permits Peter Sternlight, Manager of the Federal Reserve System Open Market Account, to be in close contact with the government securities dealers with whom the Federal Reserve System engages in purchases and sales of securities. Every morning of the work week he meets with one or more of the securities dealers and gets the "feel of the market," as the opening handshakes (firm or limp? dry or sweaty palms?) telegraph whether the market is likely to be a tic tighter or easier. On occasion Sternlight has been known to shock the market by the judicious use of one of those little hand buzzers (the kind you used to be able to get in novelty shoppes).

Feedback from the securities dealers is only one component of the vast array of data and information marshaled by the Account Manager in mapping his plans for open market operations on any given day. The starting point, of course, is the directive issued by the FOMC at its last meeting. This expression of the proposed stance of monetary policy, together with the more precise range of desired movements in money market conditions and the monetary aggregates, provide the ultimate target for open market operations. Sternlight must still decide, however, how much to sell or buy, to or from whom, and when.

Money market conditions (particularly short-term interest rates) and the monetary aggregates are directly affected by the reserves available to the banking system, as we've seen in earlier chapters. Each workday morning, a little after 9:30, Sternlight receives a report on the reserve position of the banking system as of the night before.

A sensitive indicator of pressure in this market is provided by the Federal funds rate.

The Federal funds rate, as just indicated, is the rate charged on reserves loaned from one bank to another. On any given day, some banks have excess reserves and other banks have reserve deficiencies. There are brokers who bring such banks together to arrange for a loan (called a purchase and sale) from banks with surplus reserves to banks with deficient reserves. The agreed upon interest rate is called the Federal funds rate. It can rise significantly when there are few banks with excess reserves and lots with reserve deficiencies, and it can drop just as precipitously when the reserve-rich banks outnumber the poor. Thus it acts as a sensitive barometer of conditions in the reserves market. Federal funds are available to the recipient on the same day they are transferred. There is no clearing time as is typically needed with checks drawn on commercial banks.

The Federal funds market has grown tremendously in recent years and has played a crucial role in commercial bank liability management, as pointed out in Chapter 10. It also extends beyond the exchange of reserves between commercial banks, to include other financial institutions as well. But to the manager of the System open market account it serves primarily as an information source: the earliest available indicator of bank reserve conditions.

A little later in the morning, but before the 11:15 conference call, the Account Manager is provided with a detailed projection by the research staff. It covers movements in various items that can affect the reserve position of the banking system—including currency holdings of the public (which show considerable seasonal variation), deposits in foreign accounts at the Federal Reserve Banks, and other technical factors. A change in any of these can cause reserves to go up or down and thereby affect bank lending capabilities, interest rates, and growth in the money supply. For example, as the public cashes checks in order to hold more currency, commercial banks must pay out vault cash and thereby suffer a loss in reserves. As foreign accounts at Federal Reserve banks increase—that is, as they present checks for payment drawn against commercial banks—reserves of commercial banks are transferred to foreign accounts at the Fed.

A call is also made to the U.S. Treasury to determine what is likely to happen to Treasury balances in tax and loan accounts at commercial banks—deposits of the U.S. government generated by tax payments of the public and receipts from bond sales—and to find out what is likely to happen to Treasury balances at the Federal Reserve Banks, from which most government expenditures are made. As funds are

193

shifted from Treasury tax and loan accounts in commercial banks to Treasury balances at the Federal Reserve, the commercial banking system loses reserves.[1]

By 11:00 A.M., Peter Sternlight has a good idea of money market conditions, including what is happening to interest rates, and of anticipated changes in the reserve position of the banking system. He also knows what the FOMC directive calls for. If the FOMC had asked for moderate growth in reserves to sustain moderate growth in the monetary aggregates, and all of the other technical factors just discussed are expected to pour a large volume of reserves into the banking system, he may decide that open market *sales* are necessary to prevent an excessive (more than moderate) expansion in reserves. If, on the other hand, he expects to find reserves going up too little or even declining as a result of these other forces, he may engage in significant open market purchases. It is clear, therefore, why knowledge of the amount of government securities that the Federal Reserve bought or sold on a given day or during a given week, in itself tells us almost nothing about the overall posture or intent of monetary policy. Many of them may be bought or sold mainly to offset technical influences on reserves.

At the 11:15 conference call with a member of the Board of Governors in Washington and one of the Federal Reserve Bank presidents, Sternlight outlines his plan of action for the day and explains the reasons for his particular strategy. Once his decision is confirmed, the purchase or sale of securities (usually Treasury bills) takes place. The Account Manager instructs the traders in the trading room of the Federal Reserve Bank of New York to call the thirty-five or so government securities dealers and ask them for firm bids for stated amounts of specific maturities of government securities (in the case of an open market sale) or for their selling price quotations for stated amounts of specific maturities (in the case of an open market purchase). While the Federal Reserve does not engage in open market operations to make a profit, it still insists on getting the most for its money, and it is assured of that by vigorous competition among the various dealers in government securities.

It takes no more than thirty minutes for the trading desk to complete its "go-around" of the market and to execute the open market purchase or sale. By 12:30 the Account Manager and his staff are back to watching the situation and, if necessary, buying or selling additional amounts of government securities to implement the original objective.

---

[1] The discussion of the last two paragraphs on the impact of various items on bank reserves will be explained in detail in the next chapter.

Suggestions for Further Reading

An explanation from A to Z on the formulation and execution of open market operations is found in Paul Meek, *Open Market Operations* (Federal Reserve Bank of New York, 1978). While Meek is close to the center of the action, the trials and tribulations of trying to control the money supply can be gotten straight from the horse's mouth, former Account Manager Alan Holmes, in "Operational Constraints on the Stabilization of Money Supply Growth," in *Controlling Monetary Aggregates* (Federal Reserve Bank of Boston, 1969). An excellent review of the FOMC directive is by Stephen Axelrod, "The FOMC Directive as Structured in the Late 1960's: Theory and Appraisal," in *Open Market Policies and Operating Procedures* (Board of Governors of the Federal Reserve System, 1971). For a more recent analysis within a historical context see Edward J. Kane, "All for the Best: The Federal Reserve Board's 60th Annual Report," *American Economic Review* (December 1974).

Chapter 15

Factors Affecting Bank Reserves: A Framework for Monetary Control

EXACTLY WHAT was it the Watergate burglars were looking for on that fateful night in June 1972? Was it a key that would crack the secret code of the Transylvanian foreign office? A government document telling how many UFOs have landed here? A map of the Paris sewer system?

No, it was none of these. What they were *actually* after—and remember, you heard it here first—was a copy of the Federal Reserve's balance sheet and the latest scoop on the member bank reserve equation. Ah, if they had only taken a course in money! Then they could have saved themselves a lot of woe, because they would have learned that both of these, since they are crucially important in the practical interpretation of current monetary policy, are published in part every Friday in the *Wall Street Journal* and in full every month in the *Federal Reserve Bulletin.*

What's so important about the Fed's balance sheet? For one thing, discounting, which we discussed in Chapter 13, appears directly as a central bank liability. Thus to see how much reserves commercial banks are borrowing, since we don't get to look at all member bank balance sheets every week, we must look at the balance sheet of the Fed. Moreover, open market operations, the most important tool of the Fed, directly affects the Fed's holdings of government securities. Thus, the net effect of open market operations is recorded in the Fed's balance sheet. But more importantly, as suggested in the last chapter, there are other items which buffet bank reserves—some of which pop up elsewhere in the Fed's assets and liabilities and others which slip in via the U.S. Treasury.

Back in Chapter 3 it was a simple matter to write up or down member bank reserves. Pluses or minuses in T-accounts did the job magnificently. As in so many explanatory techniques, however, that's a simplification—useful but deceptive. Now's the time to elaborate on the nitty-gritty of member bank reserves. In that way, we can flesh out the assumptions underlying Federal Reserve control over reserves. More concretely, we can pinpoint the Fed's activities that are needed just to keep reserves where they were yesterday (if that's what the Fed wants); as we'll see, sometimes that takes quite a bit of doing.

The Fed's Balance Sheet

Table 1 is the somewhat simplified balance sheet of the Federal Reserve System at the end of 1978.[1] Each of the items on both the assets and liabilities sides deserves some explanation, since each of them reflects something that has an effect on member bank reserves.

The general proof of that last statement—that every item on the Fed's balance sheet has an effect on member bank reserves—is so obvious it's easy to overlook. So here it is:

1.   By definition, on *any* balance sheet total assets = total liabilities (including net worth or "capital accounts").

2.   With respect to the Fed, its total liabilities include member bank reserves—they are "member bank deposits" in the Fed plus that part of "Federal Reserve notes outstanding" which is in member bank vaults.

[1] If you look in the back of the *Federal Reserve Bulletin,* you will find the Fed's balance sheet in a table labeled "Federal Reserve Banks: Condition and F.R. Note Statements."

TABLE 1

The Federal Reserve's Balance Sheet

(end of 1978; in billions of $)

Assets		Liabilities & Capital Accounts	
Gold certificates (including		Federal Reserve notes	
special drawing rights)	13.0	outstanding	103.3
Cash	.3	Member bank deposits	31.2
Loans (member bank			
borrowings)	1.2	U.S. Treasury deposits	4.2
U.S. govt. and agency securities		Foreign and other	
Owned outright	117.4	deposits	1.6
Held under repurchase			
agreements	1.2		
Cash items in process of		Deferred availability cash	
collection	12.9	items	6.5
Miscellaneous		Miscellaneous liabilities and	
assets	5.1	capital accounts	4.3
	151.1		151.1

Source: *Federal Reserve Bulletin.*

3. Therefore, member bank reserves must equal total Federal Reserve assets minus all other Federal Reserve liabilities (and capital accounts) besides member bank reserves.

All of which can be put more formally:

Definition 1: Fed assets = Fed liabilities + Fed capital accounts
Definition 2: Fed liabilities = member bank reserves + other
Fed liabilities
Thus (by substitution): Fed assets = member bank reserves + other
Fed liabilities + capital accounts
Therefore (rearranging terms):
Member bank reserves = Fed assets — (other Fed
liabilities + capital accounts.)

Thus, anything that affects a Fed asset or a Fed liability has to alter member bank reserves *unless it is offset somewhere else in the balance sheet.* If total Fed assets rise, for example, and there are no changes in "other liabilities," then member bank reserves have to rise. Or if Fed liabilities other than member bank reserves rise, and no asset changes, then member bank reserves have to fall. It all follows from the fundamental accounting identity: total assets = total liabilities plus capital accounts.

However, a word of caution: We have not yet taken into account *all* of the factors that might affect bank reserves, since some of them come from *outside* the Federal Reserve. In particular, we have ignored Treasury-issued coin and currency, some of which is in member bank vaults and thus is also a part of bank reserves. We will take this into account later in the chapter, and we will then have all the ingredients for the full and complete member bank reserve equation.

But first let's take a closer look at each of the major items on the Fed's balance sheet. In so doing, we will see *how* increases in the Fed's assets result in increases in bank reserves, and how increases in "other" liabilities result in decreases in bank reserves (provided, in both instances, that they are not offset by counteracting movements elsewhere).

1. *Gold certificates (including special drawing rights)* are Federal Reserve assets that arise in connection with U.S. Treasury gold purchases, regardless of whether the gold is purchased from abroad or from domestic mines. Say the U.S. Treasury buys $100 million of newly mined gold from the Get Rich Quick Mining Company in Dodge City, Kansas. The Treasury pays for the gold with a check drawn on its deposit in the Federal Reserve; the Get Rich Quick Mining Company deposits the check in its local commercial bank, which sends it to the Fed for collection, and as a result bank reserves rise by $100 million, as we see in the following T-accounts:

| U.S. Treasury | | Federal Reserve | | Commercial Bank | |
A	L	A	L	A	L
Gold +$100 Dep. in FRB −$100		Dep. of member bank + $100 Dep. of Treas. −$100		Dep. in FRB +$100	Dep. of mining co. +$100

So far, this illustrates that if a Fed liability other than member bank reserves falls, and there are no offsetting entries, then member bank reserves have to rise. When the Treasury buys gold, it draws down its deposit at the Fed (a Federal Reserve liability), and gives the check to someone who deposits it in a member bank, thereby expanding both the money supply and bank reserves.

But when gold is involved, that is not the end of the story. The Treasury has used up part of its checking account balance at the Fed. To replenish it, the Treasury issues a "gold certificate" to the Fed (a claim on the gold), equal in value to the dollar amount of gold purchased, and the Fed in exchange credits the Treasury's deposit account by a similar amount, as follows:

| U.S. Treasury | | Federal Reserve | |
A	L	A	L
Dep. in FRB + $100	Gold certif. out- standing + $100	Gold certif. + $100	Dep. of Treas. + $100

In this latter transaction, Federal Reserve assets (namely, gold certificates) have risen but member bank reserves are not affected, because a liability other than member bank reserves (namely, Treasury deposits) has risen simultaneously.[2] However, the net result of both of these transactions is still an increase in bank reserves and an equal increase in the money supply. (A gold *sale* by the Treasury would *reduce* bank reserves and the money supply, with all the above entries being the same except opposite in sign).[3]

2. *Cash* on the asset side of the Federal Reserve balance sheet consists of coin and currency issued by the U.S. Treasury (a liability of the Treasury) that the Fed happens to have in its vaults. Mostly it consists of coins. If a member bank sends a truckload of pennies to the Fed, cash goes up on the asset side of the Federal Reserve's balance sheet and member bank reserves go up on the liability side.

3. *Loans* (or member bank borrowings) have been previously examined in detail via T-accounts (see pp. 33–34 in Chapter 3). When member banks borrow from the Fed the banks' reserves rise, and when they repay such debts their reserves decline.

4. *U.S. government and agency*[4] *securities* are acquired by the Fed when it engages in open market operations, with which we are familiar by now (for the relevant T-accounts, see pp. 35–37). When the Fed buys securities bank reserves expand, and when the Fed sells securities bank reserves contract.[5]

[2] As you can see, this step is nothing more than a sterile bookkeeping operation (as opposed to the virile variety, which actually does something), since this "monetization of gold" comes *after* the gold stock has already affected bank reserves. In fact, some gold purchases are not "monetized" by the Treasury (i.e., no gold certificates are issued for them), and yet they affect bank reserves just the same. A gold purchase can be "sterilized"—kept from affecting bank reserves —by the Fed engaging in open market sales of securities to deplete bank reserves by as much as the gold purchase increased them. This is an example of "defensive" open market operations, as discussed later in the chapter.

[3] We will discuss "special drawing rights" (SDRs) in Chapter 36. They comprise only $1.3 billion of the $13.0 billion in Table 1. SDRs result from international monetary arrangements made in recent years. They are a supplement to gold in international finance, and an increase in U.S. holdings of SDRs affects bank reserves exactly the same as an inflow of gold.

[4] Agency issues are securities of government-sponsored institutions, such as the Federal Home Loan Banks and the Federal National Mortgage Association (see Chapter 27). Agency obligations account for only about $8 billion of the $117.4 billion in Table 1.

[5] There is a story, possibly apocryphal, that when a System Account Manager died suddenly, many years ago, his aides pried open his locked top desk drawer. In it was a handwritten card reading:
To increase reserves, buy
To decrease reserves, sell

5. *Cash items in process of collection* on the asset side of the Fed's balance sheet is an entry that arises in the course of clearing checks (as does "deferred availablity cash items" on the liability side). To see what they involve, let's take an example. Say you have an account in the Safe & Sound National Bank and you see in the local newspaper that for only $100 you can get an antique spittoon and bedpan (matching set, last one left, accept no substitutes!). So you rush downtown and are lucky enough to get them, paying the $100 by check. The antique dealer has his checking account at the Last Laugh National Bank, in a neighboring town. He deposits your check in Last Laugh, which sends it in to the Fed for collection.

So far so good, and indeed we saw all this before in Chapter 2. But in the real world things are just a bit more complicated than we made them back in the T-accounts on page 21. There, we said that the Fed would simply add $100 to the Last Laugh Bank's deposit in the Fed, deduct that amount from your Safe & Sound Bank's reserve account, and that would be that. But in reality, although the end results are accurate enough, the mechanics are not quite that simple, as the T-accounts below indicate:

Federal Reserve Bank

	A		L	
(a)	Cash items in process of collection: Safe & Sound Bank +$100		Deferred availability cash items: Last Laugh Bank +$100	
(b)			Deferred availability cash items: Last Laugh Bank − 100 Member bank deposits: Last Laugh Bank + 100	
(c)	Cash items in process of collection: Safe & Sound Bank −$100		Member bank deposits: Safe & Sound Bank −$100	

When the Fed receives your check from Last Laugh, it doesn't *immediately* credit Last Laugh's reserve account and reduce Safe & Sound's reserve account. What it does is give Last Laugh "deferred availability" credit, meaning that Last Laugh's reserve account will be credited in due time, according to a prearranged time schedule. At the same time it considers the check "in process of collection" from Safe

& Sound. Thus the first pair of entries, labeled (a), in the Fed's T-account above.

Next step: After a day or two, depending on the time schedule, Last Laugh will formally receive an addition to its reserve account—the pair of entries labeled (b) above. Notice that, for the moment, *after* step (b) but *before* step (c), "cash items in process of collection" on the Federal Reserve's balance sheet exceeds "deferred availability cash items" by $100. This $100 difference is known as Federal Reserve *float,* and it adds to total bank reserves because it means that one bank's reserves have been increased, but so far no other bank's reserves have been reduced.

Finally, when the check is actually collected from Safe & Sound, then Safe & Sound's reserve account will be reduced, which is step (c). At that time, "cash items in process of collection" will also decline, and both float and total reserves will fall by $100, returning to their original amounts.

Float—the difference on the Fed's balance sheet between the asset item "cash items in process of collection" and the liability item "deferred availability cash items"—arises because many checks are not collected within the time period established for crediting the reserves of banks depositing checks with the Fed. According to the time schedule now in use, all checks must be credited to a depositing bank's reserve account no later than two days after they are received by the Fed. As Table 1 indicates, Federal Reserve float was $6.4 billion at the end of 1978, representing an addition of that amount to total bank reserves.

With respect to its effect on bank reserves, the importance of float is not so much that it exists but that it fluctuates considerably. Float usually rises, for example, when bad weather grounds planes and causes delays in the mails, since this interferes with the delivery of checks en route for collection. A rise in Federal Reserve float increases total bank reserves, but such gains are temporary since subsequent declines in float reduce reserves.[6]

Note: On the Fed's balance sheet, the sum of member bank borrowing, U.S. government and agency security holdings, and Federal Reserve float is frequently referred to as "Federal Reserve credit."

6. *Federal Reserve notes outstanding* are most of our $1, $2, $5, $10, and $20 bills (and so on up the ladder), an asset to those of us who are fortunate enough to have any. But to the Fed they are just another liability. When your local bank finds itself running short of currency, it cashes a check at its regional Federal Reserve Bank and

[6] For details on float, see Arline Hoel, "A Primer on Federal Reserve Float," *Monthly Review* of the Federal Reserve Bank of New York (October 1975).

the Fed sends an armored car to deliver some more tens and twenties. This is recorded as follows:[7]

	Federal Reserve Bank		Commercial Bank	
A	L	A		L
	F.R. notes outstanding +$100	Cash in vault +$100		
	Dep. of member bank −$100	Dep. in FRB −$100		

When commercial banks ship currency back to the Fed, of course, the entries are the same but opposite in sign. Which means that when the Fed receives an inflow of Federal Reserve notes, its assets do not rise; instead, its Federal Reserve note liabilities decline, because there are fewer Federal Reserve notes *outstanding*. Federal Reserve notes in the possession of the Federal Reserve are just so much paper—if they are frayed or worn, they are burned; if they are still serviceable, they are stored awaiting the day when member banks will want them again.[8]

So when the item "Federal Reserve notes outstanding" rises, member bank deposits at the Fed fall, and vice versa. But these transactions—shipments of currency back and forth between commercial banks and the Federal Reserve Banks—do not in themselves alter bank reserves. They just exchange one kind of reserve (a deposit at the Fed) for another (cash in vault). However, if the *public* decides to hold more currency—perhaps because Christmas is approaching and people need more coins and bills to spend—then bank reserves fall dollar for dollar with the currency drain:

---

[7] What if the Fed includes in its shipment some Treasury-issued coin or some Treasury-issued $5 or $10 bills? To the extent that this occurs, then instead of the Fed liability "Federal Reserve notes outstanding" rising, what happens is that the Fed asset "cash" falls. In *either* case, member bank deposits at the Fed fall.

[8] If you have in your own pocket a piece of paper on which you have written a promise to pay the bearer $1 million, you are not by that token a millionaire. Similarly, a Federal Reserve Bank which holds its own promise to pay the bearer so much, which is what a Federal Reserve note amounts to, is not wealthier because of it.

Commercial Bank		Public	
A	L	A	L
Cash in vault −$100	Demand deposits −$100	Demand deposits −$100	
		Currency +$100	

When currency is returned to the banking system, as in the weeks after the Christmas season ends, then bank reserves rise dollar for dollar with the currency reflow. The T-accounts are the same as above, except opposite in sign. If the currency is then shipped back to the Fed, the commercial banks are merely exchanging reserves in the form of currency for reserves in the form of deposits at the Fed. As Table 1 indicates, at the end of 1978 about $103 billion of Federal Reserve Notes were outstanding, part of which was held by member banks as vault cash (about $10 billion) and the rest of which was held by the public.

7. *U.S. Treasury deposits* are just what the name implies: deposits of the Treasury held in the Federal Reserve Banks. The Treasury keeps most of its working balances in "tax and loan accounts" at many commercial banks throughout the country. This is where tax payments and the receipts from bond sales are initially deposited. But when the Treasury wants to spend the money, it first shifts its funds to a Federal Reserve Bank and then writes a check on its balance at the Fed. When the Treasury shifts its balances from commercial banks to the Fed prior to making payments, in effect it writes a check on its balance at commercial banks and gives the check to the Fed. As a result, Treasury deposits at the Fed rise and bank reserves fall:

U.S. Treasury		Federal Reserve Bank		Commercial Banks	
A	L	A	L	A	L
Dep. in comm. bank −$100			Member bank dep. −$100	Dep. in FRB −$100	Dep. of Treasury −$100
Dep. in FRB +$100			Treasury dep. +$100		

However, when the Treasury actually spends the funds, then its deposits at the Fed fall and member bank reserves rise again. Say the Treasury spends $100 on paper clips. It pays a supplier of paper clips with a check drawn on its balance at the Fed, the supplier deposits the check in his local commercial bank, the bank sends it in to the Fed, and—*voilà!*—as Treasury deposits at the Fed decline, bank reserves are increased:

Factors Affecting Bank Reserves

U.S. Treasury		Federal Reserve Bank		Commercial Banks	
A	L	A	L	A	L
Dep. in FRB −$100			Member bank dep. +$100	Dep. in FRB +$100	Demand dep. +$100
Paper clips +$100			Treasury dep. −$100		

The U.S. Treasury's Monetary Accounts

In addition to the items recorded on the balance sheet of the Federal Reserve, many transactions of the U.S. Treasury also affect bank reserves. Some of these transactions we have already discussed, but they bear repeating from the independent viewpoint of the Treasury; while others—like the issuance of Treasury currency—we have not yet taken into account.

1. First of all, strictly speaking, it is the Treasury, not the Fed, that officially buys and sells gold on behalf of the government. As we have seen, after it buys some gold, the Treasury usually issues an equal amount of gold certificates (a Treasury liability) and hands them to the Fed (for whom they are an asset), so that the Treasury can replenish its deposit account at the Fed. However, as the T-accounts at the beginning of this chapter show, it is really the gold purchase that increases bank reserves, not the subsequent issue of gold certificates. Since gold, per se, does not appear on the balance sheet of the Fed, we had to talk about the gold certificates while we were confining ourselves to the Fed's balance sheet. But now that we are bringing the Treasury explicitly into the picture, we can go right to the heart of the matter: When the Treasury buys gold, bank reserves rise, and when the Treasury sells gold, bank reserves fall.[9]

2. A second aspect of Treasury operations that affects member bank reserves is changes in the Treasury's deposits at the Federal Reserve Banks. When the Treasury shifts its deposits from its tax and loan accounts at commercial banks to its account at the Federal Reserve, prior to making disbursements, Treasury deposits at the Fed

[9] See the T-accounts on p. 199. You can confirm the ultimate significance of gold rather than gold certificates by noting that if you were to consolidate the balance sheets of the Treasury and the Fed, gold certificates would cancel out—since they are a liability of the Treasury and an asset of the Fed—leaving only the gold itself.

FED MOVES ON RATES NOW TIED TO FACTORS OF TECHNICAL NATURE

CHECK CLEARING PROBLEM SEEN

Week's Increase in Money Supply Held Not Enough to Warrant Tightening of Policy

By JOHN H. ALLAN

The turmoil in the securities markets earlier this week that resulted from the perception that the Federal Reserve might have tightened monetary policy another notch may have been for nought.

That was the conclusion indicated by statistics released yesterday afternoon by the central bank at its weekly news conference. The nation's basic money supply rose $1.4 billion in the week ended Oct. 26, a fairly sizable increase but probably not enough to make the Fed change its policy.

Instead, the central bank's action last Monday appeared to be based more on offsetting some difficulty in clearing checks within the banking system.

'Float' Soars to Record

Because O'Hare Airport in Chicago was fogged in late last week, Federal Reserve "float"—extra reserves in the banking system resulting from checks in the process of collection—soared to a record $6.2 billion on Friday.

Consequently, the Fed drained reserves from the banking system on Monday by arranging so-called matched sale-pur-chase agreements and by selling Treasury bills for its own account.

The credit markets regard outright bill sales as something of a signal of monetary policy, and they jumped to the conclusion that the Federal Reserve was increasing short-term interest rates another notch in order to slow down what was presumed to be another big jump in the nation's money supply.

A spokesman for the New York Federal Reserve Bank described the credit markets' response to the Fed's action Monday as "fairly extreme" and acknowledged that the sale of Treasury bills "made more of an effect than it usually does."

The Federal Reserve System, he emphasized, "never tries to create such a situation; it tries to calm things."

Securities Markets Rally

Late yesterday afternoon, the Government securities markets rallied on this turn in the ongoing interpretation of the Federal Reserve's current strategy.

Still, the Fed yesterday reported that the basic money supply, which is known as M-1 and is made up of currency in circulation and mos checking-account balances, expanded to a record $334.6 billion in the latest week, while the broader money supply, known as M-2, increased $2.1 billion to average a record $801 billion.

As a result, M-1 showed an annual rate of growth over the latest 52 weeks of 7.6 percent and M-2 a 10.3 percent annual rate. Both presumably are higher than the maximums set by the Federal Reserve on Oct. 18 for the 12 months from the third quarter of 1977 to the third quarter of 1978, targets to be disclosed next Wednesday.

Since late July, the Federal Reserve has been nudging short-term interest rates higher in an effort to slow down the rate of growth of the money supply. Such growth, the monetary authorities contend, will make inflation worse.

This policy has drawn criticism from the Carter Administration and others. Yesterday, for example, Senator Hubert H. Humphrey asserted that monetary policy was not providing enough stimulus to the economy.

NEWS ITEM / Even the Weather Can Cause "Defensive" Operations

SOURCE: *New York Times*, November 4, 1977

rise and member bank reserves fall; and then when the Treasury actually spends the funds, its deposits at the Fed decline and bank reserves are replenished. We have just seen the T-accounts illustrating this process, so there is no need to repeat them.

3. Finally, we have to take account of the fact that the Treasury also issues a small amount of our currency and all of our coins. Actually, the Bureau of Engraving and Printing operates the printing presses for currency (this is not the same thing as the Government Printing Office, although for all practical purposes maybe there isn't much difference), and the Bureau of the Mint manufactures the coins in three coin factories that are located in Denver, Philadelphia, and San Francisco. Both of these bureaus are departments of the U.S. Treasury.

Until the early 1960s all of our $1 bills were issued by the Treasury; they were called silver certificates. However, since then $1 bills have been issued by the Federal Reserve, in the form of Federal Reserve notes. Nevertheless, there are a couple of hundred million dollars worth of silver certificates still in circulation and these remain a liability of the Treasury. You may run across one from time to time; if you do, save it, because—unlike most of our money—it will probably increase in value (as a collector's item.) The only currency the Treasury still issues on a current basis is called United States notes; they were first printed during the Civil War, when they were popularly known as "greenbacks." Since 1878 they have been limited by law (they still are) to a total of $347 million outstanding.

With respect to bank reserves, there is no difference whatsoever between currency that is in the form of Federal Reserve notes and currency (such as United States notes or silver certificates) and coin that is issued by the U.S. Treasury. Regardless of who issued it, all coin and currency in bank vaults counts as part of reserves. When the public decides it wants to hold more currency—because when going to the supermarket a $50 bill is needed rather than a $20—then bank reserves fall dollar for dollar with the drain of currency out of bank vaults into the purses of the public. It doesn't matter whether the currency leaving the banks is in the form of Federal Reserve notes or Treasury-issued money. And conversely, when the public redeposits its change—nickels, quarters, and a few dollar bills—back in the banking system, bank reserves rise dollar for dollar with the currency reflow regardless of the type of currency being redeposited.

Indeed, we saw the T-accounts for this back on page 204. There we assumed that it was Federal Reserve notes that we were dealing with, but now we realize that the T-accounts for the public and the commercial banks would be exactly the same regardless of what kind of currency is involved.

The Member Bank Reserve Equation

We have now become acquainted with all of the factors that affect member bank reserves and we can put them all together in a full and complete "member bank reserve equation." The member bank reserve equation is actually rather simple to visualize conceptually, as long as you remember the accounting at the beginning of this chapter plus the fact that Treasury currency in bank vaults also counts as reserves.

Namely, member bank reserves = total Fed assets *minus* all Fed liabilities and capital accounts *other than* those Fed liabilities that comprise member bank reserves *plus* Treasury currency in member bank vaults. This is usually put more formally, as in Table 2, but it amounts to the same thing.[10]

Table 2, the member bank reserve equation, looks a bit different

TABLE 2

The Member Bank Reserve Equation

(end of 1978; in billions of $)

Factors supplying reserves:		
Federal Reserve credit:		
U.S. govt. and agency securities	118.6	
Loans to member banks	1.2	
Float	6.4	
Miscel. Federal Reserve assets	5.1	
Gold stock (including SDRs)	13.0	
Treasury currency outstanding	11.8	
		156.1
Less factors absorbing reserves:		
Currency in circulation (i.e., outside the Federal Reserve, the Treasury, *and member bank vaults*)	104.3	
Treasury cash holdings	.2	
Treasury, foreign, and other deposits with Federal Reserve Banks	5.8	
Miscel. Federal Reserve liabilities and capital	4.3	
		114.6
Equals member bank reserves:		
Member bank deposits with F.R. Banks	31.2	
Currency in member bank vaults	10.3	
		41.5

Source: *Federal Reserve Bulletin.*

[10] You can find the member bank reserve equation in the *Federal Reserve Bulletin* in a table labeled "Factors Affecting Member Bank Reserves."

from Table 1, the Fed's balance sheet, but the differences are really minor. "Factors supplying reserves" in Table 2 correspond roughly to Federal Reserve assets, and "factors absorbing reserves" correspond roughly to Federal Reserve liabilities, and in addition Treasury-issued coin and currency is also incorporated into Table 2. In brief, Table 2, the member bank reserve equation, amounts to nothing more than the consolidation of the Fed's balance sheet with the Treasury's monetary accounts.

Look first at "factors supplying reserves" in Table 2 and notice the similarity with the Fed's assets in Table 1. The category "Federal Reserve credit" includes the Fed's holdings of government securities, member bank borrowings, Federal Reserve float, and miscellaneous Federal Reserve assets. Remember that Federal Reserve float is the excess of the Fed asset "cash items in process of collection" over the Fed liability "deferred availability cash items." Gold stock in Table 2 replaces gold certificates in Table 1 because, as we have seen, it is the purchase or sale of the gold itself that affects bank reserves, not the issuance of gold certificates. "Treasury currency outstanding" in Table 2, the only really new item as compared with Table 1, includes all Treasury-issued coin and currency regardless of who holds it; that is, it is counted here whether it is held by the public, commercial banks, the Federal Reserve, or even the Treasury itself. Since the figure for "Treasury currency outstanding" includes the Treasury-issued currency that is held by the Federal Reserve, the item "Cash" on the Fed's balance sheet (which, as we saw on p. 200, is nothing more than Treasury-issued currency held by the Fed) drops out to avoid double-counting when we consolidate the Fed's balance sheet with the Treasury's monetary accounts into Table 2.

Turn now to the "factors absorbing reserves" in Table 2 and notice the similarity with the Fed's liabilities in Table 1. "Currency in circulation," a new entry, includes both Federal Reserve notes outstanding *and* Treasury-issued coin and currency. Currency in circulation *absorbs* reserves because it refers to currency held by the nonbank public —that is, to currency that is *outside* the Federal Reserve, the Treasury, and member banks. Any currency of any sort that may be held by the Treasury is included in the figure for "Treasury cash holdings."[11]

---

[11] For more detail on the consolidation of the Fed's balance sheet with the Treasury's monetary accounts, see David H. Friedman, *Glossary: Weekly Federal Reserve Statements* (Federal Reserve Bank of New York, 1975). However, to *really* understand the accounting nitty-gritty you'll have to dig into the *Supplement to Banking and Monetary Statistics*, Section 10 (Board of Governors of the Federal Reserve System, 1962), pp. 1–13.

We should mention that in the member bank reserve equation as actually published by the Federal Reserve, the term "currency in circulation" is defined as Federal Reserve Notes and Treasury-issued coin and currency held outside the

Putting It All to Use

How is the member bank reserve equation used? In Chapter 2, when we related demand deposits to reserves via the very simple deposit expansion multiplier (demand deposits = total reserves times the reciprocal of the demand deposit reserve ratio), we assumed that the Fed could control the volume of reserves by judicious use of open market operations. But from the member bank reserve equation (Table 2), we see that this is no simple matter. Movements in float, gold, Treasury deposits, currency in circulation, and the other variables listed in Table 2 have to be forecast and monitored. Only then can Fed open market operations hope to come close to the mark in terms of bank reserves. Open market operations, therefore, cannot be fully understood, or properly executed, without the member bank reserve equation.

For example, if reserves are rising because of a temporary decline in the Treasury's balance at the Fed, open market sales may be used to *offset* such influences. Open market operations of this type are called *defensive* because they are aimed at defending a target level of reserves from "outside" influences. Another example would be increased purchases of government securities during December in order to offset seasonal increases in currency holdings by the public. December may mean mirth and cheer to most of us, but to practitioners of the dismal science in the Fed's trading room it means "pump up reserves to offset currency drains."

There is a special type of open market operation that particularly lends itself to defensive uses, namely government securities bought under repurchase agreements. Under a "Repo" the Fed buys the security with an agreement that the seller repurchase it on a specific date in the future (usually within fifteen days). As Table 1 indicates, $1.2 billion of government securities were held under repurchase agreements at the end of 1978. A "reverse Repo" is designed to sop up reserves over a short interval; that is, the Fed sells government securities

---

Fed and the Treasury. In other words, "currency in circulation" as published by the Fed includes currency held by the banks as well as that held by the nonbank public. From the point of view of member bank reserves this is illogical, as the Fed itself admits. It is illogical because "currency in circulation" is treated as an entry that reduces reserves in the member bank reserve equation, but in fact currency held by banks is part of their reserves. The Fed's published version winds up with reserves held in the form of deposits at the Fed, to which vault cash is added back in to get total reserves. Our version corrects the structure of the member bank reserve equation, redefining "currency in circulation" as only that currency held by the nonbank public. The Fed's reasons for its form of presentation are mainly historical, as explained on page 7 of the *Supplement to Banking and Monetary Statistics* mentioned above.

and agrees to repurchase them at some date in the near future (this is also called a matched sale-purchase agreement). By their very nature, "Repos" and "reverse Repos" are *temporary* injections or deletions of reserves and might be interpreted as always being in the defensive category. But that would be falling into the well-known pitfall of identifying a specific Federal Reserve action with a particular objective. Never, never, never, do that. Once you do, the Fed denies it and then makes sure you're wrong by going out and doing just the opposite —using "Repos" and "reverse Repos" continuously to change reserves over a long period of time. In fact, in terms of volume of transactions, Repos and reverses far outweigh outright purchases and sales by a factor of 20 or 30 to 1.

Which brings us to the *dynamic* variety of open market operation. Dynamic open market operations are aimed at either increasing or decreasing the overall level of bank lending capacity by changing the level of bank reserves. Even here, the volume of purchases or sales must be undertaken in light of movements in all the other factors affecting bank reserves. For example, if an increase in reserves is desired and the member bank reserve equation shows that all other sources of reserves will be expanding, open market purchases may be completely unnecessary. For these reasons, it is not really possible for an outsider to distinguish defensive from dynamic open market operations, because the Fed is usually buying and/or selling on a continuing basis—sometimes offsetting "outside" influences on reserves, sometimes changing the total level of reserves, and sometimes even offsetting the offsetting changes. It is generally agreed, however, that the bulk of the Fed's open market operations are in the defensive category, making up as much as 80 or 90 percent of total purchases and sales.

Member Bank Reserves or the Monetary Base?

There has been considerable controversy over what variable the Fed should try to control in order to regulate the money supply. The control variable is often called an operating target, because it is the *immediate* objective of open market operations. Although we will return to this subject in the next chapter, we can make a first pass at it here.

Bank reserves are only one possible control variable. A frequently

Billions of Dollars

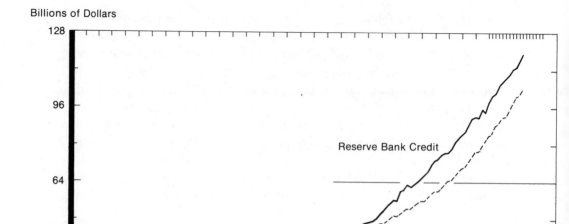

CHART 1 / Reserves and related items of member banks, averages of daily figures, quarterly. Source: Federal Reserve Chart Book.

proposed alternative as an operating target is the monetary base—total reserves plus currency held by the nonbank public. The member bank reserve equation can be altered quite easily to focus on the monetary base; just shift "currency in circulation" down to the bottom of Table 2, to join member bank reserves. Then, in terms of Table 2, what we would have is (Federal Reserve credit + gold stock + Treasury currency outstanding) *less* (Treasury cash holdings + Treasury, foreign, and other deposits with the Federal Reserve Banks + miscellaneous Federal Reserve liabilities and capital) = the monetary base (i.e., member bank reserves + currency in circulation).

It is interesting to note, as we pointed out in the Appendix to Chapter 3, that an open market operation of $1 billion does not change bank reserves by $1 billion. An open market purchase of that amount from commercial banks will *initially* change bank reserves by $1 billion, but subsequently some of these reserves leave the banking system because of increased currency holdings by the public; it is closer to the truth to say that a $1 billion open market purchase changes the monetary *base* by $1 billion.

Even here, of course, other changes can throw this off, such as fluctuations in float, gold, Treasury deposits, and member bank borrowing from the Fed.[12] Nevertheless, by and large a $1 billion open market operation can be more closely associated with a change in the monetary base (reserves plus currency held by the nonbank public) than with a change in reserves alone, all of which suggests that the base might be a better target than reserves. But there are even more problems, as you'll see in the next chapter within the context of searching for an indicator of monetary policy.

Suggestions for Further Reading

The best sources for details on the Federal Reserve's balance sheet and the factors affecting member bank reserves are Dorothy M. Nichols, *Modern Money Mechanics* (Federal Reserve Bank of Chicago, 1975), and David H. Friedman, *Glossary: Weekly Federal Reserve Statements* (Federal Reserve Bank of New York, 1975). Both are available for the asking. See also Chapter 3 of *The Federal Reserve System: Purposes and Functions* (Board of Governors of the Federal Reserve System, 1974). Current and historical data can be found in the monthly *Federal Reserve Bulletin.* A formal analysis of factors affecting reserves is William G. Dewald and William E. Gibson, "Sources of Variation in Member Bank Reserves," *Review of Economics and Statistics* (May 1967).

Three other Federal Reserve publications contain advanced discussions of how the Fed might go about controlling monetary aggregates. They are *Controlling Monetary Aggregates* (Federal Reserve Bank of Boston, 1969), *Open Market Policies and Operating Procedures* (Board of Governors of the Federal Reserve System, 1971), and *Controlling Monetary Aggregates II: The Implementation* (Federal Reserve Bank of Boston, 1972).

The distinction between defensive and dynamic open market operations was first made by Robert V. Roosa in *Federal Reserve Operations in the Money and Government Securities Markets* (Federal Reserve Bank of New York, 1956). This is still a useful booklet, but unless your library has it you are out of luck, because it is out of print.

---

[12] An example of the problems created by bank borrowing is as follows. Member banks borrow reserves at their own initiative. They also respond to interest rates in their borrowing from the central bank. For example, as interest rates on bank loans and investments rise (relative to the discount rate) during a business upswing, banks borrow more from the discount window in order to expand their loans. Similarly, as interest rates fall, perhaps because of a slowdown in economic activity, banks repay their borrowings at the Federal Reserve. Unless the Fed undertakes (defensive) open market operations to offset these movements in discounting, the money supply will vary with commercial bank borrowing from the Federal Reserve (in response to interest rates). In other words, unless the Federal Reserve is trying to control the base—unless the base is an operating target—the money supply will vary with interest rates and economic activity. Instead of the money supply merely affecting interest rates and GNP, the reverse would also be true.

Chapter 16

How to Decipher What the Federal Reserve Is Doing

TWO EXECUTIVES talk in a treasurer's office, deep inside the headquarters of an American corporation. Their topic: "Has monetary policy become less restrictive since last month?" Financial statistics lie scattered around the room.

"Look what's happened to the Treasury bill rate: It's gone down three-eighths of a point. The Fed's easing up."

"But the Federal funds rate (and they pay a lot of attention to that because it's what banks pay to borrow money overnight) hasn't budged. I don't see how you can say monetary policy has eased any."

"Okay, but the money supply grew at a 5-percent rate this month, and that's according to the Fed's own press release. Last month, it only grew at 4 percent. Policy looks easier to me."

"But free reserves fell. I thought that meant conditions were tighter."

"So did I. But total reserves went up. That doesn't look like the Fed is tightening any. How can conditions be tighter if the banks have more reserves?"

"I'm confused."

This hypothetical conversation is typical of what goes on in corporate and bank offices throughout the country, as people try to figure out what the Federal Reserve is doing, especially when a turning point in Fed policy seems at hand. If the Fed had been tightening—squeezing bank reserves and raising interest rates—a turnaround in monetary policy suggests falling interest rates (higher bond prices): someone who correctly anticipates the turnaround in Fed policy could buy securities immediately and make handsome capital gains on rising bond prices.

But what if you guess wrong? What if, instead of easing, the Fed tightens even more? Then interest rates continue to rise (bond prices fall). If you buy bonds now, all you'll get are capital *losses* as their prices drop.

With stakes so high, it's no wonder the game of Fed watching has become so popular in recent years.

Federal Reserve Disclosure

One reason there's a guessing game in the first place is because the central bank—like central banks everywhere—is reluctant to disclose exactly what it is doing now and what it is likely to do next. Until 1967, the Federal Reserve disclosed what took place at its monthly Federal Open Market Committee meetings only once a year (at the end). Starting in 1967, it released the FOMC monetary policy directives 90 days after each meeting; it reduced this delay to 45 days in 1975 and then to 30 days in 1976.

The motivation behind reducing the secrecy period to 45 days, and then to 30 days, was that in 1975 David Merrill, a young law student at Georgetown University, instituted a lawsuit against the Fed under the Freedom of Information Act. He charged that the central bank had no right to keep its monetary policy directives secret, not even for 45 or 30 days—that the directives should be made public *immediately* following each FOMC meeting. He won in Federal District Court and in the U.S. Court of Appeals, but in 1979 the Supreme Court ruled against him (by a vote of seven to two). The Fed won the case on the argument that immediate publication of the directive would give sophisticated investors an edge, permit speculators to gain unfair profits, and interfere with the execution of monetary policy.

215

A Step Back

As a first step in figuring out how to decipher what the Fed is doing, let's pause a moment and survey the terrain. After five chapters on the intricacies of Fed policy-making the details have taken over and we are in danger, to coin a phrase, of losing the forest for the trees.

The ultimate purpose of the Federal Reserve is to influence total spending and GNP. But it has no way of directly altering GNP, so it has to exert its influence indirectly—through the supply of money and credit and various interest rates, mostly medium-term and long-term rates. However, these variables—let's call them the Fed's intermediate objectives—are not directly under the Fed's control either. So it has no choice but to aim at an *operating target*, perhaps several different ones, hoping that if it hits these operating targets they will eventually nudge the intermediate objectives and thereby get the job done.

This game plan is illustrated schematically in Chart 1. Notice the distinctions between operating targets, intermediate targets, and ultimate objectives. Much of the confusion regarding Fed policy arises because these distinctions are ignored.

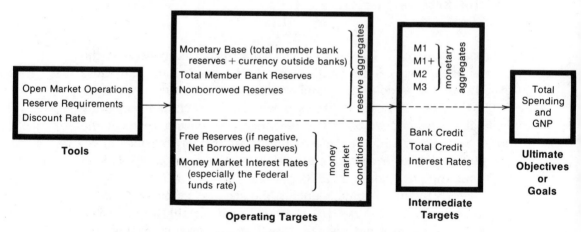

CHART 1 / The Fed's game plan.

Notice also what is included in the concepts you will often encounter in the financial pages of your newspaper: the monetary aggregates, money market conditions, and the reserve aggregates.

The *monetary aggregates* are intermediate targets; the phrase includes M1, M1+, M2, and M3. Other intermediate objectives are bank credit, total credit, and medium-term and long-term interest rates.

Money market conditions are one set of possible operating targets; the phrase refers to free reserves and money market interest rates—especially the Federal funds rate and to a lesser extent the three-month Treasury bill rate.[1]

The *reserve aggregates* are another group of possible operating targets; the phrase includes a wide variety of bank reserve measures, such as the monetary base, total reserves, and so on. Chart 2 summarizes the arithmetic relationships among the various reserve measures. (Interestingly, the last of these in Chart 2—namely, free reserves—is usually considered an indicator of money market conditions rather than as one of the reserve aggregates.)

MONETARY BASE (= total reserves + currency outside banks)
Minus Currency outside banks

= TOTAL RESERVES

Minus member bank borrowing from the Fed

= NONBORROWED RESERVES

Minus required reserves

= FREE RESERVES (or, if negative, NET BORROWED RESERVES)

CHART 2 / Relationships among alternative reserve measures.

In recent years, the Fed has been putting its plan into operation this way (more or less): It specifies its intermediate objective in terms of a desired range for monetary growth over the year—say an increase in M1 of from 5 to 8 percent. Then it sets an operating target for bank reserves that it figures will produce this rate of monetary growth—say an increase in total reserves or perhaps in nonborrowed reserves of from 2 to 4 percent over the year. Simultaneously, it sets another operating target—the Federal funds rate—that is thought to be consistent with the desired rate of increase in reserves.

The Federal funds rate has been used by the Account Manager as an indicator of the state of bank reserves. If reserves are growing too rapidly, the Federal funds rate will fall below target, signaling the

[1] Until mid-1977 the "bank credit proxy" was also a frequently mentioned indicator. It consists of total deposits at member banks, and was used as a substitute for developing trends in bank credit, since data on deposits become available earlier than data on bank loans and investments.

Account Manager to intervene and drain reserves by open market sales. Alternatively, if reserves are growing too slowly, the Federal funds rate will rise above target, alerting the Account Manager to intervene and supply reserves by open market purchases.

This is the way it was until October 1979, when the Federal Reserve shifted its emphasis away from the federal funds rate as an operating target, turning its attention to reserves instead. Whether this shift in favored operating targets is temporary or permanent is uncertain. And that cannot help but confuse matters for Fed-watchers.

With this as background, let's return to the main theme of the chapter: the search for a reliable indicator that will tell us what the Fed is really up to. Such an indicator should have two characteristics. It should be subject to the Fed's control, so that when it changes we know that it is not chance but the Fed that caused the change. And it should have a fairly predictable impact on economic activity, so that changes can be expected to produce results.

Both of these features are important for a meaningful indicator. Clearly, if the Federal Reserve has little control over a variable, it doesn't do any good to monitor it in hopes of evaluating the stance of monetary policy. But even if the Federal Reserve controls something perfectly, it may not be *worth* monitoring if it has only a tenuous relationship with economic activity.

A Pride of Lions, a Gaggle of Geese, and a Plethora of Indicators

To judge by the press, many financial observers rely on movements in the discount rate to indicate the current stance and future course of monetary policy. A change in the discount rate is heralded on the front page of *The New York Times* and solemnly announced in respectful tones by Walter Cronkite on the evening news. It is implied that when the Federal Reserve raises the discount rate, tight money is being ushered in, and when the discount rate is lowered, easy money is entering from the wings. However, most Federal Reserve officials and academic economists agree that the discount rate is a follower rather than a leader, as we saw in Chapter 13.

The two powerhouses in the monetary arsenal—reserve requirements and open market operations—also will not do, and for diametrically opposed reasons. Reserve requirement changes are not of much assistance because they are used so seldom; open market operations are not very helpful because they are used too frequently. Weekly data on Federal Reserve open market operations are released every Thursday afternoon and published in Friday's papers. But the knowledge that the Fed bought or sold so many government securities during any week, or even over a succession of weeks, is in itself of limited value; the vast majority of open market operations are of the defensive variety, as we saw in the two previous chapters.

Since it is widely understood that weekly data on open market operations alone give an inadequate picture of what is going on, many financial observers rely more on movements in interest rates for clues to the current stance of monetary policy. Of all yields, the ones most quickly responsive to monetary policy are probably the Federal funds rate and the rate on short-term Treasury bills.

However, as reliable indicators of what the central bank is doing, interest rates have serious limitations. It should be obvious that they are susceptible to change for reasons other than Federal Reserve policy; this makes it dangerous to read them as though they were determined exclusively by the Federal Reserve. The central bank has substantial influence over the supply of credit, but only limited influence over the demand for it, so interest rates may fluctuate for reasons that have nothing to do with the Federal Reserve's actions. Tight money generally means a rise in interest rates, but a rise in interest rates does not necessarily mean tight money. Indeed, as we will see in Chapter 20, excessively *easy* money might also produce a rise in interest rates.

Given the shortcomings of all the "orthodox" indicators—the discount rate, open market transactions, and the behavior of interest rates—the Federal Reserve, always helpful, releases a truckload of numbers each Thursday afternoon along with the data on open market operations. It presents current statistics on a wide variety of alternative indicators. You can take your pick!

It lists weekly figures on all of the following: the monetary base, total member bank reserves, the volume of member bank discounting from the Federal Reserve, free reserves, the money supply (M1), the money supply plus passbook savings deposits (M2), business loans at large commercial banks, and a few hundred other numbers just for good measure.

With this smorgasbord of indicators, plus the orthodox ones on the back burner, you can select those that best suit your individual taste. Free reserves attained some degree of popularity a few years ago but have fallen from favor. The main trouble is that a given level of free reserves is compatible with many different levels of the money supply and bank credit. The figure for free reserves has fluctuated within roughly the same limits for the past 20 years, while the money supply and bank credit have grown considerably during that interval.

Weeding Out the Weak, Cultivating the Strong

Interest rates are downgraded as indicators of Federal Reserve policy, because as just mentioned they are not under the firm control of the central bank. Another leading candidate, the money supply, is said to suffer from the same malady—that it is influenced by commercial bank behavior in conjunction with swings in economic activity, and that it can be controlled only imperfectly by the Federal Reserve. For example, we pointed out in the previous chapter (especially in footnote 12) that as interest rates on bank loans and investments rise relative to the discount rate during a business upswing, banks borrow more from the discount window, expand their loans, and increase the money supply. Similarly, as interest rates fall, perhaps because of a slowdown in economic activity, banks repay their borrowings at the Federal Reserve, reduce their loans, and cause the money supply to contract. If the central bank is solely responsible for changes in the money supply, then it is a good indicator of Federal Reserve policy. But if the money supply can change regardless of Federal Reserve intentions, using it as an indicator is likely to throw you off the track.[2]

In order to save the money supply as an indicator of monetary policy, Karl Brunner and Allan Meltzer have marshaled statistical evidence showing that it is Federal Reserve initiative—open market operations and reserve requirement changes—that is the main cause of movements in the money supply.[3] In particular, they show that the deposit multiplier is fairly stable and that movements in the monetary base are dominated by open market operations. As a concession, however, they are ready to fall back to the monetary base as a preferred

[2] If the Fed treated member bank borrowing as it would treat float or movements in Treasury currency, then *defensive* open market operations would be undertaken to keep total reserves (as calculated from the member bank reserve equation) constant whenever bank borrowing reacted to market interest rates and economic activity. The money supply would then be insulated from economic activity, it would be controlled by the Fed and restored to its status as "favored indicator." It is not really clear how the Fed behaves in such cases. In the short run, bank borrowing is certainly able to expand total reserves. But in the long run this is not likely. Unfortunately, we cannot really delineate the short run from the long run.

[3] For a good summary, see Karl Brunner, "The Role of Money and Monetary Policy," Federal Reserve Bank of St. Louis *Monthly Review* (July 1968).

indicator, because it removes one set of uncertainties from the effects of the Fed's actions (namely, changes in the size of the deposit multiplier).

Other Federal Reservologists prefer total reserves to the monetary base. For still others, total reserves must be purged of reserves arising from member bank borrowing at the discount window—leaving us with nonborrowed reserves to chart the course.

The Federal Reserve itself added to the confusion (purposely?) by announcing early in 1972 that it had begun using reserves available to support private deposits (RPDs) as an operating target. RPDs are calculated by subtracting from total reserves those reserves required against Treasury (U.S. government) deposits and interbank deposits, neither of which is included as part of the money supply.[4] What is left are RPDs, reserves available to support private nonbank deposits (both demand and time). But the Fed is fickle: early in 1976 it abandoned RPDs in favor of the monetary base, total reserves, and nonborrowed reserves, without saying which of the three indicators it prefers.

Although there has been some confusion concerning "targets" of monetary policy as opposed to "indicators" of policy, our discussion tends to blur the distinction.[5] If the Fed can control a variable, and if that variable has an impact on economic activity, then it is a good indicator. It would also be a good operating target for the Federal Open Market Committee (FOMC) to instruct the Account Manager to use in carrying out the current directive.

As we saw in Chapter 14, since early 1974 the Fed has been announcing numerical money supply targets as part of the reporting of FOMC meetings. Shouldn't such announcements be taken seriously, and used as indicators themselves? If the Fed's targets were well defined and if the Fed succeeded in hitting the mark, then we'd have no problem identifying the stance of monetary policy. But the record shows that the Fed's accuracy leaves much to be desired. In Chart 3 the shaded areas show the announced targets during 1978 for M1, M2, and the Federal funds rate. Notice that the targets are not

[4] Interbank deposits are deposits of one commercial bank with another. These are sometimes called correspondent balances, and are used by many nonmember banks to clear checks.

[5] For maximum confusion, follow this advice: first read Karl Brunner and Allan H. Meltzer, "The Meaning of Monetary Indicators," in *Monetary Process and Policy*, ed. George Horwich (Homewood, Ill.: Irwin, 1967); then read Thomas R. Saving, "Monetary Policy Targets and Indicators," *Journal of Political Economy* (August 1967). For a super-duper indicator, see Dennis R. Starleaf and James Stephenson, "The Monetary Full Employment Interest Rate," *Journal of Finance* (September 1969). Also see Benjamin M. Friedman, "Targets, Instruments and Indicators of Monetary Policy," *Journal of Monetary Economics* (October 1975).

FOMC Ranges for Short-run Monetary Growth and for the Federal Funds Rate, 1978

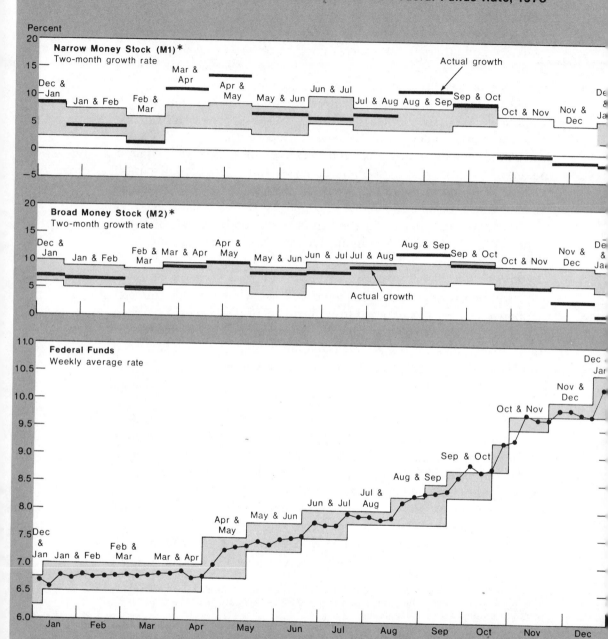

Shaded bands in the upper two charts are the FOMC's specified ranges for money supply growth over the two-month perio indicated. No lower bound was established for M1 at the October and November meetings. In the bottom chart, the shaded bands are the specified ranges for Federal funds rate variation. Actual growth rates in the upper two charts are based on data available at the time of the second FOMC meeting after the end of each period.

*Seasonally adjusted annual rates.

Source: Federal Reserve Bank of New York.

especially narrow, reflecting the well-known proverb—Big Target Means Sharp Shooter. Even so, only the Federal funds rate target is hit with any degree of consistency. If Sitting Bull had had the same accuracy, Custer would still be using Clairol.

This is pretty discouraging, to say the least. Some indicators aren't very good because the Fed can't (or won't) control them. Some are no good because, even though the Fed has them under its thumb, they don't have any consistent link with economic activity. Can anything be salvaged from this mass of confusion? Read on.

Some Helpful Hints

Where does all this leave someone trying to make an honest buck evaluating the posture of monetary policy? Instead of responding with a cliché (as is our custom)—such as "Life is tough for everyone"—we offer a series of helpful hints (HHs) to aid in interpreting Federal Reserve behavior.

1.   Divide the indicators into two groups: *the monetary and reserve aggregates*—including the money supply (M1), money supply plus passbook savings deposits (M2), the monetary base, total reserves; and *money market conditions*—especially the Federal funds rate and the interest rate on Treasury bills.

2.   Do not conclude that, because there has been an increase in the aggregates, monetary policy has embarked on a wild expansion. The money supply, for example, must increase with a growing economy to provide funds for the increased transactions associated with a larger GNP. The money supply has, in fact, increased in every year since 1950 save one (1960), although it can and has declined over shorter intervals (such as three or six months).

3.   Try to judge whether the aggregates, say the money supply, are growing faster than normal (expansionary policy) or slower than normal (restrictive policy). What is normal? The money supply grew at an annual rate of 4.0 percent during the twenty years from 1955 through 1975. From 1955 through 1965, however, its growth was only 2.2 percent a year, and from 1966 through 1975 it was 5.9 percent. Take your pick.

4.   If interest rates are falling at the same time as the aggregates are increasing at a faster-than-normal rate, it is a good bet that the Federal Reserve has embarked on a course of monetary expansion.

And if interest rates are rising at the same time as the aggregates are growing at a slower-than-normal rate, it is an equally good bet that the Federal Reserve has begun to exercise restraint.

5. The Federal Reserve publishes what transpired at the monthly FOMC meetings with a 30-day delay. Read them. If the Federal Reserve decided on increased monetary ease a month ago and your reading of the indicators shows it has not succeeded, look for signs of further easing as the Fed tries harder. If tighter monetary policy was decided upon a month ago and your reading of the indicators shows that the Federal Reserve hasn't succeeded—call your broker and sell (see Chapter 26 first).

Naturally, we assume no responsibility for the misfortunes brought down upon you when following these HHs. But we insist on 10 percent of the profits. Lotsa luck.[6]

Suggestions for Further Reading

We are indebted for the opening remarks in this chapter to William N. Cox III, "Measuring Monetary Policy," *Monthly Review* of the Federal Reserve Bank of Atlanta (December 1970). An advanced theoretical treatment of monetary policy indicators is Karl Brunner and Allan H. Meltzer, "The Meaning of Monetary Indicators," in *Monetary Process and Policy*, ed. George Horwich (Homewood, Ill.: Irwin, 1967). An empirical evaluation of alternative indicators is Michael J. Hamburger, "Indicators of Monetary Policy: The Arguments and the Evidence," *American Economic Review* (May 1970). An entire book devoted to constructing the ideal indicator is Patric H. Hendershott, *The Neutralized Money Stock* (Irwin, 1968). For instructions from the Fed itself (be careful), see "Numerical Specifications of Financial Variables and Their Role in Monetary Policy," *Federal Reserve Bulletin* (May 1974).

A great deal of useful background material on targets and indicators is contained in *Improving the Monetary Aggregates: Report of the Advisory Committee on Monetary Statistics* (Board of Governors of the Federal Reserve System, June 1976); and "A Proposal for Redefining the Monetary Aggregates," *Federal Reserve Bulletin* (January 1979).

---

[6] For those who would like to see how some indicators have charted Fed policy in the past, do not skip Chapter 37 simply because it's called "Post-World War II Federal Reserve History."

PART IV

Monetary Theory

Chapter 17

The Classical School

THE FIRST QUESTION we asked in this book was: What is the "right" amount of money? The answer depends on how money influences the economy . . . which in turn depends on how it influences spending. Classical and Keynesian economists have different views of the world in general and money in particular. This chapter and the two that follow explore the analytical foundations that underlie their differences.

The Classical school was housed in a big white building. Like most big white buildings that are meant to impress those on the outside, it was supported by two huge pillars, giving it a fortress-like appearance. At the base of one pillar the cornerstone read "Say's Law." On the other was inscribed "The Quantity Theory." All in Greek letters, naturally. This school, resembling a temple at times and an ivory tower at others, was the dominant force in macroeconomics from the eighteenth century until 1936, when John Maynard Keynes put on his Samson's wig and pulled down the huge pillars supporting the Classical structure.

But Keynes, and especially his disciples, made one miscalculation; they didn't build the Keynesian school with the ruins of the Classical edifice. Instead, they built and furnished the "modern structure" with entirely new materials. This provided the opportunity for tradition-loving academics at the University of Chicago to reconstruct the Classical school, rename it the Monetarist approch (a well-learned lesson from advertising), and mount a determined challenge to Keynesian economics in the 1960s and 1970s.

What did Classical economics have to say about macroeconomics —the determination of GNP? How did money influence economic activity in that system? What was going on inside that big white building that made it last so long and permitted its resurrection so quickly?

Say's Law

Jean Baptiste Say (1767–1832) summarized the Classical school's income and employment theory with the now familiar maxim, "Supply creates its own demand." Dubbed Say's law (by Mrs. Say), it meant quite simply that the economy could never suffer from underemployment or succumb to Thomas Malthus' fear of underconsumption. Total spending (demand) would always be sufficient to justify production at a full employment GNP (supply). Here's why:

Given current technology, potential output of the economy is determined by the size of the labor force available to work with the existing stock of capital goods (plant and equipment). This production function, in technical terms, defines the total supply of goods and services that can be produced. Say argued that actual output would be at the full employment level, since spending would always be great enough to buy all the goods and services that could be produced. Why? Because of the interplay of market forces, guided by Adam Smith's invisible hand.

If someone who wanted to work couldn't find a job, he would offer his services for less money and thereupon be snapped up by eager entrepreneurs. Entrepreneurs, finding it difficult to sell slow-moving items (chastity belts in the 1980s), would promptly lower their prices and watch their inventories disappear (at only $1 per belt you might hang it on the wall to stimulate conversation when your parents come to visit). Flexible wages and prices assured that all markets would be cleared, all goods sold, all people employed—except economists, who had nothing to do, since everything worked just fine without them. The interplay of market forces under the guiding principle of *laissez-faire* (noninterference). The best of all possible worlds.

The Reverend Thomas Malthus (1766–1834) once entered the

big white Classical school and, finding nothing inside (he couldn't believe that *he*, a man of the cloth, was unable to see the invisible hand), departed and proceeded to launch a sustained and vigorous attack on it. Spurning the microeconomic infrastructure (use that on your friends majoring in sociology), Malthus argued as follows: While the production of goods and services generates *income* in the same amount as total output (as we indicated in Chapter 4), there does not seem to be anything to force *spending* to equal total production. Supply might create its own purchasing power (income), but not its own demand (spending). In particular, if people try to save too large a fraction of their income—more than firms want to invest—part of the goods produced will be left unsold, entrepreneurs will cut back their production, and unemployed labor and capital will result. This argument was later refined and formalized by Keynes, as we shall see in the next two chapters.

However, the Classical economists were not to be disposed of so simply. People save part of their income, but such funds do not disappear. They are borrowed by entrepreneurs to use for capital investment projects. Savers receive interest on their funds and borrowers are willing to pay, as long as they expect to earn a return on their investment in excess of the rate of interest.

But what made the Classical economists so sure that all saving would actually be invested by entrepreneurs? If saving went up, would investment go up by the same amount? In Classical economics, *the rate of interest* is the key; according to Classical theory, the interest rate would fluctuate to make entrepreneurs *want to invest* what households *wanted to save*. As we explained in Chapter 4, this equality between desired saving and desired investment is sufficient to maintain production at the assumed level, in this case, full employment. The next section explains in greater detail this Classical theory of interest rate determination. It is really an elaboration of one of the market mechanisms underlying Say's law.

Classical Interest Theory

Saving, according to Classical economics, is a function of the rate of interest. The higher the rate of interest, the more will be saved (see Figure 1), since at higher interest rates people will be more willing to forgo present consumption. The rate of interest is an inducement to save, a reward for not giving in to one's baser instincts for instant gratification by consuming all one's income. It does not pay, by the way, to make too much of this Classical assumption, because Classical interest theory worked just as well if saving did not depend on the interest rate—i.e., if saving were a vertical line in Figure 1.

As long as investment is a function of the rate of interest, increasing as the rate of interest declines (as illustrated by the negatively sloped investment line in Figure 1), Classical interest theory and Say's

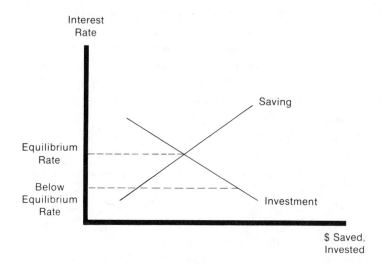

FIGURE 1 / Classical interest theory.

law remained alive and well. Let's take a closer look at why the amount of investment should increase with a fall in the rate of interest.

Investment in physical capital is undertaken because capital goods—buildings, machines, or anything which is not used up (consumed) immediately—produce services in the future. A new plant or machine is used by an entrepreneur to produce goods and services for sale. A businessman increases his capital stock (invests) if he expects that his rate of return will execeed the rate of interest he must pay on the funds he borrows to make the investment. A lower rate of interest induces entrepreneurs to undertake more investment. They will accept projects of lower expected profitability, because the cost of borrowing funds is less.[1]

---

[1] The entrepreneur need not borrow in order for the interest rate to be important in his calculation. If he already has funds, his alternative to increasing his capital equipment is to lend the funds at the going rate of interest. At a lower rate of interest, lending becomes a less attractive use of the entrepreneur's funds and real investment becomes more attractive. The rate of interest *must* fall to elicit more investment spending because of our old friend from microeconomics, the law of diminishing returns. More investment means a larger capital stock, and, given the labor force and current technology, there is reduced marginal productivity (profitability).

Figure 1 includes a supply of funds curve (people's saving) and a demand for funds curve (entrepreneurs' demand for investment). The rate of interest is in equilibrium at the point of intersection between saving and investment, where total saving is equal to investment: Everyone who wants to borrow funds is able to, and everyone who wants to lend can do so. If the rate of interest were below equilibrium, as shown in Figure 1, entrepreneurs would want more funds than savers are ready to provide and competition would force the price (interest rate) upward. If the rate of interest were above equilibrium, savers would want to lend more funds than entrepreneurs want to invest, and competition would force the price of funds downward.

But this isn't a fairy tale, so things don't stay in equilibrium for very long. If people really listened to some of the dire predictions of Thomas Malthus, they might decide to save more at every rate of interest, to provide for the day when population grows to the point where people can no longer afford to smoke grass because they must eat it. The entire saving function would then shift to the right (Figure 2). At the old equilibrium interest rate, desired saving now ex-

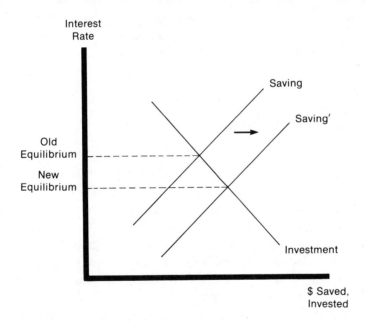

FIGURE 2 / Increased saving calls forth increased investment.

ceeds the amount of investment that entrepreneurs are ready to make. That is precisely what Thomas Malthus said was wrong with the Classical system—people would spend too little in the form of consumption, they would save too much (more than entrepreneurs cared to invest), and disaster would follow.

But not really. The excess of saving over investment puts downward pressure on the rate of interest, as savers try to lend out their funds. Some people will give in to their baser instincts as the rate of interest declines and spend a greater part of their income (saving less and enjoying it more). At the same time, the decline in the rate of interest encourages businessmen to expand their investments. As Figure 2 shows, the rate of interest will settle at a lower equilibrium, at which point all that is saved out of current income is still invested by entrepreneurs.

But where in all of this does money fit in? The interest rate is influenced only by the saving of the public (determined by their habits of thriftiness) and by capital investment of entrepreneurs (determined by the productivity of capital). Money plays no role in this area of the Classical system. It influences neither employment, the rate of interest, nor GNP. Real things are determined by real forces: Total goods and services produced and total employment are determined by the supply of capital, the labor force, and existing technology; the interest rate is determined by the thriftiness of the public and the productivity of capital. Money plays no role in the real sector of the economy. Instead it is treated separately—via the second pillar of the classical edifice, the Quantity Theory—where it determines the price level.

The Quantity Theory of Money

Money, according to the Classicists, is a veil to be pierced by the analytical mind of the economist examining the determinants of real economic activity. Money affects the price level, but nothing else. An increase in the supply of money leads to an increase in the prices of all goods and services, but everything else—most notably the level of real economic activity, the rate of interest, and people's real income —remains unchanged. This conclusion expresses the quantity theory of money. The logic behind it is as follows.

We start with the *equation of exchange*, which is not the quantity theory but simply an *identity*, a truism:

$$(1) \qquad\qquad\qquad MV = Py$$

where M is the supply of money, V is velocity or its rate of turnover, P is the price level, and y is the level of *real* income.

The physical output of goods and services is represented by (lower-case) y; that is what is produced by labor and capital given

"Now for those lessons I promised you . . .
when saving exceeds investment. . . ."

the technology currently available. Putting that in value terms (in dollars) requires that it be multiplied by an average level of prices for these goods and services—an index of prices[2]—represented by P. In other words, P times y is the total *value* of goods and services produced in the economy, namely GNP—it is usually represented by upper-case Y (see Chapter 4). On the left-hand side, the stock of money (in dollars) is represented by M. When multiplied by its velocity, the number of times such dollars are used in the purchase of goods and services, the product MV also equals total spending, or

[2] Price indices are constructed using complicated weighting schemes, to take into account the relative importance of different items produced in the economy. See Paul Samuelson, *Economics*, 10th ed. (New York: McGraw-Hill, 1976), pp. 182–83.

GNP. That is the equation of exchange. It says that total spending *(MV)* equals the value of what is bought *(Py).*[3]

The equation of exchange was originally put forth in a slightly different form. The level of real income on the right-hand side was replaced by *T*, the total level of transactions. The total level of transactions exceeds the level of GNP because there are many transactions that are excluded from GNP. Purchases and sales of *financial* assets and of *existing* assets—such as stocks and bonds, old homes, and works by the Great Masters (the 1952 Marilyn Monroe calendar) are not part of current production and hence are not included in GNP.[4] When the equation of exchange is written as:

$$(2) \qquad\qquad MV = PT$$

the velocity figure on the left-hand side is called transactions velocity.

Equation (1) is the most frequently used version of the equation of exchange. It is really the most meaningful approach, since our main concern is with GNP and not with total transactions. Thus all of our subsequent discussion will be in terms of equation (1) and the "income" velocity of money. Irving Fisher, the brilliant Yale economist who is unfortunately known for his advice to buy just before the stock market crashed in 1929, was the most eloquent expositor of the equation of exchange as we have just presented it.[5]

There is still another version of the equation of exchange, however, associated with economists at Cambridge, England. So before discussing how we progress from the simple identity expressed by equations (1) or (2) to the quantity theory as used by Fisher and other Classical economists, let us give equal time to our friends across the Atlantic.

The economists at Cambridge viewed the equation of exchange in a slightly different light. Instead of concentrating on the rate of turnover of a given stock of money during the year (its velocity), they concentrated on the fraction of GNP that people hold in the form of money. Simple algebraic manipulation of equation (1) produces the Cambridge "cash-balance approach" to the equation of exchange:

$$(3) \qquad\qquad M = kPy$$

where k is the fraction of GNP that people have command over in the form of money balances. Obviously $k = 1/V$, so equations (1) and

---

[3] As we saw in Chapter 1 velocity is *defined* as GNP ÷ M, or, in these terms, $Py \div M$. Substituting $Py \div M$ for V on the left-hand side of (1) yields $Py = Py$, which is accepted as a truism even by those from Missouri.

[4] See Samuelson, *Economics*, chap. 10, for a summary of GNP accounting.

[5] See Irving Fisher, *The Purchasing Power of Money* (New York: Macmillan, 1911).

(3) are equivalent from an algebraic standpoint (for some unknown reason, when the Cambridge economists divided both sides of equation (1) by V they changed $1/V$ to the letter k). And (3), like its predecessors, is still a truism—an identity that must be true by definition.

This latest version does represent a different orientation, however. In fact, equation (3) readily lends itself to interpretation as a *demand for money equation,* where people *want* to hold cash balances in a certain ratio to the value of GNP (say, one-third or one-fourth of GNP), to use in carrying out the anticipated level of transactions associated with that level of GNP.

But we are running a bit ahead of ourselves. It is time to convert the equation of exchange, whatever its form, from an algebraic identity—which it has been so far—into an analytical tool. Let's move, in other words, from the *equation of exchange* (an identity) to the *quantity theory of money* (a cause-and-effect hypothesis).

We started this section by saying that the quantity theory implied that increases in the supply of money cause increases in the price level. We can now be even more precise: According to the quantity theory of money, a change in the money supply produces a *proportionate* change in the price level—for example, if the money supply doubles, so does the price level. This cause-and-effect conclusion follows from two basic propositions (a nice word for assumptions) of the Classical school. First, on the right-hand side of equation (1), $MV = Py$, y is assumed fixed at full employment (now you know why we started out with Jean Baptiste Say). Second, velocity is assumed to be fixed by the payment habits of the community, or, in the Cambridge cash-balances version, k is fixed because of the stable proportion of GNP that people want to hold in the form of money balances. If $MV = Py$ and V and y are assumed to be fixed, then if M doubles it follows that P *must* double. For example, if V and y are fixed at 4 and 100 respectively, then a supply of money equal to 25 is consistent with a P equal to 1. If M doubles to 50, P must double to 2.

To understand the process involved, we need only recall the discussion in Chapter 1 of how people react to changes in the money supply brought about by central bank operations. Start out in equilibrium, with everyone satisfied with the liquidity of his portfolio. Assume the Federal Reserve doubles the money supply. Liquidity rises.[6] If people were formerly satisfied with their liquidity position, now they will try to get rid of their excess money balances by spending more. This increase in the demand for goods and services drives prices up, because total real output cannot expand—it is fixed at the full employment level by virtue of Say's law. If people were in equilibrium

[6] See p. 13 in Chapter 1.

before a doubling of M, they will stop trying to spend the increased money balances only after their total expenditures have also doubled. Since real output is fixed, a doubling of total spending must cause prices to double. End result: Money stock held by the public has doubled, *money* GNP has doubled, the price level has doubled, V is the same as before, and so is *real* GNP (i.e., y).

The two versions of the quantity theory, $MV = Py$ and $M = kPy$, are algebraically equivalent and also produce the same cause-and-effect implications for the relationship between money and prices. For explaining the transmission mechanism as we just have, and for what is to come later, the cash-balance version $(M = kPy)$ is superior (in keeping with the best British tradition). The cash-balance equation can be interpreted as a demand for money function, as we mentioned above. Assume that $k = \frac{1}{4}$. Then if Py or GNP equals $400, this means that people want to hold one fourth of GNP, or $100, in cash balances; if GNP climbs to $600, the amount of money demanded rises to $150; and if GNP doubles to $800, money demand doubles to $200.

The fraction of GNP that people want to hold in the form of money, k, is determined by many forces. It is essentially a *transactions demand* for money. Money is used as a medium of exchange, so that the value of k is influenced by the frequency of receipts and expenditures; if you are paid weekly, you can manage with a smaller daily average cash balance than if you are paid monthly. The ease with which you can buy on credit and an increase in the use of credit cards permit people to reduce the average balance in their checking accounts. Money is also used in this context as a temporary abode of purchasing power—waiting in the wings until you summon it and exercise control over real goods and services. As an individual you may hold more or less, depending upon whether you expect to be out of a job for four months or two months of the year. For the community as a whole, so the argument goes, all of these factors average out and are fairly stable, hence the public winds up wanting to hold a stable and/or predictable level of money balances relative to GNP.

Looking at the cash-balance version of the quantity theory ($M = kPy$) as a demand for money equation, it is easy to see that the doubling of prices (and hence money GNP) produced by a doubling of the money supply follows directly from the equilibrium condition that the amount of money demanded must equal the supply. When M doubles, people have twice as much money as they want to hold (money supply exceeds the amount demanded), given that nothing else has changed. So they start to spend it. They stop spending when they want to hold the increased money supply (when the amount of money demanded grows into equality with the supply). That occurs when money GNP has doubled.

It is also possible to look at this new equilibrium position in a slightly different way. Namely, the *real* amount of money that people hold is the same in both the initial and final positions. The real amount of money is given by the nominal money supply deflated by the price level, or M/P, where that tells you the amount of real goods and services that is "controlled" by the cash balances people hold. For example, if you hold a $1,000 checking account and the price index is unity, you control $1,000 worth of goods and services; if you have a $2,000 checking account but the price level has doubled, you still control the same real volume of goods and services ($M/P = 2M/2P$ is a famous theorem in advanced Boolean algebra). The cash-balance version of the quantity theory emphasizes that people are concerned with their *real* money balances, and not just the dollar value of their cash holdings.

Short-Run Versus Long-Run and Monetarist Roots

You've read Chapter 1 and you have just read what the Classical economists had to say. There are some obvious differences. According to Chapter 1 (pp. 12–14), the supply of money should influence interest rates and not just the price level. Furthermore, GNP does not always stay at its full employment level. Irving Fisher did not distinguish himself as a stock market oracle, but he was a brilliant economist; could he have been so far afield in his discussion of the quantity theory?

To some extent these are the things that sparked the Keynesian revolution, as we will see in subsequent chapters. But to leave it at that would sell Classical macroeconomics short. The Classicists were concerned with long-run analysis—decades and a score of years—rather than months or even a few years. In that context they were on much safer ground. In the long run, market forces might very well work the economy toward full employment, so a fixed level of real income determined by the supply of labor, capital, and technology might not be a bad assumption. Similarly, movements in velocity might perhaps be determined by the basic payment habits of the community, and much less buffeted by other more transitory factors. Under such circumstances, an increase in the money supply would, indeed, be reflected in higher prices.

The modern Monetarists, led by Milton Friedman, view themselves as the intellectual heirs of the Classical quantity theory approach, but they have applied that analytical framework to *short-run* problems rather than concentrating on long-run trends. The Monetarists may not contend that velocity is stable in the short run, only that it is predictable. They also do not contend that changes in M will be reflected only in P. If the economy is not operating at full employment (for whatever reason), the increase in M would be reflected in movements in real output, y, as well as in the price level, P. This short-run versus long-run issue recurs throughout subsequent discussions. The persistently nagging question that never really gets answered satisfactorily is: how long is the short-run or, looked at another way, how short is the long-run? A somewhat more profound way of putting it is: is a short long-run equivalent to a long short-run (or is it vice versa)?

Suggestions for Further Reading

Two books by Irving Fisher, *The Theory of Interest* (Macmillan, 1930) and *The Purchasing Power of Money* (Macmillan, 1911) are the most comprehensive treatments of Classical interest theory and the quantity theory, respectively. More recently, Milton Friedman has "modernized" the quantity theory; see "The Quantity Theory of Money—A Restatement" in his *Studies in the Quantity Theory of Money* (University of Chicago Press, 1956).

Chapter 18

The Keynesian Framework: I

JOHN MAYNARD KEYNES, first baron of Tilton (1883–1946), did many things differently. We are not concerned here with his ability to make a fortune speculating in the market while simultaneously teaching at King's College, Cambridge; nor with his infatuation with the finer things in life—ballet, drama—or his editorial supervision for many years of the technical *Economic Journal;* nor with his unique abilities in the fields of mathematics, philosophy, and literature. Rather, we are concerned with his contribution to economics in his book, *The General Theory of Employment, Interest, and Money,* published in 1936; how it revolutionized the thinking of all economists since, how it replaced Classical economics as the conventional wisdom, and how it led to a different outlook on employment, interest, and money.

Before going into the details of Keynes's contributions to macro-economics and monetary theory and the refinement of his ideas at the hands of other economists (collectively labeled Keynesians), it will be helpful to set the stage by noting an essential difference in Keynes's outlook compared with that of his Classical teachers. Keynes was concerned with the short-run, while Classical economists, as noted in Chapter 17, were preoccupied with the long-run. Keynes's attitude toward the concern of his Classical mentors is best illustrated by his now-famous dictum: "In the long run, we are all dead."

As casually suggested at the end of the previous chapter, it is difficult to delineate the borderline between the short and long run, but the six years of worldwide depression preceding the publication of Keynes's magnum opus was deemed too long to wait for Classical market forces to restore full employment. The length of the Great Depression sowed the seeds for the fantastic success of the *General Theory*. The most brilliant graduate students of the time (Paul Samuelson, for example) were converted to the New Faith while they listened to the lectures of their Classically trained teachers. Indeed, many of the teachers themselves became instant apostates.

Keynes was preoccupied with what determined the level of economic activity during those lengthy recession or depression intervals between the full employment points of the Classical school. Therefore, he had to introduce a new set of analytical tools to deal with the problem, since Classical economics had almost nothing to say about such matters. Keynes wanted to design a model of GNP determination that would explain how economic activity could be in equilibrium at *less* than full employment. Who or what was to blame for a depressed level of economic activity? To what extent is money the culprit?

A model is like a map. It does not include every detail of the actual terrain, but incorporates only those characteristics that are essential in explaining how to go from one point to another. Don't be turned off, therefore, if Keynes' model appears to be highly aggregative, ignoring many specifics and making many heroic assumptions. That is precisely what models are supposed to do: strip away the superfluous detail and get down to basics. The ultimate test, of course, is whether that simplified view of the world cuts through to explain actual behavior.

When Saving Doesn't Equal Investment

Chapter 4 showed that for GNP to be at an equilibrium level —that is, no tendency for change—all that is produced must be sold to consumers or willingly added to the capital stock as investment by business firms. We also said that this equilibrium condition could be stated in a different way: Total saving *desired* by households must equal total investment *desired* by firms. In that way the leakage out of the spending stream in the form of saving would be made up by desired investment spending by firms, and everyone could continue along his merry way.

In Chapter 4 we also mentioned that ex post (after all is said and done) saving is always equal to investment. Only in the ex ante (desired) sense is equality of saving and investment an equilibrium condition. Let's take a very specific example of these relationships to set the stage for our discussion in the rest of the chapter.

Assume entrepreneurs produce $1,000 billion of output (Y) at full employment and expect to sell $800 billion to consumers (C) and want to use the remaining $200 billion for investment (including inventory accumulation). They will continue producing at that rate only if their sales are realized. If consumers plan to buy $800 billion in consumer goods and services and therefore *desire* to save $200 billion, all is well. But what if consumers decide they want to spend only $700 billion on consumer goods, which means they want to save $300 billion? What will give?

Assuming that consumers succeed in implementing their spending plans, entrepreneurs will wind up selling only $700 billion, although they have produced $800 billion in consumer goods and services. Clearly their selling plans have been disappointed, and they wind up with an *extra* $100 billion in (unwanted) inventories. In fact, they *wind up* investing $300 billion (the same as saving): their planned capital accumulation of $200 billion plus $100 billion of *unintended* inventory accumulation. Saving (S) equals investment (I) ex post, but *desired* savings exceeds *desired* investment by $100 billion.

The key Classical-Keynesian confrontation revolved about precisely such circumstances: What happens when *desired* saving exceeds desired investment? The Classics had a series of simple answers based on a single principle—*prices adjust* when there is an excess supply of or demand for any good (or all goods together). Therefore, when there is an excess supply that isn't being sold, entrepreneurs reduce their prices to get rid of unsold inventories, workers lower their wage demands to stave off unemployment, and the rate of interest (the *price* of borrowing) decreases when saving exceeds investment. The fall in the interest rate lowers desired saving (increasing desired consumer spending directly) and raises desired investment, until desired saving and investment are again equal and entrepreneurs are content with their previous (full employment equilibrium) level of production.

But Keynes was not sympathetic. Prices are sticky and probably wouldn't decline as inventories piled up.[1] Wages are notoriously resistant to decreases and, even more important, fluctuations in the rate of interest do not equilibrate desired saving and desired investment. The rate of interest is determined in the money market; it

---

[1] We will relax the Keynesian assumption of downward inflexibility in prices and wages in the last section of Chapter 19.

equilibrates the supply and demand for money, not saving and invest-ment. All this will be discussed in greater detail below.

Assuming that the rate of interest doesn't bring saving into equality with investment, what happens as a result of the undesired inventory accumulation? Keynes thought that the level of output, rather than prices, would respond most quickly. Entrepreneurs with unwanted accumulating inventories (our old friend with the chastity belts) would probably cut back production. Output would fall as long as desired saving exceeded desired investment (and those useless belts kept on piling up). How far would output fall? Until desired S equaled desired I, when a new equilibrium income, lower than before, would be reached. To help us see how far GNP would fall when desired saving exceeds desired investment, Keynes invented the consumption function (or, looked at another way, the saving function).

Consumption and Simple GNP Determination

Let's start out with an equilibrium level of GNP so that we can see how discrepancies between desired saving and investment force changes in that level. Figure 1 is the familiar Keynesian cross dia-gram. (There was exactly one diagram in all of Keynes' *General Theory,* and it was a description of Classical interest theory! The figure shown here was made popular by Paul Samuelson.) The level of pro-duction or income (in dollars) is measured on the horizontal axis, and expenditures (in dollars) on the vertical axis. The line drawn from the origin at an angle of 45° marks off equal magnitudes on each axis (remember isosceles triangles from basic geometry?); hence, it traces the equilibrium condition $E = Y$, or expenditure equal to production.

Expenditure takes two forms: consumption and investment (we'll ignore the government for a while). Keynes argued that consumption spending (C) depends mainly on the level of income (Y)—more income, more consumption. In Figure 1, therefore, desired consumption is a simple linear function of Y:

$$C = a + bY$$

The letter b is the slope of the line, or $\Delta C/\Delta Y$, the change in consump-tion per unit change in income (see point X in the figure). It is called the marginal propensity to consume and is assumed to be less than 1.

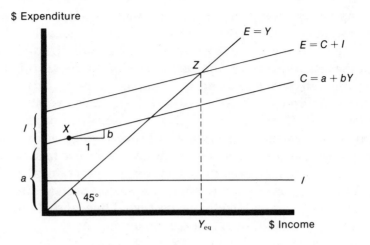

FIGURE 1 / Spending determines income.

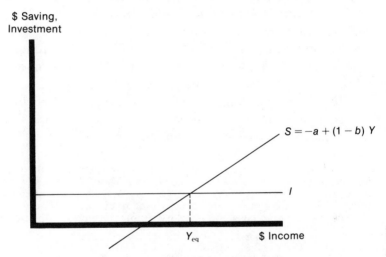

FIGURE 2 / Saving and investment determine income.

For example, if b is .8, that means an increase in Y of $100 raises C by $80. (It also means that saving goes up by $20.)

The a in the consumption function is the constant term. It records the level of C if Y were zero (presumably people eat even if they have no income—many of us have relatives like that), and it also sums up all other influences on consumption besides income. For example, if you owned Xerox when it was Haloid (only as far back as 1958), you would now be consuming a lot more than if you owned Penn Central when it was Solvent (1969). Thus, the consumption function might shift up or down, recorded by larger or smaller values for a, if people are wealthier or poorer, although our equation still says they would consume $8 out of every $10 *increment* in earned income.

As far as investment *(I)* is concerned, Keynes agreed with the Classics that it is a function of the rate of interest on bonds. Entrepreneurs compare the expected rate of return on a prospective investment with the rate of interest.[2] They invest as long as the rate of return exceeds the rate of interest and continue up to the point at which the expected return on the last investment just equals the rate of interest. If the rate of interest declines then investment projects with lower expected returns become profitable, hence investment will increase. For now we take the rate of interest as given. We also take expectations as given, which is an even more questionable proposition. Under such conditions, assume that investment is some constant amount (say $200 billion), as indicated by the horizontal line labeled *I* in Figure 1.

Equilibrium output is represented by the line $E = Y$, where total desired expenditure *(E)* equals total production Y. Total desired expenditure is the sum of desired C and desired I, or, in Figure 1, line $E = C + I$, which is the vertical addition of C $(= a + bY)$ and I. The point at which the total desired expenditure line $(E = C + I)$ crosses the expenditure-equals-production line $(E = Y)$ is equilibrium income (Y_{eq}). Point Z in Figure 1 is an example. At the level of production Y_{eq} desired expenditure equals production.

It is also true that *desired* saving equals desired investment at that same income level. Desired saving is given by the difference between income and desired consumption (i.e., $S = Y - C$). It can be

---

[2] The rate of return on an investment is determined by the expected future dollar revenues on the project and the current cost of the investment. In particular, if an investment is expected to yield $105 next year and requires a cash outlay of $100, we can calculate the rate of return quite simply. It is that rate of discount which equates the expected future revenues with the current cost, or $100 = \dfrac{105}{1 + q}$, where q is the rate of discount or, in our terminology, the rate of return. In our case it is clearly equal to .05, or 5 percent. We call q the rate of discount because it reduces (discounts) the $105 that is due next year to its current value (time is money). See Chapter 5 for a similar discussion.

Looked at another way, $100 put out at 5 percent for 1 year (100×1.05) produces $105 one year hence. This perspective also gives a clue as to how one ought to treat revenues two years hence. Namely, $100 left at 5 percent for two years produces 100×1.05 after one year, or $105, which is then reinvested and generates $110.25 after the next year ($105 \times 1.05 = $110.25). In general, therefore, if R_2 is the expected revenue two years from now, it must be discounted twice, or

$$C = \frac{R_2}{(1 + q)(1 + q)} = \frac{R_2}{(1 + q)^2}$$

The general formula for the rate of return is as follows. If revenues of $R_1, R_2 \ldots R_n$ are expected over the next n years, then the rate of discount q which equates C, the current cost, to the expected stream of revenues, as in

$$C = \frac{R_1}{(1 + q)} + \frac{R_2}{(1 + q)^2} + \cdots + \frac{R_n}{(1 + q)^n}$$

is called the rate of return on the investment project. Relax—you have at least 13 seconds to perform the necessary computations.

measured by the vertical difference between the 45° line and the consumption function. In Figure 1 the only point at which saving (the vertical difference between the 45° line and the consumption function) equals investment (the difference between the $E = C + I$ line and the consumption function) is at income Y_{eq}.

In Figure 2 we have plotted the saving function explicitly, where Y is measured along the horizontal axis and dollars saved or invested are on the vertical axis. Saving is defined as $Y - C$, so that desired saving, S, equals $Y - (a + bY)$. Rearranging terms (and factoring the Y term) gives:

$$S = -a + (1 - b)Y$$

which is called the saving function. The marginal propensity to save equals 1 minus the marginal propensity to consume (out of each dollar increment in Y, one spends b cents and saves $1 - b$ cents). From Figure 2 it is also clear that only at income Y_{eq} is desired saving equal to investment. At higher levels of income, desired saving exceeds desired investment; at lower levels of income, desired saving is less than desired investment.

Changes in GNP

Will production and income stay at level Y_{eq} in Figure 1 forever? It will if the consumption function (and hence the saving function) remains where it is, and if desired investment is also unchanged. Is that good? Yes, *if* Y_{eq} is the full employment level of economic activity. But Keynes not only wouldn't guarantee that it would be full employment, he was convinced that it would only be a fortuitous accident if it were. He reasoned that the level of economic activity is subject to wide swings because the level of investment is highly unstable. The consumption function was quite stable—you could always count on the dumb household sector to consume a predictable percentage of its income. But if entrepreneurs got uptight about future sales prospects—especially about what other businessmen were planning to do—then desired investment spending would decline and GNP would fall.

There are two ways to see *how far* GNP declines when desired investment spending falls. Let us first look at what happens in terms of total spending (investment and consumption) when desired investment falls—the wide angle approach of Figure 1. We can then

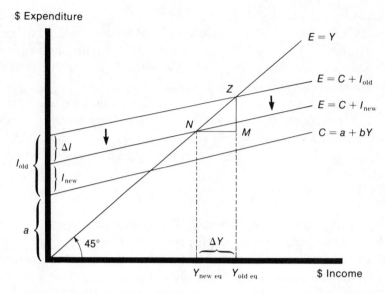

FIGURE 3 / A decline in investment spending reduces Y by a multiple of the change in investment.

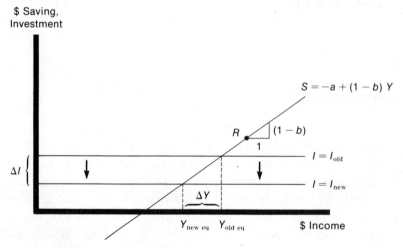

FIGURE 4 / A decline in investment spending reduces Y by a multiple of the change in investment.

look at it from the standpoint of the investment-saving relationship—the isolated-camera on S and I of Figure 2.

In Figure 3 we have replotted Figure 1's equilibrium point Z and the equilibrium income associated with the old total spending function $E = C + I_{old}$. If desired investment now falls to I_{new}, then the total desired spending function declines to $E = C + I_{new}$, the new equilibrium point is at N, and income declines to $Y_{new\ eq}$. The decline in income is written as ΔY (the change in Y), and is measured by the change in income along the horizontal axis or by the distance MN

(constructed parallel to the horizontal axis). As can be seen in Figure 3, the decline in income *exceeds* the decline in investment: the decline in income is ZM, which is equal to MN by construction, while the drop in investment is only part of ZM.

Why does income change by some *multiple* of the change in investment spending? Quite simply, because when investment changes and income begins to decrease (or increase), there is a further *induced* change in consumer spending. Consumption is a function of income, and whenever there is a change in Y, consumption spending is affected by the amount $b\Delta Y$, where b is the marginal propensity to consume.

How large is the ΔY associated with a particular ΔI? GNP will change by the sum of the changes in both components of expenditure, namely $\Delta I + \Delta C$. Algebraically:

$$\Delta Y = \Delta I + \Delta C$$

But we know that, after all is said and done, $\Delta C = b\Delta Y$ (from our consumption function). Substituting $b\Delta Y$ for ΔC we have:

$$\Delta Y = \Delta I + b\Delta Y$$

We can now solve for the unknown value of ΔY by isolating the ΔY terms on the left side. We do this by subtracting $b\Delta Y$ from each side, which yields:

$$\Delta Y - b\Delta Y = \Delta I$$

Factoring the ΔY terms on the left side gives us:

$$\Delta Y(1 - b) = \Delta I$$

Dividing both sides by $(1 - b)$ produces:

$$\Delta Y = \Delta I \frac{1}{1 - b}$$

where $1/(1 - b)$ is known as the *multiplier*. If b, the marginal propensity to consume, equals .8, then the change in income will be 5 times the initial change in investment. If $b = .5$, the change in income will be 2 times the initial ΔI.[3]

---

[3] The multiplier is sometimes derived by more explicit use of the successive rounds of consumption flowing from the initial ΔI. This is called period analysis, and it goes something like this. Initially ΔI produces a direct change in income, ΔY, equal to the ΔI. But then consumption changes by $b\Delta Y$ (which is equal to $b\Delta I$). This leads to a further change in consumption, $b(b\Delta I)$. This goes on, with the successive additions to GNP getting smaller and smaller because b is less than unity, hence b^2 is smaller than b, b^3 is smaller than b^2, and so on. The total ΔY is equal to the initial change in investment plus all of the subsequent changes in consumption (which stem from the initial $\Delta I = \Delta Y$). Or $\Delta Y = \Delta I + b\Delta I + b^2\Delta I + b^3\Delta I + \ldots + b^n\Delta I$. The right-hand side is a geometric progression whose sum is given by

$$\Delta I \times \frac{(1 - b^n)}{(1 - b)}$$

(*see next page*)

The second way of looking at this process is to impose our desired S equals desired I condition for equilibrium. In Figure 4 we see that at income $Y_{old\ eq}$ investment I_{old} equals desired saving. When investment falls to I_{new} and income is still at $Y_{old\ eq}$, desired saving exceeds desired investment and income must fall. Income falls enough to reduce desired saving until it is equal to investment. But we know from our saving function (see point R in Figure 4) exactly how much saving changes per unit ΔY:

$$\Delta S = (1 - b)\Delta Y$$

Since desired ΔS must equal desired ΔI in equilibrium, we can impose the following condition:

$$\Delta I = \Delta S$$

and then directly relate ΔI to ΔY by substituting $(1 - b)\Delta Y$ for ΔS. Hence:

$$\Delta I = (1 - b)\Delta Y$$

Dividing both sides by $(1 - b)$ produces:

$$\Delta Y = \Delta I \frac{1}{1 - b}$$

which, to our great chagrin, is the same multiplier formula as before.

Autonomous Versus Induced Changes in GNP

Figures 3 and 4 suggest that anything that shifts the *position* of the total desired spending function will alter GNP. Such shifts in the position of the spending function are produced by *autonomous* spending changes (autonomous = independent—in our case, independent of GNP). The larger the size of the autonomous change in spending, the greater will be the change in economic activity.

Since b is less than unity, b^n approaches zero as n gets large, hence we have

$$\Delta Y = \Delta I \times \frac{1}{(1 - b)}$$

which (surprisingly enough) is the same expression we derived in the text! These successive rounds of consumption were lumped together in the text into one $b\Delta Y$, by saying "after all is said and done," while here we build it up from each round of ΔY.

But the multiplier story was based on the fact that autonomous spending changes also *induce* further changes in spending—in our case, via the consumption function. The larger the propensity to spend out of increments in income, or the larger the *slope* of the spending function (the larger is b), the greater will be the induced change in spending, and thus the greater will be ΔY.

Now you can see why Keynes divided spending into the two categories of consumption and investment. What he was really interested in was induced versus autonomous spending decisions. He argued that consumption spending is largely induced, while investment spending is largely autonomous (independent of income, but a function of the expected rate of return on capital and the rate of interest). Of course, investment prospects might be influenced by sales (current and future), which are certainly related to GNP. Similarly, desired consumption may change independently of current income—the constant term in the consumption function, a, shifts when Xerox goes from $1 per share to $100 per share. Nevertheless, Keynes still felt consumer spending was largely induced (by Y), while investment spending was largely independent (of Y).

It is worth noting that the multiplier expression derived above can be modified quite simply to take account of other sources of ΔY. In particular, ΔY is related to *any* autonomous change in spending (ΔA) by the same $1/(1 - b)$ factor. Or:

$$\Delta Y = \Delta A \, \frac{1}{1 - b}$$

For example, if the consumption function shifts upward, then A equals the difference between the old and new levels of autonomous consumption spending. Just like ΔI, this produces a direct change in Y which then causes further changes in Y via the conventional reaction of consumption to income.

The great problem of macroeconomics, according to Keynes, was that changes in autonomous spending would spark fluctuations in economic activity—rather wide fluctuations, via the multiplier, if the induced component of expenditure were large. These wide fluctuations in GNP would be associated with unemployment when GNP fell below its full employment level as a result of a decline in autonomous spending, and with inflation if there were an increase in autonomous spending at a time when GNP was already at the full employment level. What to do? The Classical response to such a situation was to do nothing—laissez-faire. Keep hands off and let the long-run work things out. But that was not the Keynesian response.

Government to the Rescue

Keynes was the first of the big-time spenders. If the private sector doesn't spend enough to keep everyone employed, "let George do it" (King George, of course). Government spending and taxation could be manipulated to offset the autonomous forces buffeting GNP and thereby restore full employment.

It is not very difficult to add government expenditure and taxes to our simple model. GNP was defined in Chapter 4 as equal to the total of all expenditures in the economy—consumption, investment, and government:

$$C + I + G = Y$$

Assuming that government spending is some fixed level, G, we can simply add another line to Figure 1 for autonomous government spending. This is done in Figure 5, where $Y_{new\ eq}$ is the new equilibrium level of income when government spending is added.

"There are plenty of jobs around. People just don't want to work."

Drawing by Drucker; © 1972 The New Yorker Magazine, Inc.

If the original level of economic activity was already full employment, then government spending equal to G would be inflationary. The government, therefore, usually finances such expenditures by taxation. Taxes do not lower spending directly, in the same sense that government expenditure directly changes spending. Rather, taxes reduce the amount of income that households have available for consumption expenditure. Consumption is not so much a function of GNP but of *disposable* income, where that is defined as equal to income minus taxes $(Y - T)$. We have, therefore, a new consumption function, written as:

$$C = a + b(Y - T)$$

To see how taxes affect GNP, let's carry out the multiplication of b times Y and T. We can then write the consumption function as:

$$C = a + bY - bT$$

It is easy to see from either way of writing the consumption function that when taxes go up by \$10, consumption declines by b times that amount (or if $b = .8$, by \$8). The reason is quite simple: People treat a dollar of income taken away by the government the same way as any other decline of a dollar's worth of income—they reduce consumption expenditure by the marginal propensity to consume times the change.

Taxes, as we pointed out in Chapter 4, introduce the same type of leakage between income and spending as does saving. In fact, from the standpoint of our model it makes no difference whether people reduce their consumption because they just happen to feel like it or because the government says it would be nice if they did (curiously, if you don't feel like it in the second case, you wind up getting a striped uniform and free room and board for between one and five years). In either case, the consumption function shifts downward. Figure 6 shows the equilibrium levels of GNP with and without taxes. Figures 5 and 6 also suggest that changes in both government spending and taxes produce multiplier effects on GNP. In this respect they are just like any other kind of autonomous expenditure. But there is one big difference: Both taxes and government spending can be changed by government policy.[4]

The moral of the model of GNP including government expenditure and taxation is that the economy need not be buffeted about by autonomous changes in investment spending. Entrepreneurs may cut their desired investment spending if they get nervous, but nothing

---

[4] We will ignore the fact that taxes vary with the level of income. It does change the nature of the model slightly, but for our purposes we are better off without that complication.

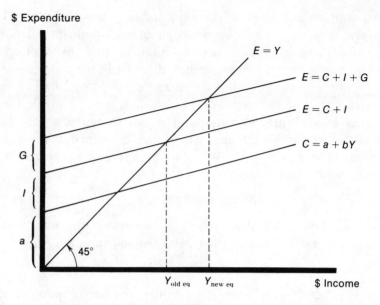

FIGURE 5 / Adding government spending raises income.

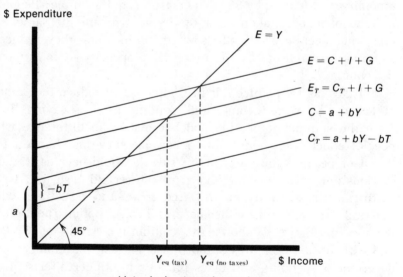

FIGURE 6 / Introducing taxes lowers income.

need happen to GNP as long as the government keeps its collective head and either increases *its* spending, or lower taxes so that consumers can increase theirs. In either case, the autonomous decline in investment spending could be offset by government *fiscal policy* (fiscal means pertaining to the public treasury or revenue, from the Latin *fiscus*). Whether or not the timing and magnitude of changes in *G* and *T* would be appropriate, given the institutional setup, is another matter (and will be discussed in later chapters). But the possibility of improving on the workings of the free market is certainly evident.

This returns us to an issue mentioned earlier: Is fiscal policy even necessary? Why doesn't income remain at full employment, with desired saving and investment brought into equality via fluctuations in the rate of interest, as the Classical economists said would happen? Why did Keynes, a truly Classical economist before he became a Keynesian, reject the Classical theory of interest rate determination? And what did he put in its place?

Money and the Rate of Interest

Our exposition of the Keynesian model so far is very much like its Classical counterpart in at least one respect—money doesn't matter. While the Classics said economic activity was set at the full employment level, and Keynes said it would settle at the point where total desired expenditure equaled production—which might be less than full employment—up to this point *neither* model has the money supply affecting real economic activity. The Classics, as we saw in the previous chapter, deflected its impact to the price level. Keynes, the financial wizard of Cambridge, took a bolder position: The rate of interest is a monetary phenomenon. It is not determined by saving and investment, the way the Classics said, but by the supply of and demand for money. Keynes also said that money might affect the level of economic activity, but only to the extent that it first influenced the rate of interest. Changes in the rate of interest would then alter desired investment spending, and thereby change the level of GNP.

The first order of business in investigating the rate of interest is to establish the framework by noting how Keynes divided the decision-making in his model of macroeconomic activity. So far, the analysis of income and expenditure revolves around two decisions— (1) household choice between spending income or saving it, with the latter simply defined as nonconsumption; (2) business firm decisions regarding the level of investment spending. These parts of the Keynesian system deal only with *flows:* consumption, saving, investment, and income over a given time period. It is, in the accountant's terminology, the "income statement" of the economy, with an implicit time dimension. We have also noted that none of these decisions involve any financial transactions; they deal only in *real* goods and services.

Money introduces an entirely new dimension to the macro model. Money is a *financial asset,* which is held in an individual's portfolio just as one holds a savings account at a bank, a corporate equity, or a Treasury bond. In other words, money is part of an individual's wealth—part of his balance sheet, in accountant's terms. The interest rate is determined by the third decision in the Keynesian scheme of things—(3) decisions of the public regarding the composition of its financial asset holdings.

Let's divide the public's portfolio into two types of assets: money and everything else. As we've seen before, money can be defined in many specific ways. For our purposes, the main distinction is that money has a fixed rate of interest, without any risk. Sometimes the rate is fixed at zero, as with currency; but that's not necessarily so, as with demand deposits. The key is that no capital losses or gains are incurred on the asset called money. Money is also used as the medium of exchange (to finalize transactions). Thus money is the most liquid of all assets, where liquidity is defined as the ability to turn an asset into the medium of exchange quickly with little or no loss in value. For lack of a better name, we'll call all other assets "bonds." The price of a bond can vary in terms of the medium of exchange, so the owner can suffer capital losses or reap capital gains. The realized rate of interest on a bond can be above or below what was expected at the time it was purchased, as we saw in Chapters 5 and 6.

Money is a riskless asset, and bonds are risky assets. If people are risk averters—that is, if they dislike risk—then they will demand a higher expected return (interest rate) on risky assets compared with riskless assets. Thus a choice is necessary: How much of one's portfolio should go into money and how much into bonds?

It is important to note that the more bonds and less money held in a portfolio, the greater the uncertainty over total portfolio yield. For example, if I have $100, all in cash, my return is certain. If I put it all into bonds yielding 10 percent, I expect my return to be just that: 10 percent. But if interest rates rise substantially after my purchase, my $100 bond might be worth (could be sold for) only $75. In this case my expected 10 percent yield turns out to be minus 15 percent— the $10 in interest minus the capital loss of $25. If I had held $50 in cash and invested only $50 in bonds, I would have lost only half as much. Thus, more bonds in a portfolio means more risk.

Our composite bond in this analysis includes all risky assets— equities, corporate bonds, municipals, even long-term government bonds. We'll assume that an efficient combination of risky assets has been derived—using the principles of Chapter 6. In Chapters 30 and 31 we'll return to the structure of yields on risky securities. For now we are concerned only with the choice between money and the composite bond of Keynes. It is this decision that determines the overall expected return—the "average" interest rate on bonds.

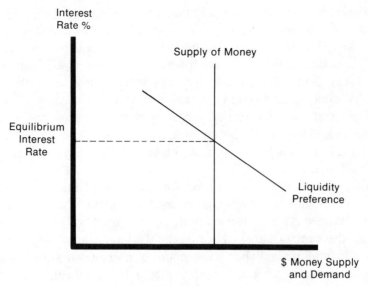

Interest
Rate %

Supply of Money

Equilibrium
Interest
Rate

Liquidity
Preference

$ Money Supply
and Demand

FIGURE 7 / Keynesian interest theory.

The demand for money, called *liquidity preference* by Keynes, is a function of the rate of interest. In Figure 7 the horizontal axis measures the quantity of money, while the rate of interest is on the vertical axis. The demand-for-money function is negatively sloped— the smaller the rate of interest, the larger the amount of money demanded.

There are a number of reasons for this negative relationship between quantity of money demanded and rate of interest. Keynes argued that people had an idea of some "normal" rate of interest, as though the rate of interest were attached to its "normal" level by a rubber band. When the rate of interest *declines*, more and more people become convinced that it will snap back to its "normal" level, i.e. that interest rates *will rise in the future*. If they hold bonds when rates are rising, they will suffer capital losses. In other words, the public, trying to avoid capital losses, would want to hold fewer bonds —and more money—as interest rates decline. This relationship has been called the speculative demand for liquidity because people are speculating on future bond prices.

A less restrictive approach to the negative relationship between demand for speculative money balances and the interest rate stresses interest rates as compensation for risk bearing.[5] A high rate of interest

[5] This approach was first formally presented in James Tobin's article, "Liquidity Preference as a Behaviour Toward Risk," *Review of Economic Studies* (1958). It is less restrictive than Keynes's original discussion, because it does not require people to expect a "normal" level of interest rates. It also puts the money versus bonds decision within a general model of portfolio choice, as we saw in Chapter 6.

means that the cost of being liquid and safe (holding money) is great, in terms of the interest forgone. A high interest rate is an inducement to hold a large portion of one's assets in bonds (bond demand is high) and only a little in cash. At lower interest rates, the opportunity cost of (what one gives up by) holding money is much less. Since it feels good to be liquid, the amount of money demanded is greater at lower rates of interest. In more formal terms, people are risk averse—they don't like risk. There must be an inducement to hold a riskier portfolio, i.e., one with a larger amount of bonds. The inducement is a higher rate of interest.

Either approach to the demand for money explains its negative relationship to interest rates (as interest rates fall the amount of money demanded rises). Coupled with a fixed supply of money, determined by the central bank (a rather bold assumption), the rate of interest is in equilibrium when the amount of money demanded equals the supply. We know that the interest rate is in equilibrium then (as in Figure 7), because below the equilibrium rate the demand for money exceeds the fixed supply. If the rate of interest momentarily fell *below* the equilibrium rate, people would want more money than they have and would try to sell bonds to get it. The attempt to sell bonds drives down bond prices and interest rates up, until—at the equilibrium rate—everyone is satisfied with their portfolio of money and bonds.

At a rate of interest *above* the equilibrium rate, people would have more money than they want. They would try to get rid of their excess money balances by purchasing bonds. Bond prices would be driven up and interest rates down, until the natives are no longer restless and are again happy with their holdings of money and bonds. This is at the equilibrium interest rate, of course.[6]

---

[6] It should not be too difficult to see why Keynesian analysis can look at the supply of and demand for money, rather than looking at the bond market directly, and say that the rate of interest is determined by equilibrium in the money market. As long as the total size of the public's portfolio, its wealth, is fixed—and in the short-run this is a reasonable assumption—then a change in the demand for money relative to supply would be reflected in a one-to-one relationship by an opposite change in the demand for bonds relative to supply. In other words, if the demand for money goes up, it necessarily implies that people want to hold fewer bonds, and vice versa. Looking only at the supply and demand for money does not cost us any information in this scheme of things. A change in one market is automatically reflected in the other.

A more sensitive assumption embedded in this analysis is that money and bonds are substitutes only for each other: An excess demand for one means there is an excess supply of the other. Neither are considered direct substitutes for real goods and services. This turns out to be a crucial distinction between Monetarists and Keynesians, as we shall see in Chapter 20.

Monetary Policy

What causes the rate of interest to change? Clearly, if either the demand for money or the supply of money shifts position, the equilibrium interest rate would change. For now, assume that the money demand function is given, and let us examine the impact of changes in the money supply on interest rates and economic activity.

In Figure 8, let's start out with the money supply at $60 billion

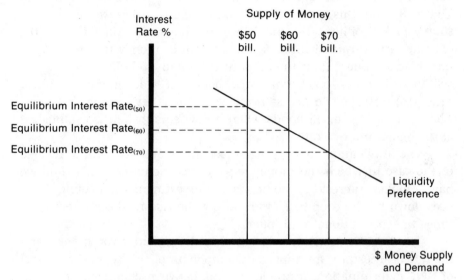

FIGURE 8 / Effect of changing the money supply on the interest rate.

and the equilibrium interest rate as indicated. Assume the central bank increases the money supply (the magic word, as Captain Marvel said, is Shazam) from $60 to $70 billion. At the old rate of interest, the amount of money that people are now holding (thanks to central bank largess) is greater than the amount they want to hold. People try to dispose of their excess money balances (reduce their liquidity) by buying bonds, driving up the price of bonds and the interest rate down until the interest rate has fallen sufficiently to make people content to hold the new level of cash (and stop trying to buy bonds). This happy state of affairs occurs at the lower equilibrium interest rate $_{(70)}$, when the amount of money demanded now equals the new supply.[7]

[7] Since some forms of money balances pay interest—such as some demand deposits—it is at least conceivable that the larger supply of money could be absorbed by a higher interest payment on money balances rather than a lower interest rate on bonds. The excess supply of money requires only a decrease in the differential between the rate on bonds and the rate on money (so that people are induced to hold relatively more of the latter). One reason all bond

The implications of the increased money supply for economic activity are clear—a lower interest rate on bonds means higher investment spending, *ceteris paribus* (a key phrase meaning everything else held constant, often used by economists to produce unexpected results and confound the man in the street). In terms of our GNP-determining diagrams earlier in the chapter, the investment line shifts up and GNP goes up by the increase in I (induced by the decline in the interest rate) times the multiplier.

A decrease in the money supply produces just the opposite results. We start once again with a money supply of $60 billion in Figure 8, and this time let the central bank *decrease* the money supply to $50 billion (the magic word is obviously Mazahs). At the old equilibrium rate of interest, the amount of money that people are now holding is less than the amount they want to hold. People try to sell bonds in order to get more cash, bond prices decline, and interest rates rise until people are satisfied with their new money balances. They stop trying to sell bonds when a new equilibrium is established at the higher interest rate (50).[8]

The implications for aggregate economic activity are the reverse of the case in which the money supply was increased. This time we have a higher interest rate on bonds and investment will decline; GNP goes down by the drop in I (induced by the rise in the interest rate) times the conventional multiplier.

The negative relationship between the demand for money and the rate of interest is an important component of the Keynesian model of GNP determination. It provides a link between changes in the supply of money and the level of economic activity.

But what Keynes giveth, Keynes can taketh away. If an increath

---

rates fall, rather than the rate on money rising, has to do with the zero interest rate on currency and the fact that currency and demand deposits exchange on a one-to-one basis. Thus, the rate of interest paid by banks on demand deposit balances cannot wander very far from the zero rate paid on currency. As a result, the major burden of adjustment to changes in the supply of money falls on all other rates of interest, rather than the own-rate on money. For a similar discussion, see James Tobin "A General Equilibrium Approach to Monetary Theory," *Journal of Money Credit and Banking* (February 1969).

[8] An interesting sidelight: When the interest rate is above the equilibrium level, the public has more money than it wants and it tries to get rid of its excess cash (by buying bonds). When the interest rate is below the equilibrium level, the public wants more money than it has and it tries to get its hands on more cash (by selling bonds). *But it never succeeds, because the supply of money—which is the amount the public has—is determined not by the public but by the Federal Reserve.* When people buy or sell bonds to one another, all they do is shuffle the money supply around among themselves, moving it from one pocket to another. What the public *does* succeed in doing is changing the price of bonds—or the interest rate—until it reaches the (equilibrium) level where people are *content* to hold the same amount of money they held all along. This probably has deep philosophical implications, but we are not sure what they are.

in the money supply does *not* lower the interest rate, investment spending will not be affected. Keynes proceeded to question the efficacy of monetary policy under certain conditions. He argued, for example, that at very low interest rates the money demand function becomes completely flat. In Figure 9 it is easy to see that a very flat demand for

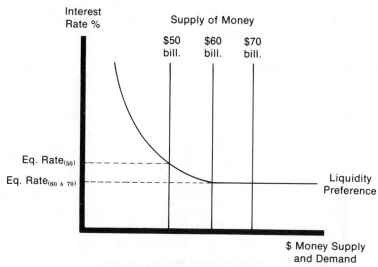

FIGURE 9 / Keynesian liquidity trap.

money function means that increases in the money supply could no longer reduce the rate of interest. In particular, an increase in the money supply from $50 billion to $60 billion lowers the interest rate, but a further increase to $70 billion fails to produce any additional decline.

What causes the money demand function to enjoy the horizontal position? Keynes argued that at very low interest rates everyone would expect interest rates to rise to more "normal" levels in the future. In other words, everyone would expect bond prices to fall, therefore no one would want to hold bonds and the demand for liquidity (money) would be infinite. Any increase in money supply would simply be held by the public (hoarded), and none of the increased liquidity would spill over to the bond market. No one, in fact, would willingly hold bonds. In this "liquidity trap," as Keynes referred to the flat portion of the money demand function, monetary policy does not alter interest rates and therefore is completely ineffective.

More generally, the flatter the liquidity preference function, the less effective is monetary policy in changing interest rates, hence in influencing GNP. In Figure 10 there are two money demand functions, one of which is relatively flat and the other relatively steep. The demand for money is much more sensitive to a change in the rate of interest when the liquidity preference function is relatively flat. Points X and Y illustrate this quite clearly; for equal changes in the interest rate, the change in the amount of money demand is larger when the demand for money is flat.

If we start out with a money supply of $50 billion and increase it

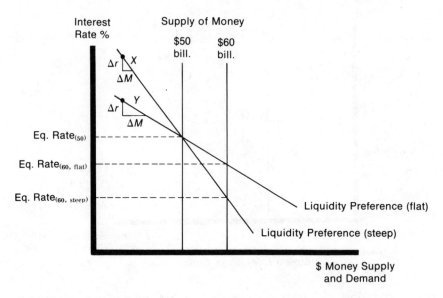

FIGURE 10 / Monetary policy and the slope of the liquidity preference function.

to $60 billion, the decline in the rate of interest is much less with the flat demand function. The reason is as follows: When the money supply increases, there is an excess of supply over demand at the old rate of interest. The interest rate falls as long as supply exceeds demand. But with a highly interest-sensitive (flat) demand for money function, even a small decline in the rate of interest increases the demand for money a lot. The equality between the amount of money demanded and the supply is restored, therefore, with a smaller decline in the interest rate. With a relatively interest-insensitive (steep) demand for money function, it takes a greater change in the interest rate to expand the amount demanded until it equals the new supply.

It should also be obvious that monetary policy will have a larger impact on GNP if *investment* is very responsive to changes in the rate of interest. A highly interest-sensitive investment function means that for a small change in the rate of interest the amount of investment spending changes a lot. For a given change in the rate of interest due to a change in the money supply, therefore, the level of GNP changes more with a highly sensitive investment function.

260

Most simple economic models assume that expectations are exogenous variables; that is, they are determined outside the system. This one is no exception. An important implicit assumption is that changes in the money supply are imposed by our central bank, the Federal Reserve, and that such policy changes are unanticipated. Under such circumstances, monetary policy alters the interest rate by more or less, depending upon the various slopes just described.

But whether an increase or decrease in the stock of money causes a *simultaneous* movement in interest rates in the predicted direction depends *crucially* on whether or not the change in policy was anticipated. In particular, if everyone expects the Federal Reserve to cut back on the money supply next week or next month, a change in interest rates is likely to occur beforehand, with little or no effect at the time the money supply is actually altered. The reasoning is simple: if everyone expects the Fed to reduce the money supply in the future—and therefore expects interest rates to rise—then profit-maximizing bondholders will try to sell bonds *now* to avoid expected capital losses. Bond sales will drive down bond prices, driving up interest rates until they just equal the expected rate next period. Thus, when the money supply is, in fact, cut back next week or next month, rates don't move at all.

Incorporating expectations about policy movements in our model is possible but cumbersome. It is illustrated by a shift in the demand for money function at every interest rate. In our particular example, when saying that bondholders want to sell to avoid capital losses, we are saying, in effect, that the demand for bonds decreases—or, in terms of our picture, that the demand for money increases at every rate of interest. That means the money demand function shifts to the right, as in Figure 11 in the next section, increasing the rate of interest with the same supply of money.

Thus, an anticipated monetary policy will change interest rates before it is implemented. This is not especially surprising once it is put into the framework of our model, but it can be troublesome for policy makers when portfolio managers get into the habit of forecasting stabilization behavior. More on this in the chapters on Monetarists versus Keynesians.

Transactions Demand and Monetary Policy

The concept of a speculative demand for money, related to the rate of interest, was a Keynesian innovation. Prior to Keynes, Classical

economists had emphasized that the only reason people would want
to hold money was for transactions purposes—to buy goods and services—as we saw in the previous chapter. An increase in GNP leads to
an increase in the amount of money demanded (at every rate of
interest), because people need more cash to carry out the higher
level of transactions. Keynes also acknowledged this transactions demand, although he did not himself appear to realize all of its implications.[9] One implication is that one cannot, as Keynes did, take the
interest rate as fixed when income changes, for a change in income
will alter the demand for money and thereby alter the interest rate.

Figure 11 shows how a change in the demand for money
(at every rate of interest) affects the interest rate. We start out with
a given money supply and a given money demand (liquidity preference) function. Together they determine the equilibrium interest rate.

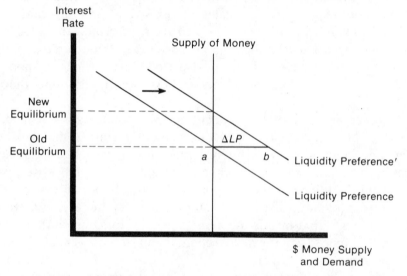

FIGURE 11 / A shift in the demand for money changes the interest rate.

Now suppose that people become more nervous than normal, perhaps
because they expect a decrease in money supply. They seek ultimate
relief by building up the proportion of cash in their portfolios. In other
words, at every rate of interest people want more money (and fewer
bonds) than before. Say the demand for money increases (ΔLP) by
the amount ab. This happens at each rate of interest, so that we now
have a new money demand function to the right of the old. At the
old equilibrium rate of interest, there is now a larger amount of money

---

[9] Keynes also discussed a precautionary demand for money: People hold
cash to provide for unforeseen contingencies. This demand was considered constant or was lumped together with transactions balances.

demanded than the fixed supply. To get more cash, people try to sell bonds, driving bond prices lower and interest rates higher until a higher equilibrium interest rate is established. The case of a decrease in the demand for money can be treated symmetrically. The money demand function shifts to the left and the interest rate declines.

Something similar happens when the level of income changes. Say income rises. People now demand more money balances at every rate of interest to carry out the higher level of transactions, the demand for money function shifts to the right, and the rate of interest rises. In an economy that is growing, perhaps because investment spending is rising, the rate of interest would rise because of the increase in transactions demand for money. Unless, of course, the central bank expands the supply of money to provide for those transactions balances.

Now you know why we said back in Chapter 1 that "easy" or "tight" money is not really a matter of increases or decreases in the money supply in an absolute sense, but rather increases or decreases relative to demand. In a growing economy, the money supply is likely to increase because the demand for money will rise along with the growth in GNP. Unless the central bank increases the money supply, interest rates will rise.

The transactions demand for money is probably affected by the interest rate as well as by income. It is very likely that higher interest rates reduce the demand for transactions balances. For example, assume you are paid $2,000 monthly (probably dropped out of school and became an apprentice plumber). You deposit the entire amount in the bank, spend it evenly over the month, and wind up at zero. Your *average* daily cash balance is $1,000. This is your transactions demand. But if interest rates on bonds were sufficiently high, you'd be willing to go to the cost and trouble to take half your salary at the beginning of the month ($1,000) and buy a bond, put the other $1,000 in your bank to be spent during the first fifteen days, and then when that runs out sell the bond and spend the second $1,000 over the last half of the month. What this means is that your average daily cash balance is only $500 (you go from $1,000 to zero evenly over fifteen days). What you gain from this is the higher interest on the funds invested in the bond market. And as long as the gain exceeds the costs, it's worth doing.

Your initial reaction might be: It would take an awfully high rate of interest to make me go through such shenanigans. That could be—but if you were a large corporation with a few million dollars in idle cash, the investment of that money could be very profitable. Most economists agree that the transactions demand for money, like the speculative demand, is a function of the rate of interest.[10] For some purposes it can be ignored or played down—but not when discussing long-run trends in velocity (see Chapter 24) and not if you are a corporate treasurer.

An interesting sidelight to the transactions demand discussion is the role played by credit cards. The easiest way to look at this is that credit cards permit a transaction to take place without holding a cash balance. In other words, one could theoretically invest all one's cash at the beginning of the month in bonds, pay for everything via those little plastic cards, and then at the end of the month sell the bond, put the proceeds into the bank, and write one check to the credit card company (which may even be the bank itself!). While this is an extreme example, it indicates how credit cards get into the model and how their growth affects the economy. Greater use of credit cards reduces the demand for money (at every interest rate), thereby lowering interest rates, permitting investment and GNP to increase.

Keynes and the Classical Economists

We have a number of apparent conflicts between the Keynesian analysis of this chapter and the Classical school discussed in the previous chapter. The latter maintained that total desired spending in the Keynesian sense would automatically tend toward that level which we call full employment. Keynes rejected that notion. The Classical economists were adherents of Say's law, while Keynesian economists concentrate on the determinants of consumption and investment expenditure in order to pinpoint the level of economic activity. The impact of money on the economy is described by Classical economists via velocity and the quantity theory, while Keynesians use liquidity preference theory.

Macroeconomics courses spend an entire semester analyzing these

---

[10] The interest sensitivity of transaction demand was first pointed out by William J. Baumol, "The Transactions Demand for Cash: An Inventory Theoretic Approach," *Quarterly Journal of Economics* (November 1952). For an application of modern cash management techniques stemming from Baumol, see Rita M. Maldonado and Lawrence S. Ritter, "Optimal Municipal Cash Management," *Review of Economics and Statistics* (November 1971). A somewhat more general treatment of household behavior is Robert J. Barro and Anthony M. Santomero, "Household Money Holdings and the Demand Deposit Rate," *Journal of Money, Credit, and Banking* (May 1972).

issues. In the end, the simple Classical and Keynesian analyses wind up as special cases of a highly complex world. Some of these details are discussed in the next chapter. But it is of sufficient interest to note that at least the conflict involving use of monetary velocity as a conceptual tool is more apparent than real.

In Chapter 1 the change in GNP relative to a change in the money supply was called the velocity of money. While the previous chapter suggested that velocity was a uniquely Classical concept, it can just as easily be used in the Keynesian framework. To Classical economists, velocity was fixed by the payment habits of the community. To Keynesians, it is influenced by the sensitivity of the demand for money to the interest rate and by the interest-responsiveness of investment spending, both of which determine the impact of money on GNP. Those who can't wait to see the implications of such factors for the monetary-fiscal policy debates between the Monetarists and Keynesians can go directly to Chapter 20. For those who prefer to formalize some of the analysis, Chapter 19 is a worthwhile investment (i.e., the discounted present value of the returns exceeds the costs).

Suggestions for Further Reading

Keynesian ideas all stem, of course, from John Maynard Keynes, *The General Theory of Employment, Interest, and Money* (New York: Harcourt, Brace, 1936). Having become a true classic (defined as a book that is no longer read, just referenced), it has been interpreted on many levels. One of the best is Alvin Hansen, *A Guide to Keynes* (New York: McGraw-Hill, 1953). A more advanced treatise is Axel Leijonhufvud (pronounced Leijonhufvud), *On Keynesian Economics and the Economics of Keynes* (Oxford University Press, 1968).

Chapter 19

The Keynesian Framework: II

WHY CONFUSE THINGS with a more sophisticated model of GNP determination? Is it worth the effort? Haven't we said that a good model is like a good map—it tells you how to get from one place to another without detailing every curve in the road, every bump in the terrain? True enough. But sometimes a few complications make life more interesting. Versatility is the password. Being able to put the model to more than one use is a desirable characteristic.

The more complex model of GNP determination set forth below is, indeed, multipurposed. Among its many attractions, it shows how monetary and fiscal policy interact with each other; it shows what determines the relative effectiveness of each; it provides a partial integration of the Classical and Keynesian systems into one conceptual framework; and it demonstrates the fundamental features distinguishing the Classical and Keynesian outlooks.

Money, Interest, and Income

In Chapter 17 we noted that the Classical economists stressed the transactions demand for money. Keynes, as we saw in the last chapter, also discussed this transactions demand, although he did not himself appear to have realized all of its ramifications. In particular, because transactions demand increases with income, the rate of interest rises as income rises. Thus, not only does the interest rate help to determine income, but in addition income helps to determine the interest rate.[1] Causation runs both ways—from the interest rate to income and from income to the interest rate. Fortunately, this is not an insurmountable problem. The economy winds up with a determinate level of each, but our model must be reformulated to take this into account.

We begin in Figure 1, with three alternative money demand functions, each associated with a different level of economic activity.[2] The liquidity preference function associated with Y_1 is for a level of GNP which is less than Y_2, which in turn is less than Y_3. Each level of GNP has its own liquidity preference function, because at higher income levels more money is demanded for transactions purposes (at every rate of interest). The horizontal distance between any two demand-for-money functions is equal to the difference in the demand for money at the two levels of GNP. If we use the classical formulation coming out of Cambridge (as discussed in Chapter 17), we can write:

$$\text{demand for money} = kY$$
$$\text{or}$$
$$\Delta \text{ demand for money} = k\Delta Y$$

The latter implies that the demand for money will change by k times the change in the level of GNP (where k equals, for example, .25). In terms of Figure 1, that means the horizontal distance between any two liquidity preference curves equals $k\Delta Y$.

The demand for money is really a function of two variables— income and the interest rate. The equilibrium condition (amount of money demanded = money supply) no longer provides an interest rate; rather, it provides combinations of income (Y) and the interest rate (r) which satisfy the condition that money demand equals money supply, *when the money supply is fixed.* In fact, according to Figure 1, a positive relationship between Y and r is needed to keep the amount of money demanded equal to the fixed money supply. A higher level of GNP (compare Y_2 with Y_1) is associated with a higher interest rate (r_2 versus r_1). This relationship between Y and r that satisfies the equilibrium condition in the money market is plotted in Figure 2, where the interest rate is still on the vertical axis but now we have

---

[1] The one exception is the liquidity trap, introduced in the last chapter, where the rate of interest is given and is independent of everything except the psychological state of the public.

[2] The discussion in the remainder of the chapter will be based on geometric analysis. For those who prefer algebra, the chapter appendix presents the entire model, and its implications, in equation form.

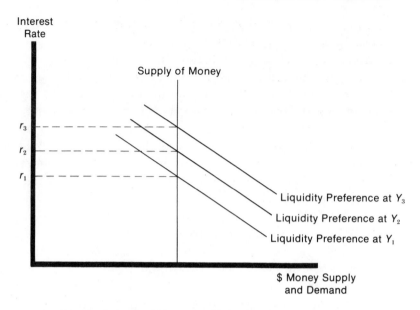

FIGURE 1 / How to derive the *LM* curve: at higher levels of income, the demand for money rises and so do interest rates.

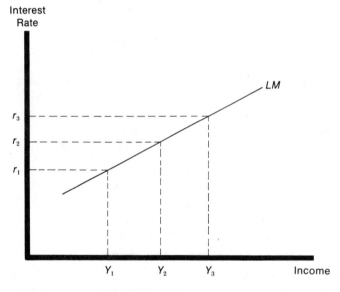

FIGURE 2 / The *LM* curve.

income on the horizontal axis. The line is labeled *LM* because it is the locus of combinations of Y and r that satisfy the *l*iquidity-preference-equals-*m*oney-supply equilibrium condition.

How should you "read" the *LM* curve? In either of two ways. For a series of alternative interest rates, it tells you what the resulting income would have to be to make the demand for money equal to the (fixed) supply of money. *At higher interest rates,* there is less money demanded, *so income must be higher* to increase the demand for transactions balances if the total demand for money is to remain equal to the (fixed) supply. *Or*, for a series of alternative income levels, it tells you what the resulting interest rate would have to be to make the demand for money equal to the fixed supply. *At higher income levels*, there is more transactions money desired, *so the interest rate must be higher* to shrink the demand for money balances if the total demand is to remain equal to the fixed supply.

Before you write to the folks back home and tell them that the wise men from Wall Street said that an increase in the interest rate raises GNP, or that an increase in GNP raises the interest rate, rest assured that nothing of the sort has been said—so far. In fact, we can't even determine Y and r as yet, much less say anything about how each of these economic variables changes. All we have is one relationship (equation or equilibrium condition) and two variables, Y and r, and you remember enough high school algebra to know that you need at least two equations to determine the equilibrium values of two variables.

We *will* produce another relationship between Y and r—based on the equilibrium condition in the market for goods and services (the $C + I + G = Y$ or the $I = S$ equilibrium condition). This great unification and solution, which will nearly blow your mind, is scheduled to take place in about ten pages. But before that cataclysmic experience, it will be helpful for subsequent policy discussions to elaborate on the factors determining the slope of the *LM* curve and shifts in its position. Both of these help determine the relative effectiveness of monetary and fiscal policy.

All About *LM*

The determinants of the slope of the *LM* curve are best illustrated by going over the reasons for its positive slope. Take point A in Figure 3. Assume that the amount of money demanded equals the fixed money supply at that point, hence combination Y_1 and r_1 lies on the *LM* curve. To see whether a second (Y, r) combination that also satisfies the equilibrium condition (money demand = money supply) lies above and to the right of A (like point B), or below and to the right (like point D), let us first pick a point C which differs from A only in the level of income.

At point C, the rate of interest is still r_1 but income is Y_2 (above Y_1). Since income is higher at point C than at point A, the transactions demand for money is greater at C. Since nothing else is changed, point *C* must have a larger demand for money than the (fixed) supply. To set matters right and restore equilibrium, the interest rate must *rise,* in order to reduce the demand for money and thereby restore the equality between demand and supply.

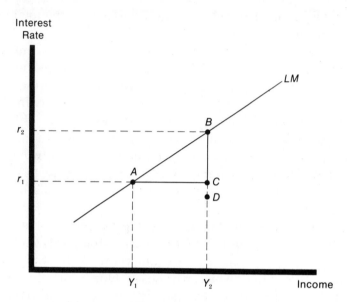

FIGURE 3 / The slope of the *LM* curve.

The slope of line *AB* (the *LM* curve) in Figure 3 is determined by two factors. *The first is the size of the gap between money demand and supply at point C.* If the increment in the amount of money demanded per unit ΔY is large, then the amount demanded will be a lot higher at *C* than at *A,* and the increase in *r* needed to restore equilibrium (to lower the amount demanded) will be large. In other words, if transactions demand is great, then the level of *r* needed to maintain demand-supply equality at Y_2 will be great, point *B* will be higher than otherwise, and the slope of the *LM* curve will be steeper.

The second factor influencing the slope of the LM curve is the interest-sensitivity of money demand. For a given excess of money demand over supply at point *C* in Figure 3, the greater the interest-sensitivity of liquidity preference, the *smaller* the necessary increase in the rate of interest to restore equilibrium. This is so because when liquidity preference is highly interest-sensitive, then even a small increase in *r* reduces the amount of money demanded by a lot. In other words, at Y_2 the rise in *r* needed to insure demand-supply equality will be smaller the greater is the sensitivity of demand to *r;* point *B* will be lower than otherwise, and the slope of the *LM* curve will be flatter.

To summarize: The slope of the *LM* curve will be steeper the greater is the income-sensitivity of the demand for money, and the less is the interest-sensitivity of demand for money; the *LM* curve will be flatter the less is the income-sensitivity of the demand for money, and the greater is the interest-sensitivity.

Monetary Policy and the *LM* Curve

What causes the *LM* curve to shift *position* (in contrast to a change in its slope)? It does get boring in the same position, so the monetary authorities come to the rescue. An increase in the supply of money moves the *LM* curve to the right, and a decrease in the money supply moves the *LM* curve to the left. By shifting the position of the *LM* curve, the Federal Reserve can increase or decrease the potential equilibrium level of GNP associated with a given interest rate. Let's see why a change in the money supply shifts the *LM* curve.

In Figure 4 we start with the *LM* curve associated with money supply M_1. All points on that curve satisfy the condition that the amount of money demanded $= M_1$. Take point a, with interest rate r_1 and income Y_1. Now increase the money supply to M_2. At point a the new larger money supply now exceeds the demand for money. What can restore equilibrium between the demand for money and money supply? Clearly, if *income* rises the transactions demand for money would go up, hence some point to the right of a, say point b, would now represent equilibrium between demand and supply. Therefore, the new *LM* curve, $LM(M_2)$, the one with combinations of Y and r that satisfy demand equal to the new larger money supply, must be to the right of the old *LM* curve. (A similar argument shows that the *LM* curve must shift to the left if there is a decline in money supply.)

We can say exactly how far to the right (or to the left) the new *LM* curve must be. If the supply of money increases by ΔM, the amount of money demanded must change by the same amount in order to restore equilibrium. But we know that the transactions demand for money changes by k times the change in income ($k\Delta Y$). So income must change until $k\Delta Y$ equals ΔM (assuming nothing else changes, which is what we are doing by looking at the horizontal differences between two *LM* curves—namely, the interest rate is being held constant). The demand for money will increase to match the enlarged supply when $k\Delta Y = \Delta M$, or when $\Delta Y = \Delta M/k$, which we can also write as $\Delta Y = 1/k \times \Delta M$. In other words, the horizontal distance between two *LM* curves is equal to $1/k \times \Delta M$, or the difference in Figure 4 between Y_1 and Y_2 is $1/k \times \Delta M$.[3]

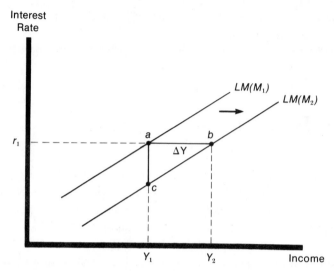

FIGURE 4 / An increase in the money supply shifts the *LM* curve to the right.

But a change in income is not the only way for a change in the money supply to be absorbed into the economy. The interest rate can fall, and this would also raise the amount of money demanded. This is represented in Figure 4 by point *c*, which lies directly below point *a*—i.e., we are still at income Y_1, *but this time it is the interest rate that has fallen* to restore equilibrium between the amount of money demanded and the new (larger) supply of money.

Unfortunately, we cannot as yet say exactly where the new increased money supply leads us. *Will it all be absorbed by increases in GNP, or will it all be absorbed by declines in the interest rate?* That question is a biggie! Our introductory discussion of Chapter 1 suggested that expansion in *M* will lead to *both* a higher GNP and a lower interest rate. Hence, if we start out at point *a* in Figure 4, the new equilibrium of the economy lies somewhere *between* points *b* and *c*. The Classical economists, however, said an increase in *M* would all be absorbed by transactions demand—i.e., GNP will increase and the economy will go to point *b*. We cannot yet answer the question because we don't really know where we started from. (We are lost.) In order to find out where the devil we are, we must introduce the real sector of the economy—saving and investment.

[3] Recall from Chapter 17 (the section "The Quantity Theory of Money") that when there is no interest-sensitivity of the demand for money, then $1/k$ equals velocity. Under those conditions, the horizontal distance (which holds the rate of interest constant) between the two *LM* curves equals ΔM times velocity. This will be important for subsequent discussions.

The Real Sector

Economic activity and interest rates are affected by behavior in the real sector as well as in the monetary sector. The counterpart to the money-demand-equals-money-supply equilibrium condition is the equilibrium between desired saving and investment (or total desired expenditure equals production). The equilibrium levels of GNP and interest rate must satisfy two equilibrium conditions: the condition that $I = S$ as well as money demand = money supply; which is a good thing, because with two variables, Y and r, we need two equations if both variables are to be determined (simultaneously).

The discussion at the end of the previous chapter already indicated the potential relationship between Y and r as far as total spending is concerned—or, looked at another way, as far as saving and investment are concerned. Desired investment spending is negatively related to the rate of interest; a fall in the rate of interest raises the level of investment spending. A higher level of investment spending, in turn, implies a higher level of GNP. These relationships are best depicted graphically. We will then discuss them in more general terms.

In Figure 5(a) the saving function is drawn together with three alternative levels of investment, each one associated with a different rate of interest. "Investment (r_1)" assumes rate of interest r_1, "investment (r_2)" assumes rate of interest r_2 (a higher rate than r_1), and so on. Figure 5(b) depicts the same situation, but from the total expenditure point of view. The three total expenditure lines are associated with the three different levels of investment.

The alternative levels of investment are derived from the investment function in Figure 6, where the rate of interest is measured on the vertical axis and the level of investment is on the horizontal axis. Interest rate r_3 is the highest rate and is associated with the lowest level of investment $I(r_3)$; interest rate r_1 is the lowest rate and is associated with the highest level of investment $I(r_1)$. The change in the amount of investment per unit change in the rate of interest $(\Delta I/\Delta r)$ measures the sensitivity of investment spending to changes in the rate of interest.

It should be obvious from Figures 5(a) and 5(b) that there is a negative relationship between Y and r as far as the real sector of the economy is concerned. Lower interest rates are associated with higher income levels as long as the equilibrium condition—saving equals investment—is satisfied. This relationship between Y and r is summarized in Figure 7, with r measured on the vertical axis and Y on the horizontal axis. (At this point, *we* are having difficulty distinguishing the horizontal from the vertical and who's on what—so keep your

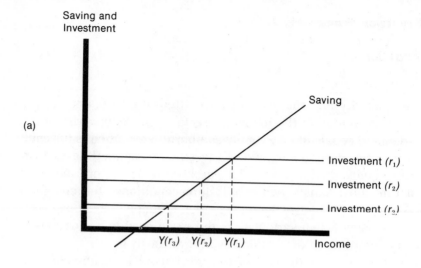

(a)

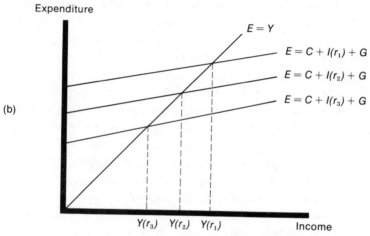

(b)

FIGURE 5 / How to derive the *IS* curve: at lower rates of interest the level of investment is higher, and so is the level of income.

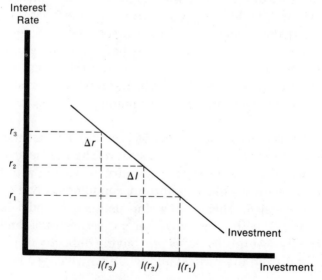

FIGURE 6 / The investment demand function.

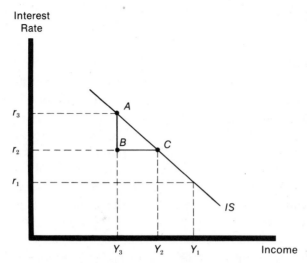

Interest
Rate

FIGURE 7 / The *IS* curve and its slope.

eyes open.) The locus of points satisfying the investment-equals-saving equilibrium condition is called the *IS* curve.

How should you "read" the *IS* curve? As with the *LM* curve, in either of two ways. For a series of alternative interest rates, it tells you what the resulting income would have to be to make saving equal to investment. *At higher interest rates*, there is less investment, *so income must be lower* to shrink saving (which is a function of income) to the point where it equals the smaller volume of investment. *Or*, for a series of alternative income levels, it tells you what the resulting interest rate would have to be to make saving equal to investment. *At higher income levels*, saving is larger, *so the interest rate must be lower* to expand investment to the point where it equals the larger volume of saving.

Perhaps now you can appreciate our advice earlier in the chapter, with respect to the *LM* curve, suggesting that you not pass on that particular information about the relationship between *Y* and *r*. Now there are two relationships between *Y* and *r*. While more of a good thing is usually better, it can lead to embarrassing situations. In our case, however, it will rescue our model from indeterminacy. But before presenting the Missouri Compromise (named after those who refused to believe it was possible), let's take a quick look at the factors that determine the slope and position of the *IS* curve; these are the things, along with the factors that determine the slope and position of the *LM* curve, that influence the effectiveness of monetary and fiscal policy.

All About *IS*

To see why the *IS* curve looks the way it does, what makes it flatter or steeper, what moves it to the right or to the left, let us examine its negative slope in greater detail. Take point *A* in Figure 7 and assume that combination (r_3, Y_3) satisfies the condition saving equals investment: hence *A* lies on the *IS* curve. Now let us move to point *B*, which differs from *A* only in having a lower interest rate (r_2 compared with r_3). But a lower rate of interest implies a higher level of investment. Hence, if $I = S$ at point *A*, then *I* must *exceed* *S* at point *B*. In order to restore equilibrium, saving must be brought up to equality with investment. There's no better way to do it (in fact, no other way at all in our model) than for income to rise, say to Y_2, which raises saving (by the marginal propensity to save times ΔY). At point *C* saving is once again equal to investment, and it too is admitted to that select group of points on the *IS* curve.

The slope of the *IS* curve is determined by the size of the discrepancy between *I* and *S* at point *B*—that is, by the sensitivity of investment to a unit change in the interest rate—and by the responsiveness of saving to increases in income (the marginal propensity to save). For example, if investment is very sensitive to changes in *r* (in Figure 6, if the investment function were flatter, so that ΔI per unit Δr were larger), then investment would exceed saving by a lot at point *B* in Figure 7. In order to increase saving by a lot, income would have to rise a lot; point *C* would be further to the right than it is, and the *IS* curve would be flatter. If the marginal propensity to save were very large, however, the increase in *Y* need not be very large to restore equilibrium, point *C* would be more to the left, and the *IS* curve would be steeper.

All of this could be said in somewhat less formal terms. The fall in the rate of interest at point *B* compared with point *A* raises investment spending. This ΔI, in turn, raises the level of GNP by ΔI times the multiplier, $1/(1 - b)$, of the last chapter. This increase in GNP is measured from point *B* to point *C*. (Note that this assumes quite explicitly that the rate of interest remains the same both before and after the increase in *Y*; and that is accomplished by drawing a *horizontal* line from *B* to *C*.) Hence the slope of the *IS* curve is flatter the more sensitive is investment spending to changes in the rate of interest, and the larger is the multiplier effect. This is perfectly consistent with the story just told in terms of the marginal propensity to save, because the larger is the marginal propensity to save ($= 1 - b$), the smaller is the multiplier of the simple Keynesian model.

To summarize: A *highly* interest-sensitive investment function and a *low* marginal propensity to save (high "simple" multiplier) imply a flat *IS* curve; a low interest-sensitivity of investment and a high marginal propensity to save (low "simple" multiplier) imply a steep *IS* curve (pretty soon the multiplier won't be so simple).

The *position* of the *IS* curve (in contrast to its slope) is altered by any change in autonomous spending, e.g., government spending, private investment that is independent of the rate of interest, or private consumption spending that is independent of income (or, looked at from another standpoint, private saving that is independent of income, such as changes induced by government taxation). Such shifts in autonomous spending disturb the $I = S$ (or $E = Y$) equilibrium condition. The equilibrium combinations of Y and r will, therefore, be altered. This can be seen by looking either at saving equals investment equilibrium or output equals expenditure equilibrium. We will spare you the agony of doing it both ways (just this once), and concentrate on the expenditure equals output approach.

In Figure 8 let's start out with *IS* curve $IS(G_1)$. At every point, saving equals investment and desired total expenditure equals income. Now assume government spending goes up, from G_1 to G_2. From Figure 5(b) it is clear that under such conditions each of the total expenditure functions would shift upward, producing a higher level of Y for each interest rate. In Figure 8, therefore, an increase

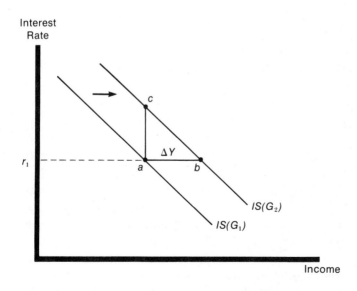

FIGURE 8 / An increase in government spending shifts the *IS* curve to the right.

in G implies a shift to the right of the IS curve, say to IS (G_2), i.e., a higher level of Y for each rate of interest.[4]

Similar shifts in the IS curve would be brought on by increases or decreases in investment spending that are independent of the rate of interest. How does something like that come about? If entrepreneurs suddenly expect higher future dollar returns on investment projects, the rate of return discussed in the last chapter will increase and some investment spending will be undertaken that otherwise would not have been. Keynes felt that such shifts would, in fact, occur quite often and in substantial magnitude. Entrepreneurs are a fickle group, very sensitive to anything (war and peace) and anyone (presidents and reporters) that might influence the future profitability of their investments. Their actions tend to shift the investment demand function (Figure 6) to the right or left, thereby shifting the IS curve to the right or left as well.

We can also say exactly how much the IS curve shifts to the right or left due to a change in autonomous spending. A change in autonomous spending, ΔA, produces a change in GNP by the amount ΔA times the Chapter 18 multiplier, $1/(1 - b)$, assuming no changes in other categories of spending (besides consumption via the change in income). In Figure 8, the horizontal distance between two IS curves—e.g., point a to point b—measures the difference between two levels of income, assuming some type of autonomous spending has increased but the rate of interest remains constant. That would equal ΔA times our old multiplier friend, $1/(1 - b)$. Therefore, an increase in autonomous spending—such as a change in government spending—shifts the IS curve to the right by ΔA times $1/(1 - b)$, while a decrease in autonomous spending shifts the IS curve to the left by ΔA times $1/(1 - b)$.

But there really is *another* possibility. The increase in autonomous spending need not raise GNP if some other category of spending simultaneously contracts. If, at the same time that government spending goes up, private investment spending is discouraged (because the rate of interest rises), it is conceivable that GNP could remain unchanged! This possibility is recognized explicitly in Figure 8 by point c, which is directly above a, implying no change at all in GNP. Instead, the rate of interest has risen sufficiently so that total spending remains the same: Income equals desired expenditure at point c as well as point b, saving equals investment at both points, and so both are on the new IS curve.

---

[4] An increase in taxes, on the other hand, implies a lower level of consumption in Figure 5 (b), hence each of the total expenditure lines is lower than before and the level of Y associated with each rate of interest is less. Result: The IS curve shifts to the left.

Keynesians seem to agree that a change in government spending will raise GNP a lot, hence we will wind up near point b when G goes up. The Classical economists, on the other hand, felt that the level of output would be unaffected by changes in any particular category of expenditure. The economy was already at full employment (Say's law); hence an increase in G would be accompanied by a decrease in some other kind of spending, leaving income unchanged (we would move to point c). We can't really tell what will happen (we are lost again) until we bring the IS curve together with the LM curve, derive equilibrium Y and r simultaneously, and then examine the way these variables respond to monetary and fiscal policy within that *general* equilibrium framework.

The Simultaneous Determination of Income and Interest: IS and LM Together

The equilibrium levels of GNP and the interest rate must satisfy equilibrium in the money market (money demand = money supply or $LP = M$), *and* in the product market ($I = S$). In Figure 9 we have drawn an LM curve for a given money supply, and an IS curve for a given level of government expenditure and taxation and a given investment function (relating I to r). The equilibrium Y and r must be at the intersection point of the IS and LM curves, point E, since only at that point does saving equal investment *and* liquidity preference (LP) equal the money supply. At any other point, one or both of these equilibrium conditions are violated, and dynamic forces will be set in motion to move income and the interest rate toward point E.

Let's see what happens if the economy is not at point E in Figure 9. Take point A on the IS curve. Saving equals investment, but money demand is less than money supply. (The latter is so because point A is directly above point B, which is on the LM curve. At point B we know $LP = M$. Since point A has a higher rate of interest, the amount of money demanded is less, and with a given money supply we have LP less than M.) People want to hold less money than they have at point A. To get rid of the money they start to buy bonds, driving bond prices higher and the interest rate lower. As the interest rate falls, investment rises and so does income—and, believe it or not, we are sliding down the IS curve toward E.

At point B, money supply equals money demand because we are on the LM curve, but investment exceeds saving (point B is directly

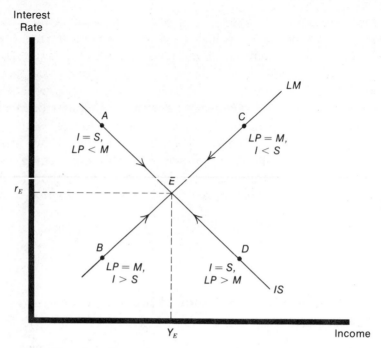

FIGURE 9 / The simultaneous determination of income and interest. (Fantastic!)

below A; at A we know $S = I$; at B the interest rate is lower, hence I exceeds S). The excess of I over S leads to an increase in production as entrepreneurs try to replenish falling inventories. As income rises, the rate of interest is driven up because the money supply is fixed and people start to sell bonds in order to get transactions balances. We are now climbing up the LM curve toward E.

At points to the right of E, dynamic forces would lead to a fall in the level of income. At C we have $LP = M$, but desired investment is less than desired saving (see if you know why—hint: compare with D). Entrepreneurs cut back their production in order to reduce inventory accumulation. As GNP falls there is a reduction in the need for transactions balances, people start buying bonds with the extra cash, bond prices rise, and interest rates decline—we return to E by sliding down the LM curve. Finally, at point D investment equals saving, but LP exceeds M. People try to sell bonds to get more cash, bond prices fall, interest rates rise; investment spending starts to fall and income falls along with it—we climb the IS curve until we get to E.

Equilibrium point E has the nice property that if the economy is not there, dynamic forces will restore that combination of Y and r. It is a *stable* equilibrium. As long as the IS and LM curves remain in the same position, any deviation of income from Y_E will set forces in motion to restore that level of output; the same is true of interest rate r_E.

"Look, the point is that where the LM *and* IS *curves intersect you get equilibrium in* both *the money market* and *the product market."*

But there is nothing sacred about income Y_E. It may or may not be a full employment level of output. We have noted no tendency for the economy to insure that Y_E is full employment, although we will suggest a few things later on. If Y_E happens to be full employment, all is well. But if it isn't, and the army of unemployed is becoming restless, the government may step in to produce full employment. As we noted in the previous chapter, it could use monetary policy or fiscal policy. We have all the tools to do a complete analysis of the impact of such policies on GNP.

Monetary and Fiscal Policy

Monetary Policy: We have now reached the point where we can put all of our slopes and shifts to good use. Figures 10, 11, and 12 summarize the way monetary policy influences economic activity, and the factors affecting its strength, within the *IS–LM* framework.

In Figure 10, if we start with *LM* and *IS*, the equilibrium level of income is Y and the interest rate is r. An increase in the money sup-

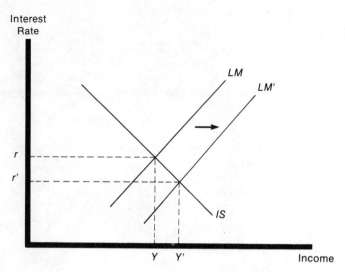

Interest
Rate

LM

LM'

r

r'

IS

Y   Y'   Income

FIGURE 10 / An expansionary monetary policy.

ply, for example, shifts the *LM* function to *LM'*, reducing the interest rate to *r'* and increasing GNP to *Y'*.[5]

Figure 11 shows that an increase in money supply (*LM* shifts to *LM'*) raises GNP by more, the *flatter is the IS curve*. With the relatively steep *IS* curve, the increase in income is only to Y_s, while with the flatter *IS* curve the increase is to Y_f. The flatter *IS* curve can be due to a highly interest-sensitive investment function. Hence, the fall in *r* due to an increase in *M* raises the level of investment by a lot. The impact of monetary policy on GNP is more powerful under such conditions.

Figure 12 is somewhat more complicated. It illustrates that an increase in the money supply is more powerful *the less the sensitivity of money demand* to changes in the interest rate. If the demand for money is rather insensitive to changes in the rate of interest, the *LM* curve is steeper. An increase in money supply would shift LM_{steep} to LM'_{steep} or LM_{flat} to LM'_{flat}.[6] The former implies an increase in GNP from *Y* to Y_s, while the latter implies a shift from *Y* to Y_f. The explanation is simple: The *less* the interest-sensitivity of the demand for money, the *larger* the decline in the rate of interest when money

[5] All of the examples are in terms of increases in the money supply. A decrease would simply shift the *LM* curve to the left and all of the changes would be just the reverse.

[6] Notice that the *horizontal* distances between the two sets of curves are identical because the income-sensitivity of the demand for money is the same in both cases; hence the *potential* increase in GNP due to the increased money supply is the same (at the old equilibrium interest rate).

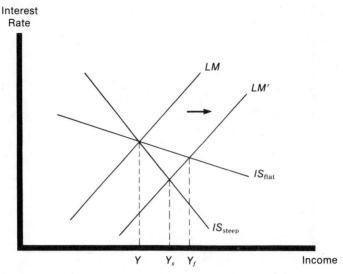

FIGURE 11 / Monetary policy is more effective the flatter the *IS* curve.

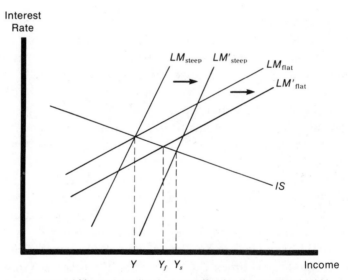

FIGURE 12 / Monetary policy is more effective the steeper the *LM* curve.

supply is increased (because the amount of money demanded increases only slightly when there is only a small fall in r); therefore, with a big drop in r (needed to increase money demand), the induced increases in investment spending and GNP are large.

Fiscal Policy: The nature of the impact of fiscal policy on GNP is summarized in Figures 13, 14, and 15. An increase in government

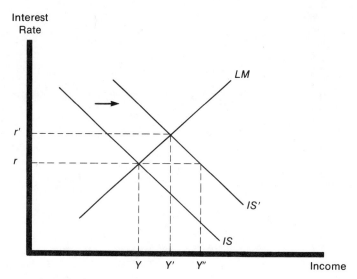

FIGURE 13 / An expansionary fiscal policy.

spending (or a decrease in taxes) shifts the *IS* curve to the right.[7]
In Figure 13 there is a shift from *IS* to *IS'*. Equilibrium GNP goes from
Y to Y' at the same time that the interest rate is driven *up* from r to r'.
The interest rate goes up because there is an increased transactions
demand for money associated with the rise in GNP and, with a fixed
money supply, r must rise to keep $LP = M$.

This interest rate effect has been suppressed until now in evaluating the impact of ∆G (or any change in autonomous spending) on
economic activity. It has significant consequences, however. It *reduces*
the size of the autonomous expenditure multiplier, hence the power
of fiscal policy, because the increase in the interest rate reduces investment spending at the same time that government expenditure is
going up. If the rate of interest had remained unchanged, the increase
in GNP would have been to Y". The size of the horizontal shift in the
IS curve is equal to ∆G times $1/(1 - b)$, and the increase from Y to Y"
is equal to that. But the actual increase in GNP is less (only to Y'),
because the interest rate goes up and investment spending is reduced
somewhat (now you know why we called $1/(1 - b)$ the "simple"
multiplier). In fact, this decrease in investment when government
spending rises has come to be known as the "crowding out" effect.
More on this in Chapter 21.

The size of the government expenditure multiplier (and thus the
effectiveness of fiscal policy) is greater, the smaller is the offsetting
effect of rising interest rates on investment spending. In Figure 14

[7] A decrease in government spending or an increase in taxes shifts the *IS*
curve to the left, and all of the impacts are the reverse of those in the text.

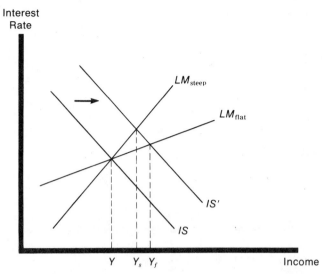

FIGURE 14 / Fiscal policy is more effective the flatter the *LM* curve.

the rightward shift in the *IS* curve has a smaller impact on GNP with the steeper *LM* curve compared with the flatter *LM* curve. When a steep *LM* curve is due to small interest-sensitivity of liquidity preference, for example, the increased transactions demand for money as GNP rises requires a large increase in the rate of interest to bring total money demand back into equality with money supply. The large rise in the rate of interest cuts off a large amount of private investment—there is a large "crowding out" effect—hence the net impact on GNP is relatively small.[8]

Figure 15 is another rather complicated diagram. It indicates that the less the interest sensitivity of investment, the larger is the government expenditure multiplier, and thus the more effective is fiscal policy. If investment spending is insensitive to changes in the rate of interest, the *IS* curve is steeper. An increase in government spending either shifts IS_{steep} to IS'_{steep}, raising GNP to Y_s, or shifts IS_{flat} to IS'_{flat}, raising GNP to Y_f. The increase in the rate of interest cuts off more investment the greater the sensitivity of investment to the rate of interest; hence the rise in income is smaller under such circumstances.[9]

[8] The steep *LM* curve can also be due to a large transactions demand for money. In this case, the increase in *Y* produces a large rise in the demand for money, forcing the rate of interest to rise by a lot in order to bring money demand back into equality with the fixed money supply.

[9] Notice that the horizontal distances between the two sets of *IS* curves are identical. This is so because, holding the rate of interest constant, the *potential* increase in GNP due to an increase in government spending is the same (because the marginal propensity to consume is assumed to be the same).

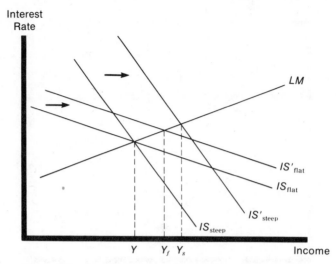

FIGURE 15 / Fiscal policy is more effective the steeper the *IS* curve.

As a reward for reading this far and still remaining conscious (check your pulse), Table 1 summarizes the factors influencing the relative effectiveness of monetary policy and fiscal policy. Start at the top of columns (1) and (2), with the statement, for example, "If *LP* is very sensitive to *r*" and then proceed to the extreme left-hand column for "*Then* (A), (B), (C) and (D)." The implications of each statement for *IS–LM* analysis and monetary and fiscal policy are recorded in the table.

TABLE 1

	(1)	(2)
Then	If *LP* is very sensitive to *r*	If *I* is very sensitive to *r*
(A) The *LM* curve is	flatter	—
(B) The *IS* curve is	—	flatter
(C) Monetary policy is	less effective	more effective
(D) Fiscal policy is	more effective	less effective

Keynes and the Classics

Velocity, one of the cornerstones of the Classical system, seems to have disappeared from our Keynesian framework. Where has all the velocity gone? It has disappeared behind the *LM* curve. Since a particular *LM* function is drawn for a *given* money supply, as one moves up along an *LM* function, the income velocity of money is necessarily going up. Income is rising but the money supply is constant, so Y/M $(= V)$ has to rise. In Figure 16, three different *IS* curves produce three different levels of GNP, as well as three different levels of velocity: V_1 (equal to Y_1/M) at *a*; V_2 ($= Y_2/M$) at *b*; and V_3 ($= Y_3/M$) at *c*. V_3 is greater than V_2, which is greater than V_1.

The rightward shifts in the *IS* curve in Figure 16, associated with (for example) increased levels of government spending, succeed in raising GNP by raising velocity. In fact, velocity goes up because the demand for money is sensitive to the rate of interest. The rise in the rate of interest induces the public to hold less speculative balances (or, more generally, make more economical use of all money balances), permitting more cash to be used for carrying out transactions.

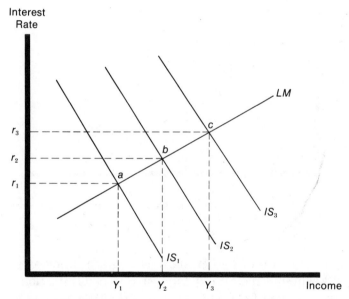

FIGURE 16 / When the *IS* curve shifts, both income and velocity rise.

If the demand for money were totally *insensitive* to the interest rate, then velocity would be constant and GNP would not be affected by shifts in autonomous spending. An interest-insensitive demand for money means that money demand depends *only* on income. For a given supply of money, there is only one level of income at which the equilibrium condition, $LP = M$, is satisfied. The *LM* curve is vertical at that level of GNP, as shown in Figure 17—implying that no matter how high government spending rises, the level of GNP cannot go up because then *LP* would exceed *M*.

It is the fixed money supply that prevents GNP from rising under such circumstances. If autonomous spending goes up, illustrated by the rightward shifts in the *IS* curve in Figure 17, the result is an increase in the rate of interest, cutting off investment spending. The rate of interest rises until the fall in interest-sensitive investment spending is equal to the autonomous increase in spending, resulting in no increase in GNP. The "crowding out" effect is complete. (We will return to the implications of a vertical *LM* curve in subsequent chapters.)

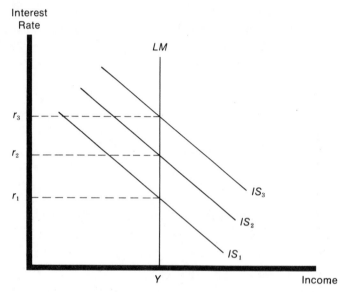

FIGURE 17 / When the *LM* curve is vertical, shifts in the *IS* curve raise neither income nor velocity.

Another feature of *IS–LM* analysis is that it integrates the Classical and Keynesian theories of interest rate determination. In Chapter 18 the simplified Keynesian view was that the interest rate was a purely monetary phenomenon, determined by the supply and demand for money. The Classical school, on the other hand, argued that the interest rate was a "real" phenomenon, determined exclusively by saving and investment. In our current treatment both monetary factors, embodied in the *LM* curve, and real factors, embodied in the *IS* curve, affect the interest rate. An increase in the money supply, by shifting the *LM* curve to the right, lowers the rate of interest, as Keynes suggested. An increase in autonomous investment, by shifting the *IS* curve to the right, raises the rate of interest, as the Classics suggested.

This partial rehabilitation of Classical interest rate theory forces us back to the question we raised earlier: Why don't variations in the rate of interest automatically bring about full employment in the Keynesian system, as the Classical economists argued would happen? Having resurrected this much of Classical theory, can we bring Say's law back to life as well?

When Will Full Employment Prevail?

When Joe Namath announced, "I'll guarantee victory," before the Jets' Super Bowl encounter with the Baltimore Colts (1970), people refused to believe him. They also laughed at Robert Fulton. But they were incredulous when the Classical economists guaranteed that the economy would generate full employment if only it were left to its own devices. (Incredulity set in right after the Great Depression; before that it was common knowledge that the economy could hit the full employment target with both hands tied behind its back—making sole use of the invisible one.)

The Classical argument can be put into the Keynesian *IS–LM* framework quite simply. Figure 18 shows an equilibrium level of income Y and interest rate r associated with *IS* and *LM*. Let's assume

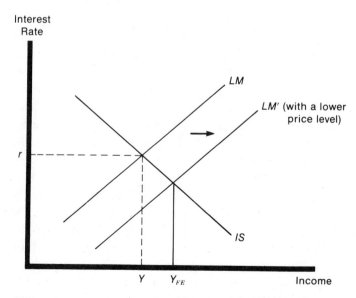

FIGURE 18 / The Classical position: Lower prices shift the *LM* curve to the right and automatically produce full employment.

that the level of GNP that would generate full employment is Y_{FE}. Quite clearly, economic activity at Y is too low to justify employing all those who want to work at the going wage rate. Unemployment is the result.

The Keynesian apparatus makes it perfectly clear that the only way employment will increase is if aggregate economic activity increases; only if desired spending increases will GNP increase beyond Y toward Y_{FE}. So far we have no reason to suspect that either the *IS* curve or the *LM* curve will shift to the right all by itself, hence no reason to suspect that output Y will not remain at that level from now until Kingdom come—unless, of course, the King comes and increases government spending or the money supply.

But the Classical economists said we needn't wait for divine intervention. With less than full employment, workers would lower their wage demands and prices would be lowered as entrepreneurs tried to sell the output they produced with the increased labor that they hired (more workers would presumably be hired at lower wage rates). However, if both prices *and wages* are falling, there is no reason to expect consumers to spend more—goods cost less but individuals receive less money for their work, so their *real* income hasn't increased. Investment spending is also not likely to be affected directly. Entrepreneurs pay less for their inputs because of the decline in prices, but they must also expect to receive a smaller dollar return on outputs; the two are likely to cancel each other out and expected profitability should be more or less unchanged. Indeed, all of our behavioral relationships are in *real* terms; people see through falling prices accompanied by falling incomes, so consumption, investment, and money-holding decisions are unaffected by equal movements in dollar incomes and prices. If no one is induced to increase spending, aggregate demand will remain at its old level, workers just hired will be fired, and the level of employment will be back where it started.

Nevertheless, the Classical economists had an ace in the hole: one thing clearly affected by a fall in the price level is the real value of the supply of money. As we saw in Chapter 17, if the money supply is fixed at $1,000 and the price level is unity, its real value (in purchasing power) is the same as if the money supply were $2,000 and the price level were doubled. But if we start out with a $2,000 money supply and the price level is cut in half—Presto, the real money supply doubles (e.g., from $2,000/2 to $2,000/1)! This increase in the real value of the money supply due to falling prices is the mechanism through which the economy would move itself from a position of less than full employment to full employment. Here's how.

In terms of Figure 18, falling prices shift the *LM* curve to the right for the same reason that an increase in money supply does—

falling prices increase the real value of the money supply and thereby create an excess of (real) money supply over the demand for money. Falling prices continue as long as people are unemployed, so that the increased real value of the money supply continues to shift the *LM* curve to the right, lowering the interest rate and increasing desired investment. This process would continue until the *LM* curve in Figure 18 is shifted from *LM* to *LM′* (the latter associated with a lower price level than at the original position), at which point economic activity is at full employment.

The Keynesian attack on this Classical mechanism was not confined to the argument that prices and wages are sticky and inflexible and not likely to fall very promptly. The Classical school, in fact, stressed that unemployment was the result of such downward inflexibility in wages and prices. Keynes said, however, that there were at least two other circumstances that would stall the move toward full employment. First, at the end of the last chapter we noted that in the case of a *liquidity trap* an increase in the money supply would not lower the interest rate. As long as the liquidity preference function is perfectly horizontal, an increase in the money supply, real or nominal, is associated with the same rate of interest. The *LM* curve is flat under such conditions,[10] and no matter how far the price level declines, the interest rate won't fall, investment spending will remain unaltered, and so will aggregate output and employment. This situation is depicted in Figure 19.

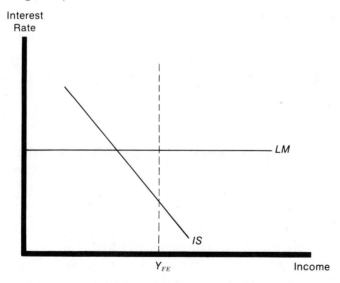

FIGURE 19 / An extreme Keynesian position: A liquidity trap.

[10] Recall that the *LM* curve is flatter the greater the interest-sensitivity of money demand. In the liquidity trap, money demand is infinitely interest-elastic, hence the *LM* curve becomes totally flat.

The second case in which falling prices fail to work is when investment is highly *insensitive* to the rate of interest. The *IS* curve is very steep. Under such conditions, declining prices and the induced reduction in the rate of interest will be unable to raise investment to a sufficiently high level to generate full employment spending, as in Figure 20.

But Classical economics wasn't built on such a fragile link between the monetary sector and real spending. The Classical argument that we have just presented based the automatic tendency toward full employment on the rightward shift *in the* LM *curve,* due to increases in the real value of the money supply. This is a thoroughly "Keynesian" mechanism, in the sense that money affects the economy only through the interest rate. But falling prices not only lower the interest rate —they also make people's money balances worth more and this might have a more direct impact on economic activity. People would be wealthier in addition to being more liquid. And if more liquidity wouldn't help (because of, say, the liquidity trap), more

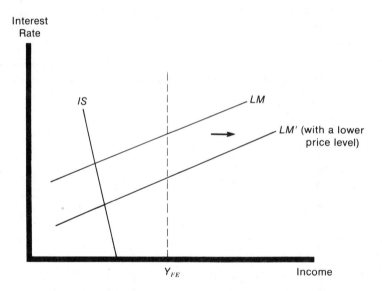

FIGURE 20 / Another extreme Keynesian position: Investment unresponsive to the interest rate.

wealth certainly would. A cash balance of $10 may not mean you're very rich if the price level is unity. But if the price level fell to 1/10 of what it was, you'd have $100 in purchasing power; a drop to 1/100 would make your $10 bill worth $1,000 (in purchasing power); and a decline in the price level to 1/100,000 of what it was would make you a millionaire!

As we noted in our discussion of the consumption function in Chapter 18, an increase in wealth raises desired consumption at every level of income. In terms of Figures 19 and 20, *the IS curve* would now shift to the right until it intersects the *LM* curve at the full employment level of GNP. Prices then stop falling, and all those who want jobs are employed (with so many millionaires, perhaps the unemployment problem would be eliminated by the army of the wealthy pulling out of the labor force!). In other words, the complete classical argument has *both* Keynesian curves, the *IS* and *LM*, moving to the right as a result of falling prices. Changes in the real value of money balances affect the rate of interest and indirectly influence investment spending (the rightward shift in *LM*), but they may also affect consumption spending directly (the rightward shift in *IS*).

Keynes would say all this is fine, but by the time it comes about all those who wanted jobs will have passed through the Great Unemployment Window in the Sky. The classical "do it yourself" path to full employment is lengthy and arduous. Unemployment can last a very long time if the economy is left to its own devices, with no help from its friends. So the Keynesian prescription is fiscal policy. The Monetarists, while Classical economists at heart, might agree that some form of stabilization policy is better than a prolonged period of falling prices (and depressed economic activity). But their remedy is monetary policy. Who is right? Read the next few chapters and then you tell us (write to Ritter, he likes to get mail).

Suggestions for Further Reading

The original presentation of the *IS–LM* model was in John R. Hicks, "Mr. Keynes and the 'Classics': A Suggested Interpretation," *Econometrica* (April 1937). Most macroeconomic texts (such as Dornbusch and Fischer, and Edward Shapiro, cited at the end of Chapter 4) present extensive analyses of monetary and fiscal policy within the *IS–LM* framework. An advanced treatment of Classical versus Keynesian macroeconomics is Don Patinkin, *Money, Interest, and Prices* (New York: Harper & Row, 1965), especially Chapters 9–14. A good advanced survey of topics in monetary theory is Harry G. Johnson, "Monetary Theory and Policy," *American Economic Review* (June 1962). An updating of Johnson's survey is Stanley Fischer, "Recent Developments in Monetary Theory," *American Economic Review* (May 1975).

The Simple Algebra of Income Determination

For the algebraically inclined, much of the discussion of Chapters 18 and 19 can be summarized succinctly in equation form. The economy is divided into two sectors: the real sector, comprising the demand for goods and services; and the monetary sector, comprising the demand for and supply of money.

The Model

The *real sector* of the economy can be described by four functional relationships (behavior equations) and one equilibrium condition (an identity). All the functional relationships are assumed to be linear, an assumption that simplifies exposition without doing excessive damage to real world applications. The functional relationships:

(1) $C = a + b(Y - T)$ Consumption (C) function
(2) $I = d - n(R)$ Investment (I) function
(3) $T = e + t(Y)$ Tax (T) function
(4) $G = \bar{G}$ Government spending (G)

and the equilibrium condition:

(5) $C + I + G = Y$ *or* $S + T = I + G$

where Y stands for GNP (income) and R for the interest rate. In each equation, the first lower-case letter represents the constant term of the function, and the second lower-case letter the coefficient of the independent variable (or the slope of the function); i.e., b is the marginal propensity to consume $(\Delta C/\Delta(Y - T))$, and n is the interest sensitivity of the investment function $(\Delta I/\Delta R)$. Government spending is indicated by $\bar{G}$, and is exogenously fixed (imposed on the system from outside).

The Simple Algebra of Income Determination

The *monetary sector* of the economy consists of two functional relationships and one equilibrium condition:

(6) $L = f - h(R) + k(Y)$ Liquidity preference (L) or demand-for-money function

(7) $M = \bar{M}$ Money supply (M)

(8) $L = M$ Equilibrium condition

The *IS* and *LM* Functions

By solving equations (1) through (5), we find the *IS* function:

(9) $Y = \dfrac{a - be + \bar{G} + d}{1 - b + bt} - \dfrac{n}{1 - b + bt} R$

By solving equations (6) through (8), we find the *LM* function:

(10) $Y = \dfrac{\bar{M} - f}{k} + \dfrac{h}{k} R$ *or* $R = \dfrac{kY + f - \bar{M}}{h}$

Equilibrium Income and Interest

By solving (9) and (10) simultaneously, we obtain equilibrium income (Y) and interest rate (R):

(11) $Y = \dfrac{1}{1 - b + bt + \dfrac{nk}{h}} \left(a - be + d + \bar{G} - \dfrac{nf}{h} + \dfrac{n\bar{M}}{h} \right)$

(12) $R = \dfrac{1}{h(1 - b + bt) + nk} [ka - kbe + kd + k\bar{G} + f(1 - b + bt)$
$- \bar{M}(1 - b + bt)]$

Multiplier Effects: On Income

From (11) one can derive the multiplier effects on income, and from (12) one can derive the multiplier effects on the interest rate, that follow from a change in government spending (ΔG), an autonomous shift in the consumption or investment function (Δa or Δd), a shift in the tax function (Δe), a change in the money supply (ΔM), or an autonomous shift in the demand for money (Δf).

The multiplier effects on income, from (11), are:

(13)
$$\frac{\Delta Y}{\Delta G \text{ or } \Delta a \text{ or } \Delta d} = \frac{1}{1 - b + bt + \dfrac{nk}{h}}$$

(14)
$$\frac{\Delta Y}{\Delta e} = -\frac{b}{1 - b + bt + \dfrac{nk}{h}}$$

(15)
$$\frac{\Delta Y}{\Delta M \text{ (or } - \Delta f)} = \frac{n}{h(1 - b + bt) + nk}$$

Multiplier Effects: On the Interest Rate

The multiplier effects on the interest rate, from (12), are:

(16)
$$\frac{\Delta R}{\Delta G \text{ or } \Delta a \text{ or } \Delta d} = \frac{k}{h(1 - b + bt) + nk}$$

(17)
$$\frac{\Delta R}{\Delta e} = -\frac{kb}{h(1 - b + bt) + nk}$$

(18)
$$\frac{\Delta R}{\Delta M \text{ (or } - \Delta f)} = -\frac{(1 - b + bt)}{h(1 - b + bt) + nk}$$

Policy Implications

A number of policy implications are contained in the above multiplier formulas. Among the more important are the following:

1. As (13) indicates, in the complete Keynesian system the multiplier effect on income of a change in government spending is *smaller* than the simple $\dfrac{1}{1-b}$ that is typically taught in beginning economics courses. It is smaller by the addition of $bt + \dfrac{nk}{h}$ to the

denominator. Here's what it means: t represents tax rates (they cut back consumer spending); k is the transactions demand for money (as income rises, the amount of transactions money desired increases, raising interest rates); n is the interest-sensitivity of investment spending (as interest rates rise, they cut back investment spending); modified by h, the interest-sensitivity of the demand for money (if liquidity preference is very responsive to interest rates, it will take only a small rise in rates to induce people to reduce their cash holdings enough to provide the additional money needed for transactions purposes).

2. Compare (13) and (14): as long as b is less than unity, an increase in government spending will increase income by more than an equal increase in taxes will lower income. The multiplier for a change in government spending is larger than the multiplier for a tax change.

2a. It follows from the above that a simultaneous and equal increase in both government spending and taxes—that is, a balanced budget change in government spending (financed entirely by higher taxes)—will not leave income unchanged, but will increase it. Balanced budgets are not neutral with respect to income.

3. Equation (15) indicates that monetary policy will be *less* powerful in affecting income the larger is h (the responsiveness of liquidity preference to interest rates) and the smaller is n (the responsiveness of investment spending to interest rates).[1]

3a. As a special case of the above, if h is *infinite* (Keynesian liquidity trap) *or* n is *zero* (investment completely insensitive to interest rates), then the multiplier for $\Delta M = 0$ and monetary policy is useless.

3b. Under such circumstances ($h = \infty$ or $n = 0$), it follows that fiscal policy is the only alternative.

4. Conversely, (15) also indicates that monetary policy will be *more* powerful in affecting income the smaller is h and the larger is n.

4a. As a special case of the above, if h is *zero* (liquidity preference completely insensitive to interest rates), then—from (13)—the multiplier for $\Delta G = 0$ and fiscal policy is useless.

---

[1] The effect of changes in h, n, or any of the other coefficients on the size of the multipliers can be verified by numerical examples (putting in actual numbers for each coefficient, calculating the multiplier, and then changing one of the coefficients and recalculating the multiplier), or by using calculus (take the derivative, for example, of $\Delta Y/\Delta M$ with respect to n, h, or k). Note also that the points made under 3a, 3b, 4a, and 4b are not discussed in this chapter. They correspond to points that will be made in the next three chapters.

4b. On the other hand, under such circumstances ($h = 0$) monetary policy is both necessary *and sufficient* to control income. If $h = 0$, equation (15) indicates that the multiplier for $\Delta M = \dfrac{1}{k}$; so long as k is constant in the liquidity preference function, a change in the money supply will always change income by the constant $\dfrac{1}{k}$. That is, $\Delta M \times \dfrac{1}{k} = \Delta Y$, which is—surprise!—the same as the quantity theory of money ($M \times$ velocity $= Y$, with velocity constant and equal to $\dfrac{1}{k}$).

PART V

The Monetarist-Keynesian Debate and Its Policy Implications

Chapter 20

The Monetarists
Versus the Keynesians

AT AN ECONOMICS CONFERENCE in the late 1960s, Robert Solow, a prominent Keynesian from MIT, commented as follows on a paper presented by Milton Friedman: "Another difference between Milton and myself is that everything reminds Milton of the money supply; well, everything reminds me of sex, but I try to keep it out of my papers."

Monetarists do, in fact, make so much of the money supply that they are rather easy to caricature. It appears frequently in their professional papers circulated among economists; it figures prominently in their policy recommendations to the government; and some have even shown how it can make money in the stock market. But so far, at least, no evidence has been presented on its qualifications as an aphrodisiac. Don't, however, rule out the possibility.

The President of the United States will use very different approaches in economic policy-making depending on whether his orientation is Keynesian or Monetarist. As a Keynesian, he and the chairman of his Council of Economic Advisers would spend considerable time pressing the Congress for countercyclical tax and expenditure legislation. If he were a Monetarist, he would spend more effort trying to convince everyone that things will get better by themselves; but if something simply must be done, then he would turn to the Federal Reserve. The Eisenhower administration followed essentially a Monetarist course, while the orientation of economic policy under Kennedy and Johnson was primarily Keynesian. The Nixon, Ford, and Carter administrations have used a little bit of everything.

How do the underlying theoretical differences between these schools affect their policy recommendations? Why have recent administrations followed a more eclectic approach than earlier ones?

The Monetarist View of Money

The Monetarists used to be called Quantity Theorists. Their lineage can be traced at least as far back as Jean Bodin in the sixteenth century, through John Locke, David Hume, David Ricardo, John Stuart Mill, up to Irving Fisher in the 1920s and 1930s, and now Milton Friedman in the 1960s and 1970s. Historically, as we pointed out in Chapter 17, they used to be concerned primarily with the relationship between the quantity of money and prices, viewing the money supply as the main determinant of the price level. The modern Quantity Theorists—or Monetarists—no longer believe changes in the money supply affect only the price level. As they see it, the role of money can be much broader than that; in the *short run* it is the crucial determinant of economic activity.

According to the Monetarists, there is a direct and reliable link between the money supply and GNP. That link is the predictability of monetary velocity. Because of it, a change in the money supply will change aggregate spending and GNP by a predictable amount.

If the money supply is increased during a recession, the increased spending primarily will raise employment and real output; on the other hand, if the economy is already close to full employment, then the increase in GNP will consist mainly of higher prices.

How high will GNP go? The answer, according to a simple version of Monetarism, is that spending on real goods and services will continue to climb until GNP has risen to the point where the relationship between it and the money supply becomes the same as it had been before the money supply was increased by the Federal Reserve. That relationship, of course, is exactly what we mean by monetary velocity (GNP/M). When GNP has reached the point where it once again stands in its previous ratio to the money supply, the public will finally be satisfied to hold the increased stock of money as a medium of exchange, and spending will level off.

Figure 1 presents this simple Monetarist position geometrically. The quantity of money is on the horizontal axis and income is on the vertical axis. The line drawn from the origin shows at every level of

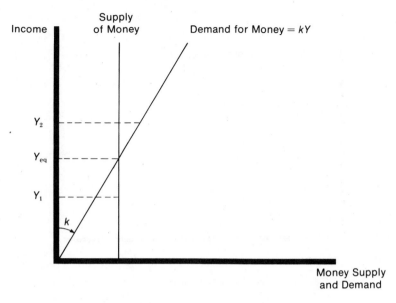

FIGURE 1 / The Monetarist view of income determination.

income how much money is demanded; people want to hold money equal to a specified fraction (k) of their income; the Monetarists, in other words, concentrate on transactions demand to explain people's holdings of money balances. The money supply is also in the diagram. Equilibrium income, Y_{eq} (be careful, it is on the vertical axis), occurs where the amount of money demanded equals the supply. If people have more money than they want (as at Y_1), they will spend it and Y will rise; if they have less money than they want (as at Y_2), they will reduce their spending and Y will fall.

An increase in the money supply causes Y to rise, because with an initial excess supply of money people start to spend and continue until money demand is brought into equality with money supply. Income continues to rise until all of the increased money supply is absorbed into increased transactions demand. This is illustrated in Figure 2. When the money supply increases from $50 billion to $60 billion, equilibrium income rises from $Y_{eq\ 50}$ to $Y_{eq\ 60}$. Nothing is said about whether interest rates rise or fall. And that's the way hard-core Monetarists like it—short, to the point, and somewhat mystical—a sure winner.

Notice the implications of the above with respect to velocity. Since the demand for money is simply a fraction (k) of income, the amount of money demanded will equal the supply of money *only* when income is a specific multiple of the money supply. That multiple is the reciprocal of k, which is also—in this particular case—the veloc-

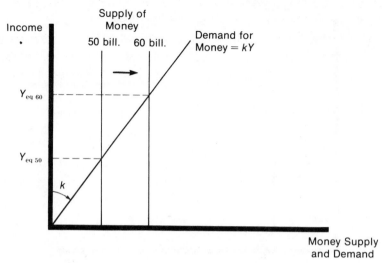

FIGURE 2 / An increase in money raises GNP: A Monetarist view.

ity of money. Velocity remains constant so long as k is unchanged.[1]

This particular view of the money-GNP relationship is quite inflexible. Most Monetarists would insist only that velocity be predictable, not necessarily a fixed and unchanging number—in other words, as money supply goes up, GNP rises by a predictable amount because the demand for money is related in a reliable way to GNP. Money demand might even depend on interest rates, but that relationship is predictable and stable as well. In either case, it is clear where the Monetarists got their name. The *ideal* situation for the central bank is a stable velocity, or at least one that is changing slowly and predictably over a period of time, and this is precisely *the* main assumption of the Monetarists. If velocity is stable (our example) or predictable (as reasonable Monetarists argue), the Federal Reserve can induce almost any volume of spending it wants simply by adjusting the money supply to the known velocity. For example, the velocity of the (narrowly defined) total money supply is now about 6. If an *addition* to the money supply also turns over 6 times a year in the purchase of goods and services, then the Federal Reserve knows for sure that if it increases the money supply by a billion dollars the end result will be an increase in GNP of $6 billion. In that case, the Federal

[1] Say the money supply is $100 billion and the demand for money equals ¼Y. Then the amount of money demanded will equal the $100 billion supply only when income is $400 billion, or 4 times the money supply. The 4 is the reciprocal of k, which is ¼. Since velocity is defined as Y/M, or 400/100, 4 is also the velocity of money. It cannot change so long as k remains unchanged.

Reserve has it made; monetary policy alone would be both necessary *and sufficient* to control aggregate spending.[2]

In the Monetarist world, there is no need to pay any attention to fiscal policy (the Keynesians' pet). Changes in the money supply can do the whole job, and stabilization policy should concentrate on that alone. No wonder Monetarists blame the Federal Reserve whenever *anything* goes wrong! Of course, there's still the question of whether we really *need* an active stabilization policy—a subject we'll discuss below.

The Keynesian View of Money

The gospel according to Saint John—the late John Maynard Keynes, that is—is that the channels through which the money supply affects GNP are rather different, as we saw in Chapter 16. They are less direct and also less reliable, primarily because velocity is not viewed as very stable in either the short or the long run. Here's why. Assume once more that the Federal Reserve increases the money supply by open market purchases of government securities. This increases the liquidity of the public, but people *may* want simply to hold this additional liquidity. The entire process might end right there, almost before it has begun. The public gets additional money and hoards it. Period. The money supply has increased but GNP is unaffected. Velocity has fallen. This is the liquidity trap case, shown in Figure 9 near the end of Chapter 18.

Another way an increase in the money supply can be short-circuited out of the income stream occurs when the increase is accompanied by a simultaneous shift in the demand for money. In Figure 3 the money demand function shifts to the right at the same time that the money supply is increased. As a result, the equilibrium interest rate remains unchanged. (A Monetarist would argue that the demand

---

[2] At the other extreme, the *worst* situation from the point of view of the monetary authorities is if velocity fluctuates randomly or perversely. If velocity moves randomly, up and down without rhyme or reason, it would be impossible to gauge the impact on GNP that might result from a change in the money supply. Under such circumstances, monetary policy would be close to useless as a tool of national economic policy.

for money is highly stable, even if it is a function of the interest rate; hence such shifts would rarely occur.)

Suppose the Monetarists have a point: that people do *not* want to hold the additional cash. Finding themselves with more money, they proceed to spend it. In the Monetarist world they are likely to spend it on *real* assets, on real goods and services, thereby directly driving up GNP. In the Keynesian world, however, they would spend it not on real assets but on *financial* assets, such as stocks and bonds —and that is why the Keynesian geometry of Figure 3 plots money and interest rates in the same diagram, while the Monetarist Figure 1 charts money in relation to income.[3] The Monetarists stress the transactions motive for holding money while the Keynesians stress the speculative motive.

In the Keynesian world, when people increase their demand for financial assets, the prices of securities rise and interest rates fall. But even so, GNP still has not been affected. This drop in interest rates *may,* then, induce some business firms or consumers to borrow and purchase real goods and services. *Finally,* GNP has been affected.

To summarize the main Keynesian view: A change in the money supply can only affect aggregate spending and GNP if it *first* changes interest rates, and *then* only if business or consumer spending is sensitive to those changes. In this way of looking at things, there's many a possible slip 'twixt the cup and the lip.

There are two other components of monetary policy that have been discussed by Keynesians, in addition to the interest rate effect on borrowing and investment spending. First, lenders are likely to make available more or less credit as the money supply is increased or decreased. Such credit *availability* effects are discussed in greater detail in Chapters 24 and 37. In addition, it has also been noted that while monetary policy does not alter wealth directly (as we pointed out in Chapter 3), it may very well produce a wealth effect through its impact on interest rates and securities prices. Lower interest rates mean higher securities prices, and higher interest rates mean lower securities prices. Capital losses are familiar to us all, and perhaps capital gains as well—even if only on paper. Such changes in the

[3] The Monetarists' chart would substitute the price level for income when the economy is at full employment. Milton Friedman has often used this issue to distinguish Monetarists from Keynesians. In particular, what is the appropriate "price of money"—the interest rate or the price level? Actually, no one really argues that the interest rate is the price of money, everyone knows that the interest rate is the price of credit (of borrowing). Similarly, everyone recognizes that increases in the price level reduce the value of money, as we pointed out in Chapter 1. The distinction is, which variable—the price level or the interest rate—fluctuates most in the short-run, and hence belongs most prominently in the picture.

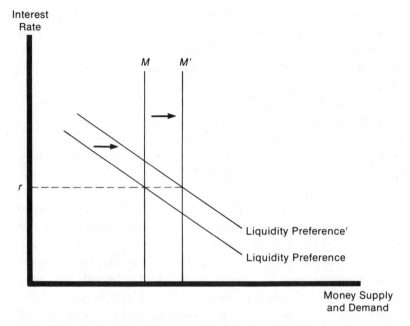

FIGURE 3 / An increase in the demand for money can offset an increase in supply, leaving the interest rate unchanged.

values of stocks and bonds in an individual's portfolio may alter his spending on real goods (a new home) or even on real bads (pornography). This indirect wealth effect provides another link between monetary policy and GNP for modern Keynesians.

One long-standing Keynesian objection to monetary policy deserves passing mention, even though it does not seem to be heard as frequently today as in the past. That is the view that monetary policy is a dangerous weapon, especially when used to fight inflation—that it cannot be used in moderation, and if it is effective at all it is likely to be *too effective*, setting off a financial crisis and an ensuing recescesion. Paradox of paradoxes!

Thus, Alvin Hansen, for years the foremost American Keynesian, wrote in 1949:

The monetary weapon has the peculiar characteristic that it is scarcely at all effective unless the brakes are applied so vigorously as to precipitate a collapse. Those who glibly talk about controlling inflation by monetary policy have failed to consider that moderate monetary measures by themselves alone are relatively ineffective, while drastic measures may easily turn the economy into a tailspin.[4]

---

[4] Alvin H. Hansen, *Monetary Theory and Fiscal Policy* (New York: McGraw-Hill, 1949), p. 161.

A decade later, in 1959, in a report for the Joint Economic Committee of the Congress, practically the same thesis was reasserted by Warren Smith, who several years later was to become a member of President Johnson's Council of Economic Advisers: "It is perhaps just as well that monetary controls have not been very effective; if they had been, they might have been disastrous."[5]

Ten years later, in 1969, the same views were put forth by others, particularly the labor unions, as soon as monetary policy tightened in the early months of the year. And, as if such episodes were scheduled decennially, tight money during 1979 was again attacked by organized labor as courting potential disaster.

Assessments of monetary policy along these lines are paralyzing. In fact, such caveats by Keynesians are reminiscent of arguments by some Monetarists that countercyclical monetary (and fiscal) policies are more harmful than helpful. Thus, as we'll see in Chapter 25, Milton Friedman argues against any and all economic fine tuning. In partial anticipation of those arguments, let's examine a crucial determinant of one's predisposition towards active monetary and fiscal policies, namely the stability of the private sector of the economy. In recent years this has become the prominent element in Monetarist-Keynesian debates.

Is the Private Sector Inherently Stable?

Monetarists tend to believe that GNP will be relatively unaffected by autonomous shifts in investment spending. Keynesians argue that unless there is an active attempt at stabilization, the level of economic activity and unemployment will fluctuate considerably when buffeted by entrepreneurial animal spirits. While these beliefs have often taken on a religious fervor, they are grounded in the rather prosaic mechanisms of Chapters 17 and 18.

Monetarists, reflecting their Classical ancestry, argue that any exogenous decrease in investment spending would be countered automatically by either increased consumption or endogenous investment spending. The mechanism could be attributed, somewhat mysteriously, to the fixed money stock, hence a relatively fixed level of total spending based on the quantity theory. Or, in keeping with Classical interest

[5] Warren L. Smith, "Monetary Policy and Debt Management" in *Staff Report on Employment, Growth and Price Levels* (Joint Economic Committee, 1959), p. 401.

theory (see Chapter 17), to a reduction in interest rates that would follow a downward shift in the investment function. The drop in interest rates would, in turn, stimulate investment spending, reduce saving (thereby increasing consumption) and make up for the initial drop in investment.

As long as that mechanism worked, there would be no need to intervene by pushing policy buttons, neither monetary nor fiscal. The level of nominal GNP would not be buffeted by exogenous shocks.

Keynesians are less impressed with the automatic offsets to gyrations in investment spending. First, the mysterious quantity theory linkage between money and nominal GNP is simply not part of the picture. Moreover, the interest rate does not necessarily respond to a drop in investment (remember, from Chapter 18, it is determined primarily in the money market). And even if the interest rate did decline, there's no guarantee that it will induce very much investment. You can forget about any help from consumption—if anything, it makes matters worse by declining with falling GNP. Thus, according to Keynesians, it is essential for the government to step in and stabilize GNP.

Fluctuations in the price level are another source of stability, according to Monetarists. If, for example, consumption and investment didn't rise fast enough to offset the initial decline in investment spending, the resulting unemployment would drive down prices. A fixed money stock with lower prices means a larger real supply of money. This could stimulate spending directly via the quantity theory. Alternatively, the larger real supply of money would lower interest rates—in good Keynesian fashion—and investment spending would increase still further. The Keynesian response to such price effects is twofold: first, prices rarely decline; and second, the spending effects are too slow to rely upon to restore full employment.

The Monetarist-Keynesian confrontation on the need for an active stabilization policy rests on empirical assessments of the speed and power of the natural stabilizers in the economy—fluctuating interest rates and prices. It would seem a rather straightforward task to measure such real-world characteristics and to ascertain who is correct. But, as we'll see in Chapter 24, that is simply not the case.

"Mr. Semple, who wants to stimulate the economy, help the cities, and clean up the environment, I'd like you to meet Mr. Hobart, who wants to let the economy, the cities, and the environment take care of themselves. I'm sure you two will have a lot to talk about."

Drawing by Stan Hunt; © 1976 by The New Yorker Magazine, Inc.

The Interest Rate: Where Does It Go and Why?

Returning to the monetary mechanism, it is obvious that, to Keynesians, one of the keys to the effectiveness of monetary policy is what happens to interest rates on financial instruments. Unless the increased liquidity produced by an expanding money supply lowers interest rates (and unless the decreased liquidity produced by contracting the money supply raises interest rates), monetary policy is probably impotent.

Even the wealth effect of monetary policy, mentioned earlier, which has been invoked by latter-day Keynesians, operates through interest rates: Higher interest rates imply lower securities prices, and lower interest rates imply higher securities prices. Such changes in wealth may or may not have a significant impact on spending. But if an expansionary monetary policy is to carry with it a wealth effect, it must lower interest rates; if a contractionary monetary policy is to have wealth effect, it must raise interest rates.[6]

Monetarists, however, do not view interest rates on securities as a major link in the transmission belt between a change in the money supply and the ultimate impact on spending. Indeed, in one version of Monetarism, if financial market interest rates do not change at all it probably indicates a very *powerful* monetary policy, since presumably the entire change in liquidity is spent *directly* on goods and services and none at all on financial assets.

The controversy between Monetarists and Keynesians over interest rates is even more complex. Milton Friedman has argued that an *expansionary* monetary policy *raises* interest rates and a *contractionary* monetary policy *lowers* interest rates; just the reverse of standard Keynesian analysis. How does Milton do it? Here's the point: An increase in the money supply *may initially* lower interest rates, if the increased liquidity is spent on financial assets. But that is only the beginning. Once GNP responds to the increased money supply (as it must in the Monetarist world) the transactions demand for money will increase, thereby driving interest rates upward. But this is hardly new. Mainstream Keynesians certainly wouldn't disagree. The Monetarists argue, however, that the "income effect" of the increased money

---

[6] Those who have read Chapter 19 may note that the wealth effect can be introduced in the *IS–LM* framework by making the *IS* curve flatter than otherwise, thereby increasing the impact of a change in money supply on GNP. The wealth effect makes the *IS* curve flatter for the following reason. A decline in the rate of interest not only increases investment spending, but also increases wealth, and thereby induces consumers to spend more. For a given decline in the rate of interest, therefore, both investment and consumption go up, which then cause income to rise by a larger amount.

supply will overwhelm the initial "liquidity effect" so that the interest rate snaps back past its original level.

If pressed on this last point, Keynesians might even acquiesce as well: After a while interest rates *could* pass the original equilibrium, but it all depends on the speed and strength of the response in GNP to monetary expansion. Keynesians would focus their attention on the interim period—before GNP expands. And this interim period is sufficiently long to justify the following statement: Expansionary monetary policy *means* lower interest rates, and contractionary policy *means* higher rates

But there's more. Until now we've ignored inflation (the Monetarist-Keynesian debate on inflation will be explored in Chapter 23), but it plays a key role in the response of interest rates to monetary policy. In particular, if expectations of inflation are generated by an expansionary monetary policy, then this will cause a *further* increase in the level of interest rates. The reason is as follows: A credit instrument promises to repay the principal of the loan after a certain time period plus an interest payment as a reward to the lender. The interest and principal are fixed in dollar terms. For example, a $1,000 one-year note which promises $50 in interest yields 5 percent. This is the nominal yield. If the rate of increase in prices during the year is 2 percent, then it takes $1,020 at the end of the year to buy, in terms of real goods and services, what $1,000 would have purchased a year earlier. Thus, in *real* terms the lender is receiving an interest return of only 3 percent. It is simply a fact of life, therefore, that the nominal rate of interest minus the rate of inflation equals the real rate of interest.

But financial experts aren't dumb. If lenders expect prices to rise by 2 percent during the next 12 months and want to receive 5 percent in real terms, they will demand 7 percent from borrowers. As long as borrowers expect the same rate of inflation, they will go along with the higher nominal rate of interest. After all, if they were ready to pay 5 percent with no inflation, they should be equally eager to borrow money at 7 percent with 2 percent inflation—they will be paying off the loan in "cheaper" dollars.[7]

What might lead *both* borrowers and lenders to expect inflation and then arrive at a higher nominal rate of interest? You guessed it— an expansionary monetary policy! When such inflationary expecta-

---

[7] Borrowers would like to pay only 5 percent. But competition for funds forces them to pay what lenders demand, unless they are willing to pass up some investment projects. But inflation will increase the expected *dollar* returns on investments so that if a project was worth undertaking before it would be just as worthwhile with inflation and the higher nominal interest rate.

tions are tacked on to the income effect, Monetarists contend that it is virtually certain that these two will dominate the initial liquidity impact and expansionary monetary policy will lead to higher interest rates. An analogous argument can be made for contractionary monetary policy lowering interest rates.

Notice, by the way, that the Classical foundations of Monetarism are clearly visible in these arguments. Increases in money lead to inflation via the quantity theory. The interest rate (the *real* interest rate—the Classicists never spoke about fake rates) is determined by savers and investors. They "pierce the veil" of money and refuse to let inflation interfere with their agreed-upon *real* rate of interest. Thus an "inflation premium" is added to the real rate and increases in money supply raise the nominal rate of interest (the one that is recorded on bonds and other credit instruments).

The story just told of interest rates rising due to the inflationary expectations generated by expansionary monetary policy has taken on an added dimension called rational expectations. In particular, inflationary expectations that incorporate the predictions of economic models, such as the quantity theory of money, as well as the predictable behavior of policy makers, are called rational expectations. They are rational in the sense that all potentially relevant information is brought to bear on the formulation of expectations. Nothing is left out.

The consequences of such apparently innocuous logic are simply amazing. In particular, if policy makers are expected to increase the money supply in an effort to lower interest rates, there will, in fact, be no effect at all on real interest rates since such anticipated money stock movements will have been already incorporated in portfolio decisions. For example, the liquidity effect of the anticipated increase in money stock will have already raised bond demand to take advantage of anticipated capital gains; thus no further bond price increases occur when the money stock actually increases. All that's left is the quantity theory effect which says that increases in money stock raise prices. Thus, the anticipated rate of inflation generated by expansionary monetary policy pushes up nominal interest rates. There simply aren't any intermediate steps. Rational expectations provide a closer link between money and prices and between money growth and inflation and severs the usual Keynesian connection between money and interest rates.[8]

Lest this be dismissed as idle theorizing, the *New York Times* article reprinted here lends credibility to the entire mechanism. Of course, journalists are at least as gullible as the rest of us—their

---

[8] For an exposition, see Frederic Mishkin, "Efficient Markets Theory: Implications for Monetary Policy," *Brookings Papers on Economic Activity* (1978:3).

discussions should receive no more weight than pedantic academic analyses.

Nevertheless, the rational expectations story sounds convincing. Remember, however, the simple quantity theory operates only at or near full employment. At lower levels of economic activity, there is considerable slippage between money and prices. Even near what we designate as full employment there are wage and price rigidities because of contractual arrangements that render simplistic the proportional relationship between money and prices.

Can we really be this far in a book on money and not be sure which way interest rates respond to monetary ease or stringency? Yes and no—unequivocally.

Most Monetarists and Keynesians generally agree that *initially* an expansionary policy lowers interest rates (and a contractionary policy raises them). But for how long? If the impact on real spending is strong, or if expectations of price changes are generated, the initial interest rate change will be reversed and rates may very well snap back past what they had been originally. Thus interest rates could be either lower or higher at some point after an expansionary monetary policy, depending on the speed and strength of the response in GNP and on what happens to expectations regarding inflation. (Similarly, interest rates could be either higher or lower at some point after tight money begins, depending on the same factors.)

Is It Money or Credit?

A subsidiary but important debate between the Monetarists and the Keynesians is whether the Federal Reserve, in conducting monetary policy, should look only at the money supply or at overall credit conditions as well.

The Keynesian analysis is a *credit,* as opposed to a strictly *monetary,* chain of causation. In a sense, money per se is seen as not too important until it finds its way into the hands of a potential spender. To a Monetarist, anyone holding money is a likely spender. But to a Keynesian, a loan transaction may be necessary to move money from its current owner, who may be holding it idle, to a borrower who wants to spend it. Thus the Keynesians take a credit view, concerned with financial assets, credit availability,.the direction of interest rates, the reaction of lenders and borrowers to rate changes, and the role of financial markets as conduits for funds.

WALL STREET FEARS OVER MONEY SUPPLY ARE SAID TO WORSEN

SHARP RISE COULD LIFT RATES

'Considerable Alarm' Is Expected if Bulge Develops at It Did in '77 —Inflationary Effect Seen

By JOHN H. ALLAN

Many of Wall Street's money market economists are beginning to worry that the nation's money supply is about to mushroom, touching off a sharp rise in interest rates this spring.

A year ago, when the basic money supply expanded $5.4 billion in early April, short-term interest rates were quick to respond. The rate on three-month Treasury bills jumped a half-point to 5 percent by mid-May.

Overly rapid growth in the money supply is regarded as one of the chief ingredients of an inflationary economy, and the behavior of money is watched closely for clues to the future behavior of business activity and prices. Over the past several years, the Federal Reserve has frequently responded to faster money supply growth by encouraging short-term interest rates to rise.

Indicators Due Out

Jeffrey A. Nichols, chief economist at Argus Research Corporation, warned that when the monetary indicators come out this Thursday, they could show "substantial" rise. The money supply has increased sharply during the first week of each of the past four quarters, he noted, adding that he "would not be at all surprised" if it happened again this week.

Seasonal distortions continued "to plague the reported data" even after the Federal Reserve's recently announced revisions in the statistics, Mr. Nichols observed. The revisions were made to take into account money deposit at banks that do not belong to the Federal Reserve System, as well as seasonal shifts.

According to Allen Sinai of Data Resources, a Lexington, Mass., investment advisory concern, growth in the money supply has already begun a series of increases that will raise it toward the upper limits of the Federal Reserve's short-run targets.

'Considerable Alarm' Seen

"Within a couple of weeks, there will be considerable alarm over the monetary growth rates," Mr. Sinai predicted.

Last Thursday afternoon, the Federal Reserve reported that the basic money supply, which is known as M-1 and which consists of money on deposit in checking accounts at commercial banks plus currency in circulation, rose $600 million to average. That took it to an estimated seasnally adjusted $341.3 billion in the week ended March 29. (The figures are reported after a one-week lag.)

With this $600 million increase, M-1 showed a two-month growth rate of 1.2 percent, well within the Federal Reserve's targeted range of 1 percent to 6 percent. For the latest 52 weeks, however, M-1 has shown a 6.9 percent growth rate, compared with the 6.5 percent maximum that the Federal Reserve would like to promote for the year from the fourth quarter of 1977 to the final three months of 1978.

The concern among some money market economists is that M-1 will soon begin to expand more rapidly, pushing the growth rate above the Fed's short-run target and further above the long-term maximum as well.

"The financial markets are ticking away like a time bomb," Mr. Sinai declared, asserting that the pressure of a rebounding economy, diminished liquidity and tighter money would push interest rates "significantly higher" over the next few weeks.

Some Express Optimism

This pessimistic outlook is not universal, of course.

The money-supply figures for this week "should not be as excessive as at the beginning of (recent) quarters," William E. Gibson, money market economist at Smith Barney, Harris Upham & Company said.

Higher interest rates in response to "surging monetary growth" can be expected late in April or early in May, not sooner, he indicated.

The Federal Reserve early last week "made every effort to convince the markets that short-term rate policy had not been changed," Mr. Gibson noted.

According to Alan C. Lerner, vice president at Bankers Trust Company, confidence in the Carter Administration's anti-inflation strategy "has all but evaporated" as the Federal budget deficit has continued so large so late in the current business expansion.

With G. William Miller, the Federal Reserve chairman, forecasting higher inflation and with the President not expected to offer a strong anti-inflation program when he speaks tomorrow, the stage may be set for a move toward tighter monetary policy, Mr. Lerner reasoned.

Aubrey G. Lanston & Company said in its highly regarded weekly letter this week, "the Administration can't be expected to urge greater monetary restraint." "It would be nice, however," the firm concluded, "if the Administration should indicate that it no longer will stand in opposition to such action."

NEWS ITEM / Money Supply and Expectations—
Confounding the Conventional Wisdom

SOURCE: *New York Times*, April 10, 1978

To a Monetarist, all this is excess baggage, more harmful than helpful (Monetarists love that phrase; it seems to fit just about anything Keynesians do). It is money per se that counts, and its effects on GNP are not roundabout but direct. To look at anything else is only a distraction.

As an illustration of a case where the two views diverge, assume that funds move from an individual to a business firm in a loan transaction (such as the purchase of a newly issued corporate bond). The money supply remains the same; the corporation now has more, but the individual has less. To a Monetarist there will be no net change in spending, since there has been no change in the money supply; the business firm, with more money, will increase its spending, but this will be offset by the lender, with less money, decreasing his. A Keynesian, on the other hand, would say that the result is more likely to be a net increase in spending; the lender is probably parting with what were idle balances, which in the till of the borrowing corporation will now be activated.[9] The money supply is unchanged, but its velocity will increase.

The Federal Reserve adheres essentially to a credit, rather than a strictly monetary, approach. Indeed, it frequently shies away from the term *monetary policy* in favor of the broader *monetary and credit policy*. Open market operations, reserve requirement changes, and discount rate movements affect credit conditions at least as much as they affect the money supply. Credit conditions include, among other things, interest rates on a wide variety of securities, the volume of activity in the various financial markets, bank reserve positions, credit extensions by commercial banks, and the flow of funds into and out of other financial institutions. The Federal Reserve considers all such credit conditions as well as the money supply when it decides what action it should or should not take.

In fact, for many years the Federal Reserve's Board of Governors in Washington seemed to consider changes in the money supply only incidentally, perhaps not even on a par with other financial variables. Recently, prodded by the Monetarist-oriented Federal Reserve Bank of St. Louis, the money supply has become more prominent in board deliberations. Nevertheless, the skeptical attitude toward excessive emphasis on the money supply remains, as revealed by the label the board's research staff has pinned on the maverick St. Louis Bank's analytical framework—Brand X.

---

[9] Note that the theoretical Keynesian models of Chapters 18 and 19 are too narrow even for a Keynesian in this case. Even the *IS–LM* analysis of Chapter 19 is not broad enough, or complex enough, to handle most loan transactions.

Nonbank Financial Intermediaries

One of the earliest confrontations between modern Monetarists and Keynesians focused on the influence of nonbank financial institutions, such as savings and loan associations and savings banks, on the efficacy of monetary policy. Since savings deposits could not have checks written on them, they were technically not part of the narrowly defined money stock. But they seemed sufficiently close to demand deposits to warrant the question: Should monetary policy be concerned with such nondemand deposit liabilities of financial intermediaries in gauging the impact of monetary policy?

Recent changes in regulations have blunted much of the debate. Some savings deposits have direct checking privileges while others can be automatically transferred to checking accounts. The distinctions between commercial banks, S&Ls, and savings banks are less pronounced than they once were, as was stressed in Chapter 7. Nevertheless, the controversy survives in the form of the various definitions of money that are promulgated by different schools of thought. Let's go to the original source of the debate and then see what lessons can be drawn for the current situation.

John G. Gurley and Edward S. Shaw of Stanford University wrote a series of articles in the mid-1950s that eventually became known as the Gurley-Shaw thesis.[10] They emphasized that the deposit liabilities of savings and loan associations, savings banks, and other financial intermediaries are, after all, not much different from the demand deposit liabilities of commercial banks, even though we generally call only the latter "money." It is true that we can spend demand deposits, and that we cannot spend a savings and loan share without cashing it in first. But cashing it in is a simple matter, easily accomplished; thus savings and loan shares and savings deposits, whether at commercial banks or at savings banks, are for all practical purposes almost as liquid as demand deposits.

Gurley and Shaw conclude that since these near-monies are outside the jurisdiction of the Federal Reserve, they make the successful execution of monetary policy difficult. Controlling liquidity only through the narrowly defined money supply will not work very well, since liquidity can also be provided by near-monies. For example, assume the Federal Reserve reduces the narrowly defined money supply to inhibit spending on real and financial assets. Interest rates on securities rise. Now the intermediaries go into action. Aware of the

---

[10] The general exposition of their arguments is in *Money in a Theory of Finance* (Washington, D.C.: Brookings Institution, 1960).

higher yields and the profits they imply, savings and loan associations raise the rate they offer on deposits in an effort to attract more funds, which they can then invest in the higher-yielding securities. The increase in deposit rates induces some individuals to put more funds in savings banks, savings and loan associations, and so on. Financial intermediation shifts into high gear.

The individuals switching money to the intermediaries may use funds they formerly had invested directly in securities, thus rebuilding their liquidity; they also may use what were idle money balances, now coaxed out of hiding by the attractive rates posted and widely advertised by the intermediaries. As long as the latter occurs to some extent, there will be a net expansion in the demand for market securities (by the intermediaries), a consequent moderation in the rise in interest rates, and—most important of all—the channeling of previously idle money balances into the eager hands of ultimate borrower-spenders.

We can illustrate the above with our now familiar money-supply-money-demand model of interest rate determination. Financial intermediaries partially offset monetary policy as follows. In Figure 4, let's

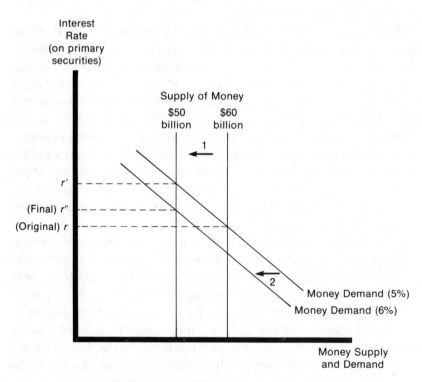

FIGURE 4 / Financial intermediaries can shift the demand for money to the left and thereby partly offset the effect of tight money on market interest rates.

start out with a narrowly defined money supply of $60 billion and a demand for money that is specified for a particular interest rate on saving deposits, say 5 percent. The equilibrium interest rate on primary securities is r. To tighten monetary policy, the Fed reduces the money supply to $50 billion. The interest rate on securities should rise to r', with the usual effects on investment and GNP. But as open market rates begin to rise from r to r', financial intermediaries raise the rate they offer on saving deposits (say from 5 to 6 percent). With higher rates available on these deposits, the public reduces its demand for narrowly defined money (at every open market rate), thus the demand for money shifts to the left, as Figure 4 indicates. The result is that the rate of interest on primary securities rises from r only to r'' instead of r'.

The behavior of financial intermediaries therefore partially offsets the impact of monetary policy on interest rates. Rates still rise as a result of tight money, but less than they would have without the intermediaries. Investment spending goes down, but by less than if market rates had gone all the way up to r'. The Fed has difficulty in controlling inflation because it can't control nonbank financial intermediation and the creation of near-monies.[11]

The Gurley-Shaw hypothesis, first developed in the mid-1950s here and at about the same time in England by the Radcliffe Committee, seemed vindicated by the experience of the 1950s and early 1960s. At that time, tight money invariably was accompanied by the mobilization of idle balances, an expansion in intermediation by financial institutions other than commercial banks, and consequent financing of the boom by these intermediaries. Debate raged as to whether the Federal Reserve should have the power to set reserve requirements for savings banks and savings and loan associations, and congressional hearings were held to explore ways to solve the problem.

As we will see in Chapter 27's discussion of housing and disintermediation, the tight-money episodes of 1966, 1969 and 1974 ran counter to the Gurley-Shaw thesis. But concern over whether monetary policy should monitor savings deposits at S&Ls and savings banks continued, and led to the popularization of the by-now-familiar ex-

---

[11] Tight money and higher open market rates can never be *completely* offset because of financial intermediary activity for the following reason: The intermediaries lower the public's demand for money by raising their deposit rates. But they raise their deposit rates only because rates on primary securities go up. If open market rates drop all the way back to the original interest rate, r, intermediaries will be paying more to their depositors but receiving no more on their assets (primary securities). Faced with a profit squeeze, they would then lower their deposit rates and the demand for money function will shift back to the right.

panded monetary aggregates. In some sense, M2 and M3 owe their existence to Gurley and Shaw.

The recent regulatory changes which have blurred the distinctions between saving and checking accounts create still greater uncertainties over what to include and what to exclude from monetary aggregates. Most Monetarists favor a narrower definition of money, arguing that if nonchecking account liabilities of financial intermediaries are included, why not add other liquid assets, such as short-term Treasury bills, to the definition. Since a line must be drawn to delineate an operational target that the Fed can focus on to influence GNP, many Monetarists stop with the medium of exchange characteristic. Now that savings banks and S&Ls can issue checking accounts, those liabilities should be included in the definition of money. Other liabilities are no better (nor worse) than Treasury bills, and therefore should be excluded. Keynesians, on the other hand, downgrade the importance of any *single* measure of monetary policy. In keeping with the precept that confusion to your enemy is bliss in your heart, they enjoy the lengthy list of Ms that currently populate monetary analysis.

A Compromise?

Monetarists claim that monetary policy should be conducted only for the purpose of controlling the money supply. Keynesians argue that interest rates and credit availability are at least as significant, maybe even more so. Monetarists contend that changes in the money supply are the major reason for fluctuations in GNP. Keynesians maintain that credit conditions are more important than the money supply, and, in any event, that fiscal policy is more important than either. The following chapters discuss still other areas of disagreement between Monetarists and Keynesians.

Ultimately, these differences can be settled only by empirical tests. As is often true in economic research, however, the factual evidence necessary to resolve the issues has been ambiguous at best and misleading at worst. There are credible (and incredible) empirical studies by eminent economists that come to diametrically opposite conclusions. In Chapter 24 we will explore the available evidence regarding the strength of monetary policy.

In its usual posture of deep humility, the Federal Reserve has refused to declare either interest rates or the money supply as the supreme channel through which monetary policy influences real economic activity. As the Federal Reserve sees it, concentrating solely on money market conditions and interest rates can lead to uncontrolled and even perverse movements in the money supply. Similarly, by focusing only on the money supply and related aggregates, interest rates are seen as subject to wider fluctuations than otherwise.

In a world of uncertainty, the Federal Reserve can never be perfectly sure of the source of the decline in economic activity that it seeks to prevent, or the cause of the inflationary pressures it seeks to thwart. Under such circumstances, it feels obliged to focus on *both* monetary aggregates *and* interest rates in the formulation and execution of monetary policy. These points are sufficiently important to warrant further elaboration by way of some examples.

Assume that a decline in economic activity is on the horizon, precipitated by a reduction in business investment spending. The correct course to follow would be expansionary monetary policy: lower interest rates, increase the rate of growth in the monetary aggregates to pump liquidity into the economy, and thereby thwart the impending contraction with both barrels. If the Fed looked at interest rates as its only guideline, it would observe a fall in rates simply because business firms have decided to spend less and borrow less and because there is a diminished need for cash with a decline in economic activity. The Fed might simply do nothing, since interest rates are already falling—in which case the money supply would not increase at all.

Or, if the decline in economic activity is sufficiently great and interest rates fall by more than anticipated, policy makers may be induced to cut back on the money supply, thereby lessening the decline in rates but *lowering* the monetary aggregates. By requiring, under such circumstances, faster growth in the aggregates as a target of monetary policy, the Fed guards against such a perverse outcome.

Suppose, on the other hand, that the decline in economic activity is precipitated by an increased demand for liquidity by households— they want to hold a greater percentage of their portfolio in the form of cash. This would lead to less spending and lending by households, hence higher interest rates, and on both counts lower economic activity. The correct course to pursue is, once again, expansionary monetary policy to increase bank reserves and the money supply at a faster rate in order to provide for the increased demand for liquidity and to lower interest rates to encourage spending. If the Fed learned its lesson from the previous example and therefore concentrates only on the aggregates, it will expand the money supply. But if households' demand for liquidity is increasing at a faster rate, their spending will still decline, they will lend less, interest rates will continue to rise, and the contraction in economic activity will not be prevented. By requiring, under such circumstances, lower interest rates as a target of monetary policy, the Fed guards against such errors.

As long as there is uncertainty over the cause of fluctuations in economic activity, *both* interest rates and monetary aggregates must be used as targets of monetary policy. A Monetarist places more emphasis on money supply and related aggregates, since he views velocity and the public's demand for liquidity as relatively stable and predictable. Keynesians rely more on interest rate targets because they are less convinced of a stable demand for liquidity and a predictable velocity. The Federal Reserve—also known as the Great Compromiser —uses both.

Suggestions for Further Reading

A good summary of the modern Keynesian view of money, in contrast with the modern Quantity theory, is Lawrence S. Ritter, "The Role of Money in Keynesian Theory" in *Banking and Monetary Studies*, ed. Deane Carson (Homewood, Ill.: Irwin, and Dorsey Press, 1963). A presentation of both sides of the Monetarist-Keynesian dispute on several issues is in Yung Chul Park, "Some Current Issues in the Transmission Process of Monetary Policy," International Monetary Fund *Staff Papers* (March 1972). The "credit versus money" debate is set forth in William L. Silber, "Monetary Channels and the Relative Importance of Money Supply and Bank Portfolios," *Journal of Finance* (March 1969). Finally, for an explanation by some of the protagonists themselves see Warren L. Smith, "A Neo-Keynesian View of Money," in *Controlling Monetary Aggregates* (Federal Reserve Bank of Boston, 1969); and Milton Friedman and Anna J. Schwartz, "Money and Business Cycles," *Review of Economics and Statistics* (February 1963 Supplement). An excellent survey of the points of disagreement between Monetarists and Keynesians is the discussion among Leonall C. Andersen, Lawrence R. Klein, and Karl Brunner in the September 1973 issue of the Federal Reserve Bank of St. Louis *Review*. In an attempt to settle matters once and for all a conference was held at Brown University in 1974. The proceedings are now available in Jerome L. Stein, ed., *Monetarism* (New York: North-Holland, 1976). Their only request is that you identify your affiliation so you can be certain to get the correct unexpurgated version in the appropriate binding (red for Keynesians, blue for Monetarists).

Chapter 21

Financial Aspects
of Fiscal Policy

FISCAL AND MONETARY POLICY are usually thought of as independent alternatives. In practice, however, the use of fiscal policy often carries monetary implications. As a result, the impact of government spending on the economy cannot be fully assessed until we know how the government *finances* its spending. Where does it get the money from? Does it raise the funds by taxation or by selling securities (i.e., by borrowing), and if the latter, who does it borrow from? To see how and why the method of financing government spending matters, let's start out by examining the relevant T-accounts. We will then proceed to see what the Monetarists and Keynesians have to say on the subject.

Financing Government Spending

The federal government can finance its expenditures in any of five alternative ways. It can raise the funds it needs by (1) taxation, (2) borrowing from the nonbank public, (3) borrowing from the commercial banking system, (4) borrowing from the Federal Reserve, or

(5) printing money. Each method has somewhat different implications for bank reserves and the money supply.

1. *Taxation.* Assume the government decides to spend an additional $100 million on water pollution control equipment, and chooses to raise the money by levying taxes on everyone who takes more than one shower a week. As the taxes are collected, they are initially deposited in the Treasury's accounts at commercial banks throughout the country, called the Treasury's "tax and loan accounts." Thus demand deposits (DD) at commercial banks are transferred from private ownership to Treasury ownership. The relevant T-accounts look as follows:

T-Accounts for Taxation

U.S. Treasury		Fed. Res. Banks		Commercial Banks		Nonbank Public	
A	L	A	L	A	L	A	L
DD in comm. bank + $100					DD of Public − $100	DD in comm. bank − $100	Taxes due − $100
Taxes due − $100					DD of Treasury + $100		

As a result of this step alone, the money supply falls by $100 million since government deposits are not counted in the money supply.[1] Bank reserves, however, are not yet affected. But before the Treasury spends the money, it first shifts the funds from the commercial banks to a Federal Reserve Bank so that it can make its disbursements from a central account. *This* step depletes total bank reserves by $100 million, as the following T-accounts show:

T-Accounts for Shifting Funds to the Federal Reserve

U.S. Treasury		Fed. Res. Banks		Commercial Banks		Nonbank Public	
A	L	A	L	A	L	A	L
DD in comm. bank − $100			Member bank dep. − $100	Dep. in FRB − $100	DD of Treasury − $100		
DD in FRB + $100			Treasury deposit + $100				

[1] The money supply is defined as currency and demand deposits owned by the nonbank public, because it is designed to measure the *private* sector's liquidity.

Having raised $100 million and shifted it from commercial banks to its account at the Federal Reserve, the government now spends it. When expenditures are made, the Treasury writes checks on its demand deposit account at the Fed to pay its suppliers. The suppliers deposit the checks in commercial banks, and the banks send the checks to the Fed for collection. The result is that the money supply *and* bank reserves go back up by $100 million:

T-Accounts for Government Spending

U.S. Treasury		Fed. Res. Banks		Commercial Banks		Nonbank Public	
A	L	A	L	A	L	A	L
DD in FRB — $100			Member bank deposit + $100	Dep. in FRB + $100	DD of public + $100	DD in comm. bank + $100	
Goods & services + $100			Treasury deposit — $100			Goods & services — $100	

By combining all the effects of acquiring funds via taxation and spending the money, we see that neither the money supply nor bank reserves are altered. The money supply falls when taxes are collected, but it rises by the same amount when the government spends the proceeds. Similarly, bank reserves at first decline when the Treasury shifts the funds to its account at the Fed, but then reserves are replenished when the Treasury spends the money.[2]

2. *Borrowing from the nonbank public.* Alternatively, suppose people who take more than one shower a week amount to a substantial voting bloc (not very likely), and Congress decides it would be the better part of valor not to tax them. Instead, the Treasury finances its spending—now *deficit* spending—by borrowing, specifically by selling bonds to the nonbank public. The T-accounts are the same as for taxation, except this time people get a government security for their money instead of a receipt saying they paid their taxes:

---

[2] While the end result of the government's taxation and spending is to leave the money supply and bank reserves unchanged, the *timing* of the shifting of funds from tax and loan accounts at commercial banks to the Fed, and of subsequent expenditures, create management problems for commercial bankers and for the Federal Reserve, as we saw in Chapters 14 and 15.

T-Accounts for Borrowing from Nonbank Public

U.S. Treasury		Fed. Res. Banks		Commercial Banks		Nonbank Public	
A	L	A	L	A	L	A	L
DD in comm. bank + $100	Debt outst. + $100				DD of Public − $100	DD in comm. bank − $100	
					DD of Treasury + $100	Govt. bond + $100	

Again, as with taxation, this reduces the money supply, transferring it from the pockets of the public to the accounts of the Treasury. When the Treasury shifts the funds to the Fed, bank reserves are also reduced, but as soon as the government spends the funds the money supply and bank reserves bounce back to where they had been originally (we have already seen the T-accounts for both of these transactions). The net result: After all is said and done, just like the taxation case, neither the money supply nor bank reserves are altered (although this time the public does wind up with more government bonds than before).

3. *Borrowing from the commercial banking system.* The Treasury need not sell its securities to the nonbank public. Instead of the public buying the securities, the commercial banks might buy them. The ultimate net effects of this depend on whether the commercial banks are (a) fully loaned up to begin with (zero excess reserves) or (b) have excess reserves. To see why this is so, let's examine each possibility.

(a) If the banking system is fully loaned up to begin with, it will not be able to buy the government securities unless it first disposes of other assets. This is because the purchase of the government securities would result in an increase in Treasury demand deposits at commercial banks, against which required reserves must be held. To release sufficient reserves, private deposits have to be reduced by a corresponding amount. By selling $100 million of other investments to the public, the banks can now buy $100 million of government bonds from the Treasury. The relevant T-accounts are as follows, with the banks' liquidation of other investments above the dashed line and their subsequent acquisition of government securities below it:

T-Accounts for Borrowing from the Commercial Banking System
(zero excess reserves)

U.S. Treasury		Fed. Res. Banks		Commercial Banks		Nonbank Public	
A	L	A	L	A	L	A	L
				"Other" securities − $100	DD of Public − $100	DD in comm. bank − $100	
						"Other" securities + $100	
DD in comm. banks + $100	Debt outst. + $100			Govt. bonds + $100	DD of Treasury + $100		

These transactions, by themselves, decrease the money supply, because the public has less deposits. (Although the Treasury has gained deposits, we have pointed out above that Treasury deposits are not counted as part of the money supply.) But, as in our previous cases, the Treasury shifts its funds to its account at the Fed and then spends them. When the funds are spent, the public's money holdings are restored to their former level. So after all is said and done, once again there is no change in either total bank reserves or the money supply.

(b)   On the other hand, if banks have excess reserves to begin with, then they will not have to dispose of other securities or call in loans in order to make room for their new purchases of Treasury securities. Thus, that part of the T-accounts above the dashed line would not be necessary. The banks buy the Treasury bonds, open up a new deposit for the Treasury, the Treasury shifts its balance to the Fed, and then spends the money. When the Treasury spends, individuals receive brand new demand deposits (for which they give up goods and services). Under these circumstances, financing a deficit by borrowing from the banks *increases the money supply* by as much as the deficit (but it does not alter total bank reserves).

4.   *Borrowing from the Federal Reserve.* The Treasury[3] still has

---

[3] In ordinary circumstances, the Treasury does not sell securities *directly* to the Federal Reserve. Rather, newly issued Treasuries are brought to market through auctions held by the Federal Reserve Banks. The Fed acts as the Treasury's fiscal agent—distributing issues to ultimate buyers (see the Appendix to Chapter 30 for a more complete discussion). Securities dealers such as those encountered in Chapter 14's open market operations, buy newly issued Treasury obligations for their inventory, to distribute to their customers. Our example in the text would be implemented if the Federal Reserve bought back some of these newly issued securities from dealers.

two options remaining. For one, it could borrow the money directly from the Federal Reserve:

T-Accounts for Borrowing from the Federal Reserve

U.S. Treasury		Fed. Res. Banks		Commercial Banks		Nonbank Public	
A	L	A	L	A	L	A	L
DD in FRB + $100	Debt outst. + $100	Govt. bonds + $100	Treasury deposit + $100				

In this case the Treasury does not have to shift the funds to the Federal Reserve prior to spending them; they are already there. Also, this method of borrowing reduces neither the money supply nor bank reserves. The government merely sells some bonds to the Fed, gets a checking account for them, and is in business. Painless. Also, as you might suspect, potentially inflationary if carried too far. Because when the Treasury *spends* the funds, the public winds up with more demand deposits and the banks with more reserves, as our T-accounts for government spending (that we saw earlier) show. Indeed, this way of financing is every bit as inflationary as the fifth method, printing greenbacks.

5. *Printing money.* Instead of borrowing from the Federal Reserve, the Treasury could do virtually the same thing by printing currency, depositing it with the Fed, and then spending from its account at the Fed. The T-accounts for printing money are almost identical with those for borrowing from the Fed; the only difference is that the Treasury gives the Fed non-interest-bearing currency instead of interest-bearing bonds. But that is a meaningless difference, since at the end of the year the Federal Reserve turns over most of its earnings to the Treasury anyway.

T-Accounts for Printing Money

U.S. Treasury		Fed. Res. Banks		Commercial Banks		Nonbank Public	
A	L	A	L	A	L	A	L
DD in FRB + $100	Currency outst. + $100	Treasury currency + $100	Treasury deposit + $100				

Since printing money and borrowing from the Fed are practically the same, why doesn't the government just print money when it wants to instead of borrowing from the Fed? Because then the inflationary consequences of the government's finances would be too visible and too many people would complain. Borrowing from the Federal Reserve is more complicated. Since most people don't understand that it is the same thing as printing money, they don't criticize what is happening.

Having gone through each of the five ways the government can finance its spending, let's summarize how each affects the money supply. At one end of the spectrum, taxing, borrowing from the non-bank public, and borrowing from commercial banks with zero excess reserves leaves the money supply and bank reserves unaltered after the government spends. In the middle are the net effects of spending money acquired by borrowing from banks with excess reserves: the money supply rises by the amount of the deficit, but total bank reserves do not change. At the other end of the scale are the net effects of borrowing from the Fed or printing money: in each of these cases, both the money supply and total bank reserves rise by the amount of the deficit.

Keynesians Versus Monetarists on Fiscal Policy

As we have seen, the way government spending is financed has monetary implications, and these are likely to influence fiscal policy's ultimate effect on aggregate spending and GNP. For example, when government spending rises and GNP goes up as a result, the public's need for day-to-day transactions money is likely to rise along with GNP. If the supply of money does not increase simultaneously, the public will find itself short of cash, will presumably sell off some financial assets in order to try to get additional money, and will thereby drive up interest rates. This so-called "crowding out" effect may inhibit private investment spending and home building, partly offsetting the expansionary impact of the government's spending. In brief, both the execution and net impact of fiscal policy appear to be inextricably bound up with monetary implications.

The Keynesian position on these matters is that any fiscal action, no matter how it is financed, will have a significant effect on GNP. Keynesians do not deny that interest rates are likely to rise as GNP goes up, unless new money is forthcoming to meet cash needs for day-to-day transactions. Thus, they admit that a deficit financed by money creation is more expansionary than one financed by bond sales to the public, and that both are more expansionary than increased government spending financed by taxation. However, Keynesians do not believe that the decrease in private investment spending caused by higher interest rates will be great enough to offset fully the government's fiscal actions. They think that the net effect will be significant, and in the right direction, regardless of what financing methods are used.

One reason for this conclusion is that higher interest rates have dual effects. They may reduce private investment spending, but they may also lead people to economize on their cash balances, thereby supplying part of the need for new transactions money from formerly idle cash holdings. Put somewhat differently, even if an expansion in government spending is not financed by new money, the velocity of existing money will accelerate (in response to higher interest rates) so that the old money supply combined with the new velocity will be able to support a higher level of spending and GNP.

The Monetarist view is that unless an increase in government spending is financed by new money creation, it will not alter GNP. Since velocity is seen as more or less stable, a direct link exists between the money supply and GNP. In order for GNP to rise, the money supply must expand.

If an increase in government spending is financed by borrowing from the Fed or by printing money, it will indeed increase spending and GNP. But according to the Monetarists, it is not the deficit that is responsible—it is the additional money. Furthermore, a deficit is a very clumsy way to go about increasing the money supply. Why not simply have the Federal Reserve engage in open market operations? That would accomplish the same purpose, a change in the money supply, without getting involved in budget deficits or surpluses.

As the Monetarists see it, a fiscal deficit financed in any other way—as by selling bonds to the public—will not affect aggregate GNP. True, the government will be spending more. But others will wind up spending less. Net result: No change in total spending or in GNP. The rise in government spending will *initially* increase GNP. However, this will increase the demand for cash for transactions purposes and drive up interest rates, and bond sales to finance the government's expenditures will drive up rates still further. The public will be buying government bonds and financing the government, instead of buying corporate bonds and financing business firms. Business firms will be "crowded out" of financial markets by the government. The rise in interest rates will reduce private investment spending by as much as government spending is increased, and that will be the end of the story. Government fiscal policy, unaccompanied by changes in the supply of money, merely changes the proportion of government spending relative to private spending.[4]

Another way to express Monetarist objections to the Keynesian emphasis on fiscal policy is to think in terms of the long run versus the short run. As Monetarists see it, Keynesians concentrate too much on first-round (or short-run) effects, and tend to ignore subsequent long-run financial implications. The magnitude of the long-run financial aspects of a fiscal deficit or surplus is, in fact, much greater than the direct spending impact.

For instance, assume a budget deficit is produced by an increase in government spending financed by money creation. The increase in government spending is a once-for-all expansion. But the deficit must be financed continuously. After a year, if the deficit is financed by creating money, the change in the money supply will equal the increase in government spending. But if the deficit persists through the next year, the money supply will again rise by the same amount. The same will hold true in the next year and the next. In other words, as the Monetarists view it, deficit spending may work eventually not because of its direct spending effects, but rather because of the long-run monetary effects that deficits produce.

How to Decipher the Stance of Fiscal Policy: A Footnote

Time and again, in this chapter as well as in many others, we have discussed expansionary and contractionary fiscal policy in terms of deficits and surpluses in the federal budget. A budget deficit is ex-

---

[4] Anti-inflationary fiscal policy encounters similar objections from the Monetarists. An increase in tax rates that generates a fiscal surplus reduces private income and consumer spending. If the government destroys or simply holds the money (the tax revenue it has collected over and above its expenditures), the surplus is accompanied by a reduction of the money supply in private pockets. Both Keynesians and Monetarists would agree that this is anti-inflationary, although for different reasons—the Keynesians because of the direct fiscal impact on consumer spending (with the tax increase reducing people's take-home pay) and the Monetarists because of the contraction in the money supply.

But if the government uses the surplus to retire part of the national debt, the funds flow back into the economy. The government retires debt by buying back its bonds. Bond prices are driven up, interest rates fall, and private investment spending increases. Keynesians would argue that GNP will still decline, that the debt retirement is a minor ripple on a huge wave. Monetarists, however, would say that private investment spending will increase until it replaces the cutback in consumer spending, leaving no net effect on GNP. For more on the mechanics of debt retirement, see Lawrence S. Ritter, "A Note on the Retirement of Public Debt During Inflation," *Journal of Finance* (March 1951).

HOW TO SCORE (OLD-TIMERS' DAY)

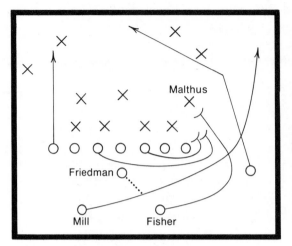

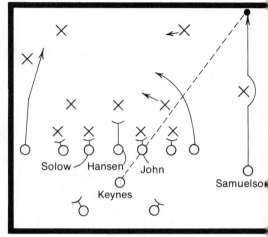

Monetarist Power Sweep

Milty Friedman hands off to J. S. Mill—who streaks down the right sideline behind a big block (actually a clip) by Swifty Irving Fisher that completely upends Big Tommy Malthus.

Keynesian Long Bomb

J. M. Keynes hits Poor Paul Samuelson with a TD pass—fantastic blocking by the unsung heroes of the front line, led by Bob Solow, Alvin Hansen, and Elton John (betcha didn't know he was a closet Keynesian).

pansionary and a surplus is contractionary. However, it is time to point out that there are serious limitations to using the *current* deficit or surplus as a guide to the stance of fiscal policy.

The problem of interpreting the stance of fiscal policy stems from the fact that tax receipts, hence the size of the deficit or surplus, vary passively with GNP. Congress sets tax *rates*, not receipts; receipts then go up and down with GNP. Given the level of government spending, when GNP rises tax receipts automatically increase and surpluses are automatically created (or deficits reduced). When GNP falls, tax receipts decline and deficits automatically result.[5] Thus, it is impossible to draw any meaningful conclusions regarding the stance of fiscal policy by comparing a budget surplus in one year at one level of GNP, with a deficit in another year at a *different* level of GNP.

For example, the existence of a deficit during a recession suggests, at first glance, that fiscal policy is expansionary. It may be, however, that the tax structure is so steep that it drives income (and thereby tax receipts) down to recession levels. A deficit may thus actually be the result of a *contractionary* fiscal policy. The tax cut of 1964 was enacted primarily on the basis of such thinking; its inten-

[5] In this respect tax receipts are very much like interest rates. As we pointed out in the previous chapter, they are not fully under the control of the government.

332

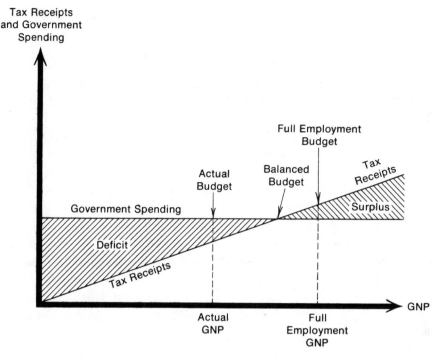

FIGURE 1 / The full employment budget.

tion was to reduce the "fiscal drag" on the economy. It was argued that the overly restrictive tax structure—with taxes rising too rapidly as GNP went up—made it virtually impossible for a rise in GNP to make any sustained headway.

The budget concept that *is* useful as an indicator of the posture of fiscal policy is called the full employment budget. The main problem in comparing deficits or surpluses in year X with year Y is that there are different levels of GNP in both years. As Figure 1 indicates, the idea of the full employment budget eliminates this problem by sticking to one concept of GNP, namely the full employment GNP. The full employment budget is defined as what the federal budget surplus (or deficit) *would be,* with the expected level of government spending and the existing tax structure, *if the economy were operating at the full employment level of GNP throughout the year.*

This calculated measure, the full employment budget, can be used to evaluate the effects and the performance of fiscal policy more meaningfully than the actual state of the budget, whatever it might be. As an illustration, in 1962 GNP was well below its full employment potential. As Figure 1 indicates, a low level of GNP produces a poor tax harvest and, consequently, a deficit in the actual budget. Nevertheless, fiscal policy was hardly expansionary. In fact, it was quite the opposite; if GNP had been at the full employment level, or close to it, tax revenues would have risen so greatly that the *full employment budget* would have had a substantial surplus. Conclusion: The fundamental stance of fiscal policy was restrictive, not expansionary, and one reason for the high level of unemployment in 1962 stemmed from fiscal policy—even though the actual budget showed a deficit.

Thus, in a rare example of fiscal bravery, a tax cut was passed by Congress in 1964 despite the existence of a current budget deficit. A reduction in tax rates swings the tax receipts line (in Figure 1) downward and diminishes the full employment surplus. An increase in government spending also shrinks the full employment surplus. A tax rate increase or a drop in government spending, both of which are restrictive actions, enlarge it. It is clear that changes in the *full employment budget* reflect basic *discretionary* changes in fiscal policy, as contrasted with movements in the actual budget that can be the *passive* result of fluctuations in GNP. The full employment budget is, therefore, a better indicator of the stance of fiscal policy than the actual budget.

Suggestions for Further Reading

For more on the monetary implications of fiscal policy, see Lawrence S. Ritter, "Some Monetary Aspects of Multiplier Theory and Fiscal Policy," *Review of Economic Studies* (1956). Also see David I. Fand, "Some Issues in Monetary Economics: Fiscal Policy Assumptions and Related Multipliers," Federal Reserve Bank of St. Louis *Review* (January 1970); and Roger W. Spencer and William P. Yohe, "The 'Crowding Out' of Private Expenditures by Fiscal Policy Actions," Federal Reserve Bank of St. Louis *Review* (October 1970). An advanced treatment of the monetary effects of fiscal policy is James Tobin, "An Essay on Principles of Debt Management," in *Fiscal and Debt Management Policies* by the Commission on Money and Credit (Englewood Cliffs, N.J.: Prentice-Hall, 1963). For a further note see D. H. Keare and your old buddy, William L. Silber, "Monetary Effects of Long-Term Finance," *American Economic Review* (June 1965). For an advanced treatment of the entire subject that should become a classic, read Alan S. Blinder and Robert M. Solow, "Analytical Foundations of Fiscal Policy," in *The Economics of Public Finance* (Washington, D.C.: Brookings Institution, 1974). Finally, a superb exposition of the subject is found in Benjamin M. Friedman, "Crowding Out or Crowding In? Economic Consequences of Financing Government Deficits," *Brookings Papers on Economic Activity*, 1978:3.

Appendix

Should We Worry About the National Debt?

Deficit spending is at the heart of Keynesian fiscal policy. We have just seen that deficits create government debt, in one form or another. There are many who think this is the sure road to perdition. Let's see if they're right.

Debt worriers are fond of statistical computations. We now have a national debt of some $800 billion (in the form of marketable and nonmarketable government securities, held by the public and by government agencies) and a population of about 220 million. Conclusion: Every man, woman, and child in this country owes about $3,635, whether he knows it or not. Every newborn infant starts life not only with a pat on the back but also with a $3,635 share of the national debt hanging over his head.

Is the situation really all that bad? Are the debt worriers right when they warn us that, by passing on a national debt of $800 billion, we are burdening future generations with a weight it will be almost impossible for them to bear? Are they correct in cautioning us, with stern voices, that we are penalizing those as yet unborn by forcing them to pay for our own vices and follies?

This is of direct concern to monetary policy for two reasons. First, the interest rate that the government pays on its debt is frequently cited as one of the key burdens passed on to future generations. If so, the monetary authority might be convinced to keep that cost to a minimum, in order to hold down the burden. In fact, this has happened in the past.[1] Second, the existence of the debt makes life more complicated for the Federal Reserve, because the Treasury must refinance part of the debt as it comes due. The Treasury often likes help on such occasions, and the Fed—while formally independent from the Treasury—still likes to maintain friendly relationships.

---

[1] See Chapter 37 for a discussion of the Fed's pegging of the interest rates on government securities.

The National Debt Equals the National Credit

The national debt is essentially the net result of past and present fiscal policy, mostly past. It is the sum of all past deficits, less surpluses, in the federal budget. A budget deficit requires that the government either print money or borrow to cover the deficit, and most modern governments choose to borrow (that is, sell government securities). As a result, we acquire a national debt, embodied in the form of government bonds; the total of government securities outstanding *is* the national debt. It is increased by every additional deficit we incur and finance by issuing more bonds.

If the national debt is a debt, we must owe it to someone. Indeed we do—mostly to ourselves. Most of our government's bonds are internally held, that is, they are owned by citizens of the United States. Thus, while we the people (as the United States) *owe* $800 billion, we the people (as owners of government securities) are simultaneously *owed* close to the same amount. A government bond is, after all, an asset for whoever buys it.

All evidences of debt must appear on two balance sheets, and government securities are no different from any other IOU in this respect. Every IOU appears on the balance sheet of the debtor, as a liability; but it also turns up, not surprisingly, on the balance sheet of whoever is holding it, its owner, this time as an *asset*. Thus, every liability necessarily implies the existence of a financial asset owned by someone else. For the same reason, every *financial* asset implies a corresponding liability on the part of someone else.

This accounting gem has interesting ramifications. It means, for one, that merely creating money cannot, in and of itself, make a country richer, a conclusion that always pleases conservatives. After all, money is a financial asset, which implies that somewhere else there is a corresponding liability. If liabilities go up as rapidly as assets, the country as a whole (including both the government and the private sector) can be getting no richer.

Most of our money is in the form of demand deposits, which are liabilities of commercial banks. The part of our money that is in the form of coin or currency is a liability of either the United States Treasury or the Federal Reserve, depending on which agency issued it.

Thus merely creating money can hardly make a nation richer, no matter how much it creates. To become richer—to increase its net worth—a country must increase its output of *real* assets, its production of real goods and services. As conservatives like to point out, if we want to become wealthier we must work harder and produce more. Printing money, per se, will not do it.[2]

By the same token, however, exactly the same logic also implies that one of the conservatives' favorite incantations is equally false: the belief that increasing the national debt makes a country poorer. Government bonds are liabilities to the government but are financial assets to whoever owns them. If the national debt increases, someone's financial assets go up as much as the government's liabilities. If domestically held assets rise along with liabilities, the country as a whole can be getting no poorer.

The very term *national debt* is thus a half-truth. If it is a domestically held debt, it could just as well be called the *national credit*. Both labels are half-truths. As with all liabilities, it is *both* a debt (to the borrower) *and* a credit (to the lender).

To become poorer—to reduce its net worth—a country must reduce its holdings of real assets, curtail its production of *real* goods and services. Increasing the national debt, no matter how high, cannot in and of itself make a country poorer so long as it is owned internally. (Actually, about $125 billion of our $800 billion national debt is held by foreign citizens and institutions.)

Nor does an increasing national debt, just because of its size, impose a burden on future generations. As long as the debt is held internally, neither the interest nor the principal represents a dead weight on the backs of our children and grandchildren. The taxes that must be raised to pay the interest are merely transfers from one group within the economy, the taxpayers, to another group, the bondholders. Future generations inherit tax liabilities, but they also inherit bonds and the right to receive the interest on them.

Even if the debt had to be paid off, future generations, as inheritors of the bonds, would be making payments of the principal to themselves. In fact, of course, the federal debt never has to be fully repaid any more than does the debt of any going concern, public or private. As parts of the debt come due, they can be repaid with fresh borrowings. Continuous refinancing is typical of the modern successful corporation, because confidence in the company's ability to earn future income makes holding its bonds both safe and profitable. Similarly, confidence in the continuing viability and taxing power of the federal government eliminates the need for net repayment of principal, either currently or in the future.

---

[2] While the country as a whole does not get richer when the government prints money and spends it, the *private* sector's wealth does go up. This has been discussed in the literature in connection with the wealth effect of "outside money" (where outside money refers to money that is not offset *within* the private sector of the economy). This is the subject of extensive analysis in pure monetary theory and can safely be ignored for now. For bedside reading, see Don Patinkin, *Money, Interest, and Prices*, 2nd ed. (Harper & Row, 1965).

The Real Burden of the Debt: I

Does this mean that the debt worriers are completely off the track? Not quite, and therein lies the story of the *real* burden of the debt as contrasted with the imaginary burden.

In the first place, holdings of government bonds are not evenly distributed among the population. Some of us have more than our $3,635 share, much more; some have less, much less. Thus current interest payments on the debt, while "only" an internal transfer from taxpayers to bondholders, may create problems of legitimate concern to the public. If taxpayers are largely from the lower- and middle-income groups and bondholders are primarly in the upper income brackets, then the tax collection → interest payment transfer will increase the inequality of income distribution. Little is known about the pattern of interest payments on the government debt according to income of the recipient. This transfer *may*, therefore, interfere with social objectives of reducing income inequality.

Furthermore, if the federal debt grows at a faster rate than GNP, tax rates may have to be increased to meet interest payments. Higher tax rates may reduce work incentives. If so, production falls and overall economic well-being decreases. In the United States, however, the national debt has actually declined quite substantially as a proportion of GNP. In 1945 the national debt was about 130 percent of GNP; in 1955, 70 percent; in 1965, 45 percent; and in 1975, 38 percent.

Even if the debt falls as a proportion of GNP, if interest *rates* go up sufficiently, then tax rates may have to be raised to meet the interest payments, possibly reducing work incentives. Interest rates have indeed risen since 1945, but the interest "burden"—interest charges as a proportion of GNP—has not increased. Over the past 30 years, annual interest payments have fluctuated between 1½ and 2½ percent of GNP, with the most recent figure hovering at 2 percent.

The Real Burden of the Debt: II

Aside from the possible income-redistribution and work-incentive problems associated with interest payments on the national debt, there is one way in which the debt might impose a burden, a cost, on future generations. This involves not the interest, but the principal itself.

Should We Worry About the National Debt?

As we noted above, a country will become poorer only if it reduces its output of real assets, its ability to produce real goods and services. In this very meaningful sense, the wealth of future generations can be measured by the real capital stock they inherit, the real productive capacity we bequeath to them. A smaller capital stock permits less production, hence less consumption. A larger capital stock enables the economy to produce more, hence consume more.

Assume that the economy is already operating at a full capacity rate of production and that the budget is balanced. The government then increases its spending, financing its additional expenditures by sufficient new *taxation* to forestall inflation. In this case the increased use of resources by the government comes primarily at the expense of consumption. Consumers, left with less aftertax income, have to cut back their spending by as much as government spending has been stepped up.

Alternatively, under the same initial circumstances, assume that the additional government spending is *debt financed* rather than tax financed, and that a tight monetary policy is used along with debt financing to prevent inflation. Now interest rates will rise and the increased use of resources by the government will come primarily at the expense of investment instead of consumption. The higher interest rates will release resources from private investment for use by the government, with investment spending cut back by as much as government spending has been increased.

As a result, the production of new plant and equipment will be curtailed, and future generations will consequently inherit a smaller capital stock. Future productive capacity is lower than it might have been. In this limited sense, the "burden" of debt financed government expenditure is transferred to future generations.

Two qualifications are necessary. First, note that the argument assumes we start from a full capacity rate of production, roughly a full employment level of GNP. If the additional government spending were to take place during a recession, when there are idle resources available, there would be no "burden" on future generations, no matter how it was financed. During a recession there are unemployed resources that can be tapped, so the government can increase its spending without anyone else reducing theirs. There would be no reason to permit a rise in interest rates, since the danger of inflation would be minimal, and an expansion in spending and GNP would be beneficial to all.

Under such circumstances the future capital stock is not diminished. In fact, if the government's deficit spending succeeds in getting us out of the recession, the future capital stock will probably be *enlarged*. Thus increasing the national debt during a recession, instead of imposing a burden on future generations, is actually doing them a favor.

Second, the "burden" argument totally ignores what the government spends the money on. Assuming full employment, if the government's expenditure is for current consumption purposes—such as subsidizing inexpensive lunches for congressmen or schoolchildren—then total capital passed on to the future is indeed reduced. But if the government builds highways and dams or increases any type of capital asset that raises future productivity, the increased investment by the government replaces the decreased investment by private business. Future generations will inherit the same capital stock, except more will be in the form of public capital and less in the form of private capital.

Moving from theory to reality, the fact of the matter is that a significant part of our public debt stems directly from World War II military spending. In 1941 our national debt was $65 billion, and in 1945 it was $280 billion. Most of these expenditures occured during a period of full employment. Yet few would call this a burden passed on to the future. Without it, we might well have had no future.

Chapter 22

The Monetarists Versus the Keynesians (in Pictures)*

MODEST PETROVICH MOUSSORGSKY, the nineteenth-century Russian composer, published his popular *Pictures at an Exhibition* in 1874. Maurice Ravel later orchestrated these piano pieces and provided a royal introduction to *Pictures*—lots of horns (but no singing violins). Surely the Monetarist-Keynesian dispute deserves as much consideration. Unfortunately, when we suggested to Basic Books that they orchestrate a 45 rpm record with every copy of this book— perhaps the Beatles' *Taxman*, in honor of fiscal policy—they turned us down with icy stares. So we offer you the next best thing: The Monetarist-Keynesian dispute in pictures!

The last two chapters presented the Monetarists versus the Keynesians mostly in words. For those who have gone through the diagrammatic analysis of Chapter 19, it is possible to display a number of the differences between the Monetarists and the Keynesians, in both theory and policy, with that chapter's *IS–LM* model. This chapter, therefore, presents an *IS–LM* accompaniment to the last two chapters, with omissions where there is no *IS–LM* counterpart to the dispute. (In fact, one of the lessons of this chapter might be the *very* limitations of the *IS–LM* framework.)

---

* This chapter uses analytical techniques developed in Chapter 19. If you skipped Chapter 19, skip this one also.

The Monetarists on Money

Over strenuous objections from Monetarists, and recognizing that such an approach can risk doing an injustice to their cause, we can represent an oversimplified Monetarist position within the *IS–LM* framework. In fact, near the end of Chapter 19 the Monetarist "special case" in the Keynesian model was set forth: a demand for money unresponsive to interest rates—depending on income only—producing a vertical *LM* function (see Figure 17 in Chapter 19 and the discussion related to it).

In that world, things are very simple. Velocity is constant. With a fixed money supply, GNP can't change and neither does velocity. The impact of a change in money supply on the level of income equals ΔM multiplied by velocity (V). This can be seen in Figure 1. Start with *LM* and *IS* and equilibrium income Y. An increase in the money supply shifts the *LM* curve to the right by $\Delta M \times V$ (see footnote 3 of Chapter 19 and footnote 1 of Chapter 20). The new equilibrium level of income is Y' and it is obvious that the change in income from Y to Y' equals $\Delta M \times V$ *in this case.* Income continues to rise until all of the increased money supply is absorbed into increased transactions demand.

On the other hand, as Figure 2 shows, when the *LM* curve is not vertical but is positively sloped (as is the case when the demand for money that underlies it is somewhat responsive to the rate of interest), then the increase in income due to a change in the money supply will be less than in Figure 1. In Figure 2 we have superimposed a set of positively sloped *LM* curves (*LM* and *LM'*) on the Monetarist case of Figure 1. While the horizontal distance between the two *LM* curves is the same as before, the increase in income is clearly less than before.[1] Why? Because the increase in the supply of money lowers the interest rate, and at lower interest rates people will hold some of the increased money supply in the form of "idle" balances rather than for transactions purposes. Thus the velocity or rate of turnover of the *total* money supply falls (some of it is now being held "idle"). But we are running a bit ahead of ourselves; let's wait until we come to the Keynesian analysis of money to complete this part of our story.

Let us reemphasize that the Monetarists are playing the game under protest—they don't like the rules of the Keynesian *IS–LM* apparatus. It forces them into a situation where the change in money supply first lowers the interest rate, which increases investment, and thereby GNP. Figure 1 in Chapter 20 suggested a considerably more

---

[1] The horizontal distance between the two *LM* curves is the same as before, but now it is simply called $\Delta M \times 1/k$, because $1/k = V$ only when the interest-sensitivity of liquidity preference equals zero.

The Monetarists Versus the Keynesians (in Pictures)

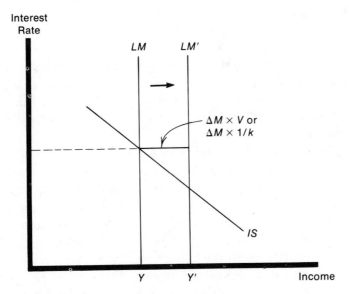

FIGURE 1 / When the *LM* curve is vertical, an increase in the money supply increases income by Δ*M* times velocity.

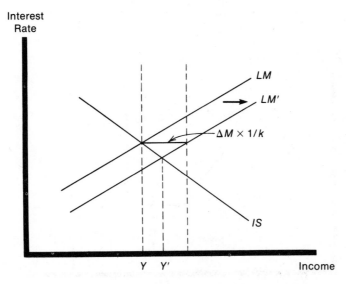

FIGURE 2 / When the *LM* curve is not vertical, an increase in the money supply is less powerful in increasing income.

direct channel, one that would be preferred by most Monetarists. While the vertical *LM* curve does convey some of the Monetarist flavor—i.e., the stability of velocity—it still leaves a Keynesian taste. Moreover, as we stressed in Chapter 20, the assumption of stability in velocity is replaced by predictability in less extreme versions of Monetarism. More on this in the next few sections.

Keynesians on Money

In terms of the *IS–LM* model, the Keynesian reservations about the potency of monetary policy can be summarized in a number of "special cases." First, an increase in money supply would not affect anything if the *LM* curve were horizontal at the relevant level of GNP, i.e., if the liquidity trap were a reality.

Figure 3's supply and demand for money functions form the basis for constructing Figure 4's *LM* functions. If we increase the money supply from *M* to *M'* in Figure 3's liquidity trap, then we get no shift in the *LM* function in Figure 4.[2] The *LM* curve with *M* (namely, *LM*) is the same as with *M'* (namely, *LM'*). As can be seen in Figure 4, when the *IS* curve intersects *LM* (or *LM'*), producing equilibrium income Y_{eq}, an increase in the money supply from *M* to *M'* does not lower the interest rate. All of the increased money supply is held as idle balances. Equilibrium income is unchanged. More money and the same level of GNP implies a decrease in velocity—the hallmark of the Keynesian critique of monetary policy.

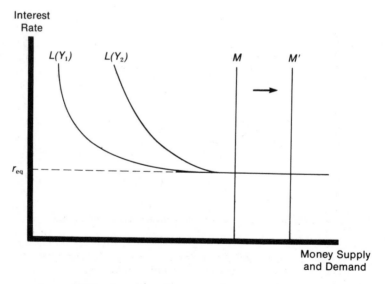

FIGURE 3 / With a liquidity trap, an increase in the money supply from *M* to *M'* does not shift the *LM* curve (see Figure 4).

[2] See p. 265 for a verbal derivation of the horizontal *LM* curve from a liquidity trap.

The Monetarists Versus the Keynesians (in Pictures)

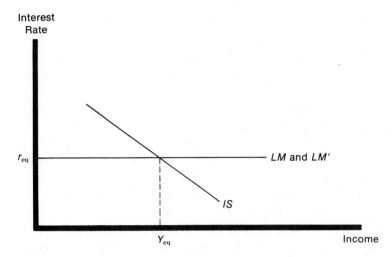

FIGURE 4 / With a liquidity trap, an increase in the money supply, since it does not shift the *LM* curve, does not change income.

A second category of pitfalls for monetary policy concerns the *IS* curve. Even if the liquidity preference function is well-behaved, so that an increase in the money supply succeeds in lowering the rate of interest, there might still be no impact on GNP if investment is completely unresponsive to the rate of interest. From Chapter 19 we know that the *IS* curve is very steep if investment has little interest-sensitivity; with zero interest-sensitivity, the *IS* curve is vertical. Under

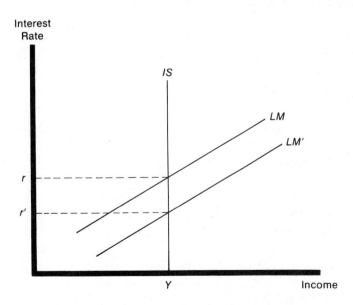

FIGURE 5 / When the *IS* curve is vertical, monetary policy is ineffective.

such conditions, changes in the money supply do not affect income even though they may change the rate of interest. Figure 5 illustrates that situation. Start with *IS* and *LM* and equilibrium income Y. Then, an increase in the money supply causes a rightward shift in the *LM* curve to *LM'*, which merely lowers the interest rate with no impact on GNP. Once again, the money supply has gone up but GNP hasn't, with velocity falling as a result.

To summarize: Monetary policy works in the Keynesian world when both the *IS* curve and the *LM* curve are "normal." Pathological cases of horizontal *LM*s and vertical *IS*s require fiscal medicine rather than monetary prescriptions to alter GNP. More generally, even when we are untroubled by horizontal *LM* curves and vertical *IS* curves, the impact of money on GNP is not the simple ΔM times a fixed velocity. For example, an increase in M may produce falling interest rates, more investment, and higher GNP. But GNP is not likely to rise in direct proportion to the change in M because interest rates decline, increasing the speculative demand for idle money along with the transactions demand. In other words, velocity is likely to decline.

Is the Private Sector Inherently Stable?

The vertical and horizontal LM curves depict extreme Monetarist and Keynesian positions, respectively. Moderate wings in both camps assert only that the LM curve is "nearly vertical" on the one hand or "quite flat" on the other. Such tendencies are sufficient to demonstrate the stability or instability of economic activity in the face of exogenous shifts in private investment.

Figure 6 shows two alternative LM curves: LM_{steep} and LM_{flat}. There are two IS curves representing shifts in autonomous investment. As can be seen in the picture, with LM_{steep} the induced fluctuation in GNP due to the shifting IS curve is S to S'. When the LM curve is LM_{flat}, however, the fluctuation in GNP is much wider, between F and F'. The key to the smaller fluctuation in GNP with LM_{steep} is that the level of interest rates fluctuates more than with LM_{flat}. Thus, when the IS curve shifts from IS' to IS, the interest rate falls a lot, inducing a large amount of endogenous investment to offset a large part of the decline in autonomous investment. With a flatter LM curve, the fall in the rate of interest is smaller and induced investment is less. Thus, a steeper LM curve stabilizes the level of economic activity associated with a particular stock of money because the interest rate

The Monetarists Versus the Keynesians (in Pictures)

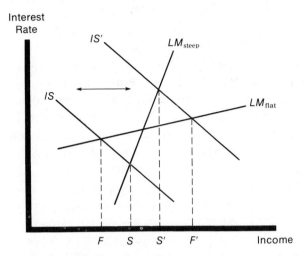

FIGURE 6 / A flatter *LM* curve means wider fluctuations in GNP due to exogenous shifts in investment.

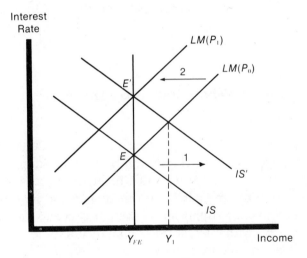

FIGURE 7 / At full employment fluctuations in the price

fluctuates more. That's not quite how Monetarists would necessarily tell the story, but it's close enough.

When the economy is operating near its full employment capacity, fluctuations in the price level help to stabilize the economy. Figure 7 shows the intersection of IS and $LM(P_0)$ at Y_{FE}. We introduced Y_{FE} at the end of Chapter 19. It represents the full employment level of GNP. The LM curve is labelled with a particular price index, P_0, since changes in the price level will affect the position of LM. Moreover, at full employment, it's quite possible that prices will change. A shift in autonomous spending pushes IS to IS' and raises aggregate demand to Y_1. When aggregate demand exceeds full employment capacity, prices rise. A rise in the price level with a fixed stock of money reduces the *real* supply of money (see the end of Chapter 19). This pushes the LM curve back towards the full employment line. This process stops once aggregate demand is back at full employment—in our picture this occurs at the intersection between IS' and $LM(P_1)$.

At the new equilibrium E' we have both a higher price level and a higher rate of interest. The higher price level reduced the real supply of money, raised interest rates, and pushed back aggregate demand to the full employment level. Thus, the fixed supply of money together with flexible prices and interest rates insulates full employment economic activity from exogenous changes in investment. The process would be reversed (lower prices and lower interest rates) if there were a decrease in exogenous investment (shifting IS to the left). Notice that Figure 7 has the elements of an inflation story. Rising prices were the result of aggregate demand (the intersection of IS and LM) exceeding full employment capacity. More on this in Chapter 23.

The Interest Rate: Where Does It Go and Why?

Some of the disagreement discussed in Chapter 20 about how the rate of interest responds to changes in the money supply can be illustrated within the *IS–LM* framework.[3] In Figure 8, let's start out with *IS* and *LM;* equilibrium is at *E* with income Y and interest rate *r*. An increase in the money supply shifts the *LM* curve to *LM'* and the new equilibrium is *E'*, with interest rate *r'* and income Y'.

How does the economy move from *E* to *E'*? Technically, this is a question in economic dynamics: the path of movement between one

[3] The distinction between nominal and real interest rates produced by inflationary expectations is not made within the simple *IS–LM* framework. Hence, that aspect of the argument discussed in Chapter 20 will not be reproduced here. As long as price expectations don't interfere, the two rates are equal; and unless stated otherwise, that is what we assume throughout the chapter. The Keynesian apparatus is not really geared to the real versus nominal rate distinction, although there have been some attempts. See William Gibson, "Interest Rates and Monetary Policy," *Journal of Political Economy* (May/June 1970); and Thomas Sargent, "Anticipated Inflation and Nominal Interest," *Quarterly Journal of Economics* (May 1972), and by the same author, "Rational Expectations, the Real Interest Rate, and the Natural Rate of Unemployment," *Brookings Papers on Economic Activity* (No. 2, 1973). See also Stephen F. LeRoy, "Interest Rates and the Inflation Premium," *Monthly Review* of the Federal Reserve Bank of Kansas City (May 1973).

The Monetarists Versus the Keynesians (in Pictures)

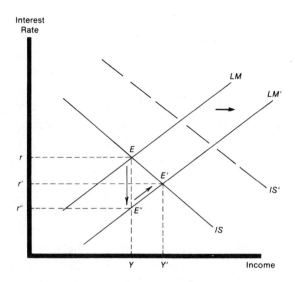

FIGURE 8 / When the money supply goes up, can the interest rate be far behind?

equilibrium and another. And while geometry is all right for comparing two equilibrium points (called comparative static analysis), as we have been doing, it has serious drawbacks in dynamics. Ever mindful of student desires, we decided to spare you the differential equations (if you promise to pay attention).

We start by assuming that immediately after the increase in money supply the level of income will remain unchanged, and the entire adjustment to the increased money supply will come in the form of a reduction in the rate of interest. This means the economy moves from E to E'' in Figure 8, and that the interest rate must initially fall to r'' to keep the amount of money demanded equal to the new supply at the same level of GNP. But E'' is not equilibrium because, although it is on the LM curve where money demand equals money supply, it is not on the IS curve, hence investment is not equal to saving. The fall in the interest rate means desired investment has gone up but so far saving hasn't. As a result—with investment greater than saving—production, income, and hence GNP begin to rise. The economy, therefore, moves up along the new LM curve toward E'.

This dynamic story suggests that even according to Keynesians the initial decline in the rate of interest (to r'') will be sharper than the ultimate response (the new equilibrium rate is at r'). Initially, the increased liquidity drives the interest rate way down. As income begins to rise, the interest rate is driven up. The liquidity effect of the increased money supply is partially offset by the income effect. Nevertheless, the negative slope of the IS curve does suggest that, in the traditional Keynesian model, the *equilibrium* interest rate after an increase in the money supply must be below the old rate. The income effect on interest rates does not swamp the liquidity effect.

There are other possibilities (even without introducing price expectations) that could lead to a *higher* interest rate after an increase in money supply without departing from the Keynesian spirit. One obvious possibility is a modestly upward sloping *IS* curve. Don't panic —we don't intend to go into this case; it introduces too many complications. We mention it just so that you are aware of it. And you can see (use your imagination) that if the *IS* curve is positively sloped, the new equilibrium interest rate will lie above the old.[4]

Another possibility is that as GNP rises entrepreneurs decide to invest more at every rate of interest. This can come about, for example, because of more exuberant expectations of future profits (as entrepreneurs extrapolate a trend in economic activity). This increase in "autonomous investment" causes the *IS* curve to shift to the right. If the shift is to *IS'* in Figure 8, the rate of interest will increase above r, despite an increase in the money supply.[5]

When the economy is operating at or near full employment, the Keynesian interest rate mechanism gives way completely to Classical/ Monetarist arguments. In particular, at full employment the rate of

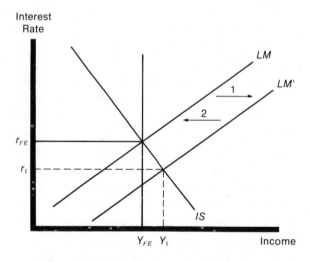

FIGURE 9 / An increase in money supply at full employment doesn't lower the interest rate.

[4] A positively sloped *IS* curve occurs under conditions that are described in Chapter 12 of Thomas F. Dernberg and Duncan M. MacDougall, *Macroeconomics*, 5th ed. (New York: McGraw-Hill, 1976). Also see William L. Silber, "Monetary Policy Effectiveness: The Case of a Positively-Sloped *IS* Curve," *Journal of Finance* (December 1971).

[5] This new position might not be considered equilibrium, however, if the rightward shift in the *IS* curve is based entirely on the *expansion* in GNP and its effect on entrepreneurs' expectations. At some point the bubble will burst, and then the *IS* curve shifts back.

interest is independent of movements in the money stock. This can be seen in Figure 9, starting with IS and LM intersecting at Y_{FE} and r_{FE}. The latter is the real rate of interest since, as usual, we are assuming the absence of any inflationary expectations. As always, an increase in money supply shifts LM to LM', apparently pushing down the interest rate from r_{FE} to r_1 and raising aggregate demand to Y_1. But the excess of aggregate demand over Y_{FE} causes prices to rise. This reduces the real supply of money, pushing LM' back towards LM. After all is said and done, prices have risen until the LM curve is back where it started, since otherwise prices would keep on rising. And when LM' is back at LM, the real rate of interest is restored to its original level. Thus, at full employment, increases in money supply cannot reduce the interest rate below r_{FE}. Similar reasoning shows that *decreases* in the money stock will not raise interest rates above r_{FE} if prices fall when aggregate demand is below full employment.

The interest rate r_{FE} has a special name. It's called the natural rate of interest and is defined as that rate which equates saving and investment at full employment. It is determined by the intersection point between the IS curve and the Y_{FE}-line. Shifts in the money stock can't change r_{FE}. Only shifts in the IS curve can, as we saw earlier in Figure 7. Thus, at full employment only saving and investment (including government spending) determine the interest rate; money has nothing to do with it. At full employment, classical interest theory pops out of the Keynesian picture!

The implications for the effect of expansionary monetary policy on interest rates at full employment are twofold: (1) The real rate of interest is unchanged by increases in money supply. (2) Nominal rates (not shown in the figures) will rise if inflationary expectations are generated by the increased money stock. The latter is quite likely especially in the long run. Borrowers and lenders recognize that excessive expansion in money stock means rising prices. This will no doubt lead them to agree upon an inflation premium attached to the real rate of interest. With the real rate fixed at r_{FE}, the net result is an increase in nominal rates by the expected rate of inflation.

The Fiscal Policy Dispute

In the beginning of this chapter we illustrated the Monetarist and Keynesian polar positions on monetary policy within the *IS–LM* framework—the vertical *LM* curve for the Monetarist power thrust and the

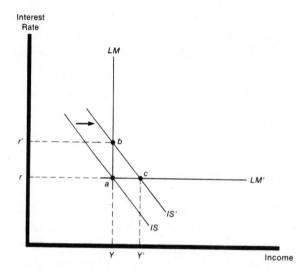

FIGURE 10/When the *LM* curve is vertical, fiscal policy is completely ineffective; when it is horizontal, it is totally effective.

horizontal *LM* curve for Keynesian monetary impotence. These polar cases have their symmetrical counterpart in that fiscal policy has a zero impact with a vertical *LM* curve, while it is completely effective (with no offsetting crowding out due to interest rate effects on private investment) with a horizontal *LM* curve.

Figure 10 illustrates these points. Let's start at point *a* with income *Y* and interest rate *r*. An increase in government spending (or a reduction in taxes) shifts the *IS* curve from *IS* to *IS'*. If the *LM* curve were *LM*, the new equilibrium would be at *b*, and the entire impact is absorbed by a higher interest rate with no increase at all in GNP. In this case there is complete crowding out, as discussed in the last chapter. But if the *LM* curve were *LM'*, the new equilibrium would be at *c* and the impact is entirely on GNP, with no rise at all in the interest rate; in fact, since the rightward shift in the *IS* curve equals ΔG times $1/(1-b)$, which also equals the change in GNP, the simple multiplier of Chapter 18 has returned in full bloom.

The general case of the positively sloped *LM* curve produces results that lie between the extremes, as we saw in Chapter 19. An increase in government expenditure raises GNP, but by less than the "full multiplier" of the simple Keynesian system. This is because the interest rate goes up, cutting off some private investment (there is partial but not total crowding out). The rise in the rate of interest does not lower investment by as much as government spending increases because the higher rate of interest also reduces the demand for money, permitting once idle speculative balances to be used for carrying out the increased transactions associated with higher levels of GNP. It would seem, therefore, that unless the economy is char-

"In theory, yes, Mrs. Wilkins. But also in theory, no."

acterized by the extreme case of zero interest-sensitivity of the demand for money (producing a vertical *LM* curve), even Monetarists would agree that fiscal policy could have some impact on GNP.

Not so fast, says Professor Friedman. The shape of the *LM* curve is only part of the story. Perhaps more important, the financing aspects of fiscal policy—especially in the long run—tend to dominate the direct impacts of a change in government spending or taxation. The *IS–LM* model is not readily adapted to illustrate such effects, despite some recent attempts.[6]

It is also important to note that at full employment an increase in government expenditure is crowded out in real terms, even if the LM curve has a positive slope. Return to Figure 7 above, which shows

[6] For example, William L. Silber, "Fiscal Policy in *IS–LM* Analysis: A Correction," *Journal of Money Credit and Banking* (November 1970), and Alan S. Blinder and Robert M. Solow, "Analytical Foundations of Fiscal Policy," in *The Economics of Public Finance* (Washington, D.C.: Brookings Institution, 1974), pp. 52–53.

a rightward shift in the IS curve at Y_{FE}. We can now use that same picture to represent an increase in government spending at full employment. Initially there is an increase in aggregate demand to Y_1, with investment demand declining (along the IS curve) to offset only part of the increase in government expenditure. A positively sloped LM curve permits such an expansion in aggregate demand. But that's not the end of the story. With aggregate demand, Y_1, exceeding full employment production, Y_{FE}, prices rise (from P_0 to P_1) pushing LM (P_0) back towards LM(P_1) and raising the interest rate still further. That process will continue until the new equilibrium E' is reached. At that point the real interest rate has increased by enough to cut off an amount of investment spending equal to the initial increase in government expenditure. How do we know? Simple. If that weren't the case, aggregate demand would still be above Y_{FE}, prices would still be rising, and so would the interest rate. (The logic is simply nauseating.)

Two points are worth noting in this example: First, the interest rate at full employment is obviously affected by shifts in the real sector of the economy, represented by the IS curve (even though it is unaffected by shifts in the monetary sector). Second, notice that nominal GNP is higher at E' compared with E. How do we know? Because real GNP is still at Y_{FE}, but prices are higher (P_1 versus P_0). Thus, while there is real crowding out at full employment even with a positively sloped LM curve, there isn't nominal crowding out as with the vertical LM curve.

The story at full employment is decidedly Monetarist-Classical, even when cloaked in a Keynesian framework. But that's not really as devastating to Keynesian protagonists as it initially seems. After all, at full employment Keynes was as Classical an economist as Milton Friedman and John Stuart Mill put together.

Suggestions for Further Reading

Two advanced articles on the complete Monetarist position, both by Milton Friedman, are: "A Theoretical Framework for Monetary Analysis," *Journal of Political Economy* (March/April 1970), and "A Monetary Theory of Nominal Income," *Journal of Political Economy* (March/April 1971). An even more recent exposition is by Karl Brunner and Allan H. Meltzer, "Mr. Hicks and the Monetarists," *Economica* (February 1973). For an interesting discussion by leading Monetarists and Keynesians over the nature of the issues, see the comments by Karl Brunner, Allan Meltzer, James Tobin, Paul Davidson, Don Patinkin, and Milton Friedman in "A Symposium on Friedman's Theoretical Framework," *Journal of Political Economy* (September/October 1972).

Appendix

Interest Rates Versus Money Supply Targets Under Uncertainty

In our discussion of the Federal Reserve compromise in the last section of Chapter 20, we indicated that the interest rate and the money supply were competing targets for monetary policy. We concluded that an optimum monetary policy strategy was to monitor both variables. This problem can be considered quite apart from the Monetarist-Keynesian dispute over the channels of monetary policy. In particular, it can be analyzed within the *IS–LM* framework under the most general circumstances—a positively sloped *LM* curve and a negatively sloped *IS* curve.[1]

The simplest point to demonstrate is that hitting a particular target in terms of the interest rate implies loss of control over the money supply, while hitting a money supply target implies loss of control over the interest rate. We don't even need *IS* and *LM* curves for that, just money demand and money supply curves. In Figure 1 let's assume that r^* is the target interest rate, and we start out with the original money supply and liquidity preference curves *M* and *LP*. If the demand for money shifts to *LP'* then the Fed must accommodate the demand by shifting the supply curve to *M'* if the rate of interest is to remain at r^*. Therefore, to peg the interest rate the Federal Reserve must be willing to relinquish control over the money supply. Figure 2 shows why keeping control over the money supply implies greater fluctuations in the rate of interest: with money supply fixed, shifts in the demand for money produce interest rates between r' and r''.

Is it always better for the Fed to specify a target for the money supply rather than the interest rate? Not necessarily. In terms

[1] The bulk of this discussion is based on an article by William Poole, "Rules of Thumb for Guiding Monetary Policy," in *Open Market Policies and Operating Procedures—Staff Studies* (Board of Governors of the Federal Reserve System, 1971). Poole also offers a simple demonstration within the *IS–LM* framework that monetary policy with an interest rate target minimizes *variability* in GNP when there are random fluctuations in the demand for money (and thus in the *LM* curve), while monetary policy with a money supply target minimizes *variability* in GNP when there are random fluctuations in the *IS* curve. This will be shown below as well.

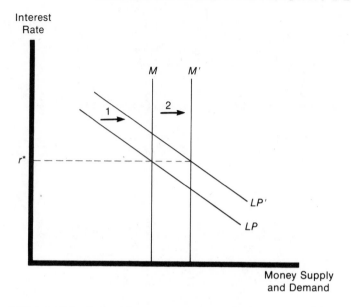

FIGURE 1 / If the Federal Reserve wants to peg the interest rate, it has to abandon control over the money supply.

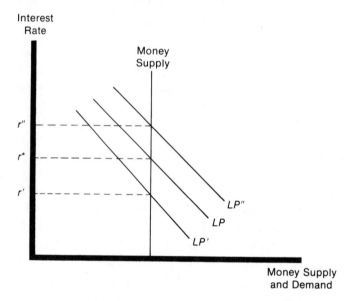

FIGURE 2 / If the Federal Reserve wants to peg the money supply, it has to abandon control over the interest rate.

of simple *IS–LM* analysis, if one knew the source of the variation in income, there would be no problem. Take the situation depicted in Figure 3. Starting out with *IS* and *LM* yields income Y and interest rate r. Now let's say the level of income starts to fall *because of a left-ward shift in the IS curve to IS'*. The equilibrium point moves from a to b. If the Fed knew what was happening, it would try to shift the *LM* curve to the right by increasing the money supply.

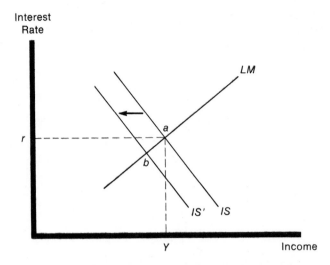

FIGURE 3 / A leftward shift in the *IS* curve lowers income. The interest rate falls, but monetary policy is not expansionary.

But with uncertainty as to the cause of the decline, the following might be the sequence of events. If the Fed takes the *interest rate* as its guide, it observes that the interest rate has fallen and concludes that monetary policy is already expansionary. Or, worse yet, if it adheres to the previous target level of the interest rate, it might even reduce bank reserves, shifting *LM* to the left, further aggravating the decline in GNP. By requiring expansionary Fed policy to provide *both* lower interest rates *and* increases in the money supply (or in a growth context, an increase in the money supply at a faster than normal rate), a rightward shift in the *LM* curve is assured.

Now take the other case: If the Federal Reserve has its sights set only on a particular *money supply,* this may also turn out to be insufficient to insure an expansionary monetary policy when GNP is declining. In Figure 4, the decline in income from Y is brought about *by a leftward shift in the LM curve to LM'* (as a result of an increase in the demand for money at every level of *r* and Y). The equilibrium point moves from *a* to *b*. If the money supply were held constant at the target level (or in a growth context, was increasing at its normal rate), the needed expansionary monetary policy would not be forthcoming. By requiring a *lower* rate of interest in this context, the money supply will have to rise (or its growth rate will have to increase) to provide the necessary stimulus—thereby shifting the *LM* curve to the right.

It appears, therefore, that the Federal Reserve would minimize its errors if it monitored *both* the interest rate and the money supply in executing a particular monetary policy: a conclusion which pleases extremists in neither camp. Rabid Monetarists insist the money supply come out a winner, and diehard Keynesians demand an interest rate

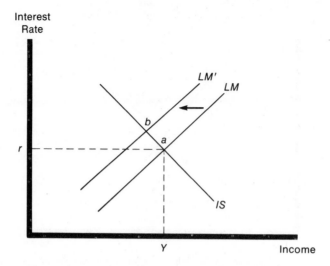

FIGURE 4 / A leftward shift in the *LM* curve lowers income. The money supply has not fallen, but monetary policy has become contractionary.

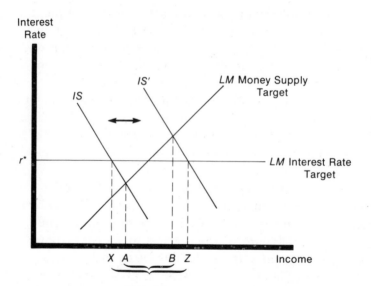

FIGURE 5 / With an interest rate target, an unstable *IS* curve leads to wider variation in GNP than if the Fed had a money supply target.

victory. Fortunately for the Fanatics, *IS–LM* analysis is sufficiently versatile to give each group what it wants—under the right circumstances.

Consider the situation where the major source of instability in GNP comes from unanticipated movements in the *IS* curve. In Figure 5 we have the *IS* curve shifting back and forth between *IS* and *IS'*. With a money supply target set by the Fed and a stable demand function for money, we have the standard money market equilibrium curve pictured in Figure 5. The level of GNP varies between *A* and *B*.

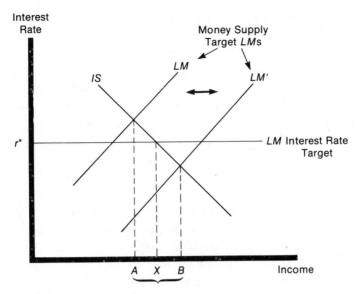

FIGURE 6 / With a money supply target, an unstable *LM* curve leads to wider variation in GNP than if the Fed had an interest rate target.

Compare this variability in GNP with what occurs when the Fed sets the interest rate as its policy target. Under such conditions we have the horizontal money market equilibrium curve in Figure 5.[2] GNP varies between X and Z. Clearly the money supply target is superior— it insures a smaller variability in GNP when the major source of instability is in the *IS* curve. A victory for the Monetarists.

When the game is played in the Keynesian ballpark, things turn out just the reverse. Here the demand for money is highly unstable. If the money supply is fixed by the Fed, and the demand for money shifts, then the *LM* curve moves between *LM* and *LM'* in Figure 6. With a fixed *IS* curve, GNP varies between A and B. But if the Fed uses an interest rate target, the relevant "*LM* curve" is again horizontal and there is no instability in GNP whatsoever. It stays put at X.

Monetarists insist that the most stable relationship in the economy (if not the world) is the demand for money. The Keynesian consumption function is much less stable. The *IS* curve is, therefore, the major source of GNP instability. Figure 5 tells the truth—a money supply target is best. Keynesians argue that if anything is unstable it is Monetarists themselves. Not being psychiatrists, they'll settle for

---

[2] The *LM* curve is flat under such circumstances because the Fed accompanies any increased demand for money with an increased supply, as we saw in Figure 1. Hence, higher levels of Y (which increase the demand for money) are associated with the same level of interest, r^*. Notice that the definition of the *LM* curve is slightly different: it is the combination of Y and r with a *given* Federal Reserve policy and not a *given* money supply. That's why we've called the *LM* curve by its formal name: the money market equilibrium curve.

an unstable demand function for money. The *LM* curve is, therefore, the major source of GNP variability. Figure 6 tells the truth—an interest rate target is best.

As in most Monetarist-Keynesian disputes the ultimate resolution lies in empirical evidence. No one believes that either the *IS* curve or the *LM* curve is perfectly stable. Unfortunately, there has been virtually no formal analysis of the *relative* stability of the underlying behavior in the real sector (*IS*) versus the monetary sector (*LM*). At least one observation does seem possible, however. Keynesians are the first to admit that investment is unstable. Hence, in order to assume a fixed or relatively stable *IS* curve, an accurately offsetting fiscal policy (such as *G* increasing whenever autonomous investment decreases) must be assumed. This makes the Keynesian case somewhat weaker than the Monetarist argument.[3] What this probably proves, in a somewhat broader context, is that if you want to win a debate you should never—but never—admit anything.

---

[3] Actually, the Monetarist case for a money supply target gets support from some Keynesians as well. The money supply acts as a built-in stabilizer, with interest rates fluctuating up and down to keep investment from rising too steeply or falling too far. There is an even more advanced argument in favor of the money supply target, based on rational expectations. See (at your own risk) Thomas Sargent and Neil Wallace, "Rational Expectations, the Optimal Monetary Instrument, and the Optimal Money Supply Rule," *Journal of Political Economy* (April 1975).

PART VI

The Effectiveness of Monetary Policy

Chapter 23

Monetary Policy and Inflation

ARTHUR F. BURNS, former Chairman of the Board of Governors of the Federal Reserve System, once told a visitor, "One of the greatest evils of inflation is that it leaves the President with no easy choices." When asked whether he thought the voters appreciate a real effort to stop inflation, he responded, "I like to think you are rewarded at the polls. But even if the reward isn't at the polls, I come from a culture where there is a belief in a reward in the hereafter."

Those of you who have been valiantly searching for the Eleventh Commandment can now rest easy; "Thou shalt fight inflation" has just been added to the scriptures!

To most of us, inflation is not something we pray for or against in houses of worship, but something we encounter in supermarkets, department stores, and, of course, doctors' offices. Needless to say, prices today are quite different even from what they were only 25 years ago. Workers and businessmen whose incomes have risen along with the rising prices can still visit their favorite stores and hospitals, although they probably can't stay as long as they used to in either place. But inflation is a more painful matter for many others, especially for the elderly and for retired or disabled people whose incomes are more or less fixed for the rest of their lives. At a sustained annual increase of 6 percent, prices will double every twelve years; at an increase of 8 percent, they will double every nine years; and if prices go up at the rate of 10 percent annually, they double every seven years.[1]

Under such circumstances, it is obvious that retirement incomes of a fixed dollar amount gradually melt away. A retirement income that is initially adequate slowly becomes marginal, and, as the years continue to unfold, approaches the level of sheer subsistence. About the only thing many older people can hope for is that they reach the hereafter before inflation does.

Who is responsible for inflation? Is money the culprit? Can we bring an inflationary spiral to a halt if we clamp down on the money supply? Can wage-price controls help?

Too Much Money Chasing Too Few Goods

The classic explanation of inflation is that "too much money is chasing too few goods." The diagnosis implies the remedy; stop creating so much money and inflation will disappear.

Such a diagnosis has been painfully accurate during those hard-to-believe episodes in history when runaway hyperinflation skyrocketed prices out of sight and plunged the value of money to practically zero. Example: Prices quadrupled in revolutionary America between 1775 and 1780, when the Continental Congress opened the printing presses and flooded the country with currency. The phrase "not worth a continental" remains to this day. Germany after World War I was even more extreme; prices in 1923 were 34 billion times what they had been in 1921. In Hungary after World War II it took 1.4 nonillion pengö in 1946 to buy what one pengö could purchase a few years earlier (one nonillion equals 1,000,000,000,000,000,000,000,000,000,-000).

Pathological breakdowns of this sort are impossible unless they are fueled by continuous injections of new money in ever-increasing volume. In such cases, money is undoubtedly the inflation culprit, and the only way to stop the avalanche from gathering momentum is to slam a quick brake on the money creation machine.

---

[1] As a special bonus, we give you "the rule of 72" for growth rates. If something (anything) is growing at a compound annual rate of x percent, to find out how many years it will take to *double*, divide 72 (the magic number) by x. For example, if prices are rising at 6 percent a year, they will double in $72 \div 6 = 12$ years. It isn't precise to the dot, but it's a useful rule of thumb. While we're on such things, there's another rule of thumb that has to do with cricket chirps and temperature. If you listen carefully to a cricket, the number of times it chirps in 15 seconds plus 37 equals the temperature in degrees Fahrenheit. Where else, we ask you, can you get such neat information?

Creeping Inflation

However, hyperinflation is not what we have been experiencing in this country in recent years. During World War II consumer prices rose by about thirty percent. In the immediate postwar years (1945–1949), after wage and price controls were removed, they climbed another 30 percent. None of this was unexpected or particularly unusual. Prices typically rise in wartime and immediately thereafter.

The unusual thing about prices and World War II is not that they rose so much during and immediately after it, but that they have never declined since. Quite the contrary—prices have continued onward and upward to this day, virtually without interruption, producing the longest period of continuous inflation in American history. In all prior wars, prices had gone up during and immediately after hostilities, but then had fallen back somewhat. Not this time. In all prior peacetimes, price increases had been interrupted from time to time by occasional corrective periods of stable or declining prices. No longer.

From 1949 through 1979, the cost of living increased in every year but one (1955). The annual rate of inflation over the entire 30-year period averages out at close to 4 percent per year. Prices are now almost triple what they were in the late 1950s, when most of you were born. They are double what they were in 1969.

This is not hyperinflation. It is not like America in 1775, Germany in 1923, or Hungary in 1946. This is a different sort of animal—nibbling away doggedly, insistently, without pause, at the purchasing power of the dollar. Prices do not skyrocket, they only creep—some years 6 percent, some years 10 percent—but always in the same direction, always up, up, up.

This type of inflation is something new. Is money the culprit here, too? Can creeping inflation, like hyperinflation, be stopped simply by slamming the brakes on the money supply? To work our way around these questions, it will be helpful to examine the recent inflation process a bit more closely.

Demand Pull

We understand fairly clearly—as well as anything is understood in economics, anyway—why the price level rises when aggregate demand exceeds the limits of the economy's full capacity output. This

365

is the orthodox inflation setting, exemplified in starkest form in war-time when we simply cannot produce enough goods and services to satisfy all would-be purchasers at existing prices. The excessive spending (in relation to the available supply of goods and services) bids up prices, thereby eliminating some potential buyers and, in effect, rationing the available short supply among those able and willing to pay more.

War thus generates the classic form of demand-pull inflation, with competition among buyers for the available goods and services driving prices higher. People are put to work producing war goods—which are bought by the government—but the incomes they receive, unless siphoned off by higher taxes, are as available as ever for the purchase of private consumer goods and services. At the same time, the output of civilian goods is curtailed as war production takes precedence.

Part of the reason for our inability to eliminate the inching up of prices is simply that we have never really brought World War II to a complete end. An entire generation has grown up that has never fully known peace. Intermittently, in the past quarter century, the financial, manpower, and matériel resources of the nation have been mobilized in an effort to produce both guns *and* butter. Budget deficits, shortages, and accelerated consumer and business buying plans have periodically converged, with the swollen aggregate demand outpacing the economy's productive capacity.

Cost Push

But that cannot be the whole story. There have been periods of relative tranquillity, primarily in the late 1950s and early 1960s, and since the Vietnam war ended, when international tensions eased and slack developed in the economy. But even then prices continued upward. For example, aggregate demand from government, business, and consumers was in no sense excessive during the years 1974 and 1975. If anything, demand was sluggish. Unemployment averaged about 7 percent of the civilian labor force during that two-year period; nevertheless, consumer prices rose by 11 percent in 1974 and by 9 percent in 1975.

Why should prices rise when spending is slow and we are far below full employment of our labor force and full capacity utilization of our industrial plant? In past years, before World War II, these were the very times when prices *fell* and the impact of prior inflation was to some extent ameliorated. Some new ingredients have evidently entered the picture since the 1930s, and drastically altered the economy's response mechanism.

One such ingredient is the economic strength of labor unions. The American Federation of Labor was founded in 1886, but the real power of trade unions to influence money-wages came with the passage of the Wagner Act and related legislation half a century later. On the basis of government encouragement of unionism as a declared principle of public policy, the expansion of the economy from the depression of the 1930s into the war boom of the 1940s carried with it an enormous growth in union membership. The ranks of organized labor jumped from 3 million members in 1933 to 9 million in 1940 and 15 million in 1946. Today, union rolls list almost 25 million members. The Taft-Hartley Act of 1947 corrected some union abuses, but it put hardly a dent in their newfound power to extract wage increases in excess of productivity growth, thereby generating round after round of higher production costs.

The second new ingredient—closely related to the economic power of organized labor, although not so recent an arrival—is the substantial market power of big business. Because of the nature of modern technology, which often results in lower unit production costs as the scale of operations expands, a few large firms dominate many major manufacturing industries. Their size enables these industrial giants to exert a degree of control over their prices that would be impossible in a thoroughgoing competitive environment, thereby permitting them, to some extent, to pass on cost increases to their customers.

The third new ingredient is the Employment Act of 1946, under which the government assumed responsibility for maintaining high employment through the use of its monetary, fiscal, and related powers. According to the Employment Act, "it is the continuing policy and responsibility of the federal government to use all practicable means . . . to promote maximum employment, production, and purchasing power." Without the support of the Employment Act, neither Big Labor nor Big Business, individually or in concert, could sustain a wage-price spiral for very long. In the absence of the Employment Act, labor would have to take more seriously the possibility that it might be jacking up money-wages too far—that excessive wage demands might force businessmen to cut back on their hiring. Businessmen would similarly have to guard against pricing their products out of the market. But such restraints are relaxed by the presence of a full employment guarantee underwritten by Big Government, standing ready to "insure prosperity" with injections of purchasing power should employment or sales decline too far.

Finally, in the past few years these three ingredients driving prices up have been joined by a fourth element: *imported* inflation. When the international oil cartel raised oil prices 400 percent late in 1973, we suddenly realized that our domestic price level has become extremely sensitive to actions quite beyond our control. Political extortion in the form of the 1973 Arab oil embargo had devastating economic impact. The prices that we have to pay for certain key imports from abroad—like oil and some other raw materials—have a pervasive influence on our own cost of living. When a well-organized international cartel, like the Organization of Petroleum Exporting Countries (OPEC), sets artificially high prices for its products and successfully limits its output to keep those prices up, the consequences include higher consumer prices in the United States (and elsewhere) regardless of the state of our domestic economy.

All of this has created an environment of inflationary expectations. And such expectations feed on themselves by forcing labor and business to enter contractual arrangements that pass on higher wages and prices in a never-ending spiral. The old-fashioned pattern of demand-pull inflation—excess aggregate spending, greater than the economy's productive capacity, pulling prices up—has not disappeared. Witness the Korean War period, the 1956–1957 episode, and Vietnam. But demand-pull (or buyers') inflation has been joined in the postwar period by a new form of inflation—cost-push (or sellers') inflation. Even when aggregate spending subsides, as from 1958 through 1964 and again in 1969–1970 and 1974–1975, prices still rise. The distinguishing feature of cost-push or sellers' inflation is a rising price level while the economy is still below a full employment (full capacity) rate of production.

Indeed, even when full employment is far distant on the horizon, Big Labor and Big Business start to turn the screws. Backed by substantial market (and political) power of their own, underwritten by a high employment guarantee that gives some immunity from the consequences of their actions, strong unions and large corporations begin throwing their weight around and marking wages and prices up even when aggregate demand is weak and anemic. As we move closer to full employment, they gradually become more aggressive until, in the immediate neighborhood of full employment, the pressure for higher wages and prices becomes literally explosive. At this point, for all practical purposes, cost-push and demand-pull become virtually indistinguishable as they interact and reinforce one another.

Actually, it is somewhat artificial to separate the two kinds of inflation to begin with; wage increases in excess of productivity growth mean higher costs for the businessman, thereby putting upward cost

*"I've called the family together to announce that, because of inflation,
I'm going to have to let two of you go."*

Drawing by Joseph Farris; © 1974 The New Yorker Magazine, Inc.

pressure on prices. Those same higher wages also mean larger incomes
for wage earners, thereby generating a step-up in consumer spending
that yanks prices up from the demand side. The stage is then set for
a new round of wage negotiations based on the increase in the cost
of living, as the process feeds on itself and continues ad infinitum. Or
is it ad nauseam?

Money and Creeping Inflation

Unlike hyperinflation, money is not so obviously the culprit when it
comes to the real problem of our times, creeping inflation. The "fit"
between the money supply and the cost of living exists, but it is rather
loose and a bit baggy.

Take, for example, the four decades from 1930 to 1970:

1. From the end of 1930 to the end of 1940, the money supply increased by 70 percent, but prices, instead of rising, fell 15 percent.
2. From 1940 to 1950, the money supply increased by 175 percent, but prices rose by only 80 percent, less than half as much.
3. From the end of 1950 to the end of 1960 provides the best fit; the money supply grew by about 25 percent and the consumer price index rose by about 20 percent.
4. However, from 1960 through 1970 the relationship sags again; the money supply increased by 40 percent, but prices by just 20 percent.

Upon further examination, even the close relationship during the 1950s turns out to be less impressive. During the first half of the decade, the money supply increased twice as fast as prices; and during the second half, prices increased twice as rapidly as the money supply. At the end of the 1960s the money supply was about 4½ times larger than it had been in 1940, but prices were "only" about 2½ times higher.

This is not meant to imply that money has nothing to do with creeping inflation. Quite the contrary, it has a great deal to do with it, if only because, sooner or later, people will not be able to continue buying the same amount of goods and services at higher and higher prices unless the money supply increases. If the money supply today were no larger than it was in 1940 ($40 billion), or even than it was in 1950 ($115 billion), prices would have stopped rising long ago—and so would real economic activity.

Over the long run, an increase in the money supply is a *necessary* condition for the continuation of inflation, creeping or otherwise.

But it is not a *sufficient* condition. Increases in the money supply will not raise prices if velocity falls (as in the 1930s). Even if velocity remains constant, an increase in the money supply will not raise prices if production expands. When we are in a depression, for example, the spending stimulated by an increase in the money supply is likely to raise output and employment rather than prices. Furthermore, in the short run at least, and sometimes the short run is a matter of several years, increased spending and inflation can be brought about by increases in velocity without any increase in the money supply.

Nevertheless, it bears repeating that inflation can persist for any length of time only by grace of the central bank. If the inflation is primarily demand-pull, a cutback—or mere stability—in the money supply will sooner or later put an end to further increases in spending, and thereby eliminate, or at least substantially moderate, the upward drift of prices. If the inflation is primarily cost-push, a cutback or stability in the money supply will sooner or later make it difficult, if not impossible, for business firms to sell their products at higher and higher prices—and thereby make it equally impossible for them to continue granting wage increases in excess of productivity growth, no matter how strong labor may be.

Let us end this section with a summary statement of the role of money in the inflation process. Does more money *always* lead to inflation? No, but it can under certain circumstances, and if the increase is large enough it probably will. Case 1: If the central bank expands the money supply while we are in a recession, the increased spending it induces is likely to lead to more employment and a larger output of goods and services rather than to higher prices. Case 2: As we approach full employment and capacity output, increases in the money supply become more and more likely to generate rising prices. However, if this increase is only large enough to provide funds for the enlarged volume of transactions accompanying real economic growth, inflation still need not result. Case 3: Only when the money supply increases under conditions of high employment *and* exceeds the requirements of economic growth can it be held primarily responsible for kindling an inflationary spiral.

The time horizon and the extent of inflation are also relevant. In the short run, an increase in monetary velocity alone (generated by increasing government or private spending), with a constant or even declining money supply, can finance a modest rate of inflation. The longer the time span, however, and the higher prices rise, the less likely that velocity can do the job by itself. Over the longer run, the money supply must expand for inflation to persist.

Conclusions: More money does not always lead to inflation (Cases 1 and 2), but sometimes it does (Case 3). In the short run, inflation can make some headway without any change in the money supply, but rising prices cannot proceed too far too long without the sanction of the central bank.[2]

Do High Interest Rates Make Inflation Worse?

Although restrictive monetary policy appears essential in controlling inflation, complaints against its use have consistently come from critics who assert that the higher interest rates produced by

---

[2] In the appendix to this chapter, we use Chapter 19's *IS–LM* framework to illustrate more formally the role of money in inflation.

tight money make inflation *worse* rather than better. Since interest is one of the costs of doing business, it is argued, higher interest rates, like higher wages, tend to *raise* rather than lower prices.

Long-time Congressman Wright Patman of Texas, who died in 1976 after 48 years in the House of Representatives, was a leading proponent of this point of view, along with spokesmen for organized labor. Surprisingly, there is possibly more truth in this position than most professional economists—who refuse to take it seriously and typically dismiss it out of hand—are willing to admit.

Higher interest rates *do* increase costs, and thereby push prices up from the supply side. They also *do* result in larger incomes for lenders, owners of savings deposits, and bond holders, enabling them to increase their spending and thereby help to pull up prices from the demand side. Cost-push and demand-pull. On the surface, at least, higher interest rates are not so different from higher wage rates. If the latter are inflationary, why not the former?

The standard response to these arguments is that interest is so small an element of business costs, and of income, that higher rates don't matter that much. But such a response raises more questions than it answers. Indeed, it goes so far that it all but destroys the orthodox case for higher interest rates made by the proponents of monetary policy themselves—which is that higher rates lower investment spending, decrease aggregate demand, and thus reduce inflationary pressures. If interest is so minute an element of business costs, then how can higher rates be expected to affect investment spending significantly, as the proponents of monetary policy claim?

The fact is that interest is *not* a negligible item in business costs. In expenditures for long-lived plant or equipment, particularly, it may be a crucial component of costs. For example, if you buy a $50,000 home (and that's cheap) and get a mortgage for the full amount at 9 percent interest for 30 years, before all is over and done with you will be paying $93,000 in interest and the $50,000 house will wind up costing you $143,000. If the interest rate increases to 10 percent, your total interest payments will add up to $105,000, and the house will cost you $155,000—more than triple its list price.

Furthermore, interest is no trivial component of national income. In recent years it has been running at about 10 percent of personal aftertax income.

The standard response, then, to the "higher interest rates raise prices" argument is wrong. If that were the only answer, the heretics would be far more correct than the traditionalists, even on the traditionalists' own grounds. The answer, if there is any, will have to be found elsewhere.

The answer to the "high interest rates raise prices" school of thought lies in a closer examination of the assumed similarity between the effects of higher wage rates and the effects of higher interest rates. Earlier in this chapter, we pointed out that higher wage rates are inflationary. Wage increases in excess of productivity gains mean higher costs, thereby putting upward cost pressure on prices from the supply side. Higher wages also mean larger incomes for wage earners, thereby generating an increase in consumer spending that pulls prices up from the demand side. Interest rates appear to do the same thing— and they do. Higher interest rates *do* raise costs and incomes, and *do* thereby generate cost-push and demand-pull inflationary pressures.

In the preceding section we also pointed out, however, that wage increases *alone* could not fully explain either cost-push or demand-pull inflation. To maintain inflation for any sustained period, wage increases must be accompanied by continued injections of new money: Permissive increases in the money supply are a necessary condition for the continuation of inflation. If the central bank does *not* increase the money supply, or actually reduces it, inflation will sooner or later peter out, regardless of the strength of unions or the monopoly power of business.

Similarly, high interest rates accompanied by monetary expansion are also inflationary. But rising interest rates attributable to tight money—monetary restriction—are not.

Rising interest rates that result from tight money should be equated *not* with higher wages plus an enlarged money supply, which is typically the equation that is implied, but with higher wage rates accompanied by a constant or lower money supply—as if every time wages increased a certain percent, the central bank automatically cut back the rate of growth in the money supply a similar percent. This, in general terms, is what happens when interest rates rise during a period of *tight* money.

Such higher interest rates, like higher wages under similar circumstances, may raise the price level briefly, but if the central bank sticks to its guns, it will not go up far or for long. With a constant or lower money supply, further increases in the price level eventually would be difficult to finance. At that point the higher interest rates will choke off spending, and total expenditures will stop rising. Then the inflation process will grind to a halt (regardless of the higher costs) as a result of tight monetary policy.

Does More Inflation Cause Higher Interest Rates?

Unlike many of the questions we have discussed, there is relatively little controversy over the proposition that an increase in the rate of inflation leads to higher interest rates. This is true whether we go from no inflation at all to a rate of inflation of 5 percent or whether the rate of inflation jumps from 5 percent to 10 percent. Irving Fisher, of Quantity Theory fame, was the first to recognize that inflation, or more precisely, expectations of inflation, would lead to higher interest rates on bonds. In particular, Fisher argued that the nominal or monetary interest rate on a bond was equal to a "real" rate plus the expected rate of inflation. A higher expected rate of inflation would lead to a higher nominal yield.

Recall our discussion in Chapter 20, where the Monetarist-Keynesian debate over the response of interest rates to monetary policy was analyzed. Part of that discussion emphasized that a lender who is satisfied with a $1000 one-year note which promises $50 in interest, will demand a higher interest payment, say $70, if the price level is expected to increase by, say, 2 percent during the year. The reason: with 2 percent inflation, it takes $1020 at the end of the year to buy what $1000 would have bought a year earlier. Thus, when expected inflation rises from zero to 2 percent, the nominal yield on a bond must rise from (say) 5 percent to 7 percent to keep lenders happy.

Who cares if lenders aren't happy? Why not let them be unhappy, with the interest rate remaining at 5 percent? Under such conditions they might very well refuse to lend their funds because they would receive only 5 percent in nominal terms, which is reduced to 3 percent in real terms by inflation. If lenders refused to part with their funds, borrowers would be unable to borrow. And that would make *them* unhappy as well. So, borrowers, realizing that they'll be repaying their loans with cheaper dollars, and to get their hands on funds with which they expect to make even more money, decide to raise the nominal interest rate on their promissory notes to lenders. That way everyone's happy, including Irving Fisher who said it all along: the nominal rate of interest rises by the expected rate of inflation.

Can we really be this far in our book and finally arrive at an issue on which everyone agrees? Don't be ridiculous! The story just told, of lenders and borrowers joyously arriving at a 2 percent increase in the nominal rate on bonds when expected inflation jumps by 2 percent, takes time to work itself out. In the short-run, lenders might be induced to accept a lower real rate of interest. Thus, instead of the nominal rate of interest rising by 2 percent, it might rise by less, in which case the real rate would fall when expected inflation jumps by 2 percent. Eventually, as lenders adjust their cash balances and borrowers alter their investment plans, the real rate returns to its long-run level and the nominal rate rises above the real rate by the expected rate of inflation.

How long is the long-run? Ah, if we only knew the answer to that question, how simple life would be. We get closer to Irving Fisher's result even in the short-run—say within six months—as the delay in borrower and lender reactions gets shorter. Furthermore, when expectations of inflation respond quickly to economic forces, the Fisher result is likely to occur still more quickly. On the other hand, when delays are long and expectations of inflation respond slowly, then it takes longer for nominal rates to rise by the full amount of the expected inflation. As a general rule, it is a good bet that an increase in nominal rates of interest will closely follow a jump in inflationary expectations, but nominal interest rates are unlikely to respond immediately by the full amount suggested by Fisher.

The Trade-off Between Price Stability and Employment

Since inflation is not something we want any more of, and since the monetary and fiscal tools to curb it are at hand, why don't we just use them and put a stop to these never-ending increases in the cost of living?

The reason we hesitate is because of an apparent conflict of national objectives. The cost of price stability—in terms of the unemployment necessary to get it—is too high. If we pursued monetary (and fiscal) policies with the determination necessary to put a total and complete brake on inflation, we would probably find ourselves with catastrophic rates of unemployment, at least in the short-run. We do not want any more inflation, but we do not want any more depressions either, and so far we have been unable to find a solution to the problem of stopping rising prices without simultaneously bringing on at least a recession.

To put the problem succinctly, it seems that we cannot have both price stability and full employment at the same time. If we want stable prices, we have to sacrifice full employment. And if we want a high level of employment, we have to give up stable prices. Exactly what are the terms of this trade-off?

THE EFFECTIVENESS OF MONETARY POLICY

On the basis of our past experience, Chart 1—known as a Phillips curve after its popularizer, Professor A. W. Phillips—gives a rough idea of the cost, in terms of unemployment, of various degrees of price stability. For example, point A (1 percent inflation, 5½ percent unemployment) represents the situation in 1963; point B (4 percent inflation, 3½ percent unemployment) represents 1968.

As the Phillips curve indicates, obtaining absolute price stability during the 1960s would have required an estimated 8 percent unemployment rate. Furthermore (and this Chart 1 does not indicate), for well over a decade the black unemployment rate has been approximately twice the national average. An overall national unemployment rate of 8 percent, which is about what it would have taken to eliminate inflation completely during the 1960s, implies a black unemployment rate at the deep depression level of 16 percent. Even worse, the black teen-age unemployment rate has been averaging six or seven times the overall jobless rate for many years; an overall national unemployment rate of 8 percent means a black teen-age unemployment rate of about 50 percent.

The optimum choice among this array of less-than-happy alternatives is not amenable to a purely economic solution. If we move to the left on the curve and choose low unemployment, some people will be hurt by the resulting inflation. On the other hand, if we move toward the right on the curve and choose something close to stable prices,

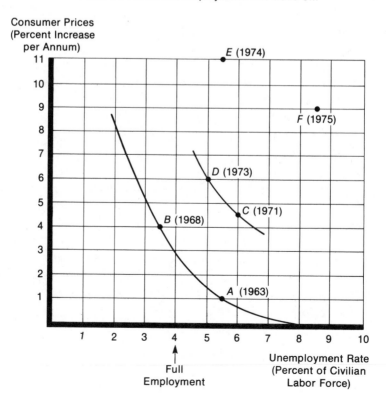

CHART 1 / Prices and employment: The trade-off.

other people will be hurt by the resulting unemployment. An economist, as an economist, has no basis on which he can judge which is better. Resolution of this conflict of interests fundamentally involves personal value judgments and assessments of the social implications of the alternatives more than it involves economics.

But things are even more complicated. Historical relationships are subject to change. In the 1970s, a bad situation has gotten even worse, as Chart 1 indicates. Today, a policymaker who looks at the 1960s Phillips curve and chooses absolute price stability will get not 8 percent unemployment but evidently lots more to boot.[3]

What happened? Where has the Phillips curve of the 1960s gone?

To the right—along with other elder statesmen—is the simplest answer, and the one that appeals to most Keynesians. The trade-off between stable prices and full employment has simply gotten worse, because of structural changes that have taken place in the economy. A changed composition of the labor force, an expansion in the demand for skilled labor but not for unskilled, more aggressive union behavior, increased market power in the hands of the large corporations, the oil situation, and other factors have all pushed the Phillips curve to the right.[4]

The Monetarist Challenge to the Phillips Curve

And yet there is a still more mind-boggling possibility—no Phillips curve at all. The trade-off between stable prices and high employment is illusory. That towering iconoclast, Milton Friedman, has pounced on another victim!

The Monetarist reasoning goes something like this: Government policies to increase employment generate rising prices; some additional employment can initially be bought with higher prices. But workers are not fools. They soon realize that rising prices are eroding the value of their pay raises. If they were satisfied with 3 percent pay raises when prices were stable, now they will want more to keep pace with inflation. If we assume 4 percent inflation has been generated, for

---

[3] Just to see how they would look, why not put in the points on Chart 1 for 1976, 1977, and 1978 yourself? In 1976 we had 6 percent inflation and 7½ percent unemployment; in 1977 6½ percent inflation and 7 percent unemployment; and in 1978 7½ percent inflation and 6 percent unemployment.

[4] A chief proponent of this argument is George L. Perry, "Changing Labor Markets and Inflation," *Brookings Papers on Economic Activity* (No. 3, 1970).

example, workers will want 7 percent pay raises to get a 3 percent *real* wage increase. If employers believe they can pass on such a wage increase in the form of higher prices, they will grant it—thereby making the inflation worse. Then, as the day follows the night, unions will want even larger money-wage increases next year to wind up with another real wage hike. Thus expectations of further inflation snowball through round after round of ever-growing wage settlements promptly followed by corresponding price increases.

This has become known as the "accelerationist" hypothesis. It implies ever-increasing rates of inflation to maintain unemployment at its lower level. It also suggests that if and when unemployment rises, the inflationary expectations that caused the spiral will remain for a while, thereby leaving us with both high unemployment and high inflation.

On such grounds, Friedman argues that there is no true trade-off between employment and prices, because in the long run you can't fool all of the people very much of the time. You may be able to buy some additional employment with higher prices for a while, but as soon as workers catch on that their pay raises are more imaginary than real, either the inflation will accelerate or businessmen will begin to lay off workers. In either case, the Phillips curve doesn't give the correct answer to the question of how high prices would rise if employment were increased by a given amount.

What should be done?

Nothing, says Friedman. Let the economy find its own "natural" rate of unemployment. Don't try to lower unemployment by counter-cyclical monetary-fiscal policies, because they'll only produce inflation. It will only help for a short while, and the more you do it the worse things will get.[5]

Is all this true? To some extent, yes. In the long run, the trade-off between employment and prices does get worse, as Chart 1 indicates. But most of the evidence points to a rather long run—such as five years—before all the employment effects of increased inflation are wiped out. We can still use inflation to buy some employment—but less than we thought and for a shorter time period.

[5] An early presentation of this argument is in Milton Friedman, "The Role of Monetary Policy," *American Economic Review* (March 1968).

Wage-Price Controls and All That

There are other means that have been proposed to help resolve the inflation-unemployment quandry. These include manpower training programs, index-linked contracts throughout the economy, escalating annuities and social security payments, wage-price guidelines and outright controls.

Manpower programs are aimed at shifting the dismal Phillips curve to the left. There is substantial agreement that the fundamental cause of the present position of the Phillips curve is the failure of labor markets to operate effectively. Less inflation would be associated with any given level of aggregate demand and employment if workers who are between jobs could be placed more quickly, if disadvantaged workers who make up the "hard-core unemployed" could be retrained with skills that are in short supply, and if artificial barriers to entry were removed from certain trades and occupations. Manpower programs designed to rectify some or all of these structural maladjustments in the way our economy utilizes its labor force might very well permit us to coexist with an unfriendly Phillips curve by pushing it to the left.

Since the basic problem with inflation is that it imposes costs—in the form of erosion of purchasing power—on certain segments of the public (widows living on pensions, and others whose income is more or less fixed in dollar terms), it is conceivable that one way to get around the problem of inflation is to compensate those who suffer most. This could be achieved by linking annuities and social security payments, and perhaps many other contracts as well, to some cost-of-living index. This has been billed as "living with inflation" by James Tobin of Yale and Leonard Ross of Columbia.[6] Brazil has often been cited as a country that successfully used widespread indexation—that is, escalator or cost-of-living clauses—as a means of softening the impact of inflation. The main drawback of such arrangements is that they do not get at the heart of the problem, the root causes of inflation, and thus they may lull us into complacency about inflation and increase the likelihood of hyperinflation.

Which brings us to wage-price controls. There are many types of wage-price policies—the strong variety, best approximated by wartime controls with stiff legal sanctions and rationing; the intermediate kind, such as voluntary wage and price guidelines with vague and largely unspecified penalties; and the weak variety, consisting of

[6] See James Tobin and Leonard Ross, "Living with Inflation," *New York Review of Books* (May 6, 1971).

"What, no Phillips curve!"

appeals to labor and business to act with restraint and integrity. Well, as the poet said, "Integrity ain't all it's cracked up to be"—so much for the effectiveness of the weak form of wage-price controls. As for the strong form of controls—few would argue, save perhaps John Kenneth Galbraith, that the benefits flowing from a full-blown set of mandatory wage-price controls would even remotely justify the bureaucratic costs and inefficiencies typically incurred in their implementation.

Wage-price controls once again involve trying to shift the Phillips curve to the left. This time, however, we merely try to suppress some of the inflation associated with a given level of employment. But the costs cannot really be escaped. Inflation is inequitable—to those living on relatively fixed incomes. But so are wage-price controls—to those who were slow in joining the inflationary wage-price spiral before the controls were imposed. Even more serious is the interference of wage-price controls with the price mechanism that is so vital in channeling resources to where they are most desired in a decentralized unplanned economy. Indeed, even centrally planned economies appear to be moving toward *greater* reliance on decentralized price-profit signals to direct resources to their best uses.

Many European countries that have experimented with rather permanent wage-price controls (called "incomes policies" across the Atlantic) have concluded that they don't really work. Methods of getting around controls are developed as time passes, making them both ineffective and more inequitable. As an interim measure, however, temporary controls may have a greater justification and a better track record. If conditions are ripe for a slowdown in inflation, but inflationary expectations have become a way of life, imposition of controls may have some shock value. By some standards, the three-month wage-price freeze of 1971 was a success, probably for this reason. Furthermore, when business and labor believe that controls are a temporary phenomenon, there is less incentive to incur the moral indignation of friends and neighbors by evasion.

Unfortunately, we cannot provide a happy ending to our story on inflation. The current state of the art does not have the solution to the confrontation of stable prices and full employment. Money is at the root of inflation in the long run but not the short run. The Phillips curve is alive and well in the short run but not the long run. Wage-price controls work in the short run but not the long run. Living with inflation, as suggested by Tobin and Ross, may be a good idea—but for how long?

Suggestions for Further Reading

The original article by A. W. Phillips describing the trade-off between inflation and unemployment is "The Relation Between Unemployment and the Rate of Change in Money Wage Rates in the United Kingdom, 1861–1957," *Economica* (1958). A classic survey of demand-pull versus cost-push inflation is by Paul Samuelson and Robert Solow, "Analytical Aspects of Anti-Inflation Policy," *American Economic Review* (May 1960). More recently, see David Laidler and Michael Parkin," Inflation: A Survey," *Economic Journal* (December 1975). Many excellent articles dealing with inflation and the controversy between the "structuralists" and "accelerationists" can be found in various issues of the *Brookings Papers on Economic Activity* since 1970.

Two good books devoted entirely to inflation are R. J. Ball, *Inflation and the Theory of Money* (Chicago: Aldine, 1965), and James A. Trevithick and Charles Mulvey, *The Economics of Inflation* (New York: Wiley, 1975). See also Morris Goldstein, "The Trade-off Between Inflation and Unemployment: A Survey of the Econometric Evidence of Selected Countries," International Monetary Fund *Staff Papers* (November 1972).

Finally, a very useful and readable small volume is G. L. Bach, *The New Inflation* (Providence, R.I.: Brown University Press, 1973).

Appendix

*IS–LM Analysis of Inflation**

The role of money in demand-pull inflation, discussed early in the chapter, can be illustrated within the *IS–LM* framework. To make matters simple (and somewhat unrealistic), let's assume that there are no price increases until the economy is at full employment—upward pressure on prices does not begin until aggregate demand exceeds the full employment income. In other words, let's abstract from the Phillips curve problem. In fact, the setting is just the same as Chapter 22's Monetarist-Keynesian dialogue at full employment.

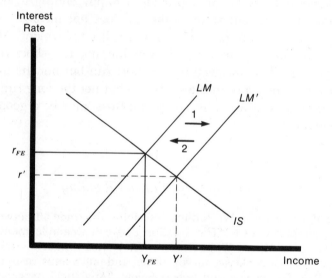

FIGURE 1 / At full employment, an increase in the money supply shifts the *LM* curve to the right and produces inflation.

Realized aggregate demand is given by the intersection of the *IS* and *LM* curves. Start, in Figure 1, with *IS* and *LM* intersecting *at the full employment income* (Y_{FE}), so that the equilibrium income and the full employment income are one and the same. Now if *either* curve shifts to the right, aggregate demand for goods and services will exceed the economy's capacity to produce such output at the current price level. Inflation will result.

* This appendix uses analytical techniques developed in Chapter 19. If you skipped Chapter 19, skip this appendix as well.

382

1.   For example, in Figure 1 assume the money supply is increased: the *LM* curve shifts to *LM'* and aggregate demand rises to Y'. Aggregate demand exceeds full employment output and prices are bid up, illustrating a classic case of demand-pull inflation. The increased price level then reduces the *real* supply of money (see the end of Chapter 19 for the impact of price changes on the real money supply), and the *LM* curve begins to shift back toward its original position. The interest rate is pushed up and investment spending is reduced. Rising prices stop when aggregate demand is back at its old level, i.e., when the *LM* curve is back where it started. Note that in this case both the money supply and the price level are higher than before, but the *real* money supply and *real* output are unchanged.

An increase in the money supply raises prices, but the inflation provides its own cure—prices stop rising once the *real* supply of money (the nominal money supply adjusted for the higher price level) falls back to its original level. Indeed, unless the nominal money supply is increased again (producing another rightward shift in *LM*), inflation has stopped. Continuous injections of money, of course, will cause continuous rightward shifts in the *LM* curve, and continuous inflation. Large and continued injections of money cause continuously large rightward shifts in the *LM* curve, and produce hyperinflation.

2.   As long as the *LM* curve is positively sloped, i.e., as long as the demand for money is sensitive to changes in the interest rate, inflation can occur even if the money supply is constant. In Figure 2, again start with *IS* and *LM* intersecting at the full employment income. This time the *IS* curve shifts to *IS'*—perhaps because of an increase in government spending. Aggregate demand, now Y', exceeds Y_{FE} and prices start rising. But here too the inflation is brought to an eventual halt *if the money supply is held constant*. Rising prices—say from P to P'—reduce the real supply of money; because of that the *LM* curve shifts to the left (to *LM'* in Figure 2), and once again aggregate demand is at Y_{FE}, at which point the inflationary pressure ends.[1]

In this case it is not increased money that causes inflation; the money supply, as we stressed, is held constant. Rather it is the in-

---

[1] How do we know that the *LM* curve will shift back to the left just far enough to again intersect the *IS* curve at the full employment income? Because until it has shifted that far back, prices will keep on rising, reducing the real value of the money supply, and *LM* will continue to move to the left. Once it has returned to its original position (i.e., where it intersects *IS* at full employment), prices will stop rising, the real money supply will no longer contract, and the *LM* curve will therefore stabilize at that point. This case also demonstrates that, at full employment, an increase in government expenditure cannot raise real GNP. This is true even with a positively sloped *LM* curve, as we noted toward the end of Chapter 22.

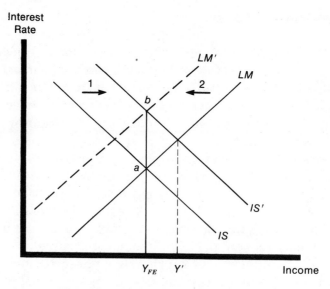

FIGURE 2 / At full employment, a shift in the *IS* curve to the right produces inflation even without an increase in the money supply.

creased government (or consumer or investment) spending that raises aggregate demand above the full employment level. But the higher level of transactions associated with the increased price level (at the same level of *real* income, Y_{FE}) must be financed in some way. Total transactions have risen from $P \times Y_{FE}$ to $P' \times Y_{FE}$. This increased level of *money* income can be financed with the existing money supply because velocity has gone up ($P' \times Y_{FE}/M$ is greater than $P \times Y_{FE}/M$). Velocity increases because the demand for money is sensitive to the interest rate. As the interest rate rises, the amount of desired speculative money balances contracts, releasing funds for transactions purposes. (In Figure 2, velocity at point b is higher than at point a).

3. While holding the money supply constant assures that the inflationary pressure of a once-and-for-all increase in the *IS* function will disappear, *continuous* rightward shifts in the *IS* curve—produced, let us say, by ever-increasing government expenditures—could *apparently* cause continuous inflation. But appearances are deceiving; inflation could not continue indefinitely, regardless of a rightward-shifting *IS* curve, if the money supply is really held constant. Here's why:

We just noted that rightward shifts in the *IS* curve can create inflation only when money demand is at least somewhat sensitive to interest rates; when the interest rate goes up, desired holdings of speculative money balances go down, permitting such funds to be used to carry out transactions. But it is generally agreed that speculative balances will eventually become depleted. In other words, the interest-sensitivity of money demand decreases with higher and higher interest rates, until it becomes zero when there are no more speculative balances left. At that point, the entire money supply is being used for transactions balances, and money GNP can rise no further.[2] Put somewhat differently, the velocity of money has reached its upper limit and can rise no further.

When this great moment arrives, the *LM* curve becomes vertical (zero interest-sensitivity), and further rightward shifts in the *IS* curve have no impact on aggregate demand. The only result is a higher interest rate. Here's the picture. Start out with *IS* and *LM* in Figure 3, intersecting again at the full employment income; shifting the *IS* curve to *IS'* produces aggregate demand *Y'*. Prices rise (say from *P* to *P'*), shifting *LM* to *LM'* and the new equilibrium to point *a*. The *LM* curve is now vertical, however, at level of real income Y_{FE} with the new price level (or at nominal income $P' \times Y_{FE}$).

Any further rightward shift in the *IS* curve, say to *IS''*, cannot raise aggregate demand because the existing money supply—remember, the money supply is being held constant—cannot support any higher level of transactions. Instead, the increased (say) government

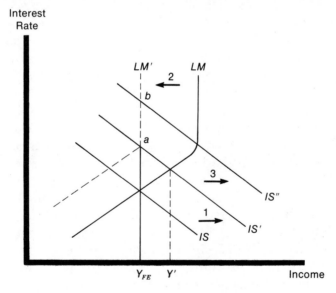

FIGURE 3 / Rightward shifts in the *IS* curve can no longer cause inflation when the *LM* curve becomes vertical.

[2] In Chapter 18 we suggested that even the transactions demand for money is sensitive to the interest rate, because at higher interest rates it pays to economize on transactions balances. While this may very well be true, it is usually assumed that the transactions demand for money is less interest-elastic than speculative demand. Or, put somewhat differently, given the technology of the payments system at any point in time, there is a maximum rate of turnover— velocity—of a particular stock of money; therefore, the *LM* curve becomes vertical at high interest rates.

spending of so many billion dollars is fully offset by the rate of interest rising high enough to *reduce* private investment by the same amount; total spending remains the same, with the increase in government spending "crowding out" an equal amount of private investment spending. The economy moves from point *a* directly to point *b* without suffering any inflation, just a higher rate of interest.

4. Our story is almost complete. The *IS–LM* analysis has demonstrated the seemingly pretentious contentions of the chapter: namely, that inflation can occur only for a short while in the absence of increases in the money supply. Sooner or later a constant money supply keeps inflation in check. But we also noted that increases in money supply do not always produce inflation, and that, too, can be illustrated in the *IS–LM* world.

The simplest case is when the *IS* and *LM* curves intersect at less than Y_{FE}. Increases in the money supply in such circumstances raise real income but not prices. Even at full employment, however, increases in money supply will not necessarily be inflationary, if we recognize that full employment GNP grows over time—as the labor force and the stock of capital grow, and as technological progress increases productivity, enabling the economy to produce more real goods and services. In terms of our picture, the Y_{FE} line shifts to the right as the productive capacity of the economy increases. Aggregate demand *must* increase if we are merely to stay in the same place as far as the unemployment picture is concerned.

In Figure 4, if we start out with *IS* and *LM*, all is well when full employment GNP is represented by Y_{FE}. But by next year full employment output becomes Y'_{FE}, and unless aggregate demand increases via rightward shifts in the *LM* and/or *IS* curves, the current level of demand will be too small to generate full employment. In a growing economy, therefore, increases in the money supply (producing rightward shifts in the *LM* curve—say to *LM'*) are needed simply to maintain full employment.[3] Only if the rightward shift in the *LM* curve intersects the *IS* curve *beyond* Y'_{FE} will the increased money supply be inflationary. In other words, only if increases in the money supply exceed the transactions needs of a growing economy will inflationary pressures be generated.

---

[3] It is also usually recommended that as output grows, not only should the money supply increase, shifting *LM* to the right, but taxes should be reduced (or government spending increased) in order to shift the *IS* curve to the right as well. Which curve does most of the shifting to accommodate growth will affect the rate of interest and therefore the *composition* of aggregate demand, in terms of the proportion of consumption relative to investment spending.

IS–LM Analysis of Inflation

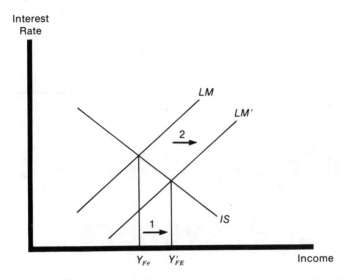

FIGURE 4 / Over time, the full employment level of income moves to the right, so that more money finances real growth rather than inflation.

5. Finally, a reminder. The *IS–LM* framework of analysis is only fully appropriate when inflation is of the demand-pull variety. Remember that at the very start of this appendix we assumed that no Phillips curve problem exists. When inflation is due mainly to supply or cost-push factors—like aggressive union wage demands or the dramatic 400 percent increase in international oil prices that was imposed in 1973–1974—then it is difficult to handle the analysis within the constraints of the *IS–LM* framework. Both Keynesians and Monetarists analyze the economy primarily in terms of aggregate demand. When cost or supply factors are the main elements influencing the economy, neither the simple Keynesian nor Monetarist analytical techniques are very helpful.[4]

[4] For a treatment of supply shocks in an extended Keynesian framework, see Rudiger Dornbusch and Stanley Fischer, *Macroeconomics* (McGraw-Hill, 1978), Chapters 11–13.

Chapter 24

Empirical Evidence on the Effectiveness of Monetary Policy

THEORY, LIKE PUNISHMENT, is said to be good for the soul. But even the most philosophical among us realize that humans—and yes, even students—also require rewards that are somewhat more concrete. Having poked into every nook and cranny of the Monetarist-Keynesian dialectic over the effectiveness of monetary and fiscal policy, the time has come to reveal the Truth (with a capital T). Since many people believe that numbers are Truth, here they are aplenty.

What are the facts about the behavior of velocity? How powerful is the impact of monetary policy on economic activity? How does it compare with fiscal policy? What particular categories of spending are most influenced by monetary policy? After all, if monetary policy is to alter GNP, it cannot do it by mystic incantations; it has to do it by changing the consumer spending of households, the investment spending of business firms, or the expenditures of governments—federal, state, or local. In contrast to the theoretical discussion of previous chapters, we now turn to the *empirical* evidence.

Living With Velocity

We have seen again and again how the Monetarist-Keynesian debate hinges on the behavior of velocity, the Monetarists contending that it is relatively stable and that any changes are highly predictable, Keynesians arguing that either contention is an exaggeration. The facts are that velocity is neither perfectly stable nor fully predictable. Unfortunately for the Federal Reserve, it does not operate in a world designed for its own convenience. With a money supply of $400 billion, a miscalculation of only 0.1 in velocity means a $40 billion swing in GNP. And with a money supply of $800 billion, the GNP jump is twice as large. But all is not necessarily lost. While velocity is not fixed, neither do its movements appear to be random or perverse. If the Federal Reserve could discover the underlying determinants of fluctuations in velocity, it might still be able to coexist with such a moving target.

With that in mind, examining the past may provide a clue to developments in the future. Chart 1 plots the historical course of three measures of velocity, each one associated with a different money

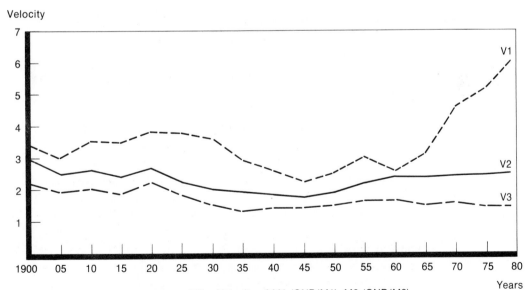

CHART 1 / The Velocity of M1 (GNP/M1), M2 (GNP/M2), and M3 (GNP/M3) between 1900 and 1980.
Sources: *Historical Statistics of The United States*, Department of Commerce, and *Federal Reserve Bulletins*.

supply concept. The velocity figures for VI are based on M1, V2 on M2, and V3 on M3. Two broad generalizations emerge from the picture. First, while none of the velocity measures has been completely stable during the twentieth century, the meanderings of V2 and V3 have been quite tame. Of course, we just pointed out that even small miscalculations in velocity mean wide swings in GNP, especially for the more inclusive definitions of money. Nevertheless, the rather narrow range of movement in V2 and V3 is impressive. The second glaring message of Chart 1 is that V1 looks like it's on a space-flight trajectory. Those who prefer the narrow definition of money have some explaining to do.

First the facts. Velocity of M1 reached a peak of about 4 with the onset of the 1920s. It fell almost continuously during the Great Depression and World War II to an all-time low of about 2 in 1946. Since then, however, V1 has skyrocketed. It rose to 2.5 in 1950, 3.5 in 1960, passed its previous peak of 4 in 1965, pushed well past 5 in 1975 and now stands at over 6. Why has the velocity of M1 gone on its own trip, apparently giving Monetarism a bad name and making life difficult for the Federal Reserve? If we have a reasonable explanation, we might be able to claim that V1's behavior is predictable, and that's enough for most reasonable people.

The main reason for the extent of the postwar rise in velocity of M1 lies in the relatively narrow historical definition of M1, demand deposits plus currency, and the increasing attractiveness of other categories of financial assets—bonds as well as stocks, savings and loan shares as well as savings accounts in commercial banks—as prudent and desirable outlets in which to invest excess cash. These assets are highly liquid, almost as liquid as money, and yet they possess an attribute missing in M1 during most of these years—the right to receive an interest income. Attractive yields on financial assets other than money have led more and more people to wonder why they should ever hold any idle cash aside from what they need for day-to-day transactions purposes. Traditional concepts about how much cash on hand is really necessary for doing business have also come under reexamination. If cash for day-to-day transactions purposes can be pared down, then some of it can be loaned out to earn interest. The money put to work earning interest moves to borrowers who can use it for current purchases. As a result, a larger volume of current spending flows from the same stock of money.

In terms of our theoretical models, this means that the demand for money is determined, in part, by interest rates. There have been many empirical studies of the demand for money, and almost all have indicated some degree of interest-sensitivity. None have come up with a liquidity trap a la Keynes, but neither have they confirmed the Classical zero interest-elasticity either.[1]

Corporate treasurers, in particular, have found that it pays dividends to scrutinize their cash holdings intensively. Could they manage to get along with somewhat less in the till than they had previously thought of as "normal," and invest a portion in high-yielding time deposits at commercial banks or in U.S. Treasury bills (short-term government securities)? Increasingly, the answer has been "yes," and imaginative new techniques of cash management have been developed to facilitate the process (as well as some not so imaginative old techniques, such as becoming "slow payers" when bills come due).

This trend has not escaped the attention of consumers. They have learned to economize on money by substituting lines of credit at retail stores and financial institutions in place of cash reserves; in addition, the growing use of credit cards has drastically reduced household needs for day-to-day transactions money. What was formerly held in the form of non-interest-bearing demand deposits or currency, for emergency use or for current payments, now shifts to interest-bearing savings deposits.

In summary, it is clear that velocity has not been completely stable, nor has it fluctuated randomly or perversely.[2] There is a discernible pattern in the movements of M1 velocity during the postwar period—a persistent long-run rise (with minor short-run dips during recessions). Even though we may not be able to pinpoint all the specific determinants, we can still see broad cause-and-effect relationships.

Higher interest rates lead to an increase in velocity by inducing business firms and households to economize on money. They hold less, lend out the excess, and others (the borrowers) can then spend it. Once learned, techniques of cash management are not easily forgotten, so that even in recessions, when interest rates fall, velocity does not drop back very far.

Furthermore, the long-run upward trend in M1 velocity over the past quarter-century suggests that fundamental structural relation-

[1] For an excellent summary of empirical studies on the demand for money, see David E. W. Laidler, *The Demand for Money: Theories and Evidence* (New York: International Textbook Company, 1969). For a first-rate examination of the interest-sensitivity of the demand for money as well as an analysis of the stability of the overall relationship, see Stephen M. Goldfeld, "The Demand for Money Revisited," *Brookings Papers on Economic Activity* (No. 3, 1973).

[2] An early attempt at demonstrating the predictability of velocity is Karl Brunner and Allan H. Meltzer, "Predicting Velocity: Implications for Theory and Policy," *Journal of Finance* (May 1963). The Goldfeld article cited in footnote 1 is a more recent inquiry into the issue.

ships between the money supply and the spending habits of the community are apparently in the process of transition. New payment methods have been introduced (credit cards and automated funds transfers are prime examples), as financial innovation occurs side by side with technological innovation in industry. Such financial innovation, however, rarely takes root overnight. Established payment habits change only gradually.

Thus, although velocity is not fixed, neither is it likely to change drastically in the short run. And this is especially true for V2 and V3. The Federal Reserve may be able to live with such moving targets. By gaining further insight into what makes velocity move, the central bank might be able to establish a range of probabilities as to where velocity is likely to be tomorrow and the day after, and act on that basis. In other words, a morning line on velocity (not unlike the one your local bookie puts out on the races at Hialeah)—provided the odds are unemotionally calculated and continuously reassessed in the light of emerging evidence—might still enable the Federal Reserve to come out a winner.

But the simple velocity approach, even with carefully calculated probabilities, leaves much to be desired as a guideline for Federal Reserve policy-making. It ignores time lags between changes in monetary policy and the impact on economic activity. It also ignores the vast statistical methodology available to zero in on a more precise estimate of the impacts of policy changes. While our "casual empiricism" on the behavior of velocity is clearly suggestive, it is far from the whole story.

Time Lags in Monetary Policy

By their own admission, Federal Reserve officials are not omniscient. If the economy starts to slip into a recession, it takes time before the experts realize what is happening so they can take steps to correct it. Similarly, if inflation begins to accelerate, it takes a while before the evidence verifies the fact.

Prompt recognition of what the economy is doing is not as easy as it sounds. For one thing, the available data are often inadequate and frequently mixed: New car orders will rise while retail department store sales are falling; farm prices may be dropping while employment in urban areas is rising. Furthermore, the economy rarely proceeds on a perfectly smooth course, either up or down. Every upsweep is interrupted from time to time by erratic dips; every decline into recession is punctuated irregularly by false signs of progress, which then evaporate. Is a change only a brief and temporary interruption of an already existing trend, or is it the start of a new trend in the opposite direction? No one is ever perfectly sure. This problem of getting an accurate "fix" on what is happening in the economy, or what is likely to happen in the near future, is called the *recognition lag* in monetary policy. In 1968–1969, for example, the Federal Reserve did not recognize that inflation was as serious a problem as it turned out to be until rising prices had gathered too much momentum to be halted. In 1975, the shoe was on the other foot: preoccupation with massive inflation continued even as the economy slipped into the worst recession since the 1930s.

As soon as the recognition lag ends, the *impact lag* begins, spanning the time from when the central bank starts using one of its tools, such as open market operations, until an effect is evident on the ultimate objective—aggregate spending in the economy. It may take weeks before interest rates change significantly after a monetary action has begun. Changes in credit availability and money supply also take time. And a further delay is probable before actual spending decisions are affected. Once monetary policy does start to influence spending, however, it will most likely continue to have an impact on GNP for quite a while. All of this was swept under the rug in the theoretical models discussed in earlier chapters. But now it's time to add some flesh to that bare-bones description of the real world.

Regarding the *recognition* lag, rough evidence suggests that the Federal Reserve generally starts to ease about half a year or more after a boom has already run its course, whereas it starts to tighten only about three months after the trough in a business cycle. This evidence is less than definitive, and it is likely that under some circumstances the monetary authorities will sense what is going on and take action more promptly than under other circumstances. Nevertheless, the inference that the central bank is typically more concerned with preventing inflation than with avoiding recession probably contains a grain of truth.

The *impact* lag is most conveniently discussed, along with the strength of monetary policy, in terms of the results that formal econometric models of the economy have produced. An econometric model is a mathematical-statistical representation that describes how the economy behaves. Such a model gives empirical content to theoretical propositions about how individuals and business firms, lenders and borrowers, savers and spenders, react to economic stimuli. After such relationships are formalized in a mathematical expression, data on past experience in the real world are used to estimate the precise behavioral pattern of each sector. A model, therefore, is based on real-world observations jelled into a formal pattern by the grace of statistical techniques. Thrown into a computer, the model simulates the economy in action and grinds out predictions based on the formal interactions the model embodies.

Our knowledge of how best to construct such a model is far from complete. The same data can produce different results depending on the theoretical propositions used to construct the model. As one cynic put it, "If one tortures the data long enough, it will confess."

A Keynesian model, for instance, would incorporate behavioral assumptions different from those of a Monetarist model, and hence grind out an alternative set of predictions. A Monetarist model might relate total GNP to money supply directly, on the basis of a predictable velocity assumption. A Keynesian model, on the other hand, would spend considerable time trying to explain the determinants of consumption spending, investment spending, and liquidity preference. In other words, a Keynesian model would try to generate empirical counterparts to the equations presented in Chapters 18 and 19 (only much more complex).

Furthermore, the data we have available to feed our models are not all that we would like. In any case, past relationships are not always reliable guides to future behavior; if they were, the favorite would always win the football game and marriages would never end in divorce.

Nevertheless, despite all their shortcomings, such models, if carefully and objectively constructed, are probably superior to casual off-the-cuff observations followed by inadequately supported generalizations—provided they are always taken with a healthy dose of skepticism.

The Federal Reserve Board, together with economists at the Massachusetts Institute of Technology and the University of Pennsylvania, developed an econometric model of the behavior of economic aggregates in the United States. Many other economists have done similar work at other universities and financial institutions. But our discussion will be based primarily on the Federal Reserve–MIT–Penn model, called the Federal Reserve model for short, which was prepared specifically to evaluate the impact of stabilization policies on economic activity.[3] The results of Monetarist models, such as the one constructed at the Federal Reserve Bank of St. Louis, will be contrasted with the Fed model.

[3] Actually, there are two versions of this model—the Fed model, which is used by the policy makers, and the MP model (a.k.a. the MPS model because of participation by the Social Science Research Council), which is played with by the academics.

The Impact of Monetary Policy on GNP

The latest edition of the Federal Reserve model—and there have been numerous editions—includes virtually every conceivable linkage (maybe) between monetary policy and real economic activity. Interest rate effects, wealth effects, and credit availability are all explicitly articulated in mathematical splendor. As a first approximation to measuring the impact of monetary policy, let us look at what the model says about the effect of changes in the money supply on spending (i.e., on GNP). An increase in the money supply of $1 billion produces an increase of $1.5 billion in GNP after six months. At the end of a year GNP rises by $2.5 billion, and at the end of two years it is nearly $6 billion above its initial level. After three years, economic activity is still rising, producing an increase of more than $10 billion in GNP above its original level.

These results imply a rather long lag before the full effects of an increase in the money supply are felt on spending. If the Federal Reserve undertakes an expansionary monetary policy now, it will have to contend with the effects of such policies well into the future. This can create serious problems for monetary policy, as we shall see later.

Monetarists, especially those of the St. Louis variety, are unhappy with the Fed model. They don't like the detailed description of the transmission mechanism between money and economic activity, suspecting that the architects of the model may have unwittingly left out some of the *direct* links between money and spending. Exactly what these links are is not for us to know—but money works in mysterious ways, so we must have faith. The Federal Reserve Bank of St. Louis pits the midwestern virtue of simplicity against the sophisticated system produced by the Boston-Philadelphia-Washington Establishment.

The simple St. Louis model relating GNP directly to money produces a much faster and initially larger impact of money on economic activity. According to the St. Louis model, an increase of $1 billion in the money supply raises GNP by over $3 billion after six months and by over $5 billion after one year, roughly double the impact derived from the Federal Reserve model over the same time intervals. After one year, however, the St. Louis model finds no additional impact of money on GNP.

The Fed economists counter that the little black box connecting money and GNP in the St. Louis model does not lend itself to scientific evaluation. It is impossible to tell how much of the change in GNP is really due to changes in money supply and how much is due to other things that are changing at the same time. In short, the St. Louis model is too simple to be trusted by Easterners.

Some economists have argued that the effectiveness of monetary policy is asymmetrical—monetary policy is more effective in stopping inflation than in getting us out of recession. They reason that the high interest rates and curtailed availablity of credit that characterize tight money cannot help but force restrictions on spending, while the low interest rates and ample credit availablity that are typical of easy money will not necessarily induce people to borrow and spend.

The Federal Reserve model provides some support for an asymmetrical response to tight versus easy money. In particular, a *decrease* of $1 billion in the money supply lowers GNP by $4 billion after one year and by $8 billion after two years. Thus the impact of tight money is more than one-third larger than the impact of easy money.[4] The St. Louis model, however, makes no distinction between periods of easy or tight money. According to the Monetarists, money is money and if you want it and don't have it, it is equally disturbing as when you have it and don't want it. (Yes, the sentence is written correctly; we checked it three times, and so did the proofreaders.)

Returning to the question of time lags, it should be noted that it takes time for an open market operation by the Federal Reserve to have an impact on the money supply. Reserves provided through open market purchases, for example, must work their way through the banking system as banks make loans and buy securities. If we take as the starting point for monetary policy an injection of about $300 million worth of reserves via an open market purchase, this raises the money supply by about $1 billion after six to nine months. Meanwhile, GNP increases by a little less than $1 billion after six months, and by about $2 billion after one year, as compared with our previous figure of $2.5 billion. If we measure the lag in monetary policy from the point in time when the Federal Reserve injects reserves through open market operations, the total lag becomes somewhat longer than was suggested in the first two paragraphs of this section.

The Effect of Monetary Policy on Interest Rates

The impact of monetary policy on interest rates is also generated by our econometric models. Here again Monetarist models differ somewhat from the Keynesian variety. *All* models show that interest rates

[4] Warning: The Surgeon General has determined that all of these numbers are dangerous—they can be and often are changed without notice. The model is very sensitive to where it starts and stops and who is playing with it. Admission is restricted to persons over eighteen with parental guidance suggested.

decline and remain below their original levels for six months to a year after an expansionary monetary policy, and that they are above their original levels for a similar period after a contractionary monetary policy. The Fed model, for example, shows that a \$1 billion increase in reserves via open market purchases by the Federal Reserve lowers the corporate bond rate by one-fourth of 1 percentage point initially; after some slight readjustment upward during the next twelve months, it levels off and remains below its original level for a considerable length of time.

The more sensitive three-month Treasury bill rate reacts with greater gyrations to an open market purchase. Immediately following a \$1 billion purchase of government securities by the Federal Reserve, the bill rate declines by more than 1 percentage point. But after a year the bill rate is only one-half of 1 percentage point below its original level, and it eventually comes to rest about one-third of 1 percentage point below its starting point. Under certain conditions, the Federal Reserve model does suggest that interest rates could rise above their original levels in response to an expansionary monetary policy: namely, when inflationary price expectations are especially strong. Even here, however, the decline in rates lasts at least through the second year of expansion. In contrast, there are some Monetarist models that show the Treasury bill rate snapping back to its original level and going above it within six to twelve months after an expansionary monetary policy.[5]

Fiscal Policy Versus Monetary Policy

The theoretical discussions of earlier chapters indicated a clear distinction between Monetarist and Keynesian views on the effectiveness of fiscal policy compared with monetary policy. It should be clear by now that this dispute can be decided only by resort to empirical evidence. The Keynesians claim, for example, that the power of fiscal policy was demonstrated by the success of the 1964 tax cut in bringing the economy up to a high level of employment. The Monetarists contend that fiscal policy alone is useless, and that it was the rapid expansion of the money supply during that period that did the job. They also point to the failure of the 1968 tax surcharge to stop inflation. The Keynesians respond by asserting that acceleration of the war in Vietnam undid the impact of the 1968 tax increase.

[5] One example is William E. Gibson, "Interest Rates and Monetary Policy," *Journal of Political Economy* (May/June 1970).

Frustrated, let us turn to Federal Reserve's model for a decision. Figure 1 shows the simulated response in nominal GNP (left side) and real GNP (right side) to a $10 billion expansion in government expenditure. In each of the pictures there are three lines, each representing alternative monetary policies accompanying the expansionary fiscal policy. The solid line shows the effect with a monetary policy that keeps the three-month Treasury bill rate unchanged. That assumption implies an expansion in the money stock to accommodate rising demand as GNP goes up. The dotted line assumes a monetary policy that keeps bank reserves (but not necessarily the money supply) unchanged. The dot-dash line simulates the results with a constant money stock.

It is evident from the pictures that this last monetary policy causes a substantial amount of crowding out, as we would expect. The fixed money stock policy forces rates of interest to rise as GNP increases and this cuts off investment spending. Note, however, that there isn't complete crowding out of nominal GNP, although in the righthand picture there is crowding out of real GNP after about two years.

The multiplier effects of government spending are much more expansionary with the two more accommodating monetary policies. Thus the Fed model confirms the crucial role of money for the size of the fiscal policy multipliers. But the Fed model maintains that complete crowding out does not take place even with a fixed money stock assumption.

The Monetarist model of the Federal Reserve Bank of St. Louis is less wishy-washy than its sparring partner: An increase of $1 billion in the money supply raises GNP by over $5 billion after one year, while a similar increase in government spending has *zero* impact on GNP over the same time period. An increase in government spending raises GNP after six months, but by the time a year has elapsed, other types of spending have been crowded out to offset the expansion in government expenditures. What other types of spending? On this the St. Louis model is silent, just as it is silent on the transmission mechanism through which money affects spending. Indeed, it is this agnosticism on the transmission process and the surprising result with respect to fiscal policy that make the St. Louis model incomprehensible to many Keynesians.

The Fed model also provides a detailed look at the impact of monetary policy on different categories of spending. Monetary policy does not have an equal impact on all kinds of spending. Until now, we have discussed its overall impact on GNP and compared it with fiscal policy. Now it is time for a more detailed examination: Which kinds of spending does monetary policy affect most, and which kinds of spending appear to be relatively immune?

398

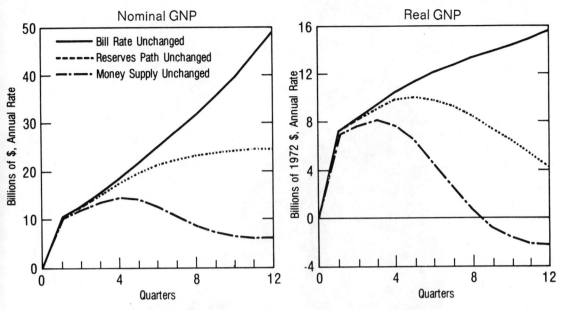

FIGURE 1 / Simulated Response of GNP to a $10 Billion Increase in Government Spending. Source: *Congressional Budget Office.*

Investment Spending

One would expect interest rates and investment spending to move in opposite directions: An increase in interest rates, for example, should lower investment spending. If the cost of borrowing rises, so our theory said, business firms should presumably be less willing to incur new debt to build new factories or buy new equipment. The historical record shows, however, that interest rates and business investment almost always move in the *same* direction. As in most cases where fact contradicts economic theory, one of them must give ground— and it is usually fact.

In the historical record, many things are happening simultaneously, so separate strands of cause and effect are not sorted out. Investment spending is influenced by a number of factors besides interest rates—sales expectations, changes in anticipated profitability, pressures from competitors who may be installing new equipment, the degree of capacity currently being utilized, the availability of internal funds (undivided profits and depreciation reserves), expectations regarding labor costs, and expectations regarding inflation, to name only some. An increase in interest rates may inhibit investment, and yet investment may, in fact, rise if a number of these other elements shift sufficiently to offset its effect.[6]

[6] Recall our theoretical discussion of the investment function in Chapters 18 and 19. The negative relationship between interest rates and investment was drawn with the explicit assumption that all other factors remained constant (*ceteris paribus* to the rescue once again!).

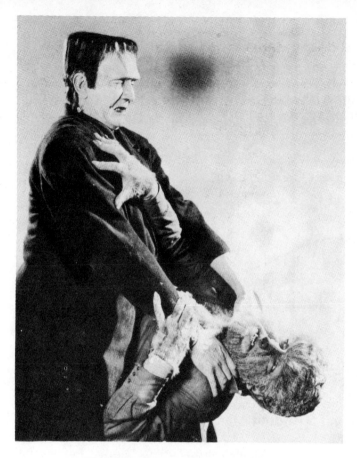

The Monetarists vs. the Keynesians

The actual change in investment spending from one year to the next reflects the net impact of *all* the variables influencing it, not just interest rates alone. We would expect, however, that if interest rates had not risen, investment would probably have expanded even further.

Econometric methods permit us to sort out the effects of individual variables, allowing us to experiment in the "laboratory" of statistical techniques. The effects of interest rates on investment, for example, can be examined holding all other influences constant. The results show that a rise in interest rates does reduce investment spending. In the Federal Reserve's model, for example, an increase of 1 percentage point (say from 8 to 9 percent) in the corporate bond rate lowers business spending on new plant and equipment by about half a billion dollars after one year, by about $2.5 billion after two years, and by $4 billion after three years.

In this instance the time lag is clearly quite substantial. Most investment decisions are not made in the morning and executed in the afternoon. Decisions regarding installation of new machinery and construction of new plants are usually made many months in advance of their actual execution. Thus an increase in rates does not promptly affect investment spending. What it does affect is *current decisions* that will be *implemented* months or years in the future.

The Federal Reserve model does reveal a category of investment spending that is extremely sensitive to a change in interest rates. That category is residential construction, which, although not business investment, is still generally considered a form of investment because of the long time horizon involved, with returns accruing for many years into the future. An increase of 1 percentage point in the interest rate lowers housing expenditures by $2 billion within nine months and by $3 billion after a year. In addition to this interest rate effect, residential construction is also affected by monetary policy through credit rationing by financial institutions engaged in mortgage lending. Some of the implications of this strong relationship between monetary policy and homebuilding are explored further in Chapter 27.

Small business perhaps deserves special mention in any discussion of the impact of monetary policy on investment expenditures. Spokesmen for small business have always contended that, during periods of tight money, commercial banks discriminate against them in their allocation of scarce loanable funds.

The evidence on this is not altogether clear, but it is likely that small firms are indeed at a disadvantage relative to large borrowers during periods when banks are short of funds.[7] Furthermore, large firms have access to the corporate bond market, the commercial paper market, and other alternative sources of funds, while small firms do not.

On the other hand, extension of trade credit (delayed payment for supplies) from large to small firms tends to offset some of these disadvantages. In effect, through their supplier-customer relationships, the large firms pass their access to funds on to the smaller firms in the form of trade credit. To some extent this alleviates the problem, although it is not likely that it eliminates it.

State and Local Government Spending and Consumer Spending

Construction expenditures by state and local governments also appear sensitive to the actions of the monetary authorities. Municipal bond flotations are often reduced, postponed, or canceled during periods

---

[7] For some empirical evidence see William L. Silber and Murray E. Polakoff, "The Differential Effect of Tight Money: An Econometric Study," *Journal of Finance* (March 1970).

Stores Squeezed By Interest Rates

By ISADORE BARMASH

Ebenezer Scrooge for retailers this year takes the form of rapidly rising interest rates.

The stores are being forced to pay increasingly more to finance their inventory purchases. This, and fears of an economic downturn, are making them extremely cautious buyers. And their moves to keep a tight rein on inventories are, on the one hand, causing friction with suppliers and, on the other, raising visions of a loss of sales caused by short supplies. There may even ben some cheaper prices for the consumer along the way.

The interest-rate squeeze has already become apparent in the third-quarter earnings reports of some retailers and is expected to have a greater impact on fourth-quarter profits because rates are higher still in that period. The situation has led retailers to devise new strategies to ease the impact of higher rates.

The problem is prevalent among virtually all varieties of retail chains and independents. They traditionally take out short-term loans to pay for seasonal merchandise needs and have to wait for consumers to pay for goods once they are sold. And since almost half of retail merchandise is bought on credit, many a merchant is carrying high-interest loans while waiting as much as 90 days for many of his customers to pay their bills.

Several major banks pushed the prime rate — the interest charged to their most creditworthy customers — to a four-year high of 11 percent last week amid indications that it would go even higher. The prime rate was at 7.5 percent at the beginning of the year and began its rise in May.

Some of the results of that rise:

- The J. C. Penney Company, the nation's third-largest retail chain in sales, last week reported a 6.8 percent decline in its third-quarter net income and attributed part of it to an 89 percent rise in its interest expense, or cost of borrowing.

- Sears, Roebuck & Company, the largest retailer, in its first such action in many years, announced that a group of 16 institutional investors had assumed ownership of $550 million of Sears consumer receivables, or about 8 percent of the company's total sales, as well as additions coming from new consumer purchases. Sears said that the proceeds of the sale would reduce short-term debt. Industry observers also saw it as a move by Sears to ease any financial pressures that might come from higher interest rates.

- Federated Department Stores Inc., which operates both Bloomingdale's and Abraham & Straus in this area, told its division heads several weeks ago to reduce their inventories for the rest of the year because it expected an economic slowdown. Inventories at Federated, the nation's largest operator of department stores, were reportedly up 15 percent at the end of the second quarter from the year before but have since declined to about 10 percent over the 1977 level. Federated's third-quarter earnings, however, rose only 1.9 percent over the year-earlier figure, the company reported last week.

NEWS ITEM / The Impact of Monetary Policy

SOURCE: *New York Times*, November 19, 1978

of high and rising interest rates. Many municipal governments have self-imposed interest rate ceilings that eliminate them from the market when rates go up. In other instances, when interest costs become too large, local voters became reluctant to approve bond issues for school construction and other projects, since the higher interest burden implies the immediate or eventual imposition of higher property or sales taxes.

The Federal Reserve model indicates that a 1 percentage point rise in the interest rate cuts state and local government spending by almost $2 billion after six months. Subsequently, however, the impact declines as the municipalities rethink their problems and, typically, proceed sooner or later with much of their planned expenditures.

Consumer spending, according to the Fed model, is affected by monetary policy directly through the wealth effect of monetary actions on the values of stocks and bonds in household portfolios, and indirectly through the impact on the level of income. About one-third of the impact of monetary policy on GNP after one year occurs through changes in consumer spending, with another third coming from residential construction, and the remainder divided between plant and equipment spending by businesses and spending by state and local governments. The effects on consumer spending continue to build up during the second and third years following a monetary action, while the impact on housing tends to stabilize as credit rationing by financial institutions becomes less important. After the first year, the thrust of monetary policy is reinforced by the delayed effects on business plant and equipment spending.

Lags Again

The evidence presented by both Monetarists and Keynesians suggests that monetary policy does have a significant impact on economic activity, with much of the impact distributed over two calendar years. There are powerful short-run effects but, at least as far as the Federal Reserve model is concerned, even more powerful long-run effects.

When the initial *recognition lag* is combined with the *impact lag*, the usefulness of monetary policy as a stabilization device becomes less obvious. Suppose a boom tops out in January but the Federal Reserve does not realize it is over until July, at which time monetary policy starts to ease. Its pre-July tightness may still be having depressing effects through the first half of the *following year*, but by then we might well be in the middle of a recession and in need of exactly the opposite medicine. The Federal Reserve will be providing that opposite medicine, but its expansionary effects may be so long delayed that they might not take hold until we are in another boom, thus once again making matters worse. Monetary policy will be a destabilizer rather than a stabilizer!

This scenario is sufficiently worrisome to warrant more detailed treatment in the next chapter.

Suggestions for Further Reading

There are four excellent references on the Federal Reserve model: Frank de Leeuw and Edward M. Gramlich, "The Federal Reserve–MIT Econometric Model," in the *Federal Reserve Bulletin* (January 1968); Robert H. Rasche and Harold T. Shapiro, "The FRB–MIT Econometric Model: Its Special Features," *American Economic Review* (May 1968); Frank de Leeuw and Edward M. Gramlich, "The Channels of Monetary Policy: A Further Report on the Federal Reserve–MIT Model," *Journal of Finance* (May 1969); and Franco Modigliani, "Monetary Policy and Consumption," in *Consumer Spending and Monetary Policy* (Federal Reserve Bank of Boston, 1971). A detailed evaluation of fiscal policy multipliers is found in the background paper of the Congressional Budget Office, *Understanding Fiscal Policy* (Government Printing Office, April 1978).

The two best expositions of the St. Louis model are Leonall C. Andersen and Jerry Jordan, "Monetary and Fiscal Policy: A Test of Their Relative Importance in Economic Stabilization," Federal Reserve Bank of St. Louis *Review* (November 1968), and Leonall C. Andersen and Keith Carlson, "A Monetarist Model for Economic Stabilization," Federal Reserve Bank of St. Louis *Review* (April 1970). For a discussion of the pros and cons of the St. Louis Monetarist approach, see the "Comment" by Frank de Leeuw and John Kalchbrenner and the "Reply" by Leonall Andersen and Jerry Jordan in the Federal Reserve Bank of St. Louis *Review* (April 1969). Also see the previously cited article by Alan Blinder and Robert Solow in *The Economics of Public Finance*, especially pp. 63–78, for an overview of the problems with the St. Louis model. For some political economy on this, see William L. Silber, "The St. Louis Equation: Democratic and Republican Versions and Other Experiments," *Review of Economics and Statistics* (November 1971).

An evaluation of the development of these empirical studies is, William C. Brainard and Richard N. Cooper, "Empirical Monetary Macroeconomics: What Have We Learned in the Last 25 Years," *American Economic Review* (May 1975). To see how they broke from the starting gate in the Monetarist-Keynesian Correlation Derby, first read Milton Friedman and David Meiselman, "The Relative Stability of Monetary Velocity and the Investment Multiplier in the United States, 1897–1958," in *Stabilization Policies* by the Commission on Money and Credit (Englewood Cliffs, N.J.: Prentice-Hall, 1963). Then read Michael E. DePrano and Thomas Mayer, "Tests of the Relative Importance of Autonomous Expenditures and Money," *American Economic Review* (September 1965), and also Donald D. Hester, "Keynes and the Quantity Theory," *Review of Economics and Statistics* (November 1964).

Finally, a simple and useful exposition of econometric techniques is Ira Kaminow's "A Non-economist's Non-mathematical Guide to Econometric Forecasting," in the Federal Reserve Bank of Philadelphia's *Business Review* (October 1970).

Chapter 25

Should a Robot Replace the Federal Reserve?

SOME MONETARISTS, most notably Milton Friedman, have abandoned countercyclical stabilization policy altogether. They never had any use for fiscal policy to begin with, and the issue of time lags in the impact of monetary policy has led them to jettison countercyclical monetary policy as well. In the previous chapter we noted that time lags do indeed make the implementation of monetary policy potentially hazardous.

"Countercyclical" monetary policy means leaning against the prevailing economic winds: easy money in recessions, to get the economy on the move again; tight money when there is a boom, to slow it down. In its most naive form, however, countercyclical monetary policy tends to ignore the complications bred by time lags.

Assume that the Federal Reserve forecasts a recession due six months from now. If the forecast is correct, and if a current expansion in the money supply would have an impact six months hence, well and good. But what if the Federal Reserve's crystal ball is not clear, and it is more than a year before the main impact of today's monetary policy is reflected in the economy? Then the effects of today's expan-

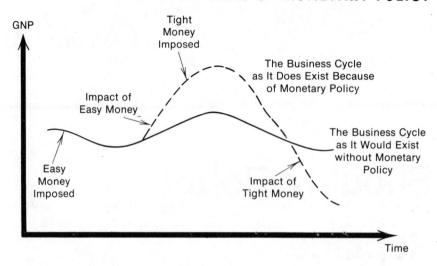

FIGURE 1 / Friedman's alleged perverse effects of countercyclical monetary policy.

sionary monetary policy are likely to be felt *after* the economy has
passed the trough and is already on its way up.

As Figure 1 illustrates, the impact of today's easy money may
exacerbate tomorrow's inflation. This is Milton Friedman's explanation
for the rampant inflation of 1969; the rapid rate of growth in the
money supply in 1968, intended to forestall recession, lit the fuse of
the inflationary time bomb that exploded the following year. Tight
money will have similarly delayed effects; it may be imposed with the
best of intentions, to curtail a boom, but its real impact, being delayed, might accentuate a recession. And this occurred in its most
reckless form in late 1974, so the argument goes. Excessively tight
money was aimed at curtailing the rampant inflation; it precipitated
the 1975 recession in the process. Monetary policy is a destabilizer
rather than a stabilizer!

On these grounds—the precarious nature of economic forecasting
and the alleged length, variability, and unpredictability of the time
lags involved—Friedman and some other Monetarists have given up
on orthodox monetary policy. Friedman argues that the economy has
been and is now inherently stable (see Chapter 20), and that it would
automatically tend to stay on a fairly straight course, as Figure 1
indicates, if only it were not being almost continuously knocked off
the track by erratic or unwise monetary policies. Conclusion: Quaran-
tine the central bank. The best stabilization policy is no stabilization
policy at all. Hasn't it all been said before:

> They also serve who only stand and wait.
>
> —John Milton

Rules Versus Discretion

What Professor Friedman proposes instead is that the Federal Reserve be instructed by Congress to follow a fixed long-run rule: Increase the money supply at a steady and inflexible rate, month in and month out, year in and year out, regardless of current economic conditions. Set the money supply on automatic pilot and then leave it alone.

The specific rule would depend· on the definition of the money supply adopted—increase the money supply by 3 percent a year if it is defined in the conventional way as demand deposits plus currency, by 4 percent a year if time deposits in commercial banks are added in as well. In either case, the particular number is not so important to Friedman as the restriction that once it is decided upon it be left alone thereafter. No tinkering! The 3 (or 4) percent figure is intended to keep prices stable and employment high by allowing aggregate demand to grow secularly at the same rate as the growth in the economy's real productive capacity (due to growth in the labor force and increased productivity).

Such a rule, it is claimed, would eliminate forecasting and lag problems and therefore remove what Friedman sees as the major cause of instability in the economy—the capricious and unpredictable impact of discretionary countercyclical monetary policy. As long as the money supply grows at a constant rate each year, be it 3, 4, or 5 percent, any decline into recession will be temporary. The liquidity provided by a constantly growing money supply will cause aggregate demand to expand. Similarly, if the supply of money does not rise at a more than average rate, any inflationary increase in spending will burn itself out for lack of fuel (as we saw in Chapter 23). Anyway, any discretionary deviations by the central bank would interfere with the natural course of the economy and only make matters worse.

The United States Congress has been impressed enough to come part of the way toward a Friedman-type rule, in preference to allowing the Federal Reserve to rely entirely on its own judgment and discretion. In March 1975 both the House of Representatives and the Senate passed House Congressional Resolution 133, which instructed the Federal Reserve to "maintain long-run growth of the monetary and credit aggregates commensurate with the economy's long run potential to increase production." It also required that the Fed report quarterly to Congress on its target monetary and credit growth rates for the upcoming twelve months. In November 1977 these provisions were incorporated into the Federal Reserve Act itself.

*"But didn't Milton say not to touch the
steering wheel once we're moving?"*

Whether one believes in a fixed rule or not, such procedures can hardly be anything but beneficial. They force the Fed to continuously assess its policies in quantitative terms without shackling it with an inflexible formula. The result should be smoother monetary growth and the elimination of the extremely high (and extremely low) monetary growth rates that have often had harmful effects in the past.

Given the present state of knowledge, it is difficult to justify legislation at the present time that would circumscribe the Federal Reserve's actions more rigidly. The fact is that so far very little is really known about the length and variability of the time lags. Such evidence as there is, and there is not much, is extremely mixed, as we saw in the last chapter. Serious research on the subject is only in its early stages, and no consensus is apparent among economists who have worked in the area. It should be noted, however, that the variability of GNP before World War II (even excluding the Great Depression) was much larger than instability since World War II, and it is only in the latter period that stabilization policy has been active.[1]

[1] See Martin N. Baily, "Stabilization Policy and Private Economic Behavior," *Brookings Papers on Economic Activity* (1978:1).

It is ironic—or perhaps instructive—that in the final analysis the extremists from both camps, Monetarist and Keynesian, have collectively ganged up on the Federal Reserve. The extreme Monetarists want to shackle it, because their concern with time lags leads them to believe it is both mischievous and harmful. The extreme Keynesians want to subordinate it to fiscal policy, because they think it is either useless or lethal.

In the middle, squabbling but making more common cause than they had thought possible, are the moderates: moderate Monetarists, who believe that the forecasting-lag problem is not so great as to negate all the stabilizing effects of countercyclical monetary policy; and moderate Keynesians, who believe that monetary policy probably does change interest rates and/or the availability of credit, and that those changes, along with fiscal policy, probably do influence spending decisions in the right way at more or less the right time. While one group concentrates mainly on the money supply and the other primarily on credit conditions, they are nevertheless in agreement that some form of countercyclical monetary policy is necessary and, on balance, beneficial.[2]

It seems clear, after all is said and done, that central banking is still at least as much art as science. We simply do not yet know enough to legislate an eternal rule, or even a rule for the next six months, that the Federal Reserve must follow under any and all circumstances. Meanwhile, for better or worse, we appear to have no alternative but to rely on our best knowledge and judgment in the formulation of monetary policy. We can only try to make sure that the decisionmakers are able and qualified men and women with open minds and the capacity to learn from experience.

Suggestions for Further Reading

For a survey of the literature on time lags, see Michael J. Hamburger, "The Lag in the Effect of Monetary Policy: A Survey of Recent Literature," *Monthly Review* of the Federal Reserve Bank of New York (December 1971). Professor Friedman's views on a rule for monetary policy are spelled out in his *A Program for Monetary Stability* (Bronx, N.Y.: Fordham University Press, 1959). The original statement on this subject was made by Henry Simons in "Rules Versus Authorities in Monetary Policy," *Journal of Political Economy* (February 1936). A formal examination of Friedman's

[2] For an eloquent defense of active stabilization policy, see Franco Modigliani, "The Monetarist Controversy," *American Economic Review* (March 1977).

hypothesis using modern control techniques is Stanley Fischer and J. Phillip Cooper, "Stabilization Policy and Lags," *Journal of Political Economy* (July/August 1973).

For opposing positions, see John M. Culbertson, "Friedman on the Lag in Effect of Monetary Policy," *Journal of Political Economy* (December 1960), and R. S. Sayers, *Central Banking After Bagehot* (Clarendon Press, 1957). The views of Harry G. Johnson, Abba P. Lerner, Paul Samuelson and others on rules versus authorities can be found in Volume 2 of the *Hearings* of the House Committee on Banking and Currency, *The Federal Reserve System After Fifty Years* (88th Congress, 1964).

Chapter 26

Does Monetary Policy Affect the Stock Market?

ANY CIVIC or social club program chairperson knows that if it is announced that next week's meeting will feature a renowned speaker on "The Crisis in America's Cities," hardly anyone will show up. But if the announcement states that the topic will be "The Outlook for the Stock Market" and mentions a speaker no one ever heard of, the hall will be packed. It would be hard to find a subject that intrigues people more than the stock market. Everyone knows about stocks: how they go up, and how they can make you rich. Forty years ago everyone knew about stocks: how they go down, and how they can make you destitute.

Why do stock prices go up and down? Not so much particular stocks, like IBM or Xerox, but why does the entire stock market soar or shudder, with all stocks more or less rising or falling together?

It is a fact of life that the total supply of stocks in existence is more or less fixed. What changes is not so much the number of shares lying around—in vaults, under mattresses, and concealed between the pages of the family Bible—but the price of each.

For example, at the end of 1978 the market value of all the pub-licly held shares of stock in existence amounted to something like $1,000 billion. In the early 1960s it was about $500 billion, and in the early 1950s less than $200 billion. And yet in the past twenty-five years corporations have raised relatively little money by issuing new stock, perhaps $150 billion or so at most. This means, and the word has obviously gotten around, that almost all of that $1,000 billion— probably at least $850 billion of it—represents price appreciation of existing shares.

The fact that the total supply outstanding is relatively fixed does not, of course, imply that the amount offered on the market need be fixed. People who have bought, and even some who haven't, can always sell. Thus in recent years stocks have been drifting out of the hands of individual investors, who on balance have been selling, into the plush suites of institutional investors, who have been buying. In 1960 pension funds, mutual funds, insurance companies, and other institutional investors held about 15 percent of the market value of outstanding shares; now they hold about 30 percent. But 70 percent or $700 billion is still held by individuals, about 25 million of them, and each and every one is out to make a killing.

Strangely enough, given the widespread interest in the stock market, economists have generally had very little to say about it. The most popular postwar college textbook, Paul Samuelson's *Economics*, is estimated to have sold over 3 million copies since it first appeared in 1948. Considering the royalties accruing to so popular an author, and a leading economist in the bargain, one would think he might have accumulated both the wherewithal and the trained experience to discover at long last the secret of what makes the market tick. But if Paul has found out, he isn't telling! The latest edition of *Economics* contains only five pages on the stock market (out of 917).

Some economists are less reticent than Professor Samuelson about letting us in on why stock prices fluctuate. Their explanations have ranged from the influence of sunspots on men's emotional be-havior to the conspiratorial machinations of shadowy figures in high places. However, the explanations that are of most interest to us here deal with money and monetary policy.

Is it true, as some claim, that the elusive clue to movements in overall stock prices is found in changes in the money supply? Or does the secret lie, as others believe, in changes in monetary policy in general? If the former are correct, and to some extent the latter, perhaps all the paraphernalia with which market analysts now so laboriously wrestle for signs of the future can be put aside; the best tout sheet might turn out to be the weekly member bank reserve statistics.

A Money Supply View of Stock Prices

The belief that fluctuations in the money supply provide the key to movements in stock prices is based on a series of cause-and-effect hypotheses that contain elements of both Monetarist and Keynesian thinking. In its simplest form, the reasoning is as follows: When the Federal Reserve increases the money supply at a faster than normal rate, the public, finding itself with more cash than it needs for current transactions purposes, spends some of its excess money buying financial assets, including stocks. Since the supply of stocks is more or less fixed, especially in the short run, this incremental demand raises their price. Some stocks will go up more than others and some may go down, depending on the prospects for particular companies, but overall the *average* of stock prices will rise.

Or the transmission process might be somewhat more complex, but with similar results. The increase in the money supply may first lead the public to step up its *bond* purchases, thereby raising bond prices. Higher bond prices imply lower interest rates. With bonds yielding less, some potential bond purchasers are likely to switch over to the now relatively more attractive stock market. The demand for stocks expands because their substitute, bonds, has become more expensive—just as the demand for Yamahas will expand when their alternative, Hondas, become more expensive (not to mention the Suzuki).

Or it could be an even more roundabout process. The larger money supply leads to lower interest rates, more investment spending, more consumer spending (through the multiplier), a higher GNP, and along with it larger corporate profits. Enlarged corporate profits spur stock purchases and higher stock prices.

In any case, the result is the same. Whether the postulated chain of causation is direct, from the money supply to stock prices, or indirect, through the bond market and interest rates, or through GNP, an increase in the money supply is seen as accelerating the demand for stocks, leading to higher stock prices.

Conversely, decreases in the money supply—or increases at a slower rate than necessary to provide for the transactions needs of a growing economy—leave the public with shortages of funds. Result: among other things, a cutback in stock purchases—again, either directly or because, with higher interest rates, bonds become more attractive buys, or because corporate profits decline as GNP falls. This reduced demand for stocks lowers their prices.

Conclusion: A rapidly expanding money supply leads to higher stock values; inadequate monetary growth leads to a bear market.

Persuasive as the underlying reasoning may seem, all too frequently the facts simply do not bear it out. Evidently too many other cross-currents simultaneously impinge on the stock market, such as business expectations and political developments. Like so many other single-cause explanations in economics, this simplified view of stock price determination contains too much truth to ignore, but not enough to make it very reliable in the clutch.

Consider 1929, and the couple of years before and after. From mid-1927 to mid-1928, the money supply increased by 1.6 percent; from mid-1928 to mid-1929, it increased by 1.2 percent. The stock market, meanwhile, going its merry way, *doubled.*

In the next two years, from mid-1929 to mid-1931, the money supply contracted by about 5 percent each year. If the stock market was merely reacting to changes in the money supply, it was by all odds the biggest overreaction in history, because the proverbial bottom dropped out and the market promptly lost all the gains it had made in the previous two years and then some.

Furthermore, it is not at all clear precisely what is cause and what is effect. Did the market crash in 1929 because, among other things, the money supply contracted? Or did the money supply contract because the market crashed (as banks called speculative margin loans and demand deposits were wiped off the books)? The latter explanation is as logical as the former.

The 1929 market collapse, as many see it, was due to a number of interrelated factors: an unwarranted mood of euphoric optimism prior to the crash, excessive speculative activity, fundamental weakness in underlying business conditions, and so on. The money supply, if it influenced the break at all, did so only as one among many causes.

None of which is meant to imply that the money supply was or is unimportant. If it had been rapidly and forcefully restored to its 1929 level by 1930, or even 1931, the depression initiated by the stock market collapse would probably not have been either as severe or as long as it turned out to be. That the Federal Reserve stood by, wringing its hands, while the money supply declined by 30 percent from 1929 to 1933 undoubtedly intensified and prolonged what we now call the Great Depression. But that is a very different thing from saying that movements in the money supply caused or could have given one even a vague idea of the heights or the depths to which stock prices went from 1927 to 1931. As a matter of fact, most of the drop in the money supply occurred *after* 1931; by that time, however, the market was too weary to do much reacting, either over or under.

To come closer to the present, in 1940 the stock market fell 15 percent even though the money supply was then rising 15 percent (on top of a similar rise the year before). In 1962, again, the market tumbled despite an increasing money supply. And in 1973–1974 the stock market fell by more than 40 percent, even though the money supply increased by 11 percent over that two-year period.

On other not infrequent occasions, however, it is true that declines in stock prices *were* preceded or accompanied by declines in the rate of growth of the money supply, as in 1957, 1960, and 1969. And often increases in stock prices were indeed associated with increases in the growth of the money supply, as in 1967, 1968, and 1975.

In at least some of these instances, however, both stock prices and the money supply might conceivably have been reacting to a third causal force, perhaps an upturn in business conditions stimulated by the outbreak of war ( ) peace ( )—check one—a spurt in consumer spending, or something else. An improvement in business conditions, regardless of cause, typically leads to an expansion in bank business loans, a larger money supply, brighter profit prospects, and thereby higher stock prices. As the history of business cycles indicates, such upswings (or downturns) are capable of generating a cumulative push that can work up considerable momentum, carrying *both* the money supply and stock prices along with it.

Chart 1 (on page 417) provides some idea of the pitfalls involved in reading a cause-and-effect relationship into two sets of statistics simply because they move together. The unbroken line indicates the movement of stock prices, annually, from the end of 1960 through the end of 1966, using stock prices at the end of 1960 as the base (= 100).

The thin dashed line, on a similar index basis, is the movement of the money supply annually, also from the end of 1960 through the end of 1966. Over this particular six-year period, changes in the money supply clearly bore little relationship to turning points in stock prices.

Finally, the chart includes a third line (W). Its movements are obviously closely related to changes in stock prices. Almost without exception, the line labeled W and the line tracing stock prices move up and down together.

Cause and effect? The line labeled W, make of it what you will, is an annual index (1960 = 100) of the number of times members of the old Washington Senators baseball team struck out each year, over the period 1960 through 1966. (Source: *The Sporting News's Official Baseball Guide and Record Book*, Annual, 1960–1966.) For at least these years, evidently, an investor trying to forecast turning points in the stock market would have been better off spending his time reading the box scores than the money supply figures.

Monetary Policy and Wall Street

Once we expand our horizon to encompass more than the money supply alone, there seems to be agreement that monetary policy, in general, frequently does have a considerable influence on the stock market. The consensus appears that it is by no means the only influence, and often is overshadowed by other forces and events; nevertheless, it is widely believed that on balance monetary policy has had a substantial effect on stock prices at times in the past, especially since the mid-1960s, and is likely to continue to do so in the foreseeable future.

This is quite aside from the power of the Federal Reserve to set margin requirements on stock purchases. In an attempt to prevent a repetition of the speculative wave, financed heavily with borrowed funds, that carried the market to dizzy heights in 1928 and until the fall of 1929, Congress in the 1930s authorized the Federal Reserve to impose margin (or minimum down payment) requirements on the purchase of stocks. If the margin requirement is 100 percent, then 100 percent cash must be put up and no borrowing at all is permitted. If the margin requirement is 80 percent, that much of one's own cash must be put up when buying a security and only the remaining 20 percent can be financed by borrowing from a bank or a broker. Of course, you could always finance the entire amount by borrowing from your brother-in-law and no one would be the wiser (except perhaps, in the long run, your brother-in-law).

High margin requirements probably have helped restrain speculation in stocks, particularly by those who could least afford it. Nevertheless, if the Federal Reserve had only this device to influence the market, it would be relying on a weak reed indeed. Margin requirements are 100 percent at Santa Anita and Hialeah racetracks, but at last report speculative activity by those who could not afford it as well as by those who could appeared unimpaired.

The impact of overall monetary policy on stock prices stems not so much from the Federal Reserve's power to set margin requirements as from its influence over the money supply, the entire spectrum of interest rates and financial markets, and current and expected business conditions. It is in the recent past, rather than 20 or 30 years ago, that the effects of monetary policy on stock prices are most clearly visible. The credit squeezes of 1966, 1969, and 1974 are prime examples.

During 1966, for instance, the money supply increased at a slower than normal rate. Bankers, businessmen, and the general public, carried away by skyrocketing interest rates, labeled the episode

Does Monetary Policy Affect the Stock Market?

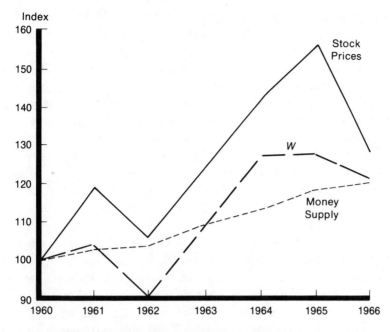

CHART 1 / Stock prices and other variables, 1960–1966.

Stock Prices: Dow-Jones Industrials, monthly closing averages for December of each year (December 1960 = 100). Money Supply: Demand deposits plus currency, monthly averages for December of each year (December 1960 = 100).

the Great Credit Crunch of 1966. Credit availability was sharply curtailed and interest rates on fixed-income securities soared. Stock prices tumbled about 20 percent during the first ten months of the year, despite booming business conditions—a rather clear indication of the potency of tight monetary policy, when applied vigorously, in affecting stock prices.

The easy money policy that prevailed during 1967 and most of 1968 was correspondingly accompanied by a rapid and lengthy upturn in the stock market. Reimposition of exceedingly tight money in 1969, however, was followed by a prompt collapse of stock prices. The Dow-Jones Industrial Average plunged from 985 in late 1968 to the 630 level in mid-1970, when it finally began to turn around.

In 1974 we again had tight money, as interest rates rose even higher than in 1966 and 1969. The bank prime rate, for example, hit a high of 12 percent in mid-1974. And stock prices, which had already fallen 20 percent in 1973, fell another 30 percent in 1974.

During the three decades from the early 1930s to the early 1960s, the reaction of the stock market to monetary policy was less prompt and less predictable than it has recently been. Stocks frequently seemed to go their own way during those years, regardless of what the central bank was doing. Not so any more; since the mid-1960s there is a rather clear cause-and-effect relationship between the general stance of monetary policy and movements in stock prices. There are two reasons for this change:

First, the central bank has recently acted with more authority than it did previously. In retrospect, during the 1950s and early 1960s, when the Federal Reserve was just testing the air after almost 20 years of virtual hibernation, a wiggle in long-term bond rates would cause it to beat a hasty retreat. It was afraid to probe too far for fear of starting a recession. An increase in interest rates on long-term government bonds from 3½ to 3¾ percent was considered a hazardous venture.[1]

The Credit Crunch of 1966, however, gave the monetary authorities a different perspective. Prices fell on long-term government bonds to the point where effective interest rates approached 5 percent —not so high by later standards, but the equivalent of Mount Everest then—and yields on some intermediate-term Treasury bonds went over 6 percent. The economy thrashed and strained, but it did not collapse. It proved to be more resilient than many had supposed.

However, something else did happen. For the first time in a generation, many investors became aware that such things as bonds existed. And under certain conditions, they were more attractive additions to one's portfolio than stocks. The rise in bond interest rates (which means a fall in bond prices) thus had repercussions in the stock market; some individual and institutional investors held off buying stocks, or sold some they had, and bought bonds instead, thereby driving stock prices down.

In theory, the prices of stocks and bonds *should* move together in precisely that way, since they are substitutes for each other in investor portfolios just as Yamahas and Hondas are on the highway (with or without monkey bars and sissy bars). As we noted earlier in this chapter, if the price of bonds falls (implying higher interest rates), some buyers will switch out of stocks and into the now relatively more attractive bonds—thus causing the price of stocks to fall too. For similar reasons, if the price of bonds rises, stock prices should rise also.

However, during the 1950s this relationship did not hold very closely. For most of that decade, interest rates on bonds were slowly rising, cautiously adjusting upward from artificially low war and postwar levels. Slowly rising bond interest rates imply slowly falling bond prices. Stock prices, on the other hand, were ebullient during most of the decade.

[1] See Chapter 37.

Does Monetary Policy Affect the Stock Market?

With yields on bonds and stocks now at more realistic levels relative to each other, the sympathetic relationship between them has reasserted itself and they are likely to continue to move together in the future. From now on, when the Federal Reserve bangs bonds around, stocks are likely to get a nosebleed.

The *second* reason monetary policy affects stock prices more today than 20 or 30 years ago is simply that the Federal Reserve has made believers out of many former skeptics. If the Federal Reserve is ineffectual, who cares? But if monetary policy is effective in influencing the course of the economy, then a lot of people care a great deal. Today, many more financial analysts and observers of economic trends are persuaded that the central bank can achieve its announced objectives, or at least come reasonably close, than thought so a few decades back.

Monetary Policy Expectations and Stock Prices

Indeed, the pendulum appears to have swung so far in recent years that expectations about the immediate future course of monetary policy have now become one of the main topics of conversation among stock market analysts. Every week stock market participants pause on Thursday morning, awaiting the release of the Federal Reserve's money supply figures that afternoon.

If the figures show that the money supply is growing *faster* than the Fed's announced guidelines—say the Fed is aiming to increase the money supply by 4 to 6 percent annually, but the weekly figures reveal that in fact it has been increasing by 9 percent—then Wall Street concludes that the Fed will soon be *tightening* to get the money supply back on the track.

Alternatively, if the figures show that the money supply is growing *more slowly* than the Fed's announced guidelines—again say the Fed is aiming to increase the money supply by 4 to 6 percent, but this time the weekly figures reveal that in fact it has been increasing by only 1 percent—then Wall Street concludes that the Fed will soon be *easing to* get the money supply back on the track.

Views on Wall Street are mixed as to precisely what such figures imply for stock prices. If the money supply has been growing faster than the Fed's target, so that tightening is in order, then some see this as heralding a fall in stock prices, but others view it as signaling an upturn. Those who see tighter money as precipitating a fall in the

Dow Off by 11.44 to 806.91 As Fears on Fed Heighten

Test of 2-Year Low May Be Near—Transportation Average Also Plunges

By VARTANIG G. VARTAN

Stock prices tumbled yesterday, with the Dow Jones industrial average dropping more than 11 points, following apparent confirmation that the Federal Reserve was permitting short-term interest rates to move higher.

The blue-chip Dow, following last week's rebound of 14 points, almost wiped out this advance in a single session as it tumbled 11.44 points to 806.91. The transportation average, made up of railroad, airline and trucking issues, also sustained a substantial loss.

By virtue of its sizable decline, the industrial average now hovers at a level that shortly might test its two-year low, set Oct. 25 at 801.54. More than 1,000 issues fell in yesterday's widespread decline.

The week's main market surprise has been the upward push in interest rates by the Fed — one that was somewhat modified yesterday, but still is considered strong — coming at a time when most analysts had believed that the nation's money manager would allow rates to consolidate for a while after recent increases.

One chief reason why stockbrokers worry about higher interest rates is that they tend to enhance the attraction of Treasury bills and other fixed-income securities at the expense of equities.

While the upward nudge in rates and fears about an economic slowdown have been factors in causing a 20 percent price decline so far this year for the Dow, analysts said that unhappiness with the policies of the Carter Administration also had weakened the fabric of the stock market.

No Great Rush to Sell

Underscoring this sense of unease is the fact that, for the first time since World War II, a Democratic President has witnessed a market decline during his first year in office. Stock prices advanced in the initial year of White House occupancy by Presidents Truman, Kennedy and Jackson.

Trading volume, meanwhile, held to a slow pace, totaling 17.17 million shares, compared with Monday's 17.07 million shares. Such light turnover indicated no great rush to sell by investors and traders, despite the decline of equity prices across a broad front.

NEWS ITEM / Monetary Policy and the Stock Market

SOURCE: *New York Times*, November 2, 1977

stock market reason that tighter money means higher interest rates (lower bond prices); this will make bonds relatively more attractive than stocks, resulting in lower stock prices as well. On the other hand, others see tighter money as signaling an upturn in stock prices on the logic that inflation has been bad for stock prices; tighter money will stop inflation, which in turn will eventually bring interest rates down and thereby stimulate higher stock prices.

The same divergence of views exists for the implications of easier money. If the money supply has been growing more slowly than the

Fed's target, so that easing is in order, some see this as likely to produce higher stock prices. They reason that easier money means lower interest rates (higher bond prices); this will make stocks relatively more attractive than bonds, resulting in higher stock prices. Others, however, come to the opposite conclusion. They see easier money as fueling inflation, which in turn will eventually bring higher interest rates and thereby depress stock prices.

By and large, the first group (tighter money will depress stock prices, easier money stimulate them) seemed to hold the predominant opinion in the early seventies. But as inflation accelerated during the decade, the second group gained adherents (tighter money will stimulate stock prices, easier money depress them).

Both groups, however, had their problems (and so have we). One problem is difficulty in interpreting the weekly Federal Reserve statistics, which are often ambiguous. One money supply measure may overshoot the target at the same time as another money supply measure undershoots it. Which measure should be used? Or the money supply may overshoot the target on the basis of the past month's data but undershoot it on the basis of the past two or three months' data. Which time span should be used?

Not to mention the potentially biggest problem of all: the Federal Reserve may have changed its target! There is a one-month delay between meetings of the Federal Reserve's Open Market Committee and release to the public of what transpired. If the Fed changed its money supply target from a 4–6 percent annual growth rate to 1–3 percent, then 1 percent is right on target and does not imply future easing. Someone who acts as though it does imply future easing could be making a serious mistake.

But then whoever said making money in the stock market is easy!

Suggestions for Further Reading

For attempts to quantify the relationship between the money supply and stock prices see Michael W. Keran, "Expectations, Money, and the Stock Market," Federal Reserve Bank of St. Louis *Review* (January 1971); K. E. Homa and Dwight M. Jaffee, "The Supply of Money and Common Stock Prices," *Journal of Finance* (December 1971); and Michael J. Hamburger and Levis A. Kochin, "Money and Stock Prices: The Channels of Influence," *Journal of Finance* (May 1972). For a critical analysis of these efforts, see the discussion by Merton H. Miller, also in the May 1972 issue of the *Journal of Finance*. Also see James E. Pesando, "The Supply of Money and Common Stock Prices," *Journal of Finance* (June 1974); and Robert D.

Auerbach, "Money and Stock Prices," *Federal Reserve Bank of Kansas City Monthly Review* (September–October 1976).

One of the early attempts to examine the relationship between money and stock prices was Beryl W. Sprinkel, *Money and Stock Prices* (Homewood, Ill.: Irwin, 1964); this has since been revised and retitled *Money and Markets: A Monetarist View* (Irwin, 1971). A recent interesting study of the relationship between stock prices and economic activity is Barry Bosworth, "The Stock Market and the Economy," *Brookings Papers on Economic Activity* (No. 2, 1975).

If this chapter has tempted you to think you can beat the market, before you try to do so read Burton Malkiel's paperback *A Random Walk Down Wall Street* (New York: Norton, 1974). Or if you have the notion that other games of chance are more in your line, at least know what the odds are against you. You'll find them all in John Scarne's *New Complete Guide to Gambling* (New York: Simon and Schuster, 1974).

Chapter 27

Selective Credit Policies and Housing

CREDIT DOES JUST ABOUT EVERYTHING these days—it buys houses and cars, provides college educations and trips abroad, and helps establish small businesses. Politicians have found that helping constituents do their favorite thing can take an apparently harmless route: make it easier to get credit. Sometimes a maximum interest rate is specified to make the borrower even happier.

These types of programs are called selective credit policies. Some are very direct, such as the Federal Housing Administration and Veterans Administration (FHA-VA) mortgage insurance and guarantee program. Some are somewhat indirect, such as the line of credit at the Treasury granted to the Federal National Mortgage Association in exchange for its mortgage market activities, or the restriction on savings and loan associations that they invest primarily in mortgages and government securities. Still others are harder to pinpoint: Regulation Q sets the maximum rate commercial banks can pay on time deposits. It apparently can be used to prevent commercial banks from competing with savings and loan associations, thereby making mortgage credit more readily available.

While the examples just given relate to mortgages and housing, there are few areas which have escaped the credit control syndrome. Consumer credit used to be regulated by the Federal Reserve Board under Regulation W; stock market credit still is (Regulations G, T, and U). The Small Business Administration makes loans to—you guessed it—small businesses. The federally sponsored Student Loan Marketing Association guarantees loans of students (not just marketing students). And the government's Export-Import Bank does something for exporters and importers—exactly what is not clear.

With all this activity out in the open, and even more going on behind the scenes, it is important to probe the depths of selective credit policies. Once we tally the pluses and minuses in general, we turn to more detailed scrutiny of the Big One: housing and its credit supporters.

A Catechism on Selective Credit Policies

QUESTION. *How are selective policies supposed to work?*

ANSWER. Their objective is to encourage (or discourage) a particular type of real expenditure—say, housing (or consumer durable goods expenditures)—by increasing (or decreasing) the volume of credit directed to such activities and/or by making the terms of credit (interest rates, down payments) easier (or more stringent). One obvious prerequisite for the effectiveness of selective credit policies is that there be a close relationship between a specific type of credit and a particular category of real expenditure. For example, if the purchase of a home is closely related to the availability of mortgage credit, it is possible to encourage housing by inducing lenders to make mortgage loans rather than other types of loans. As lenders devote more funds to mortgages and less to, say, business loans, the interest rate on mortgages should fall and people will thus be encouraged to take out mortgages and buy new homes.

But that is not the only way to use mortgage money. What if someone already has enough cash to buy a home and is ready to spend it for that purpose regardless of mortgage terms? The availability of cheap mortgage money then induces him to take out a mortgage to finance his home—freeing his other funds for more serious endeavors, like a two-year tour of the world's major red-light districts. In this case a house is not a home, and it is the former that the selective credit policy winds up financing!

A selective credit policy will be most effective in redirecting real resources when there is a rigid dollar-for-dollar relationship between a specific type of credit and a particular category of expenditure. If there is some slippage—that is, if the expenditure can be financed in other ways or the specific type of credit can be used differently—the effectiveness of the selective credit policy is impaired.

Many selective credit policies are imposed on only one sector of financial markets. The portfolio restrictions on savings and loan associations, for example, limit their assets essentially to government bonds and mortgages. Another example is the proposal that commercial banks have different reserve requirements on different types of loans. Such selective credit policies increase the flow of credit to the favored uses only so long as other (unrestricted) lenders in financial markets do not counteract their behavior. For instance, if the reserve requirement proposal were enacted and the reserve requirement against mortgage loans were low while the reserve requirement against consumer installment loans were high, banks would find it profitable to divert more funds to mortgages and less to consumer installment credit. Initially, mortgage rates would decline and consumer credit rates would go up. This is precisely the desired objective of the selective credit policy. *But* the reaction of other institutional lenders, such as life insurance companies, will be to make fewer mortgage loans and to expand credit to consumer intallment loans, which will ultimately tend to offset the impact of the selective policy. As long as this offset is incomplete, however, selective credit policies on only a few sectors of the credit market can successfully divert some funds into favored uses.

QUESTION. *Do selective credit policies, in fact, work successfully?*

ANSWER. Under most circumstances, selective credit policies seem to work. Imposing regulations and controls does appear to divert credit into desired channels. Furthermore, borrowers do tend, for the most part, to use certain types of credit for specific types of real expenditures. But as we saw in Chapter 7, in our discussion of Regulation Q, participants in financial markets are very creative when it comes to circumventing regulations. The very success of selective credit controls is likely to sow the seeds of their ultimate failure. If consumers cannot get credit from banks to finance the purchase of automobiles because, say, the banks are preoccupied with sewage bonds of local municipalities, then the auto dealers will arrange the necessary financing. How? Most probably through the auto manufacturers, who can float bonds in the capital markets and use the proceeds for anything they want, including extending loans to potential customers.

QUESTION. *What's wrong with selective credit policies?*

ANSWER. For one thing, as indicated in the preceding paragraph, their effectiveness tends to wear out with the passage of time. Another drawback is that the real costs of such programs are obscured by the financial maze. The unavoidable fact of life is that when we are already at full employment, the cost of more resources in education or housing has to be fewer resources available for other things. This lesson is delivered loud and clear when taxes must be raised to deter the other types of expenditure, with the proceeds going to the favored groups.

But favoring some borrowers (and thereby in effect squeezing others out of the credit market), while less direct than taxation, has similar social costs—less of something else. If politicians are not aware of these costs (and the proliferation of credit programs makes it doubtful that they are), indiscriminate use of selective credit policies tries to favor everyone and everything and winds up producing nothing.

QUESTION. *Why are selective credit policies so popular?*

ANSWER. Partly because they don't *seem* as painful as taxation. Those who are unable to buy new cars because they can't get financing are likely to blame fate or the world in general, while those who can't buy them because they have so little left after taxes are likely to blame the politicians in power. Also, more positively, selective credit policies do have the attractive feature of making the private sector an active partner in the process of redirecting resources. The government only provides the incentive—an interest subsidy, insurance for the lender against default, or some other feature. The bulk of the funds are still channeled through nongovernmental institutions.

The scope of activities currently receiving favorable treatment in the credit markets extends from exports and foreign economic development to community redevelopment and higher education. Housing, however, stands head and shoulders above all other activities as the spending category receiving the most credit favors. In the next two sections we explore the housing situation in detail, with special reference to the impacts of monetary policy and selective credit programs.

The Housing Story

Countercyclical monetary policy has often been accused of having "discriminatory" effects on the housing market. It is argued that tight money has its greatest impact on residential construction. In boom periods, when money is tightened and interest rates rise, home building gets strangled. Subsequently, when money eases and interest rates fall, home building zooms ahead at an unnaturally rapid pace.

As a result, employment in the construction industry is unstable; workers try to even out their incomes over time by restrictive entry requirements and work rules; and entrepreneurs are discouraged from mechanization and modernization. All of which, it is alleged, leads to lower productivity in the housing industry than elsewhere in the economy. We are in the last half of the twentieth century, but still building homes as though we were in the first half of the nineteenth. Low-cost housing seems impossible to construct and rents across the board, on both new and existing dwellings, are higher than they need be.

Is home building indeed that fickle? If so, why? Can anything be done about it? *Should* anything be done about it? What role is there for selective credit policies?

The evidence suggests that housing takes the lead in moving us into and out of recession. Chart 1 traces expenditures on new housing as a percent of GNP from 1951 through 1978. The shaded areas represent periods of recession, from the peak of the boom at the start of the shaded area to the trough of the recession at the end. Tight monetary policy and high interest rates usually occur before the shaded areas, while easy monetary policy and low interest rates follow them. Housing expenditures as a percent of GNP typically fall immediately prior to or at the beginning of a recession, and then turn upwards soon thereafter. The only major swing in housing not associated with a peak or trough is the collapse and recovery during 1966–1967. And that period was characterized by a credit crunch and mini-recession.

On the basis of the evidence, housing is indeed a foul-weather friend. When economic activity is at its low point, housing begins to recover. In boom periods, on the other hand, housing starts are curtailed. As resources turn to making automobiles, television sets, and machine tools, the construction of homes takes a back seat.

Why? What causes these fluctuations in the housing market, fluctuations that appear closely related to the actions of the central bank?

During periods of tight money and rising interest rates, the *supply of funds to the mortgage market* is drastically curtailed. This

Percent

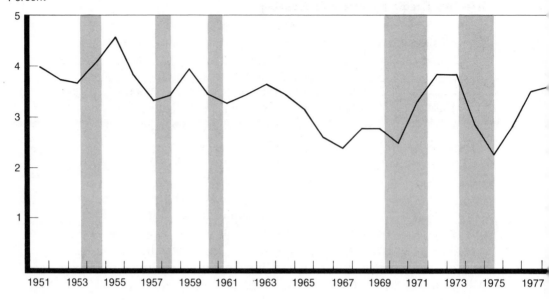

CHART 1 / New housing expenditures as a percent of GNP, 1951–1978.
SOURCE: *Annual Reports,* Council of Economic Advisors.

sharp reduction in funds available for home financing can be traced, historically, to the inability of the major mortgage lenders, savings and loan associations and mutual savings banks, to compete for funds as interest rates rise. When interest rates rise during a period of tight money, these institutions can compete for funds only so long as they can continue to move their deposit rates up in tandem with market rates. But two reasons stop them from doing so for very long.

First, the assets of these institutions are primarily long-term. Only a small portion of their portfolio turns over during any single year. Hence, when interest rates go up, they can receive a higher yield on only a small portion of their assets. Some of these financial institutions thus find it too costly to raise their deposit rates by as much as the increase in yields on government, municipal, and corporate bonds. Second, while many of the better-managed institutions might be willing to raise their deposit rates to maintain their inflow of funds, they have been prevented from doing so by the legal interest rate ceilings imposed on deposit rates.

As market rates continue to advance, but deposit rates at savings institutions do not, savers—potential depositors—start to find it more attractive to invest their funds directly in the capital markets, rather than depositing them in savings and loans or savings banks. Since individual investors are not large mortgage lenders, funds that might well have gone into the mortgage market had they been deposited in a savings and loan association now move directly into stocks or bonds.

The supply of funds available for mortgage lending dries up.

This process occurred most dramatically in 1966, when the savings and loan associations and savings banks lost funds not only to direct investment but also to commercial banks, and again in 1969 and 1974 when all deposit-type financial institutions were hard hit by outflows of funds. In the second half of 1978, on the other hand, "disintermediation" did not occur despite rising open market rates. And that's because ceilings under Regulation Q were relaxed and savings and loans were able to issue competitive money market certificates (see Chapter 7).

All this is only half the story. Another side of the coin, the nature of the *demand for housing and mortgages*, also contributes to the instability of residential construction.

In Chapter 24 we noted that residential construction spending appears to be much more sensitive to changes in interest rates than any other category of expenditure. In the Federal Reserve's econometric model of the economy, a 1 percentage point increase in long-term interest rates reduces housing demand by $3 billion after one year, while business plant and equipment spending is reduced barely half a billion dollars.

Why is the demand for housing so much more sensitive to changes in interest rates than other kinds of spending? There are probably two major reasons. First, interest is a much greater proportion of total outlay in home buying that it is in shorter-lived investments, such as inventory investment or the purchase of manufacturing equipment. The longer the investment period—that is, the longer the money will be tied up in the investment—the larger interest costs loom as an element in total costs. For example, if you buy a $50,000 home (it's cheap, grab it) and obtain a mortgage for the full amount at 9 percent interest for 30 years, you will be paying $93,000 in *interest alone*. If the mortgage rate rises to 10 percent, this will add an additional $12,000.

Second, the demand for housing is probably more sensitive to interest rate changes than other kinds of spending because families rather than business firms are undertaking the investment, and families can more easily postpone such expenditures for a few years. Business firms also invest in long-lived projects—heavy machinery, physical plant, and so on—in which interest costs bulk as large as they do in housing. But corporations face competitive pressures from rival sellers and frequently have no choice in the matter; often they must either make improvements and additions quickly or else risk losing their share of the market.

The reaction of home buyers to changes in interest rates thus reinforces the reaction of potential suppliers of mortgage money. When rates fall or rise, home buyers revise their spending plans and lenders rethink their allocation of funds Result: Feast or famine in the building industry.

Fannie Mae and Her Friends

Since housing is high on our list of national priorities and since it is, in part, the government's use of countercyclical monetary policy (producing wide swings in interest rates) that causes instability in the housing industry, there has been considerable governmental effort

Sharp Drop Is Expected In Housing

WASHINGTON, Nov. 8 (AP) — Housing construction will drop sharply in the next year because of rising interest rates, according to the Commerce Department.

In its 1979 construction forecast, made public yesterday, the department said mortgage rates would exceed 10 percent in 1979's first half. But interest rates should range from 9 percent to 10 percent in the second half, it added.

About 1.65 million new houses and apartment buildings will be built in 1979, down from two million in both 1977 and 1978, the department said.

However, strong activity is still expected in the construction of industrial and commercial buildings and new sewer systems.

Inflation Hedge Seen

Consumers will continue to view the purchase of houses as a hedge against inflation, the department said.

"The degree to which high mortgage rates will dampen demand in 1979 seems likely to be less than in the past since there will be little anticipation of a substantial fall in interest rates," the report said.

Mortgage lending will be limited by a careful screening of borrowers and a tightening of lending terms, it added.

In its five-year predictions, the department said housing construction would average 1.8 million to 1.9 million starts a year, with mortgage rates of less than 10 percent.

"The shift of construction to Sun Belt areas will continue," it added. "Fast-rising land costs in the larger metropolitan centers will also act as a deterrent to new construction."

Rising labor, construction and land costs will continue to push prices up, the report said.

More Prefabrication Expected

There will be more use of prefabricated housing and new housing designs to offset rising energy and materials costs, it added.

Despite the housing downturn, a 5 percent increase is expected in industrial construction, the department said.

"The need for more modern and energy-efficient plants is increasing," the report said. "The growing pressures to become more competitive with imports and the growing recognition that greater tax incentives to investment are needed has probably accelerated industrial projects."

Public construction also continues to be strong, particularly sewer and water projects, which are paid for by the Federal Government.

School construction may fall off because of a decline in the school-age population and possible voter resistance to taxes, the department said.

NEWS ITEM / Interest Rates and Housing

SOURCE: *New York Times,* November 9, 1978

to reduce the variability of home building. Almost all this effort takes the form of selective credit policies designed to ameliorate the impact of tight money on housing.

The Federal National Mortgage Association, popularly known as Fannie Mae, was established by Congress in 1938. It used to be part of the Department of Housing and Urban Development (HUD) but in 1968 it became a privately owned corporation with certain ties to the government. Fannie Mae buys mortgages from institutions that no longer wish to hold them as investments. Fannie finances these so-called secondary market operations primarily by issuing bonds to the public.

Fannie's performance in the mortgage market is complemented by the work of her cousin (so she says), Ginnie Mae, more properly called the Government National Mortgage Association. A relative new-comer to the mortgage market scene, Ginnie was established by Congress in 1968 as part of the Department of HUD. Initially, Ginnie worked mostly in tandem with Fannie—providing explicit subsidies to some of the purchase programs conducted. But since 1970, Ginnie Mae has made a name on her own in connection with the "pass-through program." Instead of buying mortgages and financing these acquisitions by issuing her own securities, Ginnie Mae guarantees the timely payment of interest and principle on packages or pools of mortgages that are insured by the Federal Housing Administration (FHA) or the Veterans Administration (VA). These pools of mortgages are put together by private mortgage originators such as mortgage bankers. GNMA pass-through securities are attractive to investors such as pension funds and insurance companies because of their government guarantee and liquidity (see Chapter 31). The pass-through program has made mortgages look very much like bonds to some investors, thereby broadening the source of mortgage funds.

A somewhat less direct mortgage market role is played by the Federal Home Loan Bank System, established by Congress in 1932 to regulate the savings and loan industry (see Chapter 7). It is organized along the lines of the Federal Reserve System. It has a Board in Washington (appointed by the President) and twelve regional banks which are technically owned by the savings and loan associations. The FHLBS makes loans (called advances) to S&Ls which temporarily need funds to extend mortgage credit. Unlike the Federal Reserve, however, the FHLBS cannot create money. It sells its own securities in the capital market to finance these advances to S&Ls.

In 1970, Congress established the Federal Home Loan Mortgage Corporation (FHLMC) as a subsidiary of the Federal Home Loan Bank System. Dubbed Freddie Mac by the investment community, this latest creation does just about what Ginnie Mae does, except instead of FHA-Va mortgage-backed securities, Freddie creates par-

Fannie Mae and Her Friends

ticipation certificates in conventional mortgages and sells them to ultimate investors. As with Ginnie, the objective is to attract heretofore nontraditional funds into the mortgage market by packaging individual mortgage loans into a bondlike instrument.

All these government and government-sponsored agencies are very active during periods of tight money. During 1969 and 1974 both Fannie Mae and the Federal Home Loan Bank System pumped large volumes of funds into the mortgage market in an effort to mitigate the downturn in housing. Ginnie Mae and Freddie Mac mortgage-backed securities increased dramatically during 1977 and 1978.

There has been much concern in the money and capital markets, however, over the growth of federal credit programs. As we saw earlier in this chapter, if one use of credit is favored some other use will have to be cut back. As federally sponsored agencies bid for funds in the credit market by issuing their own securities (to buy mortgages), other borrowers without federal backing are squeezed out. It is those who are squeezed out (the squeezees) who bear the burden of tight money and higher interest rates.

Should this massive federal credit effort be made to stabilize the mortgage market? It is not such a bad thing, once you think about it, for the economy to have a foul-weather friend. The fact that housing has slackened during boom periods has taken some of the extreme inflationary pressure off the boom. Equally important, the revival of housing has made our postwar recessions less severe than they might otherwise have been. From the point of view of the housing industry, its instability has caused serious problems; but from the point of view of the overall economy, it has been, at least to some extent, a blessing.

Congress, if one is to judge by its procreation of mortgage credit programs, has decided that some other sector of the economy (but not housing) should bear the brunt of anti-inflationary monetary policy. It has implemented its decision by selective credit policies aimed at sheltering housing. It could have chosen a quite different route: to prevent inflation, the medicine could be tight fiscal policy (high tax rates and cutbacks in government spending) instead of tight money. If that were done, interest rates could possibly remain relatively low across the board, and rate ceilings, being irrelevant, would not interfere with the flow of mortgage funds. In a sense, home building would be favored by a tight fiscal policy in much the same way it is hurt by a tight monetary policy. (Consumer and government spending would probably be penalized most by a tight fiscal policy, leaving home construction relatively unaffected.)

Congress, in its infinite wisdom, has opted for maintaining tight monetary policy *cum* selective credit programs, rather than tinkering with tax rates and government expenditures during periods when anti-inflationary policy is the rule. Perhaps Congress knows something we don't about Fannie Mae and her friends. Or could it be vice versa?

Suggestions for Further Reading

An excellent analysis of the allocative effects of selective credit policies was prepared for the Congressional Joint Economic Committee, *The Economics of Federal Subsidy Programs* (1972). A good survey of the activities of foreign central banks in this area was prepared for the House Banking and Currency Committee, *Activities of Various Central Banks to Promote Economic and Social Welfare Programs* (1971). A more formal analysis is in Rudolph G. Penner and William L. Silber, "The Interaction Between Federal Credit Programs and the Impact on the Allocation of Credit," *American Economic Review* (December 1973). See also Donald R. Hodgman, "Selective Credit Controls," in *Journal of Money, Credit, and Banking* (May 1972). An up-to-date volume on the subject is *Studies in*

Selective Credit Policies, ed. Ira Kaminow and James O'Brien (Federal Reserve Bank of Philadelphia, 1975).

An excellent collection of articles on housing, how it is affected by monetary and fiscal policy and the government credit programs engaged in offsetting their impact, is the aptly titled *Housing and Monetary Policy* (Federal Reserve Bank of Boston, 1970). A survey of housing activity is Craig Swan's "Homebuilding: A Review of Experience," *Brookings Papers on Economic Activity* (No. 1, 1970). For a formal analysis of Fannie Mae and her friends, see William L. Silber, "A Model of FHLBS and FNMA Behavior," *Review of Economics and Statistics* (August 1973).

PART VII

*Financial Markets
and Interest Rates*

Chapter 28

Flow of Funds Accounting: A Framework for Financial Analysis

ACCOUNTING gives off bad vibes. It is widely believed to be the world's dullest profession. Kids grow up wanting to be movie stars or athletes but never accountants. This is unfortunate, because it is easier to be an accountant than a Faye Dunaway or a Reggie Jackson. Those jobs are already taken. It is also unfortunate because accounting is often more exciting than it looks.

Flow of funds accounting, for example, was first discovered by a Swedish fashion model named Inga, who stumbled upon it while taking silicone injections to expand her assets and thereby increase her net worth. She combined her balance sheet with her income statement so well that she is now chairman of the Federal Reserve Bank of San Francisco (under a pseudonym), which explains why her seasonally adjusted statistics can be found in the *Federal Reserve Bulletin* (if you know where to look).

Flow of funds accounting, for those who have not read Inga's autobiography (*Everything You Always Wanted to Know About Flow of Funds But Were Afraid to Ask*), is used to analyze borrowing and lending in financial markets. It traces financial transactions by recording the payments each sector makes to other sectors and the receipts it receives from them—just as a family might keep track of its money by recording all its payments and receipts. Flow of funds accounting is also similar to balance of payments accounting, as we shall see in Chapter 33. The main difference is that in balance of payments accounting (as in family budgeting) the sectors are divided into "us" and "the rest of the world," while in flow of funds accounting the sectors are mostly subdivisions within a country (such as the household sector, the business sector, the government sector, and so on).

Flow of funds accounting is useful in many ways. As we shall see, it provides a useful framework for analyzing what happens in various financial markets (Chapter 29). It can also be thought of as tracing the financial flows that interact with and influence the "real" saving-investment process we discussed in Part IV. It records the maze of financial transactions underlying real saving and investment.

To appreciate all these implications, however, we will first have to learn what flow of funds accounting is all about. Specifically, it is a record of payments between and among various sectors. This is done via sector "sources and uses of funds" statements, which is what most of this chapter is devoted to explaining. You need not commit all of the accounting details to memory; it will be sufficient to understand the main concepts that emerge. Let us begin by seeing how a typical sector "sources and uses" statement is constructed.

A Generalized Sector Income Statement

A sector "sources and uses of funds" statement is nothing more than the integration of its income statement with its balance sheet. Taking first things first, a simplified income statement, general enough to apply to any sector, would look something like the following:

(1) A Generalized Income Statement for a Single Sector:

Uses of Funds (on Current Account)	Sources of Funds (on Current Account)
Current expenditures Saving (addition to net worth)	Current receipts

$$\Sigma = \Sigma$$

An income statement like the above merely lists a sector's current receipts during a period of time as a source (inflow) of funds, and its current expenditures as a use (outflow) of funds. Current receipts differ depending on which sector is involved; they consist mainly of wages and salaries for the household sector, sales receipts for the business sector, and tax revenues for the government. Similarly, the composition of current expenditures also differs, depending on which sector we are looking at.

In all cases, however, one sector's payments become another sector's receipts: as tax payments, a major *use* of funds for households and business firms, become tax receipts, a major *source* of funds for the government. As we shall see, it is this mutual interaction that gives the eventual flow of funds matrix its interlocking nature.

Saving, on the left-hand side, is defined as any excess of current receipts for a sector over and above its current spending. It is the same as our old definition of saving from Chapter 4: saving equals income minus consumer spending. When it involves the government sector it is usually called a budget surplus, and when applied to the business sector it is frequently labeled either retained earnings or addition to net worth. In any case, since it is defined as the difference between current receipts and current expenditures, it is the balancing entry on an income statement. Thus summation equality signs are at the bottom of income statement (1).

A Generalized Sector Balance Sheet

Let us leave income statements for a moment and move over to balance sheets. Income statements show current receipts and expenditures over a *period* of time (say during the year 1980), whereas a balance sheet shows not receipts and expenditures but assets and liabilities, and not over a period of time but at an *instant* in time (say on December 31, 1980). A simplified balance sheet, general enough to apply to any sector, would look something like the following:

(2) *A Generalized Balance Sheet for a Single Sector:*

Assets	Liabilities and Net Worth
Financial assets	Liabilities
a. Money	
b. Other	
Real assets	Net worth

$$\Sigma = \Sigma$$

Like income statements, the principal difference between the balance sheets of different sectors is in the characteristic items that appear under each heading—consumer durable goods such as furniture and automobiles are typical real assets for consumers, inventories and capital equipment are typical real assets for business firms, and so on. Also like income statements, balance sheets must balance, in this case because the net worth entry is defined as the difference between total assets and total liabilities. Thus our simplified balance sheet also contains summation equality signs.

On the balance sheet above, assets are divided into two broad categories, real and financial. A *real* asset, like a car or a calculator, appears on only one balance sheet, that of its owner. A *financial* asset, however, like money or bonds, always appears on two balance sheets: that of whoever owns it (as an asset), and that of whoever owes it (as a liability). This is because every financial asset is a *claim* by someone against someone else—an IOU of some sort—like a government bond (an asset to whoever owns it, a liability of the government) or a bank deposit (again an asset to the owner, a liability of the bank).[1]

While only *financial* assets appear on two different balance sheets, *all* liabilities do, because all liabilities—by definition—represent debts owed to others. Thus any time a liability is listed on anyone's balance sheet, a corresponding financial asset must be rung up on some other balance sheet.

Converting Balance Sheet Stocks to Flows: Saving and Investment

To analyze financial trends during a year we need data on flows over a period of time, not stocks on a balance sheet at an instant in time. But all is not lost. We can convert balance sheet stocks (of goods or of money) into flows by comparing two balance sheets for the same sector, two balance sheets "snapped" at different times. For example, we can take the balance sheet of a household on December 31, 1980,

---

[1] A complication arises in this connection with respect to corporate equities (corporate stocks), because they are financial assets to whoever holds them but are not, legally, liabilities of the issuing corporation. For most purposes, the simplest way to handle this is to assume that corporate stocks and bonds are roughly the same thing, despite their legal differences, and treat them both as liabilities of the corporation. (In other words, we ignore the problem.)

A related problem, which also remains unresolved, is that both bonds and stocks are traded on organized markets and change in price, so they may be valued differently by the holder and the issuing corporation. For example, a $100 bond issued by a corporation may rise in price to $120; to the holder it is now a $120 financial asset, but to the corporation it is still a $100 liability. The difference is capital gains to the bondholder, although the bondholder receives no funds inflow unless the bond is sold.

and then again on December 31, 1981. By comparing them, and seeing what *changes* have taken place in each entry, we can translate stocks into flows: we can tell how much furniture was purchased or how much cash was accumulated *during the year* 1981.

Going back to our simplified balance sheet (2), let's take the bottom pair of entries, real assets and net worth—ignoring financial assets and liabilities for the time being—and see how we can convert those stock figures, snapped at a moment in time, into flows covering a period of time. The change (Δ) between two dates could be displayed like this:

(3) *A Partial Sector Sources and Uses of Funds Statement, on Capital Account:*

Uses of Funds (on Capital Account)	Sources of Funds (on Capital Account)
Δ Real assets (investment)	Δ Net worth (saving)

Since (3) is derived from only part of the balance sheet, it need not balance, so there are no summation equality signs at the bottom. Notice also that the column headings are different from (2): "Assets" and "Liabilities and net worth" have been replaced by "Uses of funds" and "Sources of funds," the same as in income statement (1). Now, however, they refer to uses and sources of funds on *capital* rather than current account—that is, to long-term uses and sources instead of short-term.

On the uses side, the change in real assets refers to capital expenditures, as contrasted with an income statement's current expenditures. Capital expenditures involve the purchase of *real* assets with an expected useful life of a year or more; the term is synonymous with real investment spending (or simply *investment* spending), as we have been using that term throughout this book.[2] Such capital expenditures are not included in an income statement; in accordance with conventional accounting practice, income statements are confined to current expenditures—the purchase of assets with an expected useful life of less than a year.

A distinction has to be made between "investment" spending as economists use the word (it always refers to the purchase of *real* assets with a useful life of a year or more, like houses or machine tools), and the use of the word in general conversation, where it often refers to the purchase of *financial* assets, like stocks or bonds. When we say simply investment, we always have reference to buying real assets; if we want to refer to the purchase of financial assets, we will always say, explicitly, financial investment.

[2] Real investment can be recorded on either a net or gross basis, depending on whether or not depreciation is deducted from original value.

On the sources side, the change in a sector's net worth during the period is exactly the same thing as "saving" on its income statement covering that time interval. This deserves a word of explanation, since it is not immediately obvious (even though the fact that "saving" is frequently labeled "addition to net worth" should provide a clue that they are one and the same). On a balance sheet, net worth is defined as equal to a sector's total assets minus its total liabilities. A change in net worth must therefore equal any change in total assets less any change in total liabilities. On an income statement, in contrast, saving refers to an excess of current receipts over current expenditures. But any excess of current receipts over current expenditures (flows) must imply a resulting buildup of total assets or a reduction of liabilities, or some combination of the two. Conclusion: Saving on a sector's income statement must become an equivalent change in net worth on its balance sheet.

Put somewhat differently, as a "use" of funds on current account (on the income statement), saving means *not* spending. It means retention or accumulation. As such, it represents an addition to one's wealth or net worth and becomes available as a "source" of funds for capital account.[3]

Since statement (3) is derived from only part of the balance sheet, and thus does not have to balance, it follows that an individual unit or sector may or may not invest (that is, buy capital goods) just equal to its current saving. It might save more than it invests, or invest more than it saves. If a unit or sector invests an amount equal to its current saving it is called a balanced budget sector. If it saves more than it invests it is called a surplus sector, and if it invests more than it saves it is called a deficit sector. (Read this paragraph again —these will be useful concepts later on.)[4]

How could a sector invest more than it saves? One way is simply to borrow enough to finance its deficit, which brings us to the other pair of balance sheet entries—liabilities and financial assets.

---

[3] As with investment, saving can be measured on a net or gross basis, depending on whether or not depreciation is deducted. It should be noted that even if depreciation is deducted, so that saving is measured on a net basis, depreciation would still be a source of funds for capital account, since it represents a noncash "expense" rather than an actual current outlay of funds.

[4] Alternatively, a surplus unit is one that spends (on consumption plus real investment) *less* than its current income, and a deficit unit is one that spends *more* than its current income.

"Hold it, gentlemen, hold it! I had it the wrong way around. It isn't assets that are in excess of ninety-seven million. It's liabilities!"

Drawing by Chon Day; © 1969 The New Yorker Magazine, Inc.

Converting Balance Sheet Stocks to Flows: Borrowing, Lending, and Hoarding

So far we have ignored the possibility of changes in liabilities and financial assets, the remaining entries on (2), our generalized sector balance sheet. Such changes between two balance sheet dates would look like this:

(4) *A Partial Sector Sources and Uses of Funds Statement, on Capital Account:*

Uses of Funds (Financial, on Capital Account)	Sources of Funds (Financial, on Capital Account)
Δ Financial assets other than money (lending) Δ Money (hoarding)	Δ Liabilities (borrowing)

Since (4), like (3), is derived from only partial balance sheets, it need not balance and thus contains no summation equality signs. But whereas (3) dealt with nonfinancial or "real" sources and uses of funds, (4) is concerned with *financial* transactions—with *borrowing* (an increase in outstanding liabilities) as a source of funds, and with *lending* (an increase in holdings of financial assets other than money) and *hoarding* (increased money holdings) as uses of funds.

Strictly speaking, we should separate short-term financial transactions from long-term, comparable to our distinction between short- and long-term spending on real assets. However, in flow of funds

443

accounting such distinctions are rarely made with respect to financial transactions, and all borrowing and lending, regardless of duration, are typically considered as on capital account.

The three possibilities in (4)—borrowing, lending, and hoarding—do not exhaust all the potential financial sources or uses of funds open to a sector. For instance, another possible financial *source* of funds, in addition to borrowing, is selling some holdings of financial assets. Still another source of funds is *dis*hoarding. And an additional possible *use* of funds would be to repay one's debts. These alternatives do not appear on (4) because only *net* changes are considered there, and it is implicitly assumed that they are all positive. Potential negative changes would add the three just mentioned.

By convention, if the net change in any entry turns out to be negative over a period, it is kept on the side where it presently appears in (4) but preceded by a minus sign. If the net change in financial assets for a sector turns out to be minus, for example, as when a person liquidates some of his government bonds, it would be recorded on the uses side but preceded by a minus sign and referred to as a negative use of funds. But a negative use is actually a source of funds—aha! another useful concept.

A Complete Sector Sources and Uses of Funds Statement

Believe it or not, if we string together everything we've done so far we will have before us, in all its pristine glory, Inga's remarkable discovery—a complete sector sources and uses of funds statement. Lo and behold:

(5)=(1)+(3)+(4) *A Complete Sector Sources and Uses of Funds Statement:*

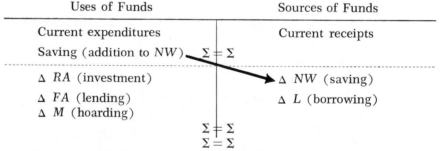

Uses of Funds	Sources of Funds
Current expenditures	Current receipts
Saving (addition to NW) $\quad \Sigma \neq \Sigma$	
$\Delta\ RA$ (investment)	$\Delta\ NW$ (saving)
$\Delta\ FA$ (lending)	$\Delta\ L$ (borrowing)
$\Delta\ M$ (hoarding)	
$\Sigma \neq \Sigma$	
$\Sigma = \Sigma$	

Above the dashed line is the income statement, below the dashed line the changes in the balance sheet. Since the income statement must balance, as must the aggregate changes in the balance sheet, the summation of all the sources must equal the summation of all the uses of funds, and therefore we have summation equality signs all over the place.

"I called in you people from Accounting because I wanted to ask you if you're having fun."

We are now able to define more precisely what we mean by a sector's sources and uses of funds:

Sources of funds consist of (a) *current receipts;* (b) any *increase in a liability* item (borrowing); or (c) any *decrease in an asset* item (selling off assets, dishoarding).

Uses of funds consist of (a) *current expenditures;* (b) *any increase in an asset* item—increased holdings of real assets (investment), of financial assets (lending), or of money (hoarding); or (c) any *decrease in a liability* item (debt repayment).

We could simplify (5) by eliminating current receipts from sources and current expenditures from uses, taking only the difference between them—saving—as a source of funds (if positive, or as a use if negative). That is what we have, in effect, if we look only below the dashed line (which is the way the flow of funds accounts are published by the Federal Reserve).

The requirement that everything below the dashed line must balance means that each sector's investing + lending + hoarding must equal its saving + borrowing. As we know, however, a sector might save more than it invests (a surplus sector), or invest more

445

than it saves (a deficit sector). If it does have a discrepancy between its saving and its investing, this necessarily implies a corresponding differential between its *financial* sources and uses of funds. To be more specific: A surplus sector, with saving greater than investment, *must* dispose of its surplus by lending, repaying debts, or hoarding (building up its cash holdings) in an amount equal to its surplus. And a deficit sector, with investment in excess of its saving, *has to* finance its deficit by borrowing, selling off financial assets, or dis-hoarding (running down its cash holdings) in an amount equal to its deficit.[5]

These conclusions flow from the fact that below the dashed line, as well as above it, the sum of all a sector's uses of funds must equal the sum of all its sources. Putting the same thing rather formally:

For any one sector:

investment + lending + hoarding = saving + borrowing

So if:

saving > investment, then lending + hoarding > borrowing

And if:

investment > saving, then borrowing > lending + hoarding

The Flow of Funds Matrix for the Whole Economy

Early in this chapter we said that flow of funds accounting records payments between and among sectors via sector sources and uses of funds statements. Since one sector's payments become another sector's receipts, when we put all these individual sector statements together we get a flow of funds *matrix* for the economy as a whole, an inter-locking grid that reveals financial relationships among all the sectors. When the flow of funds matrix was first published by the Federal Reserve in 1955, it contained the complete statements for each sector in the form of statement (5) above. Since 1959, however, it has consisted of only partial sector sources and uses statements, namely that part of (5) below the dashed line. Current receipts and current

---

[5] A deficit sector might also finance its deficit by issuing new money. However, only two sectors are legally able to exercise that unique option—banks (by creating demand deposits) and the government (by creating dollars bills). If they did so, it would be entered on their statement (5) as an increase in their liabilities (borrowing), because while money is an asset to whoever owns it, it is a liability of whoever issues it.

expenditures are not shown explicitly, but they are implicitly included in that the difference between them—saving (or dissaving)—is there.

Assuming a total of three sectors and omitting some detail, the flow of funds matrix appears essentially as follows:

(6) Flow of Funds Matrix for the Whole Economy:

	Sector A		Sector B		Sector C		All Sectors	
	U	S	U	S	U	S	U	S
Saving (Δ NW)		s		s		s		S
Investment (Δ RA)	i		i		i		I	
Borrowing (Δ L)		b		b		b		B
Lending (Δ FA)	l		l		l		L	
Hoarding (Δ M)	h		h		h		+ H	
	Σ = Σ		Σ = Σ		Σ = Σ		Σ = Σ	

NOTE: The small letters within the matrix represent the data for sector saving (*s*), investment (*i*), borrowing (*b*), lending (*l*), and hoarding (*h*), and are placed in the appropriate space where such data would be entered. The capital letters similarly represent the aggregate sum totals for the whole economy. Thus $s + s + s = S$, $i + i + i = I$, etc. (Roman "U" and "S" represent uses and sources of funds.)

This matrix is nothing more than the placing of the sector sources and uses statements side by side, each in the form of that part of (5) below the dashed line. The resulting matrix forms an interlocking self-contained system, showing the balanced sources and uses of funds for each sector, interrelations among the sectors, and the aggregate totals of saving, investment, borrowing, lending, and hoarding for the economy as a whole.

For each individual sector, as we know, its investment + lending + hoarding must equal its saving + borrowing. Since that is true for each individual sector, it is also true in summation for all the sectors taken together, i.e., for the economy as a whole.

In addition, something else is true for the economy as a whole which need not be true for any one sector taken by itself: Saving must equal investment. (Haven't we met that one somewhere before?) We developed that relationship in "real" terms in Chapters 4 and 16, and now here it is again, emerging this time from the financial side:

For the whole economy:

investment + lending + hoarding = saving + borrowing

But since one sector's financial asset is another sector's liability:

lending + hoarding = borrowing

Therefore:

investment = saving

The conclusion that saving must equal investment applies only to the entire economy taken in the aggregate, but not to any single sector taken by itself. As we have seen, any single sector may save more than it invests, or invest more than it saves. But since saving must equal investment for the economy as a whole, it follows that for each sector that saves more than it invests there must, somewhere, be other sectors that invest correspondingly more than they save.[6]

In coming chapters we shall have frequent occasion to use this framework in analyzing financial institutions and markets, and the interdependencies among them. The economic function of financial markets, after all, is to provide channels through which the excess funds of surplus units (whose saving exceeds their investment) can be transferred to potential deficit units (who want to invest more than they are saving). The flow of funds matrix enables us to trace these transactions, and see how various spending flows are financed.[7]

Suggestions for Further Reading

The best source of information on the actual construction of the accounts is *Introduction to Flow of Funds* (Board of Governors of the Federal Reserve System, February 1975). Also see A. D. Bain, "Flow of Funds Analysis," *Economic Journal* (December 1973). The usefulness of the flow of funds is exemplified by James S. Earley, Robert J. Parsons, and Fred A. Thompson, *Money, Credit, and Expenditure: A Sources and Uses of Funds Approach* (New York University, Center for the Study of Financial Institutions *Bulletin*, No. 3, 1976).

[6] This is true not only because the economy-wide total of saving must equal investment, but also because a surplus sector must dispose of its surplus, as we have seen, by lending, repaying debts, or hoarding an amount equal to its surplus. This in turn implies the existence of deficit sectors to borrow, reduce their financial assets, or dishoard.

Similarly, deficit sectors, which invest more than they save, necessarily imply the existence of surplus sectors. A deficit sector must finance its deficit by borrowing, selling off financial assets, or dishoarding. This in turn implies the presence of surplus sectors to do the lending, buying of the securities, or hoarding.

[7] By way of illustration, the appendix to this chapter shows the actual flow of funds matrix for 1977. For an alternative definition of surplus and deficit sectors, see footnote 4.

The Flow of Funds Matrix
for 1977

Table 1 is the flow of funds matrix for 1977 as presented by the Federal Reserve. Although at first glance it doesn't look very much like our simplified matrix (6), it is indeed the same thing, only more elaborate. The best way to see this is to relate Table 1 to matrix (6) column by column and line by line.

First the columns. Instead of only three sectors, the actual matrix contains four major sectors—the private domestic nonfinancial sector, the rest of the world, the U.S. government, and the financial sector. These, in turn, are subdivided into a number of subsectors, making nine in all. The names of each are self-explanatory, except perhaps for "Spons. Ag. and Mtg. Pools," which is short for federally sponsored credit agencies and mortgage pools; and the "Monetary Authority," which consists of the Federal Reserve plus the U.S. Treasury's monetary accounts. Notice that the "State and Local Governments" subsector is included in the *private* part of the economy. Some other incidental observations: the "Household" sector includes nonprofit organizations within it; "Private Nonbank Finance" includes savings and loan associations, mutual savings banks, insurance companies, pension funds, mutual funds, and credit unions.

The last two columns are new; neither of them appeared in matrix (6). The "Discrepancy" column results from the fact that deficiencies and inconsistencies often exist in the raw statistical data. Things often do not add up in the way logic tells us they should. Borrowers report liabilities of x dollars, while lenders report they are owed y dollars. Errors in data collection, omissions, differences in coverage or classification, all give rise to inconsistencies in the data. The "Discrepancy" column is the statistician's way of reconciling such problems so that the accounts balance the way they are supposed to.

We know, for example, that for "All Sectors" financial uses of funds (line 12) should equal financial sources (line 13). Thus the

449

TABLE 1 / SUMMARY OF FLOW OF FUNDS ACCOUNTS FOR THE YEAR 1977

(Seasonally adjusted annual rates; in billions of dollars)

Line	Transaction category	Households U	Households S	Business U	Business S	State and local govts. U	State and local govts. S	Total U	Total S	Rest of the world U	Rest of the world S	U.S. Govt. U	U.S. Govt. S	Financial Total U	Financial Total S	Spons. ag. & mtg. pools U	Spons. ag. & mtg. pools S	Monetary auth. U	Monetary auth. S	Coml. banks U	Coml. banks S	Pvt. nonbank finance U	Pvt. nonbank finance S	All sectors U	All sectors S	Discrepancy U	Natl. saving and investment
1	Gross saving		295.9		177.4		16.4		492.8		20.9		-54.8		12.6		.7		.2		3.2		8.4		471.5		450.6
2	Capital consumption		162.2		156.6				318.8						5.3						2.6		2.7		324.1	-2.5	324.1
3	Net saving (1-2)		136.8		20.8		16.4		174.0		20.9		-54.8		7.2		.7		.2		.6		5.7		147.3	-4.7	126.5
4	Gross investment (5+11)	329.1		150.8		8.5		488.3		21.9		-57.3		20.9		.4		.2		9.2		11.1		473.9			454.2
5	Private capital expenditures	260.4		212.0				472.5				-2.5		6.2						4.4		1.8		476.2			476.2
6	Consumer durables	178.4						178.4																178.4			178.4
7	Residential construction	76.3		15.7				92.0																91.9			91.9
8	Plant and equipment	5.8		178.3				184.1						6.3						4.4		1.9		190.4			190.4
9	Inventory change			15.6				15.6																15.6			15.6
10	Mineral rights			2.5				2.5				-2.5												-.5			
11	Net financial investment (12-13)	68.6		-61.3		8.5		15.9		21.9		-54.8		14.7		.4		.2		4.8		9.3		-2.3		2.3	-21.9
12	Financial uses	213.5		52.9		35.4		301.8		48.4		10.1		327.2		27.9		8.6		105.0		185.7		687.5			26.4
13	Financial sources		144.9		114.2		26.9		285.9		26.4		64.9		321.5		27.6		8.3		100.2		176.4		689.7	2.3	48.4
14	Gold and official foreign exchange									-.2		.3		.6				.6						*	*	-.3	
15	Treasury currency												.3					.6						.6	.3		
16	Demand deposits and currency	20.3		1.3		.9		22.5		1.9		-.5		1.6	28.6	.1			4.9	.5	23.7	1.0	1.0	25.5	28.6	3.1	
17	Private domestic	20.3		1.3		.9		22.5						1.6	25.8	.1			8.3	.5	17.5	1.0	1.0	24.1	25.8	1.6	
18	Foreign									1.9					1.9				*		1.9			1.9	1.9		
19	U.S. Government											-.5			1.0				-3.3		4.3			-.5	1.0	1.5	
20	Time and savings accounts	108.3		4.8		7.0		120.1		.7				3.5	124.5						54.6		69.9	124.5	124.5		
21	At commercial banks	39.2		4.8		7.0		51.0		.7				2.7	54.6						54.6			54.6	54.6		
22	At savings institutions	69.1						69.1						.8	69.9								69.9	69.9	69.9		
23	Life insurance reserves	8.1						8.1			.2				7.9								7.9	8.1	8.1		
24	Pension fund reserves	55.5						55.5					6.4		49.1								49.1	55.5	55.5		
25	Interbank claims													5.4	5.4			1.4	3.5	4.0	1.9			5.4	5.4		
26	Corporate equities	-5.1			2.7			-5.1	2.7	2.7	.4			6.2	.6			*			.6	6.2	*	3.8	3.8		
27	Credit market instruments	35.8	139.6	-1.5	103.3	26.4	25.9	60.6	268.7	39.5	11.9	11.8	56.8	283.7	58.2	26.9	26.3	7.1		85.8	5.5	163.8	26.5	395.6	395.6		
28	U.S. Treasury securities	1.5		-6.0		21.1		16.7		31.5			57.6	9.5		-3.4		5.8		-.9		8.0		57.6	57.6		
29	Federal agency securities	3.9		-.4		4.4		8.0				5.3	-.8	13.3			27.4	1.4		8.0		11.6		26.7	26.7		
30	State and local government securities	3.8		3.5			25.7	9.1						20.0						9.2		10.9		29.2	29.2		
31	Corporate and foreign bonds	1.1			21.0	.6		1.1	21.0	3.7	5.0			23.8	3.1					-.1		23.9	3.1	29.2	29.2		
32	Mortgages	12.5	94.1		36.9				131.0			20.0				24.0				27.4		36.1	134.0	134.0	134.0		
33	Consumer credit		35.0	3.7				3.7	35.0					31.4						17.0		14.3		35.0	35.0		
34	Bank loans n.e.c.		8.2		22.5				30.6		1.6			32.2						32.2				35.0	32.2		
35	Private s.-t. paper	8.4			16.5			9.5	16.5		2.4			18.4	3.1		4.4					9.5		19.8	19.8		
36	Other loans	8.4	2.3				.2		19.0		3.0	6.7			4.1	6.4	-1.2	1.4		4.9		5.3	4.3	25.1	25.1		
37	Security credit	1.0	3.1					1.0	3.1					3.4	1.3					.6		2.8	1.3	4.4	4.4		
38	Trade credit	1.3		24.8		1.1	1.0	30.9	27.1	1.7	.4	-.8	2.1	1.1	.7		.7			.6		1.1		33.0	29.6	-3.4	
39	Taxes payable				-1.3			1.1	-1.9			-1.6	2.1		.7									-.5	-.6	-.1	
40	Equity in noncorporate business	-17.0	.9		-17.0			-17.0	-17.0	2.1		.7	-.9	21.8	1.3		.9			14.1		7.3		-17.0	-17.0		
41	Miscellaneous	6.6	17.3	17.3	1.8	1.1		23.9	2.7	2.1	13.7	.7	-.9	21.8	36.1	1.0	1.3	-.6		14.1	14.1	7.3	20.9	48.5	51.5	3.0	
42	Sector discrepancies (1-4)	-30.1		26.7		7.9		4.5		2.5		2.5		-8.4		.4		-.6		-6.0		-2.7		-2.5		-2.5	-3.7

SOURCE: Board of Governors of the Federal Reserve System.

differences between them (line 11) should be zero. However, financial uses of funds for "All Sectors" are $687.5 billion, and financial sources are $689.7 billion. They are *not* equal. So in the "Discrepancy" column a $2.3 billion "use" is posted. *Now* they balance—well, almost; the remaining discrepancy of $0.1 billion is due to rounding. By convention, all "discrepancies" are entered on the "uses" side of the accounts, making them positive or negative as appropriate to create the equality that logic tells us should exist.

The last column, "National Saving and Investment," is merely a measure of *domestic* saving and investment. It consists of the "All Sectors" data for saving and investment, plus any discrepancies in those accounts, minus the "Rest of the World" sector. Included here is any increase in net financial claims on foreigners.

Turn now to the lines (or rows). There are two main differences between the table and matrix (6): first, a slight rearrangement of the entries (including differences in terminology); and second, the presentation of considerably greater detail.

The first line in Table 1, "Gross Saving," corresponds to "Saving" on the first line of matrix (6). The table also gives an estimate of depreciation (capital consumption, line 2) and thus data for "Net Saving" as well (line 3). Line 5 corresponds to the entry "Investment" on our model matrix. Lines 6-10 are a breakdown by type of investment. Line 12 corresponds to "Lending" on matrix (6) and line 13 to "Borrowing." Line 16 is roughly equivalent to what we have called "Hoarding."

Thus if we were to list the rows in Table 1 that correspond to the entries in matrix (6)—Saving, Investment, Borrowing, Lending, and Hoarding—they would be, in the same order, lines 1, 5, 13, 12 minus 16, and 16.[1]

Line 11, called "Net Financial Investment," refers to a sector's lending plus hoarding minus its borrowing, as we have been using these terms. And line 4, called "Gross Investment," refers to a sector's real investment plus lending plus hoarding minus its borrowing.

To see whether a particular sector is a surplus or deficit sector, we should compare the entry for that sector on line 1 with the entry on line 5. (Or, if we deducted depreciation from both saving and investment, we would compare the entry on line 3 with line 5 minus line 2.) Thus we see that during 1977 households were a surplus sector by $38.5 billion, business a deficit sector by $34.6 billion.

The remainder of the table, from line 14 down, consists of a de-

---

[1] If a money-*issuing* sector were involved, this would become 1, 5, 13 minus 16, 12, and 16. Money creation is a financial source of funds to those who issue it. See footnote 5 in the chapter.

tailed breakdown of the various forms of borrowing and lending by type of liability (or asset) involved. For example, line 33 indicates that consumers borrowed $35 billion in the form of consumer credit during 1977. Who did the lending? Line 33 also shows that $17 billion was from commercial banks, $14.3 billion from nonbank financial institutions, and $3.7 billion from nonfinancial business firms.

A word should be said about the differences between the Federal Reserve's Flow of Funds Accounts and the Department of Commerce's National Income Accounts. Three differences are of special interest. First, the National Income Accounts confine themselves exclusively to *non*financial transactions. They contain no data on borrowing, lending, or hoarding. Second, the National Income Accounts confine all *real* investment to the business sector, except for home building; with the exception of housing, neither consumers nor governments can invest. In the Flow of Funds Accounts, however, consumer purchases of durable goods are treated as (real) investment. This removes the purchase of consumer durables from the category of current (or consumer) expenditures and thereby greatly increases the volume of recorded household (and national) saving. Finally, the sectoring is more detailed in the Flow of Funds Accounts than in the National Income Accounts, making integration and reconciliation of the two rather complicated. In principle, one should be able to move easily from one set of accounts to the other, but in practice the sectoring and the treatment of various transactions are so different as to make it awkward and cumbersome to do so.

Chapter 29

Forecasting
Interest Rates

JIMMY THE GREEK operates out of Las Vegas. He sets odds on all major sporting events. He employs two dozen people, has pipelines to all sorts of confidential information, and has a lifetime of experience going for him. He knows his business. Even so, he still made the Mets 100 to 1 underdogs at the start of the 1969 baseball season (the year they wound up winning the World Series), and made Joe Frazier a 5 to 1 favorite to beat George Foreman in their heavyweight championship fight in 1973 (Foreman knocked out Frazier in the second round).

Forecasting—whether of ball games, prize fights, or interest rates —is a hazardous profession. The accuracy of predictions may have progressed some since crystal balls gave way to mathematical models and computer technology, but not as much as you might think. This perhaps explains why a lot of people are back to fiddling with tea leaves, ouija boards, and tarot cards. Be forewarned, however: No matter how you go about predicting the future, the odds are against you.

People forecast interest rates because the stakes are high, just as they try to forecast stock prices for the same reason. If stock prices are going to rise, you'll gain by buying now rather than later. If they are going to fall, you're better off selling rather than buying. The same with bonds, or with any marketable asset for that matter, so that the temptation to forecast is almost irresistible. A financial institution can't make sensible portfolio decisions without some estimate, explicit or implicit, of future trends in financial asset prices—which means, in light of the inverse relationship between asset prices and interest rates, some estimate of future trends in interest rates.

This is particularly true with respect to long-term bonds, as contrasted with short-term money market instruments, since even a small change in long-term interest rates involves a substantial change (in the opposite direction) in long-term bond prices (see pp. 65–71). A bank buying $100,000 of long-term governments at a 7 percent interest rate would suffer losses of $11,300 (on paper, anyway) were yields to rise to 8 percent. If the bank could *anticipate* such a change in long-term interest rates, it could temporarily invest the $100,000 in short-term Treasury bills, wait until long rates have risen, and *then* switch the funds from bills to bonds.

To put it briefly, economic forecasting is important because rational decision-making is impossible without some conception of the shape of things to come. Decisions regarding whether to spend or not to spend, whether to borrow (or lend) now or to postpone borrowing (or lending) for six or nine months, whether to buy securities today or to hold cash for the present, whether borrowing or lending should be short- or long-term—all these and many related business decisions hinge on what the future is expected to bring. So economic forecasting, although it is still more art than science, is inescapable.

Forecasting Techniques

We are already familiar with one method of forecasting interest rates —with an econometric model of the economy, such as the Federal Reserve model discussed in Chapter 24. Based on empirically estimated consumption and investment functions, expectations regarding fiscal and monetary polices, and interrelations among these and other factors, such models have primarily been used for GNP forecasts. In the process of grinding out their GNP numbers, however, they simultaneously spawn predictions regarding related variables, such as unemployment, price inflation—and interest rates.

But interest rate forecasts made via large-scale econometric models have been less than fully satisfactory. The theory behind them appears sound enough: Theoretical models[1] typically explain how both GNP and the interest rate are *jointly* determined by the same factors—consumer spending, investment spending, inflation, government spending, the supply of and demand for money, and so on. So, in principle, a good GNP forecast should simultaneously produce a good interest rate forecast. But knowing and doing are different things, and in practice interest rate forecasts are generally much farther from the mark than GNP forecasts. Indeed, a portfolio manager who made his

"And so, extrapolating from the best figures available, we see that current trends, unless dramatically reversed, will inevitably lead to a situation in which the sky will fall."

Drawn by Lorenz; © 1972 The New Yorker Magazine, Inc.

decisions primarily on the basis of interest rate forecasts generated by econometric models would probably be out of a job long before he finished reading all his computer printouts.

There are several reasons for the failure of econometric models in this respect. First, most such models still emphasize the "real" sector of the economy rather than the financial sector, since their main purpose has traditionally been (and still is) projecting GNP rather than interest rates. The underlying financial relationships are not nearly as fully refined in such models as the relationships regarding real spending decisions (the Federal Reserve model does, however, have a rather well developed financial sector).

Second, even in the underlying theoretical models, which also evolved with GNP in mind more than interest rates, the *immediate*

[1] Such as the *IS–LM* model in Chapter 19.

determinants of interest rates are not *explicitly* taken into account. Every participant in financial markets knows that interest rates—the price of credit—respond directly to lending and borowing pressures, or more generally to the supply of credit and the demand for credit, as any price is determined by supply and demand. None of the standard theoretical models, however, be they Classical or Keynesian, incorporate the supply and demand for credit *explicitly* into their framework.

In Classical theory, for example, the interest rate is determined by saving and investment, as we saw in Chapter 17. Classical economists were not fools; they were well aware that lending and borrowing determine interest rates. But by focusing attention on saving and investment, they thought they were getting *behind* the superficial determinants to the basic underlying forces that explain the reasons for lending and borrowing. Lending was assumed to be directly related to saving, and borrowing to investment. That might be useful for long-run analysis, but it is not very helpful when it comes to forecasting interest rates over the next six to twelve months. You can save without lending (if you hoard the money), and there can be lending without saving (banks do it all the time by creating money when they lend). Similarly, you can invest without borrowing (by using current income, or retained earnings), and you can borrow without investing (as when people borrow to speculate in the stock market). So Classical theory's determinants of interest rates—saving and investment—are far removed from the immediate determinants in the market place—lending and borrowing.

Nor does Keynesian theory do much better. In simple Keynesian analysis, as we saw in Chapter 18, interest rates are viewed as determined by the supply of money and the demand for money (liquidity preference). The supply of money, however, is a far cry from lending or the supply of credit. And the demand for money is not the same thing as borrowing or the demand for credit.

Credit and money supply, in other words, are different things. Credit is a flow concept, involving an amount over a period of time, while money is a stock, at a moment in time. In addition, they simply refer to different economic variables: If you lend a friend $10, the supply of credit is expanded, but the money supply is unaffected.

In the more complex Keynesian analysis, as in Chapter 19, saving and investment also become important in interest rate determination, and this is a step in the right direction. But lending and borrowing still remain hidden somewhere behind the scenes; our job in this chapter is to flush them out. Indeed, most practicing financial analysts approach interest rate forecasting directly via the supply of and demand for credit (or loanable funds). Let's take a closer look at how they do it. We'll then draw some comparisons with our theoretical models.

The Supply and Demand for Loanable Funds: The Level of Interest Rates

The supply and demand for credit—or loanable funds—approach to interest rate determination amounts to a straightforward application of supply and demand analysis. In any competitive market, whether for wheat, hula hoops, or tickets to rock concerts, interaction between supply and demand determines price and quantity exchanged. Financial markets are no different. The rate of interest is the price of credit or loanable funds, and whether it falls or rises depends on the relative eagerness of suppliers and demanders of loanable funds.

Take the standard supply-demand diagram (shown in Figure 1) illustrating price determination with supply and demand schedules. If, at a particular rate of interest (say 6 percent), lenders—the suppliers of loanable funds—are particularly anxious to lend, and borrowers rather reluctant to borrow, then the rate of interest will fall. On the other hand, if the rate of interest were only 4 percent, where

FIGURE 1 / Borrowing and lending determine the interest rate.

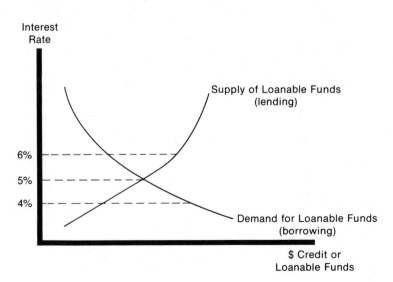

borrowers—the demanders of credit—are more eager to borrow than lenders are to lend, the rate of interest is likely to rise.[2]

Forecasting interest rates by estimating the planned (or ex ante) demand for and supply of credit thus amounts, in principle, to simply (1) projecting, at existing interest rates, the likely demand for credit (borrowing) during the coming year, (2) independently projecting, at existing interest rates, the likely supply of credit (lending), and then (3) assessing the change in interest rates that will take place in the market to bring the two into equality (since, ex post, the actual amount of borrowing will have to equal the actual amount of lending —you can't borrow unless someone else lends).

Most forecasters use a standard format for their trial-and-error worksheets. First they list, at existing interest rates, all the likely *demands* for credit—in terms of the dollar volume of various financial *instruments* that will be offered in the market as potential borrowers seek funds (such as corporate bonds, mortgages, government bonds). Second, they independently list, at existing interest rates, all the probable *supplies* of credit in terms of *who* will be wanting to lend how much. The third step is to hold your breath and compare the totals: If demand (borrowing) equals supply (lending), interest rates are likely to stay where they are and a vacation is in order; if demand exceeds supply, interest rates are likely to rise; and if supply exceeds

[2] Instead of talking about the supply of and demand for credit or loanable funds determining the rate of interest, we could talk about the same thing in terms of the demand for securities and the supply of securities determining the price of securities (see the diagram below). To supply credit (lend) is equivalent to *demanding* financial assets (securities)—financial institutions lend, for example, by purchasing financial assets. To demand credit (borrow) is the same as *supplying* securities—business firms borrow by selling their bonds or other IOUs. Look at the diagram below and compare it with Figure 1 in the text. At a price of $833 (which corresponds, let us say, to the 6 percent *yield* in Figure 1 in the text, assuming a 5 percent *coupon* on a $1,000 bond), relative eagerness to buy securities—or lend—would drive up the price of securities, just as Figure 1 shows that it would drive *down* the rate of interest. And at a price of $1,250, corresponding to a 4 percent yield, relative eagerness to sell securities—to borrow—would drive down the price of securities, just as Figure 1 shows that such circumstances would drive *up* the rate of interest.

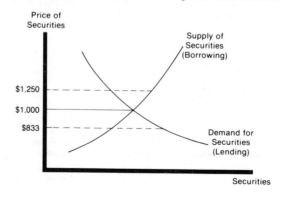

demand, interest rates are likely to fall—and in the last two cases the Caribbean cruise must be postponed, since there's more work to be done.[3]

The next step—there usually is one and it might be repeated several times—consists of making a stab at the extent of the rate changes, and then, at the new rates, adjusting the demands and supplies. Higher rates imply smaller amounts of credit demanded, larger amounts supplied. Lower rates are likely to involve larger amounts demanded, smaller amounts supplied. This has to be continued with successive iterations until the two equalize, since after all is said and done every successful borrower implies a lender, and vice versa.

The format of Table 1 illustrates the procedure. The first two steps, shown in column 1 of the table, involve the projection of likely demands for and supplies of funds at current interest rates. Demand and supply should be projected independently, of course, without reference to one when doing the other. Here the total demand for funds adds up to $160 billion, total supply only $145 billion. Conclusion: Interest rates are likely to rise.

But by how much? All we really have so far is two *points*, at existing interest rates, on a demand and supply diagram (see Figure 2A). The extent of the rate increase depends on the interest-sensitivity of demand and supply. If they both react significantly to a small change in rates (i.e., if they are both interest-elastic), a *small* rise in rates will be enough to reduce the amount demanded and increase the amount supplied so that they become equal (see Figure 2B). But if they both respond sluggishly or imperceptibly to higher interest rates (i.e., if they are interest-inelastic, as in 2C), then it will take a *considerable* rise in rates before demand and supply coincide.

Columns 2 and 3 on Table 1 are for successive approximations in demand and supply as the totals are adjusted toward equality. In

[3] This forecasting procedure implicitly assumes that financial markets are competitive, so that supply and demand pressures will be reflected in price (interest rate) changes. It rules out, therefore, the popular conspiratorial theory of interest rate determination—the view that interest rates are rigged by a few insiders with substantial market power.

It is extremely doubtful that any one person, institution, or group of institutions has anywhere near enough power to rig interest rates in this country. There are too many lenders engaged in the business of lending, and therefore too many alternatives open to most would-be borrowers, to permit any tightly knit clique of lenders (or borrowers, for that matter) to control the price of credit. Lenders charging more than prevailing rates will price themselves out of the market and lose business to their competitors. Borrowers trying to borrow at cheaper rates will find themselves outbid for funds by others who are willing to pay the market price. Even the Federal Reserve does not have enough power to set interest rates at whatever level it pleases, whenever it wishes. The central bank may control the supply of credit, but it does not control the demand, and both are involved in the determination of its price. (Actually, the central bank does not even control the supply of credit; what it controls, and only imperfectly, is the supply of bank reserves.)

TABLE 1

Credit Projections for the Year 198?

(in billions of dollars)

| | Approximation | | |
	#1	#2	#3
*Demand for credit**			
in the form of:			
Mortgages	50	——	——
Corporate bonds	20	——	——
Government securities	15	——	——
State and local bonds	10	——	——
Business loans	35	——	——
Consumer loans	25	——	——
All other	5	——	——
Total demand	160		
*Supply of credit**			
from:			
Commercial banks	55	——	——
Savings and loan associations	30	——	——
Mutual savings banks	10	——	——
Insurance companies	15	——	——
Pension funds	13	——	——
Finance companies	9	——	——
Credit unions	2	——	——
Nonfinancial business firms	6	——	——
Individuals and others	5	——	——
Total supply	145		

* Since financial institutions are *intermediaries* in credit markets, their borrowing of funds from households and others (in the form of deposits, etc.) is not included in the final demand for credit; correspondingly, the supply (lending) of funds by households and others to financial institutions is not included in the final supply of credit.

the end, the forecast for the year ahead has to have total demand and total supply equal, since that is the way they must turn out ex post. A favorite candidate for *residual* adjustment to equate supply to demand is the lender category "individuals and others," which historically —especially in recent years—has been exceedingly volatile in response to changes in interest rates. As we saw in Chapters 7 and 27, this is largely in reaction to Regulation Q rate ceilings, with households shifting to direct purchases of securities when market interest rates rise above Q ceilings, and then putting their funds back in financial intermediaries when market rates return to more normal levels. (As the footnote in Table 1 indicates, in order to avoid counting the same thing twice only the *direct* purchase of securities by households is included in the supply of credit from "individuals and others"; funds channeled by individuals and others through financial intermediaries are considered as supplied to the market by the financial institutions.)

So far we have confined ourselves to overall pressures on interest

Forecasting Interest Rates

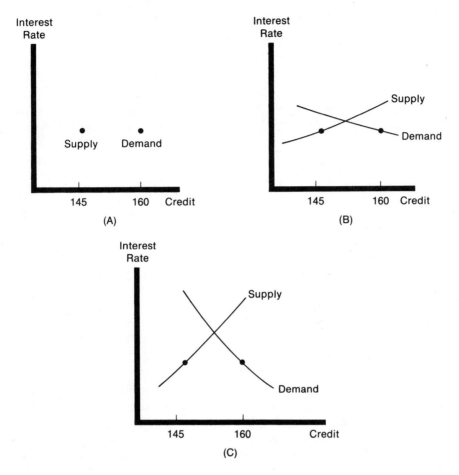

FIGURE 2 / The same initial excess of demand over supply may raise interest rates a little (B) or a lot (C).

rates. But of course there are many interest rates. In recognition of that, and to assist in thinking through the adjustment process, a matrix worksheet along the lines of Table 2 is frequently utilized. It allocates specific kinds of securities (demands for credit) among all potential purchasers (suppliers of credit). Filling it in shows how particular sectors of the financial market, and particular interest rates, are likely to be affected by supply and demand forces during the coming year.

For example, if the demand for credit by state and local governments (the supply of municipal bonds) is expected to be $10 billion during the year (from Table 1), but on the first round the matrix shows that the only likely buyers of such securities are commercial banks ($3 billion) and individuals ($2 billion), then the municipal bond area will be a prime candidate for higher yields. Other sectors may have less pressure, or even more. In this way forecasts can be

TABLE 2

Matrix Worksheet for Specific Types of Credit

Supply of Credit from	Demand for Credit in Form of							
	Mort- gages	Corpo- rate bonds	Govt. bonds	Munic- ipal bonds	Busi- ness loans	Cons. loans	All other	Total Supply ↓
Comm. banks	—	—	—	3	—	—	— =	55
Sav. & loans	—	—	—	—	—	—	— =	30
Mut. sav. banks	—	—	—	—	—	—	— =	10
Insurance cos.	—	—	—	—	—	—	— =	15
Pension funds	—	—	—	—	—	—	— =	13
Finance cos.	—	—	—	—	—	—	— =	9
Credit unions	—	—	—	—	—	—	— =	2
Nonfin. business	—	—	—	—	—	—	— =	6
Indiv. & others	—	—	—	2	—	—	— =	5
Total Demand →	50	20	15	10	35	25	5 =	160/145

made for a variety of interest rates. Of course, the matrix will have to be changed in second-and-third round iterations—with our state and local example, either the realized demand for funds will have to be reduced and/or the supply increased, until they are equal. At the end, the demand has to add up to the supply for each kind of security and also in the aggregate, in the lower right-hand corner of the matrix.[4]

In recent years one of the most important influences on interest rate forecasts has been the expected rate of inflation. Back in Chapter 20 we saw that higher rates of inflation cause lenders to demand higher nominal rates of interest as compensation for the erosion in their purchasing power. Borrowers are forced to pay higher rates if they want the funds. Most forecasters tack on an inflation premium to the interest rate forecast arrived at in the supply-demand exercise just described.

This simple inflation-adjustment procedure is based on the following implicit analysis. If inflation is expected to be two percentage points higher, say 9 percent rather than 7 percent, then at the old nominal interest rate borrowers will want more funds and lenders will offer fewer funds. This excess demand for funds puts upward pressure on nominal yields. The nominal rate of interest rises until it equates the supply of and demand for funds.[5]

[4] We have simplified both tables for illustrative purposes. Most important, we have not taken the maturity of the securities into account. If relative pressures on short-term rates versus long-term rates are of concern, then a separation should be made along such lines. That is, the demand for credit should divide government securities, for example, into short-term and long-term governments, and supply should similarly be segmented. More on the structure of interest rates in the next chapter.

[5] See Benjamin M. Friedman, "Who Puts the Inflation Premium into Nominal Interest Rates?" *Journal of Finance* (June 1978).

Do forecasters increase their nominal rate forecasts one-to-one with a jump in inflationary expectations? Sometimes. Irving Fisher's dictum that nominal rates rise by the expected rate of inflation is valid only in a world without taxes or risk. It hardly needs emphasizing that life is complicated by both. Taxes, in particular, suggest that nominal rates will go up by more than inflation to maintain aftertax yields. On the other hand, allowing for an adjustment period suggests that nominal rates go up by less than expected inflation. Thus, forecasters often take the route of least resistance—the "more thans" offset the "less thans" and the usual outcome is in the middle, a one-to-one jump.

Care must be taken, however, to match the period over which inflation is expected to accelerate with the maturity of the bond yield that is forecast. If inflation is expected to increase from 7 to 9 percent for one year and then drop back to its previous level, then only yields on one-year bonds should jump by two percentage points. Longer term maturities would reflect only one year of higher expected inflation. Thus, the near-term inflation outlook affects short-term yields while the long-run inflation outlook affects long-term yields. And that's one of the factors determining the maturity structure of interest rates, as we'll see in the next chapter.

Behind Supply and Demand

Although the supply and demand for loanable funds approach to interest rate forecasting may at first glance appear far removed from the econometric model of the economy method discussed earlier in this chapter, down deep they are based on identical factors. In order to fill in all the blanks in the two tables above, one has to bring to bear just about everything that is included, more formally, in a typical large-scale econometric model of the whole economy. Indeed, just about every subject we have discussed in this entire book becomes relevant at some point in filling in the blanks to make a loanable funds interest rate forecast.

To take the first step in the entire process—*that is, to project likely demands for credit during the coming year*—one must first forecast sector spending decisions. To estimate how much people will want to *borrow*, we first have to get an accurate idea of how much they will want to *spend* (consume and invest). To forecast spending decisions, however, means we are in effect forecasting GNP.

More than that, we also have to forecast sector sources and uses of funds statements, to discover the extent to which various kinds of spending will have to be financed by borrowing compared with other forms of financing, such as retained earnings and/or dishoarding. Some spending may also be financed by the sale of financial assets, and this should be *added* to the demand for funds (supply of securities) in financial markets. It doesn't matter, so far as interest rates are concerned, whether the government floats a new issue of Treasury bills or business firms sell some "old" Treasury bills out of their portfolios in order to finance their inventory spending. The sale of one's own liabilities (borrowing) or of someone else's liabilities (selling off financial assets) both draw funds out of financial markets; any act of borrowing *or* sale of securities adds to the demand for loanable funds and contributes to upward pressure on interest rates.

Indeed, it is this very possibility—the sale of "old" securities by their owners—that makes the prediction of interest rates so hazardous. We seem to be able to forecast real output and employment much better than we can predict interest rates. In large part this is due to the very nature of financial markets as contrasted with markets for real goods and services. There is a large supply of *existing* securities—securities that have been issued in the past—always overhanging financial markets, and decisions with respect to holding or dumping these can be made on short notice and executed rapidly. Only a small fraction of the transactions in most financial markets consist of current lending and borrowing exchanges; most transactions involve the trading of already existing securities. In addition, although financial markets are no more susceptible to waves of optimism or pessimism than other markets, in financial markets such shifts in sentiment can more easily be translated into immediate buy or sell orders. Thus, decisions with respect to buying or selling "old" securities can swamp the influence of current lending and borrowing, with consequent unforeseen effects on market interest rates. To put it briefly, forecasting interest rates is—for similar reasons—no different from predicting what is going to happen in the stock market, and even the weather man often does better than *that*.

Turning to the supply of loanable funds, we again have to use a GNP forecast, this time as a basis for estimating the flow of savings into financial institutions, which will be a significant determinant of their ability to supply credit to ultimate borrowers. Another determinant of the ability of financial institutions—especially commercial banks—to make loans and buy securities will, of course, be Federal Reserve policies. Easy money policies that expand bank reserves and the money supply will correspondingly augment the supply of loanable funds, in contrast to tight money policies that keep a lid on monetary growth. Thus money supply and money demand enter the picture.[6]

Finally, in assessing the changes in interest rates that are likely to take place due to discrepancies between ex ante demand and supply, the interest-elasticities of each kind of credit demand and supply become crucial, as noted earlier with reference to Figure 2. So also do the interest-elasticities of various kinds of spending: higher interest rates may discourage some spending from proceeding as originally planned, and lower interest rates might stimulate additional spending. These feedbacks from interest rates to spending and thereby to GNP thus require a revised GNP forecast—which means starting our method of successive approximations over again from the very beginning. So we have, in effect, come full circle. All of the forces in our theoretical model—saving, investment, money supply, money demand —are imbedded somewhere in the loanable funds framework, although not always right on the surface.

It should be pointed out that similar feedback effects take place between and among various interest rates, since financial instruments are substitutes for one another in both lender portfolios and in the options open to borrowers. If corporate bond yields rise, for example, some lenders will make marginal shifts out of government securities and into the now relatively more attractive corporates, thereby slowing the rise in corporate yields but starting an upswing in government yields. At the same time, corporations, faced with higher bond interest rates, may decide to float fewer bonds and take out more bank loans instead—which will also slow the rise in corporate bond yields, but put upward pressure on bank lending rates. Thus, because of *substitutability* on the part of both lenders and borrowers, all interest rates tend to move up and down more or less together, although the differentials among them may widen or narrow, as we will see in the next chapter.

---

[6] Debt repayment should also be added to the supply of loanable funds, just as liquidation of financial assets should be added to the demand. Debt repayment involves the purchase of one's own liabilities, compared with lending, which is the purchase of someone else's liabilities. But any purchase of securities injects funds into financial markets, regardless of whose liability the securities might represent.

Suggestions for Further Reading

Annual supply and demand for credit projections are published each year —usually in late January or early February—by Salomon Brothers (*The Supply and Demand for Credit*) and by Bankers Trust Company (*Credit and Capital Markets*). The address of the former is 1 New York Plaza, New York, New York, 10004, and the latter is Post Office Box 318, Church Street Station, New York, New York, 10015. See also William C. Freund and Edward D. Zinbarg, "Application of Flow of Funds to Interest-Rate Forecasting," *Journal of Finance* (May 1963). Also Michael J. Prell, "How Well Do the Experts Forecast Interest Rates?" in The Federal Reserve Bank of Kansas City *Monthly Review* (September-October 1973).

If you want to learn more about loanable funds interest theory and liquidity preference interest theory, a good place to start is Joseph W. Conard, *An Introduction to the Theory of Interest* (Berkeley: University of California Press, 1959). Also see Friedrich A. Lutz, *The Theory of Interest*, 2d ed. (Chicago: Aldine, 1968).

Chapter 30

The Structure
of Interest Rates

BURT REYNOLDS is not easily ruffled. He is hardly ever caught off guard. But once, while he was at one of those swinging dinner parties in Washington (actors campaigning for politicians), he met his one-time economics instructor, Dr. Mark Etz. Reynolds was standing in the corner, surveying the scene, when Etz walked up to him, puffing on his ever-present pipe, and said: "Young man, I've just realized something. There are more interest rates out there than hair on your chest." Reynolds was dumbfounded. He could hardly believe his ears. He was caught with his pants down, as it were. He had always thought there was only one—*the* interest rate that Etz had talked about all term long.

To make sure that you won't be caught in equally embarrassing circumstances, we now take note of the many different interest rates on various types of financial instruments. The structure of yields on different maturities of the *same* class of securities is explored first. We then turn to the relationship between yields on different categories of securities (such as government bonds versus corporate bonds).

The Term Structure of Rates and the Yield Curve

The relationship between yields on different maturities of the same type of security is called the *term structure* of interest rates (from "term to maturity"). For government bonds we might compare the yields on three-month Treasury bills, one-year notes, and ten-year bonds.

The relationship is sometimes depicted graphically by a *yield curve*, as in Figure 1. Often the yield curve is upward sloping—that is, short-term securities yield less than long-term securities (curve *A*). Sometimes it is rather flat—short-term yields equal long-term yields (curve *B*). And sometimes the yield curve is even downward sloping—short-term interest rates are *above* long-term rates (curve *C*).

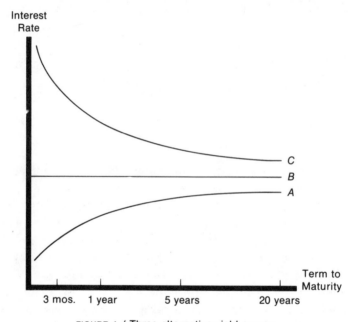

FIGURE 1 / Three alternative yield curves.

What determines the shape of the yield curve? A straightforward case can be made for a basic supply-demand approach. When the supply of short-term securities rises and the supply of longs declines, the short-term interest rate is pushed up and the long-term interest rate is driven down, and vice versa. But a simple supply-demand approach is vulnerable because it may ignore important relationships between the markets for short-term and long-term securities. The unadulterated supply-demend model is a "segmented markets" theory of the term structure.[1]

[1] The clearest exposition of this theory is John M. Culbertson, "The Term Structure of Interest Rates," *Quarterly Journal of Economics* (November 1957).

The Structure of Interest Rates

There are many—and here financial analysts and economists often find much common ground—who argue that short-term securities and long-term securities are very good substitutes for each other in investor portfolios. Not for every investor but for enough so that their decisions *collectively* make a significant impact on the market. For them, the important feature of the security they buy is what it yields over a particular period. This implies that long-term rates are related in a very special way to short-term rates. Let's illustrate that with a particular example.

Say you are the portfolio manager of a bank and you want to invest funds for two years. Assume you could buy a one-year Treasury security today yielding 5 percent, and you expect that next year the rate on one-year securities will be 7 percent. If you buy the one-year security today and reinvest in a one-year security next year, you expect an average return over the two years of about 6 percent. If you had the option of buying a *two-year* Treasury security today that yielded 6½ percent, you'd jump at it (so would everyone else). On the other hand, if two-year Treasury securities were yielding only 5½ percent, you wouldn't touch them (neither would anyone). That means, of course, that a two-year security would have to yield just about 6 percent if portfolio managers are to be content to hold them as investments (and refrain from selling them and buying one-year securties).

This suggests that the relationship between the yield on a two-year security (long-term) and a one-year security (short-term) of the same risk category (e.g., Treasury securities) depends on *expected* short-term rates. If next year's short-term rates are expected to be above the current short-term rate, long-term rates will exceed short-term rates and the yield curve will be upward sloping. If next year's short-term rates are expected to be below the current short-term rate, the yield curve will be downward sloping.

The key to this "expectations" theory of the term structure is that shorts and longs are very good substitutes for each other in investor portfolios. In fact, they're perfect substitutes—if expected yields are the same, the portfolio manager is indifferent between shorts and longs. Instead of a segmented market, there is a single market! Note in this case that if the supply of longs goes up and the supply of shorts goes down, it makes absolutely no difference as far as yields are concerned. Long-term securities will be willingly exchanged for short-term securities, with no change in yields as long as expected future short-term rates are unchanged.

There are few who argue that all investors are indifferent between short-term securities and long-term securities. It is simply a fact of life—embedded in the mathematics of bond prices—that the *prices* of short-term securities are less volatile than long-term securities. If you have to sell a security before it reaches maturity and interest rates have increased, a short-term security will have fallen in price much less than a long-term one. If you might have to sell to raise cash, you'll prefer short-term securities. Commercial banks are like that.

Recognition of the greater capital uncertainty of long-term securities leads to a modification in the expectations theory of the term structure. If most investors are like commercial banks and prefer the capital certainty of short-term securities, while most bond issuers prefer to issue long-term securities, then investors on balance will demand a premium for holding longs. This is often called a liquidity premium, but it is really a risk premium—a reward for exposure to the capital uncertainty of long-term securities. Thus, in our previous numerical example, a two-year security would have to yield more than the average of the current one-year rate and next year's expected one-year rate. Otherwise investors wouldn't want to hold the riskier two-year security.

There is evidence suggesting that there are liquidity premiums embedded in long-term interest rates. But to leave it at that would be misleading, because some investors have a *preference* for long-term securities. Life insurance companies and pension funds, for example, don't worry that much about surprising needs for cash. Their liabilities are actuarially predictable. In fact, they want to make sure they earn at least 8 (or 9 or 10) percent on their assets over the next ten (or twenty or thirty) years. That way they're sure of a profit—because they promise to pay pension holders something less than that. These institutions therefore prefer long-term securities.

Such preferred maturity ranges suggest that switches between "shorts" and "longs" take place in many portfolios whenever yields get out of line with expectations. Commercial banks, for example, require a "liquidity premium" to invest in longer-term securities. A large increase in the supply of five-year bonds may, therefore, push up the yield by more than expected. But it won't go very far. While banks and insurance companies have their *preferred* maturities, these preferences are far from absolute. Commercial banks will be lured away from their one-year notes by the increased yields on five-year bonds. And pension funds will be enticed as well. Both of these actions mitigate the upward pressure on five-year bonds.

These modifications in the expectations theory of the term structure of interest rates make the theory conform more closely to reality. A further step is to recognize that investors do not usually have precise numerical predictions of short-term rates next year, or the year after. More likely, investors form expectations of when the "level" of rates is relatively high and when the "level" of rates is relatively low. While this sounds fairly innocuous, it provides a powerful explanation of when the yield curve is likely to be upward sloping (curve *A* in Figure 1) or downward sloping (curve *B*).

When interest rates are high relative to what they have been, investors generally expect them to decline in the future. Falling interest rates mean rising bond prices, and those investors who are holding long-term bonds in their portfolio will reap their just reward—big capital gains. Therefore, when all rates are relatively high, investors will prefer to hold "longs" rather than "shorts" (because the capital gains on shorts are relatively low). This additional demand for long-term securities drives their prices up and their yields down—relative to short-term securities. Thus, long-term yields are below short-term yields when the overall level of rates is high, and the yield curve is downward sloping.

Similarly, when the general level of rates is low and yields are expected to rise in the future, investors prefer not to hold long-term securities because they are likely to incur capital losses. This drives the price of long-term securities down (and the yield up) thereby producing long-term rates above short-term rates, and an upward sloping yield curve.

Chart 1 illustrates the accuracy of these conjectures with yield curves during the mid-1970s. The actual yield curve on August 30, 1974, was downward sloping, and that's when the overall "level" of rates was quite high. On the other hand, the most sharply upward sloping curve is for January 23, 1976, when the "level" of rates was relatively low.

We could continue with more details on the term structure relationship. But we've gone about as far as we should without recognizing that nicely shaped curves such as those drawn in Figure 1 and Chart 1 hardly ever occur in nature. Not that the yield curve for any of the dates listed in Chart 1 is wrong. It's just that the yield curve depicts the relationship between yield and maturity, and there are other factors which influence yields—even on a relatively homogeneous group of securities such as governmental bonds.

There are many different issues of government bonds and each one differs in some respect (besides maturity) from the others. Some have coupons of 3 percent, others of 8 percent. Some are accepted at par (face value) in payment of estate taxes, even though they are selling well below par. These features affect the relative yields on bonds of identical maturity.[2] Chart 2 shows Chart 1's May 30, 1975,

---

[2] Take the following example. In 1958 the government issued a bond due in 1990 with a 3½ percent coupon. The bond was sold at par or face value

yield curve under a microscope. As you can see, there are little dots of different shapes around various portions of the yield curve; they represent the *precise* yields of *specific* issues. The yield curve is drawn freehand to approximate the yield-maturity relationship. In the next section, the specific features of different bonds are examined to help explain yield differentials among bonds of identical maturity.

The Risk Structure of Interest Rates

We've just seen that government securities of the *same* maturity can have different yields. Once we step away from the safety of governments, the riskiness, marketability, and tax aspects of bonds play the dominant role in explaining yield relationships. Indeed, lacking a better name, this is often called the risk structure of interest rates even though other factors besides the relative risk of default come into play. We'll take a look at the relationship between yields on governments, corporates, municipals, and mortgages, staying away from term structure influences by looking at long-term bonds only. By long-term we mean bonds with twenty years to maturity.[3]

($1,000) and yielded 3½ percent—the going rate at that time for long-term governments. In early 1975 the government issued another bond due in 1990, this time with a coupon of 8¼ percent. The yield of 8¼ percent was the going rate for long-term governments in the beginning of 1975. In May 1975 both the 3½ percent coupon and the 8¼ percent coupon had the same number of years to maturity—fifteen. They should have both yielded exactly the same thing— 8¼ percent. In particular, the price of the 3½ percent coupon bond should have fallen until the bond yielded exactly what other available government bonds of the same maturity yielded. If not, why would anyone have held the 3½'s rather than the 8¼'s? In point of fact, the price of the 3½'s fell quite a bit—you could buy $1,000 worth for only $781. But at that price, the yield was about 5.7 percent, quite a bit less than the 8¼ percent. The main reason for this is that the 3½'s are acceptable at par ($1,000) in the payment of estate taxes. Such "flower bonds," as they are irreverently called, are in great demand among wealthy elderly persons. Thus the yield is well below other government bonds of identical maturity.

It should also be noted that the 3½'s would yield less than the 8¼'s even without the estate tax feature. The coupon interest on a bond is taxed at regular income tax rates. Any appreciation in the price of a bond is treated as capital gains—which, let us assume, is taxed at half the normal rate. If I held the 8¼'s to maturity I'd have to pay income tax on the entire $82.50 (per $1,000 bond) each year. If I held the 3½'s to maturity, I'd have paid regular income tax on the $35 (per bond) each year. I'd have a capital gain of $219.00 ($1,000 paid at maturity minus the cost of $781.00) which is taxed half as much as regular income. Thus investors prefer the 3½'s to the 8¼'s; hence they would yield less even without being "flower bonds."

[3] In the good old days (1900), long-term really meant long-term—bonds of forty years maturity were common. See Benjamin Klein, "The Impact of Inflation on the Term Structure of Corporate Financial Instruments," in W. Silber, ed., *Financial Innovation* (Lexington, Mass.: Heath, 1975).

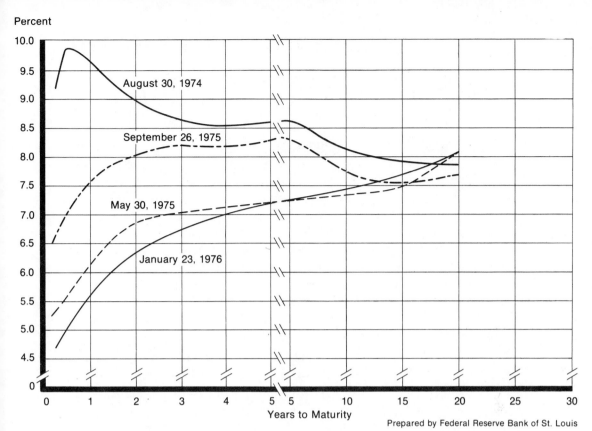

Percent

CHART 1 / Yields on U.S. Government securities. When the "level" of rates is high, the yield curve is likely to be downward sloping.

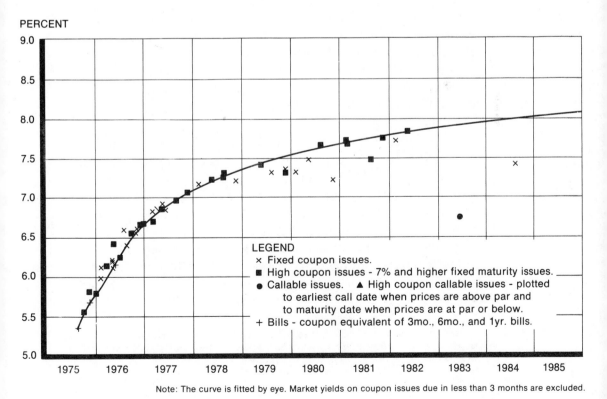

PERCENT

Note: The curve is fitted by eye. Market yields on coupon issues due in less than 3 months are excluded.

CHART 2 / Yields of Treasury securities, May 30, 1975 (based on closing bid quotations).

As with term structure theory, a straightforward supply-demand analysis can be tried in explaining yield relationships. For example, as the supply of corporate bonds rises relative to, say, governments, the yield on corporates should increase. But as with the term structure, a simplistic supply-demand approach ignores important relationships between these markets which dominate the yield structure. In particular because all bonds are substitutes for each other in investor portfolios, as soon as one yield begins to rise relative to others investors switch into that security. This substitution process holds down the widening yield differentials among securities.

In fact, when you think about it, every security entitles the holder to receive the exact same thing—a stream of dollar payments in the future. One reason investors pay a different price for each of these contracts is that sometimes people break their promises. They don't wind up doing what they said they'd do. In religion you do penance for such transgressions, in the financial world you go bankrupt. Thus, bonds are risky—they may not pay either the interest or the principal. Since the federal government has substantial taxing power and since it can always print money to pay off its bonds, there is no risk of default on government securities.[4] But for corporations, individuals, and even (especially?) municipal governments, the risk of default is prominent. Since people usually have to be paid to bear more risk, yields on corporate bonds exceed those on governments, as is evident in Chart 3. For the same reason, yields on lower quality corporate bonds exceed the yields on the issues of higher quality corporations. In fact, bond rating services such as Moody's and Standard and Poor's classify both corporates and municipal bonds into different risk classes—from AAA (the best and the brightest) to BBB (fair but fragile) to DDD (dead in default). The yields on higher rated bonds are lower than those on lower rated bonds.

Municipal bonds—the debt issued by state and local governments —have a number of interesting features. The default risk of such bonds used to be considered quite low, with the only significant bankruptcies occurring during the Great Depression. The taxing power of state-local governments is the ultimate backing for municipal bonds. But the taxing power of states and cities is limited by people's willingness to stay put and subject themselves to the burden of ever-increasing local taxes. Americans just don't sit still for very long, especially when hit by the tax prod. As a result of this and the *de facto* default of New York City in 1975, default risk considerations are

---

[4] But there is a risk of inflation if the government prints money to pay off its debt. And if the public thinks this is a real possibility, *nominal* yields will be very high even on "risk-free" governments.

The Structure of Interest Rates

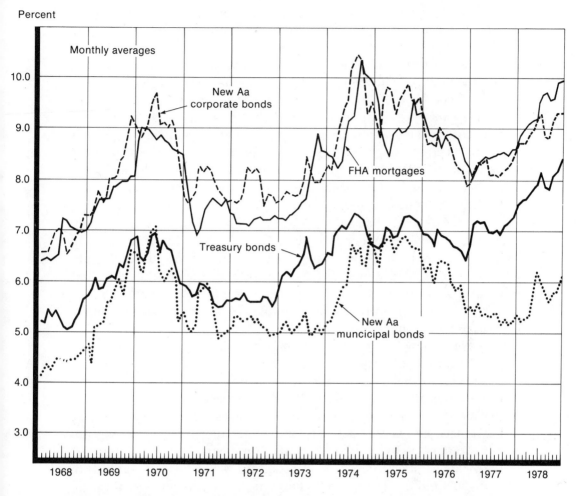

CHART 3 / Average yields of long-term Treasury, corporate, and municipal bonds and mortgages.

exerting considerable influence on the yield relationships between municipals and other bonds.

The tax-exempt status of interest payments on municipal bonds is, however, still the most important influence on municipal yields versus governments and corporates. Say you pay 50 percent of your income in taxes. If the yield on a government bond is 8 percent, you'll get $80 per $1,000 invested, but after the tax man cometh you'll wind up with only $40—or an after-tax yield of 4 percent. But if you own a municipal bond which pays $80 per $1,000 invested, you keep it all because the interest on the municipal bond is immune from the Internal Revenue Service. If the municipal bond had no chance of default and if everyone were in the 50 percent bracket, then investors would refuse to buy government bonds and would buy all the municipals they could lay their hands on if both yielded 8 percent before taxes (driving the prices of governments down and municipals up). When would investors be indifferent between the two? Clearly if the municipal bond yielded 4 percent and the government bond yielded 8 percent they both would give their owners $40 *after* taxes and the market would be in equilibrium.

Of course, everyone is not in the 50 percent tax bracket—that's reserved for rock stars and brain surgeons. At a lower income tax rate, the yield on municipals will have to be higher—say 5 percent versus 8 percent on governments.[5] Furthermore, municipal bonds ain't what they used to be in terms of their default-free reputation. This tends to push such rates even closer to the yield on fully taxable U.S. government bonds. As can be seen in Chart 3, the yields on municipal bonds have usually stayed well below comparable maturity governments, as dictated by tax considerations. But in 1970, in response to default jitters brought on by the Penn Central bankruptcy and again in 1975 due to the crisis in New York City bonds, the yields on municipal bonds were driven up to yields on fully taxable governments. These are truly classic examples of the response of interest rates to risk exposure.

Let us now turn to the yields on mortgages versus the rest. Compared with corporate bonds, mortgages are probably somewhat more risky because they are liabilities of individuals with unfamiliar credit ratings. But this cannot explain the pattern traced in Chart 3, because the mortgage rate recorded is for mortgages which are insured or guaranteed by government agencies: either the Federal Housing Administration (FHA) or the Veterans Administration (VA). And yet, the yields on such mortgages exceeded the yields on corporates until mid-1967 and are clearly well above yields on governments throughout the period. Something must be lurking in the background. And while there are a number of "special features" of mortgages, the one which is most important from our standpoint is called marketability.

Securities that are traded in organized markets such as the stock exchanges can be readily sold to someone else if the investor has to raise cash. The ready marketability of an asset is a desirable characteristic from an investor's standpoint. An individual can sell the asset on short notice without a large drop in price. Bonds with good marketability will therefore yield less than those without this characteristic. An excellent market exists for trading government bonds. It is not located in any particular building. Rather, banks and govern-

---

[5] If your tax rate is t, the yield on governments is G, and the yield on municipals is M, then after tax yields are equal when $G(1 - t) = M$. Hence, the ratio of M to G equals $(1 - t)$. With a tax rate of 37.5 percent, the yield on governments would be 8 percent compared with 5 percent on municipals.

ment securities dealers stand ready to buy and sell government bonds at quoted prices. A similar but somewhat less organized network exists for corporate and municipal bonds. Within each of these groups— governments, corporates, and municipals—some issues are more marketable than others, and yields on the less marketable securities have to be higher to make them attractive to potential purchasers. All of this will be discussed further in the next chapter.

For understanding the trends in yield differentials, we must just note that mortgages have never had any secondary market to speak of. That helps explain why FHA mortgage yields were above even the yields on corporate bonds until 1967, and have been intertwined with such rates since, despite the fact that FHA mortgages are free of credit risk. It certainly helps explain why yields on such government-insured mortgages exceed the yields on regular government obligations, although insurance fees and certain administrative headaches play a well-earned role. In recent years, most notably since 1970, government-related agencies such as the Government National Mortgage Association and the Federal Home Loan Mortgage Corporation (see Chapter 27) have fostered a secondary market in mortgages. The fact that the FHA mortgage rate recently stayed below corporate rates has been attributed by some to the development of a secondary market.

Our discussion of yield differentials has touched upon many specific features of bonds. So many, in fact, that it's hard to see how anyone can ignore them. How did we talk about interest rates for 2 chapters without mentioning each and every one? How could our analysis of movements in the *level* of interest rates have been accurate when the level is made up of so many very different parts? A quick glance at Chart 3 tells you that while rate differentials can and do change, all rates still move more or less together. Much of the *overall* movement is determined by monetary policy and the course of economic activity, as we stressed in the previous chapter. Our focus in this chapter has put those overall movements under a microscope, producing a different perspective. Sometimes one approach is preferable and sometimes the other. It depends on what you're looking for.

Suggestions for Further Reading

There are many excellent studies of the term structure of interest rates. A good survey as well as advanced material is found in Burton G. Malkiel's book *The Term Structure of Interest Rates* (Princeton, N.J.: Princeton University Press, 1966). A somewhat more difficult study is by Richard Roll, *The Behavior of Interest Rates* (New York: Basic Books, 1970). There have been numerous specific analyses as well, such as Dudley G. Luckett, "Multi-Period Expectations and the Term Structure of Interest Rates," *Quarterly Journal of Economics* (May 1967); and Edward J. Kane, "The Term Structure of Interest Rates: An Attempt to Reconcile Teaching With Practice," *Journal of Finance* (May 1970).

The risk structure of interest rates has a somewhat less organized career. An early article on the subject is Lawrence Fisher, "Determinants of Risk Premiums on Corporate Bonds," *Journal of Political Economy* (June 1959). A more recent and more general analysis is Dwight M. Jaffee, "Cyclical Variations in the Risk Structure of Interest Rates," *Journal of Money, Credit, and Banking* (July 1975). An interesting analysis of risk and term structure together is in Philip Cagan's "A Study of Liquidity Premiums on Federal and Municipal Securities," in *Essays on Interest Rates*, ed. Jack Guttentag and Phillip Cagan (New York, National Bureau of Economic Research, 1969).

A survey of rate structure issues is found in James C. Van Horne's excellent paperback *Financial Market Rates and Flows* (Englewood Cliffs, N.J.: Prentice-Hall, 1978). Finally, for the nitty-gritty on specific features of bonds such as call provisions, intermarket spreads and swap opportunities, loss recovery periods, cushion bonds, perpetuities, and the magic of compounding, see Sidney Homer and Martin Liebowitz, *Inside the Yield Book* (Englewood Cliffs, N.J.: Prentice-Hall, 1970). Don't miss the discussion on page 101 on the yield pickup swap and the net gains to the swapper.

The Nuts and Bolts
of Debt Management

The first section of this chapter discussed the relationship between short- and long-term yields on government securities. We also touched on the question of whether changes in relative supplies of government debt affect the structure of rates. We now turn to a more prosaic matter: how does the U.S. Treasury "manage" the government's obligations?

We now have a national debt—federal government securities outstanding—totaling some $800 billion. The national debt is essentially the result of past and present fiscal policy, mostly past. It is the sum of all past deficits, less surpluses, in the federal budget. Given a national debt of $800 billion, its day-to-day management has implications for the functioning of financial markets, monetary policy, and economic stability. How can the debt be refinanced most smoothly when portions of it come due? How much of the debt should be in the form of short-term Treasury bills, how much in the form of long-term Treasury bonds? First we'll discuss the statistics, then the techniques, and finally the objectives of debt management.

Of the $800 billion in government debt outstanding, only about $500 billion is in marketable form; that is, only $500 billion can be bought or sold in the open market by investors. The remaining $300 billion is divided up as follows: about $160 billion in various government trust accounts (such as social security), $80 billion in familiar U.S. savings bonds, about $30 billion in special foreign issues, and $30 billion in special state and local government series. These non-marketable issues are largely outside normal Treasury debt management considerations. This is best illustrated by savings bonds. Individuals buy and redeem them at will—with the Treasury passively accommodating the public's preferences.

Of the $500 billion in marketable government debt outstanding, about $115 billion is held by the Federal Reserve as a result of current and past open market purchases. An additional $15 billion in marketable debt is held by various government agencies. That leaves about

$370 billion of marketable government debt held by the private sector of the economy—banks, insurance companies, nonfinancial corporations, and individuals.

The magnitude of the debt management problem is best appreciated by noting that nearly $230 billion in government debt obligations come due each year and must be paid off. How? By refinancing it, of course—that is, by reborrowing the $230 billion once again, either from the same investors who choose to replace maturing issues or from others who want to get in on the act. The Treasury can replace maturing issues with short-term Treasury bills (up to one year to maturity), intermediate-term Treasury notes (one to ten years maturity), or long-term bonds (usually above ten years to maturity, sometimes twenty or thirty). And that's what debt management policy is all about: choosing the maturities to issue when replacing debt obligations.

Given the magnitude of the housekeeping details, the Treasury follows a number of well-established practices. The routine permits the financial markets to prepare properly for Treasury operations. Treasury bills are conventionally issued with original maturities of 91 days (3-month bills), 182 days (6-month bills) and 364 days (52-weeks). New supplies of 91- and 182-day bills are auctioned weekly (on Monday), while the 52-week bills are auctioned monthly.

The Federal Reserve Banks conduct these bill auctions as fiscal agents for the Treasury. Investors submit their bids to a regional Federal Reserve Bank in one of two ways: either by submitting a competitive or noncompetitive tender. Large investors (above $500,000) must submit competitive tenders: that is, they must state a bid price for a specific amount of bills. The Treasury either accepts or rejects these bids on a price priority basis. Smaller investors can submit noncompetitive tenders: that is, they state an amount they wish to buy and receive that quantity at the average price of the auction. Large banks and other government securities dealers are especially cautious in these auctions, calculating their bid prices with great care and waiting until the very last minute before submitting their orders. Small price differences can mean quite a lot when buying $100 million bills.

One popular category of bills that appears on an irregular basis is the tax anticipation bill. These bills are issued to bridge the Treasury's temporary cash flow problems. Corporations find them especially attractive because they can be used at par to pay corporate profits taxes even though their scheduled maturities are usually one week after tax payments are due. Because of this special demand by corporations, these tax anticipation bills yield somewhat less than comparable maturity bills.

Treasury notes and bonds differ from bills both because of their longer maturities and because they carry semiannual coupon payments. Bills are sold at a price discount, reflecting the interest yield, while notes and bonds are usually sold at par. The only difference between a note and a bond is that the former cannot be issued with an original maturity above ten years. These coupon issues also follow a scheduled auction pattern. Two-year notes are issued about a week before the end of every month, four-year notes are issued the last month of every quarter, with seven- and ten-year notes sometimes included in the package; bonds of fifteen- and twenty-five year maturities are also offered during these quarterly "refunding" operations.

Notes and bonds are usually issued via an auction similar to Treasury bills. In the past, the Treasury occasionally announced a subscription offering. After setting the yield and maturity on an issue, the public is invited to tender subscriptions for specific amounts. In this case, the Treasury runs the risk of setting the yield too high, resulting in an oversubscription—greater demand than the Treasury is prepared to issue. If that were an auction, it means that the yield required to sell the entire issue would be reduced. But in a subscription, the Treasury pays the stated yield and cuts back each subscription proportionally. Recent years have seen the auction method replace subscriptions as the dominant technique of Treasury refundings.

With this vast array of instruments and techniques at the Treasury's disposal, plus the network of securities dealers that make a secondary market in government obligations (to be discussed in the next chapter), it would seem relatively easy to manage even the rather large public debt currently outstanding. And in some sense it is quite easy, because Treasury obligations always get sold, and with few hangups. But while the mechanics are quite straightforward, the role and objectives of debt management are sometimes unclear.

What are the objectives of day-to-day debt management? One goal is to minimize the interest cost of the debt to the taxpayers. But this can hardly be the only objective. If it were, the Treasury could minimize the interest cost—indeed, reduce it to zero—by simply printing money and buying back all the outstanding securities. It could thus replace its interest-bearing debt (bills and bonds) with its non-interest-bearing debt (money). Obviously, the Treasury does not "monetize the debt," because to do so would probably result in massive inflation, and the Treasury also has the objective of managing the debt to promote economic stability.

These two objectives often dictate opposite policy actions. Minimizing the interest cost suggests that when we are in a recession, and interest rates are low across the board, the Treasury should refund its maturing issues with new long-term bonds, thus ensuring low interest payments for itself well into the future. During boom periods, when interest rates are typically high, the Treasury should refinance by selling short-term issues, Treasury bills, so the government does not have to continue paying high rates after yields have fallen to more normal levels.

Stabilization objectives call for just the opposite policies. When we are in a recession, the last thing we want to do is raise long-term interest rates, which is precisely what pushing long-term securities onto the market is likely to accomplish. Boom periods, when we *do* want to raise long rates (to reduce investment spending), are when we should sell long-term bonds.

Thus the objective of minimizing interest costs dictates lengthening the maturity structure of the debt (more long-term bonds relative to short-term bills) during recession periods and shortening the maturity structure during boom periods. For purposes of economic stabilization we should do the opposite—try to shorten the maturity structure during recessions and lengthen it during prosperity.

A complication that makes it difficult to lengthen the maturity structure of the federal debt is the archaic 4¼ percent legal ceiling on government bond interest rates. By virtue of a law passed in 1917, the Treasury is not allowed to pay more than a 4¼ percent interest rate on bonds with ten or more years to maturity. Since long-term market interest rates have generally been well above 4¼ percent in recent years, the Treasury has been unable to offer competitive yields on long-term securities and thus has had no choice but to borrow via shorter-maturity issues. (In a daring break with tradition, Congress recently grabbed the bull by the tail and faced the situation squarely; it modified the law and permitted the Treasury to issue up to $27 billion of bonds at rates above 4¼ percent.)

Debt management policy must be administered in coordination with monetary and fiscal policy. If minimizing the interest cost is the primary goal of Treasury debt management, then monetary and fiscal policy will have to take appropriate action to offset this counter-stabilization debt policy. If economic stabilization is the primary objective of debt management, the monetary and fiscal authorities can take this into account and reduce the forcefulness of their own actions.

Coordination between the monetary and debt management authorities is also essential on a continuing basis because of the vast magnitude of the Treasury's frequent refunding operations. When the Treasury refinances a large volume of maturing issues and issues longer-term obligations it often needs central bank help. If the Federal Reserve is pursuing a tight money policy, for example, it will often become less aggressive and resort to a policy of keeping an "even keel" in the bond markets as the date of a refinancing approaches. In effect, the central bank will mark time for a few weeks while the Treasury goes through the mechanics of the refunding operation. It is difficult enough for the Treasury to roll over so much debt without being forced to cope with additional complications resulting from actions of the monetary authorities.[1]

Monetary policy, fiscal policy, and debt management are often considered the three main tools of stabilization policy. In fact, however, debt management has typically been the runt of the litter. Perhaps that is just as well. Given the power of monetary and fiscal policy to implement national economic goals, perhaps debt management can make its most significant contribution by successfully accomplishing the more limited but not unimportant task of continuously refinancing a very large volume of government securities without unduly disturbing the nation's financial markets.

[1] For some historical perspective on "even keel," see Chapter 37.

Chapter 31

The Performance of Financial Markets

KATHARINE HEPBURN needs a script, Jackson Browne a guitar, Richard Avedon a camera, and Chris Evert a tennis racket. Each performer uses the props appropriate for the medium in question. Performances can be stimulating, comical, pleasurable, disappointing. That's how it is in the world of showbiz.

Well, it's not so different in financial markets. Brokers, dealers, specialists, and traders are the actors. Telephones, ticker tapes, and TV terminals are the props. Stocks, bonds, bills, and mortgages are the media. Performances are described as resilient, deep, broad, thin, liquid. Our task is to describe who goes with what and why. You can then decide whether to applaud or hiss after your next financial transaction.

Nature and Function of Financial Markets

As indicated near the end of the last chapter, as well as earlier in Chapter 5, financial markets facilitate exchanges of financial assets. That's not very surprising, since all markets serve precisely that function: to bring buyers and sellers together. Financial markets have received more attention than, say, the local flea market, because just about everyone transacts in some financial market. Fortunes have been made and lost in bond and stock markets and the government has closely supervised financial transactions ever since the debacle of the 1930s left millions penniless. While much of what we say is specific to financial markets, the concepts and implications extend to other areas as well.

It is useful to distinguish two distinct functions of a market: (1) the dissemination of price information and trading interests; (2) provision of facilities for executing exchange. Financial markets must provide both at reasonable costs. It is worth emphasizing at the outset that trading interests are not collected without cost: uncovering purchase and sale orders so that buyers and sellers meet at an agreeable price takes time; buyers and sellers might also be at remote locations, making it expensive to communicate such information. Geographic and temporal fragmentation make the smoothly functioning and costless trading of a theoretical Walrasian[1] auction an imaginary construct. Real-world trading at prices straddling the equilibrium price (see Figure 1 in Chapter 29) is the best we can hope for. It would be nice if actual transactions prices did a little dance around the theoretical equilibrium price.

Financial markets are organized to help us buy and sell securities and to minimize the temporary gyrations of transactions prices. For example, you can employ a broker to search for a compatible trading partner when selling a stock or corporate bond. A fee is charged to you, over and above the equilibrium price, depending in part, on the difficulty of the search and discovery. In some markets, such as for Treasury securities and corporate bonds, dealers stand ready to buy at a bid price and sell at an asked or offer price. The difference between the bid and the asked is the dealer's reward for facilitating trading. Thus, the bid-asked spread is part of the cost of transacting. It means, therefore, that the transactions price differs from the theoretical equilibrium. Moreover, searching among the various market-makers is likely to reveal price discrepancies, both of bid and offer quotations. Failure to search among all dealers, because it takes time and therefore is costly, can also add to transactions costs. Trading on a formal exchange, such as the New York Stock Exchange (NYSE), is aimed at consolidating this type of fragmentation. Buyers

[1] Leon Walras, a late-nineteenth-century French economist concerned with general equilibrium systems, conceptualized the equilibrium price as the outcome of an auction in which buy and sell orders were continuously revised until all trading occurred at a price that cleared the market. That was called the equilibrium price. The only real-world auction at which such recontracting takes place is in the London gold fixing.

and sellers meet at an open auction, with the highest bids buying and the lowest offers selling. (At least, that's the way they tell it.)

The organizational structure of a market—the existence of brokers, dealers, exchanges—as well as the technological paraphernalia—such as ticker tapes, TV quotation screens, and telegraphic communications—are all mobilized to keep transactions prices as close to true (but unknown) equilibrium prices as is economically feasible. By providing easy access to a trading forum, with many potential buyers and sellers, a security can be bought or sold quickly with little loss in value. That is what is meant by marketability—a catch-all phrase indicating low bid-asked spreads, little price dispersion, and presumably only small deviations of actual transactions prices about the true equilibrium.

Good marketability implies that a security can be sold, liquidated, turned into cash, very quickly without triggering a collapse in price. A highly marketable security is more desirable to investors, so its equilibrium price will be higher, and its yield lower, relative to less marketable securities. The rest of our discussion is devoted to describing and evaluating the marketability of various financial assets and the market structures that characterize trading.

Primary Versus Secondary Markets

Before detailing the nature of trading in securities markets, it is important to distinguish primary markets from secondary markets. Most of the popular financial markets, such as the New York Stock Exchange, are secondary markets—where existing securities are exchanged between individuals and institutions. The primary markets—markets for newly issued securities are much less well-known.

New issues of stocks or bonds to raise funds for General Motors, General Electric, or Colonel Sanders are not sold to saver-lenders on the floor of the New York Stock Exchange, the American Stock Exchange or even the Midwest Exchange. Rather, the matchmaking takes place behind closed doors, aided by Wall Street's investment bankers. The names Morgan Stanley, Goldman Sachs, Lazard Frères, and Merrill Lynch dominate the list. They often act as brokers and dealers in secondary markets as well. But in their role as investment bankers they help distribute newly issued stocks and bonds to ultimate investors—insurance companies, pension funds, and individuals throughout the country.

New Issue / May 21, 1979

$100,000,000

Northwest Bancorporation

Floating Rate Notes Due 1989

(Convertible Prior to May 1, 1988 into 8⅝% Debentures Due 2004)

Price 99.96% and accrued interest, if any, from May 31, 1979

Copies of the Prospectus may be obtained in any State in which this
announcement is circulated only from such of the undersigned
as may legally offer these securities in such State.

Salomon Brothers

Blyth Eastman Dillon & Co. Incorporated	**The First Boston Corporation**	**Goldman, Sachs & Co.**
Merrill Lynch White Weld Capital Markets Group Merrill Lynch, Pierce, Fenner & Smith Incorporated		**Bache Halsey Stuart Shields** Incorporated
Bear, Stearns & Co.	**Dillon, Read & Co. Inc.**	**Donaldson, Lufkin & Jenrette** Securities Corporation
Drexel Burnham Lambert Incorporated	**E. F. Hutton & Company Inc.**	**Keefe, Bruyette & Woods, Inc.**
Kidder, Peabody & Co. Incorporated	**Lazard Frères & Co.**	**Lehman Brothers Kuhn Loeb** Incorporated
Loeb Rhoades, Hornblower & Co.		**Paine, Webber, Jackson & Curtis** Incorporated
L. F. Rothschild, Unterberg, Towbin		**M. A. Schapiro & Co., Inc.**
Shearson Hayden Stone Inc.		**Smith Barney, Harris Upham & Co.** Incorporated
A. G. Becker Warburg Paribas Becker	**Wertheim & Co., Inc.**	**Dean Witter Reynolds Inc.**
Dain, Kalman & Quail Incorporated		**Piper, Jaffray & Hopwood** Incorporated

NEWSPAPER ADVERTISEMENT / An Underwriting Syndicate
Floats a New Issue

These distributions are called underwritings: the investment
banker guarantees an issuer of bonds a price (and implicitly a yield)
on the new issue. Often, a number of investment bankers band together in a syndicate to market a new issue; by sticking together, they
share the risk of adverse movements in interest rates between the
time an issue is bought from the corporation until it is out of the investment bankers' inventory—safely tucked away in some pension
funds' portfolio for many years to come. The idea is to get rid of the
issue as quickly as possible—within a day or two. That minimizes the
risk exposure of the investment banking firm's capital. Announce-

ments of successful underwritings, such as the one reproduced on the previous page, appear frequently in the financial press.

A number of features of this new-issue market are noteworthy. First, as with many—or most—markets, it is not located in any particular spot. Underwritings of new issues do not take place on the floor of an organized exchange. Rather, the marketplace is the conference rooms of investment banking firms, linked by telephone with each other, with corporations and with ultimate investors. Second, the most important commodity sold by these market-makers is information; information about the yield required to sell an issue and who are the likely buyers. That's one of the most important functions of markets—dissemination of price and trading information. To market the new issue, investment bankers also sell the services of their capital—buying the issue outright from the corporation, thereby ensuring that the firm pays only the agreed-upon yield. Subsequent adverse or favorable yield movements do not affect the issuing firm, just the vacation prospects of the investment bankers.

A second interesting observation focuses on the name "investment bankers." These firms can be just about anything except bankers. They do not issue demand deposits or saving deposits; nor do they make commercial loans. Indeed, commercial banks are prohibited by law from participating in underwritings of corporate securities. The Banking Act of 1933, as we saw in Chapter 9, more popularly known as the Glass-Steagall Act, separated commercial banking and investment banking, where the latter refers specifically to issuing, underwriting, selling, or distributing stocks and bonds of private corporations. Commercial banks do participate in underwriting the general obligations of states and cities; that's supposedly a safer venture. They also originate commercial loans and mortgages, sharing the latter new-issue function with savings and loan associations and mortgage bankers.[2] But commercial banks cannot underwrite corporate obligations. Underwriting and banking operations are separated by law; only the overlapping nomenclature remains from pre-Glass-Steagall days.

The near invisibility of primary markets, compared with the immense popular recognition of secondary markets for equities, does not change the fact that both serve essential functions. Moreover, there is a close interrelationship between yields on securities in secondary markets and primary markets. One important clue to the required new-issue yield on a corporation's bonds, for example, is the recent yield on the firm's obligations in the secondary market. How

---

[2] Mortgage bankers are financial firms that originate mortgages by lending to homeowners. They do not hold these mortgages, rather, they are sold to ultimate investors such as insurance companies. Mortgage bankers do for mortgages what investment bankers do for corporate bonds and stocks.

useful these yields are depends, in part, upon the "quality" of secondary market yields. Are they close to equilibrium prices or do they reflect one or two transactions that might not be representative? Only by recognizing the nature of the secondary market can the yields recorded there be evaluated. Let's start by describing some alternative types of market structure.

Equity Trading: Auctions and Dealers

The New York Stock Exchange is the most visible secondary market, in part because equities of the largest corporations are traded there. But high visibility comes, also, from the fact that you can actually see the marketplace. Trading takes place on the floor of the exchange, located at 20 Broad Street. Business is conducted by members of the exchange—those who own proverbial seats (at one time there were actual seats, but these have long since gone the way of the convertible). Transactions are recorded on the ticker tape, flashed on the floor itself as well as in brokerage offices throughout the country. This is a real marketplace, the same as the county fair, except it's a lot noisier. Nothing is left to the imagination, as is necessary in telephone markets.

Individual stocks are traded at particular locations, called posts, on the football-field floor. Traders receiving orders via telephone from brokerage offices throughout the country scurry about placing orders with particular specialists. It is the job of the specialist to maintain orderly trading for the securities he is in charge of. He can simply match publicly tendered buy and sell orders submitted at the same price. Floor traders stand at the post and bid for orders that are not matched in the specialist's "book." When none of these occur, the specialist steps in and buys for his own account (at his bid price) or sells from his inventory (at his asked price) to prevent excessive gyrations in transactions prices, and hopefully to make a handsome profit. Thus trading through specialists on the floor of the exchange is a hybrid between an open auction and dealer trading.

Stock exchanges in the United States are all modeled along these lines. In addition to the NYSE there is the American Stock Exchange (Amex), the Midwest Stock Exchange, and so on, as indicated in Table 1. As shown in the table, each exchange has its own listings—

TABLE 1
Number of Securities Listed on Exchanges
(December 31, 1977)

	Equities	Bonds
American	1,047	184
Boston	72	1
Cincinnati	6	6
Midwest	19	1
New York	1,513	2,658
Pacific	41	18
Philadelphia (PBW)	30	12
Intermountain	29	0
Spokane	24	0

Source: Securities and Exchange Commission, *Statistical Bulletin.*

securities which are traded primarily on it. Smaller companies are generally listed on the Amex and the regionals. Shares of large NYSE-listed companies are also frequently traded on regional exchanges, as can be seen in Table 2.

TABLE 2
Average Daily Volume in NYSE Listed Securities
(December 1977)

	Number of Shares (in thousands)
New York	21,474
Midwest	1,164
Pacific	731
NASD	1,032
Phila (PBW)	368
Boston	146
American	1
Cincinnati	199
Instinet*	23

* See footnote 6 below.
Source: Securities and Exchange Commission, *Statistical Bulletin.*

The markets are knitted together by electronic communications. Inter-market trading has reached a stage that effectively integrates these geographically separate market centers. Price discrepancies between General Motors quoted on the NYSE and on the Midwest exchange are arbitraged away within seconds. That means, if the price of General Motors were $50 on the NYSE but is quoted at $51 on the Midwest, an immediately profitable and riskless transaction (arbitrage) can be executed: buy at $50 in New York and sell at $51 in Chicago (that's where the Midwest Exchange is). The buying on the NYSE forces up the price, the selling on the Midwest forces down the price—with the process ending only when the prices are equalized.

Such price discrepancies rarely emerge nowadays. The regionals and the New York exchange are closely integrated. We have moved towards a national market system as mandated by Congressional legislation in 1975, although there are some further steps that might be undertaken.[3]

While exchanges nominally conduct auctions, we've just seen that specialists sometimes act as dealers—buying and selling for their own account. The vast majority of common stocks do, in fact, trade in dealer markets. To be sure, these over-the-counter (OTC) securities are usually smaller than exchange-listed stocks, with less trading interest. But currently there are nearly 2,500 stocks traded under the Automated Quotation System of the National Association of Securities Dealer, called NASDAQ. And this might be very much closer to the future of securities markets than exchange-based trading.

Trading in OTC securities used to be a relatively haphazard operation, especially when compared with organized exchanges. Individual broker/dealer firms bought and sold OTC securities for their own account—they acted as dealers. For some OTC stocks, like Anheuser-Busch and Tampax, at least half a dozen firms made a market —that is, they quoted bid and asked prices that brokers could rely upon when selling or buying for their customers. For smaller OTC securities, perhaps, only one or two firms made a market. If you placed an order with your fortune-telling stockbroker to buy Fly-by-Night Air, Inc., he would call one or two dealers, get the lowest offer, and execute the trade. But you and he could never be sure that it was the best offer— and only you really cared. One of the problems with OTC dealer markets is that trades are not automatically exposed to public bidding —as on the floor of an exchange. Moreover, the only record of market making appeared in daily pink sheets, which recorded (on pink paper) bids and offers (not trades) towards the end of the day.

Dealers still quote bids and offers on OTC securities, but just about everything else changed for the larger OTC securities when NASDAQ was introduced in 1971. TV screens replaced telephones as the communications mechanism. Market makers now enter bids and offers via a terminal linked to the NASDAQ computer, and these quotes are flashed to subscribing brokerage offices throughout the country. The hunt-and-peck method of uncovering the best bids and offers has given way to computer search—a far more efficient tech-

[3] Movement towards a centralized market started back in 1975 when the consolidated ticker-tape began reporting trades of NYSE-listed securities no matter where they were executed. Among the steps that remain to be taken: automated execution of trades based on most favorable price quotations.

nique. There were measurable improvements in the performance of OTC stock trading, as we'll see below.

A word about stockbrokers is in order. They are usually the closest contact an individual has with the stock market. Yet, in the purest sense of the word, they act only as agents, as your agent in executing your orders to buy and sell securities. They are not auctioneers, nor are they dealers in most securities. They charge a commission for filling your order at the best price. They have a fiduciary responsibility to get you the best deal. There are therefore potential conflicts of interest if your stockbroker's firm is also a dealer in an OTC security you want to sell (or buy). Legally and morally, he shouldn't sell to his firm unless it is the best bidder. But it is often difficult to monitor such responsibilities.

Bond Trading: Dealers and Brokers

The existence of New York Stock Exchange bond trading is one of the better-kept secrets on Wall Street. Compared with the immense visibility of stock transactions, bond trading is virtually invisible—even though NYSE bond transactions are recorded in the financial press alongside the stock tables. The low profile of bond transactions stems from two factors: (1) the overwhelming proportion of bond trading takes place over-the-counter, through market-making dealers; (2) bonds are held primarily by institutional investors, rather than individuals. Both of these obscure bond trading from public view.

While the bonds of some large corporations are listed on the NYSE, most corporate issues and virtually all U.S. Government, federal agency, and municipal bonds are traded over-the-counter. As shown in Table 3, the volume of OTC trading in Treasuries and agencies simply dwarfs bond trading on the NYSE.

The telephone is still the dominant mechanism for uncovering the best bids and offers of the numerous bond-dealing firms. On the other hand, most dealers maintain extensive computer-based information systems to record the holdings of bonds by ultimate investors (insurance companies, pension funds, and other institutions). This helps the dealer unearth buyers and sellers when needed.

There are so many individual corporate debt issues, that trades in a particular bond are often days or weeks apart. It does not really pay to invest in highly automated trading facilities when the volume of

TABLE 3
Comparative Stock and Bond Volume for 1977

Security	Volume
Treasuries (OTC)	Average Daily Volume of $10.8 billion; Approximate Annual Volume (assuming 250 trading days per year) = $2.7 trillion
Agencies (OTC)	Average Daily Volume of $693 million; Approximate Annual Volume (assuming 250 trading days per year) = $173.2 billion
Bonds—NYSE	Annual Volume of $4.5 billion
Equities—NYSE	5.9 billion shares traded for the year; approximate value (at an average price of 51 per share) of $300.9 billion
Equities—OTC (NASDAQ)	1.9 billion shares for the year; approximate value (even at $51 per share) of $96.9 billion

Sources: Federal Reserve Bulletin; Wall Street Journal.

transactions does not warrant the huge outlay and when the urgency for *immediate* transactions capability is lessened by the comparative stability of bond prices.

The exception is the government bond market. The volume of trading is so large (see Table 3) that computer-based trading and sophisticated communications technology now dominate the market-place. Dealers can supplement their telephone surveillance of other dealers with electronic monitoring of quotations in the brokers' market. Dealer quotes are closely intertwined by the relatively easy search process. The brokers' communications network has just about annihilated whatever fragmentation existed for large institutional investors in government bonds. If you trade in million-dollar round lots, there's virtually one marketplace.

Unlike dealers, brokers act purely as middlemen—never buying or selling for their own account—merely matching buy and sell orders. The broker actively searches for compatible trading partners, rather than passively accepting (as would a pure auctioneer) only tendered bids and offers. On the other hand, brokerage is less risky than dealing because there is no inventory to worry about. Thus the rewards to brokerage are commensurately less. Brokers earn a living by the sweat of their brow; dealer earnings must also cover the cost of ulcers.

Electronic linkage in the government securities market is provided by the brokerage firm of Garvin Guy Butler, through a subsidiary known as Garban. Bids and offers are flashed on TV terminals to the more than 35 dealers in governments. The bids can be "hit" and the offers "taken" by telephoning the office of Garban. Thus, while technology permits instantaneous search of the market, it does not, as yet, permit electronic trading.

Most other trading in the OTC bond market is still done via telephone search·among various dealer firms. An investor can search by himself—such as a life insurance company portfolio manager telephoning a number of bond dealers to locate the best bid for a corporate bond it has decided to sell. Alternatively, a property and casualty insurance company might turn to a broker in the municipal bond market to search for the most favorable price on a particular purchase or sale. Brokers in the municipal bond market typically accumulate these purchase and sale interests early during a trading day, disseminate them via teletype to their customers, and then hope for a matching set of interests. Most investors are sufficiently patient to wait at least until the end of the day before deciding where to buy or sell. Their patience is encouraged by the stability of municipal bond prices (relative to, say, common stocks) and the stiff price penalty they'd probably incur by trading with their first contact.

Money Market Trading

Short-term debt instruments, such as Treasury bills and municipals under one year to maturity, trade in the OTC market just like their longer-term relatives. So do negotiable bank certificates of deposit (CDs) and bankers acceptances. These are very active markets, with numerous dealers quoting bids and offers. It pays a trader to shop around to get the best deal—not so much because of the wide discrepancies in market quotes but because the huge dollar amounts make even small price differentials worth the extra time and effort.

Commercial paper, the short-term debt of prime-rated corporations, does not trade in a secondary market. Rather, if an investor would like to sell his paper before it comes due, he turns to the issuer who stands ready (usually) to redeem before maturity. Companies that employ dealers to sell their commercial paper are absolved of this nuisance; the dealer usually makes a limited secondary market—agreeing to buy back paper from its customers only.

The most unique form of trading structure is in the shortest of all money market instruments—Federal funds. These are unsecured one-day obligations of a commercial bank. The borrowing bank buys Federal funds and the lending bank sells Federal funds, with the transfer occurring immediately (same-day funds). There is, in essence, only a primary market. Banks deal directly with each other in buying and selling, with large money-market banks doing most of

Latest Financial Technology.

the buying. There are two major federal funds brokers: Garvin Guy Butler and Mabon Nugent. They match purchase and sale orders communicated to them via telephone.

The unique aspect of the operation is that a seller (lender) of Federal funds must approve of the buyer (borrower) because the latter has an unsecured obligation to repay the funds on the following day.[4] That's why Fed funds can't be resold—they are not negotiable. I might not mind if Citibank owed me money but would not have relished the thought of their transferring that obligation to Franklin National Bank on the eve of that bank's demise. Thus, even if the price is right, Fed funds brokers must check with the parties involved before completing a transaction. Fed funds brokers must try harder for some banks than for others.

[4] Overnight repurchase agreements with government bonds accomplish the same transfer of funds but with the bonds serving as security. The Federal funds market and the RP market are alternative sources of overnight funds for banks (see Chapter 9). The yields on these two sources move quite closely together. If they didn't, banks would arbitrage between the two markets, bringing their yields together—much as the prices of GM in New York and Chicago are held together.

Mortgage Trading: A New Industry

The secondary market for mortgages would be virtually nonexistent if it weren't for government intervention. As mentioned in Chapter 27 and towards the end of the previous chapter, the Federal National Mortgage Association and the Federal Home Loan Mortgage Corporation buy mortgages from savings and loan associations, savings banks, and mortgage bankers. But there's virtually no trading in individual mortgages. There just aren't any buyers.

The main difficulty with mortgages is the diversity of individual characteristics and the relatively small size of each issue. These preclude active market-making. A dealer would be inundated with unwanted detail if he bought and sold individual mortgage loans.

Along came the Department of HUD's Ginnie Mae (Government National Mortgage Association) and announced in 1971 that it would insure the timely payment of interest and principal on bundles of FHA-VA insured mortgages. These had to be at least $1 million lots of standardized individual mortgages—government insured, identical coupon, with a servicing fee paid to the originator of the mortgage to collect and "pass through" the interest and principal to the ultimate investor. Dealers viewed these "pass through" instruments as quite similar to bonds and began to quote bids and offers on them. The volume outstanding of these neatly wrapped mortgages grew to more than $50 billion by 1978. Trading became extremely active. The underlying mortgages thus gained marketability by disappearing into a package.

Conventional mortgages have recently joined their FHA-VA cousins in the pass-through parade. The Federal Home Loan Mortgage Corporation issues participation certificates in conventionals and a number of private firms, led by the Bank of America, have issued pass-throughs backed by conventional mortgages. The once-nonexistent secondary market for mortgages now flourishes under the multicolored packaging of pass-throughs and participation certificates.

Efficiency of Secondary Market Trading

Now that the major forms of market organization have been described, we can ask the big question: Do they measure up? How well do the various financial markets match buyers and sellers? The general criterion for performance was described earlier in the chapter: transactions prices should hover about the true equilibrium price. Since we never observe the latter, a number of proxy performance measures are used—the most popular of which is the bid-asked spread. But as we'll see, there's much more to a good performance than narrow bid-asked spreads.

Figure 1 illustrates the relationship between the bid-asked spread and the theoretical equilibrium. Sellers on the supply curve and buyers

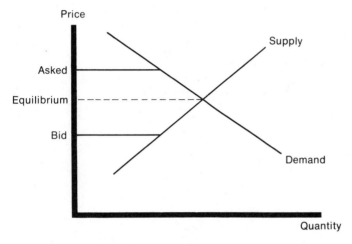

FIGURE 1 / Bid-asked spreads cause actual transactions prices to hover about the true equilibrium price.

on the demand curve could transact at the equilibrium price if they waited for each other. Impatient sellers are confronted by the bid price by a dealer who hopes to turn around and sell at the asked price to anxious buyers. The spread is the dealer's reward for holding what he's bought even though he doesn't want it. As is obvious from the figure, a smaller spread means that transactions prices will be closer to the equilibrium price.

The dealer will quote a narrow bid-asked spread if: (1) the expected volume of transactions is large; and (2) if the anticipated risk of large price changes is low. Large volume means it's easy to turn over inventory since there are frequent orders to buy and sell. Low volatility of price changes means that the risk exposure of the dealer's inventory is small. Both mean the dealer can be forced to quote narrow bid-asked spreads and still stay in business—committing his capital and skill to market making. Since dealers are no more benevolent than the rest of us, the element forcing dealers to quote narrow spreads is competitive pressure.

Table 4 shows a number of sample bid-asked quotations from the *Wall Street Journal*. First some basic explanations of the numbers. All bonds are quoted as a percent of par. Thus, on December 20, 1978, the Treasury 8 percent coupon notes due in May 1980 could be sold at $97\frac{2}{32}$ (the bid price) per $100 face value and could be bought at $97\frac{6}{32}$ (the asked price) per $100 face value. Since minimum denominations of most notes and bonds are $1,000, that means it costs $971.875 to

TABLE 4

Name of Market	Particular Issue		Bid	Ask	Spread
	Coupon	Maturity			
1. *Governments and Agencies*					
Treasury Note	8	May 1980	$97\frac{2}{32}$	$97\frac{6}{32}$	$\frac{1}{8}$
Treasury Bond	$7\frac{7}{8}$	Feb 1993	$90\frac{18}{32}$	$90\frac{26}{32}$	$\frac{1}{4}$
GNMA	$8\frac{1}{2}$	—	$92\frac{2}{32}$	$93\frac{10}{32}$	$\frac{1}{4}$
Federal Home Loan Bond	$7\frac{3}{8}$	Nov 1993	$85\frac{8}{32}$	$86\frac{8}{32}$	1
2. *Tax Exempts*					
Dallas Fort Worth Airport	$6\frac{1}{4}$	2002	92	95	3
Massachusetts	9	2001	$121\frac{1}{2}$	$123\frac{1}{2}$	2
Munic Asst Corp of NY	8	1986	98	100	2
3. *OTC Stocks*					
Anheuser-Busch		—	$23\frac{3}{4}$	$24\frac{1}{4}$	$\frac{1}{2}$
Tampax		—	$27\frac{3}{4}$	$28\frac{3}{4}$	1
Wiener Corp		—	19	21	2

Source: *Wall Street Journal*, December 20, 1978.

buy while I get $970.625 if I sell a $1,000 Treasury note. The spread (asked minus bid) recorded in the last column is $\frac{1}{8}$ or 12.5 cents per $100, or $1.25 per $1,000 transaction. In other words, if I bought a $1,000 Treasury note and decided to sell immediately because I just got a hot stock tip, it would cost $1.25 for my schizophrenia. A $2,000 round trip, as they call it, costs $2.50, a $3,000 trade, $3.75 and so on. This is a measure of the liquidity costs of the security: the transactions costs of buying and selling.

As can be seen in the first few lines of the table, government notes, bonds and GNMAs have very small bid-asked spreads. The short-term Treasury note has the narrowest spread—suggesting correctly that short-term money market instruments have the most liquid market.

The long-term bond of the Federal Home Loan Bank Board has a 1 point spread—or $10 per $1,000 bond, compared with the $\frac{1}{4}$ point or $2.50 per $1,000 round-trip transaction in the similar maturity

Treasury bond. This suggests that federal agency bonds have less liquidity than Treasury obligations. Which is true.

The tax exempt market in the second section of the table indicates $20 and $30 round-trip costs for long-term municipals. The liquidity is much less than either the Treasury market or the agency market.

The explanation for the variation in the spreads lies primarily in the volume of trading in the particular issues. Short-term Treasury bills and notes are more actively traded than Treasury bonds. GNMA volume is greater than agency trading, while the individual municipal issues trade most infrequently.

The last section of Table 4 records the bids and offers for three OTC securities. The shares of Anheuser-Busch trade on a ½-point spread, Tampax trades on a 1-point spread and Wiener Corporation on a 2-point spread. Like point spreads in football, these quotations must be scrutinized before jumping to costly conclusions. It would seem, for example, that Anheuser-Busch has a smaller liquidity cost than the Federal Home Loan Bond. In fact, the reverse is the case. Quotations in the equity market are *per share*. Thus, to buy 100 shares of Anheuser costs $2,425 (24¼ times 100), with an immediate sale netting $2,375. Thus the cost is $50 for a $2,400 transaction. A $3,000 round trip in the agency market costs only $30. The lesson is clear: bid-asked spreads must be related to the price of the security and the implied cost of trading or liquidating a fixed dollar amount. The two other OTC stocks are still worse compared with *any* of the bond markets: A round trip of about $2,800 in Tampax comes to $100 and a taste of Wiener Corp costs $200 per $2,000 trade. In general, higher bid-asked spreads on equities versus bonds reflect the greater risk of price fluctuation a dealer is exposed to.

But there's more to the story than bid-asked spreads.[5] For one thing, we haven't mentioned bid-asked spreads on the organized exchanges. The reason is that they aren't published in the newspapers even though a specialist will quote a spread at his post. Eastman Kodak, a very active NYSE security, was selling at about $60 on December 20, 1978, and was quoted on a spread of no more than ¼. That's $25 per $6,000 round trip or $12.50 per $3,000—not much more than it would cost to trade $3,000 in Treasury bonds—and considerably less than the liquidity cost in the agency market. For trades

---

[5] Even the bid-asked spread itself is not as unambiguous as it seems. In competitive dealer markets, bids and offers are quoted by each market-maker. The quotations in Table 4 are averages. Unless all quotes are identical, a potential trader is confronted with price dispersion. It pays to search among dealers for the most favorable quote, but this search adds to the cost of executing a trade. See Kenneth D. Garbade and William L. Silber, "Price Dispersion in the Government Securities Market" *Journal of Political Economy* (August 1976).

of that size, equities are just about as liquid, if not more so, than Treasury or agency securities.

The real difference between liquidity in Treasuries or agencies compared with *any* equity lies in the size of transaction that can be handled without causing either a widening of the bid-asked spread or a shift up (in the case of a buy) or down (for a sale) in the implicit equilibrium price. Quotes in equities must be good for at least a round lot—100 shares. Quotes in the Treasury market must also be good for a round lot—either $1 million or $500,000 in face value. A $5 million order in Treasuries can also be filled without much trouble. But for equities, there's simply no way to liquidate a $5 million block of stock —or even a $1 million position—without causing the specialist to back away after the purchase of 100 or 200 shares. Thus the bid-asked spread measures the liquidity cost of normal-sized transactions, and what's normal in the Treasury and agency markets would be abnormal in any common stock. In fact, blocks of stock are not brought to the auction market on the exchange floor unless a trade has been arranged beforehand by dealers. While the public auction of organized exchanges looks good and has distinct advantages, it simply cannot handle the large trades of institutional investors.[6]

This discussion suggests a somewhat more sophisticated measure of market performance; one that focuses on the ability of a market to absorb large trading volume without causing wild gyrations in transactions prices. The qualitative description of such markets is relatively easy: they have breadth, depth, and resiliency. A market is deep if it is easy to uncover buy and sell orders above and below current transactions prices; if these orders exist in large volume, then the market has breadth; if new orders quickly pour in when prices move up or down, the market is called resilient.

All of these characteristics imply low transactions price volatility. For example, even if a dealer's bid and asked quotes are good for 100 shares only, if a larger purchase order produces sales from the crowd surrounding an exchange trading post or causes institutions that continuously monitor dealer quotes to call in sell orders, then prices won't gyrate much. Markets which are *not* broad, deep, and resilient are called thin markets; only a small volume of trading can be absorbed without producing wide price swings.

Having said all that, there's not much else to do. There just aren't any good measures of this aspect of liquidity. Simply looking at price

---

[6] Institutional investors can trade among themselves through a computerized brokerage service called Instinet. Trading interests are recorded via computer terminal and then transmitted to other subscribing institutions. When there is a match, the trade is recorded and executed.

volatility is not enough—part of everyday price movements are equilibrium price changes and do not reflect poorly on a market's liquidity. One important observation can be made, however, concerning the impact of communications technology on the ability of any market to absorb large orders without becoming "disorderly." Traders who can continuously monitor quotations on TV screens like NASDAQ or Garban can participate more quickly in buying and selling if prices deviate from their view of equilibrium. When prices fall, they buy; when prices rise, they sell. This very process contributes to price stability and liquidity. Moreover, once in place, the reduction in price volatility also leads to narrower bid-asked spreads, since dealer inventories are subject to less risk.[7]

We have extended our discussion of secondary market trading efficiency, marketability and liquidity to the point of no return. Price changes should be small when trading is motivated by liquidity needs; that's the characteristic of highly marketable securities. But new information affecting the underlying value of the security should be reflected quickly in equilibrium price changes. Indeed, if prices of financial assets did not reflect news about bankruptcies, earnings trends, lawsuits, and whatever else affects the payments promised by the issuer of the financial instrument, then the market would be inefficient. Some call this aspect of a market allocational efficiency. Until now we have analyzed the operational efficiency of financial markets. Actually, the popular discussion of "efficient capital markets" focuses on allocational efficiency, without calling it by that name. We discussed some aspects of efficient capital markets in Chapter 6 in the context of portfolio theory. We'll add a few thoughts on the subject in the next section, within the framework of regulation of securities markets.

Efficient Capital Markets and Regulation

A vast literature has developed during the past fifteen years based on a relatively straightforward proposition: the current price (hence: expected yield) of a security fully reflects all publicly available in-

---

[7] See Anthony Santomero, "The Economic Effects of NASDAQ: Some Preliminary Results," *Journal of Financial and Quantitative Analyses* (January 1974), for evidence that NASDAQ significantly reduced bid-asked spreads on OTC securities.

formation. Put somewhat differently: there is no unexploited information whose recognition would lead to superior investment performance. If securities prices fully reflect all available information, the capital market is called efficient.

It's hard to argue with the statement that markets will be efficient. If securities prices didn't reflect all publicly available information, market pressures would quickly force them to do so. Suppose a news flash that an OTC-traded company discovered how to make oil out of used textbooks were ignored by dealers. Everyone else would find the price of the security relatively cheap in view of the fantastic profits the company will reap. Buy orders pour into brokerage offices and sell orders disappear. Dealers will meet their commitment to sell 100 shares at the old price and then would more than double the quoted asking price to avoid selling what they don't have at ridiculously low prices. As soon as the dealer quotes a price sufficiently high to reflect the rosy profit outlook, buy orders drop to normal (the security is no longer such a bargain), sell orders reappear (let's take some profits), and the new equilibrium price fully reflects all publicly available information.

There's nothing wrong with that story. It happens all the time. The problem arises in the implications for buying and then selling securities. The implication is: don't trade. If prices quickly incorporate all information affecting the fortunes of a company, then you can't earn above-average returns by selling so-called overvalued securities or buying undervalued ones. There aren't any bargains. Moreover, the fancy charts sold by investment advisers, suggesting that you buy when the price of a stock rises by 5 or 10 percent, aren't worth the paper they are printed on.

Needless to say, securities analysts have little use for such academic ranting and raving. How quickly do you think markets absorb new information? Within a day or two is the best estimate of academic researchers.[8] If that's the case, there is little to gain from buying or selling after reading the investment bulletins of your favorite brokerage house. By the time you've finished, there's nothing to do but watch which way the price of your security went.

Allegations that manipulation, deception, and misinformation helped turn the 1929 stock market collapse into a national disaster led Congress to enact the Securities and Exchange Act of 1934. The Act provided for the establishment of the Securities and Exchange Commission to prevent fraud and promote equitable and fair operations in

---

[8] One of the first articles testing market efficiency is Eugene Fama, Lawrence Fisher, Michael Jensen and Richard Roll, "The Adjustment of Stock Prices to New Information" *International Economic Review* (February 1969). For a general review see Eugene Fama, "Efficient Capital Markets," *Journal of Finance* (May 1970).

securities markets. The focal point of SEC regulations is the disclosure of information that might be relevant for the pricing of securities. There are two major aspects of disclosure requirements: (1) In the primary markets, corporations issuing new securities must file a registration statement with the SEC, disclosing all information that might be pertinent to investors; (2) In secondary markets, no person, especially corporate insiders, may trade on nonpublic information.

Our discussion of market efficiency made specific reference to publicly available information. It's quite possible—indeed, quite probable—that nonpublicly available information can be used to make extra profits or avoid undesirable losses. The SEC insists that no investor should be at a disadvantage when purchasing or selling securities. Not only must there be full disclosure of all pertinent information, but misinformation and dissemination of false or misleading reports are specifically prohibited.

The SEC's job is not an easy one. It has enlisted the aid of the various organized exchanges and the National Association of Securities Dealers in supervising brokers, dealers, and transactions in secondary markets. The exchanges and the NASD take these disciplinary and supervising responsibilities seriously. And with good reason. The specter of more detailed SEC involvement in day-to-day operations is more than enough to encourage vigorous self-regulation.

It would be a mistake, however, to assume that manipulation, fraud, misinformation, and deception have disappeared from financial transactions simply because the SEC plays watchdog. Markets are efficient because investors and traders scrutinize and search and screen all information for themselves. *Caveat emptor et venditor* are still the watchwords that ensure market efficiency.

Exotica: Options and Futures

Regulatory supervision of the stock and bond markets is undergoing severe testing because of the proliferation of trading in put and call options, as well as the successful innovation of futures contracts for financial assets. Neither options nor futures are new inventions. Puts and calls have traded in OTC markets since the nineteenth century, and organized commodities exchanges have traded agricultural futures for at least as long. But in the mid-1970s put and call options were standardized and trading was inaugurated on the Chicago Board Options Exchange (CBOE) and then on the American Stock Exchange.

Futures in financial instruments were innovated by the Chicago Board of Trade, the major commodity futures exchange, followed closely by the Chicago Mercantile Exchange.

Trading activity in options and financial futures skyrocketed in recent years, causing the SEC, the Federal Reserve, and the U.S. Treasury to worry about the implications of options on stocks and futures on bonds for the underlying markets. First let's briefly describe options and futures on financial assets and then turn to the legitimacy of government concern.

An option contract confers the right to buy or sell a particular stock at a specified price (the exercise or striking price) within a certain time interval. A call option gives the right to buy (call the stock) and a put option the right to sell (put the stock). Examples are: a call option to buy 100 shares of Eastman Kodak at a price of $70 per share (the exercise price) expiring 6 months from now, or a put option to sell 100 shares of Kodak at a price of $70 expiring 6 months from now.

How much, if anything, are such options worth? Well, if Kodak's stock price increases to $80, the call option is worth at least $10—because I can take it to the writer (seller) of the option and demand the stock for $70—which I could then immediately sell on the New York Stock Exchange for $80. The call option confers at least $10 in capital gains. The put option won't be worth very much since Kodak stock sells for $80, hence a contract conferring the right to sell the stock at $70 has little value. But if Kodak's price had dropped to $50, then the put option at $70 would be worth quite a bit—at least $20. The reason is: I can buy the stock at $50 on the New York Stock Exchange, take it to the writer (seller) of the put option and he must buy the stock at $70—the put entitles me to a capital gain of $20 if I choose to exercise (execute) the contract. The possibility of stock prices fluctuating up and down, plus the right to exercise the contract, give value to put and call options.

Despite rumors to the contrary, a futures contract is not an option. It is a firm agreement to deliver, at some future date, a standardized product. The price at which delivery is to be made is agreed upon now. The buyer of the futures contract is entitled to receive the product and the seller is bound to deliver it. In financial futures, the product to be delivered is securities: $1 million in U.S. Treasury bills, $100,000 in GNMAs, and so on. The precise maturity of the bills and the coupon of the GNMAs are specified beforehand.

The prices of futures contracts can fluctuate considerably. Let's make believe it's May (seasonally adjusted, that's an especially nice month). You buy a futures contract to receive next September a three-month Treasury bill. Let's say the agreed-upon price is 98—reflecting a currently expected yield of about 8 percent per annum. If Treasury bills drop in yield to 4 percent between now and September, then the futures contract you bought at 98 rises in price—to about 99. The reason is: the futures contract you bought entitles you to receive, from the writer (seller), $1 million in Treasury bills. In September, 3-month Treasury bills are, in fact, selling for 99—reflecting a yield of 4 percent per annum. That's precisely what your futures contract is worth in September. If that weren't the case—say your futures contract still sold for 98—sharp-eyed arbitrageurs would buy contracts for September delivery at 98 in the futures market, exercise the contracts, and immediately sell the bills in the Treasury bill market for 99. This arbitrage brings together the price of the futures contract and the spot price (in the underlying market) during the delivery month (September, in our example).

Futures contracts do not have to be exercised to realize a profit. You can sell your September contract for 99 without ever setting eyes on a Treasury bill. In fact the fellow who sold you the contract last May would be ready to buy it back. That way his obligation to deliver Treasury bills is canceled.

Despite clear differences in the contractual agreements, options and futures do share common features. Both are useful for speculation because they are highly leveraged instruments—that is, the amount of money that must be put up (to ensure that buyers and sellers honor their contracts) is small relative to the price swings that are experienced. Both are traded through clearing corporations which intervene between buyers and sellers—permitting each to concentrate on expected price movements and not on the reliability of the other party to fulfill the contractual obligation. Both options and futures fulfill legitimate economic functions—providing portfolio managers with additional opportunities for risk reduction.

But the most important common characteristic shared by options and futures is that each is suspected of potentially disrupting or destroying the spot markets for the commodities—in our case, the underlying stocks and bonds. Trading in stock options on the Chicago Board Options Exchange now surpasses trading in some underlying stocks on the NYSE. What will happen to the liquidity of stock trading? Will the options market dominate the stock market, with the proverbial tail wagging the dog? Do the futures markets in Treasury bills and GNMAs create greater instability in spot prices?

There is substantial concern by the Federal Reserve, the Treasury, and the SEC over these issues. All share a common interest in the viability of liquid and efficient secondary markets. But so far there is no empirical evidence demonstrating that options and futures are detrimental to the underlying financial markets. That doesn't, of course, mean these issues shouldn't be investigated most carefully. But it does mean that the regulators' reflex to curb financial innovations simply because they are new must be restrained. Until detrimental evidence is uncovered, it is best to follow the precept: let a thousand flowers bloom. Although it wasn't first enunciated to support innovative financial practices, it is a most appropriate maxim.

Suggestions for Further Reading

The classic article on the interrelationship between information and markets is George J. Stigler, "The Economics of Information," *Journal of Political Economy* (June 1961). Bid-asked spreads were brought into the picture by Harold Demsetz, in "The Cost of Transacting," *Quarterly Journal of Economics* (February 1968). A broad historical perspective on the impact of technology in financial markets is found in Kenneth D. Garbade and William L. Silber, "Technology, Communication and Performance of Financial Markets: 1840–1975," *Journal of Finance* (June 1978). An excellent description of the Government and agency markets is found in First Boston Corporation's *Handbook of Securities of the United States and Federal Agencies*. Finally, a fascinating glimpse of the underwriting process in action can be found in Ernest Bloch, "Pricing a Corporate Bond Issue: A Look Behind the Scenes," *Monthly Review* of the Federal Reserve Bank of New York (October 1961).

PART VIII

International Finance

Chapter 32

Money in International Finance

THE UNITED STATES has had a deficit in its international balance of payments almost every year since 1949, which, as everyone knows, is a Bad Thing. As a result we have lost more than half of our gold, and *this*, it goes without saying, is an even more Serious Matter. We were the proud owners of 700 million ounces of gold in 1949, and now we have only about 275 million ounces left.

What to do?

An international "balance of payments" is an accounting record of all payments made across national borders. In Chapter 33 we will examine the balance of payments in more detail, but for the moment it is enough to say that for each country it shows the payments made to foreigners and the receipt of funds from them, in the same way that a family might keep a record of all its expenditures and receipts. Americans make payments to others, for example, when we import foreign goods, buy foreign securities, lend to other countries, build factories on the outskirts of London or in the suburbs of Rome, or travel abroad on our summer vacations. On the other side of the ledger, we take in money when foreigners pay us for our exports, buy our stocks or bonds, build television factories in Illinois, or visit the Grand Canyon.

A deficit in our balance of payments is no different from a deficit in a household's budget. It means that we have been paying out more money abroad than we have been taking in, possibly because we have been importing more than we have been exporting, or because more Americans are visiting Paris and London than foreign tourists are taking in the sights of Yonkers and Yazoo City. Foreigners thereby accumulate more dollars than they need for their payments to us, and in the ordinary course of events—at least prior to August 15, 1971— many of these dollars were presented to the United States Treasury with a polite but firm request that they be exchanged for gold. Until August 15, 1971, the Treasury stood ready to honor, promptly if not happily, all official foreign requests at the rate of 1 ounce of gold for every $35 tendered, but on that date President Nixon got tired of paying out so much gold and called the whole deal off.

A nation can hardly run balance of payments deficits forever (although the United States does seem determined to prove otherwise). Sooner or later, after all, a country has to pay for its imports, and to do that it has to get the money from somewhere—for example, by borrowing from abroad or by selling some of its own products to others (i.e., by exporting). To that end, a number of suggestions are constantly made to cure our chronic deficit—to stop paying out more than we take in. One remedy that has often been proposed by many in the international financial community, and occasionally echoed by some here at home, is old-fashioned discipline, otherwise known as the time-honored hickory stick treatment.

The Discipline of the Balance of Payments

Balance of payments disciplinarians believe that to spare the rod is to spoil the child. Their recommendations as to how we should go about restoring equilibrium in our international accounts are appropriately strict. The Federal Reserve should administer the hickory stick by contracting the money supply and raising interest rates until tight money succeeds in reducing GNP and lowering wages and prices. It is difficult to estimate how much unemployment this might involve —perhaps 15 or 20 percent of the labor force, at a minimum.

With a depression-level GNP, the incomes of Americans would be so low that we would be hard put to afford such "luxuries" as travel abroad and the purchase of so many foreign products. In addition, there would be effects stemming from the change in prices here relative to prices abroad. With lower costs and prices in the United States, foreign goods become relatively more expensive, which discourages Americans from buying so many Volkswagens and Japanese transistor radios, thus reducing our imports. The lower price tags here would similarly encourage foreigners to buy more of our now cheaper goods and services, thereby expanding our exports. Less imports and more exports: we will be paying out less money abroad and taking in more, thus reducing and possibly eliminating our balance of payments deficit.

At the same time, it is expected that purely financial flows would reinforce these effects. The higher interest rates that tight money induces here would bring in some foreign money seeking our attractive-yielding securities, and domestic money that had formerly been invested in foreign securities would presumably now return home to buy bargain-priced American stocks and bonds.

This is called Defending the Dollar. Obviously it is not a pleasant process, involving as it does tight money to induce substantial unemployment—large enough to wring lower wages and prices out of the economy—and a shrinking GNP. It is clear that it is based on the well-known Rocky Marciano principle, that the best defense is a good offense: we defend the dollar by attacking the economy.[1]

Professor Marciano thus takes his place in the Annals of Economics, right behind Professor Phillips, of Phillips curve fame (see Chapter 23) and Professor E. J. Finagle, discoverer of Finagle's law ("Inanimate objects are out to get us"). Of course, like all firm discipline, the Marciano principle is administered reluctantly and only for our own good. Rest assured, it would hurt the Federal Reserve more than it would hurt the economy; the Federal Reserve said so itself when, on the basis of this sort of reasoning, it *raised* the discount rate from 1½ percent to 2½ percent on October 9, 1931 and then to 3½ percent on October 16, a week later. (By 1931 the Great Depression was something more than a speck on the horizon; GNP had already fallen 25 percent below its 1929 level, and unemployment had already risen to over 15 percent of the labor force.)

---

[1] For those of you too young to remember, Rocky Marciano (Rocco Francis Marchegiano) was world heavyweight boxing champion from September 1952 until he retired undefeated in April 1956. He never learned to box very well, but he didn't have to. He had 49 professional fights and won all of them, 43 by knockouts.

The Gold Standard

The gold standard, which was in effect throughout much of the Western world during the last half of the 1800s and the first few decades of the 1900s, represented the Marciano principle in action. What was the gold standard and how was it supposed to work?

Under the traditional gold standard, nations fixed the value of their money in terms of gold and stood ready to buy or sell gold freely at the established price. This necessarily resulted in a fixed exchange ratio of one nation's money in terms of another's, called the par (or parity) rate of exchange. Say the United States fixed 20 dollars an ounce as the price of gold and Great Britain decided upon 5 pounds an ounce: then the par rate of exchange would be 4 dollars for 1 pound, for both $4 and £1 could purchase equal amounts of gold.

This fixed rate of exchange was quite stable. It would not vary above or below par by more than the cost of shipping gold across the Atlantic. If an American importer of £100 worth of British goods (woolen underwear) found that he was being charged more than $400 plus gold shipping costs in order to get the 100 British pounds he needed to pay his supplier, he could always merely buy $400 worth of gold (20 ounces) from the U.S. Treasury and ship it to England at his own expense to discharge his obligation. Thus the price of a unit of foreign money could rise only to an upper limit, known as the gold export point, which was above the par of exchange by the amount of gold shipping costs.

Similarly, the price of foreign money could not fall below par by more than the cost of shipping gold. If an American exporter of $400 worth of snuffboxes to England found that he would be offered less than $400 minus gold shipping costs for the 100 British pounds he had coming, he could always simply request that 20 ounces of gold be shipped here at his expense. Thus the lower limit of the foreign exchange rate was called the gold import point.

Under the rules of the gold standard, the money supply of every nation was tied rigidly to its gold supply. The gold standard was then expected to be a self-equilibrating mechanism in which balance of payments deficits and surpluses are automatically corrected by flows of gold among nations. This gold flow mechanism was expected to work just like the hickory stick treatment. Say the United States had a deficit in its balance of payments because it had been importing more than it had been exporting. It would make up this deficit by shipping gold abroad. This would mean less gold here and more gold in Great Britain, which would decrease the money supply in the United States and increase the money supply in Great Britain. Tight money here and an enlarged money supply abroad would lead to lower prices and wages here and to higher prices and wages abroad. With lower prices and wages here relative to abroad, Americans would be discouraged from buying any more woolen underwear from England and the British would find our snuffboxes even better bargains than before. So our imports fall, our exports expand, and our balance of payments deficit is corrected. Precisely the same as the Marciano principle: We drive the domestic economy into recession in order to improve our international balance of payments![2]

This sacrifice of domestic stability on the alter of international stability led to the downfall of the gold standard in the early 1930s, and there is no likelihood that it will ever return. In this day and age no nation is about to abdicate control over its financial affairs in favor of gold or anything like it. Before the development of modern monetary and fiscal policies, government intervention to influence the economy was unknown; because they knew no better, nations suffered through depressions and inflations and simply waited for times to improve. But it is not possible to turn back the clock. It is an open question whether modern monetary-fiscal policies actually do more good than harm, but any administration that failed to take strong action to alleviate recessions and inflations—and tried to invoke gold as the reason for its inaction—would hardly remain long in office. Today monetary policy is expected to actively alter monetary and credit conditions to influence domestic economic activity, not to passively adapt to changes in our gold stock merely because it might restore equilibrium in our balance of international payments.

Nevertheless, one remnant of the gold standard did manage to hang on until rather recently—until 1973, as a matter of fact. At the end of World War II the nations of the world agreed to maintain

---

[2] Historically, a main function of the gold standard was to serve as a safeguard against inflation, by tying the money supply to gold and thereby providing an upper limit on the money-issuing power of the state. Insofar as governments of all sorts have a propensity to print excessive amounts of money in order to finance wars and circuses, it was thought that gold would play a useful role by forcing governments to live within their means. No more gold, no more money.

However, in reality gold has usually proved to be extremely unreliable in preventing inflation. Even in the good old days (remember them?), when coins were the sole circulating money, kings and princes found ways to circumvent any gold shortage by clipping the coins and changing the rules. And today, with most of our money in the form of demand deposits at commercial banks and with electronic money on the horizon, any conceivable connection between gold and the money supply is too tenuous to rely on as an effective means of preventing excessive monetary expansion. The need to prevent inflation is undeniable, but gold has never been dependable in that respect and is even less likely to be so today.

fixed and inflexible exchange rates, more or less as under the gold standard. This led to periodic financial crises, as we shall see in later chapters. Before turning to the performance of fixed exchange rates in the postwar period, however, let's examine another alternative: flexible (or floating) exchange rates.

Floating Exchange Rates

Another possible cure for a balance of payments deficit, one that does not clash so violently with the goals of high employment, stable prices, and economic growth, is to permit flexibility in the price of foreign money (or, what amounts to the same thing, in the foreign price of dollars). Say a Mexican peso costs Americans 5 cents and a French franc costs us 25 cents. Until early 1973, such prices of one kind of money in terms of another—or exchange rates—were rigidly fixed by international agreement under the overall supervision of the International Monetary Fund (IMF), an institution established at an international monetary conference held at Bretton Woods, New Hampshire, in 1944.

The IMF's main function was to oversee the stability of exchange rates, although it was really unable to prevent unilateral exchange rate alterations when nations individually decided it was in their self-interest to make such changes. From World War II until 1973 world monetary arrangements were based on a network of more or less fixed (or pegged) exchange rates, supervised by the IMF.

The alternative to a system of fixed exchange rates is to unpeg them, *and let them float freely in accordance with supply and demand conditions for each particular country's money.* An increase in the *supply* of Mexican pesos would lower their price, say from 5 cents to 4 cents a peso; an increase in the *demand* for French francs would raise their price, say from 25 cents to 30 cents a franc. This was not permitted under IMF monetary arrangements until 1973; actually, it wasn't *officially* permitted until 1976.

Remember that a deficit in our balance of payments means we are paying out more money abroad than we are taking in. American importers are paying out more dollars for Swiss cuckoo clocks and Scotch whisky than foreigners need to buy our exported Frisbees and Fords. Result: An excess supply of dollars (or an excess demand for foreign money, since you can look at it either way) builds up throughout the world.

When exchange rates are free to fluctuate in response to supply and demand, the excess supply of dollars—due to our spending so much abroad—depresses the price of dollars to foreigners. The dollar *depreciates* relative to other monies. (Instead of the French having to pay 4 francs to get a dollar, something *less* than 4 francs would get them that much of our money.)

Or you could look at the same thing from the other side of the transaction, in which case an excess supply of dollars translates into an excess demand for other monies. When we import toenail clippers from Hong Kong or hitchhike along the not-so-sunny coast of Portugal, we have to buy their money to make payments. You can either say we are supplying dollars or buying (demanding) foreign money. From the latter point of view, this excess demand for foreign money—due to our spending so much abroad—raises the price of foreign money to Americans. Other monies *appreciate* relative to the dollar. (Instead of Americans getting a franc for 25 cents, we would have to pay *more* to get 1 franc.)

This depreciation of the dollar (or appreciation of other monies) has two effects. First, dollars become cheaper for foreigners, so our goods and services automatically become less expensive for them even though our domestic price tags remain unchanged. After all, it makes no difference to them whether our goods are less expensive for them because our price tags are lower (the Marciano method) or because each United States dollar costs them less of their own money while our price tags stay the same (the flexible exchange rate method). In either case our goods are cheaper for foreigners to buy, and our exports are likely to expand.

Second, foreign monies now cost us more, so that foreign goods and services automatically become more expensive for us to buy. With foreign products costing us more, because foreign money costs more, our purchases from abroad—our imports—are likely to fall.

Thus the end results are the same as the Marciano route: more exports and less imports. We take in more francs and pesos as we receive payment for our enlarged exports, and pay out less dollars abroad because of our lower imports, thereby putting an end to both the deficit in our balance of payments and the depreciation of the dollar.[3] However, we achieve these results by letting exchange rates decline while keeping our economy stable, instead of by send-

[3] Actually, the price elasticities of our exports and imports are important here, but we will ignore this complication. If you want to dig further into such details, see the discussion of the Marshall-Lerner condition in any textbook on international economics. For an advanced treatment see Rudiger Dornbusch, "Currency Depreciation, Hoarding, and Relative Prices," *Journal of Political Economy* (July/August 1973).

ing the economy into a nosedive while keeping exchange rates stable.

Freely floating exchange rates are a sharp departure from international monetary arrangements as they existed prior to 1973. Until then, fixed exchange rates—called par values—ruled the roost. The 1973 crisis in international finance (to be discussed in Chapter 34) moved the world toward exchange rate flexibility. In January 1976 the IMF officially approved the present system of floating exchange rates.

Most academic economists, both Monetarist and Keynesian, lean toward floating exchange rates. Most bankers and government officials, on the other hand, seem to favor a system of fixed exchange rates; they argue that freely floating rates create so much uncertainty regarding the price of foreign money that *international* trade is seriously impaired. Advocates of rate flexibility reply that fixed rates often creat so much disruption at home—by forcing countries to adjust their economies instead of their exchange rates—that they seriously inhibit *domestic* trade (that is, GNP).

Since early 1973 flexible exchange rates have gained the upper hand. But the advocates of fixed rates have not given up the fight by any means; they are waiting in the wings, hoping that floating rates sink so that fixed rates can surface once again. We will explore fixed versus floating exchange rates further in Chapters 34 and 35; first, however, let's stop a moment and take a little closer look at the balance of payments.

Suggestions for Further Reading

Have we loaded the dice in favor of floating exchange rates? If you think so, you can redress the balance by reading Henry Wallich's "In Defense of Fixed Exchange Rates," which is reprinted in *Money and Economic Activity*, Lawrence S. Ritter, ed., 3rd ed. (Boston: Houghton Mifflin, 1967). Also see Paul Einzig, *The Case Against Floating Exchanges* (New York: St. Martin's, 1970), and M. A. van Meerhaeghe, *International Economics* (New York: Crane, Russak, 1972).

On the other side of the coin (i.e., in favor of floating rates), read Milton Friedman, "The Case for Flexible Exchange Rates," in his *Essays in Positive Economics* (University of Chicago Press, 1953). See also his *Dollars and Deficits* (Englewood Cliffs, N.J.: Prentice-Hall, 1968).

If you want to know more about how the gold standard really worked, read Arthur I. Bloomfield, *Monetary Policy Under the International Gold Standard, 1880–1914* (Federal Reserve Bank of New York, 1959).

Chapter 33

Balance of Payments Accounting

QUESTIONS ABOUT THE BALANCE of payments are asked so frequently that we feel it would be a service to mankind to correct at least a few of the major misconceptions that abound. For example, the question that arises most often is: "What color is the balance of payments?" Many people think it is purple, but that is wrong. It is generally wrong, anyway, because the balance of payments is purple only when the consumption function is lavender and, as you recall from Chapter 18, that is a special case. In fact, the balance of payments is usually a deep green, except when it has been left out in the rain too long.

The second most frequently asked question is that hardy old perennial: "How fat is the balance of payments?" It is often said that economists don't know much, and even if they do, who cares? But here is a perfect example to the contrary. Econometric studies show very clearly that the balance of payments is usually too thin for its own good, especially in the Western Hemisphere. It certainly could use more vitamins and yogurt.

The third question that comes up most often, usually at drive-in theaters, is: "Is the balance of payments male or female?" Since this is a family book, we would rather not go into that. (We know the answer; we just don't know how to say it so it won't offend anyone.)

And finally: "Does the balance of payments really balance?" The answer to that is definitely yes, unless it is shoved. But since most people seem to remain unconvinced, a further word of explanation is necessary.

Sources and Uses Once Again

Actually, a country's balance of payments is nothing more than a sector sources and uses of funds statement in disguise. Just as a sector sources and uses statement (Chapter 28) records a sector's receipts from and payments to other sectors, so a country's balance of international payments shows the country's receipts from and payments to other countries. The main difference is that in flow of funds accounting the sectors are subdivisions within a country (the household sector, the business sector, and so on), while in balance of payments accounting the sectors are divided into "our country" and "the rest of the world."

In principle we could construct a model balance of payments for a country, from the ground up, in exactly the same way we constructed our model sector sources and uses statement in Chapter 28. All you have to do is think about the United States as a sector, versus the rest of the world, and everything else follows just about the same way. In practice, however, things are a bit more complex, mainly because the entries in our balance of payments—as it is presented by the Department of Commerce—are artfully arranged so as to camouflage the fact that it is really nothing more than a simple sources and uses of funds statement. But lest you be too hard on the economists at the Department of Commerce for making life complicated, don't forget the ancient Buddhist adage: Simplicity is the enemy of Romance.

Without tearing aside the veil of mystery completely, let's return briefly to what we meant by sources and uses of funds when we were doodling with sector sources and uses statements back in Chapter 28:[1]

1. *Sources* of funds consist of (a) *current receipts;* (b) any *increase in a liability* item (borrowing); or (c) any *decrease in an asset* item (selling off assets, dishoarding).

2. *Uses* of funds consist of (a) *current expenditures;* (b) any *decrease in a liability* item (debt repayment); or (c) any *in-*

[1] See especially p. 445.

crease in an asset item—increased holdings of real assets (investment), financial assets (lending), or money (hoarding).

3. We concluded that *the sum of a sector's sources of funds must equal the sum of its uses of funds:* if a sector spends on current and capital goods more than its current receipts (deficit sector), it has to finance its deficit by borrowing, selling off assets, or dishoarding; if its consumption plus investment spending is less than its current income (surplus sector), it has no choice but to repay debts, lend, or hoard an amount equal to its surplus.

Sources and uses of funds have similar meanings and implications in a country's balance of international payments, except that now we have to adapt to the fact that in international transactions we are dealing with *another* country's money. A source or receipt of funds for us as a nation means we get an inflow of foreign money; a use or expenditure of funds for us as a nation means we part with foreign money, an outflow, as we spend abroad. So in international balance of payments accounting, sources and uses of funds become sources and uses of *foreign* monies.

What are some of our main *sources* of foreign money (or foreign exchange, as it is usually called)? Clearly, merchandise exports yield us foreign exchange. When your average Peruvian housewife subscribes to *Vogue,* she mails in some Peruvian money which can be taken to our local bank and changed into dollars. But the Peruvian money does not disappear; the U.S. bank now owns it. From the point of view of the U.S., as a nation, we have acquired foreign exchange. (A unit of Peruvian money is called a sol. Remember that. It will probably be on the final.)

The same thing applies if foreign tourists travel across the highways and byways of America in search of Paradise (Montana), Hell (Michigan), or Intercourse (Pennsylvania). They need American money if they are to get a Big Mac at McDonald's, and to get dollars they have to go to a bank and hand over some sucres, bahts, kyats, or leva—which are, respectively, the monies of Ecuador, Thailand, Burma, and Bulgaria. We similarly receive an inflow of foreign exchange when we export stocks or bonds (borrow from abroad), just as when we export goods—as when an oil sheik in Kuwait buys some U.S. Treasury bills or IBM stock (foreigners traditionally account for a little under 10 percent of the transactions on the New York Stock Exchange). In all these instances foreigners need to buy dollars, and in the process we as a nation acquire ownership of some of their kind of money.

519

Uses of funds on our balance of international payments come about when it is Americans who do the spending: when we import voodoo dolls from Haiti or love potions from Xanadu; when American tourists in blue jeans and headbands check in at the Sahara Hilton; and when Americans import stocks or bonds (lend to foreigners), as when we buy some United Kingdom Treasury bills in London. In all of these instances we have to pay with foreign money, so we go to a bank or currency exchange and buy pounds or francs or what have

TABLE 1

A Generalized Sources and Uses of Funds Approach to the Balance of Payments for the United States*

Uses of Foreign Exchange	Sources of Foreign Exchange
Current expenditures—as for:	*Current receipts*—as for:
Our merchandise imports	Our merchandise exports
U.S. tourist spending abroad	Foreign tourist spending here
Interest and dividends paid to people abroad	Interest and dividends received from abroad
Services rendered by foreign ships, airlines, etc.	Services rendered by U.S. ships, airlines, etc.
U.S. military spending abroad	Foreign military spending here
Unilateral transfers (gifts, remittances, etc.) from U.S.	Unilateral transfers (gifts, remittances, etc.) to U.S.
Decreases in liabilities (debt repayment)—such as:	*Increases in liabilities* (borrowing)—such as:
Reductions in foreign holdings of U.S. securities	Purchases by foreigners of U.S. securities
Reductions in foreign bank loans to U.S. companies	Increases in foreign bank loans to U.S. companies
Reductions in foreign holdings of U.S. money, in the form of either U.S. currency or demand deposits in U.S. banks	Increases in foreign holdings of U.S. money, in the form of either U.S. currency or demand deposits in U.S. banks
Increases in assets—such as:	*Decreases in assets*—such as:
Direct investment by American firms abroad (ownership interest)	Direct investment by foreign firms in the U.S. (ownership interest)
Our purchases of foreign securities (lending)	Reductions in our holdings of foreign securities
Increases in U.S. bank loans to foreign companies (lending)	Reductions in U.S. bank loans to foreign companies
Increases in our holdings of foreign money, in the form of either foreign currency or demand deposits in foreign banks (hoarding)	Reductions in our holdings of foreign money, in the form of either foreign currency or demand deposits in foreign banks (dishoarding)
And our purchases of gold	And our sales of gold

* In the more traditional presentations of the balance of payments, sources of foreign exchange are usually called credits (or plus items), and uses are called debits (or minus items).

you (or else use up some of the foreign exchange we have previously acquired). In the process, of course, foreigners acquire ownership of some of our kind of money.

In other words, the sources and uses of foreign exchange for the United States—our balance of international payments—correspond to the standard sources and uses of funds for a sector in domestic trade. Table 1 offers a somewhat formal presentation.

Does It Really Balance?

Does the balance of payments really balance? Of course it does. Just as on a sector sources and uses statement the sum of all a sector's sources of funds must equal the sum of all its uses, so on a nation's balance of international payments all the sources have to equal all the uses. The same logic applies to both.

Like a household, a country cannot incur a deficit by spending on current and capital goods more than its current receipts unless it finances that deficit by borrowing, selling off some assets, or drawing down its cash reserves.[2] It cannot incur a surplus by total spending less than current receipts without disposing of that surplus via debt repayment, lending, or building up its cash reserves (hoarding). In brief, if a country's uses are greater than its sources in some categories, then its sources must be correspondingly greater than its uses on the remainder of the statement.

If all this is so—if the balance of payments always balances— then why all the fuss? How can people keep talking about a deficit in our balance of payments, which implies an inequality, when such an inequality appears to be an impossibility?

Again, just like sector statements, it all depends on precisely what you are measuring. A sector's *total* sources must equal its *total*

---

[2] A complication arises in this connection with respect to certain kinds of direct foreign equity investment, similar to the complication regarding corporate equities and bonds mentioned in footnote 1 of Chapter 28. We resolved that problem by assuming that corporate stocks and bonds are roughly the same thing, and we will resolve this difficulty the same way.

Say that Volkswagen ships an entire automobile manufacturing plant, piece by piece, to Ohio. Our imports would rise, but we would *not* be financing this current deficit by borrowing, selling off assets, or dishoarding, since these imports are still owned by Germany. It is handled in the balance of payments accounts as a direct investment by foreigners in the United States (ownership interest). The simplest way to think of this, consistent with footnote 1 in Chapter 28, is to assume that Germany's equity ownership of assets in the United States is roughly the same as if Germany acquired debt claims on this country (our borrowing). In other words, once again stocks and bonds are considered roughly the same thing.

uses, but within the totals particular pairs might not match up at all: a sector's current expenditures can exceed its current receipts, or vice versa; its saving might exceed its investment, or vice versa; its borrowing might exceed its lending, or vice versa. If you measure the grand totals, they are equal. But if you look behind them, you will find that those grand totals usually are made up of many (eventually offsetting) inequalities.

The typical items that adjust to make our balance of payments "balance" are increases or decreases in foreign holdings of U.S. dollars or short-term securities, and (prior to August 1971) transfers of gold between nations. For example, say we import more than we export: We have to pay for the difference, which we could do by giving a check to the foreign seller. He deposits the check in his bank to get francs or pesos, so his bank now has the check, which means that a foreign bank now owns demand deposits in an American bank. Our balance of payments would show more imports than exports, but this would be balanced by an increase in foreign holdings of a U.S. liability (demand deposits are a liability of the U.S. bank). In effect, we have financed our imports by borrowing from abroad—the lender is the foreign bank that now owns a demand deposit in a U.S. bank.

The foreign bank might decide to exchange that demand deposit for U.S. Treasury bills, to earn some interest. But that wouldn't change anything; from the point of view of the balance of payments, that just substitutes one kind of U.S. liability for another. Or prior to August 1971 the foreign bank might, through its government, have used the demand deposit to buy some of our gold: in that case a U.S. gold sale (a source) would balance our imports (a use). No matter how you figure it, in the aggregate sources are always equal to uses.

So what does a balance of payments deficit (or surplus) mean?

Measure for Measure (or As You Like It)

Economists often talk about the *trade* deficit (or surplus), or the deficit *on current account*. Indeed, reference is frequently made to no less than *six* different balance of payments deficits—or surpluses— each of which results from selecting different categories in the payments accounts. Table 2 illustrates each of the six and their relationships to each other. Although at first glance Table 2 looks rather different from Table 1, way down deep it is the same thing.

Using Table 2 to illustrate the calculations, here are the particulars of each balancing act:

1.   The *trade balance* is the most old-fashioned of all, measuring only merchandise exports relative to imports. In Table 2 the merchandise trade balance has a $1 billion surplus, with exports $1 billion greater than imports. In Mercantilist days, in the 1600s and 1700s, this was the exclusive measure. A country with excessive imports would have to settle up by selling off some of its gold, clearly a Bad Thing. Adam Smith worked hard in his study in Edinburgh for many years and finally emerged with a big book attacking this narrow view of international finance, thereby becoming Famous. He pointed out that it was better to consume more goods than to hoard more gold, but many people are still not convinced to this very day. (In any case, he never got as Famous as Lady Godiva, who did nothing more than ride naked on a white horse through the town of Coventry, which is an indication of where people's priorities were even in those days.)

2.   The *goods and services balance* adds services, including such transactions as military expenditures, tourist spending, and interest and/or dividends paid or received for past investments. In Table 2 services transactions alone show a surplus of $5 billion, so that the surplus of goods and services, which is a cumulative balance, is $6 billion.

3.   The *current account balance* adds transfer payments, both private and governmental. Transfer payments are gifts flowing from one country to another. In Table 2 the current account balance has a $2 billion surplus, because the U.S. made $4 billion more transfer payments to the rest of the world than received from the rest of the world, thereby shrinking the $6 billion goods and services surplus to only $2 billion on current account.

4.   The *basic balance* adds long-term securities transactions to the current account figures.[3] We have a *basic* deficit in our balance of

---

[3] Securities and bank lending transactions, by the way, whether short- or long-term, are generally called capital movements. Our purchases of foreign securities are a capital outflow from the U.S., while foreign purchases of our securities are a capital inflow. Imports of foreign securities, like imports of foreign goods, are a use of foreign exchange for us; exports of our securities, like exports of our goods, provide us with foreign exchange.

Note that section D of Table 2 includes three kinds of long-term securities transactions: direct investments, portfolio investments, and long-term loans. These distinctions are rather arbitrary. Foreign purchases of U.S. stocks, for instance, are classified as direct investments only if the foreigner acquires 25 percent or more of the enterprise. Otherwise it is considered a portfolio investment. All purchases of U.S. bonds by foreigners are considered portfolio investments.

payments when the sum of our current expenditures plus our net purchases of long-term foreign securities exceeds the sum of our current receipts plus foreign net purchases of long-term U.S. securities. In Table 2, for example, our basic deficit is $1 billion.

5. The *net liquidity balance* also incorporates nonliquid short-term private capital movements, allocations of SDRs (see Chapter 36), and errors and omissions (because many international transactions go unrecorded). Adding these elements brings the net liquidity deficit to $7 billion, as Table 2 shows.

6. Finally, the *official settlements balance* brings in liquid short-term private capital movements. Table 2 indicates that foreigners bought $4 billion of short-term U.S. securities, while we bought $2 billion of theirs, yielding a $2 billion surplus in the liquid private capital accounts. Adding this to the net liquidity balance yields an official settlements deficit of $5 billion.

Why so many different measures of what constitutes a balance of payments deficit (or surplus)? Primarily to confuse the general public, one might surmise. The government can always publicize the measure that currently looks best—the one that shows the smallest deficit. In addition, however, each measure focuses on something a little different from the others.

Today, discussion centers mainly on the relative merits of the basic balance compared with the net liquidity balance and the official settlements balance. The details of these controversies are beyond the scope of this book,[4] and if you are bewildered don't feel you're the only one. In 1976 the Department of Commerce threw up its hands and announced that it would no longer publish figures on any of these three balances. Now it just publishes the numbers on all the transactions and lets people themselves compute whichever balance makes them happiest.

Sources and Uses and Foreign Exchange Rates

We can conclude this chapter by using our balance of payments analysis to formalize our more or less casual discussion in the previous chapter regarding the determination of foreign exchange rates. Anytime a transaction takes place between the residents of two different

[4] For a full discussion, see Ingo Walter, *International Economics*, 2nd ed. (New York: Ronald Press, 1975), chaps. 16 and 17.

TABLE 2

Illustrative U.S. Balance of Payments*
(in billions of dollars)

	Net Balance	Cumulative Net Balance
A. Merchandise Trade:		
1. Exports	+ 70	
2. Imports	− 69	
Merchandise Trade Balance	+ 1	*+ 1*
B. Services:		
1. Military Receipts	+ 2	
2. Military Payments	− 5	
3. Income on U.S. Investments Abroad	+ 18	
4. Payments for Foreign Investments in U.S.	− 9	
5. Receipts from Travel and Transportation	+ 9	
6. Payments for Travel and Transportation	− 11	
7. Other Services (net)	+ 1	
Balance on Services	+ 5	
Goods and Services Balance		*+ 6*
C. Transfer Payments:		
1. Private	− 1	
2. Government	− 3	
Balance on Transfer Payments	− 4	
Current Account Balance		*+ 2*
D. Long-term Capital:		
1. Direct Investment Receipts	+ 3	
2. Direct Investment Payments	− 5	
3. Portfolio Investment Receipts	+ 4	
4. Portfolio Investment Payments	− 1	
5. Government Loans (net)	− 2	
6. Other Long-term (net)	− 2	
Balance on Long-term Capital	− 3	
Basic Balance		*− 1*
E. Short-term Private Capital:		
1. Nonliquid Liabilities	+ 1	
2. Nonliquid Claims	− 5	
Balance on Short-term Private Capital	− 4	
F. Miscellaneous:		
1. Allocation of Special Drawing Rights (SDR)	0	
2. Errors and Omissions	− 2	
Balance on Miscellaneous Items	− 2	
Net Liquidity Balance		*− 7*
G. Liquid Private Capital:		
1. Liabilities to Foreigners	+ 4	
2. Claims on Foreigners	− 2	
Balance on Liquid Private Capital	+ 2	
Official Settlements Balance		*− 5*
The Official Settlements Balance is Financed by Changes in:		
U.S. Liabilities to Foreign Official Holders:		
1. Liquid Liabilities	+ 5	
2. Readily Marketable Liabilities	+ 1	
3. Special Liabilities	− 2	
Balance on Liabilities to Foreign Official Holders	+ 4	
U.S. Reserve Assets:		
1. Gold	0	
2. Special Drawing Rights	0	
3. Convertible Currencies	+ 1	
4. IMF Gold Tranche	0	
Balance on Reserve Assets	+ 1	
Total Financing of Official Settlements Balance		+ 5

* Pluses are sources of foreign exchange (or credits), and minuses are uses of foreign exchange (or debits). Official data are published monthly in the *Survey of Current Business* (U.S. Department of Commerce). This particular format was changed by the Department of Commerce in 1976, with some of the balances reduced to memorandum items and others eliminated entirely.

countries one kind of money has to be exchanged for another. An American importer of tequila would like to pay his Mexican supplier with dollars, but the Mexican wants pesos. An American exporter ships 250,000 "I'm for McGovern" bumper-stickers to Ethiopia and would prefer to get paid in dollars, but the Ethiopian importer (who must know something we don't) wants to pay with Ethiopian dollars (that's right, theirs are called dollars, too). In each instance, and in millions of similar ones, an exchange of one kind of money for another is necessary before the transaction is fully completed. In every such transaction, either the importer has to buy some money that is not his native money, or the exporter has to sell some money that is not *his* native money. (Read that sentence over a few times and see if it's right—to tell the truth, we're not all that sure ourselves.)[5]

Such exchanges of one kind of money for another are made on the foreign exchange market, which is worldwide. Many banks throughout the world buy and sell foreign monies, in the form of foreign currencies and demand deposits in foreign banks. So do foreign exchange dealers, for whom this sort of thing is their main business, and currency exchanges—which are found downtown, at airports, and at railroad stations in all major tourist centers. Under the circumstances, one would expect that the price of foreign monies, like the price of any commodity that is bought and sold, would respond to market forces of supply and demand. The only problem is to identify those forces—the determinants of the supply and demand for foreign exchange.

Our balance of payments provides the clue. All the items listed as *sources* of foreign exchange to us are just that—they increase the *supply* of foreign money on the foreign exchange market. For example, when we export goods or securities, importers abroad offer (supply) their own money—foreign money from our point of view—to buy dollars to pay for their purchases.

And all of the items listed as *uses* of foreign exchange on our balance of payments similarly give rise to a *demand* for foreign money in the same way. For example, when we import goods or securities, we have to buy (demand) foreign money to pay for our purchases.

Notice, for the sake of completeness, there is always a reciprocal exchange involved. An increased supply of foreign money always implies an increased *demand* for our money (dollars). And an increased demand for foreign money always implies an increased *supply* of our money. If you reread the two previous paragraphs, you will see that clearly, now that you are aware of it.[6]

[5] P.S.: It's right.
[6] Also see p. 515.

Probably the most concrete way to see the reciprocal nature of foreign exchange transactions is to think in terms of tourist spending, where one currency is exchanged directly for another on an individual basis; all the other transactions, although they may be somewhat more complicated, follow the same principles. Take the case of an increased tourist supply of foreign money: If a French merchant sailor comes ashore when his ship docks in New York, he has to sell francs (*to buy dollars*) before he can purchase a ticket to a Haydn chamber music recital at Carnegie Hall. Or take the case of an increased tourist demand for foreign money: If you go to Tangier, you have to buy Moroccan dirhams (*offering dollars in the process*) before you can pick up one of those rare bargains in the Casbah—like a Bulova watch (psst, just smuggled in, monsieur)—that you could have bought for half as much in your home town.

Let us return, however, to thinking in terms of the supply of and demand for foreign money (rather than the corresponding demand for and supply of our money). The supply of foreign exchange arises from the right-hand side of our balance of payments (labeled sources), and the demand for foreign exchange from the left-hand side (labeled uses). A *surplus* in our balance of payments—say on an official settlements basis—means that the supply of foreign exchange exceeds the demand for it, so *the price of foreign money should fall* (foreign money should depreciate relative to the dollar). On the other hand, a *deficit* in our balance of payments implies that the demand for foreign exchange is greater than the supply, so *the price of foreign money should rise* (foreign money should appreciate relative to the dollar).

Figure 1 says the same thing with reference to one specific kind of foreign money, German marks. The dollar price per mark is on the vertical axis, the number of marks on the horizontal. The supply and demand curves for marks have the conventional shapes: the amount of marks supplied increases as their dollar price rises, since when marks become relatively more valuable, then U.S. goods become cheaper to Germans, so that we would export more; the amount of marks demanded increases as their dollar price falls, since when marks become relatively less expensive, then German goods become cheaper to us, so that we would import more.

As drawn, the supply and demand curves for marks imply an equilibrium price of 50 cents for one mark. (Let's use convenient numbers instead of realistic ones.) At that equilibrium foreign exchange rate, the supply of foreign exchange neither exceeds nor falls short of the demand, and our official settlements balance of payments shows neither a surplus nor a deficit (at least with respect to Germany).

But what would happen if the exchange rate were *pegged* lower—say at 25 cents for one mark? Then our exports (and German imports) would shrink, our imports (and German exports) would grow, and our official settlements balance of payments would start to show a deficit. Reflecting this, the demand for marks would exceed the supply by amount *AB*, as Figure 1 indicates.

At 25 cents, the mark is *undervalued* (i.e., underpriced). With floating exchange rates, the excess of demand over supply would force the mark back up to its equilibrium level. If the price is held at 25 cents by international agreement, however, official central bank intervention is necessary to prevent market supply and demand from exerting their effects. The West German monetary authorities step in and sell marks themselves (equal to *AB*) to satisfy the excess demand and in that way hold the exchange rate below the free market equilibrium. In so doing, they acquire dollars.

Notice that instead of thinking in terms of an undervalued mark, we could just as logically refer to an *overvalued dollar*. The equilibrium exchange rate of 50 cents for a mark is the equivalent of 2 marks for a dollar. The exchange rate at which the mark is underpriced, 25 cents per mark, implies that the dollar is correspondingly overpriced, at 4 marks for a dollar. This 4:1 ratio between the two monies makes our goods expensive for Germans, thus inhibiting our

FIGURE 1 / Supply of and demand for foreign exchange and foreign exchange rates.

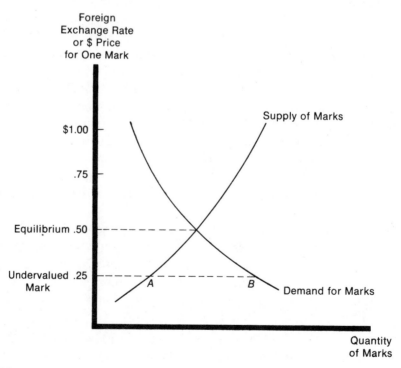

exports, but makes German goods cheap for us, thus stimulating our imports.

As noted above, the supply of marks represents a demand for dollars, and the demand for marks implies a supply of dollars. When the mark is undervalued (the dollar overvalued), we would either say that the demand for marks exceeds their supply, as we have been saying, *or we could say that the supply of dollars exceeds the demand for them.* When the German monetary authorities intervene and sell marks, to satisfy the excess demand for them and thereby prevent the price of marks from rising, they do so by buying dollars—which simultaneously mops up the excess supply of dollars and prevents the price of dollars from falling.

What would the West German authorities do with all the dollars they bought if they really wanted to keep the mark from appreciating? Until August 1971 they could, if they wished, use them to buy some U.S. gold. Well, theoretically they could—although if they had tried to buy too much, the gold store would have closed up shop even sooner. In any event, now about all they can do is hold on to the dollars (there are worse things), or use them to buy some interest-earning assets, like U.S. Treasury securities.

Aren't the West German monetary authorities silly for holding all those dollars, for which they have given up both valuable merchandise (in export goods) and financial assets on which they have to pay interest (in exporting securities as they borrowed from abroad)? Sure. But they can only dispose of the dollars by letting the mark rise to a more realistic level, which would hurt their exports, reduce jobs in their export industries, encourage imports, and generally harm employment and profits in Germany. So they prefer to hold excessive dollars instead of making the painful adjustments that would be required in converting their dollars into something of greater value. Or so it was until the beginning of 1973, when they were hit by a torrent of dollars. Crisis conditions made it impossible for them to continue, as we shall find out in the next chapter.

Suggestions for Further Reading

One of the most useful articles on balance of payments accounting is Rita M. Maldonado, "Recording and Classifying Transactions in the Balance of Payments," in the *International Journal of Accounting* (Fall 1979). Also very helpful is Norman S. Fieleke, "Accounting for the Balance of Payments," in the Federal Reserve Bank of Boston's *New England Economic*

Review (May/June 1971). An updated version has been published by the Boston Fed titled "What is the Balance of Payments?" (1976). Write to the Federal Reserve Bank of Boston, zip code 02106, for a copy. (Remember to say "please.")

Also useful is the analysis of alternative balance of payments measures in the 1970 and 1971 *Economic Report of the President*. If you really want to get down to the nitty-gritty, see the Bernstein Report, more formally titled *The Balance of Payments Statistics of the United States: Review and Appraisal*, Report of the Review Committee for Balance of Payments Statistics to the Bureau of the Budget (U.S. Government Printing Office, 1965). The chairman of the Review Committee was Edward M. Bernstein. If you have any friends abroad, have them order it, too; it costs $1.50, and that would help reduce our deficit. A helpful guide to the Bernstein Report, by the way, is in the Morgan Guaranty *Survey* (May 1965).

More recently, another committee has examined the balance of payments format, as a result of which extensive changes have been made in the way the figures are presented. See *Report of the Advisory Committee on the Presentation of Balance of Payments Statistics*; it appears in the June 1976 issue of the *Survey of Current Business*, which is published by the U.S. Department of Commerce.

Chapter 34

International Financial Crises and the Collapse of Fixed Exchange Rates

ONE THING that fixed exchange rate arrangements provided in abundance was intermittent crises in world financial markets, tremors that nearly everyone agonized over although hardly anyone was really quite sure what was going on. Just to say that exchange rates were fixed didn't necessarily make it so, especially when forces of supply and demand were constantly impinging on them. It is in the story of how they were fixed, and in what had to be done to keep them from fluctuating, that we find the reasons underlying almost every monetary crisis that erupted abroad during the past quarter century—as well as the seeds of the two Big Ones that finally exploded both at home and abroad in 1971 and 1973 and at long last brought the House of Fixed Rates tumbling down.

The Genesis of International Monetary Crises

Remember how floating exchange rates operate? When a country runs a balance of payments deficit, its money *depreciates* relative to other monies; its outflows of funds exceed inflows, pumping too much of its own money abroad, and this burgeoning supply leads to a decline in its relative value. In turn, this relative depreciation of its money should expand the deficit country's exports, contract its imports, and thereby restore its balance of payments to equilibrium.

But with fixed exchange rates, as they existed from the end of World War II until 1973, the process never got off the ground. By international agreement (under the IMF), a deficit country that saw its money start to depreciate had to step in promptly to stop the decline. It did so by buying up its own money in order to mop up the excess supply. However, it couldn't buy up its own money by offering more of the same in exchange—which, as a government, it could simply print —because that's what people were *selling*, not buying. It had to use *other* money to buy up its own, and this other money is called its international reserves.

Traditionally, international reserves have been held in the form of gold, because of its general acceptability. Since the end of World War II, however, most foreign countries have held a substantial portion of their reserves in the form of U.S. dollars, which have been just about as acceptable as gold in making international payments. They also hold other kinds of "foreign exchange" among their reserves —pounds, marks, francs, and so on—but mostly they hold U.S. dollars. Other nations acquire dollars when we run our deficits and then hold them as their reserves.

In *general*, countries use their reserves in the same way individuals and business use their cash balances—to bridge temporary gaps between the receipt and expenditure of funds, to tide them over periods when inflows of funds are slack, and to meet unexpected or emergency needs. *In particular*, with a system of fixed exchange rates, countries also used reserves to intervene in foreign exchange markets whenever the value of their money threatened to slide away from par (its agreed-upon fixed value). A foreign country generally used U.S. dollars for this purpose, paying out dollars to buy up any excess supply of its own money, thereby preventing its own money from depreciating relative to other monies. Or, if it was a surplus rather than a deficit country, selling its own money to keep it from *appreciating* relative to others.[1]

Now let us see how things used to work and watch a mini-crisis develop under a system of fixed exchange rates. A deficit foreign country—Great Britain, for example—seeing its money start to depreciate, promptly steps in to maintain the par value of the pound by paying out its reserves to buy up excess pounds. *But what if Great Britain continues to run payments deficits?* Then it must continue to shell out reserves to absorb pounds. However, its reserves are far from infinite. Sooner or later, when it runs out of reserves, its "defense of the pound" has to come to a halt. When the authorities sense that propping up the exchange value of the pound is becoming too costly in terms of the drain on reserves, and no end appears in sight, *then*, having stopped defending the pound, they start attacking the IMF—to win a decrease in the exchange rate. Great Britain devalues the pound—that is, it lowers the par value of the pound.

Once the financial community senses that devaluation is a possibility, however remote, it is likely to undertake actions that increase the probability of its occurrence. To illustrate with the same hypothetical example: Anyone who owns pounds, or liquid assets payable in pounds, and suspects that the pound may be devalued would be inclined to get out of pounds and into some other kind of money— say West German marks or Swiss francs—until the devaluation has been completed; then, with the same marks or francs, he could buy back more pounds than he originally had. Such "speculative" sales of pounds by private holders must of course also be purchased by the British monetary authorities, as they try to prevent the pound from depreciating below par. This puts an added strain on their reserves, thereby increasing the likelihood of devaluation, which in turn stimulates renewed "speculative" activity. "Keeping the faith" under such circumstances is all but impossible.

International transfers of short-term funds stemming from fears of devaluation can feed on themselves in this fashion and rapidly build up to the point where they generate massive reserve drains. Such short-term flows of funds include the purchase of Treasury securities as well as shifts of time and demand deposits. Since devaluations are an ever-present fact of life under a fixed exchange rate system, countries with balance of payments deficits have traditionally been viewed with some suspicion by those who manage large pools of mobile funds—treasurers of multinational corporations, bankers,

---

[1] This means, by the way, that since dollars are the reserves of foreign countries, the United States was in the unique position of not having to intervene itself to keep *its* money from changing in value relative to other monies; since all the other countries were intervening to keep their monies from changing in value relative to the dollar, the dollar was automatically prevented from changing relative to them.

Arab oil sheiks, financial consultants to private investors, and others with similar responsibilities. Indeed, fund managers often got nervous about holding a country's money as soon as that country's rate of inflation exceeded that of other countries, since this was taken as an early warning signal of future devaluation (a rise in prices that is more rapid than elsewhere hurts exports, encourages imports, and thereby invites balance of payments deficits).

All of this at least produced a convenient by-product for the monetary authorities *after* they devalued: they could always blame the devaluation on "the unprincipled speculators in foreign exchange who mounted a disloyal attack on the [pound] and finally, despite a staunch defense, succeeded in bringing it to its knees."

There always has to be a scapegoat!

The Special Case of the United States

The above recital of a typical European monetary crisis and ultimate devaluation is similar to American experience, except that where the United States was concerned the scenario was slightly different because of the unique role of our dollar as a reserve in world finance. As we have seen, the monetary reserves of other countries consist mainly of U.S. dollars; in turn, the reserve behind the dollar consists mainly of gold. Thus the saga of our dollar has been closely intertwined with that of gold, which calls for a moment's digression on that subject.

Gold played a pervasive role in international finance under the system of fixed exchange rates, since par values were customarily calculated with reference to it. As an illustration, suppose the dollar is defined as equal to four-tenths of an ounce of gold, while the mark is defined as equal to one-tenth of an ounce of gold. From these ratios, fixed par values emerge: in this example, $1 = 4 marks (or each mark = ¼ of a dollar).

Devaluation refers to a country formally lowering the fixed ratio between its money and gold, as if the United States were to redefine the dollar so that it would no longer be equal to four-tenths of an ounce of gold but to only two-tenths of an ounce of gold instead. As a consequence, $1 would be equal to only 2 marks (and each mark would now be worth ½ of a dollar).[2]

[2] That is, $1 would now equal 2 marks *provided* West Germany did not devalue simultaneously. If Germany *also* devalued by the same proportionate amount—from one-tenth of an ounce of gold to one-twentieth of an ounce—then we are right back where we started, with $1 = 4 marks.

In the American devaluation of 1934, to take a historical illustration, a dollar that had been worth about one-twentieth of an ounce of gold became worth only one thirty-fifth of an ounce. If United States devaluation means that $1 becomes worth a smaller fraction of an ounce of gold, then of course it takes more dollars to buy an ounce. When a dollar was equal to about one-twentieth of an ounce of gold, then about $20 = 1 ounce; with a dollar equal to only one thirty-fifth of an ounce of gold, then $35 = 1 ounce. Thus it became customary to speak of a devaluation of the dollar simply as a rise in the price of gold.

With this as background, let us turn to the main crises that involved the United States during the 1960s.

Crisis Number 1. The 1960s had hardly begun before rumors erupted that dollar devaluation was imminent—that the United States was about to raise the price of gold above the $35 an ounce that had prevailed since 1934. Underlying these reports was the hard fact that we had been running balance of payments deficits steadily through the 1950s, thereby supplying dollars to the rest of the world in excess of the foreign exchange we were taking in. Some of these foreign-held dollars were returned to the U.S. Treasury with a request to please exchange them for gold, if you don't mind. As a result, our gold stock—*our* reserves—dwindled. At the same time, many U.S. dollars were *not* presented for gold; instead, they were held by foreign countries as *their* reserves. But if they had been sent in for gold, we would have been hard put to honor them, because by 1960 our short-term dollar liabilities to foreigners had grown larger than our gold stock. We couldn't have redeemed all the outstanding claims on our gold even if we wanted to.

There was nothing secret about these facts, and they quite naturally gave a lot of people reason to suspect that we might very well devalue, thereby automatically increasing the value of our gold stock. As a result, in anticipation of gold soon being worth more than $35 an ounce, in late 1960 a heavy private demand for gold drove its price to $40 an ounce in London and Zurich, where the main free gold markets of the world, open to anyone, are located. (In financial circles this was called a "speculative attack on the dollar" and was widely regarded as un-American.)

Free market gold at $40 an ounce posed a threat to our gold reserves. Foreign central banks might be tempted to buy gold from the U.S. Treasury at the official price of $35 an ounce and then sell it in London or Zurich for $40. (Others would be tempted, too, but the Treasury would sell only to a government or a central bank.) The crisis remained on the front pages until it was resolved early in 1961, when the world's leading financial nations formally established a "gold pool" to peg the market price at $35. The central banks of the United States, Britain, Belgium, Holland, West Germany, Italy, France, and Switzerland began to act in concert, as a syndicate, to sell gold to the free market when the price threatened to rise above $35, and to buy it when it started to fall below.

Crisis Number 2. All of this worked tolerably well for several years, until the gold pool's sales (to keep the price down) drained so much gold out of their coffers that the central bankers became somewhat disenchanted at the prospect of playing the game much longer. The reason the gold pool had to keep selling, and hardly ever buying, was the same reason it had been organized to begin with: persistent U.S. balance of payments deficits, feeding dollars abroad, continued to arouse the same anticipations that had run up the price of gold in the first place.

Under the circumstances, it was only a matter of time before the next crisis. It arrived late in 1967 as the war in Southeast Asia accelerated the flow of U.S. dollars abroad. The private demand for gold was so great during 1967 that by year's end the central banks in the gold pool had almost $2 billion less in their gold reserves than they had at the start of the year. So in March 1968, to front page headlines, they called it quits.

The gold pool was replaced by a "two-tier" gold price system. This time the world's central bankers decided to build their own version of the Berlin Wall, separating once and for all the official monetary gold market from its private counterpart. In brief, they picked up what chips were still theirs and went off to play strictly among themselves, with all transactions within the fraternity to take place at the official price, then $35 an ounce, agreeing by blood oath not to sell or buy any more gold in the private market. As for the private buyers and sellers, they could do as they wished and trade at whatever price they pleased.

In one tier, the central banks agreed to buy and sell gold only among themselves and at the official price, and they agreed not to buy any newly mined gold nor to sell or buy gold on private markets. The other tier was represented by the private market, where all newly mined gold was to be channeled, and where the price was allowed to vary in response to supply and demand. Thus from March 1968 until November 1973, when the two-tier system fell apart, there were two gold prices: the official price and the free market price. The official price was the price at which all governmental and IMF settlements were recorded; this was $35 an ounce until it was increased to $38 in December 1971 and then to $42.22 in February 1973. The free market price, however, fluctuating with the tides of private supply and demand, soared to well over $100 an ounce during this 5½ year period, reaching the then-record high of $125 in mid-1973. So long as the two tiers did not deal with each other, or with intermediaries, there was no necessary relationship between the two prices—like fire trucks and bananas, they went their separate ways.

Although the two-tier system worked from early 1968 to late 1973, it contained within itself the seeds of its own demise: the higher the free market price rose above the decreed official price, the greater became the incentive for those governments with relatively large gold holdings to push for worldwide devaluation up to the market price. Or, alternatively, to sell some of their gold to the private market. Countries have violated blood oaths for much less.

So in November 1973 the two-tier gold price system collapsed under the strain of trying to keep the official and private gold markets in separate watertight compartments. Governments agreed that if any of them wished they were once again free to buy or sell gold in the lucrative private market.

But one tier or two, United States balance of payments deficits continued and even became larger.

Why Did Dollar Devaluation Take So Long?

How could this country continue to run payments deficits for over twenty years, and all that while avoid the consequences (i.e., devaluation) that other countries would face had they tried the same? As we have seen, Great Britain or France or West Germany would have had to step in much earlier and pay out reserves to stop their money from depreciating below par—pay out reserves to buy up excess supplies of their own money. Continued losses of their reserves in this fashion, accelerated by the inevitable "speculative" transfers of liquid funds into other kinds of money, would force devaluation upon them within a relatively short time. Surely it could not continue for over two decades!

But the United States was (and to an extent still is) in a uniquely fortunate position. While other countries could run deficits only so long as their reserves held out, we were able to run deficits much longer because our dollars *are* the reserves of others. Thus there has been (and still is) a rather special demand for U.S. dollars that nothing else, except gold itself, can satisfy. As a reserve money, the dollar was utilized by *other* countries, under IMF agreement, to intervene in foreign exchange markets to keep the exchange value of *their* money at par relative to the dollar. This automatically kept the dollar from changing relative to other monies, as already noted in footnote 1, without the United States having to intervene itself. If the dollar started to depreciate in relative value, then other countries would find their money *a*ppreciating relative to the dollar and *they* would step in and sell their own money (buy dollars) to keep exchange rates at their fixed par values. Which is just another way of saying that the reserve role of the dollar put the U.S. in a uniquely fortunate position, especially in a world of fixed exchange rates.

Nevertheless, even those upon whom fortune smiles risk running out of luck if they push it too far. Until mid-1971 the entire world monetary superstructure was erected on the basic premise that other countries could always come to the U.S. Treasury and exchange their dollars for gold. By the end of 1970, however, that superstructure looked precariously unstable; the U.S. gold stock ($11 billion) had become much smaller than foreign central bank holdings of U.S. short-term Treasury securities plus U.S. bank deposits ($20 billion), with the differential widening. It was evident the United States was at long last in danger of running out of *its* reserves.

In light of our diminishing gold reserves, both absolute and relative to our commitments, other countries became increasingly reluctant to hold the additional dollars spewed forth by our payments deficits. But instead of getting smaller, U.S. balance of payments deficits grew larger; as a consequence, worldwide expectations of impending American devaluation grew at an even faster pace, despite (because of?) repeated official denials that the United States would ever think of such a thing.

By 1970 the view had become commonplace that the dollar was "overvalued" relative to other monies—that is, at prevailing (fixed) exchange rates a dollar was able to buy too many Dutch guilders, too many West German marks, too many Japanese yen. To put it the other way, others could get too *few* dollars for their money.[3] This contributed to our payments deficits by encouraging us to import too much (foreign goods were relatively cheap for us, partly because foreign money was so cheap) and export too little (foreigners found our goods relatively expensive, partly because our money was so expensive).

The particular sequence of events that set off the inevitable explosion was sparked by vast international transfers of short-term funds in 1970 and the first half of 1971, actually at first more in

---

[3] See Figure 1 in the previous chapter.

response to intercountry interest rate differentials than to nervousness over imminent U.S. devaluation. International capital movements, whether in response to interest rate differentials or because of expectations with respect to exchange rate alterations, of course contribute to balance of payments deficits (or surpluses) just like imports (and exports) of goods and services. That is, the purchase by Americans of foreign securities or foreign bank deposits, for whatever reason, involves our making payments abroad (like U.S. imports), and the purchase by foreigners of U.S. Treasury bills or deposits in American banks involves our receiving payments from abroad (like U.S. exports). During 1969, short-term money had moved *to* the United States, attracted by the high interest rates here during that tight money period. In 1970 and 1971, however, with recession in the United States and interest rates lower here than abroad, funds moved back to Europe, contributing to our payment deficits.

Eurodollars

It is useful to mention in passing at this point that international capital movements have been given added impetus in recent years by the rapid growth of Eurodollars. These unusual creatures are deposits in foreign banks, mostly in Europe, that are on the foreign banks' books as payable in U.S. dollars, rather than in the money of the country where the bank is located. For example, Eurodollars are born when an American transfers his dollar deposit from an American bank to a foreign bank and keeps it there *in dollars* (rather than switching to pounds, say, if the bank to which he transfers his money is in England). They are similarly created when a foreign holder of a deposit in an American bank does the same thing, as when a French exporter gets paid with a check on an American bank and deposits it in his local bank outside Paris with instructions to retain it as a dollar deposit (instead of exchanging it into the equivalent amount of francs). For that matter, anyone in another country can create Eurodollars by exchanging his local money for dollars and then depositing them in his local bank, with instructions to keep the deposit in dollar form. The original Eurodollar deposit can then serve as the basis for dollar loans by the foreign bank, and if redeposited the process can be repeated, thereby creating additional Eurodollars.

Close to E$400 billion are now on the books of commercial banks abroad, including the overseas branches of American banks, and they represent a particularly mobile pool of interest-sensitive funds. Indeed good old Regulation Q had a great deal to do with the growth of Eurodollars: The interest rate ceilings on deposits in the United States induced many corporate and institutional depositors in American banks to shift their deposits to foreign banks, to get higher yields, but to keep them payable in dollars for the sake of convenience.

In the tight money years 1966 and 1969, when the Federal Reserve was putting severe pressure on bank reserve positions, its policies were partially offset by Eurodollar transactions. Unable to compete effectively for domestic funds because of Regulation Q, American banks borrowed large amounts of Eurodollars from their overseas branches to restore the lending power the Federal Reserve was just as diligently trying to deplete. Suspicion that Eurodollar borrowings blunted the bite of monetary policy induced the Federal Reserve in mid-1969 to impose reserve requirements on them in an effort to restrain their growth.

The Real Storm: 1971

But to return to our unfolding story. We left the particular sequence of events that set off the inevitable explosion (that brought down the house that IMF built) just as we were mentioning that it was sparked by vast international transfers of short-term funds in 1970 and the first half of 1971, at first more in response to the attraction of higher interest rates abroad than to nervousness over imminent U.S. devaluation. These interest-sensitive short-term capital outflows worsened our already weak balance of payments position, so apprehension rapidly mounted with respect to possible dollar devaluation. A flight from the dollar ensued during the first half of 1971, including large-scale conversions of Eurodollars into other monies, especially the "strong" ones most likely to appreciate (such as West German marks, Swiss francs, and Japanese yen).

To maintain the fixed par values of their own money, as required by the IMF, the central banks of these "strong money" countries had no choice but to buy up the flood of dollars offered in the market, for that purpose paying out their own money (see Figure 1 in the previous chapter). To give you an idea of the enormous magnitudes involved: at the end of January 1971 foreign central bank dollar holdings amounted to $20 billion, *already a historic high*; by the end of May, only four months later, they had swollen to $32 billion. In only four months, foreign central banks had bought up $12 billion, almost none of which they really wanted!

Such an avalanche of dollar purchases by these central banks, like any other open market buying by a central bank, laid the basis for an enormous expansion of their domestic money supplies—in most cases contrary to the prevailing monetary policies of the countries involved. Forced to buy up vast amounts of dollars, and shoveling out their own money to pay for them, other countries were rapidly expanding the reserves of their own banks and losing control over their domestic money supplies. In the process of maintaining the *external* value of their money, they were losing their grip on its *internal* value.

West Germany wanted out first. In early May 1971, after buying up several billion dollars in the first few days of the month, West Germany ceased its dollar purchases, abandoned fixed exchange rates, and let the mark float to find its own level. Holland did the same. For a short while the crisis seemed to have been weathered successfully. During June and July there was actually a fair demand for dollars, and foreign central banks were able to get rid of about 5 billion of them.

But that turned out to be only the calm before the *real* storm. In the first half of August there was again a feverish rush to convert dollars into other monies—by mid-month, foreign central bank dollar holdings soared to close to $35 billion, well above the May peak. And then it was, on August 15, 1971, that President Nixon ended the convertibility of the dollar into gold.

Faced with jittery and panic-prone international financial markets, with $35 billion in the hands of foreign central banks, obligated to pay out gold to any central bank that wanted to exchange its U.S. dollars for it—but with only $10 billion worth of gold left in the Treasury—Nixon announced that the game was over. There weren't enough chips left.

Actually, the termination of the dollar's convertibility into gold caused little disarray in international finance. Everyone had known for the better part of a decade that the commitment of the United States to pay out gold in exchange for dollars was more symbolic than real. If it had ever been put to a real test, it would have ended years before. Fixed exchange rates also went out the window for four months after August 15. Most major countries joined West Germany and Holland and permitted exchange rates to float, with each country's money finding its own value relative to the others on the basis of supply and demand conditions, à la Figure 1 in the previous chapter. And do you know what? International trade did not come to a halt!

But good things rarely last. In mid-December 1971, the leading nations resurrected fixed exchange rates as part of a "new look" in

"O.K. The forward rate for marks rose in March and April, combined with a sharp increase in German reserves and heavy borrowing in the Euro-dollar market, while United States liquid reserves had dropped to fourteen billion dollars, causing speculation that the mark might rise and encouraging conversion on a large scale. Now do you understand?"

international financial arrangements. The December 1971 Smithsonian Agreement provided that exchange rates could fluctuate a little (but not much) more than before. Previously, exchange rates had been permitted under IMF rules to fluctuate by 1 percent above or below par before a central bank was required to intervene to stabilize them. The Smithsonian Agreement widened those limits to 2¼ percent on either side of par. The world's Financial Authorities felt this was such a drastic change it deserved a new name to memorialize the event; they decided that from then on the fixed rate would no longer be called the par value, but rather the "central" value.

Par—pardon, central—values were simultaneously realigned, to produce an average depreciation of the dollar of about 12 percent against the major trading nations, with the expectation that this would inhibit U.S. imports, stimulate U.S. exports, and thereby help remedy our payments deficit. Also as part of the Smithsonian Agreement, the dollar was *finally* devalued, for the first time since 1934—from the equivalent of one thirty-fifth of an ounce of gold to one thirty-eighth of an ounce. This raised the official price of gold from $35 to $38 an ounce.

But for a number of reasons, things didn't work out as planned. Within fourteen months—in February 1973—the United States devalued again, this time raising the official price of gold an additional 11 percent, to $42.22 an ounce.

1973 and the Collapse of Fixed Exchange Rates

The Smithsonian Agreement of December 1971 was hailed by President Nixon as "the most significant monetary agreement in the history of the world." However, again words didn't necessarily make it so; by February 1973, only fourteen months later, the Smithsonian Agreement had almost completely disappeared, leaving hardly a trace.

The basic premise of the Smithsonian Agreement was that fixed exchange rates are a viable foundation for an international financial system, that the trouble lay not in fixed rates per se but in the particular levels at which the rates had been fixed. Conclusion: Realign the rates, fix them at new, more "realistic" levels and then everything will be just fine. But it didn't work out that way. With exchange rates pegged once more, and thereby prevented from reflecting shifting supply and demand pressures, the lid blew off again in early 1973.

A minor event sparked the explosion. In late January, Italy established new exchange rules for the lira. Fearing that the value of their money would decline, many Italians sold lira for dollars and then exchanged the dollars for Swiss francs. The inflow of dollars panicked the nervous Swiss monetary authorities, who stopped buying dollars and let the Swiss franc float. This brought the treasurers of multinational corporations and the Arab oil sheiks into action. Sensing that another flight from the dollar might be imminent, they promptly proved it, dumping dollars for German marks and Japanese yen.[4] Within a week the West German Bundesbank had to (reluctantly) buy $6 billion, and the Bank of Japan had to swallow over $1 billion, to keep the dollar from falling below (or the mark and yen from rising above) agreed-upon levels.

On February 12, 1973, not unwillingly, the United States announced that it was again devaluing the dollar, raising the price of gold from $38 to $42.22 an ounce. The news was fresh that in 1972

[4] It was no longer profitable to move into the Swiss franc, since it had floated upward to the point where it was not a bargain anymore.

we had run a $6 billion deficit on current account—devaluation against the mark and yen could help correct that imbalance.[5] Even so, large-scale selling of dollars—in anticipation of *further* devaluation—broke out again within weeks. Finally, in the so-called Brussels Agreement of March 12, 1973, Germany and the major Western European nations decided they had no choice but to let their monies float vis-à-vis the dollar, and so they abandoned fixed exchange rates.

Since March 1973 the international monetary system has been characterized mainly by floating exchange rates. Several Western European nations fix the value of their monies relative to each other, permitting only limited fluctuations above or below par. And almost all small less-developed countries peg the value of their money to that of a larger country, typically a major trading partner. But by and large floating rates are the order of the day, with demand and supply continuously moving exchange rates up and down.

Strictly speaking, floating rates existed "illegally" for almost three years, since the IMF's regulations still required fixed par values until early in 1976. However, no one seemed to worry about such technicalities. Finally the rules of the game were officially changed at the IMF's meetings in Kingston, Jamaica, in January 1976. At those meetings the entire structure of mandatory fixed exchange rates, erected at Bretton Woods near the close of World War II, was formally dismantled and a new international monetary system was constructed in its place, one that permits flexible exchange rates (although it does not require them). None of the participants at the Jamaica meetings, by the way, appeared to think it strange that the new exchange rate regulations were being drawn up almost three years *after* they had been put into practice.

The Jamaica Agreement also altered the nature of the International Monetary Fund, from an exchange rate supervisor and regulator to a forum for debate and an agency to assist the underdeveloped nations. In addition to legalizing floating rates, it was agreed to "demonetize" the international monetary role of gold by terminating the concept of an "official" gold price. The IMF also agreed to sell 25 million ounces of its own gold on the open market and use the proceeds to aid the poorer nations.

---

[5] Cooperation from Germany and Japan was necessary so that they did not simultaneously devalue in terms of gold. A number of other nations—Mexico, South Korea, Israel, Greece, Turkey, Yugoslavia—devalued along with us, so as to leave the relationship between their monies and the dollar unchanged.

544

Floating Rates: Success or Failure?

Have floating exchange rates been a success? In some respects they undoubtedly have been an improvement over fixed rates. Had fixed rates still been in existence late in 1973, for example, it is not hard to imagine the financial crises of vast proportions that would have exploded when the Organization of Petroleum Exporting Countries (OPEC) announced a fourfold increase in oil prices. Floating rates have absorbed the shocks of that and similar episodes remarkably well.

But floating rates have nevertheless fallen far short of expectations. In the last section of Chapter 32 we noted that floating rates would hopefully end a persistent balance of payments deficit without destabilizing the economy in the process. Unfortunately, things have not worked out quite that way. The dollar has depreciated rather steadily on international financial markets since floating began early in 1973, but our economy has been far from stable. What has resulted is a worsening of inflation here at home. We have to pay more for imports (since foreign money costs us more) and the amount of our exports demanded by foreigners has increased (since our goods are cheaper for them because our money is cheaper). For both reasons—cost-push and demand-pull—inflation in the United States has been exacerbated by the depreciation of the dollar.

At the same time, the decline of the dollar relative to foreign monies has *not* wiped out our chronic balance of payments deficit. If there was anything floating rates were expected to do, it was to rectify that situation by making our imports more expensive and our exports more competitive. But in fact our payments deficit has grown *larger* rather than smaller. We seem to have gotten ourselves into the worst of all possible worlds: a falling international dollar, a rising domestic price level, and a balance of payments deficit larger than ever.

There are several explanations for this unhappy state of affairs, none of them entirely satisfactory. One is that the balance of payments corrective process takes time—that although the payments deficit may get worse for a while in response to depreciation, eventually it will get better. Economists often refer to this as a J-curve phenomenon: at first things deteriorate, but at some point they turn around and improve dramatically. Things get worse initially because imports are resistent to the price increases caused by the depreciation of the dollar, implying that imports actually rise in dollar volume in the short run; similarly, it takes time before exports are stimulated. In the short-run, therefore, the depreciation of the dollar is likely to enlarge the balance

Fed Sold Marks To Help Dollar

By MARIO A. MILLETTI

The Federal Reserve Bank of New York, attempting to support a skidding dollar, intervened heavily in the foreign-exchange markets from August to October by selling the equivalent of $236.8 million in West German marks, Fed officials said yesterday.

The officials, in their regular quarterly report, stressed that the intervention was not directed at maintaining a specific level for the dollar but was aimed instead at quelling disorderly or unsettled market conditions.

The Fed's operations, which amounted to a total of around $400 million, involved mainly buying and selling marks. "We haven't intervened in yen," said Scott E. Pardee, a vice president at the New York Fed. The mark and the Japanese yen recently have been the strongest currencies against the dollar.

Particularly Unsettled in October

The Fed's intervention occurred at about the same time that Treasury Secretary W. Michael Blumenthal made statements suggesting that the Government's policy was not to prop up the dollar, although he said that a strong and stable dollar was a necessity.

The currency markets were particularly unsettled in October, when most of the Fed's intervention took place, said Mr. Pardee and Alan R. Holmes, executive vice president in charge of the New York Fed's foreign desk.

Mr. Pardee attributed much of the market conditions to "more of a gambling atmosphere than we've had in really more than a year or so." Foreign-exchange dealers, he said, were ignoring favorable economic forces in the United States. He added that market actions often were determined by rumors—such as the one that Arthur F. Burns, chairman of the Federal Reserve Board, had resigned—and by unfavorable news stories.

"I thought the Government securities market was subject to rumor-mongering, but I must say the exchange market goes them one better because it is more international in scope," commented Mr. Holmes.

The Fed's October actions, which amounted to the equivalent of around $200 million, were one of its two or three largest monthly interventions, Mr. Pardee said. "We've had to operate more forcefully than we have had to since early 1975," he added.

The Fed's total market dealings from August to October were submerged in the record $30 billion of gross market interventions by all major central banks throughout the world, the Fed's report showed. The overall figure reflects, among other things, an unsuccessful major attempt by the Bank of England to limit a rise in the pound.

In the prior May through July period, Fed intervention amounted to the equivalent of $300 million compared with total major central bank interventions of $22 billion, a spokesman said.

NEWS ITEM / Dirty Float

SOURCE: *New York Times,* December 1, 1977

of payments deficit rather than contract it. *Eventually,* however, there will be a meaningful turnaround.[6]

An alternate explanation is that we have never really given floating rates a sufficient chance to float freely, so they could produce their results. Instead, nations have continuously intervened in foreign exchange markets, nudging exchange rates higher or lower, refusing to let the free market operate. Instead of "clean" floats, we have had managed or "dirty" floats.

[6] See Rudiger Dornbusch and Paul Krugman, "Flexible Exchange Rates in the Short Run," *Brookings Papers on Economic Activity* (No. 3, 1976).

For example, in November 1978, President Carter and the Federal Reserve announced a barrage of measures intended to stop further foreign exchange depreciation of the dollar. These measures included the authority to borrow $15 billion worth of marks, yen, and francs from foreign central banks in order to buy dollars, higher commercial bank reserve requirements, and a 1 percent increase in the discount rate (to attract foreign funds by raising short-term interest rates here). This massive support of the dollar was aimed at combating inflation at home—since, as noted above, a continuously depreciating dollar accentuates both cost-push and demand-pull inflationary pressures. Nevertheless, we can't have it both ways: if we want floating rates, we have to let them float.

So far, then, the verdict is mixed. Floating foreign exchange rates are neither a clear success nor an unmitigated disaster. Everything considered, they have probably been an improvement over fixed rates since they came into being in 1973. Many bankers and business executives would still prefer to return to fixed rates,[7] but the likelihood appears slim that it will happen in the near future.

Suggestions for Further Reading

For two excellent insiders' views of the events discussed in this chapter, see Charles A. Coombs, *The Arena of International Finance* (New York: John Wiley & Sons, 1976); and Robert Solomon, *The International Monetary System, 1945–1976* (New York: Harper and Row, 1977).

On speculative flows of funds and international financial crises, see Donald L. Kohn, "Capital Flows in a Foreign Exchange Crisis," *Monthly Review* of the Federal Reserve Bank of Kansas City (February 1973); and Philip Rushing, "Reciprocal Currency Arrangements," *New England Economic Review* of the Federal Reserve Bank of Boston (November/December 1972).

In more general terms, see Abba P. Lerner, "What Would We Do Without the Speculator?" in his *Everybody's Business* (East Lansing: Michigan State University Press, 1961); and Milton Friedman, "In Defense of Destabilizing Speculation," in his *The Optimum Quantity of Money and Other Essays* (Chicago: Aldine, 1969). Also see the article by Friedman,

[7] For an expression of views along these lines, see "The Drift Back to Fixed Exchange Rates: Floating Rates Are Being Viewed Worldwide as a Costly, Failed Experiment," *Business Week* (June 2, 1975), pp. 60–63.

"The Case for Flexible Exchange Rates," in his *Essays in Positive Economics* (University of Chicago Press, 1953).

For more advanced discussions regarding speculation, see William J. Baumol, "Speculation, Profitability, and Stability," *Review of Economics and Statistics* (August 1957), and Lester G. Telser, "A Theory of Speculation Relating Profitability to Stability," *Review of Economics and Statistics* (August 1959).

If you want to learn more about Eurodollars, read Milton Friedman, "The Eurodollar Market: Some First Principles," Morgan Guaranty *Survey* (October 1969), and *Eurodollars: The Money Market Gypsies* by Jane Sneddon Little (New York: Harper & Row, 1975). Also Geoffrey Bell, *The Eurodollar Market and the International Financial System* (New York: Halsted Press, 1973).

Chapter 35

Independent Domestic Stabilization Policies Under Fixed and Floating Exchange Rates

O N A NUMBER of occasions in the preceding few chapters we have mentioned that a country's freedom to pursue its own *internal* (or domestic) stabilization policies may be limited by what kind of *external* foreign exchange rate arrangements are in effect. With fixed exchange rates, for example, we have noted that a country's domestic stabilization policies may be constrained by the requirement that it maintain external exchange rate stability. With floating rates, on the other hand, nations are freer to adopt whatever domestic stabilization policies they wish because external factors—such as balance of payments deficits and surpluses—will be taken care of automatically by fluctuations in exchange rates. The purpose of this chapter is to present these arguments in more systematic fashion.

Under the Gold Standard

The best place to begin is with the old-fashioned gold standard, because it is in many ways the most simple and straightforward of all international arrangements. Under the gold standard, nations decided upon a price for gold and then stood ready to buy and/or sell unlimited quantities at that price. This necessarily resulted in a fixed rate of exchange between one nation's money and another's: if France established 20 francs an ounce as the price it would pay for gold, and the United States decided upon $10 an ounce, then the par rate of exchange would be 2 francs = $1, since both 2 francs and $1 could buy equal amounts of gold. The market rate of exchange would not vary above or below par by more than the relatively slight cost of shipping an ounce of gold between the two countries. *In addition, and extremely important, each nation agreed to tie its money supply rigidly to its gold stock.* Here's how it worked:

Assume that the United States, with an excess of imports over exports, has a deficit in its balance of payments, while France has a surplus. We are paying out more than we are taking in. The resulting excess supply of dollars on world financial markets will lead to depreciation of the dollar relative to the franc, and the exchange rate will start to slide from 2 francs = $1 to say 1.96 francs = $1. But if it costs 2 cents to ship $1 of gold from New York to Paris, the exchange rate will not slide lower than 1.96 francs = $1, because if it starts to do so gold itself will be shipped from New York to Paris. In particular, if an American importer of 200 francs worth of French perfume is told by his local Brooklyn banker that he can get only 195 francs for his $100, he will turn around and buy $100 worth of gold from the U.S. Treasury and ship it to France at his own expense (which would be $2). With his $100 of gold now in Paris, he discharges his 200 franc obligation. The total cost: $102. This is cheaper than operating through the foreign exchange office of his local bank. Thus the dollar could depreciate no lower than the gold export point—that is, the point where it became cheaper to ship gold rather than buy foreign money.

As the United States loses gold its money supply will shrink and as France gains gold its money supply will expand, assuming no offsetting actions by the respective central banks. Prices and employment are likely to fall here and rise in France. *This process will automatically tend to correct our balance of payments deficit:* our imports will decline (because French goods now carry higher price tags and our depressed income makes us too poor to buy them anyway), and our exports will grow (because our goods now carry lower price tags and the French, in a booming prosperity, are in a good position to splurge anyway). Simultaneously, the process also tends to correct France's balance of payments surplus, because her exports will fall and her imports will increase.

In addition, these balance of payments effects will be reinforced by purely financial flows of funds. International capital movements affect balance of payments deficits and surpluses just as movements of goods and services do. The purchase by foreigners of U.S. securities means we receive an inflow of funds (like U.S. exports), and our purchase of foreign securities means we are making payments abroad (like U.S. imports). With tight money here interest rates will rise, while with the money supply expanding in France interest rates will fall there (at least for a while). So French residents will start buying the now higher-yielding U.S. Treasury bills, and Americans who were buying French securities will cut back and start shifting over to U.S. securities. Thus purely financial transactions will also operate to redirect funds away from France and toward the U.S., thereby eliminating France's balance of payments surplus and America's deficit.[1]

Under such a system, what freedom do individual nations have to pursue their own independent domestic stabilization policies, such as the use of monetary and fiscal policy to promote high domestic employment and stable domestic prices? Virtually no freedom at all, because to do so, even modestly, would break the rules of the gold standard game and interfere with the international balance of payments adjustment process. That adjustment process operates in large part through domestic *instability*: balance of payments deficits are corrected by recessions and surpluses are corrected by inflationary booms.

What if gold flows out of a deficit country and that country reacts by deliberately keeping its money supply from contracting, or actively uses fiscal policy to alleviate the recession? It could thereby prevent the adjustment process from running its course. Which means it could continue to run balance of payments deficits *until it ran completely out of gold*. But when that happens, the game would have to end, at least for the deficit country. If it tries to continue importing more than it exports, it will be unable to pay for its net imports. Thus the old-fashioned gold standard provides no freedom for individual nations to pursue domestic stability, since the gold standard requires domestic instability if it is to work. No wonder it is long gone, never to return.

[1] We are implicitly assuming less than perfect capital mobility. Otherwise, interest rate differentials disappear immediately through arbitrage. See Dornbusch and Fischer, *Macroeconomics* (New York: McGraw-Hill, 1978), Chapters 18 and 19.

551

With Fixed Exchange Rates

Fixed or pegged exchange rates are not so different from the gold standard. (After all, the gold standard is a pegged rate system, with exchange rates fixed by relative gold prices and limited in their variation by the cost of shipping gold.) Under the fixed exchange rate system, relative money values are decided upon—usually with reference to gold, but that is not necessary—and those agreed-upon *par values* are then maintained by government intervention in foreign exchange markets to keep exchange rates stable. Some slight variation is usually permitted above and below par. This intervention in foreign exchange markets to maintain par values takes the form of a country using its international reserves—typically gold and dollars—to buy up its own money when it starts to depreciate; or selling its own money —which can just be printed up—when it starts to appreciate. *Government intervention replaces gold shipment as the mechanism which keeps par values in line.*

Assume that Great Britain, with an excess of imports over exports, has a deficit in its balance of payments, while West Germany has a surplus, and that the par value between the two monies is 4 marks = 1 British pound. Great Britain is paying out more than it is taking in. The resulting excess supply of pounds on world financial markets will lead to depreciation of the pound relative to the mark and the exchange rate will start to slide from 4 marks = 1 pound to say 3.95 marks = 1 pound. But it is permitted to slide no lower— this time not because the exchange rate has reached the gold export point, but because it has reached the "buy" intervention point. Great Britain steps in and uses its dollar and gold reserves to buy pounds, while Germany possibly steps in and sells some marks (by buying pounds). Thus the pound depreciates no lower and the mark appreciates no higher. Exchange rates are kept stable.

Does all of this help to correct payments imbalances? The answer is: not very much. To a certain extent there may be some impact, because when the Bank of England sells dollars (to buy up pounds) it contracts its money supply, while when Germany's central bank buys pounds (sells marks) it increases its money supply.[2] This should lead to higher interest rates in England, lower interest rates in Germany, and thereby to financial flows of funds from Germany to

---

[2] When a central bank sells *anything* it contracts bank reserves and the money supply, and when it buys *anything* it increases bank reserves and the money supply. Central bank sales or purchases of foreign exchange, in other words, have the same effects as ordinary open market operations conducted with Treasury bills.

London—which will reduce both Germany's balance of payments surplus and Great Britain's deficit.

But these money supply effects are frequently offset by the central banks themselves. They can neutralize (usually called sterilize) the bank reserve effects of foreign exchange operations by open market purchases or sales of securities, because there is no requirement that a country tie its money supply rigidly to its international reserves the way a country is supposed to tie its money supply to its gold stock under the gold standard. With pegged exchange rates, but none of the other rules of the gold standard, there simply is no automatic adjustment process that can eliminate balance of payments deficits and surpluses. Fixed exchange rates without the real substance of the gold standard are like the Cheshire Cat in Lewis Carroll's *Alice in Wonderland*: the cat has vanished and only the grin remains.

Since there is no automatic balance of payments adjustment process, what is to stop Great Britain from going its merry way and running payments deficits forever (merely stepping in to buy pounds whenever the pound threatens to depreciate below 3.95 marks = 1 pound)? The answer is not so different from the gold standard answer: *eventually Great Britain will run out of international reserves* —gold and (in this case) dollars. And then, again, the game will have to end, for England at least. When that time arrives, or actually well before it, Great Britain will have to devalue—that is, change par to say 3 marks = 1 pound—and then, perhaps with a loan of international reserves from the IMF to tide Britain over, the game can possibly begin again. (But of course if Great Britain devalues, then fixed rates have certainly not remained fixed, have they?)

Under such a system, how much freedom do individual nations have to pursue their own independent domestic stabilization policies? Not very much, it turns out. Can Great Britain inflate its money supply and try to live the good life regardless of what is happening elsewhere? If it did, interest rates would fall in London (at least initially) and funds would start flowing abroad in search of higher yields. Also, rising prices and higher incomes relative to other countries would hamper Great Britain's exports and stimulates its imports. On all counts, its balance of payments deficit would worsen and it would wind up desperately buying up pounds to stop the pound from depreciating below 3.95 marks, in the process using up its scarce international reserves.

Under fixed exchange rate arrangements, with no automatic external mechanism to take care of payments imbalances, nations have to take deliberate *internal* measures to do the job. Which means that a chronic deficit nation sooner or later has no choice but to take

domestic steps—in terms of domestic monetary and fiscal policies—
to contract its imports, expand its exports, and attract financial investments from abroad. Not surprisingly, these measures generally
bear more than a slight resemblance to what happens under the old-
fashioned gold standard. To successfully contract imports and expand
exports requires holding down wages and prices at home, or at
least holding the rate of inflation below that of other countries (so
domestic products become relatively less expensive), and quite possibly inducing at least a mild domestic slump. To attract financial
flows from abroad requires tight money and higher interest rates at
home. The process may not be as abrupt as under the gold standard,
and steps can be taken that to some extent postpone and cushion the
impact, but in the final analysis the medicine is roughly the same. If
a chronic deficit nation decides it would rather not take such measures,
it will run out of reserves as it tries to prevent its money from depreciating on international financial markets. So under fixed exchange
rates, as under the gold standard, freedom of individual domestic
action is severely limited by balance of payments considerations.

There is one exception to this principle, at least for a while:
namely, a nation that is in the uniquely fortunate position of having
its money used as reserves by the rest of the world. Say the United
States runs continuous balance of payments deficits. What would soon
be viewed as an excess supply of that country's money on world
financial markets in any other case, is not so promptly thought of as
excess in the case of the dollar—since other countries want dollars to
hold as part of their reserves. Until other countries start to feel that
enough is enough, a reserve money country, such as the United States,
can run balance of payments deficits with virtual impunity. In effect,
since dollars represent a U.S. liability, everyone else is happily (?)
lending to the United States. But eventually this tolerance comes to
an end, and when that happens the dollar also starts to depreciate
and then the U.S. is in the same boat as everyone else. Then our freedom to pursue strictly domestic objectives is also constrained, and
"the discipline imposed by the balance of payments" becomes universal.

One illustration of this is the dilemma that intercountry interest
rate differentials have posed for the Federal Reserve during recessions
since the early 1960s. In a recession, should the Fed attempt to *lower*
interest rates at home to stimulate domestic spending—and then see
the balance of payments worsen as short-term funds move abroad in
search of higher yields? Or should the Fed attempt to *raise* interest
rates at home to attract funds from abroad, or at least deter
funds from leaving, thereby bolstering the balance of payments—but
then see the recession worsen as domestic spending is curtailed by

high interest rates? At times the Federal Reserve's response to this problem has been to try to *twist* the structure of interest rates here at home, lowering long-term rates to encourage domestic business expansion while simultaneously keeping up short-term rates to prevent an outflow of funds abroad. However, as the Fed has discovered, it can twist the interest rate structure only so far. Under most circumstances it simply is not possible to lower long-term interest rates beyond a certain point without dragging short-term rates down with them.[3]

The desire to keep short-term interest rates from falling too far, because of balance of payments considerations, has thus checked the vigor of easy money in the past couple of decades. If there is a lesson to be learned from this—and there is—it is not that the Federal Reserve lacks the power to make interest rates whatever it wishes, although that is true enough (as we pointed out in Chapter 20). The more important lesson to be learned, the one applicable to international monetary affairs, is that no central bank can conduct an independent, wholly domestically oriented monetary policy within the framework of fixed exchange rates.

With Floating Exchange Rates

Floating or flexible foreign exchange rates are generally hailed as the one system that permits a country to pursue independent domestic policies, unhampered by external balance of payments considerations and irrespective of policies other countries are following. And we have certainly joined that chorus in the preceding pages. The reasons for the acclaim are not hard to find.

With floating exchange rates, relative money values are determined by forces of supply and demand and are left to seek their own level. They are stabilized neither by flows of gold nor by central bank intervention to maintain par values. Let's start out, as before, with an exchange rate between West Germany and Great Britain at 4 marks = 1 pound. Also assume that Great Britain, with an excess of imports over exports, starts to run a deficit in its balance of payments, while Germany starts to run a surplus. England is paying out more than it is taking in. The resulting excess supply of pounds on world financial markets will lead to depreciation of the pound relative to the mark

---

[3] For a possible explanation, see our discussion of the term structure of interest rates in Chapter 30.

and the exchange rate will start to slide from 4 marks = 1 pound to say 3.95 marks = 1 pound.

Only this time the Bank of England does *not* step in to stop the slide, so that if England continues to run payments deficits and Germany continues to run surpluses, the pound will continue to depreciate —to 3.90 marks = 1 pound, 3.80 marks = 1 pound, and so on.

This depreciation of the pound—or appreciation of the mark, if you prefer to look at it that way—does not occur under the gold standard, because of gold flows, nor does it occur under pegged exchange rates, because of central bank intervention. Now, however, currency depreciation (or appreciation) is permitted to run its course, *and in the process automatically generates corrective pressures that rectify payments imbalances*. England's exports of goods, services, and securities will grow—because pounds have become cheaper for foreigners, thereby automatically making British goods (and securities) cheaper for foreigners even though the price tags on these goods and securities may not have changed at all. And England's imports will contract—because foreign money has become more expensive for the British, thereby automatically making foreign goods (and securities) more expensive for them even though foreign price tags may not have changed. For the same reasons, West Germany's imports of goods, services, and securities will rise and its exports will fall. Great Britain's balance of payments deficit and Germany's surplus are both wiped out by fluctuations in the exchange rate. *Equilibrium is restored by instability in the exchange rate rather than by instability in the two economies.*

Under this system, nations have much more freedom to pursue their own independent domestic stabilization policies. A deficit country can continue to use monetary and fiscal policies to maintain a prosperous economy. It does not have to induce a recession at home in order to make its exports more attractive and cut back on its imports; depreciation of its money on world financial markets will automatically take care of that.

All of which sounds too easy. There must be a catch. And sure enough, there is. It is true that deficits (and surpluses) will eventually be taken care of by exchange rate movements. But do *not* leap from that to the further conclusion that the adjustment process will be painless. Because it might be very painful indeed!

Think for a moment of what that adjustment process involves for a deficit country (say Great Britain): it means, for one thing, that her imports will cost more, because England, with her money depreciating, will have to pay more to acquire the marks and francs she needs for her imports. If these imports are "essential"—like food for Great Britain or oil for the United States—the cost of living will rise and living standards will fall in the deficit country. This is inflation. If you have to pay a lot more for food, or for gasoline, you will have a lot less left over for other things. In addition, there will be less "other things" available, because England's exports are likely to expand. Since other countries can obtain pounds cheaply, foreigners will take a larger fraction of Great Britain's output—leaving less for the home folks. On both grounds—more expensive imports and more exports—life will become less comfortable in Great Britain. She will get rid of her payments deficit, but will find her standard of living declining in the process.

Unwilling to face this reality, many deficit countries try to pursue domestic policies that forestall such painful adjustments. A typical scenario goes somewhat as follows. As the cost of living rises in England, because of more costly essential imports, unions insist on correspondingly larger wage increases in an effort to maintain real wages. This drives up business costs, which are already higher because imported raw materials cost more. Result: a higher wage-price level in England. *The central bank now expands the money supply by enough to support these higher wages and prices, and thereby nullifies the effects of the pound's depreciation.*

On the export side, the higher British prices wipe out the export advantages of the depreciated pound: if the pound has depreciated by 10 percent but British price tags rise by 10 percent, foreigners find British goods no cheaper than before. And on the import side, if the pound depreciates by 10 percent then home goods look more attractive to British residents than the now more expensive foreign products, but if British price tags rise by 10 percent then foreign goods are no more expensive (relative to British goods) than before. In brief, inflation in Great Britain—because of a refusal to lower living standards—has offset the balance of payments corrective effects of the pound's depreciation. The result: continued deficits and further depreciation of the pound, until sooner or later measures are taken that effectively cut back imports and stimulate exports—or, in other words, that reduce Britain's standard of living.[4]

---

[4] Britons *have* to lower their standard of living in the sense that they must consume less, produce less capital goods for home use, or accept fewer government services. GNP $= C + I + G +$ exports $-$ imports. Assume that $C + I + G = 110$ and exports $= 10$ and imports $= 20$. Thus GNP $= 100$. Keeping GNP at 100 but forcing exports to equal imports, say at 15 each, requires that $C + I + G$ equal no more than 100, as compared with 110 before. This assumes, however, that the British balance of payments deficit is due to an excess of merchandise imports; if it is due to excessive lending abroad (importing foreign securities), then the British can balance their books by lending less abroad.

Thus, while nations have considerably more freedom to pursue their own independent domestic stabilization policies with a system of floating exchange rates than they have with a system of pegged rates, this freedom is far from unlimited. If a country wants to import from abroad it ultimately has no choice but to maintain a price level at which its products are competitive in export markets. Otherwise it cannot get the foreign exchange it needs to pay for its imports. This implies that a deficit nation cannot long permit inflation to continue at home at a faster rate than is taking place in the countries with which it trades. This necessity cannot be ignored in deciding upon domestic monetary and fiscal policies, regardless of what kind of international monetary system may be in effect. Evidently the "discipline of the balance of payments" (see Chapter 32) is unavoidable, whether we like it or not.

Suggestions for Further Reading

A lucid analysis of some of the issues involved in this chapter is presented by Janice M. Westerfield in "Would Fixed Exchange Rates Control Inflation?" in the Federal Reserve Bank of Philadelphia's *Business Review* (July/August, 1976). Also see Marina n. V. Whitman, "Global Monetarism and the Monetary Approach to the Balance of Payments," *Brookings Papers on Economic Activity* (No. 3, 1975); and Paul A. Volcker, "The Political Economy of the Dollar," Federal Reserve Bank of New York *Quarterly Review* (Winter, 1978–79). Also valuable is Thomas M. Humphrey, "The Purchasing Power Parity Doctrine," in the Federal Reserve Bank of Richmond's *Economic Review* (May/June 1979).

Chapter 36

What About Gold?

ONCE UPON A TIME, long ago and far away, the natives of a small island in a remote part of the world had a monetary system of which they were extremely proud. Although they lacked commercial banks and had no Federal Reserve, they had something many people consider much more important—a monetary standard. It was not a gold standard, but it was somewhat similar. It was a rock standard. Near the southeastern edge of the island, on a high cliff, sat a handsome and enormous rock, awesome to behold and thrilling to touch, and it was this that they decided should serve as "backing" for their money.

Naturally, the rock was too heavy, and indeed too valuable, to use as an actual means of payment. Instead, for circulating media itself, corresponding to our coins and dollar bills, they used special clamshells. People had confidence in these because boldly inscribed on them were the words:

Will Pay to the Bearer on Demand One Dollar in Rock

The very fact that this statement was made meant that no one ever demanded any rock. The assurance that it was there was sufficient.

For many years all went well. The economy was simple but prosperous, and those from the Great Civilizations across the sea who occasionally visited the island marveled at its stability and its thriving commerce. The natives were not reluctant to explain the reasons for their prosperity: hard work, thrift, clean living, and, above all, sound money. Sound as a rock.

Unfortunately, one night a severe storm struck the island. The inhabitants awoke the next morning to find the rock gone, evidently hurled into the sea by the furies of nature. Consternation! Panic! Luckily, however, they were saved from the potential consequences—worthless money and economic collapse—by an accident of fate that took place within the week. One of the younger natives, a child of no more than eight, perched on the very cliff where the rock had once been, was looking at a rainbow arching far out over the horizon. Following it down, he suddenly saw—or thought he saw—the rock, fathoms deep, under the water.

After much excitement, it was finally ascertained that on very clear days, when the sea was calm and the sun at a certain angle, some who had especially strong eyes could see it. Those who could not, which included almost everyone, were assured by those who could that the outlines of the boulder were indeed discernible. And so, the backing still there, confidence in the money was restored, and in a short while the island became more prosperous than ever.

Of course, all the outstanding clamshells had to be called in, so that the elders of the community could strike out the words:

Will Pay to the Bearer on Demand One Dollar in Rock

In their place was painstakingly inscribed:

Will Pay to the Bearer on Demand One Dollar
in Lawful Money

Now if anyone brought in a clamshell to be redeemed, it would simply be exchanged for another clamshell. As it turned out, however, no one bothered. After all, with the backing assuredly there, the money obviously was as good as rock.

Gold at Home

Our own monetary system, of course, has always been much more rational. Until the early 1930s all of our money was redeemable in gold at the United States Treasury. Every dollar bill, and for that matter every demand deposit as well, actually or implictly bore the following inscription:

The United States of America
Will Pay to the Bearer on Demand One Dollar in Gold

Then overnight, in 1933, it was declared illegal for anyone in this country to have gold in his possession, except for industrial or numis-

"Then it's agreed. Until the dollar firms up,
we let the clamshell float."

matic purposes. Gold ownership by Americans was made illegal by an executive order issued by President Franklin D. Roosevelt on April 5, 1933. The prohibition was formalized by the Gold Reserve Act of 1934. Accordingly, the inscription on the currency was solemnly, officially, and duly altered to:

The United States of America
Will Pay to the Bearer on Demand One Dollar
in Lawful Money

In 1947 a literal-minded citizen of Cleveland, A. F. Davis, sent the Treasury a $10 bill and respectfully requested, in exchange, the promised $10 in "lawful money." He received back, by return mail, two $5 bills.

Seventeen years later, in 1964, the venerable inscription was finally removed from our currency. All that remains is an unpretentious observation: "This note is legal tender for all debts, public and private." Also (in considerably larger print): "In God We Trust."

Pursuing the same theme somewhat further, until 1965 the

Federal Reserve was required to hold reserves in the form of warehouse receipts for gold, called gold certificates.[1] The amounts required were 25 percent behind member bank deposits at the Federal Reserve Banks (member bank reserves) and also 25 percent behind all outstanding Federal Reserve notes (most of our currency). These gold certificate reserves were considered the ultimate backing behind our money, both demand deposits and currency. Indeed, economics textbooks were fond of portraying our monetary system as an inverted pyramid, with a base of gold that supported an equal volume of gold certificates, above that a fourfold expansion of member bank reserves and currency, and atop that a further multiple expansion of demand deposits. It was clear to any conscientious reader that without its Atlas-like foundation of gold the entire U.S. monetary system would collapse.[2]

But then, as the U.S. gold stock dwindled from over $20 billion in 1958 to less than $16 billion at the end of 1964, the gold backing behind member bank deposits at the Fed was quietly eliminated by Congress and the President on March 3, 1965. Three years later, on March 19, 1968, the corresponding gold reserve against currency was also abolished, just as casually. No one seems to care. The newspapers hardly mentioned it. Is somebody covering up?

All of which raises an intriguing question. There is, we are told, billions of dollars worth of gold buried deep beneath the surface of the earth in heavily guarded Fort Knox, Kentucky. Have you ever seen it? Do you know anyone who has?

Why don't you write a letter to the Federal Reserve or the Treasury, tell them you're going to be in Kentucky anyway, and ask them to let you stop by and take a look at the gold in Fort Knox? On second thought, don't bother. We did, and got back a rather chilly reply: "With reference to your inquiry relating to Fort Knox, all the gold is stored in sealed compartments and no visitors are allowed."

Sealed compartments? No visitors allowed? It sounds more like King Tut's tomb or Count Dracula's crypt than a twentieth-century monetary system. A curse on all who shall enter here! Do you *really* believe there is any gold there? Does it really matter?

[1] Encountered in Chapter 15, in connection with the Federal Reserve's balance sheet.

[2] You will find the famous inverted pyramid in the 8th edition of Paul A. Samuelson's *Economics* (McGraw-Hill, 1970), p. 306. But it is nowhere to be found in the 9th edition (1973) or thereafter.

Gold Abroad

We seem to have broken free from our superstitious attachment to gold here at home. We appear perfectly capable of transacting business without using little gold coins of the kind we had before 1933. And although U.S. citizens are once again allowed to have gold in their possession—since the beginning of 1975—the change in the law created less excitement than the rumor that the Rolling Stones were planning to replace Mick Jagger with Frank Sinatra. In this country, so far at least, the demand for gold for private hoards can be described as modest at best.

However, the same cannot be said of the world at large. Private citizens still hoard gold in many countries where there is no law against it, and in some countries where there is. And nations do the same, since they continue to settle up their net debts among themselves by playing house with small gold bars of a specified purity and weight. (Each bar, about the size of an ordinary brick, contains 400 ounces of 99.5 percent fine gold, which at $42.22 an ounce—the last "official" price—makes a typical bar worth almost $17,000.) In fact, you can even see some of this gold. Foreign governments store much of their gold in the basement of the Federal Reserve Bank of New York. A guided tour takes you down to the crypts. You can even hold one of the bars. Curious, isn't it?—we can touch theirs but not ours.

The "official" price of gold is worth a brief historical recapitulation. When gold was truly the legal basis of our monetary system, the official price was the price that the U.S. Treasury would pay for gold and at which dollars were redeemable back into gold. That is, with full convertibility at $20.67 an ounce, for example, you could turn in $20.67 and receive in exchange one ounce of gold. The official price was set at $20.67 an ounce by the Gold Standard Act of March 14, 1900, and it remained there until it was raised to $35 an ounce by President Roosevelt on January 31, 1934, even though, starting in 1933, U.S. citizens were no longer permitted to have gold. In August 1971, President Nixon stopped selling gold to foreigners as well, but the official price stayed at $35 until December of that year when it was raised to $38 as part of the Smithsonian Agreement. It was hiked once again by President Nixon in February 1973 to its final figure of $42.22 an ounce.

But dollars have not been redeemable into gold domestically since 1933 or internationally since 1971. The two-tier gold price system fell apart late in 1973, and ever since 1968 the free market price has been well above the official price, making the latter sort of academic. The free market price has ranged between $100 and $700 an ounce since late 1973, so no one would sell at the official price of $42.22. It became a little silly to talk about an official price of $42.22 when there was no longer any buying or selling taking place at that "price." So in January 1976 the concept of an "official" price was formally abolished at the IMF meetings in Kingston, Jamaica. The price of gold is now simply whatever it brings on the open market. We keep referring to $42.22 here only because it is convenient to use that figure as a reference point. A more realistic present-day figure would be about fifteen times that, or around $600 an ounce, which has been the recent free market price.

There is probably about $1,500 billion worth of gold in existence in the world today (calculated on the basis of the free market price)—roughly 2½ billion ounces, at $600 an ounce. Actually, estimates range from 2 to 3 billion ounces, which at $600 an ounce implies a dollar value between about $1,200 and $1,800 billion. So much of the estimating approaches sheer guesswork, however, that one might as well slice it down the middle and settle for $1,500 billion as a reasonable figure. For instance, none of the Communist-bloc nations will reveal its gold holdings; private hoarders, regardless of their politics, are even more discreet.

The United States has stashed away about $160 billion (at $600 an ounce), we are told, and other governments and central banks outside the communist sphere have close to $600 billion. The Soviet Union is estimated to have official gold holdings somewhere between $70 and $200 billion (most likely in the neighborhood of $140 billion), and other Communist countries, including China, perhaps $60 billion. Finally, there are substantial private hoards secretly squirreled away, some from the dawn of time, by peasants and potentates from France and Switzerland to India, Kuwait, and Tibet. Lord only knows what these amount to, but brave men calculate between $480 and $600 billion, with around $540 billion a likely figure (which includes a few billion in private hoards in the Communist countries).

With 2½ billion ounces in existence, and each brick-size bar containing 400 ounces, that amounts to about 6¼ million bars. That much could fit into one ocean liner and still leave enough room for 100,000 copies of *Mad* magazine.

The annual production of newly mined gold adds relatively little to this stock—about 50 million ounces emerges annually from the bowels of the earth. About 70 percent of this, sometimes more, comes from South Africa, a little over 10 percent from the Soviet Union, and 5 percent from Canada, the three largest gold producers. In many years this is not enough to satisfy all the *nonmonetary* demands for gold, not to mention the monetary ones. Jewelers, dentists, and manufacturers use a considerable amount every year, and hoarders frequently acquire and then promptly rebury at least as much. So even though newly mined gold adds about 2 percent to the total supply every year, some years end with *less* gold on hand for worldwide monetary uses than was available when the year began.

Paper Gold?

The ending of the external convertibility of the dollar into gold in 1971 and the formal abandonment of fixed exchange rates (and an official gold price) in January 1976—both discussed in the previous chapter—have severely ruptured the umbilical cord connecting international finance and chemical element 79.[3] But the attachment has by no means been severed. Many governments are still convinced that, of all possible stores of value, gold is the safest, the least susceptible to manipulation by other governments, and the most likely to appreciate in value over the long pull. The spectacular rise in the price of gold on the free markets of London and Zurich in recent years, to well above the old official fixed price, only reinforces many foreign governments' desire to hold on to what gold they have and to get as much more as they can. General de Gaulle was no doubt articulating the views of more central bankers than would care to admit it when, in 1965, he rhapsodized over the beauty and desirability of gold, which "does not change its nature, has no nationality, and is eternally and universally accepted as the unalterable fiduciary value par excellence."

In fact, gold does indeed frequently change its nature; it can be refined, melted, molded, minted, sweated, and has often been debased. In terms of its nationality, it is no different from hula hoops, turnips, or aardvarks. It is universally acceptable only because of the belief that it will continue to be so. And its value is certainly not unalterable, as recent history dramatically attests. Gold is not a help but more a nuisance, and frequently a considerable handicap, in international monetary affairs, as nations discovered long ago with respect to their domestic finances.

[3] While we're getting technical, we might as well mention that gold— chemical element 79—melts at 1063° centigrade, boils at 2600° centigrade, has a specific gravity of 19.3, and has an atomic weight of 196.967 (whatever that means).

All of which gives us a chance to bring up another neat Rule of Thumb— this time, how to convert temperature from Celsius to Fahrenheit. Take degrees in Celsius, multiply by 1.8, and add 32. So if you're in London and you hear that the temperature in Trafalgar Square is 20°, multiply that by 1.8 (=36), add 32, and you know it's 68° Fahrenheit.

In 1970 the potentially most hopeful step of all, away from gold, was hesitantly taken with the introduction into the world's monetary system of International Monetary Fund Special Drawing Rights (SDRs)—more commonly known as "paper gold." Actually, SDRs were agreed upon in principle several years earlier, at the 1967 annual meeting of the IMF in Rio de Janeiro, but it took two years before international consensus could be reached regarding their details, and still another year before they could be implemented. (Only three years of study, debate, discussion, and hassling around the conference table is tantamount, in international monetary circles, to acting on impulse.)

SDRs are a new form of money, an international reserve asset, usable (only by central banks and governments) to settle international debts in much the same way as gold. But instead of having to be panned, dredged, or mined from the earth, they are created out of thin air—just like demand deposits—by a purely man-made entry on the books of the IMF. About $20 billion of SDRs have thus far been made available for member nations of the IMF to draw upon when needed.

SDRs were originally valued in terms of gold, but since mid-1974 they have been valued in terms of a weighted average of exchange rates for the monies of the major trading nations. As a result, some international trading contracts have been drawn up calling for payment in the dollar or pound equivalent of SDRs rather than simply in dollars or pounds, because the value of an SDR is likely to be more stable in terms of worldwide purchasing power than the value of any single kind of money. If the dollar depreciates, for instance, it will take more dollars to equal one SDR and a foreign seller who has priced his goods in terms of the dollar equivalent of SDRs will therefore get more dollars for his goods. In other words, the pricing of internationally traded products in terms of the dollar equivalent of SDRs, rather than in terms of just dollars, gives the seller some protection against any depreciation of the dollar vis-à-vis other monies. This commercial use of SDRs has enhanced their prestige in recent years.[4]

One purpose of SDRs is to assist those countries with balance of payments or reserve difficulties: a nation with a shortage of reserves, currently running a balance of payments deficit (e.g., Brazil), can draw on its SDR allotment to meet its payments needs. When it receives its SDRs, Brazil can then transfer them to a strong reserve position country, say West Germany, that is "designated" by the IMF to "purchase" them. In exchange, Brazil will receive West German marks, which it can either convert into U.S. dollars or other foreign exchange, or use directly in making necessary payments. Countries

[4] In late 1979, for example, one SDR unit was worth $1.30.

"designated" by the IMF to buy SDRs do not have to accept them above a specified limit.

The term "paper gold" is, strictly speaking, a misnomer. SDRs are still far from the true equal of gold in terms of general acceptability. Countries "designated" by the IMF to surrender some of their money for SDRs are not nearly so enthusiastic about the transaction as they would be had they been "designated" to receive gold itself.

It is obvious that if SDRs are to be a success, they will require continued cooperation among nations. Nevertheless, they represent an inching away from mysticism in international monetary affairs —one small step for mankind. Provided they receive tender loving care, they may hopefully grow and prosper; but by any realistic assessment, it does not appear likely that they will soon topple gold from its pinnacle.

Is Gold a Good Investment?

Since it is legal for Americans to own gold once again (ever since the beginning of 1975), and since it is highly unlikely that gold will soon disappear from the world monetary stage, the question naturally arises: Is gold an attractive investment? Is buying gold a wise way to get rich or a dumb way to go broke?

Because gold earns no interest or dividends, it immediately suffers in comparison with such alternatives as savings accounts, bonds, stocks, and rental property—although in this respect it is similar to diamonds, stamps, rare coins, art objects, and non-income-producing real estate. Because it yields no current income, the wisdom of buying gold thus depends entirely on the prospect for future price appreciation.

If gold can be expected to rise in price by more than about 5 to 10 percent annually, which is roughly what one can earn in a savings account or in bonds or stocks, then it is worth considering seriously as an investment. But if it is not likely to match that rate of price appreciation, one can do better—and with greater safety—in one of the more customary forms of investment. In terms of this criterion, the historical record indicates that there have been only three periods in the past hundred years when an investment in gold would have paid off. One was the period just prior to 1934, the second was the period from the end of 1967 to the end of 1974, and the third was from mid-1976 through 1979.

In January 1934, President Roosevelt increased the price of gold by 69 percent, from $20.67 to $35 an ounce. Thus anyone who had the foresight to buy gold at $20.67 from February 1929 through February 1933, and who sold it at $35 in February 1934, would have been rewarded with a compound rate of return of anywhere between 11 and 70 percent per annum, the exact figure depending on when it was bought. In recent years gold buyers have done even better: The free market price of gold rose from $35 an ounce in 1967 (unchanged since 1934) to a peak of almost $200 in December 1974, a compound annual rate of price increase close to 30 percent for the entire seven-year period. Indeed, between late 1972 and late 1974 the price of gold more than *tripled!* And from mid-1976 to early 1980 it rose from $105 an ounce to well over $700 an ounce.

But be careful, because these figures greatly exaggerate the likely profits obtainable from gold in recent years. The free market price did not rise without interruption from 1967 through 1974. During much of 1971, for example, the price was below 1969 levels, and similarly from June through November 1973 the price of gold fell by 30 percent. Or how do you think people felt who bought gold at $195 an ounce in January 1975, as soon as ownership by Americans became legal, and then watched it fall to $105 by July 1976? That's a 45 percent drop in value in just a year and a half.

Supply and demand factors make the price of gold highly volatile. With respect to supply, new production adds to the existing stockpile at the rate of only about 2 percent a year. This means that the overwhelming element on the supply side is not the amount of current ore production but uncertainty as to how much holders of the existing stockpile might try to unload. For instance, the U.S. Treasury deliberately (and successfully) cracked the price spiral in January 1975 by selling 750,000 ounces from its gold hoard, and then auctioned off another 500,000 ounces in June 1975. Similarly, at the January 1976 IMF meetings in Kingston, Jamaica, the IMF agreed to sell 25 million ounces of its gold on the open market and use the proceeds to aid developing countries. Since then there have been periodic sales of gold by both the U.S. Treasury and the International Monetary Fund. In other words, sales by large holders, including the Soviet Union, are always a threat to break the price.

On the demand side, again, a significant portion of the demand for gold is not for current industrial or artistic use but rather is motivated by psychological considerations—in particular, by fear regarding an uncertain social and economic future. Gold has traditionally been thought of as a hedge against inflation; when prices threaten to rise rapidly the private demand for gold expands, but when infla-

I was born in 1929, when gold was selling for $20.67 an ounce...I married in 1968, in an outwardly happy marriage. That was the year gold began to go up again...For the past few years my wife has been having an affair with another man...

...Six months ago she went off to live with him...If I had bought gold in 1929 I could sell it today at 9 times the price at $180 an ounce, up from $20.67 then...Last week she came back 'To give our marriage another chance,' she says...'To give our marriage another chance?' I tell her, 'Until next time you leave, you mean'...

Some say gold stocks yes, gold bars no. I say gold bars yes, gold stocks no... Yesterday she left 'forever'...This morning she's back again...'I want to say something,' she says...

tion subsides that demand often vanishes overnight. This sort of demand typically fluctuates erratically on short notice, and rather small changes in supply or demand can produce wide price swings.

Thus gold is a highly speculative investment in which the warning *caveat emptor* is particularly appropriate. Large gains can occasionally be made, but large losses are just as likely on the basis of the historical record over the past hundred years. It is appropriate to end this chapter as we began, with a story: A man on a sinking ship ran to fetch his gold hoard before jumping overboard. When he landed in the water, the weight of the gold made floating impossible, so down he went. The crucial question is: Did he have the gold, or did the gold have him?

Suggestions for Further Reading

Those of you who want to become full-fledged gold bugs can start by reading the following: Miroslav A. Kriz, *Gold: Barbarous Relic or Useful Instrument?* (Princeton Essays in International Finance, 1967); Jack L. Davies, *Gold: A Forward Strategy* (Princeton Essays in International Finance, 1969); Fritz Machlup, "Speculations on Gold Speculation," *American Economic Review* (May 1969); and Robert Mundell, "Real Gold, Dollars, and Paper Gold," *American Economic Review* (May 1969). A quick way to bring yourself pretty much up to date is to read the Winter 1974–1975 issue of The Federal Reserve Bank of San Francisco *Business Review*, which is devoted entirely to the subject of gold; it contains articles on gold by Hang-Sheng Cheng, Nicholas Sargen, Kurt Dew, Michael Keran, and Michael Penzer.

Also required reading: Milton Friedman, "Commodity-Reserve Currency," in *Essays in Positive Economics* (University of Chicago Press, 1953), not to mention John Maynard Keynes, *A Treatise on Money* (New York: Harcourt Brace, 1930), vol. 2, pp. 289 ff. This time Friedman and Keynes are on the same side of the fence.

Actually, you'll probably get a better appreciation of the role of gold in human affairs if you go to the movies and see Alec Guinness in *The Lavender Hill Mob* or Humphrey Bogart in *Treasure of the Sierra Madre*. And don't miss W. C. Fields in the Klondike in *The Fatal Glass of Beer*.

PART IX

*The Past
and the Future*

Chapter 37

Post-World War II Federal Reserve History

IN GRADE SCHOOL, history was stories: Columbus sailing on the Santa Maria, George Washington chopping down the cherry tree, Abraham Lincoln going from a log cabin to a white house, and Theodore Roosevelt charging up (and down) San Juan hill. In high school, history was dates: 1066, 1492, 1776, 1789, 1812, 1848, 1914, 1929, 1941, and, if you went to a good high school, 1984. By the time college rolled around, you were sick of history because it sometimes resembled math—all those numbers to regurgitate on the weekly quizzes. So college history returned to the grade-school approach— which never should have been abandoned—history as ideas: the Judeo-Christian ethic, the benevolent despot, the Enlightenment, and 173 isms, ranging from romanticism and communism to masochism and sexism.

All of which goes to prove that history can be fun if you don't pay too much attention to when things happened. So what if you think that Occam's razor is a close competitor of Gillette's, as long as you know that Sir William of Occam insisted that you shave away all that extra stubble from your theories. So what if you don't know when the feudal lord's *Jus Primae Noctis* was introduced, as long as you recognize that it was the seminal concept behind modern group marriages.

With such an introduction to a discussion of Federal Reserve policy in the post-World War II period, it is not too difficult to conclude that we will be short on dates and long on stories. Actually, there are even better stories about the Federal Reserve that we are holding back. (Will anyone who was at the 1967 Christmas party of the Federal Reserve Bank of Kansas City ever forget?) But after all, we have to leave some material for the advanced courses.

The Accord

The financing of World War II was done by both federal taxation and selling government securities. The latter accounted for a huge chunk, as evidenced by the growth in the national debt from $65 billion in 1941 to $280 billion in 1945. To encourage banks, financial institutions, and individuals to buy government bonds, the Treasury and the Fed adopted a fixed structure of interest rates on government securities. The Treasury issued securities with yields ranging from three-eighths of 1 percent on short-term Treasury bills to 2½ percent on long-term bonds; the Federal Reserve did its part by *pegging* the price of the securities at par. In other words, the Fed was a "buyer of last resort" in case a holder wanted to sell government bonds but could not find a buyer at the fixed price. This meant that government securities had zero capital loss risk and were, therefore, bought willingly by banks and others at the very low pegged yields.

This situation was good for the Treasury, because it was able to finance the federal debt at very low cost. The situation was not so good for the Federal Reserve, because (as we saw in Chapter 20) when the central bank pegs the interest rate it loses control over the money supply. In this case, since the Federal Reserve had to keep the price of government securities from falling, it had to buy governments whenever any holder wanted to sell—and when the Fed buys it increases bank reserves. This meant that any upward pressure on the interest rate would be met with increases in the money supply, which was not too good for anti-inflationary policy. While minimizing the cost of the federal debt may or may not be an important objective,[1] the inability of the Federal Reserve to use open market sales of securities to sop up bank reserves meant that anti-inflationary stabilization policy was robbed of its most significant weapon—monetary policy.

[1] See the appendix to Chapter 21 for the importance of the interest cost of federal debt.

After World War II, the Federal Reserve agreed to continue the low interest rate support policy because the threat of recession loomed as a consequence of the cutback in government spending. As it turned out, inflation, not recession, was the problem: pent-up demands that had been suppressed by wartime rationing and shortages were turned loose on the economy just as it was converting to peacetime production. The Fed was still holding down interest rates, however, in deference to the Treasury's demands to minimize the cost of the federal debt, as well as because it was thought to be unfair to impose capital losses (that would result from rising interest rates) on the patriotic citizens who had bought bonds to finance the war.

The conflict in Federal Reserve policy was relieved by the 1949 recession—low interest rates were the right thing in that context. But with the outbreak of the Korean war in 1950, and the resurgence of inflation as the problem of stabilization policy (consumer prices rose 8 percent between May 1950 and March 1951), the controversy was brought to a head. On March 4, 1951, the Federal Reserve and the treasury reached a compromise that became known as the Treasury—Federal Reserve Accord. A joint statement was issued which read:

The Treasury and the Federal Reserve System have reached full accord with respect to debt management and monetary policies to be pursued in furthering their common purpose to assure the successful financing of the Government's requirements and, at the same time, to minimize monetization of the public debt.

The key phrase for the Fed was the last one, "to minimize monetization of public debt." When the Federal Reserve was preventing rates from rising, it had been forced to buy government securities, thereby adding to bank reserves and monetizing (turning into money) the national debt. The Accord said that such monetization should be held to a minimum. But the 41 words preceding that last clause were a typical attempt at high-level obfuscation of the crucial concessions extracted by the Treasury in the process of the Fed gaining its "freedom."

What Hath Pegging Wrought?

Although the Accord meant that the Fed no longer had to peg interest rates, that it could pursue countercyclical monetary policy without such a constraint, the legacy of the pre-Accord period was felt long after its demise. At least four characteristics of Federal Reserve policy during the 1950s can trace their roots to pegging. The "availability doctrine" and "bills only" can be viewed as Federal Reserve reactions to pegging, while "orderly conditions in the government securities market" and "even keel" are extensions of it—with the Treasury smiling broadly.

In an effort to gain support for abandoning the pegging policy, a number of Federal Reserve officials, primarily associated with the Federal Reserve Bank of New York, presented a series of arguments to show that tight monetary policy could be pursued effectively even if the resulting increase in interest rates were minimal. These arguments became known as the *availability doctrine*.[2] As the name implies, tight money would hold back spending not because the rise in interest rates would make borrowers want to borrow less and spend less. Rather, tight money would induce *lenders* to cut back the availability of credit to borrowers.

There were two main components of the availability doctrine: nonprice credit rationing and the lock-in effect. First, it was argued that banks might very well prefer to keep interest rates relatively constant during tight money and, instead, ration the *amount* of their lending to certain customers. Second, slightly higher interest rates would also produce capital losses in the government bond portfolios of commercial banks. Since they would be embarrassed to realize capital losses, banks would be "locked-in" to their holdings of governments— and would be unwilling to sell them off to get reserves with which to make business loans.[3]

The second Federal Reserve reaction to the pre-Accord support program for bond prices was a severe allergic response to buying long-term government bonds. Beginning in early 1953, *bills only* was the rule. It meant that the Federal Reserve would no longer carry out open market operations with long-term securities—just Treasury bills. By avoiding long-term securities, the Fed indicated that it would not be easily roped into a bond-support program again.

But the Federal Reserve wasn't completely victorious in the fireworks of '51. The Treasury–Federal Reserve Accord devoted much of

---

[2] Robert V. Roosa, then a vice-president at the Federal Reserve Bank of New York, wrote an influential article on the subject entitled, "Interest Rates and the Central Bank," in *Money, Trade, and Economic Growth: Essays in Honor of John Henry Williams* (New York: Macmillan, 1951). Allan Sproul, then president of the New York Fed, expressed similar views in the same volume.

[3] The availability doctrine was given great attention in the professional economic literature. A good summary is Assar Lindbeck, *The "New" Theory of Credit Control in the United States* (Stockholm: Almqvist and Wiksell, 1962). While the lock-in aspect of the doctrine received little empirical support, the nonprice credit rationing argument has been formalized and shown to be empirically relevant. See Dwight M. Jaffee and Franco Modigliani, "A Theory and Test of Credit Rationing," *American Economic Review* (December 1969).

its verbiage to the "successful financing of the government's requirements." The Federal Reserve agreed to "maintain orderly conditions in the government securities market" and somewhat later switched to "correcting disorderly situations in the government securities market." This concern with erratic movements of prices in the government bond market was especially evident during periods of large Treasury financing. The Federal Reserve promised to avoid tightening monetary conditions during sizable Treasury financing operations. Monetary policy was set on an "even keel" during those periods. As a matter of fact, even today the Federal Open Market Committee still adds, when relevant, "taking account of Treasury financing" to the directive issued to the manager of the System Open Market Account.

A Decade of Free Reserves Fighting the Business Cycle

From 1951 to 1961 there were three cycles in economic activity—marked by the recessions of 1953–1954, 1957–1958, and 1960–1961. Countering cyclical fluctuations in aggregate GNP is what stabilization policy is all about. Let us see how well the Federal Reserve did in countering the inflationary pressures associated with cyclical peaks and the high levels of unemployment associated with cyclical troughs.

To evaluate Federal Reserve behavior during this period requires two separate yardsticks—one to measure what the Fed was actually doing, and one to measure what it *should* have been doing. To measure what the Federal Reserve was actually doing, we will use an indicator from each class of indicators described in Chapter 16. The rate of growth in the money supply will serve as the representative of the monetary aggregates, and the Treasury bill rate will represent money market conditions. The Fed's favorite during this period, free reserves (which belongs in the money market group), will also be used. To indicate when a change in central bank policy should have taken place, we will use the turning points in the business cycle as designated by the unofficial arbiter of such things, the National Bureau of Economic Research (NBER).[4]

Before looking at the statistics, it would be nice to know whether the Federal Reserve expressed concern with the problems of combating inflation and fighting recession during the 1951–1961 period. A

[4] For a comprehensive discussion of how the NBER decides on peaks and troughs, see G. H. Moore and J. Shiskin, *Indicators of Business Expansions and Contractions* (New York: National Bureau of Economic Research, 1967).

quick review of the minutes of the Federal Open Market Committee[5] should be sufficient to convince even those (like certain members of Congress) who see the devious hand of Machiavelli in every Federal Reserve gesture, that our friendly central bank at least spoke of the virtues of anti-inflationary and anti-recessionary objectives during the 1950s. Phrases such as "with a view . . . to restraining inflationary developments" and "with a view . . . to mitigating deflationary [recessionary] tendencies" populate the directives issued by the FOMC throughout the 1950s. Now let's see whether they did what they said they wanted to do, and when they did it.

Charts 1, 2, and 3 plot for the 1951–1961 period the three-month Treasury bill rate, the annual rate of growth in M1 (demand deposits plus currency outside banks) over the previous two quarters, and the level of free reserves. The contraction phase of each of the business cycles is indicated by the shaded area, with the beginning signified by the peak in business activity (P) and the end designated by the trough (T). The recession beginning in the second half of 1953 and extending through the first half of 1954 is generally associated with the end of the Korean War, the contraction beginning in July 1957 and ending in April 1958 has been attributed to reduced inventory investment by businessmen, and the recession of May 1960–February 1961 has been connected in one way or another with the steel strike of 1959.

The periods immediately before each of the contractionary phases start are the ones of greatest inflationary pressures. If the Fed has been doing its job, it will have embarked on anti-inflationary policies well before the peak. From peak to trough the unemployment rate is increasing, and if the Fed is on top of the problem it will begin a policy of ease immediately at the peak (or, if its crystal ball is really good, some time before it.)

The path of the Treasury bill rate in Chart 1 suggests high grades for the Fed. The bill rate rose throughout the expansionary phases and declined at or even slightly before the onset of each contraction, except for 1957 when the Fed seems to have waited too long. But, as we saw in Chapter 16, unless the monetary aggregates are growing at an above-average rate, cyclical movements in interest rates are a poor guide to an *actively* expansionary or contractionary monetary policy. And Chart 2 does, indeed, paint a rather grim picture of Fed performance as far as the money supply is concerned. Monetary growth rates should be relatively high in recessions and relatively low in the expansionary phases. Instead, the picture that emerges is almost the reverse. The growth rates do seem to slow down right before the peaks,

[5] The Annual Reports of the Board of Governors of the Federal Reserve System contain discussions of FOMC meetings.

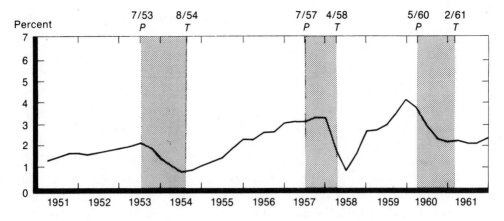

CHART 1 / Level of 3-month Treasury bill rate, 1951–1961.

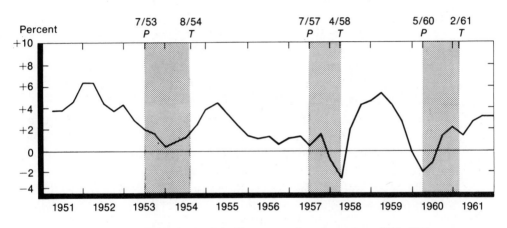

CHART 2 / Rate of growth in M_1 over previous 2 quarters, 1951–1961.

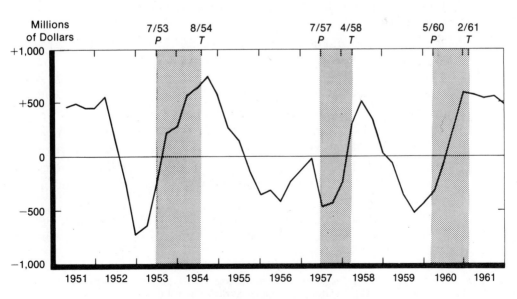

CHART 3 / Level of free reserves, 1951–1961.

and that saves the Fed from a failing grade, but it has clearly not done a very good job as far as the aggregates go.

This failure of the monetary aggregates to move as they should during periods of recession is not surprising. In those days, the Federal Reserve viewed the level of free reserves as the primary conduit for monetary policy. Fed expansionary policy meant open market purchases, increasing Federal Reserve credit and bank reserves until excess reserves were pushed up and/or bank borrowing at the Fed was reduced, so that the level of free reserves (excess minus borrowing) rose. The FOMC would raise the target level of free reserves during contractionary phases of the business cycle (expansionary monetary policy) and lower the target level during expansionary phases of the business cycle (contractionary monetary policy).

Chart 3 shows that the free reserves indicator behaved pretty much as it should have. Free reserves dropped during the inflationary pressures of 1951 and 1952 and rose sharply with the onset of the 1953 recession. There was a blunted upward movement in free reserves in 1956, when the Fed "erred on the side of ease" as it misread an emerging contraction—which partially accounts for subsequent Fed caution and hence the late rise in free reserves when the "real thing" started in the second half of 1957. Free reserves also climbed immediately before and during the 1960 recession.

Doing so well on the free reserves scale, however, almost guaranteed poor performance with the aggregates. The Fed wasn't keeping an eye on money supply growth while it was doing its thing with free reserves. This meant, for example, that as the economic expansion gathered steam and there was an increase in the demand for bank loans and demand deposits, required reserves would rise along with the increase in demand deposits, and excess reserves would drop. Free reserves would, therefore, also decline. If the Fed adhered to a target level of free reserves, open market purchases would be ordered to supply the reserves required to support the increase in demand deposits. The result: a validation of the money supply growth during a boom period. The reverse would occur in the recession phase of the cycle. Free reserves would go up as business borrowers repaid loans and reduced their demand deposits. To adhere to the target level of free reserves, the Fed would sop up reserves and validate the decline in demand deposits.[6]

This particular sequence didn't have to occur, of course. The Fed could have been twice as smart and altered its free reserves target by

---

[6] The disadvantages of free reserves as a target are set forth explicitly in Jack Guttentag, "The Strategy of Open Market Operations," *Quarterly Journal of Economics* (February 1966).

even more than it did during booms and recessions. Money supply growth might also have been monitored explicitly. But neither was done. The historical record of the first decade after the Accord suggests that the Fed didn't do too well as far as the aggregates are concerned, even though its heart and operating arm were in the right places at the right time (free reserves moved in the correct direction and with fairly good timing). The next decade brought a new set of problems and, quite naturally, a new set of policy weapons and concerns.

Twist, Growth, and Inflation

From 1951 through 1961 monetary policy was obsessed with free reserves. From 1962 through 1971 monetary policy lost its hang-up about free reserves and outgrew its allergic reaction to long-term government bonds—it deviated from the bills-only policy it had adopted in response to the pegging experience. Without a real business cycle to keep it busy from early 1961 until late 1969, the Federal Reserve turned its attention to fostering growth and helping the battle against the Gnomes of Zurich in the international arena until about 1965, after which the growth objective gave way to curbing inflation. Let's take a closer look at why the Fed changed its weapons, after a decade of fighting rather than switching.

The recovery from the 1960 trough was slow and deliberate. Unemployment remained above 5 percent through 1964. Fears of a new era of stagnation were heard throughout the eastern seaboard (a euphemism for "Boston to Washington"). Stimulating growth became a key objective of government policy. Since a high level of investment is one of the keys to a growing economy, the Kennedy administration and a Democratic Congress passed the 7 percent investment tax credit in 1962. A complementary monetary policy would have been low interest rates to stimulate investment spending. Charts 4 and 6, however, reveal higher Treasury bill rates and reduced levels of free reserves throughout the first three years of an acknowledged sluggish recovery in the level of economic activity.

The ambivalence of the Federal Reserve toward an all-out war against sluggish economic activity can be traced to concern over the balance of payments, gold outflows, and the international value of the dollar. Low interest rates at home aggravate these international problems because when interest rates abroad are higher than interest rates here, dollars tend to move abroad to get the better yields. The Federal

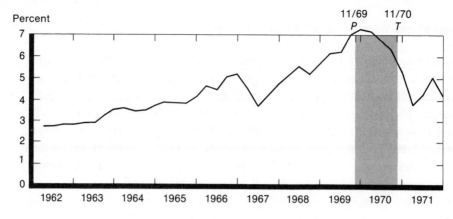

CHART 4 / Level of 3-month Treasury bill rate, 1962–1971.

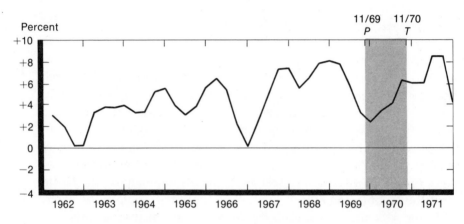

CHART 5 / Rate of growth in M₁ over previous 2 quarters, 1962–1971.

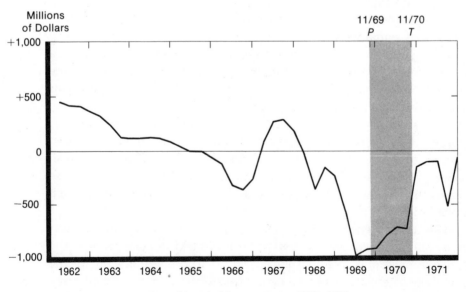

CHART 6 / Level of free reserves, 1962–1971.

Reserve was, therefore, torn between the need for lower interest rates to encourage domestic economic expansion, and the need for higher interest rates to alleviate our balance of payments deficits.

As a compromise, the Federal Reserve adopted an expansionary monetary posture that would put *downward* pressure on *long-term* interest rates (to encourage domestic investment), while at the same time putting *upward* pressure on *short-term* interest rates (to discourage outflows of funds abroad). "Operation twist" was carried out from 1961 through 1963. Twisting had just emerged as part of the rock-and-roll scene and the Fed, ever susceptible to new fads and fashions, was swept along with the beat.

"Operation twist" refers to the attempt to twist the term structure of interest rates—lowering the yield on long-term securities while raising the yield on short-term issues. "Twist" is also used to characterize the type of open market operation used to further that objective. Open market purchases of long-term securities, rather than short-term Treasury bills, were instituted. The idea was that, in addition to providing reserves, the actual purchase of securities in an open market operation tends directly to drive up the price (lower the yield). And it was the yield on long-term securities that the Fed wanted to see go down, not the yield on short-term securities. Hence, the Fed bought long-term securities and dropped its ten-year-old policy of buying and selling only bills.

There was much dispute over whether purchases of longs instead of shorts actually did anything to the interest rate structure.[7] The data in Table 1 do suggest that something was pushing short rates up but keeping long rates down. And there were at least two other things the Fed did which might have helped produce such a response, aside from the normal pattern of short-term rates going up by more than long-term rates during economic expansion. The first was a series of increases in Regulation Q, the maximum rate commercial banks can pay on time deposits. This permitted commercial banks to increase the time deposit part of their liabilities (i.e., they were able to lengthen the average maturity of their liabilities). Banks

---

[7] There are two parts to the doubts about the efficacy of open market operations in longs versus shorts. The first is that the change in the supply of the security bought or sold as part of an open market transaction is only a small ripple on a huge wave. The increase in reserves, not what kind of security is purchased, is the dominant factor (this is the very logic behind the bills-only policy). Hence, buying longs instead of shorts does little to keep short-term rates from falling. Second, there are many theories of what determines the term structure of interest rates. It is quite possible that changes in the relative supplies of shorts and longs have little effect on the structure of yields. The reason is that shorts and longs may be very good substitutes for each other, implying that their relative prices don't change very much. See p. 468 for a fuller explanation.

TABLE 1

	Yields On:			
	3-Month Treasury Bills	10-Year Treasury Bonds	Corporate Bonds	
			Aaa	Baa
1961	2.38	3.90	4.35	5.08
1962	2.78	3.95	4.33	5.02
1963	3.16	4.00	4.26	4.86

Source: *Federal Reserve Bulletin.* All yields are annual averages.

could, therefore, increase their holdings of long-term assets (bonds), bidding up their prices and lowering their yields.

The second Federal Reserve action was the failure to lower the discount rate as part of the expansionary monetary posture. The discount rate was reduced from 4 to 3 percent in 1960, and kept at that level through mid-1963, when it was increased. Banks in need of reserves would therefore sell Treasury bills (driving down their price and raising their yield) instead of borrowing at the Fed, as long as the bill rate was below the discount rate.

Whether or not "operation twist" did what it was supposed to, and despite the fact that balance of payments problems continued to plague the U.S. economy throughout the 1960s, the conflict in Fed policy more or less disappeared. The cure emerged as the sluggish level of economic activity gave way to inflationary pressures associated with escalation in Vietnam. From the beginning of 1965 until the end of the decade, the Fed's primary concern was price stability, so that domestic and international objectives both called for similar policies. Charts 4 and 6 show a sharp rise in interest rates and a sharp decline in free reserves from the beginning of 1965 through the end of 1966, as the Federal Reserve tightened the screws. In fact, credit became extremely tight in 1966 and interest rates rose to then-record levels, providing new-found evidence of the potency of monetary policy. The use of Regulation Q as a countercyclical policy weapon was also introduced —*not* raising it even though market interest rates were all moving up.

The battle against inflation was interrupted at the end of 1966 as a mini-recession developed, not enough of a slowdown to qualify by NBER standards but sufficiently noticeable to produce expansionary monetary policy—as evidenced by high levels of free reserves and lower interest rates throughout 1967. At this point it is worth recalling from Chapter 14 that it was during 1966 that the Fed decided to exercise some control over monetary aggregates. Money market conditions and free reserves were no longer, by themselves, good enough targets.

Chart 5 plots the annual rate of growth in money supply (over the previous two quarters) from 1962 through 1971. The very tight monetary policy of 1966 is characterized by a reduced rate of growth in M1, and even in the fourth quarter of that year, when ease had already been decided upon, money supply growth continued to decline (no doubt a result of the sharp slowdown in economic activity). The easy monetary policy of 1967 was characterized by an increased rate of growth in the money supply. So far, so good.

With the battle against inflation escalating to an all-out war in 1968, however, the record is somewhat less rosy. Free reserves dropped sharply in 1968, save for a small upward jump in the second half of the year to prevent the recession that was expected to emerge as a result of anti-inflationary fiscal policy (in the form of the income tax surcharge). Still so far, so good. The money supply, on the other hand, was putting on its own show—by growing at near record rates. It was only in the second half of 1969 that money supply growth was checked—with free reserves hitting the lowest levels in the postwar period, and interest rates skyrocketing to unheard of heights—making the Crunch of 1966 seem like a lovers' embrace. But by this time a slowdown in economic activity was more than a possibility; it was already here.

Unlike the recessions of the 1950s, the 1969–1970 contraction was induced deliberately by stabilization policy, mostly monetary. Inflation was out of control. Everyone, even the Democrats who had been turned out of office in 1968, was ready to accept some unemployment to take the pressure off an overheated economy. The very tight monetary policy of the second half of 1969 produced the recession that began officially in November of that year (the NBER has 20:20 hindsight).

The return to easy monetary policy was quick and double-barreled —both free reserves and money supply growth, especially the latter, turned upward and stayed there throughout 1970. Renewed emphasis on control of the aggregates early in 1970 as Arthur Burns took over as chairman of the Federal Reserve Board, seems to have helped. Money supply growth finally appeared to be moving counter-cyclically, in contrast with its perverse procyclical movements in the 1950s.

But the economy and economic policy were far from out of the woods. Inflation had still not been licked by mid-1971. Further, the recovery in 1971 was far from vigorous. Rapid inflation with considerable unemployment—the worst of all possible worlds—had become a reality. Monetary policy remained expansionary through the first half of 1971. But by then the Fed's old nemesis, our balance of payments deficit, reared its head again and stayed up, as sharply lower interest rates here encouraged huge outflows of funds abroad. All three at once—inflation, unemployment, and balance of payments deficits. Any bright ideas?

Controls, Collapse, and Continued Inflation

The solution to the inflation unemployment combination came in the form of wage-price controls, introduced on August 15, 1971, as part of Nixon's New Economic Program. The 1970 recession had been engineered to induce the demise of inflation, but prices weren't submitting fast enough. The temporary freeze on wages and prices was shock treatment in its most blatant form—to break the inflation psychology and allow economic expansion to proceed.

The initial results were quite favorable, with the inflationary fires apparently snuffed out by the deep freeze. As the freeze gave way to a formal program of wage-price controls, the monetary authorities decided that the major order of business was to get the economy moving vigorously. The Fed took aim at the 6 percent unemployment rate by voting for still faster growth in the monetary aggregates at the last meeting in 1971. Money market conditions were eased to promote more growth in the aggregates. The balance of payments problems that would normally accompany lower interest rates were dealt with in the international aspects of the NEP,[8] including foreign import controls and suspension of convertibility of the dollar into gold.

Chart 7 shows the three-month Treasury bill rate during the 1972–1978 period and Chart 8 shows annual rates of M1 growth over the previous two quarters during the same period. We don't need our free reserves chart anymore because the Fed finally abandoned this relic of bygone days. Its favorite money market indicator is no longer free reserves but rather the federal funds rate, which for our purposes is adequately represented by the three-month Treasury bill rate.

The year 1972 produced just about what Dr. Burns and his operating team prescribed. Money supply growth accelerated throughout the year. The Treasury bill rate was held at very low levels for the first half of the year and was then permitted to increase relatively slowly with the sharp advance in economic activity. The protection against inflation afforded by wage-price controls let the monetary authorities do their expansion act with little reservation. The economy did, indeed, move ahead. Unemployment dropped to the 5 percent range in late 1972 and inflation seemed to be restrained.

But the Fed was nervous. In the second half of 1972, money

[8] The NEP of August 1971 is not to be confused with the NEP of March 1921. The former was introduced by Richard Nixon in the United States, and the latter was introduced by Vladimir Ilyich Lenin in Russia. Actually, *ours* was a New Economic Program; *theirs* was a New Economic Policy. You could never mix them up.

growth proceeded at rates which, if continued, would have surely rekindled inflation. Furthermore, the stranglehold of wage-price controls had to be broken as shortages developed in some industries, misallocations became more obvious, and the incentive to cheat became more widespread. In the beginning of 1973, the Fed decided to restrain the growth in monetary aggregates, just as the administration began its phase-out of wage-price controls. The Fed once again used rising interest rates as a vehicle for restraining M1 growth. As can be seen in Chart 8, money supply growth did in fact slow throughout the year. But the Fed kept on chasing a moving target, as the desired rate of money supply growth was lowered in every meeting but one of the Federal Open Market Committee between January and September.

It is hard to say what happened next and why. The battle against

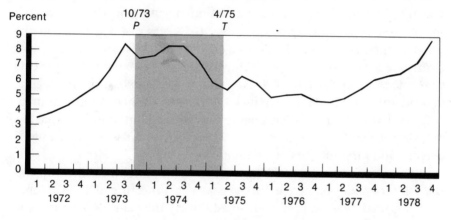

CHART 7 / Level of three-month Treasury bill rate, 1972–1979.

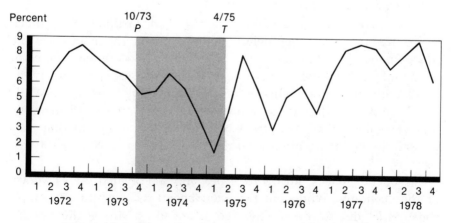

CHART 8 / Rate of growth in M1 over previous two quarters, 1972–1979.

inflation had already gone bad. The rate of increase in prices during the first half of 1973 was more than double the annual 3 percent inflation between August 1971 and December 1972. Was the increase in inflation because of the rapid growth in M1 in 1972 and the failure to cut back quickly in the first few months of 1973? Was it because of pent-up price increases that had been submerged by stiff controls during 1972, only to surface with the decontrol of 1973? Would the Fed's efforts to lower M1 growth have succeeded if the Big Shock of 1973 hadn't occurred? Would the 1927 Yankees have won a World Series against their 1978 descendants?

We'll never really know the answers to these questions (except for the last one which is definitely yes). The Arab oil embargo launched in October 1973 helped turn an uncertain economic situation into a disaster area. And the Fed, along with everyone else, was confused. Price increases, which had been accelerating—skyrocketed. The natural slowdown in the expansion during mid-1973 sputtered further due to lack of fuel. November 1973 was the beginning of the worst economic collapse in post–World War II history; but that was hardly obvious back then. Inflation was still public enemy Number One well into the summer of 1974. Not only was the extent of the decline in economic activity unanticipated, but the simultaneous jump in inflation made the 1971 inflation-unemployment combination look like the promised land. By the end of 1974, unemployment was more than 7 percent and inflation was 10 percent.

It is clear from the FOMC deliberations that fighting inflation was the primary policy objective until the very last meeting of 1974. Money supply growth was, in fact, restrained during the year, as is obvious in Chart 8. But the Fed was plagued by continued shortfalls in its M1 targets (see Chapter 16). Money supply growth kept on slipping below the desired "moderate growth" objective, which only made the economic slowdown worse.

Criticism of the Fed on these grounds seems justified. While much was going on at the time, including concern over the stability of the entire financial system due to the Shock of 1974—the bankruptcy of the Franklin National Bank—the Fed couldn't seem to justify its consistently inaccurate pursuit of the monetary aggregates. While money market conditions are supposed to be only a means to an end— the aggregates—there is a grain of truth to the argument that they mislead the Fed more often than not, as in the good old days of free reserves.

Monetary policy during 1974 probably aggravated the slowdown in the economy. While the recession began as a result of "supply constraints" due to the oil embargo, it ended up vintage Keynesian:

insufficient aggregate demand. While many critics have faulted the Fed for staying with the anti-inflation policy for so long, if only those without sin were permitted to cast the first stone, the rock-throwing would hardly begin. Just about everyone except some extreme Keynesians was hung up on inflation through the middle of 1974. The more appropriate criticism is that the Fed was more contractionary than *it* wanted, at least as measured by the monetary aggregates.

The recovery began, as always, when least expected. Amidst predictions of the collapse of capitalism and warnings of a depression to rival the Big One, the level of economic activity turned upward in early 1975, spurred by a classic Keynesian tax cut and an actively expansionary monetary policy. And economic activity moved ahead quite vigorously, with real growth quickly wiping away the 9 percent unemployment rate hit in May 1975.

As the nation prepared to enter its Bicentennial year, Congress reasserted its own independence by requiring that the Federal Reserve announce annual target ranges for the monetary aggregates. The objective was twofold: to provide congressional committees with a yardstick for evaluating Fed performance and to reduce the public's uncertainty over the future course of monetary policy. The Congressional resolution also established firmly the primacy of the monetary aggregates in gauging monetary policy's effectiveness.

The first target range prescribed growth in M1 of between 5 and 7½ percent from the first quarter of 1975 through the first quarter of 1976. Actual M1 growth during that interval amounted to 4.95 percent—not too bad. As can be seen in Chart 8, however, the two-quarter growth rates in M1 were quite erratic. In fact, during the last half of 1975 and the first quarter of 1976, M1 grew much more slowly than had been specified—giving rise to the now celebrated "case of the missing money."[9] Financial developments such as money market mutual funds, telephone transfers between savings deposits and demand deposits, and extensive use of repurchase agreements by corporate treasurers have made the M1 statistics less useful and less reliable than they once were. It's somewhat ironic that just as the monetary aggregates are getting long-overdue attention, the old standard-bearer, M1, loses some of its value.

Indeed, after a reasonably successful 1976, the M1 growth record

---

[9] Those unfamiliar with this infamous conundrum can partake in the confusion by reading the following: Stephen M. Goldfeld, "The Case of the Missing Money," *Brookings Papers on Economic Activity* (1976:3); and Gillian Garcia and Simon Pak, "Some Clues in the Case of the Missing Money," *American Economic Review* (May 1979).

leaves much to be desired. The economic objectives were to sustain the recovery and to simultaneously wind down inflationary pressures; a tall order by any standard. Fed policy during 1977 and 1978 was, therefore, aimed at moderate growth in the aggregates to encourage economic activity, but with a gradual reduction in the tolerable ranges. Instead, as is evident from Chart 8, M1 growth during 1977 pushed beyond its 1973-1974 peaks—hardly what the doctor ordered to keep down inflation.

There is little doubt that the excessive rate of monetary expansion had something to do with the 9 percent rate of inflation experienced during 1978. Not far behind as an explanation is the drop in unemployment to below 6 percent. Skilled labor is in short supply at such utilization rates, and the upward pressure on prices is hard to contain. One reflection of the jump in inflation during 1978 is the sharp rise in the Treasury bill rate towards the end of the year, as shown in Chart 7. That's a classic example of newly generated inflationary expectations pushing up nominal rates of interest.

As the decade came to a close, we seemed almost back where we started. Wage-price guidelines were formulated in 1979, and the government's Council on Wages and Prices (COWPS) was invigorated. The similarity with 1971 is quite striking, even though there was a Republican in the White House back then and a Democrat in 1979. But there is an unfortunate distinction. Confidence in the efficacy of stabilization policies still lingered at the onset of the 1970s; a legacy of the short-run successes of the 1960s. As we enter the 1980s, the humility acquired during the 1970s is in danger of turning to cynicism. We have a long road to travel before convincing evidence surfaces regarding our ability to conduct a responsible fiscal and monetary program.

Suggestions for Further Reading

A number of historical studies have been made of Federal Reserve policies. Broadest in scope and historical range is Milton Friedman and Anna J. Schwartz, *A Monetary History of the United States, 1867–1960* (Princeton, N.J.: Princeton University Press, 1963). Going back to the start of the Federal Reserve System, see Seymour E. Harris, *Twenty Years of Federal Reserve Policy* (Cambridge, Mass.: Harvard University Press, 1933), and H. Parker Willis, *The Theory and Practice of Central Banking* (New York: Harper & Row, 1936). Also see Elmus R. Wicker, *Federal Reserve Monetary Policy, 1917–1933* (New York: Random House, 1966).

For the 1930s and 1940s, see Lester V. Chandler, *American Monetary*

Policy, 1928–1941 (New York: Harper & Row, 1971), and Marriner Eccles' autobiography, *Beckoning Frontiers* (New York: Knopf, 1951).

For the post–World War II period, the availability doctrine is analyzed in Assar Lindbeck, *The "New" Theory of Credit Control in the United States* (Stockholm, 1959). Regarding free reserves versus total reserves and money supply, see Jack Guttentag, "The Strategy of Open Market Operations," *Quarterly Journal of Economics* (February 1966). A formal statistical analysis is presented by Michael W. Keran and Christopher T. Babb, "An Explanation of Federal Reserve Actions, 1933–1968," *Federal Reserve Bank of St. Louis Review* (July 1969). A post-mortem on the previous year's monetary policy is presented annually in the January (or February or March) issue of the Federal Reserve Bank of St. Louis *Review*. For all you spectral analysis fans, don't miss Charles Schotta and Vittorio A. Bonomo, "A Spectral Analysis of Post-Accord Federal Open Market Operations," *American Economic Review* (March 1969).

For history of a different sort (much better), read Lawrence S. Ritter and Donald Honig, *The Image of Their Greatness: An Illustrated History of Baseball from 1900 to the Present* (New York: Crown, 1979).

Chapter 38

Is Money Becoming Obsolete?

WHAT MIGHT the financial system look like in the year 2000? Buck Rogers and Flash Gordon are passé, Jules Verne is old hat (around the world in *eighty* days), and 1984 draws too close for comfort. The science fiction of yesterday has become the reality of today. An excursion into financial science fiction for the Brave New World ahead should provide a fitting ending for this book.

The Decline of Demand Deposits

"He spends money," they say, "as though it's going out of fashion." And perhaps money is indeed going out of fashion.

When checkbook money first began to gain popularity in this country, in the nineteenth century, it took decades before people finally realized what was happening. For a long time checking accounts were not even considered part of the money supply. They were viewed as proxies or substitutes for "real" money, namely hard cash. Somewhere in the vaults of the banks, it was thought, nestled the coin and currency, dollar for dollar, behind every checking account.

As a matter of fact, even coin and currency were suspect. Dimes and dollar bills were considered mere stand-ins for the *really* genuine article—gold coin or bullion. That, and only that, was truly money. Anything less was, like Daylight Saving Time, a violation of the Lord's will.

Today, demand deposits are gradually losing their monetary importance, just as currency did a century ago. Checking accounts still constitute the bulk of our money supply, but the money supply itself has been diminishing in importance in our evolving financial system. Thirty years ago the money supply—M1—amounted to half of our GNP; twenty years ago it was equal to around a third of GNP; today it has shrunk to about one-sixth of GNP. We are carrying on more and more business, both financial and nonfinancial, with a relatively smaller and smaller supply of money.

Just as a hundred years ago coin and currency gradually gave way to the convenience and efficiency of demand deposits, so today demand deposits, as we have known them, are gradually giving way to even more convenient and efficient payment mechanisms. The growth of credit cards, for example, has made it unnecessary to write 25 checks when making 25 purchases. One check, at the end of the month, will do for all. And often that check is not even needed, since your friendly neighborhood bank can make an automatic debit to your account at regular intervals, relieving you of the need to write it.

If you have your paycheck sent directly to your bank by your employer, and make most of your purchases with that bank's credit card, with payment settled up at stated intervals by the bank automatically reducing your account by the amount of the charges incurred, you will soon find your checkbook obsolete.

If we combine the essence of this already realistic payments system with the potentialities of the high-speed computer, magnetic tape storage, remote feed-ins, and satellite transmission, it does not take too much imagination to make a stab at the shape of things to come.

Debits and Credits in the Year 2000

A few decades from now, coins will probably still be with us for inserting into vending machines that we can then shake and bang to release our aggressions. But checks may well have vanished as quickly as they came. Check payment is really nothing more than a bookkeeping operation to begin with. As a method of information dispersal as to how the books should be kept, checks are—in light of present and foreseeable technology—notoriously cumbersome, slow, unreliable, and inefficient.

More in keeping with the twenty-first century will be a vast nation-wide balance sheet and clearing system in which debits and credits can be rung up virtually instantaneously by electronic impulse. Every individual and every transacting organization of whatever sort will be tagged at birth with a number and a slot on the "books" of a computerized nationwide accounting and payments system, a National Ledger, as it were.

Credits and debits to each individual account will be made by the insertion of a twenty-first century version of a credit card into a twenty-first century version of a telephone or teletype. Instead of a written piece of paper instructing a bank to credit this account and debit that one—that is, a check, with its necessary physical routing from place to place—the insertion of a plastic card into the appropriate receptacle will automatically credit and debit both accounts instantaneously. It should not be too difficult to devise a system whereby the proper code will serve as a means of verifying the validity of the electronic instructions to the Great Master Bookkeeper in the Sky.

Eliminating checks would be only one of the many advantages that would emerge from such a system. All financial assets are nothing more than a representation of someone else's liability or evidence of equity. Current practice, which consists of inscribing same on embossed parchment, has been absurd for at least two generations. There is no need for stocks and bonds to look like Pronouncements of State by King Henry VIII. As everyone is fully aware, a simple computer print-out would do just as well. However, by the year 2000 even that will not be necessary, since it will all be recorded automatically on the magnetic tape of the National Ledger as soon as a stock or bond is sold or a transaction made.

An even more important advantage will be the saving in time and effort currently devoted to keeping the books in a society slowly but surely being inundated by paper work. We are only kidding ourselves if we think we have made much progress in this area since quill pens replaced whatever it was they replaced.

In any event, manpower will have to be saved somewhere to provide personnel for the army of computer repairmen who will in all certainty be busy around the clock answering customer complaints and fixing breakdowns in the equipment. One supply source for repairmen, of course, will be the cadres presently known as the Monetarists and the Keynesians. Their hard-learned skills will be obsolete in the twenty-first century. After spending a lifetime accumulating regressions and correlation coefficients designed to test the role of money in economic activity, what else will they be able to do when money itself becomes no more than a historical *curiosa*?

A National Ledger payments system will be possible in a surprisingly few years. Already its introduction depends more on costs and financial evaluations regarding its profitability than on purely technological considerations. It remains to be seen whether the necessary services will be provided by one firm, an association of private financial and nonfinancial firms, or the government, alone or in partnership with private enterprise.

There are obvious advantages inherent in its being a governmental function. For example, for many years employees of the Communist Party USA were not permitted to receive social security benefits. If they and other malcontents could similarly be denied access to the National Ledger, and thus barred from making or receiving payments of any sort, the American Way of Life could be made even more Secure.

Implications for Financial Markets

With methods of communication and the dissemination of information perfected to the ultimate degree by the year 2000, in all likelihood financial markets will finally take on the characteristics of the purely competitive markets that economists have been talking about in classrooms since the days of Adam Smith. Instead of simple buy and sell orders, or bid and offered quotations, potential buyers and sellers of financial assets will be able electronically to transmit complete demand and supply schedules to a central clearing computer, specifying the amounts of various securities they wish to buy or sell at a range of alternative prices.

Of course, this in itself would not be quite sufficient to meet classroom standards for a purely competitive market, since one of the prerequisites for such a market is that the participants possess perfect foresight regarding the future as well as perfect knowledge of the present. But even that might be incorporated by feeding probability forecasts into the Giant Maw of the computer. Is it too farfetched to suggest that such forecasts might even involve some of the parapsychological techniques—like clairvoyance and precognition—currently under intensive study at some of our most prestigious universities and on several all-night radio programs?

Judge Refuses Man's Request
To Let Him Become a Number

MINNEAPOLIS, Feb. 13—A district court judge today denied the request of a Minneapolis man who wanted his name changed to a number, saying that it would be "an offense to basic human dignity."

Michael Herbert Dengler filed a petition in October seeking to assume legally the name 1069, which he said he had used for more than four years. Mr. Dengler cited philosophical reasons for his request, saying that each of the numerals had symbolic significance to him. Taken together, he said, the numerals "describe what is inherent in me."

He was out of town and could not be reached for comments on the ruling.

Mr. Dengler, a 32-year-old former resident of North Dakota, had twice been denied such permission by courts in that state. The North Dakota Supreme Court conceded that "One Zero Six Nine" might qualify as a name, but balked at his use of numerals instead of words.

Opened Checking Account

However, after Mr. Dengler moved to Minnesota he opened a checking account as 1069, and he displays a Social Security card also identifying him by number. He said he had little trouble passing checks bearing the unusual name.

"I just write the check and say, 'Would I write a bad check with a name like this?'" he said.

But Mr. Dengler said that he had been discriminated against by potential employees and utility companies that refused to accept his number as a name. In an interview for a job at a large corporation, a personnel officer reportedly told him: "You come in here with a name. We'll give you a number."

Mr. Dengler's attorney, Timothy Geck, said at a court hearing in Minneapolis that several utilities had refused to give his client services as 1069 without a court order making it official. The Northwestern Bell Telephone Company, for example, would give Mr. Dengler only an unlisted telephone number as 1069, Mr. Geck said.

Judge Donald Barbeau of Hennepin County District Court said he believed Mr. Dengler was sincere in his philosophical motives for requesting the change, but said that he could not "in good conscience add to today's inhumanity by giving it the stamp of judicial approval."

"Dehumanization is widespread and affects our culture like a disease in epidemic proportions," Judge Barbeau wrote in his opinion. "To allow the use of a number instead of a name would only provide additional nourishment upon which the illness of the dehumanization is able to feed and grow to the point where it is totally incurable."

Mr. Geck said, after learning of the decision, that "there is a very good likelihood" that Mr. Dengler would appeal the ruling to the Minnesota Supreme Court.

NEWS ITEM / The Twenty-First Century

SOURCE: *New York Times*, February 14, 1978

Implications for the Economy

Economic policymaking, Monetarist or Keynesian, will also mean something quite different in the twenty-first century from what it means today. Monetary and fiscal policy are far too uncertain in their impact for use in the Century of Efficiency that will follow the present Century of Progress.

By that time, all assets and liabilities as recorded on the National Ledger will be subject to increase or decrease by any given percentage by Executive Order, thereby instantaneously altering the wealth of every individual and every business firm in the country. If aggregate spending does not respond promptly in the direction and amount desired, further asset-valuation adjustments can be fine-tuned until the reaction on the part of the private sector conforms to what is deemed necessary to assure the Good Life for all.

Given human nature, this may possibly give rise to the problem of "valuation evasion"—that is, an illegal market in which assets are valued and transactions effected at prices other than those recorded on the National Ledger. The result would be the accumulation of unrecorded wealth for those involved in such dealings. If this gains currency, so to speak, an entire underground financial system—complete with (unreported) deposits, handwritten checks, and a subterranean check-routing network—is likely to spring up in opposition to the more efficient computerized and satellite-supervised official payments system.

The most effective remedy to prevent such undermining of the common welfare would be to bar all participants in Financial Subversion from access to the National Ledger. Practitioners of too-private enterprise would thus be consigned, along with employees of the Communist Party USA, to deserved financial ostracism as Subverters of the National Happiness.

Such a solution would have the self-evident virtue of safeguarding the Sinews of our Efficiency, while at the same time being consistent with the preservation of our Cherished Freedoms.

Suggestions for Further Reading (and Viewing)

Two books, both available in paperback—Aldous Huxley's *Brave New World* (New York: Harper & Row, 1932), and George Orwell's *1984* (New York: Harcourt, Brace, 1949). And two movies—Stanley Kubrick's *2001: A Space Odyssey*, and Charlton Heston in *Planet of the Apes*.

Also (less interesting): Lawrence S. Ritter and Thomas R. Atkinson, "Monetary Theory and Policy in the Payments System of the Future," *Journal of Money, Credit, and Banking* (November 1970); Mark J. Flannery and Dwight M. Jaffee, *The Economic Implications of an Electronic Monetary Transfer System* (Lexington, Mass.: Lexington Books, 1973); and William Silber, "Towards a Theory of Financial Innovation," in Silber, ed., *Financial Innovation* (Lexington Books, 1975).

Index

Earley, James S., 448
Eastburn, David P., 156
Eccles, Marriner S., 111, 148, 156, 182, 591
Econometric models, 394
  of Federal Reserve Bank of St. Louis, 395–396, 400, 401, 403, 428
  FMP. *See* FMP model
  interest rate forecasting and, 454–455
Economic forecasts. *See* Forecasts
Economic growth, and intermediation, 59–60
Einzig, Paul, 17, 516
Eisenhower, Dwight D., 301
Electronic banking, 594
Employment. *See* Full employment; Unemployment
Employment Act of 1946, 367
Equation of exchange, 232–237
Equity capital of banks, 122–124
Equity trading, 489–492
Eurodollars, 539–540
European-American Bank, 105*n*
Evert, Chris, 484
Exchange rates
  fixed, 551–554
    domestic stabilization policies and, 551–554
    international monetary crisis and, 532–534
    See also Gold Standard
  floating, 514–516
    domestic stabilization policies and, 524–529, 550, 554–557
    Jamaica Agreement on, 544, 563, 569
    success or failure of, 545–546
    sources and uses of funds statements and, 524–529
Expected yield, 75
Expenditures. *See* Spending
Export-Import Bank, 424

Fama, Eugene, 502*n*
Fand, David I., 334
Fannie Mae, 64, 200*n*, 423, 430–433
Farwell, Loring C., 71

Federal Advisory Council, 146
Federal Deposit Insurance Corporation (FDIC), 102–105
  assessment rates for, 104
  bank failures and, 89
  creation of, 102–103
  Federal Reserve conflicts with, 99–101
  membership in, 98, 99
  mutual savings banks and, 87
  taking over failed banks by, 103–104, 105*n*
Federal Financial Institutions Examination Council, 101
Federal funds, 66
Federal funds market, 135–136
Federal funds rate, 218
Federal Home Loan Bank Board, 86, 101
Federal Home Loan Bank System, 64, 86, 199*n*, 431–432
Federal Home Loan Mortgage Corporation (FHLMC), 431, 477
Federal Housing Administration (FHA) mortgages, 64, 422, 431, 476, 477, 496
Federal National Mortgage Association (Fannie Mae), 64, 199*n*, 422, 430–431
Federal Open Market Committee (FOMC), 146, 148, 150, 577, 578, 580, 587, 588
  directive of, 185–192
    execution of, 192–194, 221
    proviso clause of, 190–191
  disclosure by, 215
  as indicator of Federal Reserve policy, 224
  power and authority of, 150
  RPDs as operating target of, 221
Federal Reserve Act (1913), 97, 144, 148, 151, 152, 407
  discounting mechanism under, 170, 172, 174
Federal Reserve Bank of New York, 562, 576
  Account Manager of System Open Market Account at, 150, 184–185, 192–194, 218, 221
  President of, 151
Federal Reserve Bank of St. Louis, 316

PICTURE CREDITS

Page 20—From the film *Dracula* (Universal, 1931); page 62—from the film *Gone With the Wind* (M-G-M, 1939); page 100—from the film *Why Worry?* (1923); page 153—from the film *Comedy of Terrors* (American International, 1963); page 168—from the film *Son of Frankenstein* (Universal, 1939); page 186—from the film *Treasure of the Sierra Madre* (Warner Bros., 1948); page 233—from the film *Horse Feathers* (Paramount, 1932); page 281—from the film *Dr. Jekyll and Mr. Hyde* (Paramount, 1920); page 380—from the film *Dr. Jekyll and Mr. Hyde* (Paramount, 1932); page 400—from the film *Frankenstein Meets the Wolf Man* (Universal, 1943); page 408—from the film *Air Raid Wardens* (M-G-M, 1943); page 432—from the film *Bride of Frankenstein* (Universal, 1935); page 495—from the film *Seven Chances* (M-G-M, 1925).